Developmental Dyslexia

The
DYSLEXIA
Foundation

The Extraordinary
BRAIN
series

Developmental Dyslexia
Early Precursors, Neurobehavioral Markers, and Biological Substrates

edited by

April A. Benasich, Ph.D.
Center for Molecular and Behavioral Neuroscience
Rutgers, The State University of New Jersey
Newark, New Jersey

and

R. Holly Fitch, Ph.D.
University of Connecticut
Storrs, Connecticut

·P A U L·H·
BROOKES
PUBLISHING CO.®

Baltimore • London • Sydney

Paul H. Brookes Publishing Co., Inc.
Post Office Box 10624
Baltimore, Maryland 21285-0624
USA

www.brookespublishing.com

Typeset by BLPS Content Connections, Chilton, Wisconsin.
Manufactured in the United States of America by
Sheridan Books, Inc., Chelsea, Michigan.

The following was written by a U.S. government employee within the scope of his
or her official duties and, as such, shall remain in the public domain: Conclusion/
Next Steps. The opinions and assertions contained herein are the private opinions
of the authors and are not to be construed as official or reflecting the views of the
U.S. Government.

Library of Congress Cataloging-in-Publication Data

Developmental dyslexia : early precursors, neurobehavioral markers, and biological
substrates / edited by April A. Benasich and R. Holly Fitch.
    p.   cm.
Includes bibliographical references and index.
  ISBN-13: 978-1-59857-186-8 (hardcover)
  ISBN-10: 1-59857-186-9 (hardcover)
  1. Dyslexia.   2. Neurobehavioral disorders.   3. Behavior genetics.
  I. Benasich, April.   II. Fitch, R. Holly.

RC394.W6D48 2012

616.85'53—dc23   2012001963

British Library Cataloguing in Publication data are available from the British Library.

2016   2015   2014   2013   2012

10   9   8   7   6   5   4   3   2   1

Contents

About the Editors

April A. Benasich, Ph.D., Professor of Neuroscience, Director of the Infancy Studies Laboratory, Center for Molecular and Behavioral Neuroscience, Rutgers, The State University of New Jersey, 197 University Avenue, Newark, NJ 07102

Dr. Benasich is Professor of Neuroscience and Director of the Infancy Studies Laboratory at the Center for Molecular and Behavioral Neuroscience. Her research focuses on the study of early neural processes necessary for typical and disordered language development. Specifically, she studies the development of temporally bounded sensory information processing (shown to be a major predictor of language impairment and dyslexia), the neural substrates that support these developing abilities, and the relations seen with emerging language and cognitive abilities from infancy through early childhood.

R. Holly Fitch, Ph.D., Associate Professor, Behavioral Neuroscience Division, Department of Psychology, University of Connecticut, 406 Babbidge Road, Unit 1020, Storrs, CT 06269

Dr. Fitch received her B.S. from Duke University and her Ph.D. in biobehavioral sciences (concentration in developmental psychobiology) from the University of Connecticut. Her research centers on understanding how the disruption of early brain development underlies subsequent cognitive disabilities, with a particular focus on risk factors for language-relevant skills. Topics of research include animal models of brain damage typical of premature and term birth insult, as well as animal models for genetic risk factors associated with cognitive disability.

Contributors

Jessica M. Black, Ph.D.
Assistant Professor
Graduate School of Social Work
Boston College
McGuinn Hall
140 Commonwealth Avenue
Chestnut Hill, MA 02467

Bharath Chandrasekaran, Ph.D.
Assistant Professor
University of Texas at Austin
1 University Station, A1100
Austin, TX 78712

Michelle YH Chang, M.Ed.
Research Study Assistant
Children's Hospital Boston
1 Autumn Street, AU613
Boston, MA 02115

Alicia Yue Che, M.S.
Graduate Assistant
Physiology and Neurobiology
University of Connecticut
75 North Eagleville Road
Storrs, CT 06269

Naseem Choudhury, Ph.D.
Associate Professor of Psychology
Ramapo College of New Jersey
    and Center for Molecular and
    Behavioral Neuroscience,
    Rutgers University
505 Ramapo Valley Road
Mahwah, NJ 07430

Elise de Bree, Ph.D.
Assistant Professor
Utrecht University
Department of Pedagogical
    Sciences/Utrecht Institute of
    Linguistics OTS
Postbus 80.140
3805 TC
Utrecht, The Netherlands

**Jean-François Démonet, M.D.,
    Ph.D.**
Lausanne University Hospital
    and University of Lausanne
Leenaards Memory Center
Department of Clinical
    Neuroscience
CHUV & University of Lausanne
Rue du Bugnon 46
CH-1011 Lausanne
Switzerland

Andrea Facoetti, Ph.D.
Assistant Professor
Dipartimento di Psicologia
    Generale, Università di Padova
Via Venezia 8
35131
Padova, Italy

Nadine Gaab, Ph.D.
Assistant Professor of Pediatrics
Harvard Medical School
Children's Hospital Boston
Department of Medicine
Division of Developmental
   Medicine
Laboratories of Cognitive
   Neuroscience
Office 611
1 Autumn Street, Mailbox #713
Boston, MA 02115

Ellen Gerrits, Ph.D.
Professor
HU University of Applied
   Sciences Utrecht
Faculty of Health Care
Post Office Box 85182
3508 AD
Utrecht, The Netherlands

P. Ellen Grant, M.D.
Chair in Neonatology, Children's
   Hospital Boston
Founding Director, Fetal-Neonatal
   Neuroimaging & Developmen-
   tal Science Center
Director of Fetal and Neonatal
   Neuroimaging Research, Chil-
   dren's Hospital Boston
Affiliated Faculty of the Harvard-
   MIT Division of Health Sci-
   ences and Technology
Children's Hospital Boston
Department of Medicine, Divi-
   sion of Newborn Medicine
Department of Radiology, Divi-
   sion of Neuroradiology
300 Longwood Avenue
Boston, MA 02115

Elena L. Grigorenko, Ph.D.
Associate Professor
Yale University
230 S. Frontage Road
SHMI E75
New Haven, CT 06519

Nancy L. Hayes, Ph.D.
Associate Professor, Director of
   Clinical Foundations
Florida State University College
   of Medicine
1115 West Call Street
Tallahassee, FL 32306-4300

Martha R. Herbert, M.D., Ph.D.
Assistant Professor, Neurology
   (Pediatric)
Harvard Medical School
Massachusetts General Hospital
TRANSCEND Research
149 13th Street, Room 10.018
Charlestown, MA 02129

Fumiko Hoeft, M.D, Ph.D.
Instructor of Psychiatry, Associate
   Director of CIBSR
Stanford University School of
   Medicine
401 Quarry Road
M/C 5795
Stanford, CA 94305-5795

Nina Kraus, Ph.D.
Hugh Knowles Professor
   (Communication Sciences;
   Neurobiology & Physiology;
   Otolaryngology)
Director, Auditory Neuroscience
   Laboratory
Northwestern University
2240 Campus Drive
Evanston, IL 60208

Christiana M. Leonard, Ph.D.
Emeritus Professor
University of Florida
Department of Neuroscience
McKnight Brain Institute
100 S. Newell Drive
Gainesville, FL 32611

Joseph LoTurco, Ph.D.
Professor of Physiology and
  Neurobiology
University of Connecticut
Department of Physiology and
  Neurobiology
75 North Eagleville Road
Storrs, CT 06269-3156

Ben A.M. Maassen, Ph.D.
Clinical Neuropsychologist
Full Professor in Dyslexia
University of Groningen
Center for Language and Cogni-
  tion Groningen (CLCG) &
  University Medical Centre
Post Office Box 716
9700 AS
Groningen, The Netherlands

Cecilia Marino, M.D., Ph.D.
Eugenio Medea Scientific In-
  stitute, Department of Child
  Neuropsychiatry
Via don Luigi Monza 20
Bosisio Parini, 23842
Lecco, Italy

Sara Mascheretti, M.Sc.
Ph.D. Student
The Academic Centre for
  the Study of Behavioural
  Plasticity,
Vita-Salute San Raffaele
  University
Via Stamira d'Ancona, 20
20127 Milan, Italy

Natasha M. Maurits, Ph.D.
Professor of Clinical
  Neuroengineering
University Medical Center
  Groningen
Department of Neurology, AB51
Post Office Box 30001
9700 RB
Groningen, The Netherlands

Bruce D. McCandliss, Ph.D.
Patricia and Rodes Hart Chair
  of Psychology and Human
  Development
Vanderbilt University
Department of Psychology and
  Human Development
Peabody College #552
230 Appleton Place
Nashville, TN 37203-5721

Peggy McCardle, Ph.D., M.P.H.
Chief, Child Development and
  Behavior Branch
Eunice Kennedy Shriver National
  Institute of Child Health and
  Human Development
6100 Executive Boulevard, Suite
  4B05
Rockville, MD 20852-7510

Brett Miller, Ph.D.
Program Director, Reading,
  Writing and Related Learning
  Disabilities Program
Eunice Kennedy Shriver National
  Institute of Child Health and
  Human Development, Nation-
  al Institutes of Health
6100 Executive Boulevard, Suite
  4B05
Rockville, MD 20895-7510

Massimo Molteni, M.D.
Child Neuropsychiatrist
Head of Child Psychopathology
  Unit—Health and Safety
  Manager
IRCCS "Eugenio Medea"—Ass.
  La Nostra Familglia
Via Don Luigi
Monza, 20
23842 Bosisio
Parini (LC)
Italy

Richard S. Nowakowski, Ph.D.
Randolph L. Rill Professor and
    Chair
Florida State University, College
    of Medicine
Department of Biomedical
    Sciences
1115 West Call Street
Tallahassee, FL 32306

Cyril R. Pernet, Ph.D.
Academic Fellow
Brain Research Imaging Centre
Language and Categorization Lab
Division of Clinical Neurosciences
University of Edinburgh
Western General Hospital
Crewe Road
Edinburgh
EH4 2XU
Scotland, United Kingdom

Elena Plante, Ph.D.
Professor
University of Arizona
Department of Speech, Language,
    & Hearing Sciences
1131 E. 2nd Street
Tucson, AZ 85721-0071

Nora Maria Raschle, M.S.
Ph.D. Student
Children's Hospital and Har-
    vard Medical School Boston
University of Zurich,
    Switzerland
Division of Developmental
    Medicine
Laboratories of Cognitive
    Neuroscience
1 Autumn Street, AU 612
Boston, MA 02215

Glenn D. Rosen, Ph.D.
Associate Professor of Neurology
Beth Israel Deaconess Medical
    Center
Department of Neurology,
    E/CLS-643
330 Brookline Avenue
Boston, MA 02215

Margaret J. Snowling, Ph.D.
Professor of Psychology
University of York
Department of Psychology
Heslington
York YO10 5DD
United Kingdom

**John Stein, M.A., M.Sc.,
    B.M.B.Ch., FRCP**
Emeritus Professor of
    Neuroscience
Magdalen College, Oxford
    University
Sherrington Building
Parks Road
OX1 3PT
United Kingdom

Patrice L. Stering, M.Ed.
Graduate Student
Children's Hospital Boston
University of Massachusetts,
    Amherst
Department of Psychology
403 Tobin Hall
135 Hicks Way
Amherst, MA 01003

Caitlin E. Szalkowski, M.A.
University of Connecticut
Department of Psychology
406 Babbidge Road
Unit 1020
Storrs, CT 06269

Aarti Tarkar, B.S.
Doctoral Student
University of Connecticut
75 N. Eagleville Road
Unit 3156
Storrs, CT 06269

Petra van Alphen, Ph.D.
Utrecht Institute for Linguistics
   OTS, Utrecht University
Trans 10
3521 JK
Utrecht, The Netherlands

Aryan van der Leij, Ph.D.
Professor of Special Education
University of Amsterdam
Nieuwe Prinsengracht 130
1018 VZ
Amsterdam, The Netherlands

Frank Wijnen, Ph.D.
Professor of Psycholinguistics
Utrecht University, Utrecht In-
   stitute of Linguistics OTS
Trans 10
3512 JK
Utrecht, The Netherlands

Yuliya N. Yoncheva, Ph.D.
Postdoctoral Researcher
Vanderbilt University
Department of Psychology and
   Human Development
Peabody College #552
230 Appleton Place
Nashville, TN 37203-5721

Jennifer Zuk, M.Ed.
Research Assistant
Children's Hospital Boston
1 Autumn Street, Room 612
Boston, MA 02115

Frans Zwarts, Ph.D.
Full Professor in Linguistics
Faculty of Arts, Linguistics &
   School of Behavioural and
   Cognitive Neurosciences
   (BCN), University Medical
   Centre
University of Groningen
A. Deusinglaan 1
9713 AW
Groningen, The Netherlands

The Dyslexia Foundation and the Extraordinary Brain Series

William H. Baker, Jr., April A. Benasich, and R. Holly Fitch

This volume is a compilation of presentations from the 12th International Symposium of the Extraordinary Brain Series, which was held at beautiful Ashford Castle in Cong, Ireland, in June/July 2010. Traditionally, symposia in this series are designed to put researchers from various disciplines into a secluded environment for a week, to present their own research but also to facilitate listening to and critiquing research outside of their domain. This provides a unique perspective to researchers both within and outside the field of dyslexia per se, who, in general, associate and collaborate with members of their specific discipline. This broad interdisciplinary mix creates an appreciation for the "larger domain," encompassing topics relevant to dyslexia across participants. The weeklong conferences allow for varied formal and informal interaction and discussion, which serves to highlight novel issues and ideas that, it is hoped, will stimulate new research and inform ongoing research. For example, the current symposium included researchers spanning the domains of population genetics, genetic neuroscience (animal models), early infant development, prospective longitudinal assessment, infant/child neuroimaging, and statistical modeling. Our goal was to create a focus on the earliest potential precursors to dyslexia by shifting the emphasis away from older diagnosed populations and toward very early genetic, neural, and prelingual phenotypes (i.e., a "predyslexic" phenotype[s]). This topic provided a new direction for The Dyslexia Foundation Extraordinary Brain Series.

HISTORY OF THE DYSLEXIA FOUNDATION

The founder of The Dyslexia Foundation (TDF)—William H. Baker, Jr.—experienced the educational inadequacies of a system ignorant of the causes (and even the existence) of dyslexia. As a youngster, Baker benefited from small classes, extra attention, and compassionate parents. All of these factors helped him to successfully complete grade school and college. But in 1976 (after failing in graduate school), an astute clinician finally recognized that Baker struggled with dyslexia. These experiences spurred him to learn more about dyslexia and ultimately to work with the Orton Society—one of the few groups at that time working to enlighten the educational community with a specific, multisensory approach to teaching people with dyslexia. However, Baker felt that more evidence and knowledge were needed in order to discover the most effective ways to unlock the potential of each child, with or without dyslexia. Baker thus began the Research Division of the Orton Society. He, along with Drake Duane, gathered the small number of experts then in the field who were convinced that dyslexia was an actual condition, and together they set out to broaden the scope of knowledge regarding how language learning takes place—and, ultimately, to develop more effective educational approaches for children with impairments. The experts included Norman Geschwind, Roger Saunders, Drake Duane, Margaret Rawson, and McDonald Critchley.

At that time, Albert Galaburda and Thomas Kemper (under the mentorship of Geschwind) were taking a novel approach in studying the brains of *postmortem* dyslexics for structural/neuronal anomalies. With Geschwind's untimely passing in 1984, the Orton group feared a loss of the momentum generated by his visionary thinking. At this juncture, Galaburda put forward the transformative notion that researchers from seemingly unrelated fields could be pulled together to address the challenge. In 1987, Galaburda and Baker (with the help of Caryl Frankenberger and funding by Emily Fisher Landau) initiated this novel approach to cross-field dyslexia research integration by convening a group of renowned international experts of widely divergent disciplines in Florence, Italy. Thus The Extraordinary Brain Symposium Series was born.

Subsequently in 1989, Baker established the Dyslexia Research Foundation (later changed to The Dyslexia Foundation, or TDF). The mission of TDF is to promote scientific breakthroughs in the early detection, prevention, and remediation of dyslexia and related reading difficulties; to disseminate new findings and evidence-based reading approaches to researchers, practitioners, and families; to prevent the economic and psychological suffering caused by reading failure; and to unlock the full potential of children and adults with dyslexia so that they may personally succeed and contribute fully to society.

IN SEARCH OF EARLY PRECURSORS, NEUROBEHAVIORAL MARKERS, AND BIOLOGICAL SUBSTRATES

In recent years, research on diagnosis and treatment of dyslexia has accelerated with an increasing focus on identifying biological substrates and potential early precursors. Novel approaches within the past decade include investigations of neural and genetic mechanisms that might contribute to later patterns of disability in developmental language learning disorders (i.e., candidate genes and neurobehavioral markers), a goal that has been facilitated by new technologies ranging from gene association and linkage analyses to animal modeling.

Accordingly, an appreciation has emerged for the compelling overlap seen in core deficits across related and comorbid disorders, such as early language impairment (or specific language impairment [SLI]), autism spectrum language impairment, reading impairment, attention-deficit hyperactivity disorder, and others. Thus researchers have begun to look more closely at core deficits (or intermediate phenotypes) that span these various disorders as a way to hone in on factors (genetic, neural, behavioral) that underlie specific aspects of language and reading disruptions. One of the most common comorbidities for SLI (a.k.a. developmental dysphasia) is a subsequent diagnosis of dyslexia or reading disability (a.k.a. specific reading disability [RD], or developmental dyslexia [DD]). Both SLI and dyslexia are defined by exclusionary criteria. In the case of SLI, this condition is diagnosed when a child has delayed or disordered language development that cannot be attributed to a known cause such as hearing impairment, intellectual disability, childhood schizophrenia, infantile autism, or frank neurological disorders. For dyslexia, a general definition highlights an unexpected delay or deficit in the acquisition and performance of reading, despite an overall nonverbal IQ in the normal range. This prevalent comorbidity between SLI and dyslexia likely reflects the fact that even though most children with SLI eventually learn to understand and produce speech, acquisition of early reading skills requires that children map learned phonemes (sounds) onto orthographic representations (letters). Deficits in phonemic representation and/or phonologic processing comprise a core and persisting component of SLI; thus, it is not surprising that a large portion (>50%) of children with SLI go on to be diagnosed with dyslexia. As a result, investigators have begun to use a "merged" diagnostic category of "language learning disorder" (LLD; a.k.a. language-learning disabilities or language-learning impairments). Careful examination of the earliest identifiable precursors in infants and young children at risk for LLDs such as SLI and dyslexia may enable earlier identification and remediation of children at highest overall risk for such disorders.

Taken together, such approaches provide a mechanism to address common pathways underlying various forms of language disability, along with increased power to expand the scope of research to genetic associations with intermediate phenotypes such as memory (rather than broad diagnostic categories), as well as an opportunity to utilize animal models in which language per se is absent. As we will describe in this volume, these approaches can be further coupled with creative cognitive approaches to assessing complex higher functions (i.e., reading and literacy) in both typical and impaired populations. Finally, the integration of these different levels of analysis has been greatly facilitated by recent innovative imaging techniques that can be applied to young children and infants.

Despite the explosion of independent research examining biological substrates and neurobiological correlates of dyslexia, there are two important goals that remain unmet. First, dyslexia must be approached in a multidisciplinary, convergent manner to capitalize on the wealth of promising data from molecular, genetic, physiological, and cognitive laboratories. However, the synthesis and integration of data from research ranging from early precursors and developmental trajectories, to the role of genetics and gene–behavior associations, to the neural interplay among comorbid conditions have proved exceptionally difficult to achieve. One important reason for this failure is that the explosive expansion of research in these areas makes it difficult to keep abreast of the vast findings—much less to understand and quantify their application to the complex landscape that is now the field of dyslexia.

Second, the field of dyslexia research has not as yet developed an essential unifying focus on "predyslexic" phenotypes. It is critical, as noted in many of the chapters that comprise this volume, that the field moves away from an exclusive focus on diagnostic categories and toward a deeper investigation of the role of comorbidity and core deficits as well as intermediate phenotypes of dyslexia. We argue this point because a tighter focus on precursors—such as predyslexic populations—would enable earlier identification of those children at highest risk for later dyslexia, as well as provide insight into etiologies, common pathways, neurobiological correlates, and long-term behavioral phenotypes. Further, because developmental neuroscience clearly shows that the earlier intervention is begun the more "plastic" the brain and the greater the possibility for improvement, *early identification will certainly lead to the most promising intervention techniques for application to educational settings.* In sum, this must be a top priority.

With these factors in mind, the TDF symposium held in 2010 was developed to focus strongly on the two following themes:

- **Identifying those factors that contribute to the ability to identify the earliest predictors of later LLDs, whether they are genetic, neurobiological, or cognitive/behavioral.** This aim speaks to insights that can be obtained from research that examines putative neural mechanisms and their links with developmental LLDs, tracking early developmental trajectories in populations at risk for LLDs and identifying associations between candidate genes and behavioral phenotypes, and further, puts more specific concentration on the comorbidity of related disorders that might provide insight on the etiology of dyslexia.

- **Explicating those factors that relate to understanding the core deficits in children who will present with a diagnosis of dyslexia.** An integral and essential component of early identification relates to understanding the core deficits in young children—specifically those deficits that most effectively predict later language and reading problems in children who have not yet fully developed language or reading skills but who are amenable to diagnostic measurement. Methodologies that might assist in this endeavor can be grouped thematically and include those noted previously. In addition, recent advances in developmental imaging of young children now allow closer examination of the brain–behavior interface as well as the evaluation of the earliest effects of remediation and intervention.

In sum, our fundamental objective was to address a number of broader issues over the course of the June/July 2010 TDF symposium that hopefully would foster synergies, as well as changes in research focus, that could move the field forward and produce a lasting and meaningful impact within the fields of dyslexia, cognitive science, neuroscience, genetics, and educational research. Specifically we aimed to 1) identify unexplored potential links between brain and behavior, 2) consider novel approaches including use of cutting-edge and emerging technologies, 3) identify strategies to facilitate identifying core deficits in the prereading domain, 4) strengthen links between research and practice, and 5) address policy and funding implications. We believe that the goals of the 2010 symposium speak also to the overarching aims of TDF—to provide broader understanding of the phenomena and mechanisms of learning that ultimately allow for the development of a more effective method of educating not just children with dyslexia, but all children.

Acknowledgments

We thank Will Baker and The Dyslexia Foundation (TDF) for sponsoring the Extraordinary Brain Symposium that inspired this volume. It was an honor to have the opportunity to bring together this impressive group of top international and interdisciplinary research scientists—in an incredibly beautiful setting—to focus on biological substrates, neurobehavioral markers, and potential early precursors related to dyslexia. Needless to say, the success of the symposium and of this book rests on many shoulders. First, the diverse meeting participants from both within and outside of the dyslexia field gave exciting and thought-provoking presentations, and contributed wholeheartedly to the wide-ranging discussions that took place within the meetings, as well as at meals and sidebars. Our speakers truly provided the core content to make the meeting successful—thank you. Next, thanks to the talented cadre of moderators who facilitated and contributed to the direction of these discussions, including Naseem Choudhury, Peggy McCardle, Brett Miller, Paula Tallal, and Maryanne Wolf. (Note that emergent content from these discussions is reflected in each of the sectional introductions, as well as in the Next Steps conclusion.) Of course, a meeting of individuals coming in from around the globe to an Irish Castle—some with families in tow and other special needs—requires enormous behind-the-scenes effort and coordination. Stefany Palmieri and her husband, Kent Wallace, to whom we offer our sincere thanks—along with congratulations on the birth of their daughter, born shortly after the Ireland meeting—patiently executed the organizational details. We are so grateful for having had the benefit of their invaluable assistance. We thank Cindy Roesler and Maki Koyama, who not only presented posters but also smoothed the way for us by taking detailed notes and numerous photos and executing countless errands. We also express our thanks to Sarah Shepke and Sarah Kendall at Paul H. Brookes Publishing Co. for facilitating the production of this volume and for their patience, careful editing, and insightful suggestions.

Finally, we both would like to take a quiet moment to thank our families for their support, encouragement, and good humor while tolerating frequent disruption and occasional turmoil—first while planning and executing the conference and then during the several stages of putting this book together. The lives we lead would be impossible without their love and understanding.

In sum, we feel that this has been an extraordinary adventure that firmly focuses attention on the earliest potential precursors to dyslexia and that, it is hoped, will provide a new direction for The Dyslexia Foundation Extraordinary Brain Series and for the dyslexia field.

Brain Development, Genes, and Behavior Phenotypes

Introduction

R. Holly Fitch

A major overarching objective of The Dyslexia Foundation (TDF) conference held at Ashford Castle, Cong, Ireland, in July 2010 was to embrace the notion that the study of dyslexia *should* and *can* be addressed in a multidisciplinary, convergent manner using the wealth of research emerging from molecular, genetic, physiological, and cognitive laboratories. One clear benefit from this approach can be seen in the nascent success of elucidating genetic mechanisms contributing *not only* to the complex diagnostic phenotype of "dyslexia" overall, but also more specifically to core underlying deficits or "intermediate phenotypes" associated with dyslexia—and possibly also to comorbid and/or overlapping disorders such as language impairment. In fact, a variety of approaches to the identification of critical genetic–neural–behavioral links or associations are currently in progress (many to be discussed in this volume), with ongoing work expected to reveal more specific dynamics between genes, neural systems, and delineated core deficits contributing to clinical language disorders. Such expanded approaches are also allowing us to move beyond an exclusive research emphasis on diagnosed older human populations, toward the study of at-risk prereaders (<6 years), and even to the study of core phenotypes below the level of reading that can be effectively modeled in animals.

In this section, meeting attendees/authors lay out preliminary steps to approach the goal of dissociating the genetic–neural–behavioral underpinnings of dyslexia, specifically by addressing the fundamental mechanisms regulating the construction and development of the brain and individual variation therein (Chapter 1). In so doing, researchers provide a window to the fundamental genetic "code" modulating early processes of neural progenitor proliferation, neural and glial migration and differentiation, synaptogenesis, myelination, and synaptic pruning. Although the sequential order of these events remains largely consistent across species and across brain regions, each of these critical components of neural development also exhibits regional and temporal *variation* that is genetically regulated. For example, higher mammalian and primate species experience a relative expansion and elaboration of cortical development that stems from a genetically regulated increase in subdivisions of cortical progenitors, leading in turn to a substantially larger cortical–subcortical ratio (Finlay, Hersman, & Darlington, 1998). Similarly, cortical neuronal migration in higher mammalian species has evolved to include both radial and tangential migration of cells destined to become excitatory glutamatergic and inhibitory GABAergic cortical neurons, respectively (Diaz & Gleeson, 2009). These complex dynamics are regulated by an enormous number of protein factors, coded in turn by genes—all engaged in the interactive process of "putting the brain together." Homing in on aspects of this process that may go awry in the early stages of brain construction in "predyslexic" fetal and postnatal development will be key to any comprehensive understanding of associated neural and functional anomalies, as well as the eventual behavioral expression of difficulties.

Although the basic role for regulatory genetic mechanisms in normative brain development is being investigated largely from one side of the research framework—through animal research—human epidemiological and genetic association studies also continue to reveal new putative genes that may be associated with an overall dyslexia diagnosis (Chapters 4 and 5). Not surprisingly, many of these "candidate dyslexia-risk genes" (CDSGs) in turn appear to play a major role in early brain development (Chapters 2 and 10). Through the process of applying the study of these identified CDSGs to animal research with techniques like RNAi and knockout models, we can see the approach come full circle, permitting the assessment of the effects of genetic manipulations of CDSGs identified in human populations (using animal homologs) on core behavioral deficits identified in human diagnosed populations (but also assessed in animal models; Chapter 11). Animal research on language disability has truly come a long way.

In subsequent sections, the authors elaborate on how to identify these core behavioral phenotypes amenable to modeling in a nonhuman species, as well as to early screening in prelingual and/or prereading infant and child populations. Such core features include (but are not limited to) 1) motor/articulation problems (contributing to expressive language disorders), 2) rapid auditory processing and auditory memory deficits (contributing to speech perception difficulties), 3) phonological processing and phonemic awareness disorders, 4) short-term and/or working-memory disorders (which include verbal and nonverbal components) 5) visual memory deficits (which may contribute more heavily to surface or "orthographic" dyslexia) and 6) visuospatial attention deficits. Across various studies these key behavioral components have been utilized to predict or correlate with diagnostic criteria of language dysfunction, as well as to show association with genetic factors of language disability and/or to distinguish among subcategories of individuals with diagnosed language disorders. Studies of these patterns of deficits have also been used to address questions such as whether dyslexia reflects a dysregulation of specific neural subsystems across a variety of regions and modalities (e.g., a general "magnocellular deficit"; Chapter 3).

Thus, through such scientific cross-pollination from seemingly disparate fields—ranging from clinical psychology to epidemiology to genetic analysis to behavioral neuroscience in animal models—it may be possible to eventually paint a picture of dyslexia that begins with genetic alterations and ends in a clinical diagnosis. Doing so opens the door for earlier diagnoses, improved screening, improvement in our understanding of the neural substrates of typical and atypical reading, and above all, the potential for better treatment and remediation of variations in brain development that lead to unnecessary lifelong difficulties in school and life.

REFERENCES

Diaz, A.L., & Gleeson, J.G. (2009). The molecular and genetic mechanisms of neocortex development. *Clinics in Perinatology, 36,* 503–512. doi:10.1016/j.clp.2009.06.008

Finlay, B.L., Hersman, M.N., & Darlington, R.B. (1998). Patterns of vertebrate neurogenesis and the paths of vertebrate evolution. *Brain, Behavior and Evolution, 52,* 232–242. doi:10.1159/000006566

CHAPTER 1

Overview of Early Brain Development

Linking Genetics to Brain Structure

Richard S. Nowakowski and Nancy L. Hayes

The developing brain begins as a tube with a hollow core, and like any tube, the neural tube has length, circumference, and thickness. This basic analogy serves to illustrate the relatively simple anatomical organization of the neural tube shortly after it closes at ~8 weeks of gestation (Figure 1.1). The differentiation of the neural tube along its length gives rise to the major subdivisions of the brain and spinal cord, with differentiation around its circumference leading to regional variation. Moreover, differentiation throughout the thickness of the neural tube wall produces the additional cytoarchitectonic variability of the different regions of the brain.

The driving force behind this last process is cell proliferation in the ventricular zone (VZ). In its appearance the VZ appears as a simple pseudostratified columnar epithelium that is histologically uniform throughout the central nervous system (CNS) and also throughout the developmental period but also it is a dynamic epithelium. There is, however, an underlying complexity in both the movement of the nuclei of the VZ cells (see details later in this chapter) and as by microarray studies that show that thousands of messenger RNA (mRNA) species are expressed in the VZ and that many hundreds are developmentally regulated (i.e., change systematically during the developmental period). Thus, possible mechanisms for the genetic basis for variation among individuals exist from the earliest stages of brain development.

To link the action of specific genes to brain structure, we have developed a new method of quantifying individual differences in brain structure. Our analysis shows that, in general, a significant proportion of the differences in the size and shape of any specific brain structure is regulated by a small number of genetic loci (although usually more than one). So far our work with this new method has been confined to mice, but both the anatomical methods and the SNP-association method can be easily adapted to humans. Finally, comparisons of genetic data from mice and humans suggest that variation in gene expression in humans is at least as diverse as it is in mice.

EARLY BRAIN DEVELOPMENT

Early brain development sets the stage for the production and elaboration of diversity in the CNS (Nowakowski & Hayes, 1999). Despite the complexity of the adult brain, in the embryo, topologically it is derived from a simple hollow tube (Figure 1.1). Like any tube, the neural tube has three dimensions. For convenience, instead of X, Y, and Z (the usual Euclidean dimensions), it is easier to think about the neural tube as having a length, circumference, and radius. During the early gestational period, the differentiation of the neural tube along its length, circumference, and radius contributes differently to the final form of the adult brain. The processes characteristic of each of these three dimensions are described in the following paragraphs.

The longitudinal differentiation of the neural tube produces the major subdivisions of the brain and spinal cord. In the brain, the names of these subdivisions are derived from the Greek word *enkephalos*, which means "brain." Each subdivision is further named for its position relative to the front of the brain, or for the shape of the ventricle it surrounds (Figure 1.2): the prosencephalon (*pro* = front), which becomes the telencephalon (*telos* = end = cerebrum) and diencephalon (*dia* = between = thalamus); the mesencephalon (*mesos* = middle = midbrain); and the

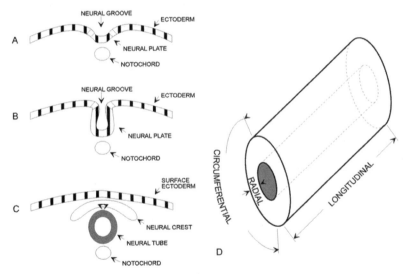

Figure 1.1. Neurulation. The process of neurulation begins at the end of the third week after conception. During the next few days, the outer surface of the embryo (or ectoderm) folds in upon itself to form the neural tube. A) At the beginning of neurulation, a shallow groove appears to mark the position of the neural plate. B) Subsequently, the groove deepens and C) the lateral edges of the neural plate fuse to become the neural tube. A small group of cells just lateral to the edge of the neural plate and some cells from the dorsal-most portion of the neural tube (arrows in C) become the neural crest. The neural tube is the forerunner of the central nervous system (CNS) (i.e., the brain and spinal cord), whereas the neural-crest cells produce most of the peripheral nervous system. Together the neural tube and the neural crest are often referred to as the neuroectoderm. D) Once closed, the neural tube, like any other tube, can be considered to have three dimensions: length or a longitudinal dimension, a circumferential or tangential dimension, and a radial dimension. Differentiation of the neural tube along these three dimensions is a useful way to conceptualize the primitive organization of the mammalian CNS. (From Nowakowski, R.S., & Hayes, N.L. [1999]. CNS development: An overview. *Development and Psychopathology, 11*[3], 395–417; reprinted by permission.)

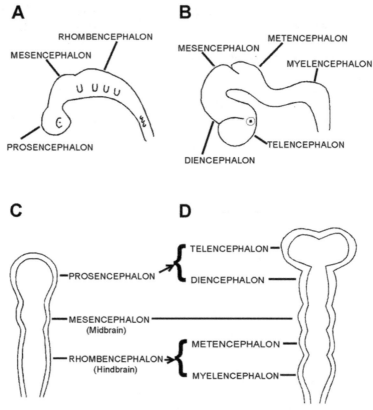

Figure 1.2. Longitudinal differential of the neural tube. A) A drawing of a lateral view of the brain of a 4-week-old human embryo. This is only shortly after neurulation, and already the three primary brain vesicles (the prosencephalon, mesencephalon, and rhombencephalon) are present. B) A stretched-out and cut-away dorsal view of the 4-week-old brain as seen in A. C) A drawing of a lateral view of the brain of a 5-week-old human embryo. At this age the prosencephalon has become divided into the telencephalon and diencephalon, and the rhombencephalon has divided into the metencephalon and myelencephalon. D) A stretched-out and cutaway dorsal view of the 5-week-old brain as seen in C. (From Nowakowski, R.S., & Hayes, N.L. [1999]. CNS development: An overview. *Development and Psychopathology, 11*[3], 395–417; reprinted by permission.)

rhombencephalon (*rhombus* = rhomboid, the shape of the IVth ventricle, which it surrounds), which becomes the metencephalon (*meta* = behind = pons) and myelencephalon (*myelos* = marrow = medulla and spinal cord) and also gives rise to the cerebellum.

After the closure of the neural tube, the brain grows rapidly. In humans, by far the fastest growing part of the brain is the telencephalon—in particular, the cerebral cortex. The driving force behind this rapid growth is cell proliferation (Caviness Jr. et al., 2003; Caviness Jr., Takahashi, & Nowakowski, 1995; Nowakowski & Hayes, 1999). In most regions of the CNS, it is cell proliferation within a region directly adjacent to the ventricles—the VZ—that drives the production of both the correct number of cells and the correct cell classes. The VZ is histologically uniform throughout the CNS and also throughout the developmental period. However, the VZ is also a dynamic epithelium. With each pass through the cell cycle, the nuclei of the VZ cells move away from the ventricular surface to replicate their DNA and then return to the ventricular surface to further divide (mother cells). Early in each cell cycle, some daughter cells exit the cell cycle and VZ to become neurons (Figure 1.3).

REGIONAL ANATOMY

Regional anatomy is also significantly affected by variation in cell proliferation and migration in the wall of the neural tube (i.e., along its radial dimension). When the neural tube closes, the entire thickness of its wall comprises the VZ (Figure 1.4). As cells proliferate, the wall gets thicker and a marginal zone (MZ; a thin cell-free area) appears beneath the pial surface. Shortly afterward, the first neurons are produced, as daughter cells leave the VZ and migrate into the MZ to form the intermediate zone (IZ).

Although this early sequence of events is common to the entire neuraxis, subsequent events vary in each of the major subdivisions of the nervous system. The simplest pattern occurs in the spinal cord and retina, in which the VZ is the only proliferating population. Here the neurons exit the proliferating population to occupy the inner part of the MZ. In

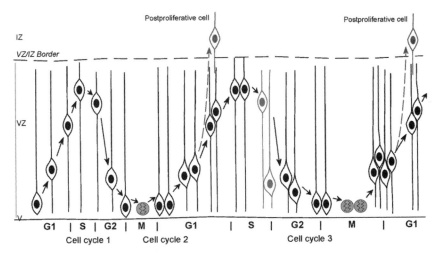

Figure 1.3.   The cell cycle in the ventricular zone of the developing central nervous system. This schematic diagram illustrates the interkinetic movement of the nuclei of the cells comprising the proliferative ventricular epithelium of the ventricular zone (VZ). With each pass through the cell cycle, the nucleus of a single cell moves from its starting position at the ventricular surface at the beginning of G1 to the border of the VZ, where it enters S. During G2, the nucleus again moves down to the ventricular surface, where it enters M and divides to form two cells. With each pass through the cell cycle, some postmitotic neurons are produced. The postmitotic neurons migrate away from the VZ to produce the structures of the adult brain (in this case, the cerebral neocortex). During the production of the neocortex in mice, the cell cycle lengthens with each cell cycle, and there are a total of 11 cell cycles. (From Nowakowski, R.S., & Hayes, N.L. [1999]. CNS development: An overview. *Development and Psychopathology, 11*[3], 395–417; reprinted by permission.)

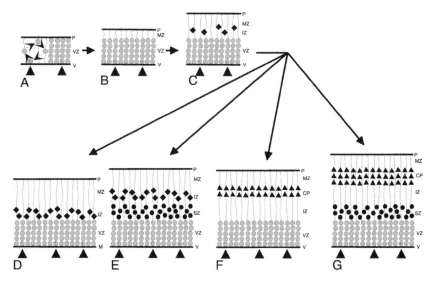

Figure 1.4. Radial differentiation of the neural tube: A, B, and C are schematic diagrams of the early stages of the radial differentiation of the neural tube through which every part of the central nervous system (CNS) passes. D, E, F, and G are schematic diagrams of various options for the later stages of the radial differentiation of the neural tube. Each of these options is characteristic of a different part of the neural tube. A) At the time of closure of the neural tube, its wall consists of a population of proliferating cells organized into a pseudostratified columnar epithelium, known as the ventricular zone (VZ). In this proliferative zone the nuclei of the cells are stratified, but also each cell has processes that contact the ventricular (V) and pial (P) surfaces of the neural tube. As diagramed on the right-hand side of the drawing, mitosis occurs at the pial surface (arrowheads), and during the cell cycle, the nucleus of each cell moves to a different level. DNA synthesis, for example, occurs in the outer half of the VZ. This to-and-fro movement of the cell nuclei is known as interkinetic nuclear migration and means that all cells, even though they are apparently at different levels, are part of the proliferative population. B) The next zone to appear during the radial differentiation of the neural tube is the marginal zone (MZ) that is an almost cell-free zone between the VZ and the pial surface. C) The intermediate zone (IZ), which contains the first postmitotic cells in the nervous system, is the next to form. This zone is located between the VZ and the MZ. D) In some parts of the neural tube, such as the spinal cord, the postmitotic cells derived from the VZ aggregate and mature in a densely populated IZ. E) In some areas, such as the dorsal thalamus, a second proliferative zone, the subventricular zone (SVZ), is formed between the VZ and the IZ. In the SVZ, interkinetic nuclear migration does not occur, instead mitotic figures (arrowheads) are found scattered throughout the thickness of the zone. (DNA synthesis also occurs throughout the thickness of the SVZ.) The postmitotic cells derived from both the VZ and SVZ aggregate and mature in a densely populated IZ. (Note, however, that any cells derived from the VZ must cross the SVZ.) F) In the hippocampus, the postmitotic cells derived from the VZ migrate across a sparsely populated IZ to form a cortical plate. G) In the cerebral cortex, postmitotic cells derived from both the VZ and SVZ migrate across a sparsely populated IZ to form a cortical plate. (From Nowakowski, R.S., & Hayes, N.L. [1999]. CNS development: An overview. *Development and Psychopathology, 11*[3], 395–417; reprinted by permission.)

the thalamus and midbrain, a second proliferating population appears, called the subventricular zone (SVZ). In these regions of the nervous system, the neurons exit the proliferating populations to occupy the inner part of the MZ. In the hippocampus (part of the archicortex), only the VZ forms, whereas in the neocortex, both the VZ and SVZ appear. In these two cortical regions, migration is an active process. The early born neurons occupy the deepest regions of the cortex, and the later born neurons occupy progressively more superficial regions of the cortex (thus moving past earlier migrated cells). It is important to note that in late development, just before birth in mice, in all of the CNS the proportion of daughter cells leaving VZ increases from 0% to 100%, at which point the VZ "disappears" (Nowakowski, 1987; Nowakowski & Rakic, 1981).

Through a series of experiments in which the cell cycle, its length, and the length of its phases have been measured systematically over the period of time during which neurons are produced, the basic quantitative features of neocortical development have been established (Caviness, Bhide, & Nowakowski, 2008; Caviness Jr. et al., 2003; Caviness Jr., Nowakowski, & Bhide, 2009; Nowakowski, 2006; Nowakowski, Caviness, Takahashi, & Hayes, 2002). These experiments have established that the mouse neocortex is produced in 11 cell cycles over a 6-day period. During this period, the cell cycle lengthens from about 8 hours to approximately 18 hours. Three of the phases of the cell cycle—S, G2, and M (see Figure 1.5)—remain approximately constant in length; however, G1 lengthens significantly, almost four fold.

Another aspect of the cell cycle that changes significantly during this 11–cell cycle period is the proportion of daughter cells that exits during each iteration of the cell cycle. This proportion increases systematically, and this increase is the crucial determinant of final regional neuron number. Understanding the coordinated change of cell-cycle length and cell-cycle exit fraction has allowed the development of a mathematical model that accounts for many of the major features of neocortical development (Nowakowski et al., 2002). Extrapolation of mouse neocortical development to the human

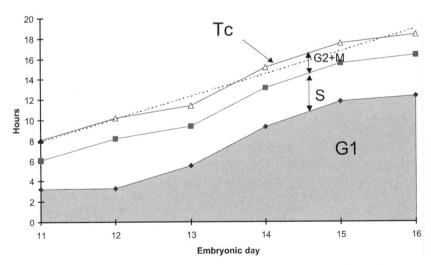

Figure 1.5. In the developing neocortex the cell cycle lengthens systematically over the course of the 6-day period during which neurons are produced. At the onset of E11, the length of the cell cycle (Tc) is ~8 hours and by the end of the E16 Tc it is over 18 hours. During this time the length of G2+M and S phases of the cell cycle do not change systematically, and, hence, most of the lengthening is within the G1 phase of the cell cycle. From these data, the total number of cell cycles during this period is calculated to be 11. (From Caviness Jr., V.S., Takahashi, T., & Nowakowski, R.S. [1995]. Numbers, time and neocortical neuronogenesis: A general developmental and evolutionary model. *Trends in Neurosciences, 18*[9], pp. 379–383; reprinted with permission.)

neocortex indicates that ~35 cell cycles would be necessary to make the much larger human neocortex. At each pass through the cell cycle, not only are different numbers of neurons produced but also the cell class and laminar destination of the neurons produced change systematically. The first neurons produced occupy the deep layers of the neocortex, whereas the later produced neurons occupy progressively more superficial layers. These features taken together indicate that the VZ changes dynamically during the period of neuronogenesis (whether 11 cell cycles in mice or 35 cell cycles in humans). The histological features of the VZ are constant throughout this period and, indeed, throughout the neuraxis. In other words, even as the quantitative and qualitative output of the VZ constantly changes, its own appearance with respect to how the cells look in a microscope remains relatively unchanged. However, the complexity of the VZ as revealed by microarray studies of gene expression shows that thousands of mRNA species—perhaps as many as one third of the genome—are expressed in the VZ and that many hundreds of these are developmentally regulated (i.e., change systematically during the developmental period; Nowakowski et al., unpublished results).

GENES AND BRAIN DEVELOPMENT

The involvement of thousands of mRNA species during neocortical development provides an enormous opportunity for genetic variation in the genome (i.e., mutations or polymorphisms) to significantly influence neocortical development. Advances in both mouse and human genetics have paved the way for an analysis of how this genomic variation could be related to variation in the structure of individual human brains (Altshuler et al., 2010; Frazer et al., 2007).

Given the fact that there are 25,000–40,000 genes in the mammalian genome, performing an analysis of the underlying genetic basis of brain structure variation is a daunting task. Nevertheless, mouse genetic resources allow us to begin this analysis. To begin to link the action of specific genes to brain structure, we have developed a new method of quantifying individual differences in the structure of the brain. We then use both specialized mouse genetic resources (recombinant inbred [RI] strains) and single nucleotide polymorphism (SNP) association to map genes that affect the size and shape of specific brain structures.

We have begun our analysis on the mouse hippocampus for two reasons. First, the hippocampus has a well-characterized morphology that is highly conserved in its basic organization across the mammalian species. Second, microarray data are available for 100 different inbred strains, including two sets of RI strains (CXB and BXD) and a small mouse diversity panel that consists of 8 of the 15 available sequenced strains of mice. We began by analyzing the online microarray data set, which consists of measured gene expression levels in the mouse hippocampus from 45,000 genes for 100 strains (Overall et al., 2009). We constructed a statistical screen to identify genes that exhibit only two levels of expression—that is, high and low. Such a dichotomous pattern is consistent with monogenic control of expression levels (Figure 1.6A). Using this screen, we identified 459 candidates (Figure 1.6B). This is approximately 1%–2% of the genome. Our statistical criteria were relatively stringent, so this represents a low estimate of the incidence of such monogenically controlled expression patterns. Moreover, it should be noted that the database used contains measurements only of genes expressed in the adult hippocampus.

In order to estimate the effects of genetic diversity on the morphology of a complex system, we developed a procedure for quantifying the

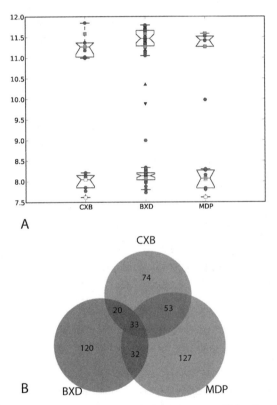

Figure 1.6. Gene expression differences in the hippocampus of inbred strains of mice. A) An example of the gene expression of a single transcript messenger RNA (mRNA) (for peroxiredoxin 2, Prdx2, Affymetrix probe # 1430979_a_at) as measured in the hippocampus of 99 different inbred strains of mice comprising three genetic groups. Only two levels of gene expression are found that is consistent with monogenic control of gene expression in all three groups. The graph shows the data for the CXB and BXD sets of recombinant inbred strains and for a mouse diversity panel (MDP) consisting of several other inbred strains. Strains with a high level of gene expression are shown with dark dots, and strains with a low level of gene expression are shown with a lighter dot. For the BXD strain there are also two F1 hybrids that show, as might be expected, an intermediate level of gene expression. The difference between the high and low gene expression levels is approximately 4 log (base 2) units or approximately 16-fold. B) A Venn diagram of all 490 transcripts (of ~45,000) that were found to have a pattern of monogenic control. The pattern in which all three genetic groups show the high/low dichotomy (as shown in A) was found for 33 transcripts.

morphological differences in the hippocampus (Mo & Nowakowski, 2012). This analysis was performed in the 13 CXB RI strains and the 2 progenitor strains C57BL/6J and BALB/ByJ. All mice were males, 60 days of age. The hippocampus in each of the 15 strains was characterized by making 96 measurements on a single horizontal section passing through the posterior commissure. These measurements were sufficient to distinguish without error all 15 strains from one another using a discriminant analysis (Table 1.1). We then treated each of the 96 measurements as a phenotype or trait. Genomewide association of the morphological data with SNP data showed that of the 96 traits analyzed, 73 were associated with one or more significant or suggestive quantitative trait locus (QTL). It is interesting to note that only 1 of the 96 traits is possibly monogenic; the others showed a heritability pattern that is probably oligogenic, and most indicated a digenic pattern. Many of the traits were well correlated with several other traits, and many of the correlated traits were associated with the same significant or suggestive QTL.

This analysis clearly shows that the genetics underlying the morphological differences in the CXB mice are significantly more complex than the genetics of mRNA expression in that most of the morphological differences appear to be controlled by two to three different loci. Despite these limitations, our analysis shows that, in general, a significant proportion of the differences in the size and shape of any specific brain structure is regulated by a small number of genetic loci (although usually more than one).

This morphological work has so far been confined to mice, but also both the anatomical methods and the SNP-association method are easily adapted to humans. Preliminary studies on human brains indicate that the range of morphological variation in humans is at least as great as what we have observed in mice. Also, the genes that affect morphological traits such as size and shape of structures are likely to be active during the developmental period, indicating that genetic diversity can literally change the anatomy of the brain.

This analysis in mice can be extended to humans by considering the relationship between an inbred strain and the wild-type condition. Generally, mice bred for use in the laboratory have been inbred by brother–sister mating for many generations. Many dozens of inbred strains have been created in this way (Beck et al., 2000). The process of inbreeding forces genes to homozygosity. This means that any given inbred strain is homozygous at virtually every locus in the genome. Humans and wild-type mice are, in contrast, heterozygous at many loci. This means that an inbred strain has, in effect, half of the genetic diversity found in any wild-type mouse or individual human. In other words, each inbred strain of mouse equals one half of a human, at least from this simple genetic perspective. Conversely, this means that two different humans will be at least twice as diverse as the difference between two inbred strains of mice. It stands to reason that we should expect at

Table 1.1. Discriminant analysis classification table. This discriminant analysis table shows that the 96 measured morphological traits are sufficient to uniquely identify all of the members of the CXB set of recombinant inbred strains.

Strain	BALB/c	C57BL/6	CXB-01	CXB-02	CXB-03	CXB-04	CXB-05	CXB-06	CXB-07	CXB-08	CXB-09	CXB-10	CXB-11	CXB-12	CXB-13	Correctly classified
BALB/c	12	0	0	0	0	0	0	0	0	0	0	0	0	0	0	1
C57BL/6	0	12	0	0	0	0	0	0	0	0	0	0	0	0	0	1
CXB-01	0-	0	12	0	0	0	0	0	0	0	0	0	0	0	0	1
CXB-02	0	0	0	12	0	0	0	0	0	0	0	0	0	0	0	1
CXB-03	0	0	0	0	12	0	0	0	0	0	0	0	0	0	0	1
CXB-04	0	0	0	0	0	12	0	0	0	0	0	0	0	0	0	1
CXB-05	0	0	0	0	0	0	12	0	0	0	0	0	0	0	0	1
CXB-06	0	0	0	0	0	0	0	12	0	0	0	0	0	0	0	1
CXB-07	0	0	0	0	0	0	0	0	12	0	0	0	0	0	0	1
CXB-08	0	0	0	0	0	0	0	0	0	12	0	0	0	0	0	1
CXB-09	0	0	0	0	0	0	0	0	0	0	12	0	0	0	0	1
CXB-10	0	0	0	0	0	0	0	0	0	0	0	12	0	0	0	1
CXB-11	0	0	0	0	0	0	0	0	0	0	0	0	12	0	0	1
CXB-12	0	0	0	0	0	0	0	0	0	0	0	0	0	12	0	1
CXB-13	0	0	0	0	0	0	0	0	0	0	0	0	0	0	12	1
Overall correct classification rate																1

least 2%–4% of the genes expressed in the human hippocampus to have monogenic expression levels.

Moreover, results emerging from the 1000 Genomes Project study of human genetic variation (Altshuler et al., 2010) indicate that the human population is at least twice as variable in terms of the simple measure of SNP variants (15 million versus 8 million found in mice) (Frazer et al., 2007). The combination of genomewide heterozygosity and twice as much population variance suggests that in humans the number of genes with such monogenically controlled expression levels is likely to be much higher than the murine level 1%–2% of the genome, perhaps as high as 4%–8%.

CONCLUSION

We envision that it will be possible to use genetic differences in inbred strains of mice, as well as in humans, as a sort of "Rosetta Stone" to translate information collected in various ways and with a variety of methods, that is, across a variety of traits, including mRNA expression levels, morphological traits, pathologies, and even behaviors. To make this translation, a comprehensive analysis of quantitative traits could be used to match each of the various types of traits to the genome (Figure 1.7). Traits that map to different sites in the genome—that is, that are *not* colocalized—would definitively be shown to be under the control of different genetic loci. In contrast, traits that map to the same genetic loci, that is, that are colocalized, would be candidates for coordinated control by that single locus. The tremendous homology between the mouse and human genome, and among vertebrate species in general, potentially provides a way to bridge the gap between basic science research and

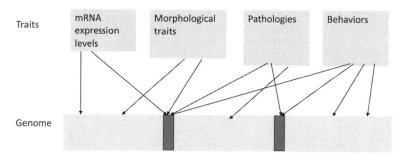

Colocalization → Candidates for causality

Lack of colocalization → Definitively unrelated!

Figure 1.7. Genome as the Rosetta Stone. Genotype/phenotype analysis makes it possible to use the genome as the "Rosetta Stone"—that is, as a platform upon which causal relationships between phenotypes can be eliminated or established. Phenotypes that colocalize to the same genetic locus are candidates for having a common cause. In contrast, phenotypes that localize to different genetic loci are thereby shown to be definitively unrelated.

translational research quickly. The combination of genomewide approaches to understand the development and function of the human brain and approaches using human genetics (Skiba, Landi, Wagner, & Grigorenko, 2011), as well as the use of animal models such as mouse knockouts and knockins (see Chapter 2), will in the next few years contribute significantly to the understanding of dyslexia and other disorders of reading and language.

REFERENCES

Altshuler, D., Durbin, R.M., Abecasis, G.R., Bentley, D.R., Chakravarit, A., Clark, A.G., … Cartwright, R.A. (2010). A map of human genome variation from population-scale sequencing. *Nature, 467*(7319), 1061–1073. doi:10.1038/nature09534

Beck, J.A., Lloyd, S., Hafezparast, M., Lennon-Pierce, M., Eppig, J.T., Festing, M.F., & Fisher, E.M.C. (2000). Genealogies of mouse inbred strains. *Nature Genetics, 24*(1), 23–25.

Caviness, V.S., Bhide, P.G., & Nowakowski, R.S. (2008). Histogenetic processes leading to the laminated neocortex: Migration is only a part of the story. *Developmental Neuroscience, 30*(1–3), 82–95. doi:10.1159/000109854

Caviness, V.S., Jr., Goto, T., Tarui, T., Takahashi, T., Bhide, P.G., & Nowakowski, R.S. (2003). Cell output, cell cycle duration and neuronal specification: A model of integrated mechanisms of the neocortical proliferative process. *Cerebral Cortex, 13*(6), 592–598. doi:10.1093/cercor/13.6.592

Caviness, V.S., Jr., Nowakowski, R.S., & Bhide, P.G. (2009). Neocortical neurogenesis: Morphogenetic gradients and beyond. *Trends in Neuroscience, 32*(8), 443–450. doi:10.1016/j.tins.2009.05.003

Caviness, V.S., Jr., Takahashi, T., & Nowakowski, R.S. (1995). Numbers, time and neocortical neuronogenesis: A general developmental and evolutionary model. *Trends in Neuroscience, 18*(9), 379–383.

Frazer, K.A., Eskin, E., Kang, H.M., Bogue, M.A., Hinds, D.A., Beilharz, E.J., … Cox, D.R. (2007). A sequence-based variation map of 8.27 million SNPs in inbred mouse strains. *Nature, 448*(7157), 1050–1053. doi:10.1038/nature06067

Mo, Z., Hayes, N.L., & Nowakowski, R.S. (2012). Phenomic analysis of the mouse hippocampus and dentate gyrus.

Nowakowski, R.S. (1987). Basic concepts of CNS development. *Child Development, 58*(3), 568–595. doi:10.2307/1130199

Nowakowski, R.S. (2006). Stable neuron numbers from cradle to grave. *Proceedings of the National Academy of Sciences, USA, 103*(33), 12219–12220. doi:10.1073/pnas.0605605103

Nowakowski, R.S., Araki, K.Y., Stein-O'Brien, G.L., Cai, L., Bhide, P.G., and Caviness, V.S., Jr. (2009). The transcriptome of the murine neocortical PVE. Unpublished.

Nowakowski, R.S., Caviness, V.S., Jr., Takahashi, T., & Hayes, N.L. (2002). Population dynamics during cell proliferation and neuronogenesis in the developing murine neocortex. *Results and Problems in Cell Differentiation, 39,* 1–25.

Nowakowski, R.S., & Hayes, N.L. (1999). CNS development: An overview. *Development and Psychopathology, 11*(3), 395–417. doi:10.1017/S0954579499002126

Nowakowski, R.S., & Rakic, P. (1981). The site of origin and route and rate of migration of neurons to the hippocampal region of the rhesus monkey. *The Journal of Comparative Neurology, 196*(1), 129–154. doi:10.1002/cne.901960110

Overall, R.W., Kempermann, G., Peirce, J., Lu, L., Goldowitz, D., Gage, F.H., … Williams, R.W. (2009). Genetics of the hippocampal transcriptome in mouse: a systematic survey and online neurogenomics resource. *Frontiers in Neurogenomics, 3*(55), 1-10

Skiba, T., Landi, N., Wagner, R., & Grigorenko, E.L. (2011). In search of the perfect phenotype: An analysis of linkage and association studies of reading and reading-related processes. *Behavior Genetics, 41*(1), 6–30. doi:10.1007/s10519-011-9444-7

CHAPTER 2

Loss of the Dyslexia Susceptibility Gene DCDC2 Increases Synaptic Connectivity in the Mouse Neocortex

Joseph LoTurco, Aarti Tarkar, and Alicia Yue Che

A BRIEF HISTORY ON THE GENETICS OF DYSLEXIA

As early as 1896, W.P. Morgan noted that dyslexia tends to run in families. A genetic reason for this association was subsequently demonstrated by twin studies carried out in the 1950s showing that monozygotic twins, unlike fraternal twins, had a nearly 100% concordance for dyslexia (Hallgren, 1950; Hermann, 1956; Hermann and Norrie, 1958). Such a shared risk for twins with largely identical genes seemed to indicate a wholly genetic cause of dyslexia. Results from later and larger twin studies, however, have shown that the genetic heritability is significantly less than 100% and is actually between 30% and 60% (Alarcon & De-Fries, 1997; Bakwin, 1973; Decker & Vandenberg, 1985; DeFries, Fulker, & LaBuda, 1987; DeFries & Gillis, 1991; Harlaar, Spinath, Dale, & Plomin, 2005; Hawke, Wadsworth, & DeFries, 2006; Hohnen & Stevenson, 1999; LaBuda & DeFries, 1988; Pennington & Gilger, 1996; Stevenson, Graham, Fredman, & McLoughlin, 1987). Although still high, the large range of estimated heritability likely indicates that the genetic risk of dyslexia is complex and modifiable by a variety of interacting environmental factors. Dyslexia now serves as a familiar example of complex behavioral traits that have strong, and perhaps inseparable, genetic and environmental causes. In order to understand such traits, it becomes essential to first understand the function of risk genes and then determine how environmental experience modifies the function of such genes.

The phenomenal progress of genetic research, culminating in the sequencing of the entire human genome in 2000, made possible powerful genetic studies that have resulted in the identification of specific chromosomal regions linked to dyslexia and the identification of individual genes associated with dyslexia. Nine chromosomal loci have now been identified, *DYX1–DYX9*. Of these, four—1p34-p36 (*DYX8*), 2p (*DYX3*), 6p21.3 (*DYX2*), and 15q21 (*DYX1*)—have been replicated by several groups. More recently, single genes that code for known proteins

This work was supported by grants from the Eunice Kennedy Shriver National Institute of Child Health and Development, National Institutes of Health.

have been identified within the *DYX1* and *DYX2* loci on chromosomes 6 and 15 respectively. The three genes in these loci with the strongest association to dyslexia are *KIAA0319* and *DCDC2* on chromosome 6 and *DYX1C1* on chromosome 15. The functions of the proteins coded by these three genes are now becoming increasingly well defined. Other genes have now also been linked to dyslexia, however, as of 2011, these others still await confirmation in more than one study population and so will not be considered in this chapter.

IDENTIFICATION AND FUNCTION OF DYSLEXIA-ASSOCIATED GENES

The identification of candidate genes *DYX1C1*, *KIAA0319*, and *DCDC2* presented new opportunities to begin to test hypotheses for cellular causes of dyslexia. In a series of experiments using in utero RNAi for rodent homologs of these genes in rats, all three candidate genes were shown to play a role in neuronal migration (Burbridge et al., 2008; Meng, Smith, et al., 2005; Paracchini et al., 2006; Rosen et al., 2007; Threlkeld et al., 2007; Wang et al., 2006). In these studies, when dyslexia-associated genes were targeted by RNAi in a subset of developing neurons in the cerebral neocortex, targeted neurons would fail to migrate appropriately into the cerebral neocortex.

The results from the RNAi neuronal migration experiments have been used to support a possible common explanation for a developmental defect that could explain dyslexia. There are, however, important limitations in these experiments that must be considered before altered migration is accepted as a unifying biological explanation for dyslexia. By design, and guided by one specific hypothesis, the RNAi studies focused specifically on a function in neuronal migration and were not a comprehensive test of the biological roles for these three dyslexia-associated genes. The method used—in utero RNAi—alters only a subset of developing neurons and is therefore not a genetic manipulation that affects all of the cells in a developing organism. Studies of this type are not comprehensive and cannot identify changes besides those in migration or differentiation of neocortical pyramidal neurons. For example, the in utero RNAi method could not reveal a role in the very earliest periods of development. The results from the in utero RNAi experiments do indicate a function in developing neurons but also they should not be interpreted as indicating that the only role of dyslexia-associated genes is in neuronal migration.

Genetic knockout experiments are required to comprehensively determine the requirement of any gene in developing or mature organisms. Only recently have results from such experiments begun to emerge for dyslexia-associated genes. In our lab, in the past year we have begun to assess the effects of deleting two rodent homologs for dyslexia-associated genes in mice, *DYX1C1* and *DCDC2*, in order to comprehensively determine their functions. The initial findings using genetic deletion reveal a more complicated role for dyslexia-associated genes than solely neuronal migration.

DYX1C1: The First Dyslexia-Associated Gene

DYX1C1, the first gene linked to dyslexia, was identified when researchers discovered a chromosomal translocation and gene truncation present in some members of two Finnish families with a history of dyslexia (Nopola-Hemmi et al., 2000; Nothen et al., 1999; Schulte-Korne et al., 1998; Smith et al., 1983). Closer examination of the translocation revealed a breakpoint that disrupted the gene EKN1, which was renamed Dyslexia Susceptibility 1 Candidate 1 (*DYX1C1*). Although this initial study showed a significant association in two relatively small Finnish samples (Taipale et al., 2003), several subsequent studies in populations in the United Kingdom, United States, and Italy did not find a significant association with dyslexia risk (Cope, Harold, et al., 2005; Marino et al., 2005; Meng, Hager, et al., 2005). Studies of a German sample population and additional U.S. sample populations, however, have shown that one of the dyslexia-related single nucleotide polymorphisms (SNPs) in *DYX1C1* does associate with dyslexia (Brkanac et al., 2007; Dahdouh et al., 2009). In addition, a study of the same Italian sample, in which a family-based association between *DYX1C1*-risk alleles and dyslexia was not found, did find a significant association with verbal short-term memory (Marino et al., 2007), an endophenotype (or "intermediate phenotype") of dyslexia (Marino et al., 2007). Moreover, a study evaluating *DYX1C1*, this time in a large Australian sample population, discovered a novel missense mutation was found to reliably associate with risk for dyslexia (Bates et al., 2009). In fact this study reports the first association with dyslexia and a specific mutation that would result in an altered amino acid sequence in the protein dyx1c1. Although there has been a mixture of positive and negative results for *DYX1C1* in different populations and studies, results from more than 1,000 individuals now supports a *DYX1C1* association with dyslexia. Thus, to date, the first identified dyslexia gene, *DYX1C1*, still has the strongest support for a link to dyslexia.

A beginning understanding of the function of the *dyx1c1* protein has come from several different studies that indicate a link to multiple intracellular pathways. The protein domains of *dyx1c1* include an N-terminal p23 and three C-terminal tetratricopeptide repeat (TPR) domains. The N-terminal p23 domain of *dyx1c1* protein, when overexpressed in cell lines, can interact with Hsp70, Hsp90, and CHIP, an E-3 ubiquitin ligase, suggesting that the protein may be involved in degradation of unfolded proteins (Hatakeyama, Matsumoto, Yada, & Nakayama, 2004). Recently, *dyx1c1* has been shown to be involved in the degradation of the estrogen receptor potentially through its interaction with CHIP (Massinen et al., 2009). Expression of *dyx1c1* protein has also been shown to be predictive as a cancer biomarker, and its expression is upregulated in several types of cancer cells, including breast and colon cancer (Chen et al., 2009; Kim et al., 2008). These findings suggest that the cellular functions of *dyx1c1* protein could be diverse and linked to receptor function, protein degradation, and cell proliferation and differentiation.

In vivo RNAi studies that address the hypothesis that *DYX1C1* may play a role in migration have shown that if a cohort of newly produced neurons are transfected with plasmids that induce RNAi to knockdown *dyx1c1* expression, then neurons become arrested in their normal migration path and attain altered multipolar morphologies (Wang et al., 2006). Wang et al. went on to show that the TPR domains of *dyx1c1* are critical to migration, in that mutations missing the TPR domains failed to rescue migration in the altered cohort of neurons, whereas expression of the TPR domains alone were sufficient to restore normal migration. In a follow-up study, Rosen et al. (2007) examined what the final malformation profile would be for brains in which *DYX1C1* was knocked down. Although the embryo knockdown created a nearly uniform arrest in migration, most neurons restarted their migration and attained positions similar to control treated neurons by juvenile postnatal ages. Distinct malformation types were also found to occur with some variety in different animals treated with *DYX1C1* RNAi. These malformations included heterotopia in white matter, ectopia in layer one of the neocortex, and hippocampal heterotopia with dysplasia. Behavioral assays of animals with *DYX1C1* RNAi–induced malformations have revealed impairments in auditory processing, short-term memory, and changes in spatial learning correlated specifically with the presence of hippocampal heterotopia (Szalkowski et al., 2011; Threlkeld et al., 2007; see Chapter 11). Cooccurrence of white matter heterotopia with superficial malformations, ectopia, and microgyria have been reported in certain human malformation syndromes (Wieck et al., 2005). Overall the experiments with *DYX1C1* knockdown are in surprising agreement with the neuronal migration hypothesis of dyslexia. In particular, the occurrence of diverse malformation types, including ectopia, is consistent with dyslexia studies in humans (Galaburda, 1988; Galaburda & Kemper, 1979).

New Insights of Function from Studies of *DYX1C1* Mutant Mice

As discussed, the focused RNAi approach does not address the complete in vivo role of *DYX1C1* or any gene. The absolute and comprehensive function of a gene can only be determined by making genetic mutations. In mammals, typically such approaches and mutations are made in mice, although germline mutation approaches are now also available for rats. Our lab has now begun to study and characterize the first mutant mouse lines that have nonfunctional copies of the *DYX1C1* gene. When mice are missing one copy or this gene, they appear to develop normally with no obvious impairments in development. In stark contrast, when both copies of the *DYX1C1* gene are deleted, mice show a severe developmental defect that includes alterations in the brain and visceral organs. Dramatically, mutants lacking two functional copies of *DYX1C1* show complete situs inversus, a condition in which all thoracic organs, including the heart, liver, lung, spleen, stomach, and colon (which normally show a left–right asymmetry), are inverted such that all organs are reversed (i.e., the heart is now on the right side instead of the left). These studies reveal that indeed *DYX1C1* has a role in very early development that precedes a function in the migration of neurons.

This surprising left–right reversal in asymmetry in the *DYX1C1* knockouts may provide a link to theories of dyslexia that suggest impairment in normal asymmetry in brain function. Although situs inversus in humans is rare and does not alter the lateralization of the planum temporale or cerebral dominance (Kennedy et al., 1999), situs inversus does result in a reversal of the frontal and occipital petalia (Ihara et al., 2009; Kennedy et al., 1999). An interesting possibility, therefore, is that decreases in *DYX1C1* function may create mismatches between different brain asymmetries. Such a mismatch between neural asymmetries in different brain regions could result in neural circuits that are not optimized for learning. Given the phenotype of *DYX1C1* mutant mice, investigation of changes in brain asymmetries at different levels is warranted in dyslexic individuals carrying the *DYX1C1* alleles associated with dyslexia.

In addition to situs inversus, *DYX1C1* mutant mice develop severe hydrocephaly over the second postnatal week after birth. This type of neural phenotype is typically associated with a defect in cilia motility in the cerebral aqueduct, which is required for proper circulation of cerebral spinal fluid. In fact, both situs inversus and hydrocephaly are conditions that are often comorbid in primary cilia dyskinesias (PCDs) (Filegauf, Benzing, & Omran, 2007). Left–right asymmetry of visceral organs is determined by the action of cilia in the very early embryo at the ventral node, and cilia are similarly required for normal flow of cerebral spinal fluid. Hydrocephaly in children, even when successfully treated without significantly decreased IQ outcome, has been associated with persistent defects in reading and other reading-based impairments (Barnes, Faulkner, Wilkinson, & Dennis, 2004; Prigatano et al., 1983). Although many more analyses are yet to be done on this new mouse mutant, these early observations indicate that *DYX1C1* has many important roles in early development that go beyond a role in neuronal migration. Sorting through which of these required functions of *DYX1C1* are linked to neural functions necessary to sensory processing and learning will be critical next steps.

KIAA0319 and *DCDC2*: The Dyslexia-Associated Genes on Chromosome 6

DYX2, on chromosome 6p, is the most replicated of *DYX* loci in the genome and has been linked with both global and component phenotypes of dyslexia (Cardon et al., 1994, 1995; Fisher et al., 1999; Grigorenko et al., 1997; Kaplan et al., 2002; Smith, Kimberling, & Pennington, 1991). Two peaks of genetic association have been identified within *DYX2* that include the genes *KIAA0319* and *DCDC2* (Kaplan et al., 2002; Meng, Hager, et al., 2005).

KIAA0319   In 2002, Kaplan et al. (2002) showed a peak of association at a marker in the 5′ untranslated region of *KIAA0319*. In 2004, a study by Francks et al. showed a peak of association in a 77 thousand base pair region containing the first four exons of *KIAA0319*, and this was replicated by Cope, Harold, et al. (2005) using a dense set of SNPs to further identify a risk haplotype in the same region. The risk haplotype was later shown to be related to a selective decrease in the expression of *KIAA0319* but not other genes in the locus (Harold et al., 2006). The risk haplotype of *KIAA0319* that includes the promoter region has now been shown to confer reduced promoter activity and an aberrant binding site for the transcriptional silencer OCT-1 (Dennis et al., 2009). Genetic variation within *KIAA0319* has been correlated with the range of variation in normal reading ability (Paracchini et al., 2008), further strengthening the association between *KIAA0319* and reading.

The *KIAA0319* gene encodes an integral membrane protein with a large extracellular domain, a single transmembrane domain, and a small intracellular C-terminus. There are several splice variants of *kiaa0319* (Velayos-Baeza, Toma, da Roza, Paracchini, & Monaco, 2007), all of which are glycosylated, and one form is secreted (Velayos-Baeza, Toma, Paracchini, & Monaco, 2008). The extracellular domain has a consensus signal peptide and 5 PKD domains. PKD domains in the polycytsin 1 protein are involved in adhesion between kidney cells and so may be important to cell adhesion (Silberberg, Charron, Bacallao, & Wandinger-Ness, 2005). To date there is only one defined protein interactor of *kiaa0319* protein, adaptor protein-2 (AP-2), which is part of the endosomal pathway (Levecque, Velayos-Baeza, Holloway, & Monaco, 2009). In addition, Velayos-Baeza et al. (2009) discovered that *kiaa0319* protein in proteolyticly cleaved at the plasma membrane and so can be secreted into the extracellular space. The structure, membrane localization, and emerging cell biology of *kiaa0319* protein are consistent with it being a new class of neural cell adhesion molecule that exists as a secreted and nonsecreted form, and so may be involved in both adhesion and in signaling between cells.

KIAA0319 expression was targeted with RNAi in migrating neocortical neurons in rats to test for a potential role in migration. Similar to *DYX1C1*, RNAi knockdown of *KIAA0319* interrupted and slowed neuronal migration (Paracchini et al., 2006). However, *KIAA0319* knockdown—in contrast to knockdown of *DCDC2* and *DYX1C1*—created a distinct cellular phenotype: Disrupted neurons appeared to lose their normal radial association and radial glial fibers, and migrating neurons were often found orthogonal to the radial glia scaffold that they typically migrate along (Paracchini et al., 2006). A knockout mouse for

KIAA0319 is currently under production; however, as of now, there is no information on the effect of *kiaa0319* protein loss on overall developmental pattern and function.

DCDC2   Meng et al. (2005) reported the first association of *DCDC2* with dyslexia. These investigators identified a deletion and compound short tandem repeat (STR) in intron 2 of *DCDC2*, a gene located 500 kb from *KIAA0319*. The STR in *DCDC2* showed a significant association with dyslexia in a cohort of 153 American dyslexic families (Meng, Hager, et al., 2005), and an association with *DCDC2* was independently confirmed in a German population (Schumacher et al., 2006). In this same association study, a haplotype within *DCDC2* was identified in the German sample that showed association directly proportional to the severity of dyslexia (Schumacher et al., 2006). In a large study population of Australians with dyslexia and case controls, *DCDC2* was associated with variation in the range of reading abilities (Lind et al., 2010). Together, the genetic association studies to date provide the strongest support for *DYX1C1* and *DCDC2*, because independent research groups studying separate large populations have found the associations for these two genes.

Of the dyslexia-associated genes, *DCDC2*, by membership in a gene family of well-studied function, was suspected a priori to have a role in the migration of neurons in the cerebral neocortex. *DCDC2* is one of an 11-member group of proteins distinguished by the presence of DCX, or doublecortin domains (Coquelle et al., 2006; Reiner et al., 2006). The first characterized gene of this family, *DCX*, was identified by the discovery that mutations in *DCX* cause double cortex syndrome in females and lissencephaly in males (Barkovich & Kuzniecky, 2000; Gleeson, Lin, Flanagan, & Walsh, 1999). The dcx domain is critical for binding to and stabilizing microtubules and is regulated by phosphorylation (Gleeson et al., 1999). At least two members of this family, *DCX* and *DCLK*, have now been found to interact genetically in mice in neuronal migration in the cerebral cortex (Deuel et al., 2006; Koizumi, Tanaka, & Gleeson, 2006). Moreover, in a study comparing the biochemical and cellular functions of proteins in the *dcx* family, it was found that *dcdc2* exhibits similar molecular properties and cellular functions to *dclk* and *dcx* proteins (Coquelle et al., 2006).

Based on the similarity of structure and function between *dcdc2* and *dcx* proteins, Meng et al. (2005) hypothesized that *DCDC2* may play a role in neuronal migration. Using an RNAi approach targeting *DCDC2* expression in migrating neocortical neurons in the embryonic rat neocortex, we found that knockdown of *DCDC2* interrupted neuronal migration (Meng et al., 2005). Extending the initial RNAi studies, Burbridge et al. (2008) showed that the migration disruptions caused by knockdown of *DCDC2* resulted in diverse disruptions similar—but not identical—to those created by *DYX1C1* knockdown (Burbridge et al., 2008). Knockdown of *DCDC2* caused both scattered heterotopia within the white matter and a population of neurons to overmigrate to ectopic positions in the neocortex.

New Insights of Function from Study of *DCDC2* Mutant Mice

In order to investigate the developmental role of *DCDC2* in a more comprehensive fashion, we have produced a knockout mouse missing the *DCDC2* gene. Homozygous mutants, lacking *dcdc2* function, show a slight delay in growth in the first postnatal weeks after birth. On average, the knockout mutants are 10% smaller than animals without mutations in *DCDC2*. The mutants show no apparent disruptions in neuronal migration or neurogenesis in the neocortex. The brains display normal neuronal positions in all neocortical lamina and are indistinguishable by gross and cellular measures of morphology. This result at first would seem to contradict the results obtained with RNAi against *DCDC2* in the rat. However, *dcdc2* function may follow a precedent similar to *DCX*, a gene that when knocked out in mice shows little migration defect in the neocortex, but when targeted with RNAi in the rat shows a profound defect in migration. These findings for *DCX* have led to the conclusion that either *DCX* has a species-specific function or that RNAi reveals migration defects because only a subpopulation of neurons are targeted. To determine whether *DCDC2* has species-specific function, we attempted to reproduce the RNAi experiments in mice. We found that, whereas RNAi against *DCDC2* in embryonic rats impairs migration, the same RNAi that targets *DCDC2* expression in embryonic mouse neurons has no effect on migration. This finding indicates that indeed, similar to *DCX*, *DCDC2* has a species-specific requirement in neuronal migration. It remains unknown whether *DCDC2* plays an obligate role in migration in human neurons.

DCDC2 Function in Cellular Neurophysiology

A goal of any explanatory model for the function of dyslexia-associated genes must be to link the function of that gene to some alteration in the function of neural circuits. Such alterations could take the form of any combination of changes in connectivity, synaptic plasticity, or intrinsic electrophysiological properties of neurons—all of which could alter synaptic processing and/or learning. For example, the neuronal migration hypothesis for dyslexia susceptibility proposes that changes in neuronal placement have effects on the development of connectivity within neocortical circuits. Indeed, consistent with this link between migration and altered circuit physiologies, it is well established that disruptions in neuronal migration in the neocortex invariably result in heighted neuronal excitability and in many cases epileptiform activity. Although there is a clear association between migration abnormalities and functional circuit abnormalities, it cannot be ruled out that genes with function initially in the placement and migration of neurons may have a second fundamental function later in the development on the electrophysiology of neurons.

As already mentioned, mice lacking functional copies of the *DCDC2* gene have structurally normal brains without apparent migration abnormalities. This allows us to initiate an electrophysiological analysis without confounds related to changes in migration. We can, therefore, assess whether loss of *DCDC2* has primary electrophysiological effects in neuronal circuits.

In order to test for changes in the electrophysiology in *DCDC2*-mutant mice, we made whole-cell patch-clamp recordings from pyramidal neurons in layer 2/3 of the somatosensory neocortex. In recordings of more than 60 neurons in both *DCDC2* mutants and nonmutants, we found consistent and significant alterations in the physiology of individual neocortical neurons. These differences include elevation of the resting membrane potential, increased spontaneous synaptic activity (Figure 2.1), and changes in temporal properties of action potential firing rates (Figure 2.2). We also found significant increases in spontaneous glutamatergic synaptic activity in *DCDC2* knockouts compared with controls without mutation, but we found no significant changes in the amplitude of spontaneous synaptic events. The increased frequency of synaptic events typically reflects either increases in the number of synapses or more active synapses.

In order to determine whether neurons in *DCDC2* knockout have intrinsic differences in their responses to inputs, we delivered a series of intracellular stimulation pulses and assessed the action potential firing rates and patterns of impulses in neurons. Our reasoning was that if cells have an intrinsic change in response, independent of synaptic input, then such an intrinsic change would alter responses to nonsynaptic input. As shown in Figure 2.2A, neurons in the *DCDC2* mutant animals consistently fired more action potentials. Although such an increase in rate might be expected to enhance the detection of a stimulus, it is also possible that the increased sensitivity and response increase the "noise" in a synaptic circuit, because even nonoptimal stimuli may initiate strong responses.

A prominent and well-supported explanation for learning deficits in dyslexia and specific language impairments is that deficits in temporal processing in developing neural circuits impede the ability to make associations between speech sounds and written language (Tallal, 1980; Tallal, Miller, & Fitch, 1993). The ability to make consistent temporally based associations in any neural circuit depends on a degree of temporal precision in the firing patterns of neurons. As learning in such circuits requires cotemporaneous synaptic events, as well a consistency in the temporal signature of any repeated signal, neurons need to have a reliable temporal response to the same stimulus from trial to trial. We therefore tested whether neurons in the *DCDC2* mutant, compared with wild type, would show any difference in the trial-to-trial temporal precision in action potentials elicited by the same stimulus delivered to neurons. As shown in Figure 2.2, we have discovered a dramatic

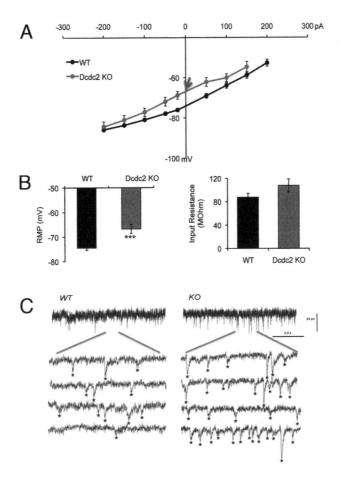

Figure 2.1. Mutation in the *Dcdc2* gene causes changes in the electrophysiology of neocortical pyramidal neurons. A) Voltage-current relationship for neurons of WT and KO mice show that the mutant cells (KO) are more depolarized but have similar passive-membrane properties. B) Bar graphs showing the significant change in the resting membrane potential in the KO relative to the WT, and a lack of a significant difference in the input resistance. C) Examples of current traces showing the spontaneous-synaptic activity in mutants and WT cells. The currents were recorded in the presence of TTX to block spontaneous action potentials and SR to block inhibitory synaptic currents. The traces show that there is a significant increase in the frequency of spontaneous-synaptic currents (*) in the KO neurons. (*Key:* KO, knockout or mutant; SR, SR-95531; TTX, tetrodotoxin; WT, wild type or nonmutant.)

difference in the temporal precision in responses in *DCDC2* mutant and nonmutant neocortical neurons. Cells in the mutant show a high degree of stimulus-to-stimulus variation. Thus, the intrinsic electrophysiological state of neocortical pyramidal neurons lacking *DCDC2* is not compatible with accurately repeatable temporal patterns of neural impulses. The significance of this alteration to sensory processing or learning is not yet known, but in models of circuit function, a loss of stimulus-to-stimulus

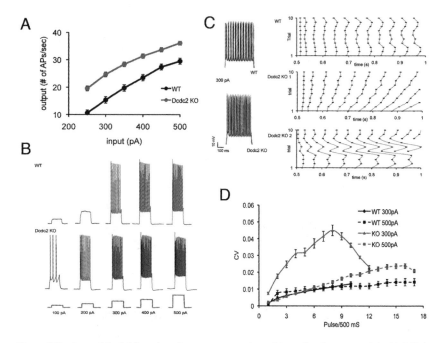

Figure 2.2.   Loss of *Dcdc2* function changes temporal precision of action potentials. A) Cells in the KO fire more action potentials to a range of inputs than do cells from WT animals. B) Example traces showing the increases in action potential firing rates. C) Example of trial-to-trial variation in KO and WT cells. The traces are 10 consecutive-overlayed responses showing an increase in variation in when action potentials occur in the KO. This increased variability is also shown in the graphs to the right that plot the time of occurrence of each action potential in 10 consecutive stimuli. Two patterns of degraded precision are shown for the knockout. In one pattern the action potentials are progressively more delayed in each consecutive trial, and in the second (lower graph in C) the action potentials occur at a range of variable rates from trial to trial. D) A plot showing the dramatic increase in the coefficient of variation in the time when action potentials in a train occur in WT and KO pyramidal neurons. (*Key:* KO, knockout; WT, wild type.)

temporal precision would be predicted to significantly degrade accurate stimulus detection and stimulus-specific learning to rapidly changing stimuli.

CONCLUSIONS AND FUTURE PERSPECTIVES

It is now clear that the disruption of genes associated with dyslexia have effects on neurodevelopment. The initial biological explanations based primarily on RNAi studies emphasized a common role of dyslexia-associated genes in the migration of neurons. These experiments, however, were deliberately designed to test only a function in neuronal migration (by transfecting only cortical migrating neurons). The first studies using more comprehensive and complete methods to eliminate the function of the two dyslexia-associated genes in mice, *DYX1C1* and *DCDC2*, now show that the functions of dyslexia-associated genes are more complex and diverse. *DYX1C1* has a primary and initial role in left–right developmental patterning, whereas a primary function of *DCDC2* appears to be in the electrophysiology of neurons, absent an early developmental role.

The identification of specific neurodevelopmental disruptions associated with the loss of function of dyslexia-associated genes is only the beginning of a mechanistic understanding of dyslexia. Functional neurophysiological studies in humans are needed to connect developmental disruptions in neuronal patterning or electrophysiology to function within cortical circuits involved in reading. Work with animal genetic models is required to define in detail the specific cellular neurophysiological and circuitry changes that follow interruption of dyslexia genes. Understanding the cellular disruptions in animal models could help to define critical periods of intervention and may identify physiological mechanisms that could be targeted to enhance early education-based remediation. For example, the changes in temporal precision in neurons in the *DCDC2* knockout could point to the value of remediation methods that involve using stimuli or training methods that make stimuli more easily distinguishable with clinical applications to human populations.

REFERENCES

Alarcón, M., & DeFries, J.C. (1997). Reading performance and general cognitive ability in twins with reading difficulties and control pairs. *Personality and Individual Differences, 22,* 793–803. doi:10.1016/S0191-8869(96)00267-X

Bakwin, H. (1973). Reading disability in twins. *Developmental Medicine and Child Neurology, 15,* 184–187. doi:10.1111/j.1469-8749.1973.tb15158.x

Barkovich, A.J., & Kuzniecky, R.I. (2000). Gray matter heterotopia. *Neurology, 55,* 1603–1608.

Barnes, M.A., Faulkner, H., Wilkinson, M., & Dennis, M. (2004). Meaning construction and integration in children with hydrocephalus. *Brain and Language, 89*(1), 47–56. doi:10.1016/S0093-934X(03)00295-5

Bates, T.C., Lind, P.A., Luciano, M., Montgomery, G.W., Martin, N.G., & Wright M.J. (2009). Dyslexia and DYX1C1: Deficits in reading and spelling associated with a missense mutation. *Molecular Psychiatry, 15*(12), 1190–1196. doi:10.1038/mp.2009.120

Brkanac, Z., Chapman, N.H., Matsushita, M.M., Chun, L., Nielsen, K., Cochrane, E., ... Raskind, W.H. (2007). Evaluation of candidate genes for DYX1 and DYX2 in families with dyslexia. *American Journal of Medical Genetics, 144B,* 556–560.

Burbridge, T.J., Wang, Y., Volz, A.J., Peschansky, V.J., Lisann, L., Galaburda, A.M., ... Rosen, G.D. (2008). Postnatal analysis of the effect of embryonic knockdown and overexpression of candidate dyslexia susceptibility gene homolog Dcdc2 in the rat. *Neuroscience, 152,* 723–733. doi:10.1016/j.neuroscience.2008.01.020

Cardon, L.R., Smith, S.D., Fulker, D.W., Kimberling, W.J., Pennington, B.F., & DeFries, J.C. (1994). Quantitative trait locus for reading disability on chromosome 6. *Science, 266,* 276–279. doi:10.1126/science.7939663

Cardon, L.R., Smith, S.D., Fulker, D.W., Kimberling, W.J., Pennington, B.F., & DeFries, J.C. (1995). Quantitative trait locus for reading disability: Correction. *Science, 268,* 1553. doi:10.1126/science.7777847

Chen, Y., Zhao, M., Wang, S., Chen, J., Wang, Y., Cao, Q., ... Li, J. (2009). A novel role for DYX1C1, a chaperone protein for both Hsp70 and Hsp90, in breast cancer. *Journal of Cancer Research and Clinical Oncology, 135*(9), 1265–1276. doi:10.1007/s00432-009 -0568-6

Cope, N., Harold, D., Hill, G., Moskvina, V., Stevenson, J., Holmans, P., ... Williams, J. (2005). Strong evidence that KIAA0319 on chromosome 6p is a susceptibility gene for developmental dyslexia. *American Journal of Human Genetics, 76,* 581–591. doi:10.1086/429131

Cope, N.A., Hill, G., van den Bree, M., Harold, D., Moskvina, V., Green, E.K., ... O'Donovan, M.C. (2005). No support for association between dyslexia susceptibility 1 candidate 1 and developmental dyslexia. *Molecular Psychiatry, 10,* 237–238. doi:10.1038/sj.mp.4001596

Coquelle, F.M., Levy, T., Bergmann, S., Wolf, S.G., Bar-El, D., Sapir, T., ... Reiner, O. (2006). Common and divergent roles for members of the mouse DCX superfamily. *Cell Cycle, 5,* 976–983. doi:10.4161/cc.5.9.2715

Dahdouh, F., Anthoni, H., Tapia-Paez, I., Peyrard-Janvid, M., Schulte-Korne, G., Warnke, A., ... Zucchelli, M. (2009). Further evidence for DYX1C1 as a susceptibility factor for dyslexia. *Psychiatric Genetics, 19*(2), 59–63. doi:10.1097/YPG.0b013e32832080e1

Decker, S.N., & Vandenberg, S.G. (1985). Colorado twin study of reading disability. In D.B. Gray & J.F. Kavanagh (Eds.), *Biobehavioural measures of dyslexia* (pp. 123–135). Parkton, MD: York Press.

De Fries, J.C., Fulker, D.W., & LaBuda, M.C. (1987). Evidence for a genetic aetiology in reading disability of twins. *Nature, 329,* 537–539.

De Fries, J.C., & Gillis, J.J. (1991). Etiology of reading deficits in learning disabilities: Quantitative genetic analysis. In J.E. Obrzut & G.W. Hynd (Eds.), *Neuropsychologocal foundations of learning disabilities: A handbook of issues, methods and practice* (pp. 29–47). London, England: Academic Press

Dennis, M.Y., Paracchini, S., Scerri, T.S., Prokunina-Olsson, L., Knight, J.C., Wade-Martins, R., ... Monaco, A.P. (2009). A common variant associated with dyslexia reduces expression of the KIAA0319 gene. *PLoS Genetics, 5,* e1000436. doi:10.1371/journal.pgen.1000436

Deuel, T.A., Liu, J.S., Corbo, J.C., Yoo, S.Y., Rorke-Adams, L.B., & Walsh, C.A. (2006). Genetic interactions between doublecortin and doublecortin-like kinase in neuronal migration and axon outgrowth. *Neuron, 49,* 41–53. doi:10.1016/j.neuron.2005.10.038

Finucci, J.M., Guthrie, J.T., Childs, A.L., Abbey, H., & Childs, B. (1976). The genetics of specific reading disability. *Annals of Human Genetics, 40,* 1–23. doi:10.1111/j.1469-1809.1976.tb00161.x

Fisher, S.E., Marlow, A.J., Lamb, J., Maestrini, E., Williams, D.F., Richardson, A.J., ... Monaco, A.P. (1999). A quantitative-trait locus on chromosome 6p influences different aspects of developmental dyslexia. *The American Journal of Human Genetics, 64,* 146–156. doi:10.1086/302190

Fliegauf, M., Benzing, T., & Omran, H. (2007). When cilia go bad: Cilia defects and ciliopathies. *Nature Reviews of Molecular Cell Biology, 8*(11), 880–893. doi:10.1038/nrm2278

Galaburda, A.M. (1988). The pathogenesis of childhood dyslexia. *Research Publications Association of Research of Nervous Mental Disabilities, 66,* 127–137.

Galaburda, A.M., & Kemper, T.L. (1979). Cytoarchitectonic abnormalities in developmental dyslexia: A case study. *Annals of Neurology, 6,* 94–100. doi:10.1002/ana.410060203

Gleeson, J.G., Lin, P.T., Flanagan, L.A., Walsh, C.A. (1999). Doublecortin is a microtubule-associated protein and is expressed widely by migrating neurons. *Neuron, 23,* 257–271. doi:10.1016/S0896-6273(00)80778-3

Grigorenko, E.L., Wood, F.B., Golovyan, L., Meyer, M., Romano, C., Pauls, D. (2003). Continuing the search for dysleixa fenes on 6p. *American Journal of Medical Genetics Part B (Neuropsychiatric Genetics), 118B,* 89–98.

Grigorenko, E.L., Wood, F.B., Meyer, M.S., Hart, L.A., Speed, W.C., Shuster, A., Pauls, D.L. (1997). Susceptibility loci for distinct components of developmental dyslexia on chromosomes 6 and 15. *American Journal of Human Genetics, 60,* 27–39.

Hallgren, B. (1950). Specific dyslexia (congenital word blindness). A clinical and genetic study. *Acta Psychiatrica et Neurologica Supplementum, 65,* 1–287.

Harlaar, N., Spinath, F., Dale, P., Plomin, R. (2005). Genetic influences on early word recognition abilites and diabilites: A study of 7-year-old twins. *Journal of Child Psychology and Psychiatry, 46,* 373–384.

Harold, D., Paracchini, S., Scerri, T., Dennis, M., Cope, N., Hill, G., ... Monaco, A.P. (2006) Further evidence that the KIAA0319 gene confers susceptibility to developmental dyslexia. *Molecular Psy-*

chiatry, 11, 1085–1091, 1061. doi:10.1038/sj.mp.4001904

Hatakeyama, S., Matsumoto, M., Yada, M., & Nakayama, K.I. (2004). Interaction of U-box-type ubiquitin-protein ligases (E3s) with molecular chaperones. *Genes to Cells, 9,* 533–548. doi:10.1111/j.1356-9597.2004.00742.x

Hawke, J.L., Wadsworth, S.J., & De Fries, J.C. (2006). Genetic influences on reading difficulties in boys and girls: The Colorado twin study. *Dyslexia 12,* 21–29.

Hermann, K. (1956). Congenital word blindness. *Acta Psychiatrica et Neurologica Scandinavica, S108,* 177–184. doi:10.1111/j.1600-0447.1956.tb01680.x

Hermann, K., & Norrie, E. (1958). Is congenital word blindness a hereditary type of Gerstmann's Syndrome? *European Neurology, 136,* 59–73. doi:10.1159/000139549

Hohnen, B., & Stevenson, J. (1999). The structure of genetic influences on general cognitive, language, phonological, and reading abilities. *Developmental Psychology, 35,* 590–603. doi:10.1037//0012-1649.35.2.590

Ihara, A., Hirata, M., Fujimaki, N., Goto, T., Umekawa, Y., Fujita, N., … Murata T. (2010). Neuroimaging study on brain asymmetries in situs inversus totalis. *Journal of the Neurological Sciences, 288* (1–2), 72–8. doi:10.1016/j.jns.2009.10.002

Kaplan, D., Gayán, J., Ahn, J., Won, T.W., Pauls, D., Olson, R., … Gruen, J. (2002). Evidence for linkage and association with reading disability on 6p21.3-22. *American Journal of Human Genetics, 70,* 1287–1298. doi:10.1086/340449

Kennedy, D.N., O'Craven, K.M., Ticho, B.S., Goldstein, A.M., Makris, N., & Henson, J.W. (1999). Structural and functional brain asymmetries in human situs inversus totalis. *Neurology, 53*(6), 1260–1265.

Kim, Y.J., Huh, J.W., Kim, D.S., Bae, M.I., Lee, J.R., Ha, H.S., … Kim, H.S. (2008). Molecular characterization of the DYX1C1 gene and its application as a cancer biomarker. *Journal of Cancer Research and Clinical Oncology, 135*(2), 265–270. doi:10.1007/s00432-008 -0445-8

Koizumi, H., Tanaka, T., & Gleeson, J.G. (2006). Doublecortin-like kinase functions with doublecortin to mediate fiber tract decussation and neuronal migration. *Neuron, 49,* 55–66. doi:10.1016/j.neuron.2005.10.040

LaBuda, M.C., & De Fries, J.C. (1988). Genetic and environmental etiologies of reading disability: A twin study. *Annals of Dyslexia, 38,* 131–138. doi:10.1007/BF02648252

Levecque, C., Velayos-Baeza, A., Holloway, Z.G., & Monaco, A.P. (2009). The dyslexia-associated protein KIAA0319 interacts with Adaptor Protein 2 and follows the classical clathrin-mediated endocytosis pathway. *American Journal of Physiology: Cell Physiology, 297*(1), C160–168. doi:10.1152/ajpcell.00630.2008

Lind, P.A., Luciano, M., Wright, M.J., Montgomery, G.W., Martin, N.G., & Bates, T.C. (2010). Dyslexia and DCDC2: Normal variation in reading and spelling is associated with DCDC2 polymorphisms in an Australian population sample. *European Journal of Human Genetics.* doi:10.1038/ejhg.2009.237

Marino, C., Citterio, A., Giorda, R., Facoetti, A., Menozzi, G., Vanzin, L., … Molteni, M. (2007). Association of short-term memory with a variant within DYX1C1 in developmental dyslexia. *Genes, Brain and Behavior, 6,* 640–646. doi:10.1111/j.1601 -183X.2006.00291.x

Marino, C., Giorda, R., Lorusso, M.L., Vanzin, L., Salandi, N., Nobile, M., … Molteni, M. (2005). A family-based association study does not support DYX1C1 on 15q21.3 as a candidate gene in developmental dyslexia. *European Journal of Human Genetics, 1–9.* doi:10.1038/sj.ejhg.5201356

Massinen, S., Tammimies, K., Tapia-Paez, I., Matsson, H., Hokkanen, M.E., Soderberg, O., … Kere, J. (2009). Functional interaction of DYX1C1 with estrogen receptors suggests involvement of hormonal pathways in dyslexia. *Human Molecular Genetics, 18*(15), 2802–2812. doi:10.1093/hmg/ddp215

Meng, H., Hager, K., Held, M., Page, G.P., Olson, R.K., Pennington, B.F., … Gruen, J.R. (2005). TDT-association analysis of EKN1 and dyslexia in a Colorado twin cohort. *Human Genetics, 118,* 87–90. doi:10.1007/s00439-005-0017-9

Meng, H., Smith, S.D., Hager, K., Held, M., Liu, J., Olson, R.K., … Gruen, J.R. (2005). DCDC2 is associated with reading disability and modulates neuronal development in the brain. *Proceedings of the National Academy of Sciences, USA, 102,* 17053–17058. doi:10.1073/pnas.0508 591102

Nopola-Hemmi, J., Taipale, M., Haltia, T., Lehesjoki, A.E., Voutilainen, A., & Kere, J. (2000). Two translocations of chromosome 15q associated with dyslexia. *Journal of Medical Genetics, 37,* 771–775. doi:10.1136/jmg.37.10.771

Nothen, M.M., Schulte-Korne, G., Grimm, T., Cichon, S., Vogt, I.R., Muller-Myhsok, B., ... Remschmidt, H. (1999). Genetic linkage analysis with dyslexia: Evidence for linkage of spelling disability to chromosome 15. *European Child and Adolescent Psychiatry, 8,* 56–59. doi:10.1007/PL00010696

Paracchini, S., Steer, C.D., Buckingham, L.L., Morris, A.P., Ring, S., Scerri, T., ... Monaco, A.P. (2008). Association of the KIAA0319 dyslexia susceptibility gene with reading skills in the general population. *American Journal of Psychiatry, 165*(12), 1576–1584. doi:10.1176/appi.ajp.2008.07121872

Paracchini, S., Thomas, A., Castro, S., Lai, C., Paramasivam, M., Wang, Y., ... Monaco, A.P. (2006). The chromosome 6p22 haplotype associated with dyslexia reduces the expression of KIAA0319, a novel gene involved in neuronal migration. *Human Molecular Genetics, 15,* 1659–1666. doi:10.1093/hmg/ddl089

Pennington, B.F., & Gilger, J.W. (1996). How is dyslexia transmitted? In C.H. Chase, G.D. Rosen, & G.F. Sherman (Eds.), *Developmental dyslexia. Neural, cognitive and genetic mechanisms* (pp. 41–61). Baltimore, MD: York Press.

Prigatano, G.P., Zeiner, H.K., Pollay, M., Kaplan, R.J. (1983). Neuropsychological functioning in children with shunted uncomplicated hydrocephalus. *Pediatric Neurosurgery, 10*(2), 112–120. doi:10.1159/000120104

Reiner, O., Coquelle, F.M., Peter, B., Levy, T., Kaplan, A., Sapir, T., ..., Bergmann, S. (2006). The evolving doublecortin (DCX) superfamily. *BMC Genomics, 7,* 188. doi:10.1186/1471-2164-7-188

Rosen, G.D., Bai, J., Wang, Y., Fiondella, C.G., Threlkeld, S.W., LoTurco, J., Galaburda, A.M. (2007). Disruption of neuronal migration by RNAi of Dyx1c1 results in neocortical and hippocampal malformations. *Cerebral Cortex, 17,* 2562–2572. doi:10.1093/cercor/bhl162

Schulte-Korne, G., Grimm, T., Nothen, M.M., Muller-Myhsok, B., Cichon, S., Vogt, I.R., ..., Remschmidt, H. (1998). Evidence for linkage of spelling disability to chromosome 15. *American Journal of Human Genetics, 63,* 279–282. doi:10.1086/301919

Schumacher, J., Anthoni, H., Dahdouh, F., Konig, I.R., Hillmer, A.M., Kluck, N., ... Kere, J. (2006). Strong genetic evidence of DCDC2 as a susceptibility gene for dyslexia. *American Journal of Human Genetics, 78,* 52–62. doi:10.1086/498992

Silberberg, M., Charron, A.J., Bacallao, R., & Wandinger-Ness, A. (2005). Mispolarization of desmosomal proteins and altered intercellular adhesion in autosomal dominant polycystic kidney disease. *American Journal of Physiology: Renal Physiology, 288,* F1153–1163. doi:10.1152/ajprenal.00008.2005

Smith, S.D., Kimberling, W.J., & Pennington, B.F. (1991). Screening for multiple genes influencing dyslexia. *Reading and Writing: An Interdisciplinary Journal, 3,* 285–298.

Smith, S.D., Kimberling, W.J., Pennington, B.F., & Lubs, H.A. (1983). Specific reading disability: Identification of an inherited form through linkage analysis. *Science, 219,* 1345–1347. doi:10.1126/science.6828864

Stevenson, J., Graham, P., Fredman, G., & McLoughlin, V. (1987). A twin study of genetic influences on reading and spelling ability and disability. *Journal of Child Psychology and Psychiatry, 28,* 229–247. doi:10.1111/j.1469-7610.1987.tb00207.x

Szalkowski, C.E., Hinman, J., Threlkeld, S.W., Wang, Y., LePack, A., Rosen, G.D., ... Fitch, R.H. (2011). Persistent spatial working memory deficits in rats following in utero RNAi of Dyx1c1. *Genes, Brain and Behavior, 10,* 244–252. doi:10.1111/j.1601-183X.2010.00662.x

Taipale, M., Kaminen, N., Nopola-Hemmi, J., Haltia, T., Myllyluoma, B., Lyytinen, H., ... Kere, J. (2003). A candidate gene for developmental dyslexia encodes a nuclear tetratricopeptide repeat domain protein dynamically regulated in brain. *Proceedings of the National Academy of Sciences, USA, 100,* 11553–11558. doi:10.1073/pnas.1833911100

Tallal, P. (1980). Auditory temporal perception, phonics, and reading disabilities in children. *Brain and Language, 9,* 182–198. doi:10.1016/0093-934X(80)90139-X

Tallal, P., Miller, S., & Fitch, R.H. (1993). Neurobiological basis of speech: A case for the preeminence of temporal processing. *Annals of the New York Academy of Sciences, 682,* 27–47. doi:10.1111/j.1749-6632.1993.tb22957.x

Threlkeld, S.W., McClure, M.M., Bai, J., Wang, Y., LoTurco, J., Rosen, G.D., & Fitch, R.H. (2007). Developmental disruptions and behavioral impairments in rats following in utero RNAi of Dyx1c1. *Brain Research Bulletin, 71,* 508–514. doi:10.1016/j.brainresbull.2006.11.005

Velayos-Baeza, A., Toma, C., da Roza, S., Paracchini, S., & Monaco, A.P. (2007). Alternative splicing in the dyslexia-associated gene KIAA0319. *Mammalian Genome, 18,* 627–634. doi:10.1007/s00335-007-9051-3

Velayos-Baeza, A., Toma, C., Paracchini, S., & Monaco, A.P. (2008). The dyslexia-associated gene KIAA0319 encodes highly N- and O-glycosylated plasma membrane and secreted isoforms. *Human Molecular Genetics, 17,* 859–871. doi:10.1093/hmg/ddm358

Wang, Y., Paramasivam, M., Thomas, A., Bai, J., Kaminen-Ahola, N., Kere, J., ... LoTurco, J. (2006). DYX1C1 functions in neuronal migration in developing neocortex. *Neuroscience, 143,* 515–522. doi:10.1016/j.neuroscience.2006.08.022

Wieck, G., Leventer, R.J., Squier, W.M., Jansen, A., Andermann, E., Dubeau, F., ... Dobyns, W.B. (2005). Periventricular nodular heterotopia with overlying polymicrogyria. *Brain, 128,* 2811–2821. doi:10.1093/brain/awh658

CHAPTER 3

The Magnocellular Theory of Dyslexia

John Stein

VISUAL REQUIREMENTS OF READING

Eighteen percent of students who exit United States (U.S.) schools are only able to read and write at a level one, a very low level (Fleischman, Hopstock, Pelczar, and Shelley, 2010). This not only consigns such students to risk for later failure, such as very low paying jobs, unemployment, and criminality, but it is also an appalling waste of talent, because in other respects these students are typically within the normal range of intelligence. They fail because reading is very difficult—the most difficult skill that most people ever have to acquire. Reading is difficult because it requires visual analysis of letters and their order, and translation of those letters into sounds. In parallel, it requires learning the phonological structure of a word and learning that continuously spoken words can be split down into phonemes (shorter sounds that may be represented by letters).

Although there is current emphasis on learning phonological skills, the very first step in reading relies on visual analysis of the text. A large proportion of the primary information processing required for reading is visual.

What, more precisely, are the visual requirements of reading? Letters have to be identified correctly; so it is often assumed that the crucial visual process for reading is the system that specializes in object identification. This depends on the small neurons (parvocellular [P] neurons) that constitute 90% of retinal ganglion cells. They signal the fine detail and color of visual targets to the ventral or "what" route that passes from the primary visual cortex toward the visual word form area that is situated in the anterior part of the fusiform gyrus on the under surface of the left occipitotemporal junction (Cohen & Dehaene, 2004).

VISUAL-MAGNOCELLULAR NEURONS

It is equally important to be able to sequence letters in the right order. People with dyslexia are less accurate and slower at sequencing letters than they are at identifying each letter individually. Correct letter sequencing depends on the properties of the other main visual subsystem, the magnocellular (M) system. The M neurons form only 10% of the ganglion cells in the retina, but they are specialized for timing visual events by signaling movement rather than form or color. When the eyes move, image motion across the retina is an important source of information about the eye movement. The M cells play a crucial part in signaling letter order. They also supply the other forward route from the primary visual cortex the dorsal "where" route, that culminates in the parietal cortex. Here, their main function is to guide visual attention and eye and limb movements (Goodale & Milner, 1992).

M cells project via the magnocellular layers of the lateral geniculate nucleus (LGN) in the thalamus to the primary visual cortex in the back of the occipital lobe and also to the superior colliculus to control eye movements (Maunsell, 1992). The axons of M cells are heavily myelinated so that the signals they project to the visual cortex arrive there approximately 10 ms before the slower ones provided by P cells.

The dendritic fields of M cells are 20 times the size of those of the P cells. As a consequence, at a reading distance of 30 cm, the M cells respond best to large blobs—around 0.5 cm in size (about half the average size of a word). Therefore, M cells cannot identify the shapes of letters, that in small print subtend only about 1 mm, nor detect letter features 0.1 mm in size. Nevertheless, they do rapidly indicate the locations and order of letters so that attention and eye movements can be directed on each in turn. This directs the P system to identify the letters (Cheng, Eysel, & Vidyasagar, 2004). Thus, if the magnocellular system is deficient, focusing attention and fixation of the eyes will be unstable and the process of sequencing letters will be slower and less accurate.

VISUAL SYMPTOMS

Such visual problems are typical complaints by many children with dyslexia who explain that "the letters blur" or "the letters move over each other, so I cannot remember what order they are meant to be in." Many children are so accustomed to letter blur and motion that they do not realize (or report) that it is abnormal unless they are specifically asked. Due to inaccurate focus of attention, many of them fail to gain a clear representation of the order of letters in a word, even without the letters appearing to move around.

Adults with dyslexia rarely complain of unstable vision in the same way. Even in well-compensated adults, the main problem is frequently a difficulty with spelling. Inaccuracies are often regularizations, or phonetic spellings of irregular words, such as "yot" for "yacht." These spelling mistakes reveal the inaccuracies of their memorized visual representations of words and may be visual-attentional in origin, and not simply phonological.

The prevailing opinion among experts is that dyslexic reading problems are mainly phonological, in large part because very few researchers test for visual symptoms as part of a standard diagnostic battery. There is wide-spread agreement that at least some children with dyslexia have visual problems, some experts put its prevalence very low—at less than 10% of all people with dyslexia (Snowling, 2000). Yet, we find that 50% of the children seen in our U.K. clinics have significant visual problems that are probably due to impaired development of their visual M system (Stein & Fowler, 2005).

MAGNOCELLULAR IMPAIRMENTS IN DYSLEXIA

A search of Pubmed shows that 90% of the studies since 2000 that have sought evidence for such M impairment in people with dyslexia have found it in at least some. Strictly speaking, visual M cells can only be rigorously defined in the subcortical visual system because only in the retina and LGN are they anatomically separated from the P system. Magno and parvo systems converge and interact strongly, so the only way to confirm that deficits in people with dyslexia are confined to the M system is to use stimuli that are selectively processed by the subcortical M neurons in the retina and LGN (Skottun, 2000).

There is strong evidence that people with dyslexia often suffer impaired development of magnocellular cells in the retina and in the LGN. In the retina, the spatial frequency doubling effect indicates the sensitivity of the M ganglion cells (Maddess et al., 1999). People with dyslexia consistently show a higher contrast threshold in this test, confirming their M cell weakness (Pammer & Wheatley, 2001). Livingstone, Rosen, Drislane, and Galaburda (1991) found that the M layers in the LGN in dyslexic brains are selectively impaired. Not only were the cells approximately 25% smaller in the dyslexic as compared to the control brains, but the M cells were not confined to their proper M layers; many had mismigrated into the adjacent konio and parvo layers of the LGN.

The cortical dorsal "where" pathway is also dominated by M input, and abnormalities have been found in people with dyslexia in this pathway as well. Specifically, anomalies have been reported in the primary visual cortex, the prestriate visual motion area (MT/V5), the posterior parietal cortex, and the ultimate goal of both M and P systems, the prefrontal cortex (Rao, Rainer, & Miller, 1997).

Sensitivity to the contrast of black-and-white gratings is mediated mainly by the primary visual cortex (VI). Since Lovegrove's first report (Lovegrove, Bowling, Badcock, & Blackwood, 1980) there have been several studies that have confirmed that the contrast sensitivity (CS) of many people with dyslexia is lower than that of control groups, particularly at the low spatial and high temporal frequencies mediated by the M system (Bednarek & Grabowska, 2002; Cornelissen, Richardson, Mason, Fowler, & Stein, 1995). Other impairments of M function in people with dyslexia involving the primary visual cortex are 1) abnormal temporal gap detection for low contrast and low spatial frequency stimuli (Lovegrove et al., 1980), 2) reduced critical flicker frequency (Chase, 1993), and 3) decreased low spatial frequency contrast sensitivity for flickering and moving stimuli (Edwards et al., 2004; Felmingham & Jakobson, 1995; Mason, Cornelissen, Fowler, & Stein, 1993; Talcott, 1998).

Ninety percent of the visual input to the motion sensitive neurons in the middle temporal visual motion area (V5/MT) is provided by the M system and only 10% comes from other sources. The best way of assessing the sensitivity of these MT neurons in individuals is to measure their responses to visual motion in "random dot kinematograms" (RDKs). Clouds of dots moving in the same direction "coherently" are progressively diluted with noise dots moving in random directions until the subject can no longer detect any coherent motion in the display. This threshold defines motion (visual dorsal stream) sensitivity for each individual. Several researchers have shown that this is reduced in many people with dyslexia (Cornelissen, et al., 1995; Downie, Jakobson, Frisk, & Ushycky, 2003; Hill & Raymond, 2002; Richardson et al., 2000; Samar & Parasnis, 2005; Talcott et al., 2000). Research has also shown reduced velocity discrimination (Demb, Boynton, Best, & Heeger, 1998; Eden et al., 1996) and elevated speed thresholds for motion-defined form (Felmingham & Jakobson, 1995).

People with low motion sensitivity can still be adequate readers (Skoyles & Skottun, 2004). Nevertheless, individual differences in motion sensitivity explain over 25% of the variance in reading ability (Talcott, et al., 2000). In other words, individual dorsal-stream performance—dominated by M cell input—plays an important part in determining how well visual reading skills develop. This observation remains true for everybody, not just those diagnosed with dyslexia.

The posterior parietal cortex (PPC) receives its main visual input from V5/MT. This input plays a crucial role in the PPC function of guiding visual attention, as well as eye and limb movements (Cheng et al., 2004). People with dyslexia have been found to be worse than good readers at cueing visual attention (Facoetti, Turatto, Lorusso, & Mscetti, 2001; Kinsey, Rose, Hansen, Richardson, & Stein, 2004), visual search (Iles, Walsh, & Richardson, 2000; Facoetti, Paganoni, & Lorusso, 2000), visual short-term "retain and compare" memory (Ben-Yehudah, Sackett, Malchi-Ginzberg, & Ahissar, 2001), and attentional grouping in the Ternus test (Cestnick & Coltheart, 1999). These findings show that dorsal stream function is impaired in dyslexia. Of course they do not prove that defects in the M system are entirely responsible, since none of the tests stimulates the peripheral magnocellular system entirely selectively, and the dorsal stream receives 10% of its input from other sources (Skottun, 2001). Nevertheless, as 90% of its input is provided by the M system, M impairment is likely to be the main cause. Moreover, many of the studies mentioned above incorporated control tests for parvo function, such as visual acuity or color discrimination—and dyslexic populations usually proved to be as good or better at these.

Taken together, this evidence suggests that poor dorsal stream performance in people with dyslexia can be mainly attributed to M system weakness, even in the presence of robust parvocellular function (Fukushima, Tanaka, Williams, & Fukushima, 2005; Skoyles & Skottun, 2004).

EYE MOVEMENT CONTROL BY THE DORSAL STREAM

Typically, the dorsal stream not only directs visual attention to a target but also redirects the eyes toward it. Numerous studies have found not only that the direction of visual attention is disturbed in people with dyslexia (Facoetti, Corradi, Ruffino, Gori, & Zorzi, 2010; Vidyasagar, 2004), and also that their eye control during reading is poor (Eden, Stein, Wood, & Wood, 1994; Kirkby, Webster, Blythe, & Liversedge, 2008; Solan, Ficarra, Brannan, & Rucker, 1998). However, it is strongly argued that these abnormalities do not cause reading problems, but are instead the result of not understanding the text. Hence, the reader has to make longer fixations and more re-inspections of previous letters to try to decode words (Rayner, 1985). Poor eye control in people with dyslexia has also been demonstrated in several nonreading situations, using tests of fixation stability (Fischer, Hartnegg, & Mokler, 2000) and of smooth pursuit and saccadic control (Crawford & Higham, 2001). These findings imply that poor eye control comes first and may be a significant cause of reading problems.

EVENT-RELATED POTENTIALS

Recording average electroencephalogram (EEG) potentials in response to a moving, low contrast, visual target provides a more objective measure of cortical dorsal stream processing than psychophysical techniques. Of recent visual event-related potential (ERP) studies in people with dyslexia, the great majority have either confirmed Livingstone's (Livingstone et al., 1991) original observation that this population has weaker responses to moving, low contrast targets than do good readers (e.g., Kuba, Szanyi, Gayer, Kremlacek, & Kubova, 2001) or have found that people with dyslexia show slower, smaller, and spatially abnormal visual attentional ERP responses in line with psychophysical results.

AUDITORY TRANSIENT PROCESSING

Although most people do so without thinking, identifying and ordering the sequences of sounds that make up speech is as difficult as sequencing letters visually. All doctors in training know this when they try to distinguish systolic from diastolic heart murmurs. Whether the murmur comes before or after the second heart sound is very difficult to decide for the novice even though these events are far slower than in average speech. Such analysis of sound sequences depends on being able to accurately detect changes in sound frequency and amplitude that are what convey information in speech. Tracking of auditory transients in real-time is mediated by a set of large neurons specialized for rapid temporal processing that may be likened to visual M cells. They contrast with smaller auditory neurons that identify different mixtures of frequencies, such as chords, by their spectral composition. These neurons work less rapidly, like visual P cells.

Thus, it appears that there are auditory equivalents of the visual M and P systems. Likewise, there are analogous dorsal "where" and ventral "what" cortical streams projecting from the primary auditory cortex toward the frontal lobe (Rauschecker & Tian, 2000). However, at no stage are the auditory M and P equivalents entirely separate or anatomically distinct, so they are not normally named M and P as in the visual system.

Paula Tallal was the first to suggest that developmental people with dysphasia and dyslexia may be poor at the auditory temporal processes required for decoding that are mediated by the auditory equivalent of the M pathways (Tallal & Piercy, 1973). Since her suggestion, there have been many hundreds of studies confirming her idea. We found that, whether dyslexic or not, children's sensitivity to changes in sound frequency and amplitude predicted their ability to read nonwords, that is, a test of phonological skill (Snowling, Goulandris, Bowlby, & Howell, 1986). Auditory M sensitivity accounted for nearly 50% of individual differences in phonological skill (Witton, Stein, Stoodley, Rosner, & Talcott, 2002).

As for the visual system, there is a wide difference in opinion of how common it is to find low-level auditory processing problems in people with dyslexia. Estimates range from 10%–70%. Psychophysical tests may not be sensitive enough to reveal the mild deficits that may cause reading problems, so it is still argued that there can be higher level phonological problems without any evidence of lower level auditory temporal processing impairments. However, using a mismatch negativity paradigm, we showed that even in the absence of a psychophysiologically demonstrable deficit, one can usually show some degree of low-level auditory processing impairment that correlates with phonological problems (Stoodley, Hill, Stein, & Bishop, 2006), and Kraus et al., make the same point in Chapter 6. Data regarding deficits in auditory processing in animal models with knock-outs or knock-downs of CDSGs (Fitch & Szalkowski, Chapter 11), as well as electrophysiological data indicating temporal coding inaccuracy in Dcdc2 knock-out mice (LoTurco et al., Chapter 2), further support this notion.

BRAIN-WIDE MAGNOCELLULAR SYSTEMS

In people with dyslexia, poor visual-magnocellular function is often accompanied by poor auditory temporal processing (Talcott et al., 2000). Processing of temporal transients is not confined to the auditory and visual systems. It is a required function throughout the nervous system. People with dyslexia have been shown to have reduced cutaneous and proprioceptive transient sensitivity (Stoodley, Talcott, Carter, Witton, & Stein, 2000) and impaired motor timing mediated by the cerebellum (Nicolson, Fawcett, & Dean, 2001). This combination of deficiencies suggests a common underlying factor. This is likely to be the kind of large neuron (magnocell) that mediates transient processing functions throughout the nervous system. All such neurons seem to come from the same lineage because they express the same surface recognition molecule to which antibodies such as CAT301 bind. This signature molecule enables them to recognize each other to make useful functional connections (Hockfield & Sur, 1990; Zaremba, Naegele, Barnstable, & Hockfield, 1990).

I have suggested, therefore, that all the features of developmental dyslexia—visual, auditory, linguistic, and motor—may be accounted for by impaired development of CAT301 type magnocellular neurons throughout the brain. The differing degree of expression of this impairment in different systems could explain the large individual differences seen among people with dyslexia—some being mainly visual, others auditory, others uncoordinated, others more purely linguistic.

Shatz and her colleagues have shown that the development of magnocells and their connections, at least in the visual system and the hippocampus, is regulated by the major histocompatibility complex (MHC) cell recognition and immune regulation gene system (Corriveau, Huh, & Shatz, 1998). Most of the 150 MHC genes reside on the short arm of chromosome 6. When M cells start information processing, MHC class 1 proteins begin to be expressed on their surfaces, probably to help them find other M cells with which to interact. If neurons do not make useful connections during development, they are eliminated by the process of apoptosis, summed up in the epithet, "Use it or lose it." Ninety percent of all the neurons generated in the germinal zones are eliminated in this way during the assembly of functional processing networks during development.

The recognition molecules on the neuronal membrane are not only important to identify each and to make effective functional connections, but also to label them as "self" so that microglia scavenging cells do not to attempt to destroy them as foreign invaders. M cells seem to be particularly vulnerable not only to genetic but also to immunological attack and other general environmental damage. Neurons within the M system also seem to be selectively damaged in prematurity, birth hypoxia, malnutrition, autoimmune diseases, and in many overlapping neurodevelopmental conditions, including dyslexia, dyspraxia, dysphasia, dyscalculia, attention-deficit/hyperactivity disorder, autism, bipolar disorder, and schizophrenia (Hari & Renvall, 2001; Stein, 2001). Perhaps the visual, auditory, memory, and motor temporal processing impairments that are seen in dyslexics are all due to underlying abnormal development of this generalized, change to central nervous system–wide, transient processing, magnocellular system.

One can take this idea a step further. Ramus showed in a small group of well-compensated undergraduates with dyslexia that only a few of them had demonstrable auditory, visual, or motor problems, whereas despite their compensation, most could still be shown to have residual phonological difficulties (Ramus et al., 2003). He attributed the latter to a higher level developmental abnormality, perhaps in the angular gyrus

(Ramus, 2004). Because the angular gyrus is an important node in the M–cell dominated dorsal visuomotor stream, clearly this impairment might also involve impaired higher level magnocellular connections.

OPPOSITION TO THE MAGNOCELLULAR THEORY

There has been vigorous opposition to the magnocellular theory (Skottun, 2000). Skottun does not contest that many people with dyslexia suffer a visual deficit, merely that it has not been clearly shown to be dependent upon impaired visual-magnocellular processing. He suggests that the visual deficit can affect both parvocellular and magnocellular systems and that it may be attributed to deficiencies in visual attention. However, since the evidence is now overwhelming that the magnocellular system dominates both bottom-up capture of visual attention and top-down orientation of visual attention that is mediated by the dorsal stream (Cheng et al., 2004), this still leaves the major visual deficit in dyslexia attributable to a magnocellular deficit.

Because there is now general agreement that dyslexia is associated with disordered temporal processing, there has been little opposition to the extension of the magnocellular theory to all kinds of temporal processing that I propose here. Final confirmation or refutation of the general magnocellular theory will only come when the genetic mechanisms controlling the development and specialization of magnocells are fully understood. In the meantime, the evidence will remain tentative and circumstantial. Emergence of insight into complex systems like this is rarely built on just one piece of conclusive evidence. Rather, observations pile on each other until, finally, everyone is convinced one way or the other, and at that point, the field will typically experience a paradigm shift.

GENETICS

Of course, the really interesting question is why people with dyslexia have impaired development of these magnocellular systems. There are three interacting factors that I will consider here: 1) genetic, 2) immunological, and 3) nutritional.

One great advantage of applying genetic techniques to the study of the development of reading skills is that reading is much easier to measure precisely than many other higher functions, such as emotion, motivation, or delusional thinking. Unlike the 600 or so genes of small effect that have been implicated in schizophrenia (Porteous, 2008), only about 10 genes with much larger effects have so far been associated with dyslexia, and their role in reading is steadily being unraveled (Williams & O'Donovan, 2006).

My colleagues and I have capitalized upon the large number of children and families with reading problems that we have seen around Oxford to carry out whole genome quantitative trait linkage (QTL) studies.

We collected nearly 400 Oxford families and replicated many of our findings in 200 Colorado families provided by Richard Olsen. I shall just discuss two new genes that these analyses have revealed.

The first of these is *KIAA0319*, situated on the short arm of chromosome 6 in the middle of the MHC complex (Paracchini et al., 2006). This appears to be under-expressed in dyslexia, and the protein it encodes is now known to be a partly extracellular, surface signature molecule. As described by Lo Turco et al. (Chapter 2), this gene and at least two others are involved in the control of neural migration early in the development of the brain. Unraveling the precise function of these genes promises to revolutionize the understanding of how dyslexia arises and, thereby, the ability to treat it successfully.

AUTOIMMUNITY

The development of M cells is under the control of the MHC gene complex with the gene *KIAA0319* in their midst. One way of identifying M cells throughout the nervous system is to stain them for their characteristic surface antigen with antibodies such as CAT301. Unfortunately, M cells, so vulnerable in other ways, seem also to be particularly vulnerable to antibody attack. Antineuronal antibodies are found in the blood in many general autoimmune conditions such as systemic lupus erythematosus (SLE). The children of mothers with lupus show a very high incidence of dyslexia and other neurodevelopmental conditions (Lahita, 1988). Benasich (2002) found that infants from families with a history of autoimmune disorders display slower auditory processing that affects their language skills. Ectopias similar to those seen in dyslexic brains are found routinely in the brains of BSXB mice, a strain of autoimmune mouse that has been bred as an animal model of lupus (Rosen, Sherman, Emsbo, Mehler, & Galaburda, 1990). It is interesting to note that children with dyslexia and their families consistently report a higher prevalence of immunological problems—not only lupus, which is rare, but also much more common conditions such as eczema, asthma, and allergies (Hugdahl, Synnevag, & Satz, 1990). We found that mothers of children with dyslexia or autism may have circulating antimagnocellular antibodies in their blood (Vincent et al., 2002).

Thus, there appears to be an association between autoimmunity, abnormal magnocellular development, and dyslexia. This provides further support for the hypothesis that magnocellular impairment may underlie the manifold symptoms of dyslexia.

NUTRITION—OMEGA-3 FISH OILS

Another chromosomal site that showed very strong linkage to reading difficulties in our Oxford and Colorado samples of families affected by dyslexia was on chromosome 18 (18p11.2), which is very close to the melanocortin receptor 5 gene (MCR5), even though this receptor is not strongly expressed in the brain. So far, we do not have any direct evidence as to how this gene may be involved in dyslexia. However, we do know that it is involved in appetite control, in particular affecting the metabolism of omega-3 essential fatty acids. The same site (18p11.2) has been implicated in susceptibility to bipolar depression (Berrettini et al., 1994).

We are particularly interested in a possible role for this gene in the metabolism of omega-3 long chain polyunsaturated fatty acids (LCPUFA) derived from fish oils. A single LCPUFA, the 22 carbon docosahexanoic acid (DHA), makes up 20% of all neuronal membranes; thus, each person has circa 100 g of DHA in his or her brain. It has just the right properties to contribute flexibility and the correct electrostatic profile to the nerve membrane. As such, it has been conserved in eukaryotic membranes throughout evolution since the Cambrian explosion 400 million years ago (Cunnane, Plourde, Stewart, & Crawford, 2007). There are cogent reasons for believing that, because humans evolved near water, their ready access to this molecule from eating fish explains how the human brain came to be so much larger in relation to the rest of the body than is the case in other animals (Horrobin, 2001). DHA seems to be particularly important for proper magnocellular neuronal function because it is "kinky" and thus prevents the lipid molecules in the membrane from packing together too tightly. This confers the flexibility in the membrane that allows ionic channels to open and close very quickly.

However, DHA is continuously removed from membranes by phospholipases because it also forms the basis of many prostaglandin, leukotriene, and interleukin signaling molecules. Likewise, another LCPUFA, eicosapentanoic acid (EPA), is the substrate for eicosanoid prostaglandins, leukotrienes, and resolvins. They all tend to be anti-inflammatory.

Our modern Western diet is dreadful, with too much of the three Ss— salt, sugar, and saturated fat. We also eat far too little oily fish, fat soluble vitamins, and minerals. Hence, a high proportion of the population, particularly from from low socioeconomic households, is dangerously deficient in these essential nutrients. In randomized controlled trials, we were able to show that simply giving deprived children supplement capsules containing EPA and DHA from oily fish, could dramatically improve their visual-magnocellular function, and thereby, their ability to focus attention and improve their reading skills (Richardson & Montgomery, 2005). We also observed that the children we were studying appeared calmer and less aggressive in the playground, perhaps because their magnocellular functions improved. We followed up this finding by giving young offenders in prison supplement capsules containing fish oils, minerals, and vitamins. In a pilot, double-blind, randomized, and controlled trial, we compared active supplements with placebo in more than 250 young men in a tough young offenders institute. The active supplements reduced the prisoner rate of offending by more than one third—"peace on a plate" (Gesch, Hammond, Hampson, Eves, & Crowder, 2002). We are now completing a much larger study, hopefully to prove conclusively that simply improving these individuals' diets can help them to exercise better self-control and to behave less antisocially. If a simple and cheap solution such as this can powerfully improve magnocellular function, it will have profound implications in society overall.

CONCLUSIONS

The genetic, developmental, nutritional, neuroanatomical, physiological, and psychophysiological evidence that I have reviewed here all support the view that fundamental phonological reading problems in people with dyslexia may be due to mild, but pervasive, impaired development of magnocellular systems throughout the brain. However, definitive proof of this will only come when there is full understanding of how genetic and environmental influences alter the development and later function of these classes of nerve cells.

REFERENCES

Bednarek, D.B., & Grabowska, A. (2002). Luminance and chromatic contrast sensitivity in dyslexia: The magnocellular deficit hypothesis revisited. *Neuroreport, 13*(18), 2521–2525.

Benasich, A.A. (2002). Impaired processing of brief, rapidly presented auditory cues in infants with a family history of autoimmune disorder. *Developmental Neuropsychology, 22*(1), 351–372. doi:10.1207/S15326942dn2201_2

Ben-Yehudah, G., Sackett, E., Malchi-Ginzberg, L., & Ahissar, M. (2001). Impaired temporal contrast sensitivity in dyslexics is specific to retain-and-compare paradigms. *Brain, 124*(7), 1381–1395.

Berrettini, W.H., Ferraro, T.N., Goldin, L.R., Weeks, D.E., Detera-Wadleigh, S., Nurnberger, J.I., & Gershon, E.S. (1994). Chromosome 18 DNA markers and manic-depressive illness: Evidence for a susceptibility gene. *Proceedings of the National Academy of Sciences, USA, 91*(13), 5918–5921. doi:10.1073/pnas.91.13.5918

Cestnick, L., & Coltheart, M. (1999). The relationship between language-processing and visual-processing deficits in developmental dyslexia. *Cognition, 71*(3), 231–255. doi:10.1016/S0010-0277(99)00023-2

Chase, C.J., & Jenner, A.R. (1993). Magnocellular visual deficits affect temporal processing of dyslexics. *Annals of the New York Academy of Sciences, 682, 326–329.* doi:10.1111/j.1749-6632.1993.tb22983

Cheng, A., Eysel, U.T., & Vidyasagar, T.R. (2004). The role of the magnocellular pathway in serial deployment of visual attention. *European Journal of Neurosscience, 20*(8), 2188–2192. doi:10.1111/j.1460-9568.2004.03675

Cohen, L., & Dehaene, S. (2004). Specialization within the ventral stream: The case for the visual word form area. *Neuroimage, 22*(1), 466–476. doi:10.1016/j.neuroimage.2003.12.049

Cornelissen, P., Richardson, A., Mason, A., Fowler, S., & Stein, J. (1995). Contrast sensitivity and coherent motion detection measured at photopic luminance levels in dyslexics and controls. *Vision Research, 35*(10), 1483–1494. doi:10.1016/0042-6989(95)98728-R

Corriveau, R.A., Huh, G.S., & Shatz, C.J. (1998). Regulation of Class 1 MHC gene expression in the developing and mature CNS by neural activity. *Neuron, 21*(3), 505–520.

Crawford, T.J., & Higham, S. (2001). Dyslexia and centre-of-gravity effect. *Experimental Brain Research, 137*(1), 122–126. doi:10.1007/s002210000659

Cunnane, S.C., Plourde, M., Stewart, K., & Crawford, M.A. (2007). Docosahexaenoic acid and shore-based diets in hominin encephalization: A rebuttal.

American Journal of Human Biology, 19(4), 578–581. doi:10.1002/ajhb.20673

Demb, J.B., Boynton, G.M., Best, M., & Heeger, D.J. (1998). Psychophysical evidence for a magnocellular pathway deficit in dyslexia. *Vision Research, 38*(11), 1555–1559. doi:10.1016/S0042-6989(98)00075-3

Downie, A.L.S., Jakobson, L.S., Frisk, V., & Ushycky, I. (2003). Periventricular brain injury, visual motion processing, and reading and spelling abilities in children who were extremely low birthweight. *Journal of the International Neuropsychological Society, 9*(3), 440–449. doi:10.1017/S1355617703930098

Eden, G.F., Stein, J.F., Wood, H.M., & Wood, F.B. (1994). Differences in eye movements and reading problems in dyslexic and normal children. *Vision Research, 34*(10), 1345–1358. doi:10.1016/0042-6989(94)90209-7

Eden, G.F., VanMeter, J.W., Rumsey, J.M., Maisog, J.M., Woods, R.P., & Zeffiro, T.A. (1996). Abnormal processing of visual motion in dyslexia revealed by functional brain imaging. *Nature, 382*, 66–69. doi:10.1038/382066a0

Edwards, V.T., Giaschi, D.E., Dougherty, R.F., Edgell, D., Bjornson, B.H., Lyons, C., & Douglas, R.M. (2004). Psychophysical indexes of temporal processing abnormalities in children with developmental dyslexia. *Developmental Neuropsychology, 25*(3), 321–354. doi:10.1207/s15326942dn2503_5

Facoetti, A., Corradi, N., Ruffino, M., Gori, S., & Zorzi, M. (2010). Visual spatial attention and speech segmentation are both impaired in preschoolers at familial risk for developmental dyslexia. *Dyslexia, 16*(3), 226–239. doi:10.1002/dys.413

Facoetti, A., Paganoni, P., & Lorusso, M.L. (2000). The spatial distribution of visual attention in developmental dyslexia. *Experimental Brain Research, 132*(4), 531–538. doi:10.1007/s002219900330

Facoetti, A., Turatto, M., Lorusso, M.L., & Mascetti, G.G. (2001). Orienting of visual attention in dyslexia: Evidence for asymmetric hemispheric control of attention. *Experimental Brain Research, 138*(1), 46–53. doi:10.1007/s002210100700

Felmingham, K.L., & Jakobson, L.S. (1995). Visual and visuomotor performance in dyslexic children. *Experimental Brain Research, 106*(3), 467–474. doi:10.1007/BF00231069

Fischer, B., Hartnegg, K., & Mokler, A. (2000). Dynamic visual perception of dyslexic children. *Perception, 29*(5), 523–530. doi:10.1068/p2666b

Fleischman, H.L., Hopstock, P.J., Pelczar, M.P., and Shelley, B.E., (2010). Highlights from PISA 2009: Performance of U.S. 15-year-old students in reading, mathematics, and science literacy in an international context (NCES 2001-004). U.S. Department of Education, National Center for Education Statistics. Washington, D.C.: U.S. Government Printing Office.

Fukushima, J., Tanaka, S., Williams, J.D., & Fukushima, K. (2005). Voluntary control of saccadic and smooth-pursuit eye movements in children with learning disorders. *Brain and Development, 27*(8), 579–588. doi:10.1016/j.braindev.2005.03.005

Gesch, C.B., Hammond, S.M., Hampson, S.E., Eves, A., & Crowder, M.J. (2002). Influence of supplementary vitamins, minerals and essential fatty acids on the antisocial behaviour of young adult prisoners. Randomised, placebo-controlled trial. *British Journal of Psychiatry, 181*, 22–28. doi:10.1192/bjp.181.1.22

Goodale, M.A., & Milner, D. (1992). Separate visual pathways for perception and action. *Trends in Neuroscience, 15*(1), 20–25. doi:10.1016/0166-2236(92)90344-8

Hari, R., & Renvall, H. (2001). Impaired processing of rapid stimulus sequences in dyslexia. *Trends in Cognitive Sciences, 5*(12), 525–532. doi:10.1016/S1364-6613(00)01801-5

Hill, G.T., & Raymond, J.E. (2002). Deficits of motion transparency perception in adult developmental dyslexics with normal unidirectional motion sensitivity. *Vision Research, 42*(9), 1195–1203. doi:10.1016/S0042-6989(02)00042-1

Hockfield, S., & Sur, M. (1990). Monoclonal antibody cat-301 identifies Y cells in the dorsal lateral geniculate nucleus of the cat. *Journal of Comparative Neurology, 300*(3), 320–330. doi:10.1002/cne.903000305

Horrobin, D. (2001). *The madness of Adam and Eve: How schizophrenia shaped humanity.* New York: Bantam Press.

Hugdahl, K., Synnevag, B., & Satz, P. (1990). Immune and autoimmune diseases in dyslexic children. *Neuropsychologia, 28*(7), 673–679. doi:10.1016/0028-3932(90)90122-5

Iles, J., Walsh, V., & Richardson, A. (2000). Visual search performance in dyslexia. *Dyslexia, 6*(3), 163–177. doi:10.1002/1099-0909(200007/09)6:3<163::AID-DYS150>3.0.CO;2-U

Kinsey, K., Rose, M., Hansen, P., Richardson, A., & Stein, J. (2004). Magnocellular mediated visual-spatial attention and reading ability. *Neuroreport, 15*(14), 2215–2218. doi:10.1097/00001756-200410050-00014

Kirkby, J.A., Webster, L.A.D., Blythe, H.I., & Liversedge, S.P. (2008). Binocular coordination during reading and non-reading tasks. *Psychological Bulletin, 134*(5), 742–763. doi:10.1037/a0012979

Kuba, M., Szanyi, J., Gayer, D., Kremlácek, J., & Kubová, Z. (2001). Electrophysiological testing of dyslexia. *Acta Medica (Hradec Kralove), 44*(4), 131–134.

Lahita, R.G. (1988). Systemic lupus erythematosus: Learning disability in the male offspring of female patients and relationship to laterality. *Psychoneuroendocrinology, 13*(5), 385–396. doi:10.1016/0306-4530(88)90045-5

Livingstone, M.S., Rosen, G.D., Drislane, F.W., & Galaburda, A.M. (1991). Physiological and anatomical evidence for a magnocellular deficit in developmental dyslexia. *Proceedings of the National Academy of Sciences, USA, 88*(18), 7943–7947.

Lovegrove, W.J., Bowling, A., Badcock, D., & Blackwood, M. (1980). Specific reading disability: Differences in contrast sensitivity as a function of spatial frequency. *Science, 210*(4468), 439–440. doi:10.1126/science.7433985

Maddess, T., Goldberg, I., Dobinson, J., Wine, S., Welsh, A.H., & James, A.C. (1999). Testing for glaucoma with the spatial frequency doubling illusion. *Vision Research, 39*(25):, 4258–4273. doi:10.1016/S0042-6989(99)00135-2

Mason, A., Cornelissen, P., Fowler, S., & Stein, J. (1993). Contrast sensitivity, ocular dominance and specific reading disability. *Clinical Vision Sciences, 8*(4), 345–353.

Maunsell, J.H. (1992). Functional visual streams. *Current Opinion in Neurobiology, 2*(4), 506–510. doi:10.1016/0959-4388(92)90188-Q

Nicolson, R.I., Fawcett, A.J., & Dean, P. (2001). Developmental dyslexia: The cerebellar deficit hypothesis. *Trends in Neurosciences, 24*(9), 508–511. doi:10.1016/S0166-2236(00)01896-8

Pammer, K., & Wheatley, C. (2001). Isolating the M(y)-cell response in dyslexia using the spatial frequency doubling illusion. *Vision Research, 41*(16), 2139–2147. doi:10.1016/S0042-6989(01)00092-X

Paracchini, S., Thomas, A., Castro, S., Lai, C., Paramasivam, M., Wang, Y., ... Monaco, A.P. (2006). The chromosome 6p22 haplotype associated with dyslexia reduces the expression of KIAA0319, a novel gene involved in neuronal migration. *Human Molecular Genetics, 15*(10), 1659–1666. doi:10.1093/hmg/ddl089

Porteous, D. (2008). Genetic causality in schizophrenia and bipolar disorder: Out with the old and in with the new. *Current Opinion in Genetics & Development, 18*(3), 229–234. doi:10.1016/j.gde.2008.07.005

Ramus, F. (2004). Neurobiology of dyslexia: A reinterpretation of the data. *Trends in Neurosciences, 27*(12), 720–726. doi:10.1016/j.tins.2004.10.004

Ramus, F., Rosen, S., Dakin, S.C., Day, B.L., Castellote, J.M., White, S., & Frith, U. (2003). Theories of developmental dyslexia: Insights from a multiple case study of dyslexic adults. *Brain, 126*(4), 841–865. doi:10.1093/brain/awg076

Rao, S.C., Rainer, G., & Miller, E.K. (1997). Integration of what and where in the primate prefrontal cortex. *Science, 276*(5313), 821–824. doi:10.1126/science.276.5313.821

Rauschecker, J.P., & Tian, B. (2000). Mechanisms and streams for processing of "what" and "where" in auditory cortex. *Proceedings of the National Academy of Sciences, USA, 97*(22), 11800–11806. doi:10.1073/pnas.97.22.11800

Rayner, K. (1985). Do faulty eye movements cause dyslexia? *Developmental Neuropsychology, 1*(1), 3–15. doi:10.1080/87565648509540294

Richardson, A.J., Calvin, C.M., Clisby, C., Schoenheimer, D.R., Montgomery, P., Hall, J.A., ... Stein, J.F. (2000). Fatty acid deficiency signs predict the severity of reading and related difficulties in dyslexic children. *Prostaglandins Leukotrienes and Essential Fatty Acids, 63*(1–2), 69–74. doi:10.1054/plef.2000.0194

Richardson, A.J., & Montgomery, P. (2005). The Oxford-Durham study: A randomized, controlled trial of dietary supplementation with fatty acids in children with developmental coordination disorder. *Pediatrics, 115*(5), 1360–1366. doi:10.1542/peds.2004-2164

Rosen, G.D., Sherman, G.F., Emsbo, K., Mehler, C., & Galaburda, A.M. (1990). The midsagittal area of the corpus callosum and total neocortical volume differ in three inbred strains of mice. *Experimental Neurology, 107*(3), 271–276. doi:10.1016/0014-4886(90)90145-I

Samar, V.J., & Parasnis, I. (2005). Dorsal stream deficits suggest hidden dyslexia among deaf poor readers: Correlated evidence from reduced perceptual speed and elevated coherent motion detection thresholds. *Brain and Cognition, 58*(3), 300–311. doi:10.1016/j.bandc.2005.02.004

Skottun, B.C. (2000). On the conflicting support for the magnocellular-deficit theory of dyslexia: Response to Stein, Talcott and Walsh. *Trends in Cognitive Sciences, 4*(6), 211–212. doi:10.1016/S1364-6613(00)01485-6

Skottun, B.C. (2001). On the use of the Ternus test to assess magnocellular function. *Perception, 30*(12), 1449–1457. doi:10.1068/p3204

Skoyles, J., & Skottun, B.C. (2004). On the prevalence of magnocellular deficits in the visual system of non-dyslexic individuals. *Brain and Language, 88*(1), 79–82. doi:10.1016/S0093-934X(03)00162-7

Snowling, M. (2000). *Dyslexia.* Oxford, England: Blackwell Press.

Snowling, M., Goulandris, N., Bowlby, M., & Howell, P. (1986). Segmentation and speech perception in relation to reading skill: A developmental analysis. *Journal of Experimental Child Psychology, 41*(3), 489–507. doi:10.1016/0022-0965(86)90006-8

Solan, H.A., Ficarra, A., Brannan, J.R., & Rucker, F. (1998). Eye movement efficiency in normal and reading disabled elementary school children: Effects of varying luminance and wavelength. *Journal of American Optometric Association, 69*(7), 455–464.

Stein, J. (2001). The magnocellular theory of developmental dyslexia. *Dyslexia, 7*(1), 12–36. doi:10.1002/dys.186

Stein, J., & Fowler, S. (2005). Treatment of visual problems in children with reading difficulties. *PATOSS Bulletin,* 15–22.

Stoodley, C., Talcott, J.B., Carter, E.L., Witton, C., & Stein, J.F. (2000). Selective deficits of vibrotactile sensitivity in dyslexic readers. *Neuroscience Letters, 295*(1–2), 13–16. doi:10.1016/S0304-3940(00)01574-3

Stoodley, C.J., Hill, P.R., Stein, J.F., & Bishop, D.V. (2006). Auditory event-related potentials differ in dyslexics even when auditory psychophysical performance is normal. *Brain Research, 1121*(1), 190–199. doi:10.1016/j.brainres.2006.08.095

Talcott, J. (1998). Temporal perception in normal and dysfunctional reading. *Physiological Society Magazine, 31,* 17–19.

Talcott, J.B., Witton, C., McLean, M.F., Hansen, P.C., Rees, A., Green, G.G., & Stein, J.F. (2000). Dynamic sensory sensitivity and children's word decoding skills. *Proceedings of the National Academy of Sciences, USA, 97*(6), 2952–2957. doi:10.1073/pnas.040546597

Tallal, P., & Piercy, M. (1973). Defects of non-verbal auditory perception in children with developmental aphasia. *Nature, 241,* 468–469. doi:10.1038/241468a0

Vidyasagar, T.R. (2004). Neural underpinnings of dyslexia as a disorder of visuo-spatial attention. Clinical and *Experimental Optometry, 87*(1), 4–10. doi:10.1111/j.1444 -0938.2004.tb03138

Vincent, A., Deacon, R., Dalton, P., Salmond, C., Blamire, A.M., Pendlebury, S., … Stein, J. (2002). Maternal antibody-mediated dyslexia? Evidence for a pathogenic serum factor in a mother of two dyslexic children shown by transfer to mice using behavioural studies and magnetic resonance spectroscopy. *Journal of Neuroimmunology, 130*(1–2), 243–247.

Williams, J., & O'Donovan, M.C. (2006). The genetics of developmental dyslexia. *European Journal of Human Genetics, 14,* 681–689. doi:10.1038/sj.ejhg.5201575

Witton, C., Stein, J.F., Stoodley, C.J., Rosner, B.S., & Talcott, J.B. (2002). Separate influences of acoustic AM and FM sensitivity on the phonological decoding skills of impaired and normal readers. *Journal of Cognitive Neuroscience, 14*(6), 866–874. doi:10.1162/089892902760191090

Zaremba, S., Naegele, J.R., Barnstable, C.J., & Hockfield, S. (1990). Neuronal subsets express multiple high-molecular-weight cell-surface glycoconjugates defined by monoclonal antibodies Cat-301 and VC1.1. *Journal of Neuroscience , 10*(9), 2985-2995.

CHAPTER 4

Investigation of Candidate Genes in Families with Dyslexia

Cecilia Marino, Sara Mascheretti, Andrea Facoetti, and Massimo Molteni

THE DYSLEXIA PHENOTYPE AND THE INTERMEDIATE PHENOTYPES APPROACH

Reading is a complex cognitive task requiring the processing of visual symbols into meaningful sounds, which are the elementary components of any language. A growing body of evidence suggests that reading relies on a multimodal and highly integrated large-scale network across phonological, attentional, memory, visual, and auditory perceptual pathways. Developmental dyslexia (DD), one of the most common neurodevelopmental disorders, is more frequent in boys than girls and is moderately heritable, with heritability estimates that typically range from 44% to 75% (Plomin & Kovas, 2005; Rutter et al., 2004). The genetic mechanisms proposed to underlie the clinical manifestation of DD are complex, and it is well known that genes are necessary—but not sufficient—to explain the risk to develop the disorder. For example, unique genotype–environment combinations occurring during crucial phases of the individual development can explain a sizable amount of such risk. Converging patterns of results across segregation studies support etiological heterogeneity, with either a single major locus (dominant or additive with sex-dependent penetrance that is higher for males), and/or a multifactorial-polygenic model, being the most parsimonious explanations for the consistently high familial aggregation rates of DD (Pennington et al., 1991). Largely prompted by these estimates, there have been dozens of genetic marker studies since 1994 conditioned on categorical diagnosis and various clinical phenotypes, such as phonological and orthographic skills. Linkages have been found to chromosome 1, 2, 3, 6, 15, and 18. *DYX1C1*, *KIAA0319*, *DCDC2*, and *ROBO1* have been consistently reported to be candidate dyslexia susceptibility genes (CDSG). The proteins encoded by these genes, though diverse, have been found to be functionally linked to pathways involved in neuronal migration and axon growth (Galaburda, LoTurco, Ramus, Fitch, & Rosen, 2006). Despite this large amount of genetic data, simple one-to-one relationships between genes and discrete or quantifiable clinical measures of DD have not emerged consistently across studies. Crucial issues for understanding the lack of consistency across studies include 1) the clinical complexity and 2) the lack of consensus regarding core impairments of DD. Furthermore, clinical phenotypes may not be optimal for genetic research, as they do not capture the true essence of the disorder, and show great intra-individual variation as a function of developmental stage and treatment. Finally, native language might determine environmental niches—in terms of orthographic transparency, graphemic complexity and direction of reading—that crucially contribute to the heterogeneity observed at the clinical level. As an alternative to clinical phenotypes, intermediate phenotypes (IPs) may be helpful, given that IPs are closer to a specific genetic abnormality than are clinical diagnoses. IPs are traits (most often neurocognitive, electrophysiological, or neuroanatomical markers) that are related to the disorder, can predate the clinical manifestation of the disease, and are shared among patients and young offspring at risk. The assumption of the IPs approach is that the genetic determination of a particular neural system dysfunction related to DD is likely to have a simpler etiological structure than the disorder phenotype, given that the latter incorporates multiple neural system dysfunctions and summarizes the influences of all susceptibility genes as well as environmental etiologic influences.

THE INTERMEDIATE PHENOTYPES
APPROACH AND GENE FINDING

In the context of the IPs approach, processes related to 1) memory, 2) rapid auditory processing, and 3) spatial attention are discussed as potential IPs, on the basis of their relationship with DD and of their simpler phenotypic structure. Short-term and working memory impairments have been found consistently in DD, with moderate to high effect sizes for short-term ($-.39$ to -1.10) and working memory ($-.37$ to $-.84$), and persist lifelong effects suggesting an impairment rather than a developmental delay model (Swanson, Xinhua Zheng, & Jerman, 2009). Genetic informative studies have shown that variation in reading performance can be explained by specific genes, as well as by a set of genes, in common with short-term and working memory (van Leeuwen, van den Berg, Peper, Hulshoff Pol, & Boomsma, 2009). Combined, short-term and working memory factors account for 29% of the genetic variability in reading performance and their contribution to the genetic covariance for reading performance is not independent from each other (van Leeuwen et al., 2009). Therefore, a common genetic factor could account for storage and manipulation of phonological relevant information, which are important aspects of short-term and working memory, as well as fundamental steps in the reading acquisition process (Baddeley, 1986).

Turning to rapid auditory processing, a growing body of evidence shows that lower-level sensory-processing mechanisms such as rapid auditory processing abilities may play a crucial role in setting up the phonological building blocks of human spoken and written language. Research has shown that individuals with impairments in phonological processing exhibit difficulties in discriminating phonetic contrasts, as well as nonspeech stimuli. Moreover, findings in 6-month-old infants using behavior measures and electrocortical activation to nonspeech stimuli revealed that infant rapid auditory processing efficiency was predictive of preschool expressive and receptive language outcome at 16, 24, and 36 months (Benasich et al., 2006; Choudhuri & Benasich, 2010; Choudhuri, Leppänen, Leevers, & Benasich, 2007).

As far as spatial attention, this ability has been shown to enhance processing not only in terms of speed but also sensitivity, possibly by reducing interactions with "near" stimuli by perceptual noise exclusion mechanisms (Dosher & Lu, 2000). Furthermore, spatial attention has been shown to modulate even the earliest sensory processing in the primary visual and auditory cortices (Poghasyan & Ioannides, 2008). Several studies have shown that visual spatial attention is a crucial component of graphemic parsing, and also that it is impaired in DD (Bucholz & McKone, 2004; Cestnick & Coltheart, 1999; Facoetti et al., 2006, 2010; Hari & Renvall, 2001; Roach & Hogben, 2007). Moreover, auditory spatial attention is rapidly oriented during speech–sound processing to enable words' segmentation (Francis, Kaganovich, & Criscoll-Huber, 2008) and to increase phonemic perception (Mondor & Bryden, 1992), and it is also impaired in DD (Facoetti, Lorusso, Cattaneo, Galli, & Molteni, 2005; Renvall & Hari, 2002) as well as in specific language impairment (Stevens, Sanders, & Neville, 2006).

In summary, based on the assumption that genes influencing liability to DD likely impinge on multiple neural systems that mediate a number of neural domains, some recent genetic association and linkage studies adopted the IP approach and implemented neurocognitive/neurophysiological trait impairments as phenotypes. For example, we recently investigated the relevance of the brain nicotinergic system upon the discrete neurocognitive mechanism of spatial attentional orienting. Attentional orienting is mainly mediated by nicotinic cholinergic receptors in the parietal cortex (Thiel & Fink, 2008), with the $\alpha4$-$\beta2$ receptor being the most common nicotinic receptor in the human cerebral cortex. Human studies showed that the $\alpha4$ subunit gene (*CHRNA4*) modulates accurate and rapid spatial attentional orienting (Greenwood, Fossella, & Parasuraman, 2005; Parasuraman, Greenwood, Kumar, & Fossella, 2005), early event-related potential components in both visual and auditory modalities (Espeseth, Endestat, Rootwelt, & Reinvang, 2007) and parietal-attentional network function as revealed by fMRI (Winterer et al., 2007). We addressed the question of whether a dysregulation of the nicotinergic system resulting in alterations of visual and auditory attentional orienting may ultimately predispose individuals to the clinical manifestation of DD.

In this study, 143 offspring from 119 nuclear families of DD probands were assessed on a spatial attention cueing task (Posner, 1980), and participants were measured in both the visual and auditory modality, as well as for DD/related phenotypes and genotyped for CHRNA4 markers. Marker-trait association analyses were performed by the quantitative transmission disequilibrium test as modeled by Abecasis, Cookson, &

Cardon (2000) for DD, as a discrete trait, and quantitative phenotypes—word and nonword reading, word and nonword spelling, orthographic choice and spatial attention measures (cueing effect). Significant associations were found between the "cueing effect" in the auditory modality and rs3827020TC, and between rs1044397GA rs1044396GA and both word and nonword reading. In a similar attempt, some investigators tested the association of central auditory speech processing (mismatch negativity, MMN) in a whole-genome data set of nuclear families of DD and found that the late component (300–600 ms)—a correlate of reduced auditory memory span—was associated with the rs4234898 genetic marker; it is interesting to note that variation at this marker was found to be correlated to the expression of the gene *SCL2A3* which belongs to the family of facilitative glucose transporters strongly expressed in the brain (Roeske et al., 2009). Recent studies have reported evidences that GRIN2B, a gene coding for a subunit of the ionotropic glutamate receptor, is associated with short-term memory both in general population (de Quervain & Papassotiropoulos, 2006) and DD families. Moreover, this latter effect is even stronger when only maternal transmission is considered (Ludwig et al., 2010). This same gene is located within a region (12p12-p13) that has been linked again to a memory phenotype in a genome scan of DD families (Brkananc et al., 2008).

Finally, the *DYX1C1* gene, located in the 15q region, is a further example supporting IPs as a successful approach to achieve consistency across studies. A number of association studies in different samples followed the original association finding (Taipale et al., 2003) with inconsistent results. Four of these studies did not find any association between *DYX1C1* variants and DD phenotypes (Bellini et al., 2005; Cope et al., 2005b; Marino et al., 2005; Meng et al., 2005a). Three studies found associations of DD with the same markers reported by Taipale et al. (2003), but the associations were in the opposite direction (Brkanac et al., 2007; Scerri et al., 2004; Wigg et al., 2004). It is interesting to note that three recent independent family-based association studies consistently found a significant association between a measure of short-term memory and *DYX1C1* (Bates et al., 2009; Dahdouh et al., 2009; Marino et al., 2007).

Candidate Dyslexia Susceptibility Genes for *DYX2* (6p21.3 Region): *KIAA0319* and *DCDC2*

The first evidence for a quantitative-trait locus in the 6p21.3 region was found in two independent U.S. samples (Cardon et al., 1994, 1995). The original Cardon et al. (1994, 1995) results prompted four independent cohort studies whereby linkage was replicated in one U.K. (Fisher et al., 1999) and two U.S. (Gayán et al., 1999; Grigorenko et al., 1997, 2003; Grigorenko, Wood, Meyer, & Pauls, 2000) samples, while a Canadian study failed to provide evidence for replication (Field & Kaplan, 1998; Petryshen, Kaplan, Liu, & Field, 2000). Successive association studies of DD employed progressively finer maps of the 6p21.3 region and identified CDSG—*VMP*, *DCDC2*, *KIAA0319*, *TTRAP*, and *THEM2*—in different samples (Cope et al., 2005a; Deffenbacher et al., 2004; Francks et al., 2004; Kaplan et al., 2002; Meng et al., 2005b; Platko et al., 2008; Turic et al., 2003). Inasmuch as most support was in favor of *DCDC2* and *KIAA0319*, a number of studies followed in which systematic linkage disequilibrium screens were performed for either one or both genes (Brkanac et al. 2007; Couto et al., 2009; Dennis et al., 2009; Harold et al., 2006; Ludwig et al., 2008; Wilcke et al., 2009). Overall, findings were surprisingly consistent in pointing to *KIAA0319* and *DCDC2* as the most relevant CDSGs. We tested for association between two *DCDC2* markers, i.e. BV677278 and rs793862, and reading, spelling, and memory measures in 210 nuclear families of DD (297 offspring) of Italian ancestry. We found significant associations between BV677278 deletion and word and nonword reading. A significant association was also found between a memory composite (backward/forward spans) and BV677278 allele 10 (Marino et al., 2011). No associations were evident between rs793862 and any measures.

Pleiotropic Effects of Candidate Dyslexia Susceptibility Genes

Converging evidence indicates that early developmental problems in oral language may predate and/or be associated with features of DD, with varying degrees of persistence and severity (Snowling, Bishop, & Stothard, 2000). In addition, the correlation between mathematics and reading is well known (Markowitz, Willemsen, Trumbetta, van Beijsterveldt, & Boomsma, 2005). When a correlation is observed between two traits whose heritabilities are substantial, one cause of such correlation is that the same genes influence both traits, an effect called pleiotropy. Behavioral genetics studies have shown strong genetic correlations for language and reading traits (Bishop, 2001) as well as for the covariation of reading and mathematics traits (Kovas et al., 2007). These data support the view that there is a degree of overlap in the genetic susceptibility across co-morbid domains. Subsequently, investigating the extent to which the same genes operate between disabilities has been one of the major efforts in the field of molecular genetics research, addressing the issue of the generality of genetic effects (Plomin & Kovas, 2005). Significant linkage results have been reported for speech sound disorder and specific language impairment to chromosome 3 and 1p34-p36, 6p22, and 15q regions (Miscimarra et al., 2007; Rice, Smith, & Gayán, 2009; Smith, Pennington, Boada, & Shriberg, 2005; Stein et al., 2006)—all of which have been previously implicated in linkage studies of DD.

In a genetically informed study of families ascertained via a child with DD, we explored the hypothesis that the CDSGs *DCDC2* and *DYX1C1* could be associated with comorbid language and mathematics skills across the whole distribution of liability. The sample consisted of 180 nuclear families, all of Italian ancestry and native language. Two hundred forty-nine offspring (mean age 10.8 ± 2.6 years, male:female sex ratio 3:1) were assessed for language (semantic comprehension, token test, syntactic comprehension, word and nonword repetition, rapid automatized naming, semantic fluency) as well as mathematics (mental calculation, written calculation, number dictation, numerical facts) phenotypes. Participants were scored for *DYX1C1*, i.e. -3GA, 1249GT, and 1259CG, and DCDC2, i.e. BV677278, markers. Our data showed that markers at both genes were associated with mathematics skills: numerical facts was linked to *DCDC2* BV677278 marker, while mental calculation, accuracy with *DYX1C1* -3GA and 1249GT markers. No statistically significant associations were found between *DCDC2* or *DYX1C1* markers and language phenotypes. In summary, these findings likely indicate shared biological or cognitive processes that underlie reading and mathematics but not language and represent primary evidence in favor of a pleiotropic effect of the *DCDC2* and *DYX1C1* genes on mathematics skills in a sizable sample of families ascertained for DD.

EXTRAGENETIC INFLUENCES AND GENE X ENVIRONMENT INTERACTIONS IN DEVELOPMENTAL DYSLEXIA

Despite mounting evidence for a genetic aetiology of DD, it is clear that the heritability of the disorder will not be 100%, a fact that points to the importance of environmental variables in mediating the degree of genetic influence upon individual differences in DD and related neuro-psychological domains (Byrne et al., 2002; Gayán & Olson, 2001, 2003; Grigorenko et al., 2007; Hayiou-Thomas, 2008; Olson, 2002, 2006; Petrill, Deater-Deckard, Thompson, DeThorne, & Schatschneider, 2006; Walker, Greenwood, Hart, & Carta, 1994). Among the most commonly described environmental factors are 1) socioeconomic status (SES), 2) familial structure and demography, 3) parental educational level, and 4) home literacy environment (see Grigorenko, 2001).

There is a large body of research establishing that SES accounts for child's language development and that it is related to the nature of mother's talk to child (e.g., the amount of speech addressed to children, the richness of the vocabulary used, the length of utterances) that can then be considered a positive predictor of child's language abilities. In representative samples, children from lower SES show slower rates of development and poorer communication skills than do children from higher SES. Moreover, lower SES mothers have consistently been found to talk less, to use a smaller vocabulary, to be more directive, and to ask their children fewer questions than higher SES mothers (Hoff & Tian, 2005).

In addition to growing evidence that marital instability is associated with behavior and emotional problems in childhood (see e.g., Amato, 2001; D'Onofrio et al., 2005; Nobile et al., 2009; O'Connor, Caspi, De Fries, & Plomin, 2000, 2003), disruption of the family structure is also associated with academic achievement and learning (Jee et al., 2008;

O'Connor et al., 2000). Having consistent relationships with parents who nurture the exploration of new skills is intuitively important for a child exposed to reading. Conversely, reliance upon only one parent may hamper this process. More broadly, a single-parent family may imply diminished parental support and higher psychosocial stress, which in turn could enhance learning difficulties. A significant impact of family structure on the development of cognitive and learning impairments was reported by O'Connor et al. (2000) studying a Colorado Adoption Project study subsample, and concluding that children who experience parental separation by the age of 12 have worse academic achievement. Recently, Jee et al. (2008) found that children who are separated from parents for more than one month have worse learning and preliteracy outcomes, as well as more learning difficulties and preliteracy problems at their entrance to kindergarten.

Similarly, there has been an increasing concern about the short- and long-term effects of early parenthood on children's intellectual, behavioral, and social development. A number of studies showed that the offspring of younger mothers are at increased risk of cognitive disadvantage and educational underachievement and that the disadvantages experienced by these children are likely to persist into adolescence and early adulthood (Fergusson & Lynskey, 1993; Fergusson & Woodward, 1999). Fergusson and Woodward (1999) already commented on the social, economic, and personal factors associated with teenage parenthood (e.g., educational underachievement, socioeconomic disadvantage, early psychosocial difficulties), which can generate greater life stress. A second and possibly more pertinent issue relates to the quality of parenting and early family life experiences associated with younger maternal age, whereby very young mothers are more likely to be less experienced and have less knowledge about developmental milestones, provide less verbally stimulating environments and home environments that are more frequently characterized by higher levels of stressful factors.

It is widely believed that there are complementary links between reading achievement and reading exposure (Bus, Van IJzendoorn, & Pellegrini, 1995; Scarborough & Dobrich, 1994) and that genetic and environmental influences contribute to individual differences in reading exposure (Harlaar, Dale, & Plomin, 2007). The evidence for genetic and environmental influences on reading exposure provides a window on its links with reading achievement. It could be the case that common genetic and environmental influences on individual differences in reading exposure reflect genetic and environmental risk factors on reading achievement. In a recent study, Harlaar et al. (2007) document that reading exposure has environmentally mediated effects on children's later reading performance beyond genetic transmission. This finding suggests that improving levels of early reading achievement may go toward fostering engagement in reading, and weakening the cycle of poor reading achievement that can arise when children do not spend time in reading.

Substance abuse, birth weight and gestational problems are additive, possible risk factors. In a study of 131 9- to 12-year-old children ascertained for prenatal exposure to different types of drugs, Fried, Watkinson, and Siegel (1997) found a significant linear dose-dependent association between prenatal cigarettes exposure and child postnatal exposure to maternal smoke and lower language and reading scores after controlling for potentially confounding prenatal factors. Most studies focusing on reading achievement have reported a much higher rate of more subtle difficulties such as minor neurological problems, learning disabilities and behavior problems among extremely premature infants at school age (Bowen, Gibson, & Hand, 2002), and impairments in reading skills among very low birth weight children compared with term controls (Samuelsson et al., 2006). Finally, in a case-control study Gilger, Pennington, Green, Smith, and Smith (1992) found some evidence of higher rate of miscarriage in families selected through a proband with reading disability. Even if the precise biological meaning of the miscarriage finding is debatable, it suggests that there may be some transmissible component in families with DD affecting early development in utero.

As more is learned about the genetic and environmental influences affecting DD/reading phenotypes, a question that remains largely unaddressed is whether analyzing gene-by-environment (GxE) interactions can better explain the contribution of genetic factors or environmental factors in isolation. A GxE interaction is a specific form of interplay, whereby genetic susceptibility conferred by a specific allele is modulated by a measurable environmental factor (see, e.g., Rutter, Moffitt, & Caspi, 2006). The direction of change in heritability along the full liability distribution may be explained by two different, yet complementary, theoretical models: 1) the bioecological model (Bronfenbrenner & Ceci, 1994), which suggests that genetic influences on behavior should be most evident when the environment is supportive, because there is greater actualization of genetic potential in supportive environments than in poor environments and 2) the diathesis-stress model (Rende & Plomin, 1992), which suggests that heritability for a disorder should be greater in poorer environments, whereby stressors lead to increased influence of deleterious alleles that would otherwise remain undetected in more supportive environments. That the strength of a genetic signal on DD/reading phenotypes may not be homogenous along the full liability distribution and across different ecological niches is suggested by the data of Kremen et al. (2005), who showed that parental education modulates the heritability of word recognition in a sample of 347 middle-age male twin pairs. Consistently, an extended De Fries and Fulker regression analysis of twin scores showed that the heritability of a weighted composite measure of word recognition, spelling, and reading comprehension increased significantly with increasing levels of parental education (Friend, De Fries, & Olson, 2008). According to the findings of several recent studies, both the bioecological and the diathesis-stress models of GxE are plausible accounts for explaining the interplay between genetic susceptibility conferred by a specific allele and a measurable environmental factor (Asbury, Wachs, & Plomin, 2005; Friend et al., 2008; Kremen et al., 2005; McGrath et al., 2007; Pennington et al. 2009; van den Oord & Rowe, 1998). In spite of the potential importance of molecular genetic approaches to GxE (Rutter et al., 2006), no study has so far taken into account the conjoint role of CDSG and measured environmental factors upon DD/reading phenotypes. The only possible exception, however, is the McGrath et al. (2007) study about the interaction between two chromosomal regions (i.e., 6p22 and 15q21 locations) and specific environmental hazards (e.g., maternal education, and parents' oral reading to child) on speech sound disorder related phenotypes (e.g., semantics, phonemic awareness, and rapid serial naming), by a sib pair linkage design. Because of the recent explosion of interest in studying GxE interaction across the whole of medicine and the great importance of molecular genetic approaches to GxE (Moffitt, Caspi, & Rutter, 2005; Rutter et al., 2006), we recently applied a general test for GxE interaction in sib pair-based association analysis of quantitative traits (van der Sluis, Dolan, Neale, & Posthuma, 2008) to: 1) three reading phenotypes (i.e., reading, spelling, and memory), 2) a set of common putative factors that have been described as potentially hazardous for DD/reading phenotypes as the environmental moderators, and 3) two CDSG genes (*DYX1C1* and *DCDC2*) variants, in a sample of 59 nuclear DD families with more than one offspring and complete phenotypic information. Results show several significant interactions between specified environmental moderators (i.e., smoking during pregnancy, risk of miscarriage, birth weight, parental marital status, father's and mother's age at childbirth) and both *DYX1C1* and *DCDC2* markers upon reading phenotypes. These findings suggest that several environmental factors can enhance the genetic susceptibility to reading impairment. More specifically, we can broadly consider these environmental factors as indicating poorer and less supportive environments with regard to reading achievement. From this perspective, our results are consistent with the diathesis-stress rather than the bioecological model of GxE interactions (Asbury et al., 2005; Rende & Plomin, 1992; van der Oord & Rowe, 1998) whereby a less supportive familial environment may lead to greater genetic liability from detrimental *DYX1C1* and *DCDC2* alleles, which would remain undetected in more supportive environments.

CONCLUSION

This is a new era in which conjoint advances in molecular genetics and dissection of the DD phenotype enable rapid progress with multiple gene discoveries and explain the necessary and sufficient conditions for overt illness manifestation. Although encouraging, the bulk of such findings raises considerable challenges for investigators attempting to unravel the etiological complexity of DD. First, accumulating evidence supports the existence of multiple genes and some overlap in genetic susceptibility across the traditional nosological divide. How is pleiotropy conceptualized? How do these genes coalesce in influencing liability to overt expression of DD and comorbid conditions? Are their effects additive or interactive? Second, there is an explanatory gap between the findings of statistical association of a gene variant with the disorder and the understanding of pathogenesis, with regard to specific illness phenomena. This gap might be easier to bridge by employing IPs in the domains of cognition, neurophysiology, or neuroanatomy. Finally, the theory that genes and environment combine to confer susceptibility to the development of diseases developed in the last century, but the use of such a framework for exploring the etiology of DD is starting to surface now. How do genes confer increased susceptibility to DD related to environmental hazards? This fascinating work is at an early stage but has the potential to change our conception of learning disabilities as well as our understanding of the pathogenesis of complex mental disorders.

Overall, it is important that researchers enter an interactive process using identified genetic factors to guide the refinement of the phenotype, and the refined phenotype in turn allowing increased power to detect further genetic signals. To facilitate this approach, it will be important to collect samples that have a full representation of DD subcomponents across phonological, memory, attentional, and visual and auditory perceptual pathways as well as detailed, high-quality phenotypic assessments—preferably using measurements that incorporate quantitative units of analysis that are amenable to assessment in the laboratory.

REFERENCES

Abecasis, G.R., Cookson, W.O., & Cardon, L.R. (2000). Pedigree tests of transmission disequilibrium. *European Journal of Human Genetics, 8,* 545–551. doi:10.1038/sj.ejhg.5200494

Amato, P.R. (2001). Children of divorce in the 1990s: An update of the Amato and Keith (1991) meta-analysis. *Journal of Family Pychology, 15,* 355–370. doi:10.1037//0893 -3200.15.3.355

Asbury, K., Wachs, T.D., & Plomin, R. (2005). Environmental moderators of genetic influence on verbal and nonverbal abilities in early childhood. *Intelligence, 33,* 643–661. doi:10.1016/j.intell.2005.03.008

Baddeley, A.D. (1986). *Working memory.* London, U.K.: Oxford University Press.

Bates, T.C., Lind, P.A., Luciano, M., Montgomery, G.W., Martin, N.G., & Wright, M.J. (2010). Dyslexia and DYX1C1: Deficits in reading and spelling associated with a missense mutation. *Molecular Psychiatry, 15,* 1190–1196. doi:10.1038/mp.2009.120

Bellini, G., Bravaccio, C., Calamoneri, F., Donatella Cocuzza, M., Fiorillo, P., ... Pascotto, A. (2005). No evidence for association between dyslexia and DYX1C1 functional variants in a group of children and adolescents from Southern Italy. *Journal of Molecular Neuroscience, 27,* 311–314. doi:10.1385/JMN:27:3:311

Benasich, A.A., Choudury, N., Friedman, J.T., Realpe-Bonilla, T., Chojnowska, C., & Gou, Z. (2006). The infants as a prelinguistic model for language learning impairments: Predicting from event-related potentials to behaviour. *Neuropsychologia, 44,* 396–411. doi:10.1016/j.neuropsychologia.2005.06.004

Bishop, D.V. (2001). Genetic influences on language and literacy problems in children: Same or different? *Journal of Child Psychology and Psychiatry, 42,* 189–198. doi:10.1111/1469 -7610.00710

Bowen, J.R., Gibson, F.L., & Hand, P.J. (2002). Educational outcome at 8 years for children who were born extremely prematurely: A controlled study. *Journal* of Paediatrics and Child Health, 38, 438–444. doi:10.1046/j.1440-1754.2002.00039

Brkanac, Z., Chapman, N.H., Igo, R.P. Jr., Matsushita, M.M., Nielsen, K., Berninger, V.W., ... Raskind, W.H. (2008). Genome scan of a nonword repetition phenotype in families with dyslexia: Evidence for multiple loci. Behavior Genetics, 38, 462–475. doi:10.1007/s10519-008-9215-2

Brkanac, Z., Chapman, N.H., Matsushita, M.M., Chun, L., Nielsen, K., Cochrane, E., ... Raskind, W.H. (2007). Evaluation of candidate genes for DYX1 and DYX2 in families with dyslexia. American Journal of Medical Genetic Part B Neuropsychiatric Genetics, 144B, 556–560.

Brofenbrenner, U., & Ceci, S.J. (1994). Nature-nurture reconceptualized in developmental perspective: A bioecological model. Psychological Review, 101, 568–586.

Buchholz, J., & McKone, E. (2004). Adults with dyslexia show deficits on spatial frequency doubling and visual attention tasks. Dyslexia, 10, 24–43. doi:10.1002/dys.263

Bus, A.G., Van IJzendoorn, M.H., & Pellegrini, A.D. (1995). Joint book reading makes for success in learning to read: A meta-analysis on intergenerational transmission of literacy. Review of Educational Research, 65, 1–21. doi:10.2307/1170476

Byrne, B., Delaland, C., Fielding-Barnsley, R., Quain, P., Samuelsson, S., Hoien, T., ... Olson, R.K. (2002). Longitudinal twin study of early reading development in three countries: Preliminary results. Annals of Dyslexia, 52, 49–74. doi:10.1007/s11881-002-0006-9

Cardon, L.R., Smith, S.D., Fulker, D.W., Kimberling, W.J., Pennington, B.F., & DeFries, J.C. (1994). Quantitative trait locus for reading disability on chromosome 6. Science, 266, 276–279. doi:10.1126/science.7939663

Cardon, L.R., Smith, S.D., Fulker, D.W., Kimberling, W.J., Pennington, B.F., & DeFries, J.C. (1995). Quantitative trait locus for reading disability: Correction. Science, 268, 1553. doi:10.1126/science.7777847

Cestnick, L., & Coltheart, M. (1999). The relationship between language-processing and visual-processing deficits in developmental dyslexia. Cognition, 71, 231–255. doi:10.1016/S0010-0277(99)00023-2

Choudury, N., & Benasich, A.A. (2011). Maturation of auditory evoked potentials from 6 to 48 months: Prediction to 3 and 4 year language and cognitive abilities. Clinical Neurophysiology, 122(2), 320–338. doi:10.1016/j.clinph.2010.05.035

Choudury, N., Leppänen, P.H., Leevers, H.J., & Benasich, A.A. (2007). Infant information processing and family history of specific language impairment: converging evidence for RAP deficits from two paradigms. Developmental Science, 10, 213–236. doi:10.1111/j.1467-7687.2007.00546

Cope, N., Harold, D., Hill, G., Moskvina, V., Stevenson, J., Holmans, P., ... Williams, J. (2005a). Strong evidence that KIAA0319 on chromosome 6p is a susceptibility gene for developmental dyslexia. American Journal of Human Genetics, 76, 581–591. doi:10.1086/429131

Cope, N.A., Hill, G., van den Bree, M., Harold, D., Moskvina, V., Green, E.K., ... O'Donovan, M.C. (2005b). No support for association between dyslexia susceptibility 1 candidate 1 and developmental dyslexia. Molecular Psychiatry, 10, 237–238. doi:10.1038/sj.mp.4001596

Couto, J.M., Gomez, L., Wigg, K., Ickowicz, A., Pathare, T., Malone, M., ... Barr, C.L. (2009). Association of attention-deficit/hyperactivity disorder with a candidate region for reading disabilities on chromosome 6p. Biological Psychiatry, 66, 368–375. doi:10.1016/j.biopsych.2009.02.016

Dahdouh, F., Anthoni, H., Tapia-Páez, I., Peyrard-Janvid, M., Schulte-Körne, G., Warnke, A., ... Zucchelli, M. (2009). Further evidence for DYX1C1 as a susceptibility factor for dyslexia. Psychiatric Genetics, 19, 59–63. doi:10.1097/YPG.0b013e32832080e1

Deffenbacher, K.E., Kenyon, J.B., Hoover, D.M., Olson, R.K., Pennington, B.F., De Fries, J.C., & Smith, S.D. (2004). Refinement of the 6p21.3 quantitative trait locus influencing dyslexia: linkage and association analyses. Human Genetics, 115, 128–138. doi:10.1007/s00439-004-1126-6

Dennis, M.Y., Paracchini, S., Scerri, T.S., Prokunina-Olsson, L., Knight, J.C., Wade-Martins, R., ... Monaco, A.P. (2009). A common variant associated with dyslexia reduced expression of the KIAA0319 gene. PloS Genetics, 5, e1000436. doi:10.1371/journal.pgen.1000436 de Quervain, D.J., & Papassotiropoulos, A. (2006). Identification of a genetic cluster influencing memory performance and hippocampal activity in humans. *Proceedings of the National Academy of Sciences, USA, 103,* 4270–4274. doi:10.1073/pnas.0510212103

D'Onofrio, B.M., Turkheimer, E., Emery, R.E., Slutske, W.S., Heath, A.C., Madden, P.A., & Martin, N.G. (2005). A genetically informed study of marital instability and its association with offspring psychopathology. *Journal of Abnormal Psychology, 114,* 570–586. doi:10.1037/0021-843X.114.4.570

Dosher, B.A., & Lu, Z.L. (2000). Mechanisms of perceptual attention in precuing of location. *Vision Research, 40,* 1269–1292. doi:10.1016/S0042-6989(00)00019-5

Espeseth, T., Endestad, T., Rootwelt, H., & Reinvang, I. (2007). Nicotine receptor gene CHRNA4 modulates early event-related potentials in auditory and visual oddball target detection tasks. *Neuroscience, 147,* 974–985. doi:10.1016/j.neuroscience.2007.04.027

Facoetti, A., Lorusso, M.L., Cattaneo, C., Galli, R., & Molteni M. (2005). Visual and auditory attentional capture are both sluggish in children with developmental dyslexia. *Acta Neurobiologiae Experimentalis (Wars), 65,* 61–72.

Facoetti, A., Trussardi, A.N., Ruffino, M., Lorusso, M.L., Cattaneo, C., Galli, R., ... Zorzi, M. (2010). Multisensory spatial attention deficits are predictive of phonological decoding skills in developmental dyslexia. *Journal of Cognitive Neuroscience, 22,* 1011–1025. doi:10.1162/jocn.2009.21232

Facoetti, A., Zorzi, M., Cestnick, L., Lorusso, M.L., Molteni, M., Paganoni, P., ... Mascetti, G.G. (2006). The relationship between visuo-spatial attention and nonword reading in developmental dyslexia. *Cognitive Neuropsychology, 23,* 841–855. doi:10.1080/02643290500483090

Fergusson, D.M., & Lynskey, M.T. (1993). Maternal age and cognitive and behavioural outcomes in middle childhood. *Pediatric and Perinatal Epidemiology, 7,* 77–91. doi:10.1111/j.1365-3016.1993.tb00604

Fergusson, D.M., & Woodward, L.J. (1999). Maternal age and educational and psychosocial outcomes in early adulthood. *Journal of Child Psychology and Psychiatry, 43,* 479–489. doi:10.1111/1469-7610.00464

Field, L.L., & Kaplan, B.J. (1998). Absence of linkage of phonological coding dyslexia to chromosome 6p23-p21.3 in a large family data set. *American Journal of Human Genetics, 63,* 1448–1456. doi:10.1086/302107

Fisher, S.E., Marlow, A.J., Lamb, J., Maestrini, E., Williams, D.F., Richardson, A.J., ... Monaco, A.P. (1999). A quantitative-trait locus on chromosome 6p influences different aspects of developmental dyslexia. *American Journal of Human Genetics, 64,* 146–156. doi:10.1086/302190

Francis, A.L., Kaganovich, N., & Criscoll-Huber, C. (2008). Cue-specific effects of categorization training on the relative weighting of acoustic cues to consonant voicing in English. *The Journal of the Acoustical Society of America, 124,* 1234–1251. doi:10.1121/1.2945161

Francks, C., Paracchini, S., Smith, S.D., Richardson, A.J., Scerri, T.S., Cardon, L.R., ... Monaco, A.P. (2004). A 77-kilobase region of chromosome 6p22.2 is associated with dyslexia in families from the United Kingdom and from the United States. *American Journal of Human Genetics, 75,* 1046–1058. doi:10.1086/426404

Fried, P.A., Watkinson, B., & Siegel, L.S. (1997). Reading and language in 9- to 12-year olds prenatally exposed to cigarettes and marijuana. *Neurotoxicology and Teratology, 19,* 171–183. doi:10.1016/S0892-0362(97)00015-9

Friend, A., De Fries, J.C., & Olson, R.K. (2008). Parental education moderates genetic influences on reading disability. *Psychological Science, 19,* 1124–1130. doi:10.1111/j.1467-9280.2008.02213.x

Galaburda, A.M., LoTurco, J., Ramus, F., Fitch, R.H., & Rosen, G.D. (2006). From genes to behavior in developmental dyslexia. *Nature Neuroscience, 9,* 1213–1217. Review. doi:10.1038/nn1772

Gayán, J., & Olson, R.K. (2001). Genetic and environmental influences on orthographic and phological skills in children with reading disabilities. *Developmental Neuropsychology, 20,* 483–507.

Gayán, J., & Olson, R.K. (2003). Genetic and environmental influences on individual differences in printed word recognition. *Journal of Experimental and Child Psychology, 84,* 97–123. doi:10.1016/S0022-0965(02)00181-9

Gayán, J., Smith, S.D., Cherny, S.S., Cardon, L.R., Fulker, D.W., Brower, A.M., ...

DeFries, J.C. (1999). Quantitative-trait locus for specific language and reading deficits on chromosome 6p. *American Journal of Human Genetics, 64,* 157–164. doi:10.1086/302191

Gilger, J.W., Pennington, B.F., Green, P., Smith, S.M., & Smith, S.D. (1992). Reading disability, immune disorders and non-right-handedness: Twin and family studies of their relations. *Neuropsychologia, 30,* 209–227. doi:10.1016/0028-3932(92)90001-3

Greenwood, P.M., Fossella, J.A., & Parasuraman, R. (2005). Specificity of the effect of a nicotinic receptor polymorphism on individual differences in visuospatial attention. *Journal of Cognitive Neuroscience, 17,* 1611–1620.

Grigorenko, E.L. (2001). Developmental dyslexia: An update on genes, brains, and environments. *Journal of Child Psychology and Psychiatry, 42,* 91–125. doi:10.1111/1469-7610.00704

Grigorenko, E.L., Deyoung, C.G., Getchell, M., Haeffel, G.J., Klinteberg, B.A.F., Koposov, R.A., ... Yrigollen, C.M. (2007). Exploring interactive effects of genes and environments in etiology of individual differences in reading comprehension. *Development and Psychopathology, 19,* 1089–1103. doi:10.1017/S0954579407000557

Grigorenko, E.L., Wood, F.B., Golovyan, L., Meyer, M., Romano, C., & Pauls, D. (2003). Continuing the search for dyslexia genes on 6p. American Journal of Medical Genetics Part B: *Neuropsychiatric Genetics, 118B,* 89–98. doi:10.1002/ajmg.b.10032

Grigorenko, E.L., Wood, F.B., Meyer, S.B., Hart, L.A., Speed, W.C., Shuster, A., & Pauls, D.L. (1997). Susceptibility loci for distinct components of developmental dyslexia on chromosome 6 and 15. *American Journal of Human Genetics, 60,* 27–39.

Grigorenko, E.L., Wood, F.B., Meyer, M.S., Pauls, D.L. (2000). Chromosome 6p influences on different dyslexia-related cognitive processes: Further confirmation. *American Journal of Human Genetics, 66,* 715–723. doi:10.1086/302755

Hari, R., & Renvall, H. (2001). Impaired processing of rapid stimulus sequence in dyslexia. *Trends in Cognitive Science, 5,* 525–532. doi:10.1016/S1364-6613(00)01801-5

Harlaar, N., Dale, P.S., & Plomin, R. (2007). Reading exposure: A (largely) environmental risk factor with environmentally-mediated effects on reading performance in the primary school years. *Journal of Child Psychology and Psychiatry, 48,* 1192–1199. doi:10.1111/j.1469-7610.2007.01798

Harold, D., Paracchini, S., Scerri, T., Dennis, M., Cope, N., Hill, G., ... Monaco, A.P. (2006). Further evidence that the KIAA0319 gene confers susceptibility to developmental dyslexia. *Molecular Psychiatry, 11,* 1085–1091. doi:10.1038/sj.mp.4001904

Hayiou-Thomas, M. (2008). Genetic and environmental influences in early speech, language and literacy development. *Journal of Communication Disorders, 41,* 397–408.

Hoff, E., & Tian, C. (2005). Socioeconomic status and cultural influences on language. *Journal of Communication Disorders, 38,* 271–278. doi:10.1016/j.jcomdis.2005.02.003

Jee, S.H., Conn, K.M., Nilsen, W.J., Szilagyi, M.A., Forbes-Jones, E., & Halterman, J.S. (2008). Learning difficulties among children separated from a parent. *Ambulatory Pediatrics, 8,* 163–168. doi:10.1016/j.ambp.2008.02.001

Kaplan, D.E., Gayán, J., Ahn, J., Won, T.W., Pauls, D., Olson, R.K., ... Gruen, J.R. (2002). Evidence for linkage and association with reading disability on 6p21.3-22. *American Journal of Human Genetics, 70,* 1287–1298. doi:10.1086/340449

Kovas, Y., Haworth, C.M.A., Harlaar, N., Petrill, S.A., Dale, P.S., & Plomin, R. (2007). Overlap and specificity of genetic and environmental influences on mathematics and reading disability in 10-year-old twins. *Journal of Child Psychology and Psychiatry, 48,* 914–922. doi: 10.1111/j.1469-7610.2007.01748

Kremen, W.S., Jacobson, K.C., Xian, H., Eisen, S.A., Waterman, B., Toomey, R., ... Lyons, M.J. (2005). Heritability of word recognition in middle-aged men varies as a function of parental education. *Behavior Genetics, 35,* 417–433. doi:10.1007/s10519-004-3876-2

Ludwig, K.U., Roeske, D., Herms, S., Schumacher, J., Warnke, A., Plume, E., ... Hoffmann, P. (2010). Variation in GRIN2B contributes to weak performance in verbal short-term memory in children with dyslexia. *American Journal of Medical Genetic Part B: Neuropsychiatric Genetics, 153B,* 503–511.

Ludwig, K.U., Roeske, D., Schumacher, J., Schulte-Körne, G., König, I.R., Warnke, A., ... Hoffmann, P. (2008). Investigation of interaction between DCDC2 and KIAA0319 in a large German dyslexia sample. *Journal of Neural Transmission, 115,* 1587–1589. doi:10.1007/s00702-008-0124-6

Marino, C., Citterio, A., Giorda, R., Facoetti, A., Menozzi, G., Vanzin, L., ... Molteni, M. (2007). Association of short-term memory with a variant within DYX1C1 in developmental dyslexia. *Genes, Brain and Behavior, 6,* 640–646. doi:10.1111/j.1601-183X.2006.00291

Marino, C., Giorda, R., Lorusso, M.L., Vanzin, L., Salandi, N., Nobile, M., ... Molteni, M. (2005). A family-based association study of the DYX1C1 gene on 15q21.1 in developmental dyslexia. *European Journal of Human Genetics, 13,* 491–499.

Marino, C., Meng, H., Mascheretti, S., Rusconi, M., Cope, N., Giorda, R., ... Gruen, J.R. (2011). DCDC2 genetic variants and susceptibility to developmental dyslexia. *Psychiatric Genetics,* in press.

Markowitz, E.M., Willemsen, G., Trumbetta, S.L., van Beijsterveldt, T.C., & Boomsma, D.I. (2005). The etiology of mathemathical and reading (dis)ability covariation in a sample of Dutch twins. *Twin Research and Human Genetics, 8,* 585–593. doi:10.1375/183242705774860132

McGrath, L.M., Pennington, B.F., Willcutt, E.G., Boada, R., Shriberg, L.D., & Smith, S.D. (2007). Gene x environment interactions in speech sound disorder predict language and preliteracy outcomes. *Development and Psychopathology, 19,* 1047–1072.

Meng, H., Hager, K., Held, M., Page, G.P., Olson, R.K., Pennington, B.F., ... Gruen, J.R. (2005a). TDT-association analysis of EKN1 and dyslexia in a Colorado twin cohort. *Human Genetics, 118,* 87–90. doi:10.1007/s00439-005-0017-9

Meng, H., Smith, S.D., Hager, K., Held, M., Liu, J., Olson, R.K., ... Gruen, J.R. (2005b). Dcdc2 is associated with reading disability and modulates neuronal development in the brain. *Proceedings of the National Academy of Sciences, USA, 102,* 17053–17058. doi:10.1073/pnas.0508591102

Miscimarra, L., Stein, C., Millard, C., Kluge, A., Cartier, K., Freebairn, L., ... Iyengar, S.K. (2007). Further evidence of pleiotropy influencing speech and language: Analysis of the DYX8 region. *Human Heredity, 63,* 47–58. doi:10.1159/000098727

Moffitt, T.E., Caspi, A., & Rutter, M. (2005). Strategy for investigating interactions between measured genes and measured environments. *Archives of General Psychiatry, 62,* 473–481. doi:10.1001/archpsyc.62.5.473

Mondor, T.A., & Bryden, M.P. (1992). On the relation between auditory spatial attention and auditory perceptual asymmetries. *Perception & Psychophysic, 52,* 393–402. doi:10.3758/BF03206699

Nobile, M., Rusconi, M., Bellina, M., Marino, C., Giorda, R., Carlet, O., ... Battaglia, M. (2009). The influence of family structure, the TOH2 G-703T and the 5-HTTLPR serotoninergic genes upon affective problems in children aged 10–14 years. *Journal of Child Psychology and Psychiatry, 50,* 317–325.

O'Connor, T.G., Caspi, A., De Fries, J.C., & Plomin, R. (2000). Are associations between parental divorce and children's adjustment genetically mediated? An adoption study. *Developmental Psychology, 36,* 429–437. doi:10.1037//0012-1649.36.4.429

O'Connor, T.G., Caspi, A., De Fries, J.C., & Plomin, R. (2003). Genotype-environment interaction in children's adjustment to parental separation. *Journal of Child Psychology and Psychiatry, 44,* 849–856. doi:10.1111/1469-7610.00169

Olson, R.K. (2002). Dyslexia: Nature and nurture. *Dyslexia, 8,* 143–159. doi:10.1002/dys.228

Olson, R.K. (2006). Genes, environment, and dyslexia: The 2005 Norman Geschwind memorial lecture. *Annals of Dyslexia, 56,* 205–237. doi:10.1007/s11881-006-0010-6

Parasuraman, R., Greenwood, P.M., Kumar, R., & Fossella, J. (2005). Beyond heritability: Neurotransmitter genes differentially modulate visuospatial attention and working memory. *Psychological Science: A journal of the American Psychological Society / APS, 16,* 200–207.

Pennington, B.F, Gilger, J.W., Pauls, D., Smith, S.A., Smith, S.D., & DeFries, J.C. (1991). Evidence for major gene transmission of developmental dyslexia. *JAMA: The Journal of the American Medical Association, 266,* 1527–1534. doi:10.1001/jama.266.11.1527

Pennington, B.F., McGrath, L.M., Rosenberg, J., Barnard, H., Smith, S.D., Willcutt, E.G... Olson, R.K. (2009). Gene x environment interactions in reading disability and attention-deficit/hyperactivity disorder. *Developmental Psychology, 45,* 77–89.

Petrill, S.A., Deater-Deckard, K., Thompson, L.A., DeThorne, L.S., & Schatschneider, C. (2006). Reading skills in early readers: Genetic and shared environmental influences. *Journal of Learning Disabilities, 39,* 48–55. do i:10.1177/00222194060390010501

Petryshen, T.L., Kaplan, B.J., Liu, M.F., & Field, L.L. (2000). Absence of significant linkage between phonological coding dyslexia and chromosome 6p23-21.3, as determined by use of quantitative-trait methods: confirmation of qualitative analyses. *American Journal of Human Genetics, 66,* 708–14. doi:10.1086/302764

Platko, J.V., Wood, F.B., Pelser, I., Meyer, M., Gericke, G.S., O'Rourke, J., ... Pauls, D.L. (2008). Association of reading disability on chromosome 6p22 in the Afrikaner population. *American Journal of Medical Genetics Part B: Neuropsychiatric Genetics, 147B,* 1278–87. doi:10.1002/ajmg.b.30774

Plomin, R., & Kovas, Y. (2005). Generalist genes and learning disabilities. *Psychological Bulletin, 131,* 592–617. doi:10.1037/0033-2909.131.4.592

Poghosyan, V., & Ioannides, A.A. (2008). Attention modulates earliest responses in the primary auditory and visual cortices. *Neuron, 58,* 802–813. doi:10.1016/j.neuron.2008.04.013

Posner, M.I. (1980). Orienting of attention. *The Quarterly Journal of Experimental Psychology, 32,* 3–25. doi:10.1080/00335558008248231

Rende, R., & Plomin, R. (1992). Diathesis-stress models of psychopathology: A quantitative genetic perspective. *Applied and Preventive Psychology, 1,* 177–182. doi:10.1016/S0962-1849(05)80123-4

Renvall, H., & Hari, R. (2002). Auditory cortical responses to speech-like stimuli in dyslexic adults. *Journal of Cognitive Neuroscience, 14,* 757–768. doi:10.1162/08989290260138654

Rice, M.L., Smith, S.D., & Gayán, J. (2009). Convergent genetic linkage and association to language, speech and reading measures in families of probands with

Specific Language Impairment. *Journal of Neurodevelopmental Disorders, 1,* 264–282. doi:10.1007/s11689-009-9031-x

Roach, N.W., & Hogben, J.H. (2007). Impaired filtering of behaviourally irrelevant visual information in dyslexia. *Brain, 130,* 771–785. doi:10.1093/brain/awl353

Roeske, D., Ludwig, K.U., Neuhoff, N., Becker, J., Bartling, J., Bruder, J., ... Schulte-Körne, G. (2011). First genome-wide association scan on neurophysiological endophenotypes points to trans-regulation effects on SLC2A3 in dyslexic children. *Molecular Psychiatry,* 16(1), 97–107. doi:10.1038/mp.2009.102

Rutter, M., Caspi, A., Fergusson, D., Horwood, L.J., Goodman, R., Maughan, B., ... Carroll, J. (2004). Sex differences in developmental reading disability: New findings from 4 epidemiological studies. *JAMA: The Journal of the American Medical Association, 291,* 2007–2012. doi:10.1001/jama.291.16.2007

Rutter, M., Moffitt, T.E., & Caspi, A. (2006). Gene-environment interplay and psychopathology: Multiple varieties but real effects. *Journal of Child Psychology and Psychiatry, 47,* 226–261. doi: 10.1111/j.1469-7610.2005.01557

Samuelsson, S., Finnström, O., Flodmark, O., Gäddlin, P.O., Leijon, I., & Wadsby, M. (2006). A longitudinal study of reading skills among very-low-birthweight children: Is there a catch-up? *Journal of Pediatric Psychology, 31,* 967–977. doi:10.1093/jpepsy/jsj108

Scarborough, H.S., & Dobrich, W. (1994). On the efficacy of reading to preschoolers. *Developmental Review, 14,* 245–302. doi:10.1006/drev.1994.1010

Scerri, T.S., Fisher, S.E., Francks, C., MacPhie, I.L., Paracchini, S., Richardson, A.J., ... Monaco, A.P. (2004). Putative functional alleles of DYX1C1 are not associated with dyslexia susceptibility in a large sample of sibling pairs from the UK. *Journal of Medical Genetics, 41,* 853–857. doi:10.1136/jmg.2004.018341

Smith, S.D., Pennington, B.F., Boada, R., & Shriberg, L.D. (2005). Linkage of speech sound disorder to reading disability loci. *Journal of Child Psychology and Psychiatry, 46,* 1057–1066. doi:10.11 11/j.1469-7610.2005.01534

Snowling, M., Bishop, D.V., & Stothard, S.E. (2000). Is preschool language impairment a risk factor for dyslexia in adolescence?

Journal of Child Psychology and Psychiatry, 41, 587–600. doi:10.1111/1469-7610.00651

Stein, C.M., Millard, C., Kluge, A., Miscimarra, L.E., Cartier, K.C., Freebairn, L.A., … Iyengar, S.K. (2006). Speech sound disorder influenced by a locus in 15q14 region. *Behavior Genetics, 36,* 858–868. doi:10.1007/s10519-006-9090-7

Stevens, C., Sanders, L., & Neville, H. (2006). Neuropsychological evidence for selective auditory attention deficits in children with specific language impairment. *Brain Research, 1111,* 143–152.

Swanson, H.L., Xinhua Zheng, & Jerman, O. (2009). Working memory, short-term memory, and reading disabilities: A selective meta-analysis of the literature. *Journal of Learning Disabilities, 42,* 260–287. doi:10.1177/0022219409331958

Taipale, M., Kaminen, N., Nopola-Hemmi, J., Haltia, T., Myllyluoma, B., Lyytinen, H., … Kere, J. (2003). A candidate gene for developmental dyslexia encodes a nuclear tetratricopeptide repeat domain protein dynamically regulated in brain. *Proceedings of the National Academy of Sciences, USA, 100,* 11553–11558. doi:10.1073/pnas.1833911100

Thiel, C.M., & Fink, G.R. (2008). Effects on the cholinergic agonist nicotine on reorienting of visual spatial attention and top-down attentional control. *Neuroscience, 152,* 381–390. doi:10.1016/j.neuroscience.2007.10.061

Turic, D., Robinson, L., Duke, M., Morris, D.W., Webb, V., Hamshere, M., … Williams, J. (2003). Linkage disequilibrium mapping provides further evidence of a gene for reading disability on chromosome 6p21.3-22. *Molecular Psychiatry, 8,* 176–185. doi:10.1038/sj.mp.4001216

van den Oord, E.J., & Rowe, D.C. (1998). An examination of genotype-environment interactions for academic achievement in a U.S. national longitudinal survey. *Intelligence, 25,* 205–228. doi:10.1016/S0160-2896(97)90043-X

van der Sluis, S., Dolan, C.V., Neale, M.C., & Posthuma, D. (2008). A general test for gene-environment interaction in family-based association analysis of quantitative traits. *Behavior Genetics, 38,* 372–389.

van Leeuwen, M., van den Berg, S.M., Peper, J.S., Hulshoff Pol, H.E., & Boomsma, D.I. Genetic covariance structure of reading, intelligence and memory in children. *Behavior Genetics, 39,* 245–254. doi:10.1007/s10519-009-9264-1

Walker, D., Greenwood, C., Hart, B., & Carta, J. (1994). Prediction of school outcomes based on early language production and socioeconomic factors. *Child Development, 65*(2), 606–621. doi:10.2307/1131404

Wigg, K.G., Couto, J.M., Feng, Y., Anderson, B., Cate-Carter, T.D., Macciardi, F., … Barr, C.L. (2004). Support for EKN1 as the susceptibility locus for dyslexia on 15q21. *Molecular Psychiatry, 12,* 1111–1121. doi:10.1038/sj.mp.4001543

Wilcke, A., Weissfuss, J., Kirsten, H., Wolfram, G., Boltze, J., & Ahnert, P. (2009). The role of gene DCDC2 in German dyslexics. *Annals of Dyslexia, 59,* 1–11. doi:10.1007/s11881 -008-0020-7

Winterer, G., Musso, F., Konrad, A., Vucurevic, G., Stoeter, P., Sander, T., & Gallinat, J. (2007). Association of attentional network function with exon 5 variations of the CHRNA4 gene. *Human Molecular Genetics, 16,* 2165–2174. doi:10.1093/hmg/ddm168

What Educators Should Know About the State of Research on Genetic Influences on Reading and Reading Disability
Elena L. Grigorenko

THE GENETICS OF READING AND READING DISABILITY: THE STATE OF THE ART

However referred to, defined, diagnosed, or measured, reading disability (RD) has always been viewed as a condition whose pathogenesis involves hereditary factors. This idea was initially presented in the description of the first documented case of RD in the late 19th and early 20th century, and although it has been challenged, it has gradually won full (or near-full) acceptance (Fletcher, Lyon, Fuchs, & Barnes, 2007). Although this assumption has been dominant for a while, what has changed over the century-long period of scientific inquiry into RD is the field's understanding of the magnitude of the impact of these heritable factors and the biological and genetic machinery behind them.

These changes in understanding have paralleled the emergence of the view that reading is a complex system of cognitive processes that is supported by multiple areas of the brain (Pugh & McCardle, 2009). Reading engages different cognitive representations that are rooted in various anatomical areas of the brain, each characterized by particular architecture. In addition, the geography of reading in the brain assumes the establishment of adequate connectivity among various reading-related areas. In short, a complex multiprocess cognitive system of reading is supported by a developmentally emergent amalgamated functional brain system. The current view asserts that this functional brain system is, in turn, established under the influence of and contributed to by complex genetic machinery. This brain system can be "broken" in more than one way, causing RD (Pernet, Andersson, Paulesu, & Démonet, 2009).

Author Note: The preparation of this chapter was supported by funds from the USA National Academy of Sciences and National Institutes of Health (DC07665 and HD052120). Grantees undertaking such projects are encouraged to express freely their professional judgment. This chapter, therefore, does not necessarily represent the position or policies of the National Institutes of Health and no official endorsement should be inferred. I express my gratitude to Ms. Mei Tan for her editorial assistance and to *Psykhe* for permission for this text to overlap with Grigorenko, E.L. (2011). At the junction of genomic and social sciences: An example of reading ability and disability. *Psykhe, 20*, pp. 81–92.

Correspondingly, it is plausible to assume that the malfunctioning of the brain system that supports reading may be caused by multiple deficiencies in the corresponding genetic machinery (Grigorenko, 2009).At this point, researchers have only a general sketch of what the components of this machinery are and how they operate. Yet, there are some clear elements of this sketch that are quite permanent.

It is widely accepted that reading is a skill that requires socialization. In other words, the overwhelming majority of people acquire the skill of reading in the presence of social "others"—either people who have already acquired the necessary skills and can transmit the knowledge (e.g., teachers) or social tools that can aid the acquisition of reading by capitalizing on crystallized knowledge of how this skill can be transmitted (e.g., computers). While attempting to understand the genetic machinery behind reading, researchers assume the presence of adequate schooling—inquiries into the genetic factors underlying reading are conducted under the assumption that deficient reading performance cannot be explained by the absence or the quality of teaching.

Yet, pretty much any characteristic of reading (e.g., reading speed, reading accuracy) or any reading-related process (e.g., phonemic awareness, lexical retrieval) is continuously distributed in the general population or, in other words, is marked by a wide range of individual differences. Investigations of the sources of these individual differences indicate that a substantial portion of variation among people in both characteristics of reading and reading-related processes can be attributed to the variation in their genetic endowments—that is, their genomes. The estimates of the magnitude of this portion suggest that, on average, they are somewhere between 40%–60% (Grigorenko, 2004), but they vary 1) across the life span, 2) for different languages, and 3) for different societal groups. These estimates are typically derived from studies of relatives and are called *heritability estimates.* To obtain heritability estimates, researchers recruit different types of genetic relatives, for example, identical (monozygotic) and fraternal (dizygotic) twins or other family members (e.g., parents and offspring, siblings, members of extended families). When the degree of genetic relatedness is known, participating relatives can be assessed with reading or related tasks and the degree of their genetic similarity can be compared with the degree of similarity with which they perform these tasks. Multiple statistical techniques have been developed to obtain heritability estimates from different types of relatives. There is no single perfect method for obtaining these estimates; therefore, researchers often use multiple types of relatives and multiple statistical approaches in order to minimize errors and maximize precision. In completing these studies, researchers have made a number of observations. First, although consistently attributing differences in performance to differences in the genome at the average of 40%–60%, they noticed some systematic fluctuations in these estimates. Specifically, these estimates are lower if they are obtained earlier in the development of the individual (e.g., among preschoolers in early grades). These estimates also tend to vary depending on the language in which they are obtained and the specific characteristics of reading they are obtained for, suggesting that there is a tremendous variation in how genetic factors manifest themselves in the different languages in which reading is acquired. Finally, these estimates tend to diverge depending on the characteristics of the sample in which they were obtained; these characteristics include socioeconomic status (SES), ethnic constellations, and quality of schooling. In summary, when characteristics of reading (e.g., speed, accuracy) and performance on reading-related tasks (e.g., tasks of word segmentation, object naming) are considered in the general population, a substantial portion of the related individual differences can be attributed to genetic differences among people. Thus, typical variation in reading is associated with genetic variation.

The genetic influences appear to be of even greater magnitude when people with reading disabilities are considered. In a number of studies, researchers obtained heritability estimates in samples selected through poor readers. Limiting variation (often relatives of poor readers demonstrate similar levels of performance) typically results in higher heritability estimates. Moreover, in these selected samples, researchers used different statistics, such as relative risk estimates, in addition to heritability. These estimates provide an approximation of the likelihood that a relative of a poor reader will also be a poor reader compared with the general population risk. Specifically, it has been estimated that the prevalence of reading disability is estimated at 5%–12% of school-age children (Katusic, Colligan, Barbaresi, Schaid, & Jacobsen, 2001). Relative risk statistics suggest that the prevalence of RD among relatives of individuals who suffer from this disorder is substantially higher than the general population estimates. These findings also attest to the important role of genes in the development and manifestation of RD. To obtain relative risk statistics, researchers recruit families of individuals with RD (so-called RD probands). Multiple types of family units can be utilized in this research: sibling units, nuclear families, and extended families. Once again, there is no single method that is ideal; working with different constellations of relatives is associated with various strengths and weaknesses and, similar to heritability studies, to maximize the accuracy and precision of findings, researchers utilize multiple approaches.

Although the literature is replete with data supporting the hypothesis that genetic factors are important for understanding individual differences in reading acquisition and reading performance, a clear delineation of the specifics of these factors has been challenging. As of the spring of 2011 the literature contained references to about 20 (Schumacher, Hoffmann, Schmal, Schulte-Korne, & Nothen, 2007) potential genetic susceptibility loci (i.e., regions of the genome that have demonstrated a statistically significant linkage to RD; typically these regions involve more than one and often hundreds of genes) and six (Grigorenko & Naples, 2009) candidate genes for RD—genes located within susceptibility loci that have been statistically associated with RD—but none of these loci or genes have been either fully accepted or fully rejected by the field.

The information that has contributed to the identification of susceptibility loci and candidate genes for RD has been generated by so-called molecular studies of reading and reading-related processes. Unlike heritability and relative-risk studies, in which participants need to be characterized only behaviorally—through their performance on reading and reading-related tasks—these studies assume the collection of genetic material DNA. Furthermore, they can be subdivided into a number of major overlapping categories, by the type of samples they engage—genetically unrelated cases/probands and matched controls or family units such as siblings or nuclear and extended families—and by the type of genetic units they target (i.e., specific genes, specific genetic regions, or the whole genome).

The first molecular-genetic study of RD was completed with a number of extended families of individuals with RD (Smith, Kimberling, Pennington, & Lubs, 1983). In such studies, families of individuals with RD (typically, severe RD) are approached and their members are asked to donate both behavior indicators of their performance on reading and reading-related tasks, as well as biological specimens. The task, once again, is to correlate the similarities in performance to similarities in genes. Now, the genetic similarities are not estimated, but also measured using special molecular-genetic (i.e., genotyping and sequencing) and statistical (i.e., linkage and association analyses) techniques. Family units can vary from pairs of siblings to large extended families. Correspondingly, this affects the sample size that is needed for enough statistical power to distinguish a true genetic signal from noise. Extended families are generally harder to identify and harder to work with, but also tend to have more power to identify the genetic source of RD (at least in these families). Smaller familial units such as nuclear families or pairs of siblings are easier to identify and recruit, but also the requirements for sample size are much greater.

The literature has illustrations of different types of samples used in the molecular-genetic studies of RD (Grigorenko, 2005), as well as examples of the utilization of different genetic units as targets. The very first molecular-genetic study of RD was a whole-genome scan, in which the genome in its entirety was considered in screening for linkage with RD, although that study had very few markers and they were protein markers (the technology then did not allow work with DNA markers). As of the spring of 2011, nine genome-wide screens for RD (Brkanac et al., 2008; de Kovel et al., 2004; Fagerheim et al., 1999; Fisher et al., 2002; Igo et al., 2006; Kaminen et al., 2003; Meaburn, Harlaar, Craig, Schalkwyk, & Plomin, 2008; Nopola-Hemmi et al., 2002; Raskind et al., 2005) had been reported. These studies utilized hundreds, thousands, and hundreds of thousands of markers, as technology and cost permitted.

There are also studies that focus on particular regions of the genome. The selection of these regions is typically determined either by a previous whole-genome scan or by a theoretical hypothesis capitalizing on a particular aspect of RD. Yet, some of the studies settled on candidate regions through different means, such as through a known chromosomal aberration. Denmark, for example, has a health policy of screening all of its newborns for macro-chromosomal changes (e.g., large rearrangements). In these cases, researchers screen individuals who have such rearrangements for the presence of RD. The hypothesis then is that a gene that is affected by such an aberration is somehow related to RD. As indicated previously, currently ±20 different genomic regions are entertained as harboring candidate genes for RD. In addition, as the goal of this work is, ultimately, to identify specific genes whose function is related to the transformation of a brain into a reading brain—that is, the establishment of brain networks supporting the different types of cognitive representations required for the acquisition of reading—there are studies of specific candidate genes.

As of the spring of 2011, there are six candidate genes being evaluated as causal genes for RD: *DYX1C1, KIAA0319, DCDC2, ROBO1, MRPL2,* and *C2orf3*. At this point, the field contains both support and lack of support for the involvement of each of these genes; thus, the findings are somewhat difficult to interpret, merely indicating that more time and effort are needed to understand the involvement of each of these genes with reading and its related processes.

NAVIGATING THE LANDSCAPE OF FINDINGS

In short, the accumulated findings, as of the spring of 2011, can be separated into definite and tentative. One definitive conclusion that the field has made pertains to the fact that individual differences in the ways people acquire and practice reading are associated with differences in their genomes. In other words, reading, in its typical and atypical forms, is genetic. The association between reading and the genome appears to be stronger for those individuals who experience difficulties attempting to acquire and exercise reading compared with those individuals who do it seamlessly (assuming, of course, the proper developmental stage and that adequate learning and teaching conditions are in place). This observation is widely accepted in the field and can be perceived as a fact. However, there are caveats. It appears that the strength of the connection between reading and the genome is variable, being weaker in early childhood and gradually getting stronger through the school years and into adolescence and adulthood. Virtually nothing is known, however, about reading in older adults—there simply have not been enough studies to investigate the dynamics of heritability estimates for reading and reading-related processes as they continue to develop in old and very old adults.

From this ultimate statement—that reading is, at least partially, controlled by genes—the degree of certainty in interpreting the observations in the field drops off rather quickly. Yes, the heritability estimates are high, but what specific genetic mechanisms generate and substantiate them? The transition from statistical estimates of the role of genetic factors to the identification of these factors has proven to be difficult. This is not specific to studies of reading only; in fact, there is a coined phrase about "missing heritability," referring to the rather common situation of multiple not-so-fruitful attempts to translate the high heritability estimates obtained for a variety of complex human conditions—that is, disorders such as diabetes, attention-deficit/hyperactivity disorder (ADHD), and autism, into underlying genetic foundations (Avramopoulos, 2010). The field of understanding the genetic bases of reading has the imprint of the field of the genetics and genomics of complex disorders in general. Specifically, many initial positive findings are often followed by nonreplications, suggesting either a high level of heterogeneity of the involved genetic mechanisms or a high level of false positive results. Either interpretation is difficult to grapple with. The former logically leads to a supposition of the field's inability to generalize effectively from specific deficiencies that might be characteristic of specific families, or from specific samples to the general population. The latter assumes that the initial samples were too small and lacking statistical power to differentiate true and false findings, and that much larger samples are needed to weed out the initial field of promising results by marking a number of them as "false positives."

Needless to say, neither of these perspectives appeals. Although these two possibilities are the most obvious ones, they are not the only alternatives. The first possibility pertains to the fact that the last few years of studies in genetics and genomics (i.e., since the completion of the first draft of the human genome in 2000) have resulted in breath-taking discoveries that have exceeded all expectations raised in the 20th century. Among these discoveries, three arguably deserve the most attention: 1) other, in addition to previously known, sources of structural variation in the genome; 2) the role of epigenetic mechanisms in understanding how the genome changes throughout development, and in different contexts and experiences (e.g., experiences ranging from diet to schooling); and 3) the role of unstable or movable elements in the genome. Although it is not possible to discuss these "new" genetic mechanisms in this overview in detail, it is important to note that none of them had been considered in the studies of the genetic bases of reading and RD. Clearly, there is much to do there!

The second possibility is related to the attempt of the field to sift through the findings and, putting aside their inconsistent nature, try to hypothesize about various underlying theoretical considerations that might bring these findings together. Thus, although, at first glance, the collection of the six candidate genes for RD seems quite disparate, they all appear to be contributing, to different degrees, to the process of brain maturation and neuronal migration (Galaburda, LoTurco, Ramus, Fitch, & Rosen, 2006). Thus, through further investigations, it is possible that the emergent system will lead the field toward the involvement of particular genetic pathways, rather than specific genes.

WHY SHOULD ANYBODY CARE?

Recent rapid progress in cellular and molecular technologies, and the speedy application of these technologies in research, has generated considerable hype in the scientific community and numerous subsequent remarkable discoveries. These discoveries are fueling hopes and expectations regarding radical changes in the ways prevention, treatment, and remediation-recovery are carried out in the fields of medical conditions and neuropsychiatric disorders. Some of these discoveries have already generated practical implications, mostly in the areas of diagnostic and pharmaceutical medicine (Guttmacher & Collins, 2002). A new field has emerged called public health genomics (PHG)—a rapidly developing multidisciplinary research and practice area whose objective is to bring, responsibly and effectively, genome-based knowledge into public health with the goal of improving population health (Brand, Schroder, Brand, & Zimmern, 2006; Brand, 2007; Burke, Khoury, Stewart, Zimmern, & Bellagio Group, 2006). This genome-based knowledge is referred to as the "-omics" of today (Tan, Lim, Khan, & Ranganathan, 2009) and is characterized by an overabundance of data and information, along with the enormous opportunities associated with the utilization of these data.

It may be accurate to say that the hype is still mostly limited to the scientific community. Practitioners rarely use these discoveries in their everyday operations and, moreover, often lack understanding of the current discoveries and developments in the field (Chen & Goodson, 2007). Similarly, interactions with the general public reveal the lack of depth in understanding the general scope of recent discoveries in genetics and genomics, prevalent misconceptions reflective of a deficiency of knowledge (Chapple, May, & Campion, 1995; Condit, 2001; Richards & Ponder, 1996; Walter, Emery, Braithwaite, & Marteau, 2004), negative biases toward particular terms (e.g., mutation; Condit, Dubriwny, Lynch, & Parrott, 2004), and the presence of strong personal, moral, and global concerns (Barns, Schibeci, Davison, & Shaw, 2000; Bates, Lynch, Bevan, & Condit, 2005; Henneman, Timmermans, & van der Wal, 2004) about the use and abuse of genetic and genomic information (Hahn et al., 2010). Yet, the very success of the integration of genome-based knowledge into public health relies on the public's ability to understand the need to collect and apply family history that is relevant to diseases and disorders, and the public's ability to consult with knowledgeable healthcare providers and self-trigger and self-monitor health-related behaviors in an informed manner (Charles, Gafni, & Whelan, 1999; Sheridan, Harris, & Woolf, 2004).

It is fair to say that very little (if any) of these discoveries, at least at this point, have made their impact on either behavioral therapy or education. Although there are no data that have been collected specifically with or from educators or other types of providers in the sphere of education (e.g., educational tutors, occupational and behavior therapists), there is no reason to believe that their level of mastery of this knowledge is any different from that of the general public. Yet, although more distant from recent genome-based discoveries, educators are only a step away from healthcare practitioners. Indeed, developmental disorders, especially common developmental disorders such as LDs in general and RD in particular, are public health issues that are serviced, primarily, by educators.

If, indeed, RD is recognized as a public health condition, then current thinking with regard to PHG, as with other common conditions, can be applied to understanding the role of genetics and genomics in issues pertaining to RD. In this context, a number of other useful parallels can be drawn connecting the literature on PHG and RD.

The essence of PHG is to personalize health care to maximize the well-being and longevity of each individual. The essence of quality education is the individualization of teaching and learning to maximize productive accomplishment and life satisfaction. Both personalized medicine and individualized education show similar trends in their utilization of technology and multimedia, engaging multiple sources of information and knowledge, and capitalizing on the usage of profiles of information rather than single data points on an individual. Both personalized medicine and education demonstrate changes in their definition of "problems." In the past, disease was defined through the presence of symptoms. Now, having accumulated a substantial corpus of data on the genomic bases of many diseases, medicine defines diseases through the presence of a genotype or a genomic signature that confers a susceptibility to these clinical symptoms (Ford et al., 2008). Similarly, education strives to find early precursors of various learning difficulties and focuses on prevention rather than on failure and subsequent remediation. Yet, although PHG has focused on the utilization of genomic information in medicine and public health since early in this century, education has largely ignored the advances in genome-based knowledge.

Similar to many common diseases in medicine, educational difficulties appear to have genetic bases. In fact, heritability estimates for academic difficulties exceed those for such common medical conditions as obesity, diabetes, and cardiovascular problems. If healthcare practitioners are applying genome-based knowledge to the understanding, prevention, and treatment of such common conditions in medicine, then why should not educators apply this knowledge to dealing with common LD, such as RD? In fact, the "preventive" logic of PHG seems totally reasonable when applied to common LD. If the genetic bases of LD are understood and there are tools and resources available for diagnostic purposes, educators might no longer have to wait for signs of academic failure. If indicators of genetic risks are identified, the specific measure aimed at preventing the onset of difficulty or failure, or at least minimizing their extent, will become increasingly powerful. And, although the initial costs of early diagnostic and preventive actions might not be negligible, subsequent remedial costs might be substantially diminished by these activities. Although this type of reasoning has not been practiced in education on a large scale, it has been present in the public health literature for more than a decade (e.g., Gibson, Martin, & Singer, 2002; Zajtchuk, 1999), and there is much to learn from this literature.

One such useful line of discourse addresses the ways and stages of translating genetic and genomic discoveries into public health applications. Although many translation paradigms have been proposed, here only one is exemplified, developed by Khoury and colleagues (Agurs-Collins et al., 2008; Khoury, Bowen, et al., 2009; Khoury, Gwinn, et al., 2007; Khoury, Valdez, & Albright, 2008). Connecting the "-omic" sciences with public health, four different stages are differentiated for the purposes of validating scientific knowledge and integrating it into disease control and prevention programs (Khoury, Bowen, et al., 2008).

At the first stage—the discovery stage, also referred to as the analytical validity stage—research attempts to connect a genetic or genomic mechanism with a particular public-health condition. At the second stage—referred to as the clinical validity phase—research appraises the value of the connection established in the first stage for health practice, validating the first-stage observations in different settings and different samples to gather evidence and assess its replicability and robustness. At this stage, evidence-based guidelines connecting a genetic or genomic discovery and a public health issue are developed. Subsequently, at the third stage—referred to as the clinical-utility phase—research attempts to apply these stage-two guidelines into health practice by mechanisms of knowledge transfer and delivery, as well as dissemination and diffusion practices.

Only having planted these practices into everyday application on a large scale can research, at stage four, access health outcomes of a genomic discovery in practice. This stage engages multiple ethical and social considerations. It is important to note that the literature today acknowledges that most current genome-based research is unfolding within stage one (Khoury, Valdez, et al., 2008). It has been estimated that only approximately 3% of published studies are conducted within stage two, and only a very few at stage three or four (Khoury, Gwinn, et al., 2007).

In the context of viewing LD (and correspondingly, RD) as a public-health problem and capitalizing on the Khoury and colleagues translational paradigm, what is today's state of affairs with respect to the relevant genetics and genomic discoveries in the field of LD in general and RD in particular? At the beginning of the 21st century, the majority of activity is still at stage one. This stage defines the analytical validity (Haddow & Palomaki, 2003) of whatever genetic or genomic test needs to be conducted so that the genotype of interest for the disorder (RD) may be measured accurately, reliably, and at a minimum expense. Although a number of specific candidate genes for RD have been identified, the field is rather far from grasping the mechanism that unifies these genes in their RD-specific action. Moreover, the field is also rather far from verifying the numerous hypotheses regarding the specific genomic regions and other candidate genes that are currently under consideration. In other words, stage one of the related work in the field of RD is far from complete. It is rapidly unfolding, but it is too early, at this stage, to ascertain the specific genetic tests that have diagnostic validity for RD.

The research on some of the candidate genes (e.g., *KIAA0319*, *DCDC2*, *DYX1C1*) has made the transition to stage two, in which the degree of association among these genes and RD is being validated in a variety of samples and contexts. The field, though, has yet to formalize the various stage-two findings into comprehensive guidelines connecting the specific genetic variants in these genes or the specific mechanisms these genes support to genetic vulnerability for RD or its specific components. These activities are crucially important for the clinical validity (Haddow & Palomaki, 2003) of a genetic or genomic finding—that is, its capacity to detect or predict the condition of interest (e.g., RD). Moreover, establishing and explicating these connections is absolutely necessary for the possibility of transitioning to stage-three practices, which should involve service providers for individuals with RD, from educators to medical doctors and career counselors. These guidelines need to be as clear and as robust as possible, presenting a list of vulnerability-genetic mechanisms and indentifying risks associated with these mechanisms. As it appears now, it is quite likely, based on the indications from the RD literature so far (Meaburn et al., 2008; Paracchini et al., 2008) and the evidence from other common disorders (Khoury, Little, Gwinn, & Ioannidis, 2007), that the relative risks associated with each of these vulnerability-genetic mechanisms is of small magnitude. Thus, the field should expect either a long list of genetic risk variants for RD or a discovery of some type of clustering for these variants that results in a substantial magnification of risk, when more than one variant is present in an individual.

Once again, the evidence in the field of RD that has been accumulated so far is rather far from being leveraged into policy recommendations. This, of course, assumes that all policy should be evidence-based and, in many cases, especially in education research, this is simply not the case. Yet, the field is working very hard both at stage one—generating new discoveries on the genetic bases of RD—and at stage two, testing the extent of the generalizability of these discoveries and their roles in various samples and contexts. A fundamental question that needs to be answered at stage two is whether an understanding of the genetic mechanism for RD may be used for pharmacological treatment of this and related disabilities—that is, so that pharmacological, but not educational, approaches can be individualized—so that educational approaches are matched to genetic mechanisms and pharmacological treatment is engaged minimally or not at all, or for both. There have been attempts to treat RD pharmacologically in Europe, but not in the United States. Whether the idea of treating RD pharmacologically will be even acceptable in the United States is not a trivial question.

At stage three, a cadre of qualified and knowledgeable providers should be able to implement the guidelines developed at stage two in their everyday practice. This phase of clinical utility is aimed at establishing the net health benefit resulting from the introduction of a particular diagnostic procedure related to genetic or genomic findings and associated with relevant interventions (Haddow & Palomaki, 2003). This stage ideally requires well-designed studies in the community. As the ultimate goal of PHG is to generate public health policies and recommendations that can be easily translated in individualized approaches for the beneficiaries of these policies, and because the major "battle" that engages individuals with RD unfolds in schooling, if there are ever PHG policies for RD, they will inevitably involve schools. At this point, it is unclear whether these policies will be delivered by educators themselves or by PHG providers placed in schools (similar to the medical outreach services delivered to schools through school nurses), but it is clear that academic activities will be a part of the PHG policies that address RD.

Finally, only when there are data collected at stage three with regard to short- and long-term outcomes of RD-related PHG will the field be able to qualify and quantify the importance and relevance of the findings described above (and the findings to be made) to RD-related outcomes. Research at this stage calls for joint efforts from public health providers, bench and education scientists, economists, policy-makers, stakeholders, and community. There is a tremendous body of literature indicating that reading failure and deficiencies in the mastery of reading are risk factors for many negative life outcomes. Correspondingly, an assessment of the impact of RD-related PHG needs to be coupled not only with short-term academic outcomes, but also with long-term life outcomes.

It is likely that the "movement" through Khoury's stages in the field of LD is not going to be easy. Even if the first-stage findings are convincingly validated at the second stage, and the variability of findings seen now is interpreted in a systematic manner such that the mechanism behind these findings is understood, the field faces the monumental tasks of completing stages three and four before being able to determine the ultimate value of genetic and genomic studies for the prevention and treatment of RD and associated deficits, and for the enhancement and promotion of literacy. Yet, many public health policies today are associated with breakthroughs and shortcuts; it has certainly been the case for many PHG applications and might well be the case for its RD-related applications. Thus, while the field is making its way through Khoury's stages, whether in a sequential or simultaneous manner, it is important to focus on tasks that connect ongoing genetic and genomic RD-associated research, at whatever stage, with the public's perception of it. There are at least three such tasks that appear to be of high priority.

The first task is that of educating the public. If traditional PHG for "conventional" health conditions such as cancer and diabetes generate so much misunderstanding and misinterpretation by the general public, the task of communicating the idea of PHG for developmental disorders, especially such common disorders as LD, will be even more difficult. It has to be done because modern public health policies count on and are targeted at an educated consumer. The literature indicates that genome-based knowledge is associated with misconceptions and misinterpretations in the public as a whole (Burton & Adams, 2009), and this appears to be particularly the case for various minority groups (Hahn et al., 2010). One of the major issues here is the removal of the negative connotation associated with the concepts of genome-based science and PHG.

The second, even more mammoth task is educating the providers—the professionals of both the fields of medicine and education—who serve individuals with LD. Here of note is a tremendous discrepancy in the literature, in which there is a large body of work on the importance of including the basic knowledge of genome-based sciences in the education of medical practitioners and virtually no work advocating the importance of the mastery of these basics by educators.

The third, and perhaps the most important, task is to trigger and stimulate substantial discourse on the intersection of PHG and education. There is a large-scale highly engaging discussion in the literature on the development of national policies on PHG in the United States and elsewhere (Gonzalez-Andrade & Lopez-Pulles, 2010; Little et al., 2009; Metcalfe, Bittles, O'Leary, & Emery, 2009), but issues concerning where and how PHG and education should meet are not part of this discussion. Because PHG is aimed primarily at common conditions directly associated with lifestyle (Agurs-Collins et al., 2008; Boccia, Brand, Brand, & Ricciardi, 2009; Khoury, Valdez, et al., 2008; Sanderson, Wardle, & Humphries, 2008), it seems that such lifelong conditions as RD, which are directly associated with life outcomes, should be a part of these discussions.

CONCLUSIONS

Completing these three tasks is crucial for the development, implementation, and evaluation of PHG for LD. Thus, engaging with them early is highly important. The observed slow rate of translation of genome-based knowledge into public health (Boccia et al., 2009) has been connected with numerous factors, such as the low relative risk for common disorders, the complexity of the four-stage translational process, and the lack of critical knowledge in the public. An unfortunate mark of the rapid development of genome-based sciences and technologies has been a popularization—to the point of hyperbole—of the scale and immediacy of the application of these developments to health-related practices (Davey Smith et al., 2005; Kamerow, 2008). Such harmful popularization, coupled with commercial potential, has often resulted in ill-justified use of genetic and genomic testing for susceptibility to complex disorders, mostly with no clear application or guidance for the proper utilization of this knowledge. It is inevitable, as any knowledge-based progress, that soon, perhaps even in the foreseeable future, the genome will become part of the common record for personalized medicine and individualized education. Thus, it is very important to prepare the general public and service providers for this transformation of the genome—from something that once cost a tremendous amount of funds to sequence, in draft, only 10 years ago, into something that will soon become just a part of the birth record for each of us.

REFERENCES

Agurs-Collins, T., Khoury, M.J., Simon-Morton, D., Olster, D.H., Harris, J.R., & Milner, J.A. (2008). Public health genomics: Translating obesity genomics research into population health benefits. *Obesity, 16,* S85–S94. doi:10.1038/oby.2008.517

Avramopoulos, D. (2010). Genetics of psychiatric disorders methods: Molecular approaches. *Psychiatric Clinics of North America, 33,* 1–13. doi:10.1016/j.psc.2009.12.006

Barns, I., Schibeci, R., Davison, A., & Shaw, R. (2000). "What do you think about genetic medicine?" Facilitating sociable public discourse on developments in the new genetics. *Science Technology & Human Values, 25,* 283–308. doi:10.1177/016224390002500302

Bates, B.R., Lynch, J.A., Bevan, J.L., & Condit, C.M. (2005). Warranted concerns, warranted outlooks: A focus group study of public understandings of genetic research. *Social Science & Medicine, 60,* 331–344. doi:10.1016/j.socscimed.2004.05.012

Boccia, S., Brand, A., Brand, H., & Ricciardi, G. (2009). The integration of genome-based information for common diseases into health policy and healthcare as a major challenge for public health genomics: The example of the methylenetetrahydrofolate reductase gene in non-cancer diseases. *Mutation Research/Fundamentals and Molecular Mechanisms of Mutagenesis, 667,* 27–34. doi:10.1016/j.mrfmmm.2008.10.003

Brand, A., Schroder, P., Brand, H., & Zimmern, R. (2006). Getting ready for the future: Integration of genomics into public health research, policy and practice in Europe and globally. *Community Genetics, 9,* 67–71. doi:10.1159/000090696

Brand, H. (2007). Good governance for the public's health. *European Journal of Public Health, 17,* 541. doi:10.1093/eurpub/ckm104

Brkanac, Z., Chapman, N.H., Igo, R.P.J., Matsushita, M.M., Nielsen, K., Berninger, V.W., ... Raskind, W.H. (2008). Genome scan of a nonword repetition phenotype in families with dyslexia: Evidence for multiple loci. *Behavior Genetics, 38,* 462–475. doi:10.1007/s10519-008-9215-2

Burke, W., Khoury, M.J., Stewart, A., Zimmern, R.L., & Bellagio Group (2006). The path from genome-based research to population health: Development of an international public health genomics network. *Genetics in Medicine, 8,* 451–458. doi:10.1097/01.gim.0000228213.72256.8c

Burton, H., & Adams, M. (2009). Professional education and training in public health genomics: A working policy developed on behalf of the public health genomics European network. *Public Health Genomics, 12,* 216–224. doi:10.1159/000200019

Chapple, A., May, C., & Campion, P. (1995). Lay understanding of genetic disease: A British study of families attending a genetic counseling service. *Journal of Genetic Counseling, 4,* 281–300. doi:10.1007/BF01408074

Charles, C., Gafni, A., & Whelan, T. (1999). Decision-making in the physician-patient encounter: Revisiting the shared treatment decision-making model. *Social Science & Medicine, 49,* 651–661. doi:10. 1016/S0277-9536(99)00145-8

Chen, L.S., & Goodson, P. (2007). Public health genomics knowledge and attitudes: A survey of public health educators in the United States. *Genetics in Medicine, 9,* 496–503. doi:10.1097/GIM.0b013e31812e95b5

Condit, C.M. (2001). What is 'public opinion' about genetics? *Nature Reviews Genetics, 2,* 811–815. doi:10.1038/35093580

Condit, C.M., Dubriwny, T., Lynch, J., & Parrott, R. (2004). Lay people's understanding of and preference against the word "mutation". *American Journal of Medical Genetics, 130A,* 245–250. doi:10.1002/ajmg.a.30264

Davey Smith, G., Ebrahim, S., Lewis, S., Hansell, A.L., Palmer, L.J., & Burton, P.R. (2005). Genetic epidemiology and public health: Hope, hype, and future prospects. *Lancet, 366,* 1484–1498.

de Kovel, C.G.F., Hol, F.A., Heister, J., Willemen, J., Sandkuijl, L.A., Franke, B., & Padberg, G.W. (2004). Genome-wide scan identifies susceptibility locus for dyslexia on Xq27 in an extended Dutch family. *Journal of Medical Genetics, 41,* 652–657. doi:10.1136/jmg.2003.012294

Fagerheim, T., Raeymaekers, P., Tonnessen, F.E., Pedersen, M., Tranebjaerg, L., & Lubs, H.A. (1999). A new gene (DYX3) for dyslexia is located on chromosome 2. *Journal of Medical Genetics, 35,* 664–669.

Fisher, S.E., Francks, C., Marlow, A.J., MacPhie, I.L., Newbury, D.F., Cardon, L.R., … Monaco, A.P. (2002). Independent genome-wide scans identify a chromosome 18 quantitative-trait locus influencing dyslexia. *Nature Genetics, 30,* 86–91. doi:10.1038/ng792

Fletcher, J.M., Lyon, G.R., Fuchs, L.S., & Barnes, M.A. (2007). *Learning disabilities.* New York: Guilford.

Ford, P., Seymour, G., Beeley, J.A., Curro, F., Depaola, D., Ferguson, D., … Claffey, N. (2008). Adapting to changes in molecular biosciences and technologies. *European Journal of Dental Education, 1,* 40–47. doi:10.1111/j.1600-0579.2007.00479

Galaburda, A.M., LoTurco, J.J., Ramus, F., Fitch, R.H., & Rosen, G.D. (2006). From genes to behavior in developmental dyslexia. *Nature Neuroscience, 9,* 1213–1217. doi:10.1038/nn1772

Gibson, J.L., Martin, D.K., & Singer, P.A. (2002). Priority setting for new technologies in medicine: A transdisciplinary study. *BMC Health Services Research, 2,* 14.

Gonzalez-Andrade, F., & Lopez-Pulles, R. (2010). Ecuador: Public health genomics. *Public Health Genomics, 13,* 171–180. doi:10.1159/000249817

Grigorenko, E.L. (2004). Genetic bases of developmental dyslexia: A capsule review of heritability estimates. *Enfance, 3,* 273–287. doi:10.3917/enf.563.0273

Grigorenko, E.L. (2005). A conservative meta-analysis of linkage and linkage-association studies of developmental dyslexia. *Scientific Studies of Reading, 9,* 285–316. doi:10.1207/s1532799xssr0903_6

Grigorenko, E.L. (2009). At the height of fashion: What genetics can teach us about neurodevelopmental disabilities. *Current Opinion in Neurology, 22,* 126–130. doi:10.1097/WCO.0b013e3283292414

Grigorenko, E.L., & Naples, A.J. (2009). The devil is in the details: Decoding the genetics of reading. In P. McCardle & K. Pugh (Eds.), *Helping children learn to read: Current issues and new directions in the integration of cognition, neurobiology and genetics of reading and dyslexia* (pp. 133–148). New York, NY: Psychological Press.

Guttmacher, A.E., & Collins, F.S. (2002). Genomic medicine—A primer. *New England Journal of Medicine, 347,* 1512–1520. doi:10.1056/NEJMra012240

Haddow, J.E., & Palomaki, G.E. (2003). ACCE: A model process for evaluating data on emerging genetic tests. In M. Khoury, J. Little & W. Burke (Eds.), *Human genome epidemiology: A scientific foundation for using genetic information to improve health and prevent disease* (pp. 217–233). New York, NY: Oxford University Press.

Hahn, S., Letvak, S., Powell, K., Christianson, C., Wallace, D., Speer, M.,

... The Genomedical Connection (2010). A community's awareness and perceptions of genomic medicine. *Public Health Genomics, 13,* 63–71. doi:10.1159/000218712

Henneman, L., Timmermans, D.R., & van der Wal, G. (2004). Public experiences, knowledge and expectations about medical genetics and the use of genetic information. *Community Genetics, 7,* 33–43. doi:10.1159/000080302

Igo, R.P.J., Chapman, N.H., Berninger, V.W., Matsushita, M., Brkanac, Z., Rothstein, J.H., ... Wijsman, E.M. (2006). Genomewide scan for real-word reading subphenotypes of dyslexia: Novel chromosome 13 locus and genetic complexity. *American Journal of Medical Genetics (Neuropsychiatric Genetics), 141,* 15–27. doi:10.1002/ajmg.b.30245

Kamerow, D. (2008). Waiting for the genetic revolution. *BMJ, 336,* 22. doi:10.1136/bmj.39437.453102.0F

Kaminen, N., Hannula-Jouppi, K., Kestila, M., Lahermo, P., Muller, K., Kaaranen, M., ... Kere, J. (2003). A genome scan for developmental dyslexia confirms linkage to chromosome 2p11 and suggests a new locus on 7q32. *Journal of Medical Genetics, 40,* 340–345. doi:10.1136/jmg.40.5.340

Katusic, S.K., Colligan, R.C., Barbaresi, W.J., Schaid, D.J., & Jacobsen, S.J. (2001). Incidence of reading disability in a population-based birth cohort, 1976–1982, Rochester, Minnesota. *Mayo Clinic Proceedings, 76,* 1081–1092.

Khoury, M.J., Bowen, S., Bradley, L.A., Coates, R., Dowling, N.F., Gwinn, M., ... Yoon, P.W. (2009). A decade of public health genomics in the United States: Centers for Disease Control and Prevention 1997–2007. *Public Health Genomics, 12*(1), 20–29. doi:10.1159/000153427

Khoury, M.J., Gwinn, M., Yoon, P.W., Dowling, N., Moore, C.A., & Bradley, L. (2007). The continuum of translation research in genomic medicine: How can we accelerate the appropriate integration of human genome discoveries into health care and disease prevention? *Genetics in Medicine, 9,* 665–674. doi:10.1097/GIM.0b013e31815699d0

Khoury, M.J., Little, J., Gwinn, M., & Ioannidis, J.P. (2007). On the synthesis and interpretation of consistent but weak gene-disease associations in the era of genome-wide association studies. *International Journal of Epidemiology, 36,* 439–445. doi:10.1093/ije/dyl253

Khoury, M.J., Valdez, R., & Albright, A. (2008). Public health genomics approach to type 2 diabetes. *Diabetes, 57,* 2911–2914. doi:10.2337/db08-1045

Little, J., Potter, B., Allanson, J., Caulfield, T., Carroll, J.C., & Wilson, B. (2009). Canada: Public health genomics. *Public Health Genomics, 12,* 112–120. doi:10.1159/000156113

Meaburn, E., Harlaar, N., Craig, I., Schalkwyk, L., & Plomin, R. (2008). Quantitative trait locus association scan of early reading disability and ability using pooled DNA and 100K SNP microarrays in a sample of 5760 children. *Molecular Psychiatry, 13,* 729–740. doi:10.1038/sj.mp.4002063

Metcalfe, S.A., Bittles, A.H., O'Leary, P., & Emery, J. (2009). Australia: Public health genomics. *Public Health Genomics, 12,* 121–128. doi:10.1159/000160666

Nopola-Hemmi, J., Myllyluoma, B., Voutilainen, A., Leinonen, S., Kere, J., & Ahonen, T. (2002). Familial dyslexia: Neurocognitive and genetic correlation in a large Finnish family. *Developmental Medicine and Child Neurology, 44,* 580–586. doi:10.1111/j.1469-8749.2002.tb00842

Paracchini, S., Steer, C.D., Buckingham, L.L., Morris, A.P., Ring, S., Scerri, T., ... Monaco, A.P. (2008). Association of the KIAA0319 dyslexia susceptibility gene with reading skills in the general population. *The American Journal of Psychiatry, 165,* 1576–1584. doi:10.1176/appi.ajp.2008.07121872

Pernet, C.R., Andersson, J., Paulesu, E., & Démonet, J.F. (2009). When all hypotheses are right: A multifocal account of dyslexia. *Human Brain Mapping, 30,* 2278–2292. doi:10.1002/hbm.20670

Pugh, K., & McCardle, P. (Eds.). (2009). *How children learn to read: Current issues and new directions in the integration of cognition, neurobiology and genetics of reading and dyslexia research and practice.* New York, NY: Psychology Press.

Raskind, W.H., Igo, R.P.J., Chapman, N.H., Berninger, V.W., Thomson, J.B., Matsushita, M., ... Wijsman, E.M. (2005). A genome scan in multigenerational families with dyslexia: Identification of a novel locus on chromosome 2q that contributes to phonological decoding efficiency. *Molecular Psychiatry, 10,* 699–711. doi:10.1038/sj.mp.4001657

Richards, M., & Ponder, M. (1996). Lay understanding of genetics: A test of a hypothesis. *Journal of Medical Genetics, 33,* 1032–1036. doi:10.1136/jmg.33.12.1032

Sanderson, S.C., Wardle, J., & Humphries, S.E. (2008). Public health genomics and genetic test evaluation: The challenge of conducting behavioural research on the utility of lifestyle-genetic tests. *Journal of Nutrigenetics & Nutrigenomics, 1,* 224–231.

Schumacher, J., Hoffmann, P., Schmal, C., Schulte-Korne, G., & Nothen, M.M. (2007). Genetics of dyslexia: The evolving landscape. *Journal of Medical Genetics, 44,* 289–297. doi:10.1136/jmg.2006.046516

Sheridan, S.L., Harris, R.P., & Woolf, S.H. (2004). Shared decision making about screening and chemoprevention: A suggested approach from the U.S. Preventive Services Task Force. *American Journal of Preventive Medicine, 26,* 56–66.

Smith, S.D., Kimberling, W.J., Pennington, B.F., & Lubs, H.A. (1983). Specific reading disability: Identification of an inherited form through linkage analyses. *Science, 219,* 1345–1347. doi:10.1126/science.6828864

Tan, T.W., Lim, S.J., Khan, A.M., & Ranganathan, S. (2009). A proposed minimum skill set for university graduates to meet the informatics needs and challenges of the "-omics" era. *BMC Genomics, 10,* S36. doi:10.1186/1471-2164-10-S3-S36

Walter, F.M., Emery, J., Braithwaite, D., & Marteau, T.M. (2004). Lay understanding of familial risk of common chronic diseases: A systematic review and synthesis of qualitative research. *Annals of Family Medicine, 2,* 583–594. doi:10.1370/afm.242

Zajtchuk, R. (1999). New technologies in medicine: Biotechnology and nanotechnology. *Disease A Month, 45,* 449–495. doi:10.1016/S0011-5029(99)90018-4

Potential Early Precursors of Specific Language Impairment and Dyslexia

Introduction

April A. Benasich

In recent years research on the diagnosis and treatment of dyslexia has accelerated with an increasing focus on identifying biological substrates and potential early precursors. A tighter emphasis on precursors, and on what we refer to here as "predyslexic" populations, should enable earlier identification of those children at highest risk for dyslexia and provide insight into the etiologies, common pathways, neurobiological correlates, and behavioral phenotypes of language learning disorders. A number of factors must also be considered in the context of early identification, including the importance of identifying associations between candidate genes and behavioral phenotypes (e.g., Newbury et al., 2011), and as discussed in Section I, broader identification of critical genetic and/or neural–behavioral links and associations. As Rosen and Fitch (Chapters 10 and 11) remind us, attempts to understand the biological substrates underlying dyslexia have led, via the work of Galaburda and colleagues (Galaburda & Kemper, 1979; Galaburda, Sherman, Rosen, Aboitiz, & Geschwind, 1985; Humphreys, Kaufmann, & Galaburda, 1990), to the use of animal models that permit the study of disruptions of neuronal migration to the cerebral cortex during early brain development. Such insights have led us to look for neurobiological markers of language learning disorders at earlier and earlier points in development.

Thus, a second and equally important overarching theme for The Dyslexia Foundation's 12th Extraordinary Brain Series Symposium was the identification of potential early precursors of language learning disorders (LLD). It is certainly the case that one of the most important goals in dyslexia research is early identification of populations at highest risk for language disorders, particularly given that current remediation relies exclusively on intervention therapies. Developmental neuroscience clearly shows that the earlier intervention is begun, the more "plastic" the brain is, and thus the greater possibility for improvement. Convergence of longitudinal behavior, anatomic, and genetic analyses (in both human and animal models) could give rise to a much-improved understanding of the etiology of dyslexia, as compared with current attempts to interpolate or reconstruct early neurobehavioral trajectories in diagnosed adults.

An integral and essential component of early identification relates to understanding the core deficits in young children—specifically those deficits that most effectively predict later language and reading problems in children who have not yet fully developed language or reading skills but who are amenable to diagnostic measurement. Thus, prospective longitudinal studies, which allow early developmental trajectories to be tracked in populations known to be at highest risk for LLDs and support identification of comorbidities that may provide important insight on the etiology of dyslexia, are critical. The chapters in this section report on studies that are designed to examine putative neural mechanisms and biological factors including the brainstem response to speech (i.e., Chapter 6) and deficits in nonlinguistic acoustic processing (i.e., Chapter 7), both neurobiological markers that could be of particular utility in the early prognosis of developmental language outcome.

Identification of early precursors logically dictates a strong focus on prospective longitudinal approaches. This technique allows populations at varying levels of risk for language disorder to be followed and compared with children without such risk factors, thus allowing careful examination of emerging perceptual and linguistic skills. In this way one can quantify qualitative and quantitative differences in developmental trajectories and their relation to subsequent language development and impairment. Several of the chapters in this section also specifically identify neurobiological markers that could be of particular utility in the early identification of children at highest risk for reading and spelling disorders (e.g., Chapter 8) and point to the utility of such early markers for early intervention and remediation.

Insights also may be gained in this domain by examining the role of comorbidities (Chapter 9) and what such perceptual, behavioral, genetic, and/or anatomical concordance might reveal about the relationship among various LLDs; for example, specific language impairment (SLI) and dyslexia (e.g., Bishop & Snowling, 2004). Such parallels are also seen when examining brain volumetrics, sensory processing, and network properties in children diagnosed with autism spectrum disorders as compared with those with developmental language disorders (Chapter 18). Here again, the question is this: How early in life can such developmental problems be detected? Also, will identifying early neurobiological correlates facilitate remediation or perhaps allow "rescue" of a less than optimal developmental trajectory?

As de Bree and colleagues discuss (Chapter 9), many children diagnosed with SLI go on to develop deficits in the acquisition of literacy milestones (e.g., Bishop, McDonald, Bird, & Hayiou-Thomas, 2009; Peterson, Pennington, Shriberg, & Boada, 2009; van Weerdenburg, Verhoeven, & van Balkom, 2006; Vandewalle, Boets, Ghesquière, & Zink, 2010) including deficits in phonological awareness, phonological (or verbal) short-term memory, and rapid naming. In addition to the link with SLI, Maassen and colleagues (Chapter 8) found that such deficits can often be identified in preschoolers who are not yet reading, and all are considered to be reliable predictors of reading difficulties. Many children with dyslexia have been shown to exhibit difficulties in the same domains that are strikingly similar to those seen in SLI, particularly when processing lower level auditory processes that may underpin the development of phonological representations (Peterson et al., 2009; Richardson, Thomson, Scott, & Goswami, 2004).

The increasing focus on identifying biological substrates and potential early precursors should enable earlier identification of those children at highest risk for dyslexia. Earlier screening methods may also open the door to earlier genetic assessments, that to date have been performed in largely adult (diagnosed) populations, as opposed to early childhood populations at higher risk for dyslexia. Coupling of early genetic assessments with early behavioral screening may also be particularly critical if it can be shown that dyslexia is polygenic and that different genes influence different core deficits, because, presumably, different core deficits would respond differentially to different interventions.

REFERENCES

Bishop, D.V.M, McDonald, D., Bird, S., & Hayiou-Thomas, M.E. (2009). Children who read words accurately despite language impairment: Who are they and how do they do it? *Child Development, 80*(2), 593–605. doi:10.1111/j.1467-8624.2009.01281

Bishop, D.V.M., & Snowling, M.J. (2004). Developmental dyslexia and specific language impairment: Same or different? *Psychological Bulletin, 130,* 858–886. doi:10.1037/0033-2909.130.6.858

Galaburda, A.M., & Kemper, T.L. (1979). Cytoarchitectonic abnormalities in developmental dyslexia: A case study. *Annals of Neurology, 6,* 94–100. doi:10.1002/ana.410060203

Galaburda, A.M., Sherman, G.F., Rosen, G.D., Aboitiz, F., & Geschwind, N. (1985). Developmental dyslexia: Four consecutive cases with cortical anomalies. *Annals of Neurology, 18,* 222–233.

Humphreys, P., Kaufmann, W.E., & Galaburda, A.M. (1990). Developmental dyslexia in women: Neuropathological findings in three cases. *Annals of Neurology, 28,* 727–738.

Newbury D.F., Paracchini S., Scerri T.S., Winchester L., Addis L., Richardson A.J., … Monaco A.P. (2011). Investigation of dyslexia and SLI risk variants in reading- and language-impaired subjects. *Behavior Genetics, 41*(1), 90–104. doi:10.1007/s10519-010-9424-3

Peterson R.L., Pennington B.F., Shriberg L.D., & Boada R. (2009). What influences literacy outcome in children with speech sound disorder? *Journal of Speech Language and Hearing Research, 52*(5), 1175–1188. doi:10.1044/1092-4388(2009/08-0024)

Richardson U., Thomson J.M., Scott S.K., & Goswami U. (2004). Auditory processing skills and phonological repre-

sentation in dyslexic children. *Dyslexia,*
10(3), 215–233. doi:10.1002/dys.276

van Weerdenburg, M., Verhoeven, L.,
& van Balkom, H. (2006). Towards a
typology of specific language impairment. *Journal of Child Psychology and
Psychiatry, 47,* 176–189. doi:10.1111
/j.1469-7610.2005.01454

Vandewalle, E., Boets, B., Ghesquière, P., &
Zink, I. (2010). Who is at risk for dyslexia?
Phonological processing in five-to-seven-year-old Dutch-speaking children
with SLI. *Scientific Studies of Reading, 14,*
58–84. doi:10.1080/10888430903242035

CHAPTER 6

Biological Factors Contributing to Reading Ability
Subcortical Auditory Function
Bharath Chandrasekaran and Nina Kraus

THEORIES OF DYSLEXIA: CORE IMPAIRMENTS

An estimated 10% of children exhibit developmental dyslexia, a disorder that affects reading and spelling skills (Démonet, Taylor, & Chaix, 2004). Although these learning problems are regarded as having a neurological basis, the nature of the core neural impairment remains unclear and debated (Démonet et al., 2004; Ramus, 2001a, 2001b). A number of studies have consistently implicated poor phonological processing as one underlying basis for reading and spelling difficulties (Carroll & Snowling, 2004; Marshall, Snowling, & Bailey, 2001; Windfuhr & Snowling, 2001). Specifically, a majority of children with impairments in reading ability exhibit difficulties on an array of tasks that measure phonological processing abilities—such as decomposing words into their constituent syllables and phonemes, deciding whether a pair of words rhyme, repeating a list of digits or nonwords, or quickly retrieving information from long-term memory. Adequate phonological skills require the explicit manipulation of speech sounds and therefore adequate representation of these sounds in the brain, as well as rapid, online access to the representations during task performance. The nature of the problems underlying poor phonological skills, and ultimately poor reading, is under debate. Here, we review three such core impairments.

Core Impairment in Processing Time-Varying Acoustic Events

Some investigators argue that the phonological impairment is an outcome of an inability to perceive *time-varying acoustic signals* (Tallal, 1980; Tallal, Stark, & Curtiss, 1976). Indeed, a significant proportion of individuals with developmental dyslexia (~50%) are also afflicted with core sensory processing impairments (Ramus et al., 2003). Auditory impairments include impaired ability to judge the temporal order of rapid auditory sequences, gap detection, detection of frequency and amplitude modulations, elevated frequency discrimination, and difficulties in auditory stream segregation (Abrams, Nicol, Zecker, & Kraus, 2006; Démonet et al., 2004; Goswami et al., 2002; McAnally, Hansen, Cornelissen, & Stein, 1997; Ramus, 2003; Tallal, Stark, Kallman, & Mellits, 1980). Comparable processing impairments in infants are predictive of their later language development (Benasich, Curtiss, & Tallal, 1993; Benasich & Tallal, 2002; Benasich, Thomas, Choudhury, & Leppänen, 2002).

Core Impairment in Excluding Background Noise

As per the noise–exclusion deficit hypothesis, the core impairment in children with learning disabilities is the inability to exclude background noise during signal processing (Sperling, Lu, Manis, & Seidenberg, 2005, 2006). Although initially proposed in the visual domain, such impairments have been shown to occur in the auditory domain as well (Ziegler, Pech-Georgel, George, & Lorenzi, 2009). According to the noise–exclusion deficit hypothesis, sensory impairments arise due to deleterious influence of background noise on sensory processing (Sperling et al., 2005).

Context-Dependent Encoding Impairment

A core impairment in context-dependent sensory processing (statistical learning) has also been identified. Children with perceptually based learning problems show reduced ability to modulate current perceptual dynamics based on prior experience. That is, children with learning problems are unable to adapt to context, resulting in poorer performance in challenging environments (Ahissar, 2007; Ahissar, Lubin, Putter-Katz, & Banai, 2006; Plante, Gómez, & Gerken, 2002).

COGNITIVE-SENSORY INTERACTION IN THE AUDITORY SYSTEM: IMPLICATION FOR DEVELOPMENTAL DYSLEXIA

The field is mired in theoretical discussions about underlying core impairments, that are nevertheless critical, because several therapeutic interventions have been devised to specifically cater to views ascribed by a certain theory (Eden & Moats, 2002; Goswami, 2006). The extant influential theories have failed to completely account for the broad cognitive, reading, and speech-in-noise perception impairments that exist in poor readers (Ramus, 2004). A critical reason why these hypotheses fail is that they are entrenched in the classic but flawed thinking that auditory processing progresses in a bottom-up manner (from sensory to cognitive processing). Consistent with mounting evidence of top-down influences, even at the lowest levels of auditory processing, there is a critical need to understand the complex-bidirectional interactions between higher-level cognitive processing and lower-level sensory encoding in poor readers. For instance, impairments in cognitive encoding can trickle down to sensory areas via a complex network of efferent feedback loops (corticofugal feedback). The broad impairments in developmental dyslexia can be a result of impaired cognitive-sensory interplay, and perhaps specifically be a result of deficient corticofugal function (Chandrasekaran, Hornickel, Skoe, Nicol, & Kraus, 2009).

Rather than get bogged down by arguments related to a causal relationship between core deficits and reading impairments, let us focus on understanding the biological correlates of the various impairments in children with reading disorders. It is important to 1) understand how biologically relevant, time-varying sounds (e.g., speech sounds that can pose perceptual challenges to children with dyslexia) are represented in the brain; 2) explore how this representation varies as a function of reading ability; and 3) understand how training and experience can modulate these representations in children with developmental dyslexia.

Brainstem Representation of Speech Sounds: A Window to Examining Cognitive-Sensory Interplay in the Auditory System

Speech sounds can be thought to consist of three basic components: pitch, harmonics, and timing (see Figure 6.1). In speech, these three elements of the acoustic signal can be differentiated based on their time scales, and they carry different informational content. In English, timing and harmonic cues convey the phonetic content of speech sounds, and are mainly responsible for the verbal message (the specific consonants and vowels). Pitch conveys intent (question versus statement), emotion, and other extra linguistic cues. Timing and harmonic cues, such as the difference in timing of voicing between /d/ and /t/, or the different release burst spectra of /d/ and /g/, are especially vulnerable to masking by background noise and pose perceptual challenges for some individuals with language and reading impairments (Hornickel, Skoe, Nicol, Zecker, & Kraus, 2009; Tallal & Gaab, 2006). Our studies have led to the development of a framework that organizes the speech signal into components that are selectively enhanced or impaired in certain populations and listening conditions (Tzounopoulos & Kraus, 2009).

Neural transcription of speech acoustics has been well studied in the auditory cortex of humans and experimental animals for stop consonants, vowels, and pitch. The focus here is on subcortical (brainstem) processing of speech sounds. The auditory brainstem response (ABR) is a noninvasive measure of far-field representation of stimulus-locked, synchronous electrical activity, originating at the brainstem (Chandrasekaran & Kraus, 2010b), that reflects the temporal and spectral characteristics of complex stimuli with remarkable precision (Skoe & Kraus, 2010). Unlike the more abstract representation of sound in the cortex, speech evokes a response in the brainstem that looks and sounds (when played back) like the evoking utterance itself (Galbraith, Arbagey, Branski, Comerci, & Rector, 1995). Responses are interpretable and meaningful in individuals. When recorded in response to a consonant or vowel syllable, the *timing* of the speech-evoked brainstem response (sABR) provides information, by fractions of milliseconds, about the onset and offset of the consonant and the vowel. The phase-locked frequency-following aspect of the response reflects spectrotemporal patterns in the evoking signal. Analysis

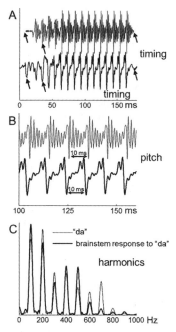

Figure 6.1. The stimulus /da/ (thin lines, upper trace in A and B) and its brainstem response (thick lines, lower trace in A and B); the brainstem response looks like the stimulus. A) The entire utterance and response with timing features indicated with arrows. B) A segment illustrating both syllable and response has a fundamental cycle of 10 ms, or 100 Hz. C) Spectral representation of the vowel portion of the stimulus. This frequency-domain representation illustrates the similarity of the harmonic structure.

of the spectral content of the response provides information about the fundamental frequency and lower harmonics, major contributors to the perceived pitch of the signal, as well as higher harmonics (including the formant structure). Several aspects of the sABR reflect language and musical experience, and short-term auditory training (Carcagno & Plack, 2011; Kraus and Chandrasekaran, 2010; Krishnan and Gandour, 2009; Russo, Hornickel, Nicol, Zecker, & Kraus, 2010; Song, Skoe, Banai, & Kraus, 2011; Strait, Hornickel, & Kraus, 2011; Tzounopoulos & Kraus, 2010), making it well suited to provide objective physiological information about speech encoding in populations with known impairments at perceptual and cognitive levels. It is important to note that higher-level cognitive processes dynamically interact with subcortical encoding of sound to shape auditory perception.

Subcortical Representation of Speech and Reading Ability

Brainstem encoding of children with language-based learning disorders reveals deficiencies in timing and harmonic shaping consistent with the phonological processing problems inherent in reading disorders (Banai et al., 2009; Hornickel et al., 2009; Hornickel, Anderson, Skoe, Yi, & Kraus, in press; Hornickel, Chandrasekaran, Zecker, & Kraus, 2011; Hornickel & Kraus, 2011; Tzounopoulos & Kraus, 2009). In evaluations of good and poor readers, it is evident that there is a relationship between the brainstem representation of speech features (timing, and harmonic structure) and reading ability, how manipulations of listening "challenge" the reader, and how contextual information affects neural encoding of speech. Together, the data show a strong association between subcortical auditory function and reading ability, and this lends credence to each of the various core impairment theories reviewed previously.

Brainstem Timing and Harmonic Encoding Is Associated with Reading Skills

A strong relationship has been observed between particular features of the speech ABR to the syllable /da/ and measures of reading skills. Significant correlations are observed between reading and subcortical timing and harmonic encoding, but not pitch encoding (see Figure 6.2). Correlational analysis between brainstem and reading indices demonstrates that reading and some phonological skills (phonological awareness and

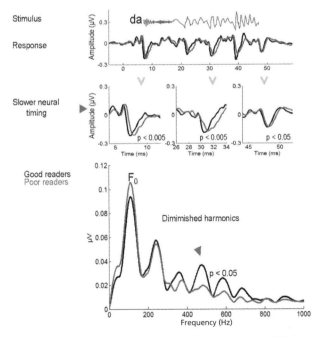

Figure 6.2. Top: Brainstem response to stimulus /da/ from good readers (black) and poor readers (grey). Middle: Key timing events in the stimulus. Poor readers show delayed-neural timing of these events. Bottom: Relative to good readers, poor readers show diminished higher-harmonic representation. (Adapted from Banai, K., Hornickel, J., Skoe, E., Zecker, S., & Kraus, N. Reading and Subcortical Auditory Function, *Cerebral Cortex*, 2009, 19, 11, pp. 2699–2707, by permission of Oxford University Press.)

phonological memory) are significantly related to subcortical timing and harmonic encoding (Banai, Nicol, Zecker, & Kraus, 2005; Banai et al., 2009; Hornickel et al., 2011; Hornickel, Anderson, Skoe, Yi, & Kraus, in press).

Consonant Differentiation

Stop consonants (e.g., in the syllables /ba/,/da/, /ga/) are especially vulnerable to misperception in poor readers (Hornickel et al., 2009; Serniclaes & Sprenger-Charolles, 2003; Serniclaes, Sprenger-Charolles, Carre, & Démonet, 2001). Timing cues evoked by acoustic differences in these syllables are present in the sABR (Johnson et al., 2008; Skoe, Nicol, & Kraus, 2011). Formant trajectories that differentiate the syllables translate into timing differences, an aspect well captured by sABRs. This is important because subcortical differentiation of stop consonants is associated with reading ability (see Figure 6.3). Specifically, children with higher phonological awareness—as measured by standardized measures—show greater differentiation among these three consonants (Hornickel et al., 2009).

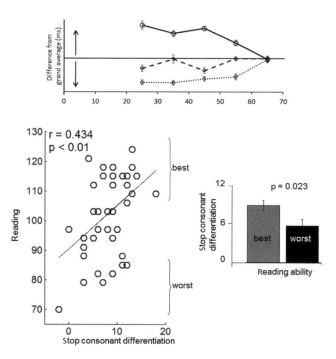

Figure 6.3. Top: Normalized response timings (x-axis represents time in milliseconds) to /ba/ (solid line), /da/ (dashed line), and /ga/ (dotted line). Timing differences persist only for the duration of the formant transition. Bottom: The subcortical differentiation score, a composite rendering of direction and extent of timing differences among responses to the three syllables, with higher scores signifying better neural differentiation, is significantly correlated with phonological awareness, and is significantly different between the top and bottom performers (inset). (*Source:* Hornickel, Skoe, Nicol, Zecker, & Kraus, 2009.)

EFFECT OF BACKGROUND NOISE ON BRAINSTEM REPRESENTATION OF SPEECH FEATURES IN GOOD AND POOR READERS

The noise exclusion hypothesis argues that background noise is particularly debilitating for poor readers, and this may represent a core impairment in some affected individuals. In an examination of the effect of background noise on the brainstem representation of speech, brainstem responses were recorded to the speech syllable /da/ in quiet and in background noise from a group of school-age children (Anderson, Skoe, Chandrasekaran, Zecker, & Kraus, 2010). The children were grouped into top and bottom readers based on standardized reading scores. Consistent with previous results (Cunningham, Nicol, Zecker, Bradlow, & Kraus, 2001), it was determined that background noise delayed the timing of the brainstem response to speech syllables in these individuals. However, children with poor reading scores showed a greater quiet-to-noise timing shift relative to good readers, suggesting that poor readers are more vulnerable to the deleterious effects of noise (see Figure 6.4).

EFFECT OF CONTEXT (STATISTICAL LEARNING) ON BRAINSTEM RESPONSES IN GOOD AND POOR READERS

The ability to tune into regularities in the auditory environment is fundamental to processing behaviorally relevant auditory signals (Suga, 2008). There is considerable evidence that even human infants are adept at extracting regularities, suggesting that the brain is exquisitely tuned to statistical properties in the auditory environment even during infancy (Saffran, Aslin, & Newport, 1996; Saffran, Johnson, Aslin, & Newport, 1999). A number of behavioral studies have shown that children with developmental dyslexia

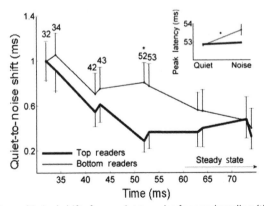

Figure 6.4.   Latency (timing) shifts from quiet-to-noise for good reading (thick black line) and poor reading (thin grey line) groups. Inset shows differences between the two groups in noise for one of the peaks. The two groups did not differ in the quiet listening condition. (Used with permission of the Society for Neuroscience, from Neural timing is linked to speech perception in noise, Anderson, S., Skoe, E., Chandrasekaran, B., & Kraus, N., *The Journal of neuroscience: The official journal of the Society for Neuroscience, 30*[14], 2010; permission conveyed through Copyright Clearance Center, Inc.)

show an impaired ability to improve sensory processing with repetition. In tasks with a large number of trials, good readers improve performance over time, but poor readers do not improve over time (Ahissar et al., 2006). This suggests that children with dyslexia are unable to use prior experience (context) to improve ongoing perception. Consistent with this proposal, it was determined that stimulus context influences encoding in the auditory brainstem (Chandrasekaran et al., 2009; Strait, Hornickel, & Kraus, 2011). Specifically, typically developing children showed enhanced spectral representation at the level of the auditory brainstem when the syllable was presented in a repetitive context, relative to when it was presented in a variable context (see Figure 6.5). In contrast, children with reading disorders showed an impairment in repetition-induced spectral fine-tuning at the level of the brainstem. Such context-dependent effects can be explained within the framework of our cognitive-to-sensory (corticofugal) theoretical model. Surprisingly, in children with dyslexia, there is enhanced spectral representation in the variable condition (relative to the repetitive context). These results are consistent with the view that in dyslexics, sensory representation may not be modulated by prior experience—a fact that may contribute to a more "creative" sensory representation. Further studies are required to disentangle the biological underpinnings of this interesting finding.

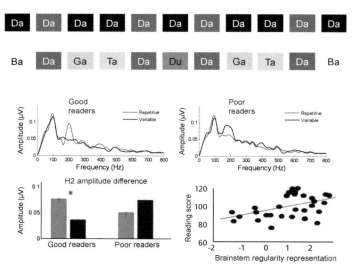

Figure 6.5. Context effects are seen for good readers but not for poor readers. The speech sound /da/ was presented in predictive (top row) and variable (second row) contexts. Grand-average spectra over the formant transition period for the good (left) and poor (right) readers show enhanced harmonic encoding in the repetitive condition in the good readers and in the variable condition in the poor readers. Bar plots of H2 amplitude support the response spectra, with greater H2 amplitude in good (left) than poor (right) readers in the repetitive condition and the opposite effect in the variable condition. The normalized difference in H2 magnitude between the two conditions reflecting brainstem regularity representation) is related to standardized scores of reading ability. Poor readers show inferior regularity enhancement in the brainstem relative to good readers. (From Chandrasekaran, B., Hornickel, J., Skoe, E., Nicol, T., & Kraus, N., [2009]. Context-dependent encoding in the human auditory brainstem relates to hearing speech in noise: Implications for developmental dyslexia. *Neuron, 64*[3], pp. 311–319. Copyright 2009 Elsevier. Reprinted by permission from Elsevier.)

BRAINSTEM-CORTICAL RELATIONSHIP IN CHILDREN WITH A WIDE RANGE OF READING ABILITY

It is well established that the left auditory cortex is specialized for processing rapid acoustic signals, and therefore crucial for speech perception (Belin et al., 1998; Niogi & McCandliss, 2006; Schwartz & Tallal, 1980; Gaab, Gabrieli, Deutsch, Tallal, & Temple, 2007). Less established is the role of the auditory brainstem in cerebral lateralization, as well as how brainstem-cortical relationships underlie speech perception ability. Auditory brainstem timing significantly predicts cerebral lateralization as measured by cortical event-related potentials (Abrams et al., 2006). Children who had atypical brainstem timing showed less cortical asymmetry, which was also associated with poor reading skills. This convergent data suggests that processing in the brainstem and the cortex are strongly linked and that subtle impairment at the level of the brainstem can dramatically alter cortical processing of speech sounds.

Training Modulates Auditory Brainstem Responses to Speech

It is well established from animal models that processing in the auditory brainstem is experience dependent and plays a crucial role in auditory learning (Bajo, Nodal, Moore, & King, 2010; Luo, Wang, Kashani, & Yan, 2008; Suga, 2008; Suga & Ma, 2003). It is important to note that brainstem encoding of speech can be ameliorated with software-based auditory training, suggesting that auditory processing in the brainstem is malleable to experience, and not hard wired (Carcagno & Plack, 2011; Russo, Hornickel, Nicol, Zecker, & Kraus, 2010; Song, Skoe, Banai, & Kraus, 2011; Song, Skoe, Wong, & Kraus, 2008). However, training does not change all aspects of the brainstem response. Rather, the plasticity is specific. For example, children with learning impairments show superior quiet-to-noise correlations after auditory training, suggesting improved fidelity of neural representation as a result of this training (Russo, Nicol, Zecker, Hayes, & Kraus, 2005).

Music as a Viable Training Approach

Music training is known to induce neuroplastic changes throughout the nervous system (Habib & Besson, 2009; Münte, Altenmüller, & Jäncke, 2002). Music training induces plastic changes that benefit music processing but also can improve processing in other domains including language and reading as well (reviewed in Kraus & Chandrasekaran, 2010). Based on this evidence, a number of researchers have argued for the viability of music as an indirect training approach in children with developmental dyslexia (Anvari, Trainor, Woodside, & Levy, 2002; Chandrasekaran & Kraus, 2010a; Overy, 2003; Strait & Kraus, in press; Tallal & Gaab, 2006). One line of research has been to evaluate the role of musical training in shaping the auditory brainstem response to musical and speech stimuli. It has been demonstrated that musical experience enhances the brainstem representation of native and nonnative speech sounds (Musacchia, Sams, Skoe, & Kraus, 2007; Wong, Skoe, Russo, Dees, & Kraus, 2007). Musical training also improves the representation of speech in noisy backgrounds (Parbery-Clark, Skoe, & Kraus, 2009). Musicians show superior stimulus-to-response correlations in noise, suggesting better fidelity of responses in challenging backgrounds. From a cognitive perspective, musicians show enhancement of a number of skills including working memory and auditory stream segregation—skills known to be deficient in children with dyslexia (Chandrasekaran & Kraus, 2010a; Parbery-Clark et al., 2009; Parbery-Clark, Strait, Anderson, Hittner, & Kraus, 2011). Taken together, these studies provide evidence for the possible utility of musical training as a potential remediation approach (Habib & Besson, 2009; Tallal & Gaab, 2006).

Theoretical Model: A Dynamic, Reciprocally Interactive, Positive-Feedback Process Between Cortex and Brainstem

Massive efferent projections from the cortex to subcortical regions form the structural basis for cognitive-to-sensory fine-tuning (Luo et al., 2008; Suga, 2008; Suga, Gao, Zhang, Ma, & Olsen, 2000; Suga & Ma, 2003; Suga, Xiao, Ma, & Ji, 2002; Winer, 2006). Efferent connections provide excitatory and inhibitory control over the brainstem nuclei. Thus, repeated stimulation by behaviorally relevant stimuli, electrical stimulation of forebrain structures, and auditory training have all been shown to induce plastic changes in the neuronal response properties in the auditory brainstem in animal models (Bajo et al., 2010; Luo et al., 2008; Suga, 2008; Suga et al., 2002). These animal studies support the view that corticofugal modulation can change processing in the subcortical structures in a behaviorally relevant manner. This forms the basis for a theoretical model that argues for a bidirectional processing scheme in the auditory system, in which sensory and cognitive factors interact to determine the end realization of a stimulus.

MODEL PREDICTIONS

In predictable contexts, the cortex is able to detect statistical regularities and modulate processing at the level of the brainstem via the selective extracting of relevant regularities, thereby improving cortical signal quality (Figure 6.6). Specifically, the feedback from the cortex fine tunes the encoding of the acoustic elements of speech at the brainstem, such that relevant aspects of the signal are enhanced and irrelevant details are suppressed, leading to an overall sharpening. This model is consistent with a proposal developed to explain cross-domain plasticity induced by musical training. This proposal suggests that subcortical plasticity may be a result of several factors, involving cortex and limbic systems (Patel, 2011). Effective efferent feedback is established in the system in predictable contexts; such plasticity occurs rapidly, persists over time, and functions to

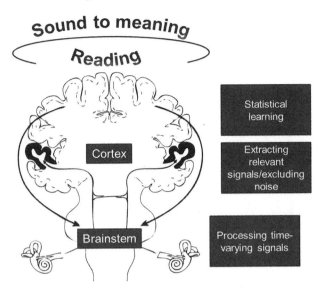

Figure 6.6. Theoretical model: The auditory system is composed of the auditory cortex and several brainstem nuclei that are connected bidirectionally (feedforward as well as feedback connections). Such interconnectivity allows for information transfer from the brainstem to the cortex, as well as feedback regulation (cortical influences on the brainstem). The cerebral cortex is adept at detecting and extracting statistical regularities in the auditory environment. Feedback from the cortex can selectively enhance relevant aspects of signal as well as suppress irrelevant signals (noise) at the auditory brainstem. Data reviewed in the main text argue for a relationship between brainstem encoding of speech and reading ability. Such a relationship reflects the cognitive-sensory nature of reading (dys)function, the biological basis for which may be the corticofugal (feedback) loops connecting the cortex and the brainstem.

improve overall signal quality in challenging backgrounds. In impaired systems (i.e., children with developmental dyslexia), our model predicts an impairment in the rapid and automatic extraction and storage of relevant auditory information (pattern detection impairment) at the level of the auditory cortex that permeates to lower-level encoding impairments via reduced feedback from the corticofugal network. Thus, in this model, both sensory and cognitive factors can contribute to ultimate reading (dys)function, mediated by an auditory system that has both feedforward as well as feedback loops. Specific contributions of various sensory and cognitive factors can explain variability in reading skills by using structural-equation modeling, a multivariate analyses technique (Hornickel et al., 2011; Strait, Hornickel, & Kraus, 2011.) The results demonstrate that specific brainstem signatures (reviewed above) contribute significantly toward explaining a high proportion of reading variance, providing a biological basis for establishing objective markers of reading ability.

CONCLUSION

Reading relies on a complex and multifaceted combination of processes that have proven difficult to disentangle. Children with reading difficulties show a broad range of impairments in cognitive and sensory processing.

The studies reviewed in this chapter show that children with reading difficulties exhibit impairments in subcortical processing of sound, as well as reduced cortical asymmetry. Finally, reading ability correlates significantly with a number of brainstem measures, including neural timing, representation of higher harmonics, resistance to background noise, and the ability to use prior experience (i.e., profit from stimulus repetition) to improve spectral representation. These factors, when incorporated in a structural-equation model, significantly predict variability in reading ability (Hornickel et al., 2011). On the basis of the studies reviewed here, we argue that the auditory brainstem response to speech serves as a significant and accessible factor underlying reading ability and impairment.

FUTURE DIRECTIONS

Future directions to further the understanding of the biological basis of reading and its application to education and clinical management include: 1) refining the subcortical neural signature for reading ability and its developmental trajectory, 2) using brainstem activity as an early neurobiological marker of reading ability, 3) integrating subcortical-neural signatures with animal physiology and genetic models, and 4) integrating information obtained through cutting-edge emerging technologies that are meaningful in individuals (i.e., subcortical physiology with structural measures, e.g., diffusion tensor imaging).

REFERENCES

Abrams, D.A., Nicol, T., Zecker, S.G., & Kraus, N. (2006). Auditory brainstem timing predicts cerebral asymmetry for speech. *Journal of Neuroscience, 26*(43), 11131–11137.doi:10.1523/JNEUROSCI.2744-06.2006

Ahissar, M. (2007). Dyslexia and the anchoring-deficit hypothesis. *Trends in Cognitive Sciences, 11*(11), 458–465. doi:10.1016/j.tics.2007.08.015

Ahissar, M., Lubin, Y., Putter-Katz, H., & Banai, K. (2006). Dyslexia and the failure to form a perceptual anchor. *Nature Neuroscience, 9,* 1558–1564. doi:10.1038/nn1800

Anderson, S., Skoe, E., Chandrasekaran, B., & Kraus, N. (2010). Neural timing is linked to speech perception in noise. *The Journal of Neuroscience: The official journal of the Society for Neuroscience, 30*(14), 4922–4926. doi:10.1523/JNEUROSCI.0107-10.2010

Anvari, S.H., Trainor, L.J., Woodside, J., & Levy, B.A. (2002). Relations among musical skills, phonological processing, and early reading ability in preschool children. *Journal of Experimental Child Psychology, 83*(2), 111–130. doi:10.1016/S0022-0965(02)00124-8

Bajo, V.M., Nodal, F.R., Moore, D.R., & King, A.J. (2010). The descending corticocollicular pathway mediates learning-induced auditory plasticity. *Nature Neuroscience, 13*(2), 253–260. doi:10.1038/nn.2466

Banai, K., Hornickel, J., Skoe, E., Nicol, T., Zecker, S., & Kraus, N. (2009). Reading and subcortical auditory function. *Cerebral Cortex, 19*(11), 2699–2707. doi:10.1093/cercor/bhp024

Banai, K., Nicol, T., Zecker, S., & Kraus, N. (2005). Brainstem timing: Implications for cortical processing and literacy. *Journal of Neuroscience 25*(43), 9850–9857. doi:10.1523/JNEUROSCI.2373-05.2005

Belin, P., Zilbovicius, M., Crozier, S., Thivard, L., Fontaine, A., Masure, M.C., & Samson, Y. (1998). Lateralization of speech and auditory temporal processing. *Journal of Cognitive Neuroscience, 10*(4), 536–540. doi:10.1162/089892998562834

Benasich, A.A., Curtiss, S., & Tallal, P. (1993). Language, learning, and behavioral disturbances in childhood: A longitudinal perspective. *Journal of the American Academy of Child and Adolescent Psychiatry, 32*(3), 585–594. doi:10.1097/00004583-199305000-00015

Benasich, A.A., & Tallal, P. (2002). Infant discrimination of rapid auditory cues predicts later language impairment. *Behavioural Brain Research, 136*(1), 31–49. doi:10.1016/S0166-4328(02)00098-0

Benasich, A.A., Thomas, J.J., Choudhury, N., & Leppänen, P.H.T. (2002). The importance of rapid auditory processing abilities to early language development: Evidence from converging methodologies. *Developmental Psychobiology, 40*(3), 278–292. doi:10.1002/dev.10032

Carcagno, S. & Plack, C.J. (2011). Subcortical plasticity following perceptual learning in a pitch discrimination task. *Journal of the Association for Research in Otolaryngology 12*(1), 89–100. Doi:10.1007/s10162-010-0236-1

Carroll, J.M., & Snowling, M.J. (2004). Language and phonological skills in children at high risk of reading difficulties. *Journal of Child Psychology and Psychiatry, 45*(3), 631–640. doi:10.1111/j.1469-7610.2004.00252

Chandrasekaran, B., Hornickel, J., Skoe, E., Nicol, T., & Kraus, N. (2009). Context-dependent encoding in the human auditory brainstem relates to hearing speech in noise: Implications for developmental dyslexia. *Neuron, 64*(3), 311–319. doi:10.1016/j.neuron.2009.10.006

Chandrasekaran, B., & Kraus, N. (2010a). Music, noise-exclusion, and learning. *Music Perception, 27*(4), 297–306. doi:10.1525/mp.2010.27.4.297

Chandrasekaran, B., & Kraus, N. (2010b). The scalp-recorded brainstem response to speech: Neural origins and plasticity. *Psychophysiology, 47*(2), 236–246. doi:10.1111/j.1469-8986.2009.00928

Cunningham, J., Nicol, T., Zecker, S.G., Bradlow, A., & Kraus, N. (2001). Neurobiologic responses to speech in noise in children with learning problems: Deficits and strategies for improvement.

Clinical Neurophysiology, 112(5), 758–767. doi:10.1016/S1388-2457(01)00465-5

Démonet, J.F., Taylor, M.J., & Chaix, Y. (2004). Developmental dyslexia. *Lancet, 363*(9419), 1451–1460. doi:10.1016/S0140-6736(04)16106-0

Eden, G.F., & Moats, L. (2002). The role of neuroscience in the remediation of students with dyslexia. *Nature Neuroscience, 5,* 1080–1084. doi:10.1038/nn946

Gaab, N., Gabrieli, J.D., Deutsch, G.K., Tallal, P., & Temple, E. (2007). Neural correlates of rapid auditory processing are disrupted in children with developmental dyslexia and ameliorated with training: An fMRI study. *Restorative Neurology and Neuroscience, 25*(3–4), 295–310.

Galbraith, G.C., Arbagey, P.W., Branski, R., Comerci, N., & Rector, P.M. (1995). Intelligible speech encoded in the human brain stem frequency-following response. *Neuroreport, 6*(17), 2363–2367. doi:10.1097/00001756-199511270-00021

Goswami, U. (2006). Neuroscience and education: From research to practice? *Nature Reviews Neuroscience, 7*(5), 406–413. doi:10.1038/nrn1907

Goswami, U., Thomson, J., Richardson, U., Stainthorp, R., Hughes, D., Rosen, S., & Scott, S.K. (2002). Amplitude envelope onsets and developmental dyslexia: A new hypothesis. *Proceedings of the National Academy of Sciences, USA, 99*(16), 10911–10916. doi:10.1073/pnas.122368599

Habib, M., & Besson, M. (2009). What do music training and musical experience teach us about brain plasticity? *Music Perception, 26*(3), 279–285. doi:10.1525/mp.2009.26.3.279

Hornickel, J., Anderson, S., Skoe, E., Yi, H., & Kraus N. (in press). Subcortical representation of speech fine structure relates to reading ability. *NeuroReport.*

Hornickel, J., Chandrasekaran, B., Zecker, S., & Kraus, N. (2011). Auditory brainstem measures predict reading and speech-in-noise perception in school-aged children. *Behavioural Brain Research, 216*(2), 597–605. doi:10.1016/j.bbr.2010.08.051

Hornickel, J., & Kraus, N. (2011). Objective biological measures for the assessment and management of auditory processing disorder. *Current Pediatric Reviews, 7*(3): 252–261.

Hornickel, J., Skoe, E., Nicol, T., Zecker, S., & Kraus, N. (2009). Subcortical differentiation of stop consonants relates to reading and speech-in-noise perception. *Proceedings of the National Academy of Sciences, USA, 106*(31), 13022–13027. doi:10.1073/pnas.0901123106

Johnson, K.L., Nicol, T., Zecker, S.G., Bradlow, A.R., Skoe, E., & Kraus, N. (2008). Brainstem encoding of voiced consonant–vowel stop syllables. *Clinical Neurophysiology, 119*(11), 2623–2635. doi:10.1016/j.clinph.2008.07.277

Kraus, N., & Chandrasekaran, B. (2010). Music training for the development of auditory skills. *Nature Reviews Neuroscience, 11*(8), 599–605. doi:10.1038/nrn2882

Krishnan, A., & Gandour, J. (2009). The role of the auditory brainstem in processing linguistically-relevant pitch patterns. *Brain and Language, 110*(3), 135–148. doi:10.1016/j.bandl.2009.03.005

Luo, F., Wang, Q., Kashani, A., & Yan, J. (2008). Corticofugal modulation of initial sound processing in the brain. *Journal of Neuroscience, 28*(45), 11615–11621. doi:10.1523/JNEUROSCI.3972-08.2008

Marshall, C.M., Snowling, M.J., & Bailey, P.J. (2001). Rapid auditory processing and phonological ability in normal readers and readers with dyslexia. *Journal of Speech, Language, and Hearing Research, 44*(4), 925–940. doi:10.1044/1092-4388(2001/073)

McAnally, K.I., Hansen, P.C., Cornelissen, P.L., & Stein, J.F. (1997). Effect of time and frequency manipulation on syllable perception in developmental dyslexics. *Journal of Speech, Language, and Hearing Research, 40*(4), 912–924.

Münte, T.F., Altenmüller, E., & Jäncke, L. (2002). The musician's brain as a model of neuroplasticity. *Nature Reviews Neuroscience, 3*, 473–478. doi:10.1038/nrn843

Musacchia, G., Sams, M., Skoe, E., & Kraus, N. (2007). Musicians have enhanced subcortical auditory and audiovisual processing of speech and music. *Proceedings of the National Academy of Sciences, USA, 104*(40), 15894–15898. doi:10.1073/pnas.0701498104

Niogi, S.N., & McCandliss, B.D. (2006). Left lateralized white matter microstructure accounts for individual differences in reading ability and disability. *Neuropsychologia, 44*(11), 2178–2188. doi:10.1016/j.neuropsychologia.2006.01.011

Overy, K. (2003). Dyslexia and music: From timing deficits to musical intervention. *Annals of the New York Academy of Sciences, 999*, 497–505.

Parbery-Clark, A., Skoe, E., & Kraus, N. (2009). Musical experience limits the degradative effects of background noise on the neural processing of sound. *Journal of Neuroscience, 29*(45), 14100–14107. doi:10.1523/JNEUROSCI.3256-09.2009

Parbery-Clark, A., Strait, D.L., Anderson, S., Hittner, E., Kraus, N. (2011). Musical training and the aging auditory system: Implications for cognitive abilities and hearing speech in noise. *PLoS ONE, 6*, e18082.

Patel, A.D. (2011). Why would Musical Training Benefit the Neural Encoding of Speech? The OPERA Hypothesis. *Front Psychol, 2*, 142.

Plante, E., Gómez, R., & Gerken, L. (2002). Sensitivity to word order cues by normal and language/learning disabled adults. *Journal of Communication Disorders, 35*(5), 453–462. doi:10.1016/S0021-9924(02)00094-1

Ramus, F. (2001a). Dyslexia: Talk of two theories. *Nature, 412*, 393–395. doi:10.1038/35086683

Ramus, F. (2001b). Outstanding questions about phonological processing in dyslexia. *Dyslexia, 7*(4), 197–216. doi:10.1002/dys.205

Ramus, F. (2003). Developmental dyslexia: Specific phonological deficit or general sensorimotor dysfunction? *Current Opinions in Neurobiology, 13*(2), 212–218. doi:10.1016/S0959-4388(03)00035-7

Ramus, F. (2004). Neurobiology of dyslexia: A reinterpretation of the data. *Trends in Neurosciences, 27*(12), 720–726. doi:10.1016/j.tins.2004.10.009

Ramus, F., Rosen, S., Dakin, S.C., Day, B.L., Castellote, J.M., White, S., & Frith, U. (2003). Theories of developmental dyslexia: Insights from a multiple case study of dyslexic adults. *Brain, 126*(4), 841–865. doi:10.1093/brain/awg076

Russo, N.M., Hornickel, J., Nicol, T., Zecker, S., & Kraus, N. (2010). Biological changes in auditory function following training in children with autism spectrum disorders. *Behavioral and Brain Functions 6*, 60. doi:10.1186/1744-9081-6-60

Russo, N.M., Nicol, T.G., Zecker, S.G., Hayes, E.A., & Kraus, N. (2005). Auditory training improves neural timing in the human brainstem. *Behavioural Brain*

Research, 156(1), 95–103. doi:10.1016/j.bbr.2004.05.012

Saffran, J.R., Aslin, R.N., & Newport, E.L. (1996). Statistical learning by 8-month-old infants. *Science, 274*(5294), 1926–1928. doi:10.1126/science.274.5294.1926

Saffran, J.R., Johnson, E.K., Aslin, R.N., & Newport, E.L. (1999). Statistical learning of tone sequences by human infants and adults. *Cognition, 70*(1), 27–52. doi:10.1016/S0010-0277(98)00075-4

Schwartz, J., & Tallal, P. (1980). Rate of acoustic change may underlie hemispheric specialization for speech perception. *Science, 207*(4437), 1380–1381.

Serniclaes, W., & Sprenger-Charolles, L. (2003). Categorical perception of speech sounds and dyslexia. *Current Psychology Letters* [Online], 10, Vol. 1, 2003, http://cpl.revues.org/index379.html

Serniclaes, W., Sprenger-Charolles, L., Carre, R., & Démonet, J.F. (2001). Perceptual discrimination of speech sounds in developmental dyslexia. *Journal of Speech, Language and Hearing Research, 44*(2), 384. doi:10.1044/1092-4388(2001/032)

Skoe, E., & Kraus, N. (2010). Auditory brainstem response to complex sounds: A tutorial. *Ear and Hearing, 31*(3), 302–324.

Skoe, E., Nicol, T., & Kraus, N. (2011) Cross-phaseogram: Objective neural index of speech sound differentiation. *Journal of Neuroscience Methods. 196*, 308–317. doi:10.1016/j.jneumeth.2011.01.020

Song, J., Skoe, E., Banai, K., & Kraus, N. (2011). Training to improve hearing speech in noise: Biological mechanisms. *Cerebral Cortex, 122*, 1890–1898. doi:10.1093/cercor/bhr196

Song, J.H., Skoe, E., Wong, P.C., & Kraus, N. (2008). Plasticity in the adult human auditory brainstem following short-term linguistic training. *Journal of Cognitive Neuroscience, 20*(10), 1892–1902. doi:10.1162/jocn.2008.20131

Sperling, A.J., Lu, Z.L., Manis, F.R., & Seidenberg, M.S. (2005). Deficits in perceptual noise exclusion in developmental dyslexia. *Nature Neuroscience, 8*, 862–863. doi:10.1038/nn1474

Sperling, A.J., Lu, Z.L., Manis, F.R., & Seidenberg, M.S. (2006). Motion-perception deficits and reading impairment. *Psychological Science, 17*(12), 1047–1053. doi:10.1111/j.1467-9280.2006.01825

Strait, D.L., Hornickel, J., Kraus, N. (2011). Subcortical processing of speech regu-

larities predicts reading and music aptitude in children. *Behavioral and Brain Functions. 7(1)*, 44. doi:10.1186/1744-9081-7-44

Strait, D.L., & Kraus, N. (in press). Playing music for a smarter ear: cognitive, perceptual and neurobiological evidence. *Music Perception.*

Suga, N. (2008). Role of corticofugal feedback in hearing. *Journal of Comparative Physiology A: Neuroethology, Sensory, Neural, and Behavioral Physiology, 194*(2), 169–183. doi:10.1007/s00359-007-0274-2

Suga, N., Gao, E., Zhang, Y., Ma, X., & Olsen, J.F. (2000). The corticofugal system for hearing: Recent progress. *Proceedings of the National Academy of Sciences, USA, 97*(22), 11807–11814. doi:10.1073/pnas.97.22.11807

Suga, N., & Ma, X. (2003). Multiparametric corticofugal modulation and plasticity in the auditory system. *Nature Reviews Neuroscience, 4*(10), 783–794. doi:10.1038/nrn1222

Suga, N., Xiao, Z., Ma, X., & Ji, W. (2002). Plasticity and corticofugal modulation for hearing in adult animals. *Neuron, 36*(1), 9–18. doi:10.1016/S0896-6273(02)00933-9

Tallal, P. (1980). Auditory temporal perception, phonics, and reading disabilities in children. *Brain and Language, 9*(2), 182–198. doi:10.1016/0093-934X(80)90139-X

Tallal, P., & Gaab, N. (2006). Dynamic auditory processing, musical experience and language development. *Trends in Neurosciences, 29*(7), 382–390. doi:10.1016/j.tins.2006.06.003

Tallal, P., Stark, R.E., & Curtiss, B. (1976). Relation between speech perception and speech production impairment in children with developmental dysphasia. *Brain and Language, 3*(2), 305–317. doi:10.1016/0093-934X(76)90025-0

Tallal, P., Stark, R.E., Kallman, C., & Mellits, D. (1980). Developmental dysphasia: Relation between acoustic processing deficits and verbal processing. *Neuropsychologia, 18*(3), 273–284. doi:10.1016/0028-3932(80)90123-2

Tzounopoulos, T., & Kraus, N. (2009). Learning to encode timing: Mechanisms of plasticity in the auditory brainstem. *Neuron, 62*(4), 463–469. doi:10.1016/j.neuron.2009.05.002

Windfuhr, K.L., & Snowling, M.J. (2001). The relationship between paired associate learning and phonological skills in normally developing readers. *Journal of Experimental Child Psychology, 80*(2), 160–173. doi:10.1006/jecp.2000.2625

Winer, J.A. (2006). Decoding the auditory corticofugal systems. *Hearing Research, 212*(1–2), 1–8. doi:10.1016/j.heares.2005.06.014

Wong, P.C., Skoe, E., Russo, N.M., Dees, T., & Kraus, N. (2007). Musical experience shapes human brainstem encoding of linguistic pitch patterns. *Nature Neuroscience, 10,* 420–422. doi:10.1038/nn1872

Ziegler, J.C., Pech-Georgel, C., George, F., & Lorenzi, C. (2009). Speech-perception-in-noise deficits in dyslexia. *Developmental Science, 12*(5), 732–745. doi:10.1111/j.1467-7687.2009.00817

CHAPTER 7

Timing, Information Processing, and Efficacy

Early Factors that Impact Childhood Language Trajectories

April A. Benasich and Naseem Choudhury

INTRODUCTION

The title chosen for the 12th Extraordinary Brain Symposium, "Developmental Dyslexia: Early Precursors, Neurobehavioral Markers and Biological Substrates," held in Cong, Ireland, in 2010, served to highlight the changing focus in the field from studying and characterizing deficits in children (and adolescents and adults as well) already diagnosed with dyslexia toward examining the earliest indicators, biomarkers, and potential precursors of developmental language disorders. Increasingly, the impetus has been on identifying those children at highest risk for language learning disorders, basically what we have termed "predyslexic" populations, in order to track developmental trajectories, facilitate early identification, and, it is hoped, provide effective and appropriate remediation. Just as important, this precursor approach promises to impart further insight into the etiologies, common pathways, neurobiological correlates, and behavioral phenotypes of dyslexia. Given the evident advantages to this approach, the basic question arises: How early might one detect reliable predictors of later language learning disorders such as dyslexia?

In this chapter, we address this question by providing an overview of a series of prospective longitudinal studies that examined the role of efficient information processing in a population of children who were at much higher risk for language learning disorders, including dyslexia, as a function of a family history of such disorders. In particular, we investigate whether infants' ability to efficiently process ongoing auditory input in the tens of milliseconds (ms) range has an impact on the developmental trajectory of language acquisition. Ongoing research in our laboratory provides evidence that the ability to perform such fine-grained acoustic analysis during infancy is one of the most powerful and significant predictors of subsequent language development and disorders. These findings have been shown using behavioral assessments of information processing (Benasich et al., 2006; Benasich & Tallal, 1996,

---

This research was supported by grants from NICHD and NSF with additional support from the Charles A. Dana Foundation, the Ellison Foundation, and the Elizabeth H. Solomon Center for Neurodevelopmental Research. We also thank the loyal parents and children who participated in this study.

2002; Choudhury & Benasich, 2003; Choudhury, Leppänen, Leevers, & Benasich, 2007), converging measures of dense-array electroencephalogram (EEG) and evoked response potentials (ERPs), as well as power analyses of resting EEG (Benasich, Thomas, Choudhury, & Leppänen, 2002; Benasich, Gou, Choudhury, & Harris, 2008; Choudhury & Benasich, 2009, 2011; Gou, Choudhury, & Benasich, 2011).

LANGUAGE ACQUISITION

Children begin to develop linguistic competence long before they can speak. During the first months of life, the infant's developing brain is involved in actively constructing a phonemic map of the sounds of his or her native language, using the inherent statistical properties of speech (Kuhl, 2000; Saffran, Aslin, & Newport, 1996). In fact, the ability to perform fine-grained acoustic analyses appears to be critical to the decoding of the speech stream and the subsequent establishment of phonemic maps (e.g., Aslin, 1989; Eimas, 1975; Eimas, Siqueland, Jusczyk, & Vigorito, 1971; Kuhl, 2004). These phonemic maps are gradually tuned to the ambient native language. In order to accomplish this, the infant brain must process and distinguish spectrotemporally modulated acoustic cues that arrive at the ear in rapid succession. For example, infants must process auditory differences in the tens of ms range, within phonemes such as /ga/ and /da/. As phonemic mapping progresses, categorical perception is enabled, leading to fast "automatic processing" of language. Most important all the components that are necessary for children to process, discriminate, and acquire language are in place at this very early, preverbal stage of development.

SPECIFIC LANGUAGE IMPAIRMENT AND SPECIFIC READING DISABILITY (DYSLEXIA)

The majority of children accomplish this complicated task with impressive ease. However, for a subset of children, language acquisition presents significant and prolonged difficulties. It is estimated that 5%–10% of children entering school (e.g., Tomblin, 1996; Tomblin, Zhang, Buckwalter, & Catts, 2000) can be classified as having a developmental language-based learning disorder referred to as specific language impairment (SLI). SLI is a diagnosis of exclusion, as it is characterized by the failure to develop typical language skills in the absence of an apparent cause; individuals have typical intelligence, hearing, and no known neurological impairments. Of interest in the broader context of language learning disorders is that more than 50% of children with SLI continue on to develop reading problems similar to those seen in people with dyslexia (Bishop & Snowling, 2004; McArthur, Hogben, Edwards, Heath, & Mengler, 2000; Tomblin et al., 2000).

Both dyslexia and SLI appear to reflect a heterogeneous group of disorders. Although controversial (Leonard, 1998; Snowling, Bishop, & Stothard, 2000), evidence supporting a continuum between oral and written language impairments has continued to mount. These investigations demonstrate that children classified as SLI and those diagnosed as having dyslexia display a variety of similar deficits in linguistic domains, including poorer performance on tasks of phonological awareness, verbal short-term memory, nonword repetition, and rapid automatized naming, thus suggesting an overlap in core deficits (see Bishop & Snowling, 2004; Leonard, 1998; Wagner & Torgesen, 1987; and Chapter 9 of this book). Whether these parallels derive from speech-specific mechanisms or from more basic processing deficits is, as of 2011, the center of continuing theoretical debate.

Added to this picture are neurobiological and neuroprognostic studies examining the genetic, neural, and perhaps "multifocal" behavioral underpinnings of language-based learning disorders (LLD) using animal models, state-of-the-art imaging, and novel statistical approaches, in an attempt to identify core underlying deficits or "intermediate phenotypes" and comorbidities (e.g., Eckert, 2004; Pennington & Bishop, 2009; Plomin & Kovas, 2005). Evidence pointing to family aggregation of both SLI and dyslexia has led to an impressive body of heritability research, including pedigree, twin, and gene-linkage investigations (see Flax et al., 2003 and Chapters 4 and 5 of this book.) Thus, careful examination of the earliest precursors for LLD, including both specific language and specific reading disorders, is an important aim that may enable earlier identification and remediation of those children at highest overall risk for LLD and provide further insight into the etiologies, common pathways, neurobiological correlates, and behavioral phenotypes of LLDs.

RAPID AUDITORY PROCESSING

The ability to decode the incoming speech stream is dependent upon the accurate perception of rapidly presented, successive acoustic signals, or rapid auditory processing (RAP). The mechanism by which RAP abilities influence language acquisition is related to the process by which speech sounds are represented, assembled, and refined in the infant brain. Difficulties in discriminating and processing brief, rapid successive auditory cues leads to distorted neural boundaries that appear to result in degraded categorical and phonemic representations (Benasich & Leevers, 2003; Cunningham, Nicol, King, Zecker, & Kraus, 2002; Elbro, 1990; Imaizumi, Priebe, Sharpee, Cheung, & Schreiner, 2010; Werker & Tees, 1987). These indistinct and perhaps overinclusive cortical representations can lead to expressive and/or receptive language delays in early childhood and subsequent reading, writing, and spelling deficits due to poor phonemic (spoken) to orthographic (visual/written) mapping (see Heim & Benasich, 2006, for a review).

Accurate and efficient decoding of language across the lifespan depends on intact RAP abilities (Benasich et al., 2002, 2006; Choudhury et al., 2007; Kraus et al., 1996; Kraus & Braida, 2002; Tallal, 2004). Difficulty in rapid processing of speech, as well as nonspeech, sounds has been shown to be associated with language impairments in adults (e.g., Heath, Hogben, & Clark, 1999; Oram Cardy, Flagg, Roberts, Brian, & Roberts, 2005), school-age children (McArthur & Bishop, 2001; Tallal, 2004), and adolescents (Weber-Fox, Leonard, Wray, & Tomblin, 2010); as we detail here, RAP abilities in the first year of life are highly associated with and predictive of later language skills (Benasich et al., 2002, 2006; Choudhury & Benasich, 2003, 2011; Choudhury et al., 2007; Kuhl, 2004; Tsao, Liu, & Kuhl, 2004; also see reviews: Heim & Benasich, 2006; Tallal, 2004). These associations have been replicated using behavioral assessments of psychophysical thresholds as well as state-of-the-art techniques such as high-density EEG/ERPs (Benasich et al., 2006; McArthur, Atkinson, & Ellis, 2009), ABRs (Basu, Krishnan, & Weber-Fox, 2010; Song, Banai, & Kraus, 2008), PET (Fiez et al., 1995), and fMRI (Gaab, Gabrieli, Deutsch, Tallal, & Temple, 2007; Poldrack et al., 2001; Tallal & Gaab, 2006; Temple, 2002; Temple et al., 2001). Thus a large body of literature implicates basic difficulties in processing brief or rapid successive auditory cues, for both speech and nonspeech stimuli, in the poor phonological skills that are observed in children with language and reading/literacy impairments. Cumulative evidence from research in our laboratory, as well as others', strongly suggests that a basic deficit in RAP of nonspeech sounds in infancy may serve as a behavior marker for subsequent LLD.

PROSPECTIVE LONGITUDINAL STUDIES: THE INFANT AS A PRELINGUISTIC MODEL

The broad objective of the research summarized here was to examine the early neural processes necessary for typical cognitive and language development, as well as the impact of atypical processing on typically developing infants and those at high risk for LLD. In all our studies, we have used converging methodologies, prospective longitudinal designs, and a developmental framework that is both prespeech and nonlanguage specific. Our initial series of behavior studies established that RAP played a significant role in both normative and atypical early language acquisition. In these studies, we used a battery of tasks, including reinforced conditioned head turning, habituation, and recognition memory paradigms, to assess auditory processing of speech and nonspeech stimuli as well as more global measures of information processing in infants across time (Benasich & Leevers, 2003; Choudhury et al. 2007; see Heim & Benasich, 2006, for more information). All of these paradigms tap processing speed as well as memory and discrimination—critical abilities for linguistic development and for more general cognitive development. In these early studies, children were seen at 6, 9, 12, 24, 36, and 48 months. We have continued to follow many of these children with yearly assessments, and a subset is now turning 8, 9, and 10 years old.

Across studies, we selected our participants based on a risk model that takes account of strong heritability for both language and reading abilities (Harlaar, Hayiou-Thomas, Dale, & Plomin, 2008; Haworth et al., 2009; Plomin & Kovas, 2005) as well as for language disorders such as SLI (Bishop, North, & Donlan, 1995; Catts, Adolf, Hogan, & Weismer, 2005; Choudhury & Benasich, 2003; DeThorne et al., 2006; Flax et al., 2003; Lewis & Thompson, 1992; Logan et al., in press; Neils & Aram, 1986; Stromswold, 2000; Tallal, Ross, & Curtiss, 1989; Tomblin, 1989; Tomblin & Buckwalter, 1998). Genetic research indicates that the rates of affected individuals in families with a positive history for LLD range from 20%–80% (Bishop & Edmundson, 1986; Flax et al., 2003; Tallal et al., 2001; Tallal et al., 1989; Tomblin, 1989). Thus infants born into such families are at increased risk to develop LLD and have comprised the target population for many of our research studies. It is important to note that none of the infants tested in these studies had a diagnosis of SLI/LLD but were at *higher risk* for developing these disorders and thus presented us with a naturally existing LLD model on which to test our hypotheses.

The findings from this early series of studies demonstrated that the RAP thresholds of infants born into families with a history of LLD were significantly poorer than those of age-matched peers from control families (Benasich & Tallal, 1996, 2002; Choudhury & Benasich, 2003; Choudhury et al., 2007). Furthermore, infant RAP abilities were shown to be highly predictive of receptive and expressive language from 12 to 36 months. Infants with poorer RAP thresholds were developing language much more slowly than those with better (lower) thresholds (Benasich & Leevers, 2003; Benasich & Tallal, 2002; Benasich et al., 2002; Choudhury et al., 2007). In addition, early RAP abilities were more robust predictors of language at 24 and 36 months of age than family history alone (Benasich & Tallal, 2002; Choudhury et al., 2007). Choudhury et al. (2007) also demonstrated the utility of a *battery* of infant tasks, uncovering multimodal processing deficits (both visual and auditory) in the same infants who were at higher risk for SLI.

In one longitudinal study, initial assessments were obtained when infants were 6–9 months of age (mean: 7½ months), and the children were then followed prospectively through age 36 months (Benasich & Tallal, 2002). In a sample of infants that included those with a family history of SLI (family history positive or FH+) as well as control infants with no such family history family history negative or FH-), psychophysical thresholds on a test of nonverbal RAP at 7½ months was the single best predictor of subsequent language outcome through 36 months of age. In every case, irrespective of group, children with poor infant RAP thresholds (150 ms interstimulus interval [ISI] or above) had significantly poorer language outcomes at 24 and 36 months. At age 3 years, RAP threshold and gender (being male) together predicted 39%–41% of the variance in language outcome. However, gender or family history alone was not predictive of outcome (Benasich & Tallal, 2002; Benasich et al., 2002).

For the same sample, a series of discriminate function analyses were conducted in order to assess how sensitive the infant measures were to individual differences in later outcome. Thirty-six-month outcomes on the Preschool Language Scale-3 (PLS-3) (Zimmerman, Steiner, & Pond, 1992) and on the Verbal Reasoning Subscales (V/R) of the Stanford-Binet (SB) (Thorndike, Hagen, & Sattler, 1986) were examined using a stringent criterion for impairment. If a 3-year-old's PLS-3 percentile score on the V/R subscales of the SB was 1 or more standard deviation below the mean, that child was classified as "impaired." We found that 6-month RAP thresholds accounted for the largest amount of variance (~29%–52%) in language scores and verbal subsets of the SB at 36 months. RAP thresholds at 6 months and male gender together accurately classified 91.4% of 3-year-olds who scored in the impaired range on the V/R subscales of the SB. Classification accuracy, at age 3 years, to impaired versus nonimpaired groups using the SB V/R subscales was 93.9% on the Verbal Reasoning Vocabulary subscale and 90.9% on the Verbal Reasoning Comprehension subscale (Benasich & Tallal, 2002; Benasich et al., 2002).

These data are striking because they so clearly demonstrate that, regardless of family history, individual differences in RAP during the first year of life significantly predict delayed language acquisition. Moreover, these findings highlight the essential role that basic nonlinguistic, central auditory processes, particularly rapid spectrotemporal processing, play in modulating early language development.

Converging Methodologies, Timing, and Developmental Trajectories

Our more recent studies have used a developmental framework and multiple methodologies to provide converging evidence for the fundamental role of temporally modulated acoustic stimuli in mounting language. This orientation allows further investigation of the question of whether the RAP deficits observed in separate studies with nonoverlapping samples, simply co-occur with the difficulties in phonological and syntactic decoding seen in children with LLD, or whether they precede and predict those impairments to be addressed.

In one longitudinal study, converging EEG/ERPs and behavioral tasks were employed to assess two groups of children (from 6 months through 24 months) using the same nonverbal stimuli used in our previous behavior studies (Benasich et al., 2006). This age range includes a very dynamic developmental period over which language abilities are progressively acquired. We were particularly interested in examining EEG/ERPs starting at the 6-month time point, given that processing abilities measured at this age in our previous behavior studies have been the strongest predictors of later language abilities (Benasich & Tallal, 2002; Choudhury & Benasich, 2003; Choudhury et al., 2007).

A series of well-defined and significant differences emerged between infants from FH+ families and control infants from FH− families. Specifically, significant group differences were observed in the speed and efficiency of preattentive information processing and discrimination abilities. Smaller mismatch responses (MMR: indexing the strength of the discrimination response) and longer latency of the N250 peak (indexing the starting point for the discriminative response) were seen in the FH+ group of infants as compared with infants without familial risk. These differences, however, were only significant for those stimuli that were rapidly successive and temporally modulated (70 ms ISI) and not for the more slowly modulated stimuli (300 ms ISI). Moreover, the latency differences in the N_{250} peak were associated with significant differences in both language comprehension and expression at 24 months of age, but only in the 70 ms ISI condition. The hemispheric pattern of response also differed between groups, again only for the 70 ms ISI condition. FH+ infants showed lower peak amplitudes in fronto-central areas of the left hemisphere as compared with the right, whereas the FH− controls showed no laterality differences. Thus, in this study we found concordance between our behavioral and electrocortical data, with both measures at 6 months reliably predicting poorer language outcomes.

Examining the Interplay of Maturation and Deviation

In a follow-up to this study, we examined the further development of RAP using converging EEG/ERPs and behavior measures in the same groups of children prospectively from 6 months through 4 years (Choudhury & Benasich, 2011). Based on prior studies (Kushnerenko et al., 2002a; Kushnerenko, Čeponienė, Balan, Fellman, & Näätänen, 2000b; Morr, Shafer, Kreuzer, & Kurtzberg, 2002), we expected to observe age-related changes in morphology, amplitude, and latency of infant long latency auditory evoked potentials (LLAEPs). However, as few have systematically documented developmental changes that take place over this age period, the direction of these changes was difficult to predict. In general, we expected to observe shorter latencies and larger amplitudes with age. Furthermore, as both FH− controls as well as FH+ infants were included, we could now begin to assess how the developmental trajectories of basic auditory processing abilities might differ as a function of "risk for LLD," even from the earliest ages, as compared with typically developing children.

A significant age-related decrease in the latency of cortical responses was observed for both FH+ and FH− infants, suggesting the expected developmental trend toward more efficient processing. Intriguingly, the morphology of the ERP response differed across age for *both* slow- (300 ms) and fast-rate (70 ms) stimuli and on both standard and deviant waveforms. This suggests that even for slower successive acoustic stimuli that appear to be easily discriminated in a behavioral context by infants at higher risk for LLD, the underlying processing strategy differs. Further, FH+ infants' responses to the fast-rate stimuli (70 ms ISI) consistently differed from those of FH– control infants at all ages, suggesting fundamental differences in RAP. Significant hemispheric differences (suppressed activation on the left) was also clearly seen (Figure 7.1) at 6, 9, and 12 months, suggesting that infants with a family history of SLI show atypical lateralization and perhaps differences in brain areas recruited when processing fast transient nonspeech auditory signals (see Choudhury & Benasich, 2011, for further discussion).

The associations between EEG/ERPs peaks and behavior were also investigated. As was seen in earlier studies, ERPs to nonspeech stimuli at 6 months (using the N_{250} as a correlate) were significantly related both

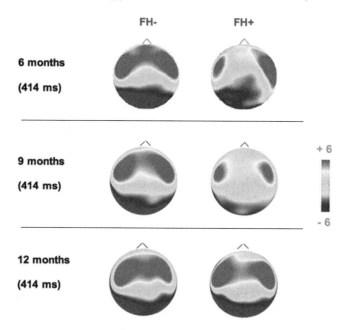

Figure 7.1. Topographic maps of the distribution of MMR amplitude at peak latency for the 70 ms ISI condition for FH–/control (left) and FH+ (right) infants at 1) 6 months, 2) 9 months, and 3) 12 months of age. The maps represent amplitude of the MMR for the 70 ms ISI stimuli, over the entire surface of the head, at peak MMR latencies. The MMR indexes the strength of the discriminative response. Anterior to posterior is represented top to bottom (nose at top). FH+ infants show significantly reduced positivities at 6, 9, and 12 months in frontal and fronto-central channels as compared to FH–/control infants, but only for the 70 ms ISI condition, not for 300 ms ISI. FH+ infants also demonstrated significantly reduced positivities in the left hemisphere as compared to FH–/controls. No laterality effect was observed in FH–/control infants. (*Source:* Choudhury & Benasich, 2011.)

concurrently and predictively to language abilities at 16, 24, 36, and 48 months in both FH+ and FH– infants but *only* in the 70 ms ISI condition. All associations were significant both within and across groups, with the R_2 in the FH+ group much stronger despite a smaller cohort.

Thus maturational trajectories of EEG/ERPs collected from 6 months through 48 months demonstrate differences that can be attributed to typical maturation as well as to maturation combined with altered or aberrant processing. Examination of our prospective longitudinal cohorts through age 7 years reveals a continuing, significant impact of atypical auditory processing in the infancy period. Early differences are also being seen in the acquisition of early reading skills such as phonological processing.

RESTING GAMMA POWER

There is now a significant literature, in both humans and animals, linking high-frequency cortical activity, specifically in the gamma range (~30–55 Hz), to a wide variety of higher cognitive processes, including perception, attention, memory (e.g., Lakatos, Karmos, Mehta, Ulbert, & Schroeder, 2008; Pesaran, Pezaris, Sahani, Mitra, & Andersen, 2002; Simos, Papanikolaou, Sakkalis, & Micheloyannis, 2002; Ursino, Magosso, & Cuppini, 2009), and language (e.g., Eulitz et al., 1996; Fukada et al., 2010; Gou et al., 2011; Korzeniewska, Franaszczuk, Crainiceanu, Ku, & Crone, 2011; Pulvermüller et al., 1996; Towle et al., 2008). In fact, it has been suggested that gamma oscillations are implicated in all higher order cortical computations (Fries, 2009). Fast oscillations, particularly in the gamma range, have been repeatedly implicated in the coincidental neural activity at the cellular level that enables perceptual binding, synaptic plasticity, and the precise temporal coordination that is key to assembling efficient networks across early development (e.g., Ben-Ari, 2001; Khazipov & Luhmann, 2006; Singer & Gray, 1995; Uhlhaas, Roux, Rodriguez, Rotarska-Jagiela, & Singer, 2009; Uhlhaas, Roux, Singer, et al., 2009).

Moreover, gamma oscillation appears to be developmentally regulated. In older children, gamma power, as measured in the EEG signal, increases significantly across age, most strikingly over frontal regions (Takano & Ogawa, 1998); activity in the lower frequency bands decreases as power in the higher frequencies increases (Clarke, Barry, McCarthy, & Selikowitz, 2001). A number of studies have also suggested that children who show EEG power indices that diverge from this normative pattern may differ as well in their maturational time course of brain development (Benasich et al., 2008; Chabot, di Michele, Prichep, & John, 2001; John et al., 1980). Specifically, it is posited that lower levels of gamma power might hinder the brain's ability to efficiently package information into coherent images, thoughts, and memories.

One particularly fascinating time period for linguistic as well as overall cognitive development occurs over the ages of 16–24 months, when an impressive developmental burst occurs. Young children in this developmental phase demonstrate striking increases in language, cognitive, and motor skills (Bates, Thal, & Janowsky, 1992; Fenson et al., 1993). Moreover, this overall surge in acquisition is also characterized by major changes in forebrain organization, including continuing maturation and myelination of temporal and frontal areas and elaboration of the extensive cortical and subcortical circuits that are thought to subserve coordinated high-frequency EEG activity (Chugani, Phelps & Mazziotta, 1987; Huttenlocher, 1990; Paus et al., 2001; Pujol et al., 2006). However, little is known about the developmental course of resting gamma power in infants and toddlers. Thus, in an ongoing series of studies we have been following the development of high-frequency brain oscillations by observing the power spectra of resting EEG across development. Our initial aim was to determine whether the development of high-frequency brain oscillations, during a time of intense learning and cortical reorganization, was related to the development of cognitive and/or linguistic abilities.

To examine this hypothesis, we studied the power spectra of resting EEG in 16-, 24-, and 36-month FH– control children as well as a group of age-matched FH+ children (Benasich et al., 2008). Artifact-free epochs of resting EEG were submitted to power spectral analysis using Fast Fourier Transform (FFT). The frequency distributions of power spectra across the scalp, as well as spectra ratios (e.g., of gamma to theta), were computed for each child.

Overall, the two groups significantly differed at both 24 and 36 months but only for frequencies within the gamma range (31–50 Hz). There were no significant group differences at any of the three ages for the lower frequencies (5–30 Hz). Furthermore, individual differences in the distribution of frontal gamma power during rest were highly correlated with concurrent language and cognitive skills for both groups of children. Gamma power was also associated with 24-month parental reports of toddler attention. Higher gamma power density functions were seen for those children who demonstrated better inhibitory control and more mature attention-shifting abilities. As a group, FH+ children showed consistently lower gamma over frontal regions, suggesting delayed maturation and/or differing recruitment of brain areas. These same children were prospectively followed in order to examine the predictive associations between resting-state cortical gamma power density across a period of intense change and developmental progress (i.e., 16, 24, and 36 months) and cognitive and linguistic performance at ages 4 and 5 years (Gou et al., 2011). We found that both 24- and 36-month gamma power were significantly correlated with later language scores, notably nonword repetition, often cited as a predictive marker for later reading impairment (e.g., Lyytinen et al., 2001; Pennington & Bishop, 2009; Smith, Pennington, Boada, & Shriberg, 2005). Moreover, resting gamma at all earlier ages (16, 24, and 36 months) was significantly correlated with standardized measures of expressive and receptive language at 4 years.

These findings suggest that variation in the capability of a particular brain to generate activity in the gamma range, or to switch into a gamma state on demand, might well index establishment of critical neural synchronies that underlie the emergence of high-frequency oscillatory activity and in turn foster efficient linguistic processing. Of course gamma power indexes basic, underlying synchronous activity of large interconnected networks of neurons, so we understand that the associations reported here do not reflect a direct cause and effect of early resting gamma power on later language outcomes. However, synchronous and efficient neural activity underlies and supports critical cognitive functions, such as attention allocation, memory formation, language development, and sensory processing. Given that we measured gamma across a dynamic period of growth and reorganization, these results also suggest that periods when new abilities are being acquired and consolidated provide a unique window into the time course of early brain maturation and may serve as an early converging marker of risk for language learning and perhaps other cognitive disorders. Lower levels of gamma power in the resting brain may provide a "red flag," indicating that a child will experience language or attention problems. Knowing that may make it possible to provide effective intervention during this critical learning period.

INTERVENTION AND REMEDIATION

Our research to date supports the premise that we can identify infants who are poor at processing rapidly changing auditory cues, whether these are speech or nonspeech sounds, and that differences in RAP thresholds are strongly related to later language outcome. Our data further suggest that even in *typical, full-term infants* without a family history of language impairment, a robust relationship exists between RAP efficiency and language (Benasich et al., 2002, 2006; Benasich & Tallal, 2002; Choudhury & Benasich, 2009, 2011). These findings support the existence of enduring differences in the ability to perform fine-grained analyses in the tens of ms range. Thus in infants, RAP impairments serve as a robust "marker" of LLD, whether examined psychophysically, with EEG/ERPs, or via power analyses, and such indicators can be used to support early identification. As noted previously, levels of gamma power in the resting brain, and significantly reduced amplitude and phase-locking of early gamma (45–75 ms) oscillations in school-age children (Heim, Friedman, Keil, & Benasich, 2011), can also serve as converging markers of risk. However, just being able to identify those children at highest risk for LLD is not sufficient. The goal is to identify and then *remediate* the child during the critical early infancy period when cortical plasticity is most active and well before the age when developmental language disorders exert negative cascading effects on language, academic, and social skills.

Much research now supports a dynamic neurodevelopmental perspective in which genes, brain, behavior, and environment interact multidirectionally throughout development, thus suggesting that changes made early in life will induce differing maturational trajectories (e.g., Dekker & Karmiloff-Smith, 2011; Karmiloff-Smith, 1998). Moreover, the neural mechanisms by which cortical plasticity are induced in the infancy period have been shown to differ from those engaged in older children and adults. Researchers who study the organization and plasticity of auditory cortex using animal models, primarily in rats, strongly suggest that there is an early "critical period" during which experience-dependent competitive modification of developing auditory cortex results in the organization of efficient temporal patterning (Bao, Chang, Davis, Gobeske, & Merzenich, 2003; Katz & Shatz, 1996; Percaccio et al., 2005; Zhang, Bao, & Merzenich, 2001, 2002). Specifically, patterned auditory inputs appear to play a crucial role in shaping neuronal processing and decoding circuits in the primary auditory cortex during early infancy. Thus, competitive neuronal activities play a particularly important and instructive role in shaping neural circuits that define the spectrotemporal structures of A1 (primary auditory cortical) neurons (Zhang et al., 2001) and may do so under the control of the nucleus basalis and cholinergic projections to basal forebrain (Bao et al., 2003; Kilgard & Merzenich, 1998). Although the boundaries of this critical period in human infants have not yet been defined, early infancy is an ideal time to guide the developing brain to set up the precise and efficient spectrotemporal pathways that are critical for language acquisition.

At this time (2011), there are no clinical screening methods or remediation technologies that can be used with human infants. We have been developing an intervention protocol that may address this gap. Our intervention technique involves a diagnostic battery followed by a progressive training task that uses an adaptive training algorithm designed to sharpen auditory discrimination abilities. The technique provides auditory/multisensory stimulation in the right spectrotemporal domain with varying stimuli of increasing complexity. Of particular importance is the very early time period chosen, when the critical process of linguistic mapping is still under way and the brain is maximally sensitive to environmental input. Preliminary evidence from our pilot studies suggests that early exposure to these specific classes of acoustic signals may well engage the ongoing experience-dependent processes that allow infants to develop more efficient fine-grained auditory processing skills and thus may "normalize" and optimize information processing in young infants well before language is acquired (Ortiz-Mantilla, Chojnowska, Choudhury, & Benasich, 2006; Roesler, Choudhury, Realpe-Bonilla, & Benasich, 2011). Our hope is that we will eventually be able to gently guide the brains of infants who are at the highest risk for LLD to be more efficient processors and perhaps avoid the cascading effects of poor processing skills on literacy.

DISCUSSION

The findings presented here illustrate the utility of examining basic processing skills early in life using converging methodologies to both validate and extend knowledge about the precursors of language and language disorder. This then provides the opportunity to investigate the interactive processes essential to language development (both normative and atypical) and for earlier identification and intervention. Such an approach also allows more general questions to be asked, specifically those relating to general prelinguistic mechanisms that might perturb emerging language in typically developing children. Across both the behavior and ERP studies, a common theme emerges: RAP abilities assessed in preverbal infants have been shown repeatedly, in different samples using different methodologies and different temporally modulated stimuli, to robustly predict variations in language abilities at later ages. These findings hold for all children irrespective of family history of LLD. Further, these results are central to the notion that there is continuity of cognitive processing abilities across the ages and that the variation in early auditory processing is measurable and meaningful and can serve as a marker for later language abilities. That is, one can reliably assess variations in RAP skills in infants that are significantly predictive of typical and atypical linguistic skills at later ages. Within the field of development RAP is one of a handful of early markers that have been shown to be a valid and reliable predictor of later abilities. These findings then have direct implications for early identification and possible remediation/prevention of one of the most prevalent forms of childhood learning disorders.

With regard to children who are born into families at increased risk of LLD because of a possible genetic risk, we have shown that they are indeed different in how they process information. We have demonstrated multimodal processing differences (both visual and auditory) between control infants and those who are at higher risk for SLI by virtue of family history. We have also shown that infants from FH+ families differ from control children with no such history in how they segment and process the auditory stream irrespective of the speed of temporal modulation. We suggest that these differences may play a significant role in the differential development of auditory discrimination abilities in the "at-risk" group for both temporally and nontemporally modulated stimuli. This "maturational lag" was also seen in the converging data examining power spectra in resting EEG. One significant advantage of prospective longitudinal studies with infants is that the method presents the opportunity to disentangle precursors of LLD from co-occurring or comorbid problems.

Although the neural mechanisms that underlie the differences observed between FH+ and FH– control infants have yet to be examined, it may be that both the electrocortical and the behavioral findings observed in our studies may emerge as a function of aberrant development of specific generators or neuronal populations (sources) that mediate discrimination and categorization of temporally modulated stimuli. Specifically, findings from our EEG/ERP studies, as well as our studies of resting and evoked gamma (Benasich et al., 2008; Gou et al., 2011; Heim, Friedman, Keil, & Benasich, 2011), are beginning to reveal patterns of development that suggest that there are meaningful divergences between FH+ and FH– controls in the rate at which specific generators "come online" and/or the rate at which neuronal ensembles are strengthened across age that may be responsible for the observed differences in children's ability to process these fast dynamic auditory signals.

As has been highlighted, the only way to meaningfully understand the "end point," that is, the adult or later childhood LLD phenotype, is to have knowledge of the developmental journey. Crucial variables that influence the trajectory of early brain development, including differences in neurogenesis, synaptogenesis, and pruning, have all been implicated in an ever-increasing number of developmental disorders that include LLD and autism (Fitch; LoTurco; Herman, see also Chapter 2). Yet, the adult phenotype provides little information about that path and does not allow one to tease apart the sequence of events. Rather than concentrate on the study of disorders solely at their end state, it is essential to study disorders in early infancy, and longitudinally, to understand how alternative developmental pathways might lead to different (or even the *same*) phenotypical outcomes (Dekker & Karmiloff-Smith, 2011; Karmiloff-Smith, 1998). Given that LLD may involve basic acoustic abilities that *support* language but are not speech specific (see also Kraus, Chapter 6), prospective studies beginning in early infancy allow the highly interactive processes essential to language development to be disentangled and allow insight into the process as it unfolds.

CONCLUSIONS

Examination of the prospective longitudinal cohorts through age 7 years reveals a continuing impact of atypical auditory processing in the infancy period on later expressive and receptive language, as well as the acquisition of early reading skills such as phonological processing and nonword repetition. Across the EEG/ERP studies, it is quite clear that developmental trajectories diverge, even when maturation is taken into account. Differences between groups occurred mainly in the left language regions of the brain, suggesting that LLDs may stem from difficulties with early perceptual-processing abilities. Analyses of the differences in the pattern and density of power spectra in resting EEG were shown for children with a family history of LLDs as compared with controls with no such history. These differences also predicted linguistic competence in domains that relate to acquisition of early reading skills, such as phonological processing and nonword repetition. Finally, putting this research into a broader context, there is a demonstrated need for the development and application of convergent assessment tools that can be applied reliably in individual infants at higher risk for developing LLDs, and thus allowing outlook for focused interventions early in development.

REFERENCES

Aslin, R.N. (1989). Discrimination of frequency transitions by human infants. *Journal of the Acoustical Society of America, 86,* 582–590.

Basu, M., Krishnan, A., & Weber-Fox, C. (2010). Brainstem correlates of temporal auditory processing in children with specific language impairment. *Developmental Science, 13*(1), 77–91. doi:10.1111/j.1467-7687.2009.00849

Bates, E.A., Thal, D., & Janowsky, J.S. (1992). Early language development and its neural correlates. In I. Rapin & S.J. Segalowitz (Eds.), *Handbook of neuropsychology: Vol. 7* (pp. 69–110). Amsterdam, the Netherlands: Elsevier.

Bao, S., Chang, E.F., Davis, J.D., Gobeske, K.T., & Merzenich, M.M. (2003). Progressive degradation and subsequent refinement of acoustic representations in the adult auditory cortex. *Journal of Neuroscience, 23*(34), 10765–10775.

Ben-Ari, Y. (2001). Developing networks play a similar melody. *Trends in Neurosciences, 24*(6), 353–360. doi:10.1016/S0166-2236(00)01813-0

Benasich, A.A., Choudhury, N., Friedman, J.T., Realpe Bonilla, T., Chojnowska, C., & Gou, Z. (2006). Infants as a prelinguistic model for language learning impairments: Predicting from event-related potentials to behavior. *Neuropsychologia, 44*(3), 396–411. doi:10.1016/j.neuropsychologia.2005.06.004

Benasich, A.A., Gou, Z., Choudhury, N., & Harris, K.D. (2008). Early cognitive and language skills are linked to resting frontal gamma power across the first three years. *Behavioural Brain Research, 195*(2), 215–222. doi:10.1016/j.bbr.2008.08.049

Benasich, A.A., & Leevers, H.J. (2003). Processing of rapidly presented auditory cues in infancy: Implications for later language development. In H. Hayne & J.W. Fagan (Eds.), *Progress in infancy research: Vol. 3.* (pp. 245–288). Mahwah, NJ: Erlbaum.

Benasich, A.A., & Tallal, P. (1996). Auditory temporal processing thresholds, habituation, and recognition memory over the first year. *Infant Behavior and Development, 19*(3), 339–357. doi:10.1016/S0163-6383(96)90033-8

Benasich, A.A., & Tallal, P. (2002). Infant discrimination of rapid auditory cues predicts later language impairment. *Behavioural Brain Research, 136*(1), 31–49. doi:10.1016/S0166-4328(02)00098-0

Benasich, A.A., Thomas, J.J., Choudhury, N., & Leppänen, P.H. (2002). The importance of rapid auditory processing abilities to early language development: Evidence from converging methodologies. *Developmental Psychobiology, 40*(3), 278–292. doi:10.1002/dev.10032

Bishop, D.V.M., & Edmundson, A. (1986). Is otitis media a major cause of specific developmental language disorders? *British Journal of Disorders of Communication, 21,* 321–338.

Bishop, D.V., North, T., & Donlan, C. (1995). Genetic basis of specific language impairment: Evidence from a twin study. *Developmental Medicine and Child Neurology, 37*(1), 56–71. doi:10.1111/j.1469-8749.1995.tb11932

Bishop, D.V., & Snowling, M.J. (2004). Developmental dyslexia and specific language impairment: Same or different? *Psychological Bulletin, 130*(6), 858–886. doi:10.1037/0033-2909.130.6.858

Catts, H.W., Adlof, S.M., Hogan, T.P., & Weismer, S.E. (2005). Are specific language impairment and dyslexia distinct disorders? *Journal of Speech, Language, and Hearing Research, 48,* 1378–1396. doi:10.1044/1092-4388(2005/096)

Chabot, R.J., di Michele, F., Prichep, L., & John, E.R. (2001). The clinical role of computerized EEG in the evaluation and treatment of learning and attention disorders in children and adolescents. *The Journal of Neuropsychiatry and Clinical Neurosciences, 13,* 171–186. doi:10.1176/appi.neuropsych.13.2.171

Choudhury, N., & Benasich, A.A. (2003). Familial aggregation in a sample of infants born into families with a history of language-based learning impairments. *Journal of Speech, Language, and Hearing Research, 46,* 261–272.

Choudhury, N., & Benasich, A.A. (2009). Infant information processing and family history of specific language impairment: Converging evidence for early auditory perceptual deficits. In H. Eswaran & N. Chatterje Singh (Eds.), *Advances in developmental neuroscience and imaging* (pp. 9–23). New Delhi, India: Anamaya.

Choudhury, N., & Benasich, A.A. (2011). Maturation of auditory evoked potentials from 6 to 48 months: Prediction to 3 and 4 year language and cognitive abilities. *Clinical Neurophysiology, 122*(2), 320–338. doi:10.1016/j.clinph.2010.05.035

Choudhury, N., Leppänen, P.H.T., Leevers, H.J., & Benasich, A.A. (2007). Infant information processing and family history of specific language impairment: Converging evidence for RAP deficits from two paradigms. *Developmental Science, 10*(2), 213–236. doi:10.1111/j.1467-7687.2007.00546

Chugani, H.T., Phelps, M.E., & Mazziotta, J.C. (1987). Positron emission tomography study of human brain functional development. *Annals of Neurology, 22*(4), 487–497. doi:10.1002/ana.410220408

Clarke, A.R., Barry, R.J., McCarthy, R., & Selikowitz, M. (2001). Age and sex effects in the EEG: Development of the normal child. *Clinical Neurophysiology, 112*(5), 806–814. doi:10.1016/S1388-2457(01)00488-6

Cunningham, J., Nicol, T., King, C., Zecker, S.G., & Kraus, N. (2002). Effects of noise and cue enhancement on neural responses to speech in auditory midbrain, thalamus and cortex. *Hearing Research, 169*(1–2): 97–111. doi:10.1016/S0378-5955(02)00344-1

Dekker, T.M., & Karmiloff-Smith, A. (2011). The dynamics of ontogeny: A neuroconstructivist perspective on genes, brains, cognition and behavior. *Progress in Brain Research, 189,* 23–33.

DeThorne, L.S., Hart, S.A., Petrill, S.A., Deater-Deckard, K., Thompson, L.A., Schatschneider, C., & Davison, M.G. (2006). Children's history of speech-language difficulties: Genetic influences and associations with reading-related measures. *Journal of Speech, Language, and Hearing Research, 49*(6), 1280–1293. doi:10.1044/1092-4388(2006/092)

Eckert, M. (2004). Neuroanatomical markers for dyslexia: A review of dyslexia structural imaging studies. *Neuroscientist, 10*(4), 362–371. doi:10.1177/1073858404263596

Eimas, P.D. (1975). Auditory and phonetic coding of the cues for speech: Discrimination of the [r-l] distinction by young infants. *Perception and Psychophysics, 18*(5), 341–347. doi:10.3758/BF03211210

Eimas, P.D., Siqueland, E., Jusczyk , P., & Vigorito, J. (1971). Speech perception in infants. *Science, 171*(3968), 303–306. doi:10.1126/science.171.3968.303

Elbro, C. (1990). *Differences in dyslexia: A study of reading strategies and deficits in a linguistic perspective.* Copenhagen, Denmark: Munksgaard.

Eulitz, C., Maess, B., Pantev, C., Friederici, A.D., Feige, B., & Elbert, T. (1996). Oscillatory neuromagnetic activity induced by language and non-language stimuli. *Cognitive Brain Research, 4*(2), 121–132. doi:10.1016/0926-6410(96)00026-2

Fenson, L.S., Dale, P., Reznick, J.S., Thal, D., Bates, E., Hartung, J.P., ... Reilly, J.S. (1993). *Technical manual for the MacArthur Communicative Development Inventory.* San Diego, CA: Singular Press.

Fiez, J.A., Raichle, M.E., Miezin, F.M., Peterson, S.E., Tallal, P., & Katz, W.F. (1995). Pet studies of auditory and phonological processing: Effects of stimulus characteristics and task demands. *Journal of Cognitive Neuroscience, 7*(3), 357–375. doi:10.1162/jocn.1995.7.3.357

Flax, J,. Realpe-Bonilla, T., Hirsch, L.S., Brzustowicz, L.B., Bartlett, C.W., & Tallal, P. (2003). Specific language impairment in families: Evidence for co-occurence with reading impairments. *Journal of Speech, Language, and Hearing Research, 46*(3), 530–543.

Fries, P. (2009). Neuronal gamma-band synchronization as a fundamental process in cortical computation. *Annual Review of Neuroscience, 32,* 209–224. doi:10.1146/annurev.neuro.051508.135603

Fukuda, M., Rothermel, R., Juhász, C., Nishida, M., Sood, S., & Asano, E. (2010). Cortical gamma-oscillations modulated by listening and overt repetition of phonemes. *NeuroImage, 49*(3), 2735–2745. doi:10.1016/j.neuroimage.2009.10.047

Gaab, N., Gabrieli, J., Deutsch, G., Tallal, P., & Temple, E. (2007). Neural correlates of rapid auditory processing are disrupted in children with developmental dyslexia and ameliorated with training: An fMRI study. *Restorative Neurology and Neuroscience, 25*(3–4), 295–310.

Gou, Z., Choudhury, N., & Benasich, A.A. (2011). Resting frontal gamma power at 16, 24 and 36 months predicts individual differences in language and cognition at 4 and 5 years. *Behavioral Brain Research, 220*(2), 263–270. doi:10.1016/j.bbr.2011.01.048

Harlaar, N., Hayiou-Thomas, M.E., Dale, P.S., & Plomin, R. (2008). Why do preschool language abilities correlate with later reading? A twin study. *Journal of Speech, Language, and Hearing Research, 51*, 688–705. doi:10.1044/1092-4388(2008/049)

Haworth, C.M., Kovas, Y., Harlaar, N., Hayiou-Thomas, M.E., Petrill, S.A., Dale, P.S., & Plomin, R. (2009). Generalist genes and learning disabilities: A multivariate genetic analysis of low performance in reading, mathematics, language and general cognitive ability in a sample of 8000 12-year-old twins. *Journal of Child Psychology and Psychiatry, 50*(10), 318–1325. doi:10.111 1/j.1469-7610.2009.02114

Heath, S.M., Hogben, J.H., & Clark, C.D. (1999). Auditory temporal processing in disabled readers with and without oral language delay. *Journal of Child Psychology and Psychiatry, 40*(4), 637–647. doi:10.1111/1469-7610.00480

Heim, S., & Benasich, A.A. (2006). Disorders of language. In D. Cicchetti & D. Cohen (Eds.), *Developmental psychopathology* (2nd ed., pp. 268–316). New York, NY: John Wiley & Sons.

Heim, S., Friedman, J.T., Keil, A., & Benasich, A.A. (2011). Reduced sensory oscillatory activity during rapid auditory processing as a correlate of language-learning impairment. *Journal of Neurolinguistics. 24*, 539–555. doi:10.1016/j.jneuroling.2010.09.006

Huttenlocher, P.R. (1990). Morphometric study of human cerebral cortex development. *Neuropsychologia, 28*(6), 517–527. doi:10.1016/0028-3932(90)90031-I

Imaizumi, K., Priebe, N.J., Sharpee, T.O., Cheung, S.W., & Schreiner, C.E. (2010). Encoding of temporal information by timing, rate, and place in cat auditory cortex. *PLoS One., 5*(7): e11531. doi:10.1371/journal.pone.0011531

John, E.R., Ahn, H., Pricep, L., Trepetin, M., Brown, D., & Kaye, H. (1980). Developmental equations for the electroencephalogram. *Science, 210*(4475), 1255–1258. doi:10.1126/science.7434026

Karmiloff-Smith, A. (1998). Development itself is the key to understanding developmental disorders. *Trends in Cognitive Sciences, 2*(10), 389–398. doi:10.1016/ S1364 -6613(98)01230-3

Katz, L.C., & Shatz, C.J. (1996). Synaptic activity and the construction of cortical circuits. *Science, 274*(5290), 1133–1138. doi:10.1126/science.274.5290.1133

Khazipov, R., & Luhmann, H.J. (2006). Early patterns of electrical activity in the developing cerebral cortex of humans and rodents. *Trends in Neurosciences, 29*(7), 414–418. doi:10.1016/j.tins.2006.05.007

Kilgard, M.P., & Merzenich, M.M. (1998). Cortical map reorganization enabled by nucleus basalis activity. *Science, 279*(5357), 1714–1718. doi:10.1126/science.279.5357.1714

Korzeniewska, A., Franaszczuk, P.J., Crainiceanu, C.M., Kuś, R., & Crone, N.E. (2011). Dynamics of large-scale cortical interactions at high gamma frequencies during word production: Event related causality (ERC) analysis of human electrocorticography (ECoG). *NeuroImage, 56*(4), 2218–2237. doi:10.1016/j.neuroimage.2011.03.030

Kraus, J.C., & Braida, L.D. (2002). Investigating alternative forms of clear speech: The effects of speaking rate and speaking mode on intelligibility. *Journal of the Acoustic Society of America, 112*(5), 2165–2172. doi:10.1121/1.1509432

Kraus, N., McGee, T.J., Carrell, T.D., Zecker, S.G., Nicol, T.G., & Koch, D.B. (1996). Auditory neurophysiologic responses and discrimination deficits in children with learning problems. *Science, 273*(5277), 971–973. doi:10.1126/science.273.5277.971

Kuhl, P.K. (2000). A new view of language acquisition. *Proceedings of the National Academy of Sciences, USA, 97*(22), 11850–11857. doi:10.1073/pnas.97.22.11850

Kuhl, P.K. (2004). Early language acquisition: Cracking the speech code. *Nature Reviews Neuroscience, 5*(11), 831–843. doi:10.1038/nrn1533

Kushnerenko, E., Čeponienė, R., Balan, P., Fellman, V., Huotilainen, M., & Näätänen, R. (2002a). Maturation of the auditory event-related potentials during the first year of life. *Neuroreport,* *13*(1), 47–51. doi:10.1097/00001756-200201210-00014

Kushnerenko, E., Čeponienė, R., Balan, P., Fellman, V., & Näätänen, R. (2002b). Maturation of the auditory change detection response in infants: A longitudinal ERP study. *Neuroreport, 13*(15), 1843–1848. doi:10.1097/00001756-2002 10280-00002

Lakatos, P., Karmos, G., Mehta, A.D., Ulbert, I., & Schroeder, C.E. (2008). Entrainment of neuronal oscillations as a mechanism of attentional selection. *Science, 320*(5872), 110–113. doi:10.1126/science.1154735

Leonard, L.B. (1998). *Children with specific language impairment.* Cambridge, MA: The MIT Press.

Lewis, B.A., & Thompson, L.A. (1992). A study of developmental speech and language disorders in twins. *Journal of Speech and Hearing Research, 35*(5), 1086–1094.

Logan, J., Petrill, S.A., Flax, J., Justice, L.M., Hou, L., Bassett, A.S., ... Bartlett, C.W. (in press). Genetic covariation underlying reading, language and related measures in a sample selected for specific language impairment. *Behavior Genetics.* doi:10.1007/s10519 -010-9435-0

Lyytinen, H., Ahonen, T., Eklund, K., Guttorm, T.K., Laakso, M.L., Leinonen, S., ... Viholainen, H. (2001). Developmental pathways of children with and without familial risk for dyslexia during the first years of life. *Developmental Neuropsychology, 20*(2), 535–554. doi:10.1207/S15326942DN2002_5

McArthur, G., Atkinson, C., & Ellis D. (2009). Atypical brain responses to sounds in children with specific language and reading impairments. *Developmental Science, 12*(5), 768–783. doi: 10.1111/j.1467-7687.2008.00804

McArthur, G.M., & Bishop, D.V.M. (2001). Auditory perceptual processing in people with reading and oral language impairments: Current issues and recommendations. *Dyslexia, 7*(3), 150–170. doi:10.1002/dys.200

McArthur, G.M., Hogben, J.H., Edwards, V.T., Heath, S.M., & Mengler, E.D. (2000). On the "specifics" of specific reading disability and specific language impairment. *Journal of Child Psychology and Psychiatry, 41*(7), 869–874. doi:10.1111/1469-7610.00674

Morr, M.L., Shafer, V.L., Kreuzer, J.A, & Kurtzberg, D. (2002). Maturation of mismatch negativity in typically developing infants and preschool children. *Ear and Hearing, 23*(2), 118–136. doi:10.1097/00003446-200204000-00005

Neils, J., & Aram, D.M. (1986). Family history of children with developmental language disorders. *Perceptual and Motor Skills, 63,* (2 Pt 1), 655–658.

Oram Cardy, J.E., Flagg, E.J., Roberts, W., Brian, J., & Roberts, T.P. (2005). Magnetoencephalography identifies rapid temporal processing deficits in autism and language impairment. *Neuroreport, 16*(4), 329–332. doi:10.1097/00001756-200503150 -00005

Ortiz-Mantilla, S., Chojnowska, C., Choudhury, N., & Benasich, A.A. (2006, October). Latency effects on infants auditory cortical evoked response as a function of varying exposure to passive and active auditory discrimination paradigms. Poster presented at the annual meeting of the Society for Neuroscience, Atlanta, GA.

Paus, T., Collins, D.L., Evans, A.C., Leonard, G., Pike, B., & Zijdenbos, A. (2001). Maturation of white matter in the human brain: A review of magnetic resonance studies. *Brain Research Bulletin, 54*(3), 255–266. doi:10.1016/ S0361-9230(00)00434-2

Pennington, B.F., & Bishop, D.V. (2009). Relations among speech, language, and reading disorders. *Annual Review of Psychology, 60,* 283–306. doi:10.1146/ annurev.psych.60.110707.163548

Percaccio, C.R., Engineer, N.D., Pruette, A.L., Pandya, P.K., Moucha, R., Rathbun, D.L., & Kilgard, M.P. (2005). Environmental enrichment increases paired-pulse depression in rat auditory cortex. *Journal of Neurophysiology, 94*(5), 3590–3600. doi:10.1152/jn.00433.2005

Pesaran, B., Pezaris, J.S., Sahani, M., Mitra, P., & Andersen, R.A. (2002). Temporal structure in neuronal activity during working memory in macaque parietal cortex. *Nature Neuroscience, 5,* 805–811. doi:10.1038/nn890

Plomin, R., & Kovas, Y. (2005). Generalist genes and learning disabilities. *Psychological Bulletin, 131*(4), 592–617. doi:10.1037/0033-2909.131.4.592

Poldrack, R.A., Temple, E., Protopapas, A., Nagarajan, S., Tallal, P., Merzenich, M., & Gabrieli, J.D.E. (2001). Relations between the neural bases of dynamic auditory processing and phonological processing: Evidence from fMRI. *Journal of Cognitive Neuroscience 13*(5), 687–697. doi:10.1162/089892901750363235

Pujol, J., Soriano-Mas, C., Ortiz, H., Sebastián-Gallés, N., Losilla, J.M., & Deus, J. (2006). Myelination of language-related areas in the developing brain. *Neurology, 66*(3), 339–343. doi:10.1212/01.wnl.0000201049.66073.8d

Pulvermüller, F., Eulitz, C., Pantev, C., Mohr, B., Feige, B., Lutzenberger, W., ... Birbaumer, N. (1996). High-frequency cortical responses reflect lexical processing: An MEG study. *Electroencephalography and Clinical Neurophysiology, 98*(1), 76–85. doi:10.1016/0013-4694(95)00191-3

Roesler, C., Choudhury, N., Realpe-Bonilla, T., & Benasich, A.A. (2011, April). Computerized auditory training accelerates the N200 response in 7-month old infants. Poster presented at the annual meeting of the Cognitive Neuroscience Society, San Francisco, CA.

Saffran, J.R., Aslin, R.N., & Newport, E.L. (1996). Statistical learning by 8-month-old infants. *Science, 274*(5294), 1926–1928. doi:10.1126/science.274.5294.1926

Simos, P.G., Papanikolaou, E., Sakkalis, E., & Micheloyannis, S. (2002). Modulation of gamma-band spectral power by cognitive task complexity. *Brain Topography, 14*(3), 191–196. doi:10.1023/A:1014550808164

Singer, W., & Gray, C.M. (1995). Visual feature integration and the temporal correlation hypothesis. *Annual Review of Neuroscience, 18*, 555–586. doi:10.1146/annurev.ne.18.030195.003011

Smith, S.D., Pennington, B.F., Boada, R., & Shriberg, L.D. (2005). Linkage of speech sound disorder to reading disability loci. *Journal of Child Psychology and Psychiatry, 46*(10), 1057–1066. doi:10.1111/j.1469-7610.2005.01534

Snowling, M., Bishop, D.V.M., & Stothard, S.E. (2000). Is pre-school language impairment a risk factor for dyslexia in adolescence? *Journal of Child Psychology & Psychiatry, 41*(5), 587–600.

Song, J.H., Banai, K., & Kraus, N. (2008). Brainstem timing deficits in children with learning impairment may result from corticofugal origins. *Audiology and Neurotology, 13*(5), 335–344. doi:10.1159/000132689

Stromswold, K. (2000). The cognitive neuroscience of language acquisition. In M. Gazzaniga (Ed.), *The new cognitive neurosciences* (pp. 909–932). Cambridge, MA: MIT Press.

Takano, T., & Ogawa, T. (1998). Characterization of developmental changes in EEG-gamma band activity during childhood using the autoregressive model. *Acta Paediatrica, Japan, 40*(5), 446–452.

Tallal, P. (2004). Improving language and literacy is a matter of time. *Nature Reviews Neuroscience, 5*, 721–728. doi:10.1038/nrn1499

Tallal, P., & Gaab, N. (2006). Dynamic auditory processing, musical experience and language development. *TRENDS in Neuroscience, 29*(7), 382–390. doi:10.1016/j.tins.2006.06.003

Tallal, P., Hirsch, L.S., Realpe-Bonilla, T., Miller, S., Brzustowicz, L., Bartlett, C., & Flax, J.F. (2001). Familial aggregation in specific language impairment. *Journal of Speech, Language, and Hearing Research, 44*, 1172–1182. doi:10.1044/1092-4388(2001/091)

Tallal, P., Ross, R., & Curtiss, S. (1989). Familial aggregation in specific language impairment. *Journal of Speech and Hearing Disorders, 54*(2), 167–173.

Temple, E. (2002). Brain Mechanisms in Normal and Dyslexic Readers. *Current Opinions in Neurobiology, 12*(2), 178–183.

Temple, E., Poldrack, R.A., Salidis, J., Deutsch, G.K., Tallal, P., & Merzenich, M.M., & Gabrieli, J.D.E. (2001). Disrupted neural responses to phonological and orthographic processing in dyslexic children: An fMRI study. *Neuroreport, 12*(2), 299–307. doi:10.1097/00001756-200102120-00024

Thorndike, R.L., Hagen, E.P., & Sattler, J.M. (1986). *The Stanford-Binet Intelligence Scale* (4th ed.). Chicago, IL: The Riverside Publishing Company.

Tomblin, J.B. (1989). Familial concentration of developmental language impairment. *Journal of Speech and Hearing Disorders, 54*(2), 287–295.

Tomblin, J.B. (1996). Genetic and environmental contributions to the risk for specific language impairment. In M.L. Rice (Ed.), *Towards a Genetics of Language* (pp. 191–210). New York, NY: Lawrence Erlbaum.

Tomblin, J.B., & Buckwalter, P.R. (1998). Heritability of poor language achievement among twins. *Journal of Speech,*

Language, and Hearing Research, 41(1), 188–199.

Tomblin, J.B., Zhang, X., Buckwalter, P., & Catts, H. (2000). The association of reading disability, behavioral disorders, and language impairment among second-grade children. *Journal of Child Psychology and Psychiatry, 41*(4), 473–482. doi: 10.1111/1469 -7610.00632

Towle, V.L., Yoon, H.A., Castelle, M., Edgar, J.C., Biassou, N.M., Frim, D.M., … Kohrman, M.H. (2008). ECoG gamma activity during a language task: Differentiating expressive and receptive speech areas. *Brain, 131*(8), 2013–2027.

Tsao, F.M., Liu, H.M., & Kuhl, P.K. (2004). Speech perception in infancy predicts language development in the second year of life: A longitudinal study. *Child Development, 75*(4), 1067–1084.

Uhlhaas, P.J., Roux, F., Rodriguez, E., Rotarska-Jagiela, A., & Singer, W. (2009). Neural synchrony and the development of cortical networks. *Trends in Cognitive Sciences, 14*(2), 72–80. doi:10.1016/j.tics.2009.12.002

Uhlhaas, P.J., Roux, F., Singer, W., Haenschel, C., Sireteanu, R., & Rodriguez, E. (2009). The development of neural synchrony reflects late maturation and restructuring of functional networks in humans. *Proceedings of the National Academy of Sciences, USA, 106*(24), 9866–9871. doi:10.1073/pnas.0900390106

Ursino, M., Magosso, E., & Cuppini, C. (2009). Recognition of abstract objects via neural oscillators: Interaction among topological organization, associative memory and gamma band synchronization. *IEEE Transactions on Neural Networks, 20*(2), 316–335. doi:10.1109/TNN.2008.2006326

Wagner, R.K., & Torgesen, J.K. (1987). The nature of phonological processing and its causal role in the acquisition of reading skills. *Psychological Bulletin, 101*(2), 192–212. doi:10.1037//0033-2909.101.2.192

Weber-Fox, C., Leonard, L.B., Wray, A.H., & Tomblin, J.B. (2010). Electrophysiological correlates of rapid auditory and linguistic processing in adolescents with specific language impairment. *Brain and Language, 115*(3), 162–181. doi:10.1016/j.bandl.2010.09.001

Werker, J.F., & Tees, R.C. (1987). Speech perception in severely disabled and average reading children. *Canadian Journal of Psychology, 41*(1), 48–61. doi:10.1037/h0084150

Zhang, L.I., Bao, S., & Merzenich, M.M. (2001). Persistent and specific influences of early acoustic environments on primary auditory cortex. *Nature Neuroscience, 4*(11), 1123–1130. doi:10.1038/nn745

Zhang, L.I., Bao, S., & Merzenich, M.M. (2002). Disruption of primary auditory cortex by synchronous auditory inputs during a critical period. *Proceedings of the National Academy of Sciences, USA, 99*(4), 2309–2314. doi:10.1073/pnas.261707398

Zimmerman, I.L., Steiner, V.G., & Pond, R.E. (1992). *Preschool Language Scale-3* (PLS-3). New York, NY: The Psychological Corporation.

CHAPTER 8

Neurolinguistic and Neurophysiological Precursors of Dyslexia
Selective Studies from the Dutch Dyslexia Programme

Ben A.M. Maassen, Aryan van der Leij, Natasha M. Maurits, and Frans Zwarts

Converging evidence suggests that developmental dyslexia (DD) is a neurobiological disorder characterized by impairments in the auditory (phonological), visual, motor, and linguistic domains. The Dutch Dyslexia Programme (DDP)[1]—a collaborative effort of the Universities of Amsterdam, Groningen, and Nijmegen—follows 180 children who are genetically at risk for dyslexia, as well as a control group of 120 children. Participants range from 2 months to 10 years of age. According to Grigorenko (2001) the at-risk children have a 40%–60% chance of being diagnosed with dyslexia, compared with approximately 4% in the population at large. Data collection in the DDP focuses on nine measurements, with different paradigms for 1) auditory and visual event-related potentials (ERPs) between 2 and 47 months, 2) assessment of environmental variables, mainly by means of parent questionnaires, 3) psychometric assessments of speech–language and cognitive development, and 4) assessments of preliteracy and reading development during kindergarten and first through third grades. At the time of this report, two thirds of the children have been tested in second grade for dyslexia. Long-term goals of the DDP are 1) to obtain a deeper understanding of the core impairment(s) of dyslexia and 2) to develop a probabilistic prognostic model for the emergence of dyslexia.

Children and adults with DD show impairments in phonological skills, a reduced phonological awareness, and poorer auditory processing (for a review, see Habib, 2000). Furthermore, subtle differences between individuals with dyslexia and typical readers (TR) have been reported in neurolinguistic, cognitive, and motor domains that suggest a diversity of underlying processing impairments related to dyslexia. In the auditory domain, people with dyslexia have been found to perform more poorly than TR when asked to discriminate and identify phonemes at the onset of consonant–vowel (CV) syllables that sound alike (e.g., /ba/-/da/; e.g., Maassen, Groenen, Crul, Assman-Hulsmans, & Gabreëls, 2001). For people with dyslexia at age 12 years, Schulte-Körne, Deimel, Bartling, and Remschmidt (1998) reported an attenuated mismatch negativity (MMN)—an indicator

[1]The DDP is funded by the Netherlands Organization for Scientific Research (NWO) in addition to the participating universities.

119

of auditory change detection—to speech stimuli on the basis of auditory event-related potentials (AERP) relative to that of their unaffected peers.

Although many relationships between secondary psycholinguistic skills (reading and spelling) and primary psycholinguistic skills (speaking and listening) have been reported, the exact nature and direction of causality of these relationships is still obscure (Nathan, Stackhouse, Goulandris, & Snowling, 2004). This chapter presents a selection of results from the DDP, with the main focus on neurophysiologic parameters that are potentially related to DD. In addition, comparisons across ages, and correlations between precursors and outcome (reading skills at school age and dyslexia diagnosis), are included.

Two types of data are presented. The first type of data (Experiment 1) consists of electrophysiological recordings taken at 2–29 months. Specifically, infants were presented with auditory stimuli and AERPs were elicited in an oddball paradigm employing a standard and deviant stimulus. Based on the literature, two hypotheses were tested. The first hypothesis said that infants who were at risk for dyslexia would show poorer auditory speech-sound perception than controls. This should result in longer latencies or lower amplitudes of the corresponding AERPs. In fact, at age 2 months such differences were found in at-risk participants (Van Leeuwen et al., 2006, 2008). In the present study, data collected at age 17 months, as well as a direct comparison with recordings at age 29 months, is presented. The stimuli comprised one-syllable Dutch words differing with respect to place of articulation of the first consonant: /b/ versus /d/, used as standard versus deviant stimulus, respectively. Some of the participants in this study have reached the age at which dyslexia can be diagnosed; for this subsample, the predictive value of the AERP data was preliminarily determined by calculating correlations. The second type of data (Experiment 2) comprises behavior–neurocognitive measures taken at age 4–5 years in relation to reading skills at second grade. This analysis focused on rapid naming of colors and pictures, which has been reported to be correlated with reading acquisition (de Jong & Van der Leij, 2003; Eleveld, 2005). Values for at-risk and control children were compared, and for the subsample of diagnosed children, correlations and predictive values of behavior measures were calculated.

EXPERIMENT 1

One of the earliest AERP studies in newborns and infants showed emerging mismatch responses (MMR) that have prognostic value regarding language development (Molfese, 2000). In addition, it was found that hemispheres are differentially sensitive to specific stimulus characteristics. In Experiment 1, at-risk and control infants at ages 17 and 29 months were examined. Earlier we reported on AERPs taken at age 2 months, showing that in the time window from 265–341 milliseconds (ms) both the at-risk and control infants demonstrated significant mismatch positivity (MMP). The MMP was larger in control than in at-risk infants; this stronger categorical response is followed—in control infants only—by a significant (late) lMMN (van Leeuwen et al., 2006, 2008).

Materials and Methods

Participants   In total, 108 children participated: 60 at risk of developmental dyslexia and 48 control children. None of these children had hearing loss or neurological problems. The at-risk children were defined by having one parent with dyslexia and at least one other family member with dyslexia related in the first degree to the parent. In the first and second assessment reported here, all children were within 2 weeks of age 17 months and 29 months, respectively.

Stimuli   One-syllable consonant–vowel–consonant (CVC) words /bɑk/ and /dɑk/ (Dutch words, meaning "tray" and "roof") were recorded (by a female speaker) in an anechoic room. The according to linear predictive coding (LPC) analyzed /bɑk/ was selected as the starting stimulus signal for a /bɑk/–/dɑk/ continuum, comprising 10 interpolation steps of second formant (F2) ranging from 1100 hertz (Hz) in /bɑk/ to 1800 Hz in /dɑk/. Categorical perception studies in adults showed that the 50% perceptual boundary was situated between levels 3 and 4. For further details on stimulus construction and perceptual validation, see van Beinum, Schwippert, Been, van Leeuwen, and Kuijpers (2005). For the present study we selected level 3 as the standard stimulus (F2 onset frequency at 1280 Hz) and level 6 as the deviant (F2 onset frequency at 1460 Hz). Deviants were randomly presented with a 10% probability in blocks comprising 500 trials; interstimulus interval (ISI) was 800 ms.

Procedure

Thirty-two-channel electroencephalography (EEG) was recorded at 500 Hz. Electrodes were placed according to the 10-20 system. The EEG was digitally band-pass filtered (1–15 Hz, 24 decibels [dB]/octave [Oct]), and artifacts exceeding + 125 μV in any channel were automatically rejected from further analysis; sleeping episodes were removed. The data were analyzed statistically in SPSS.

Analysis I

Individual grand-average ERPs were determined in a window from 125 ms before stimulus onset to 1,250 ms after stimulus onset for the standard stimulus and the deviant and for the mismatch response (deviants–standards). A peak analysis procedure was employed to extract the four early AERP components: P1, N1, P2 (for labeling of peaks see Figure 8.2), and N2. An experienced EEG technician determined the amplitudes and latencies of these components based on the averages per child, containing at least 30 epochs. Only children for whom all four peaks could be determined clearly for all conditions were included in the peak analyses. This resulted in the inclusion of 35 at-risk and 31 control children in the peak analyses. Repeated measures multivariate analyses of variance (MANOVA) were employed to test for significance of differences. To check for the presence of MMN and late MMN (lMMN), difference waveforms were calculated by subtracting AERPs to standards from those to deviants. All 108 children were included in these analyses.

Analysis II

The second analysis focused on the children from whom at least 25 epochs of the deviant AERPs were available at both 17 and 29 months of age: 35 at-risk and 28 control children. Maps of the children's scalp distribution were created for every time window based on the standard stimuli. Furthermore, grand averages were plotted for standard stimuli. Thus, it was possible to compare the data of both control and at-risk children at ages 17 and 29 months in every time window.

Results

Results Analysis I: Age 17 Months
A significant MMP was found in the control group, in that P2, with a mean latency between 234 and 255 ms, was higher in amplitude for the deviant than for the standard stimulus. These enlarged P2 peaks were present at central, as well as bilateral frontal, sites. In the at-risk children, no significant MMP effects were found (see Table 8.1). In addition, latency of peak P2 was slightly shorter for control than at-risk children, a difference that reached significance in the right hemisphere (see Table 8.2).

Table 8.3 presents amplitudes of lMMNs for central and bilateral frontal sites. The control group shows a stronger lMMN than the at-risk group, especially at right frontal sites.

Results Analysis II: Comparison of Age 17 and 29 Months
Scalp distributions of the standard stimuli show similar overall results for at-risk and control infants. At age 17 months (Figure 8.1) the pattern comprises a

Table 8.1.   Mean amplitudes in microvolts of the auditory event-related potentials peak P2 (mean latency 234–255 ms) for standard and deviant stimuli. Standard errors are in parentheses.

		Control ($n = 31$)	At-risk ($n = 35$)
Midline	standard	.51 (.29)	.54 (.27)
	deviant	1.80*(.55)	.67 (.52)
LH	standard	.61 (.32)	.61 (.30)
	deviant	1.98*(.35)	1.06 (.33)
RH	standard	.57 (.30)	.36 (.28)
	deviant	1.75*(.51)	.56 (.48)

$*p < .05$.
Key: Midline: midline electrodes; LH, RH: left, right hemisphere.

Table 8.2.   Mean P2-latency (in ms) for standard stimuli; difference between at-risk and control children is indicated.

	Control (n = 31)	At-risk (n = 35)	
Midline	234.0	238.5	
LH	250.3	255.7	
RH	242.6	254.7	(F 1.60 = 4.231, p < 0.05)

Key: Midline: midline electrodes; LH, RH: left, right hemisphere.

slightly left-lateralized positive response in the time windows around 100 ms followed by a negative field starting bilaterally (time windows 150–200 ms) and moving via central (time window 300–400 ms) to more frontal areas (time window 450–500 ms). At age 29 months (Figure 8.2) the early positive responses are of lower amplitude with at-risk infants showing a stronger, left-lateralized response than controls; the following negative responses are of higher amplitude and slightly earlier in the at-risk infants.

Figure 8.2 presents average waveforms of all standards at ages 17 and 29 months respectively for control (black curves) and at-risk (red curves) infants. The P1 and N2 are clearly recognizable at both ages for both groups. The latency of both is slightly shorter at age 29 months than at age 17 months, reflecting auditory maturation (compare Kushnerenko, 2003). A striking difference between the groups is that control infants show a much more pronounced N1-P2 complex than at-risk infants (clearest examples are circled in Figure 8.2).

Discussion

For the analysis of the mismatch responses, two time windows are of interest. The first window from 250–350 ms is the typical window in which many studies have reported mismatch responses. This mismatch response is induced by an audible difference in a repeated stimulus and is an automatic response, evoked even when the participant is not attending to the stimulus. Typically in adults the deviant evokes a more negative response than the standard, MMN, whereas in infants the difference can be inverted in polarity, resulting in an MMP (Thierry, 2005). The control children in our Experiment 1 showed a clear and significant

Table 8.3.   Late Mismatch-Negativity (LMMN) in microvolts (latency 625–725 ms) control and at-risk groups.

		Control (n = 48)	At-risk (n = 60)
Midline	Fz / FCz	−1.03*	−.88*
LH	Max.val.	−.67	−.80
RH	Max.val.	−.98*	−.53

*p < .05.
Key: Midline: midline electrodes; LH, RH: left, right hemisphere; Max. val. indicates maximum (negative) value across frontal and central sites.

124   Maassen et al.

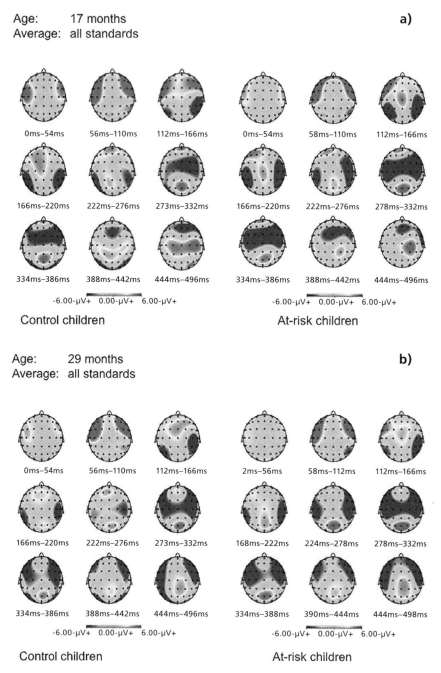

Age: 17 months   **a)**
Average: all standards

0ms–54ms   56ms–110ms   112ms–166ms   0ms–54ms   58ms–110ms   112ms–166ms

166ms–220ms 222ms–276ms 273ms–332ms   166ms–220ms 222ms–276ms 278ms–332ms

334ms–386ms 388ms–442ms 444ms–496ms   334ms–386ms 388ms–442ms 444ms–496ms

           -6.00-μV+ 0.00-μV+ 6.00-μV+   -6.00-μV+ 0.00-μV+ 6.00-μV+

Control children   At-risk children

Age: 29 months   **b)**
Average: all standards

0ms–54ms   56ms–110ms   112ms–166ms   2ms–56ms   58ms–112ms   112ms–166ms

166ms–220ms 222ms–276ms 273ms–332ms   168ms–222ms 224ms–278ms 278ms–332ms

334ms–386ms 388ms–442ms 444ms–496ms   334ms–388ms 390ms–444ms 444ms–498ms

           -6.00-μV+ 0.00-μV+ 6.00-μV+   -6.00-μV+ 0.00-μV+ 6.00-μV+

Control children   At-risk children

Figure 8.1. Topographic representations of auditory event-related potentials (AERPs) elicited by standard stimuli (time windows of 54 ms, range 0–498 ms). Left panel: control children; right panel: children at risk for dyslexia. a) The children at age 17 months. b) The children at age 29 months.

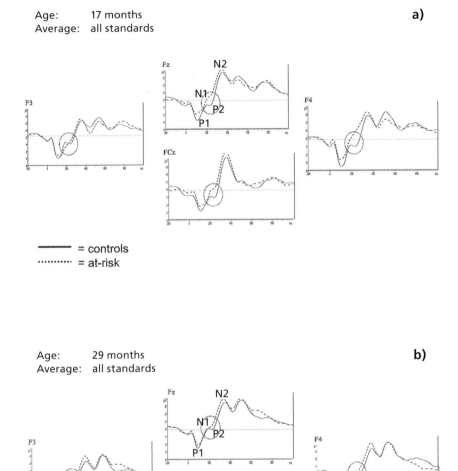

Age: 17 months   a)
Average: all standards

= controls
= at-risk

Age: 29 months   b)
Average: all standards

= controls
= at-risk

Figure 8.2. Average waveforms of standard stimuli from control (solid lines) and at-risk (dashed) children. Circles are around the significantly higher amplitude difference in the N1-P2 complex in control than in children at risk for dyslexia. Plotted are electrodes F3, Fz, FCz, F4. a) The children at age 17 months. b) The children at age 29 months.

MMP at age 17 months. In contrast, the at-risk children showed no MMP. This result can be interpreted as an indication of poor auditory information processing in the at-risk infants.

In the second window that was examined, roughly from 600 ms onward, the control infants showed a clear and significant lMMN. The lMMN is typically seen in young children and infants only, diminishing in amplitude during adolescence and hence only occasionally observed in adults. To date, it is not known what underlying process the lMMN reflects, but the fact that it occurs well after the MMP suggests it reflects higher order cognitive processing rather than sensory auditory processing. Specifically, the lMMN is enhanced in response to changes in words rather than tones or pseudowords, prompting the suggestion that the lMMN might represent detection of lexical or semantic changes (Korpilahti, Krause, Holopainen, & Lang, 2001). This conclusion seems relevant for the present study, because the standard and deviant stimuli differed not only phonologically but also semantically. Accordingly, the finding that the lMMN was only slightly reduced in our sample of at-risk children may imply that 17-month-old children at risk for dyslexia are not impaired in the later, more cognitive—lexical-semantic—stages of processing.

Scalp distributions of responses to the standard stimulus globally show similar results for at-risk and control infants, and for ages 17 and 29 months, consisting of a bilateral, frontal positivity in the epoch of 50–150 ms, followed by an early bilateral and later central negativity. A striking difference between groups is that control infants show a much more pronounced N1-P2 complex compared with at-risk infants (clearest examples encircled in Figure 8.2). In the literature there is much dispute about the maturation of the infantile P150-N250-P350 peak complex described by Kushnerenko (2003), but also one interpretation is that the infantile P350 is a precursor of adult P2, which is dependent on frequency of presentation and interstimulus interval (ISI) and seems to be modulated by expectancy (Ceponiené, Rinne, & Näätänen, 2002) or salience of the stimulus (Ceponiené, Alku, Westerfield, Torki, & Townsend, 2005).

It should be kept in mind that prior estimates would indicate that only approximately one third of the at-risk infants will eventually show dyslexia. Post hoc analyses when these children are diagnosed (with respect to reading and spelling performance) will further reveal developmental mechanisms at that time. As for now, a reduced MMP seems to indicate that the at-risk infants concerned are actually at an even higher risk of DD than predicted on the basis of family background alone. This information can be elaborated further as a clinical indication for early intervention.

EXPERIMENT 2

At preschool and kindergarten (age 4–5 years), and at the beginning and end of second grade, reading skills and cognitive functions (possibly related to early literacy development) were assessed. The main goal was to find underlying impairments predictive of dyslexia. The second goal was to come up with behavior measures that could be applied for screening and early diagnosis as soon as children enter the educational system. Use was made of reading scores at the beginning and end of second grade. Analyses of the reading scores addressed the issue of differentiating within the at-risk group children with typical reading development from those who went on to be diagnosed with dyslexia.

Materials and Methods

A total of 203 children participating in the longitudinal study were entered into the analyses—131 at risk of DD and 72 control children. Children were tested at the beginning and end of second grade (e.g., after 1 year of literacy education in first grade). Reading skills were assessed by administering the following word and nonword reading tasks, which are administered under time pressure: 1) word reading, tested at start and end of second grade with the Dutch word-fluency test (DMT, Verhoeven, 1995), and 2) nonword reading at the end of second grade, using the Klepel (van den Bos, lutje Spelberg, Scheepstra, & de Vries, 1994). Both tests are standardized and norm-referenced Dutch reading tests for use with children in elementary school. Furthermore, results of rapid serial naming tasks (colors and pictures) administered at age 59 months and in the second year of kindergarten were entered into the analyses as well.

The first statistical analyses (conducted in SPSS 16.0) comprised a factor analysis on word-reading scores at the beginning and end of second grade, followed by a two-step cluster analysis on the resulting factor scores and the nonword reading scores. Entered into the cluster analysis were the categorical variable status (at risk versus control) and the continuous variables: factor score word reading start of second grade (Reading B2) and factor score word and nonword reading end of second grade (Reading E2). The second and third analyses comprised correlation analysis of rapid naming scores and reading scores, and electrophysiological recordings and reading scores at age 17 months.

Results

Cluster analysis yielded five clusters, as presented in Figure 8.3. First, the control children were divided into two clusters. Cluster 1 comprised 35 children with above-average reading scores (1–1.5 standard deviations above the overall mean score). Cluster 3 comprised 37 control children with slightly below-average reading scores (0–0.5 standard deviation below the overall mean score). The at-risk children were divided into three clusters of almost equal numbers. Cluster 5 comprised 43 children with reading scores seriously below average (1–1.5 standard deviations below the overall mean score), and clusters 2 and 4 comprised 36 and 52 children, respectively, with reading scores paralleling clusters 1 and 3. Thus, both the control

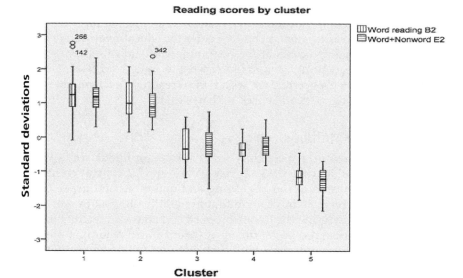

Figure 8.3. Reading scores by cluster. Cluster 1: control children, above-average readers. Cluster 2: children at risk for dyslexia, above-average readers. Cluster 3: control children, slightly below-average readers. Cluster 4: children at risk for dyslexia, slightly below-average readers. Cluster 5: children at risk for dyslexia, below-average readers.

and at-risk groups consisted of an approximately equal number of children with above-average and average to slightly below-average reading scores. In addition, approximately one third of the children in the at-risk group showed extremely poor reading scores that were in the dyslexic range.

Especially interesting were the correlations between reading scores and cluster allocation on the one hand, and performance on rapid naming of colors and pictures at age 59 months and at the end of kindergarten on the other hand. These correlations, presented in Table 8.4, were all significant.

Correlations between neurophysiologic measures at age 17 months and phonological and reading scores collected in second grade are presented in Table 8.5. The P2 latency in the left and right frontal and frontal-central sites and the amplitude difference between P2 and N1 (see Figure 8.2) on the standard stimulus showed the highest (significant) correlations. It should be noted that these are ongoing analyses; the number of participants in the latter analyses still are small.

Discussion

Based on reading scores at second grade, approximately one third of the at-risk children could be classified as having dyslexia. The remaining at-risk children were evenly divided into a subgroup of children with above-average reading skills and a subgroup with slightly below-average reading skills. A most interesting finding was that these two subgroups closely matched above-average and slightly below-average performing subgroups of children

Table 8.4. Correlations between rapid serial naming at age 59 months and kindergarten, and reading scores and cluster assignment in Grade 2.

			Start Grade 2	End Grade 2	Cluster
Age 59 months	RAN Color	r	−.36**	−.41**	.33**
		n	171	162	152
	RAN Pictures	r	−.31**	−.33**	.32**
		n	169	149	149
Kindergarten	RAN Color	r	−.48**	−.47**	.44**
		n	127	133	120
	RAN Pictures	r	−.41**	−.41**	.44**
		n	66	66	63

*$p < .05$; **$p < .01$
Key: RAN, rapid automatized naming; r, Pearson correlation coefficient; n, number of children.

from within the control group. Rapid naming scores obtained at age 59 months and at end kindergarten correlated significantly with the reading scores and with subgroups based on reading scores.

Analyses of reading scores in second grade showed significant correlations with electrophysiological recordings at age 17 months, especially P2 latency. To a lesser extent difference in amplitude between P2 and N1 at age 17 months significantly correlated with reading scores and phonological awareness in second grade.

GENERAL DISCUSSION

The aim of the DDP is, first, to obtain a deeper understanding of the core impairment(s) of dyslexia by longitudinally comparing the development of neurocognitive functions in children at risk for dyslexia with that of control children. The focus of interest is on neurophysiologic measures during the

Table 8.5. Correlations (absolute values) between AERP parameters at age 17 months and reading scores in Grade 2.

	Cluster	Reading begin Grade 2	Reading end Grade 2
P2 latency LH	$r = 0.19$	$r = 0.20$	$r = 0.28$
	$n = 36$	$n = 46$	$n = 38$
P2 latency RH	$r = 0.32$	$r = 0.31*$	$r = 0.38*$
	$n = 36$	$n = 46$	$n = 38$
FCzDVP2N1	$r = 0.42*$	$r = 0.17$	$r = 0.37$
	$n = 24$	$n = 36$	$n = 24$
FzDVP2N1	$r = 0.16$	$r = 0.38*$	$r = 0.27$
	$n = 19$	$n = 28$	$n = 19$

*$p < .05$; ** $p < .01$.
Key: Cluster: cluster assignment according to cluster analysis on reading scores Grade 2; P2 latency LH, RH: latency P2 left, right hemisphere, analysis van Herten (2008); FCzDVP2N1, FzDVP2N1: difference in amplitude (voltage) between P2 and N1 at FCz resp. Fz; r, Pearson correlation coefficient; n, number of children.

first 4 years of life and language and cognitive functions from the age of 3 years onward. In the comparisons between at-risk and control children, we earlier reported reduced mismatch responses at age 2 months (van Leeuwen et al., 2006, 2008) and delayed peaks and diminished mismatch response at age 17 months in at-risk children (van Herten et al., 2008). The present analyses added to this a reduced N1-P2 amplitude difference at age 17 and 29 months. It is most important to note that correlations between these early neurophysiologic measures and reading scores after 1 year of literacy education (beginning and end of second grade) were presented, suggesting that the auditory processes reflected in N1-P2 amplitude difference and P2 latency are specifically related to literacy development. Earlier, van Zuijen, Maassen, Been, and van der Leij (2009) reported a relationship in the study's cohort of children between mismatch response at age 2 months and reading fluency in second grade that corresponds to findings reported by Molfese (2000) and findings from the Jyväskylä Longitudinal Study of Dyslexia (JLD; Lyytinen et al., 2005). Apart from the mismatch response, the specificity of the relationship between P2 recorded from both standard and deviant stimuli and reading is striking and suggests a specific attention (Ceponiené et al., 2005) or stimulus classification impairment (Crowley, Trinder, & Colrain, 2004) in children at risk for dyslexia.

The second aim of the DDP is to develop a probabilistic prognostic model for the emergence of dyslexia. For this, in addition to neurophysiologic measures, behavior measures were also collected and correlated with reading scores. As reported previously, (Cornwall, 1992; Wolf et al., 2002) rapid serial naming of colors and pictures at the preliteracy stage provides a significant predictor of later reading acquisition. Eleveld (2005) thereby showed that nonalphanumeric rapid serial naming assessed in kindergarten is a better predictor for reading and especially spelling in first grade than is phonological awareness. Once literacy education starts, the importance of nonalphanumeric rapid serial naming diminishes, and the cognitive skills more closely related to the reading and spelling process itself—alphanumeric naming and phonological awareness—take over. A similar trend of lower correlations between nonalphanumeric rapid serial naming assessed in second grade and reading was found in our study (correlations left out of Table 8.4).

The absolute values of the correlation coefficients of the early neurophysiologic measures and reading scores are similar to rapid naming and reading scores, although the time interval between the former (4½–6 years) is much larger than between the latter (1½–3 years). Further analyses need to be conducted when the dataset is complete in order to be able to weigh the relative contribution of predictors. See for example the model by Torppa based on the JLD (Torppa et al., 2007). Implementation studies are needed to develop a protocol for screening and diagnosis that addresses questions of sensitivity and specificity of test procedures and age at which these can be most effectively administered, thereby taking the availability of effective intervention techniques into account. For a deeper understanding of the underlying impairments of dyslexia—the first question raised at the outset—further follow-up studies on the well-documented cohort of the DDP would be most interesting; the comparison between nondyslexic and dyslexic at-risk children in particular would give the unique opportunity to study normalization and compensation processes (see e.g., van Bergen et al., 2010). Furthermore, cross-linguistic comparisons are called for to study—among other questions—the issue of the role of orthographic transparency.

REFERENCES

Ceponiené, R., Alku, P., Westerfield, M., Torki, M., & Townsend, J. (2005). ERPs differentiate syllable and nonphonetic sound processing in children and adults. *Psychophysiology, 42,* 391–406. doi:10.1111/j.1469-8986.2005.00305

Ceponiené, R., Rinne, T., & Näätänen, R. (2002). Maturation of cortical sound processing as indexed by event-related potentials. *Clinical Neurophysiology, 113,* 870–882. doi:10.1016/S1388-2457(02)00078-0

Cornwall, A. (1992). The relationship of phonological awareness, rapid naming, and verbal memory to severe reading and spelling disability. *Journal of Learning Disabilities, 25,* 532–538. doi:10.1177/002221949202500808

Crowley, K.E., Trinder, J., & Colrain, I.M. (2004). A review of the evidence for P2 being an independent component process: Age, sleep and modality. *Clinical Neurophysiology, 115,* 732–744. doi:10.1016/j.clinph.2003.11.021

de Jong, P.F. & van der Leij, A. (2003). Developmental changes in the manifestation of a phonological impairment deficit in dyslexic children learning to read a regular orthography. *Journal of Educational Psychology, 95,* 22–40. doi:10.1037//0022-0663.95.1.22

Eleveld, M. (2005). *At-risk for dyslexia. The role of phonological abilities, letter knowledge, and speed of serial naming in early intervention and diagnosis.* Leuven, Amersfoort: Garant.

Grigorenko, E.L. (2001). Developmental dyslexia: An update on genes, brains and environments. *Journal of Child Psychology and Psychiatry, 42,* 91–125. doi:10.1111/1469-7610.00704

Habib, M. (2000). The neurological basis of developmental dyslexia: An overview and working hypothesis. *Brain, 123,* 2373–2399.

Korpilahti, P., Krause, C.M., Holopainen, I., & Lang, A.H. (2001). Early and late mismatch negativity elicited by words and speechlike stimuli in children. *Brain and Language, 76,* 332–339.

Kushnerenko, E. (2003). *Maturation of the cortical auditory event-related brain potentials in infancy,* (Unpublished doctoral dissertation). University of Helsinki, Finland.

Lyytinen, H., Guttorm, T., Huttunen, T., Hämäläinen, J., Leppänen, P., & Vesterinen, M. (2005). Psychophysiology of developmental dyslexia: A review of findings including studies of children at-risk for dyslexia. *Journal of Neurolinguistics, 18,* 167–195. doi:10.1016/j.jneuroling.2004.11.001

Maassen, B., Groenen, P., Crul, T.H., Assman-Hulsmans, C., & Gabreëls, F. (2001). Identification and discrimination of voicing and place-of-articulation in developmental dyslexia. *Clinical Linguistics & Phonetics, 15,* 319–339.

Molfese, D.L. (2000). Predicting dyslexia at 8 years of age using neonatal brain responses. *Brain and Language, 72,* 238–245. doi:10.1006/brln.2000.2287

Nathan, L., Stackhouse, J., Goulandris, N., & Snowling, M. (2004). The development of early literacy skills among children with speech difficulties: A test of the "critical age hypothesis." *Journal of Speech, Language, and Hearing Research, 47,* 377–391. doi:10.1044/1092-4388(2004/031)

Schulte-Körne, G., Deimel, W., Bartling, J., & Remschmidt, H. (1998). Auditory processing and dyslexia: Evidence for a specific speech processing deficit. *Neuroreport, 9,* 337–340.

Thierry, G. (2005). The use of event-related potentials in the study of early cognitive development. *Infant and Child Development, 14,* 94. doi:10.1002/icd.353

Torppa, M., Poikkeus, A.M., Laakso, M., Tolvanen, A., Leskinen, E., Leppänen, P., … Lyytinen, H. (2007). Modeling the early paths of phonological awareness and factors supporting its development in children with and without familial risk of dyslexia. *Scientific Studies of Reading, 11,* 73–103. doi:10.1080/10888430709336554

van Beinum, F.J., Schwippert, C.E., Been, P.H., van Leeuwen, T.H., & Kuijpers, C.T.L. (2005). Development and application of a /bAk/–/dAk/ continuum for testing auditory perception within the Dutch longitudinal dyslexia study. *Speech Communication, 47,* 124–142. doi:10.1016/j.specom.2005.04.003

van Bergen, E., de Jong, P.F., Regtvoort, A.G.F.M., Oort, F., van Otterloo, S., & van der Leij, A. (2011). Dutch children at family risk of dyslexia: Precursors, reading development, and parental effects. *Dyslexia, 17*(1), 2–18. doi:10.1002/dys.423

van den Bos, K.P., lutje Spelberg, H.C., Scheepstra, A.J.M., & de Vries, J.R. (1994). *De klepel.* Amsterdam, The Netherlands: Pearson.

van Herten, M., Pasman, J.W., van Leeuwen, T.H., Been, P.H., van der Leij, A., Zwarts, F., & Maassen, B. (2008). Differences in AERP responses and atypical hemispheric specialization in 17-month-old children at- risk of dyslexia. *Brain Research, 1201,* 100–105. doi:10.1016/j.brainres.2008.01.060

van Leeuwen, T.H., Been, P.H., Kuijpers, C., Zwarts, F., Maassen, B., & van der Leij, A. (2006). Mismatch response is absent in 2-month-old infants at-risk for dyslexia. *NeuroReport, 17,* 351–355. doi:10.1097/01.wnr.0000203624.02082.2d

van Leeuwen, T.H., Been, P.H., van Herten, M., Zwarts, F., Maassen, B., and Van der Leij, A. (2008). Two-month-old infants at risk for dyslexia do not discriminate /bak/ from /dak/: A brainmapping study. *Journal of Neurolinguistics 21,* 333–348.

Verhoeven, L. (1995). *Drie-Minuten-Toets (DMT).* Arnhem, The Netherlands: Cito.

Wolf, M., Goldberg O'Rourke, A., Gidney, C., Lovett, M., Cirino, P., & Morris, R. (2002). The second deficit: An investigation of the independence of phonological and naming-speed deficits in developmental. *Reading and Writing, 15,* 43–72.

CHAPTER 9
Phonology and Literacy
Follow-Up Results of the Utrecht Dyslexia and Specific Language Impairment Project

Elise de Bree, Margaret J. Snowling, Ellen Gerrits,
Petra van Alphen, Aryan van der Leij, and Frank Wijnen

D yslexia is a complex neurodevelopmental disorder that has received investigation at many levels spanning genes, brain, and behavior. This chapter presents an investigation of the cognitive deficits of dyslexia based on speech-related data.

There is now good evidence that aspects of early language development can reveal difficulties that lead to later literacy problems. These difficulties primarily include deficits in phonological awareness (PA), phonological (or verbal) short-term memory (vSTM), and rapid serial naming (RSN) (Wagner & Torgesen, 1987) and are indicative of a core phonological deficit—that is, difficulties with encoding, storing, or retrieving speech. It is important to note that studies of children with a familial risk (FR) for dyslexia—children with at least one parent with dyslexia—have demonstrated that phonological difficulties *precede* the onset of literacy instruction and therefore suggest that poor phonological skills might be precursors of dyslexia (e.g., Boets et al., 2010; de Bree, Rispens, & Gerrits, 2007; Locke et al., 1997; Lyytinen et al., 2004; Scarborough, 1990; Snowling, Gallagher, & Frith, 2003). Examination of the cognitive profiles of FR children both with and without literacy difficulties (e.g., Boets et al., 2010; de Bree, Wijnen, & Gerrits, 2010; Elbro, Borstrøm, & Peterson, 1998; Pennington & Lefly, 2001; Snowling, Muter, & Carroll, 2007) shows that the core phonological deficit affects both poor readers and typical readers in this group (indicative of a genetic liability) and that this deficit can be aggravated or compensated by other (linguistic) skills.

Coming from a different perspective, researchers exploring the underlying causes of specific language impairment (SLI) are incorporating literacy development in the frameworks proposed for this disorder. SLI is defined as an impairment in acquiring language despite normal hearing, typical nonverbal abilities, and adequate exposure (Leonard, 1998); many children with SLI develop literacy difficulties (e.g., Bishop, McDonald,

We are grateful to The Dyslexia Foundation (TDF) for hosting the 12th Extraordinary Brain Symposium. We would especially like to thank April Benasich and Holly Fitch for organizing the conference and providing feedback on the chapter. Thanks are due to the colleagues from the *Language Development and Dyslexia* project (NWO 360-70-030), Jan de Jong and Carien Wilsenach; to the students who assisted in data collection, Alice Hung, Britt Hakvoort, and Djaina Satoer; and to Elsje van Bergen for feedback on the chapter.

Bird, & Hayiou-Thomas, 2009; Vandewalle, Boets, & Ghesquière, 2010; van Weerdenburg, Verhoeven, & van Balkom, 2009). An issue that has received attention recently is whether phonological deficits in children with SLI are causally related to literacy difficulties or whether such deficits can also exist without concomitant reading problems. More specifically, there is debate as to whether children with SLI display phonological-processing difficulties or whether only those SLI children with additional literacy difficulties do so (e.g., Bishop & Snowling, 2004; de Bree et al., 2010; Catts, Adlof, Hogan, & Ellis Weismer, 2005; Rispens & Parigger, 2010; Scheltinga, van der Leij, & van Beinum, 2003; Vandewalle et al., 2010).

A direct comparison between the spoken language and literacy abilities of children with dyslexia and children with SLI is thus warranted. There has been a shift toward the investigation of the comorbidity of dyslexia and SLI rather than regarding the disorders as unidimensional and separate (e.g., Bishop & Snowling, 2004; Catts et al., 2005; Pennington, 2006; Tallal, Allard, Miller, & Curtiss, 1997). Indeed, research on children with pure disorders (dyslexia only and SLI only), comparing them with children with comorbid difficulties (dyslexia + SLI) is burgeoning (e.g., Bishop et al., 2009; Fraser, Goswami, & Conti-Ramsden, 2010; Marshall & van der Lely, 2009; Robertson, Joanisse, Desroches, & Ng, 2009).

DYSLEXIA AND SPECIFIC LANGUAGE IMPAIRMENT: A LONGITUDINAL APPROACH

A key issue pertaining to the relationship between dyslexia and SLI is the nature of the linguistic abilities of these two groups prior to the onset of literacy instruction. It is important for research to be directed toward this issue in order to map the developmental trajectory of language and literacy abilities and the mutual effect the two abilities can have on each other.

In the Utrecht longitudinal project, language abilities of children with a FR of dyslexia were compared with those of children with SLI and typically developing (TD) children without literacy difficulties in their families. The children were seen four times between their third and fifth birthdays and were presented with tasks probing speech perception and production (de Bree, 2007; de Bree et al., 2007, 2010; Gerrits, 2003; Gerrits & de Bree, 2009), morphophonology (de Bree & Kerkhoff, 2010), grammatical sensitivity (van Alphen et al., 2004; Wilsenach, 2006), and vocabulary. The preschool findings reveal similarities between the FR and SLI groups in terms of shared areas of difficulty, with respect to nonword repetition, sentence repetition, speech production, speech–sound categorization, and grammatical sensitivity. However, it is necessary to know if and how these preschool language abilities relate to subsequent literacy skills and whether this pattern is the same for affected and unaffected children in FR and SLI groups.

Follow-Up Data

A first analysis of the follow-up data was presented in de Bree et al. (2010). The nonword repetition (NWR) abilities of 4-year-old children at risk for dyslexia and children with SLI were related to their reading abilities at age 8: The SLI group obtained the lowest NWR score and the FR group performed in between the control and SLI groups. Approximately half of each of the FR and SLI groups showed reading difficulties; we will refer to these as FR poor readers (FR_PR) and SLI poor readers (SLI_PR) to distinguish them from those in each group with normal reading (NR). Whereas preschool NWR abilities correlated with literacy outcomes in the FR group, this was not the case for the SLI group. Rather, for children with SLI, phonological processing was poor regardless of literacy outcome. These findings thus lend support to the notion that dyslexia and SLI are disorders with different trajectories to literacy disorder.

The nonword-repetition data prove valuable for understanding the relationship between dyslexia and SLI. It is important, however, to also assess the performance on the related measures of speech perception, speech production, and processing in order to understand the phonological deficit in the two disorders. The questions to be addressed here are whether difficulties arise on the same tasks and to the same extent and whether they relate to literacy outcomes. The tasks that are discussed here are 1) categorical speech perception, which has found conflicting results for presence or absence in dyslexia and SLI (see, e.g., Robertson et al., 2009), 2) speech production, which only indirectly relates to literacy outcome but does mark language delay (e.g., Carroll, Snowling, Hulme, & Stevenson, 2003; Raitano, Pennington, Tunick, Boada, & Shriberg, 2004), 3) mispronunciation detection as a measure of phonological representations (e.g., Carroll & Snowling, 2004), and 4) rhyme-oddity task as a measure of phonological awareness (e.g., Goswami & Bryant, 1990). Furthermore, it is important to consider the outcome not only for literacy but also for nonword repetition at age 8. There is already a suggestion for longitudinal analysis (de Bree et al., 2010) that NWR at age 4 did not predict literacy outcome for all groups. Arguably, this might be because of the reciprocal relationship between NWR and reading development (e.g., Nation & Hulme, 2010, Rispens & Parigger, 2010), such that NWR performance is bootstrapped by reading development. In this light, it was predicted that at age 8 only SLI children with literacy difficulties (SLI_PR) should show poor NWR, and a correlation between NWR and literacy would be found at this age but not for the SLI_NR group.

A final and related issue is the role of RSN in literacy outcome. This measure contributes to literacy (e.g., de Jong & van der Leij, 2003). Moreover, Bishop et al. (2009) found that RSN was predictive of the presence or absence of literacy difficulties in a sample of 9- to 10-year-old children with SLI who had poor nonword repetition. Thus, SLI children with both NWR and RSN difficulties exhibited reading difficulties and not those

with deficits only in NWR. Vandewalle et al. (2010) extended these findings to a younger age to report that RSN skills of Flemish children with
SLI at kindergarten age predicted literacy outcome. RSN abilities thus
also need to be addressed in the Utrecht FR and SLI children to assess
whether RSN is a protective factor for literacy in these groups.

In summary, in order to gain a better understanding of the relationship between phonology and literacy and between dyslexia and SLI,
the present study assessed whether 1) phonological skills tapped between 3 and 5 years of age are early predictors of later literacy disorders,
2) NWR difficulties are persistent across ages, and 3) RSN is a protective
or aggravating factor for literacy.

Method

Participants   Three groups of children participated in this study:
children with FR of dyslexia, children with SLI, and a typically developing control group (TD control). The FR children had at least one parent with literacy difficulties as indicated by standardized reading and
phonological processing measures, including a nonword spelling task,
a timed word and timed nonword reading task, a NWR task, and an
RSN task. In order for a child to be included in the at-risk group, the
parent had to show poor performance on all the tasks, except on an additional verbal competence task, as this is often a relative strength for
highly educated people with dyslexia, in contrast with their reading and
spelling abilities. Specifically, performance on the timed word reading
or timed nonword reading task had to be in the 10th percentile, or in
the 25th percentile on both timed reading tasks, and a discrepancy of
at least 60% between verbal competence and performance on the timed
reading tasks (based on criteria from the Dutch Dyslexia Programme;
see Koster et al., 2005). The FR children did not include children whose
parents or siblings had a history of language impairment.

Children with SLI were recruited through speech therapists and
schools for children with severe speech and language difficulties. Prior
to the start of the project, they had been classified as SLI after extensive
assessment of speech and language abilities by certified speech patholo-
gists. All children had to have normal hearing, absence of neurological
difficulties, and normal nonverbal IQ (> 75). We only know of one child
in this group who had a dyslexic parent. The control children were all
without literacy and language difficulties in their family and without
language or behavioral difficulties of their own.

The children were all presented with the same test battery, but also,
as testing was free of pressure, not all children completed all tasks in one
testing phase. This means that different numbers are present for each
task (see de Bree, 2007, for more information on the samples of children).

Measures

Preschool Speech Measures
The preschool phonological process-ing tasks were speech categorization, speech production, mispronuncia-tion detection, and rhyme oddity. These are briefly described next (see also Table 9.1).

Speech categorization was tested between 3½ and 4 years of age with the traditional two alternative forced-choice categorization task. The stop-consonant acoustic continuum ranged from the word /pOp/ to /kOp/ (*doll* and *cup*). These words were natural utterances produced by a male speaker of standard Dutch. Stimuli in the continuum between the two utterances were obtained by interpolation between the relative ampli-tudes of the spectral envelopes of the words. Stimulus generation re-sulted in a continuum of seven stimuli that sounded completely natural and convincingly like utterances of the original speaker. Categorization behavior was reflected on a categorization slope with a steeper slope reflecting better categorization (see also Gerrits & de Bree, 2009).

A picture-naming and -matching task as a measure of *speech produc-tion* was also tapped between 3½ and 4 years of age. Targets included mono-, bi-, tri-, and quadrosyllabic words checked for age of acquisition. Percentages of consonants correct are reported. More data are assessed here than in Gerrits and de Bree (2009).

A *mispronunciation-detection* task was presented to the children at 5 years of age. The proportion correct was calculated of the 12 maximal mispronunciations (place of articulation, manner, and voicing; e.g., *zebra* as *pebra*) and 12 minimal mispronunciations (place of articulation; e.g., *zebra* as *vebra*) in the onset (see van Alphen et al., 2004).

Phonological awareness was assessed through a *rhyme-oddity* task at 5 years of age. Children had to select the odd one out of 20 series (e.g., *jas-glas-tas-trui*) and the proportion correct was calculated (see de Bree, 2007).

Table 9.1. Overview of preschool phonological tasks and publications.

Task	Speech categorization	Speech production	Nonword repetition	Mispronuncia-tion detection	Rhyme oddity
Age	3½–4	3½–4	4½	5	5
Source of report	Gerrits and de Bree (2009)	Gerrits and de Bree (2009)	de Bree et al. (2007, 2010)	van Alphen et al. (2004)	de Bree (2007)
Findings	TD control > FR, SLI	TD control > FR > SLI	TD control > FR > SLI	TD control > FR, SLI	No differ-ences

Key: TD, typically developing; FR: familial risk of dyslexia; SLI: specific language impairment.

Measures at 8 Years of Age Four different literacy tasks were presented to the children: two timed reading tasks—a 1-minute word reading task (Brus & Voeten, 1972) and a 2-minute nonword reading task (van den Bos, Spelberg, Scheepstra, & de Vries, 1994)—and two spelling tasks—spelling dictation (van den Bosch et al., 1993) and spelling selection (Horsley 2005).

The NWR task of de Jong (1998) was used, which contains 48 items that lead to a raw score.

The rapid digit-naming task by van den Bos, Zijlstra, and Spelberg (2002) was used for RSN, where 50 digits had to be named as quickly and correctly as possible. The RSN score was calculated as the number of symbols named per second. The higher the RSN score, the faster the naming speed.

RESULTS

Literacy Outcomes of Familial Risk, Specific Language Impairment, and Typically Developing Children at Age 8

The data of children who completed the literacy battery as well as the NWR and RSN tasks at age 8 include 24 TD control children, 44 FR children, and 17 children with SLI. A MANOVA on the literacy data in Table 9.2 (phonological data is discussed in the next section) shows significant differences among the groups on all tasks with the exception of the timed pseudoword-reading task ($p = .101$), despite clearly visible differences among the groups (but note the small effect size). On all measures the FR and SLI groups performed similarly to each other. For spelling selection, the TD control group performed better than both the FR group and the SLI group. For spelling dictation, the pattern was similar, but the differences between the TD control group and the SLI group were not statistically significant ($p = .090$). Finally, for word reading, the TD control group scored higher than the SLI group. These findings are consistent with the literature, in that both FR and SLI groups will do more poorly in terms of literacy outcomes.

A composite literacy score was computed by summing the z-scores for the four literacy tasks. A literacy deficit was defined as performance at or below one standard deviation of the mean literacy composite score for the TD control group. On this criterion, as expected, the majority of TD control children read well (19/23 = 83%), whereas fewer children in the FR (24/38 = 63%) and SLI (7/14 = 50%) groups did so. Again, these findings resemble those found in previous FR studies, where 30%–60% of FR children become diagnosed with dyslexia, as well as studies of SLI, in which a substantial percentage of children with SLI show literacy difficulties.

Table 9.2. Outcomes on the literacy and phonological measures at age 8.

	nr	Timed word reading (nr of words read per minute, max = 116)	Timed nonword reading (nr of non-words read in two minutes, max = 116)	Spelling dictation (max = 38)	Spelling selection (max = 70)	Literacy composite (z)	RSN (nr of symbols read per second)	Nonword repetition (max = 48)
		$F = 4.179$	$F = 2.360$	$F = 3.441$	$F = 8.188$	$F = 6.302$	$F = 2.791$	$F = 28.977$
		$p = .019$	$p = .101$	$p = .037$	$p < .001$	$p = .003$	$p = .062$	$p < .001$
		$\eta^2_p = 0.100$	$\eta^2_p = 0.159$	$\eta^2_p = 0.084$	$\eta^2_p = 0.179$	$\eta^2_p = 0.130$	$\eta^2_p = 0.065$	$\eta^2_p = 0.414$
TD control	24	57.5 (12.2)[a]	48.0 (13.4)	34.3 (4.1)[a]	55.3 (8.1)	-.29 (3.6)	.96 (.17)	33.0 (3.4)
FR	44	49.4 (14.6)[ab]	4.8 (17.1)	3.9 (6.6)[b]	45.3 (1.6)[a]	-4.92 (6.4)[a]	.86 (.19)	29.6 (6.5)
SLI	17	44.8 (15.4)[b]	36.9 (18.8)	29.0 (8.4)[ab]	43.4 (13.5)[a]	-5.78 (6.3)[a]	.96 (.21)	18.7 (7.9)

Note: Values with the same superscript do not differ significantly from each other on posthoc tests in cases in which a main effect is found.

Key: max, maximum; nr, number; RSN, rapid serial naming; TD, typically developing; FR, familial risk of dyslexia; SLI, specific language impairment.

Preschool Phonological Skills and Literacy Outcome

Table 9.3 shows performance on the four tasks presented at preschool age for the three groups (TD control, FR, and SLI). Significant group differences emerged for categorization slope for speech categorization, percentage of consonants correct (PCC) for speech production, and correct responses for mispronunciation detection, and there was a trend for rhyme oddity detection to differ. The pattern of performance was generally TD control > FR > SLI. However, in contrast to the NWR results (de Bree et al., 2010), this pattern is not borne out statistically in the tasks reported here. On the categorization and mispronunciation-detection tasks, the FR and SLI groups did not differ from each other. The FR group differed from the TD control group on both tasks, whereas the SLI group differed from the TD control group on categorization and marginally so on the mispronunciation-detection task (p = .052). On the speech-production task, the TD control and FR groups both performed better than the SLI group, matching the intake criteria of diagnosed language difficulties of the latter group. Effect sizes are small to medium for the preschool tasks.

In order to ascertain whether children in the FR and SLI groups carried a similar "risk" for reading difficulties that may be compensated or aggravated during development, we next analyzed performance on the phonological measures across six subgroups classified in terms of 8-year-old outcomes: control normal readers (TD_NR), control poor readers (TD_PR), FR normal readers (FR_NR), FR poor readers (FR_PR), SLI normal readers (SLI_NR), and SLI poor readers (SLI_PR; see Table 9.4). It should be kept in mind here that the number of children in each subgroup differs across the phonological tasks because of missing data.

Visual inspection establishes that the SLI_PR group always performs most poorly and that there is a gradual decline in scores from TD > FR > SLI on the speech-categorization and rhyme-oddity tasks. Consistent with the findings for NWR reported by de Bree et al. (2010), there were significant group effects on speech categorization, mispronunciation detection, and speech-production scores; differences in rhyme oddity were not significant despite discernible differences among the groups. No subgroup differences were found for the mispronunciation data, which was probably caused by the ceiling scores for the control groups and the substantial variation in the SLI groups. For speech categorization, the SLI_PR group and the FR_PR group scored less well than the control groups. For speech production, the SLI_PR group scored less well than the FR_PR and control groups. Outcomes remained the same when the TD_PR data were excluded from the analyses. Effect sizes were medium and small.

These analyses do not support a uniform connection between the preschool phonological tasks and literacy outcome at age 8. Furthermore,

Table 9.3. Results (rounded off) for preschool phonological tasks for the TD control, FR, and SLI groups.

	nr	Speech categorization (slope)	nr	Speech production (PCC)	nr	Mispronunciation detection (proportion correct)	nr	Rhyme oddity (proportion correct)
		$F = 7.792$		$F = 13.072$		$F = 11.332$		$F = 2.938$
		$p = .001$		$p < .001$		$p < .001$		$p = .059$
		Cohen's $d = .290$		Cohen's $d = .347$		Cohen's $d = .239$		Cohen's $d = .076$
		slope		PCC		% correct		% correct
TD control	12	18 (4)[a]	16	93 (4)[a]	22	99 (4)[a]	18	71 (13)
FR	23	10 (8)[a]	20	87 (11)[a]	41	95 (6)[b]	41	61 (24)
SLI	6	6 (7)[a]	16	74 (14)	12	82 (21)[ab]	15	52 (23)

Note: Values with the same superscript do not differ significantly from each other on posthoc tests in cases in which a main effect is found.

Key: nr, number of children; PCC, percentage of consonants correct; TD, typically developing; FR, familial risk of dyslexia; SLI, specific language impairment.

Table 9.4. Results on preschool phonological tasks when groups are classified according to literacy outcomes.

	nr	Speech categorization (slope)	nr	Speech production (PCC)	nr	Mispronunciation detection (proportion correct)	nr	Rhyme oddity (proportion correct)
		F 3.303		F 5.048		F 3.627		F 1.834
		p = .015		p = .001		p = .006		p = .120
		Cohen's d = .326		Cohen's d = .369		Cohen's d = .232		Cohen's d = .130
TD_NR	8 (67%)	17 (4)	11 (65%)	93 (4)	15 (72%)	99 (2)	14 (78%)	75 (9)
TD_PR	4 (33%)	20 (1)	6 (35%)	92 (6)	6 (28%)	96 (7)	4 (22%)	55 (15)
FR_NR	3 (10%)	11 (13)[b]	6 (33%)	86 (6)	12 (34%)	94 (5)	21 (58%)	64 (25)
FR_PR	19 (90%)	10 (8)	12 (67%)	88 (14)	23 (66%)	96 (6)	15 (42%)	63 (25)
SLI_NR	2 (33%)	11 (13)	3 (22%)	78 (15)	2 (20%)	90 (3)	7 (54%)	55 (22)
SLI_PR	4 (67%)	3 (4)[abd]	11 (78%)	73 (13)[abd]	8 (80%)	84 (20)	6 (46%)	47 (28)

Note: [a]significantly lower than TD_NR, [b]significantly lower than TD_PR, [c]significantly lower than FR_NR, [d]significantly lower than FR_PR

Key: nr, number of children; PCC, percentage of consonants correct; TD, typically developing; NR, normal reader; PR, poor reader; FR, familial risk of dyslexia; SLI, specific language impairment.

Table 9.5. Correlations between the preschool phonological tasks and literacy score.

		nr	Speech categorization (slope)	nr	Speech production (PCC)	nr	Mispronunciation detection (proportion correct)	nr	Rhyme oddity (proportion correct)
z-score literacy	All children	41	0.154	52	0.097	75	0.075	66	0.352**
	TD control	12	-0.725*	16	-0.138	22	0.302	18	0.698**
	FR	23	-0.076	20	-0.314	41	-0.177	41	0.176
	SLI	6	0.058	16	-0.228	12	-0.283	15	0.337

Key: nr, number of children; PCC, percentage of consonants correct; TD, typically developing; FR, familial risk of dyslexia; SLI, specific language impairment.

*$p < 0.05$, **$p < 0.01$

there were no strong correlations among the measures either within or across groups (see Table 9.5). Together, these findings suggest that there is no consistent link between the preschool phonological measures and subsequent literacy abilities.

NWR and RSN at 8 Years and Literacy Outcome

The previous section assessed whether phonological difficulties can be regarded as precursors of dyslexia that exist prior to literacy instruction. Here, we assess concurrent relationships between literacy and both NWR and RSN at age 8 (Tables 9.2 and 9.6).

First, an important question is whether NWR performance at preschool age is correlated with NWR at 8 years of age. A high positive correlation for the overall data ($r = .777$, $p < .001$) as well as a moderate correlation for the TD control ($r = .505$), FR ($r = .663$), and SLI groups ($r = .658$) separately (all with $p < .001$) attests to the stability of this measure over time.

Turning to the group differences, as expected, these were significant for both NWR and RSN: For RSN, the FR_PR group performed worse than the TD control groups. For NWR, the SLI_PR group obtained lower scores than both FR and control groups.

A second analysis ran correlation analyses between the NWR and RSN and the composite z-score of the literacy tasks. A moderate overall positive correlation existed for NWR and RSN coupled with literacy (see Table 9.7). RSN is only correlated significantly for the FR group separately, while NWR is correlated to literacy for both the FR and control groups.

Table 9.6. Outcomes on the phonological tasks when groups are classified by literacy results.

	nr	RSN (nr of symbols read per second)	NWR (nr correct, max = 48)
		$F = 4.027$	$F = 15.403$
		$p = .003$	$p < .001$
		$\eta^2_p = 0.203$	$\eta^2_p = 0.494$
TD_NR	19 (77%)	0.98 (0.17)	33.8 (3.0)
TD_PR	5 (23%)	0.93 (0.17)	29.7 (4.3)
FR_NR	21 (47%)	0.92 (0.17)	32.1 (4.7)
FR_PR	23 (53%)	0.78 (0.18)[ae]	27.2 (7.2)[a]
SLI_NR	7 (41%)	1.1 (0.20)	21.7 (9.3)
SLI_PR	10 (59%)	0,86 (0,19)	16,4 (5,6)[abcd]

Key: nr, number of groups; RSN, rapid serial naming; NWR, nonword repetition; TD, typically developing; NR, normal reader; PR, poor reader; FR, familial risk of dyslexia; SLI, specific language impairment.

[a]significantly lower than TD_NR, [b]significantly lower than TD_PR, [c]significantly lower than FR_NR, [d]significantly lower than FR_RP

Table 9.7. Correlations among RSN, NWR, and literacy at age 8.

		nr	RSN (nr of symbols read per second)	NWR (nr correct)
z-score literacy	All children	85	0.520*	0.528*
	TD control	24	0.281	0.599*
	FR	44	0.604*	0.532*
	SLI	17	0.465	0.462

Key: nr, number; RSN, rapid serial naming; TD, typically developing; FR, familial risk of dyslexia; SLI, specific language impairment.

*p < 0.01

DISCUSSION

The aim of this study was to see whether preschool phonological difficulties in children with FR for dyslexia and children with SLI flagged later literacy difficulties, whether the areas and severity of the difficulties were the same for both groups, whether phonological-processing difficulties would also be present at school age, and whether RSN might be a protective factor for literacy.

The literacy outcomes of the FR and SLI children agree with those found in the literature; of the total sample, 37% of the FR and 50% of the SLI group could be labeled poor readers. Furthermore, the FR and SLI groups performed less well than the TD control group on both the preschool and school-age measures of phonology, indicative of underlying phonological difficulties in both groups across ages. The finding of a strong correlation between preschool and school-age NWR further supports this assumption.

However, no straightforward pattern emerges when connecting the phonological measures to literacy outcome at age 8. The generalization that can be made is that the SLI_PR group performs most poorly on the phonological tasks at preschool and school age, in line with findings of other studies in which dyslexia + SLI groups performed more poorly than poor readers or SLI-only groups (e.g., Bishop et al., 2009; Marshall & van der Lely, 2009). Furthermore, the pattern of performance was that the FR normal and poor readers obtained lower scores than the control group and that the SLI normal and poor readers obtained even lower scores.

NWR at age 8 is correlated with literacy outcomes for the TD control and FR groups but not for the SLI group, although it should be kept in mind that there were missing data in this set. The findings of NWR at age 8 suggest a change in relationship to literacy compared to those found at age 4½ (de Bree et al., 2010). At age 4½, the FR_PR, SLI_PR, and SLI_NR groups performed more poorly than the control group. At age 8, however, the SLI_NR group performed like the control group on this task, suggesting "catch-up." Arguably, these findings can also be accommodated within other lines of research that find an impact of literacy on NWR, such as studies with subjects who are illiterate (Castro-Caldas, Petersson, Reis, Stone-Elander, & Ingvar, 1998) and TD children (Nation & Hulme, 2010). They can also be aligned with cognitive neuroscience models that assume a cascade of cortical circuits of phonological processing and processing of visual words (e.g., McCandliss & Noble, 2003).

It could further be proposed that NWR in the children with SLI is determined by language abilities at preschool age (e.g., proposed by Bishop et al., 2009, Conti-Ramsden & Durkin, 2007, Vandewalle et al., 2010) then shifts toward a reliance on literacy. At age 8, the normal and poor reading SLI groups do not differ significantly from each other on NWR. The expectation is that the gap between the two groups will widen as the interaction between orthography and phonological processing becomes more dominant in acquisition. A similar increase in difference on NWR performance between the FR_NR and FR_PR is expected to occur. However, future analyses will have to assess whether the poorer NWR scores of the FR group at preschool age were also determined by language development or other skills.

Similar to other recent findings (Bishop et al., 2009), RSN seems to be a protective measure for literacy difficulties; the FR_PR and SLI_PR groups showed poorer performance than the controls, and the FR_PR group was outperformed by the SLI_NR group. These findings sit well with those of de Jong and van der Leij (2003), for example, who found that children with dyslexia have poorer RSN than normal readers. The SLI_NR group showed the highest numerical scores on RSN, lending support to the idea that they can compensate for their language difficulties with RSN skills. Unfortunately, no RSN data are available for when the children were younger, but also the present findings are consistent with those of Vandewalle et al. (2010) that, in Dutch, RSN is a protective factor for literacy. An alternative interpretation, however, also deserves further investigation: It could be argued that whereas poor NWR is characteristic of SLI, RSN is unrelated to this disorder. The SLI_PR group did not show significantly lower RSN performance than the TD_NR or SLI_NR groups. To disentangle these two options, further longitudinal studies are required with larger sample sizes. In addition, the mitigating influence of orthography, predicted by letter knowledge, deserves further attention (see, e.g., Boets et al., 2010).

Another issue that needs to be addressed is the literacy score. The present study used a composite of reading fluency, timed word and nonword reading, as well as spelling dictation and spelling selection. However, it could be argued that the reading fluency and spelling need to be separated at this age (e.g., de Jong & van der Leij, 1999; Landerl & Wimmer, 2008). Analyses with a cut-off determined by the summed fluency tasks showed a similar pattern to that of the spelling and fluency literacy score for the preschool data and literacy, as well as correlations among NWR, RSN, and literacy. Nevertheless, this is an issue that warrants further attention.

Taken together, these findings lend support to a number of interpretations on language and literacy. First, the results show that phonology is a complex and multidimensional construct. Different skills have different effects on literacy (and language), and performance develops over time as the NWR data show. A second issue is that poor phonology is not sufficient for rendering poor literacy outcomes (e.g., Bishop et al., 2009; Snowling, 2008; Wolf & Bowers, 1999) as phonology was poorer in the FR and SLI groups, but poor phonology did not always lead to poor literacy skills at age 8 in these groups. RSN, arguably a measure of phonological-processing speed containing cross-modal matching of visual symbols and phonological codes (e.g., Vaessen, Gerretsen, & Blomert, 2009), proved to be one important concomitant risk factor in this study. These results are in line with proposals of dyslexia as a multifactorial deficit (e.g., Bishop & Snowling, 2004; Pernet & Démonet, Chapter 13). They stress the need for longitudinal studies into phonology and other linguistic skills and their underlying mechanisms (e.g., Flax, Realpe-Bonilla, Roesler, Choudhury, & Benasich, 2009), as well as research into potential domain-general skills required for successful literacy (e.g., Flax et al., 2009). They also underscore the need to look at individual differences and trajectories (see, Chapter 15; Snowling et al., 2003) and connect the data with findings on neuroprognosis studies (Hoeft et al., 2007, Chapters 12 and 17).

In summary, these findings show similarities and differences between children at FR for dyslexia and children with SLI on phonological measures and literacy outcome. These findings can be interpreted within multidimensional models on phonology, decoding literacy, and language that also take the role of development (age, orthographical skills) into account. They further indicate that longitudinal studies into phonology, oral language, decoding, and spelling are badly needed to gain a full picture of the potential developmental trajectories of preschool early linguistic markers and literacy.

REFERENCES

Bishop, D.V.M., McDonald, D., Bird, A., & Hayiou-Thomas, M.E. (2009). Children who read words accurately despite language impairment: Who are they and how do they do it? *Child Development, 80*, 593–605. doi:10.1111/j.1467-8624.2009.01281

Bishop, D.V.M., & Snowling, M.J. (2004). Developmental dyslexia and specific language impairment: Same or different? *Psychological Bulletin, 130*, 858–886. doi:10.1037/0033-2909.130.6.858

Boets, B., De Smedt, B., Cleuren, L., Vandewalle, E., Wouters, J., & Ghesquière, P. (2010). Towards a further characterization of phonological and literacy problems in Dutch-speaking children with dyslexia. *British Journal of Developmental Psychology, 28*, 5–31. doi:10.1348/026151010X485223

Brus, B.T., & Voeten, M.J.M. (1972). *Een-minuut test. Vorm A en B*. Nijmegen, The Netherlands: Berkhout Testmateriaal.

Carroll, J.M. & Snowling, M.J. (2004). Language and phonological skills in children at high risk of reading difficulties. *Journal of Child Psychology and Psychiatry, 45*, 631–640. doi:10.1111/j.1469-7610.2004.00252

Carroll, J.M., Snowling, M.J., Hulme, C., & Stevenson, J. (2003). The development of phonological awareness in preschool children. *Developmental Psychology, 39*, 913–923. doi:10.1037/0012-1649.39.5.913

Castro-Caldas, A., Petersson, K.M., Reis, A., Stone-Elander, S., & Ingvar, M. (1998). The illiterate brain: Learning to read and write during childhood influences the functional organization of the adult brain. *Brain, 121,* 1053–1063. doi:10.1093/brain/121.6.1053

Catts, H.W., Adlof, S.M., Hogan, T.P., & Ellis Weismer, S. (2005). Are specific language impairment and dyslexia distinct disorders? *Journal of Speech, Language, and Hearing Research, 48,* 1378–1396. doi:10.1044/1092-4388(2005/096)

Conti-Ramsden G.M., & Durkin K. (2007). Phonological short-term memory, language and literacy: Developmental relationships in early adolescence in young people with SLI. *Journal of Child Psychology and Psychiatry, 48*(2), 147–156. doi:10.1111/j.1469 -7610.2006.01703

de Bree, E. (2007). *Dyslexia and phonology: A study of the phonological abilities of Dutch children at-risk of dyslexia.* Utrecht, The Netherlands: LOT dissertation 155.

de Bree, E., & Kerkhoff, A. (2010). Bempen or bemben: Differences between children at-risk of dyslexia and children with SLI on a morpho-phonological task. *Scientific Studies of Reading, 14,* 85–109. doi:10.1080/10888430903242050

de Bree, E., Rispens, J., & Gerrits, E. (2007). Non-word repetition in Dutch children with (a risk of) dyslexia and SLI. *Clinical Linguistics & Phonetics, 21,* 935–944. doi:10.1080/02699200701576892

de Bree, E., Wijnen, F., & Gerrits, E. (2010). Non-word repetition and literacy in Dutch children at-risk of dyslexia and children with SLI: Results of the follow-up study. *Dyslexia, 16,* 36–44. doi:10.1002/dys.395

de Jong, P. (1998). Working memory deficits of reading disabled children. *Journal of Experimental Psychology, 70,* 75–96. doi:10.1006/jecp.1998.2451

de Jong, P.F., & van der Leij, D.A.V. (1999). Specific contributions of phonological abilities to early reading acquisition: results from a Dutch latent variable longitudinal study. *Journal of Educational Psychology, 91,* 450–476. doi:10.1037//0022-0663.91.3.450

de Jong, P.F., & van der Leij, D.A.V. (2003). Developmental changes in the manifestation of a phonological deficit in dyslexic children learning to read a regular orthography. *Journal of Educational Psychology, 95,* 22–40. doi:10.1037//0022-0663.95.1.22

Elbro, C., Borstrøm, I., & Petersen, D.K. (1998). Predicting dyslexia from kindergarten: The importance of distinctness of phonological representations of lexical items. *Reading Research Quarterly, 33,* 36–60. doi:10.1598/RRQ.33.1.3

Flax, J.F., Realpe-Bonilla, T., Roesler, C., Choudhury, N., & Benasich, A. (2009). Using early standardized language measures to predict later language and early reading outcomes in children at high risk of language-learning impairments. *Journal of Learning Disabilities, 42,* 61–75. doi:10.1177/0022219408326215

Fraser, J., Goswami, U., & Conti-Ramsden, G. (2010). Dyslexia and specific language impairment: The role of phonology and auditory processing. *Scientific Studies of Reading, 14*(1), 8–29. doi:10.1080/10888430903242068

Gerrits, E. (2003). Speech perception of children at risk for dyslexia and children with specific language impairment. In M.J. Solé, D. Recasens, & J. Romero (Eds.), *Proceedings of the 15th International Conference of the Phonetic Sciences* (pp. 2357–2360). Barcelona, Spain.

Gerrits, E., & de Bree, E. (2009). Speech perception and production in dyslexia and SLI: Evidence from 3–4 year olds. *Journal of Communication Disorders, 42,* 180–194.

Goswami, U., & Bryant, P.E. (1990). *Phonological skills and learning to read.* Hove, East Sussex: Lawrence Erlbaum.

Hoeft, F., Ueno, T., Reiss, A.L., Meyler, A., Whitfield-Gabrieli, S., Glover, G.H., ... Gabrieli, J.D.E. (2007). Prediction of children's reading skills using behavioral, functional, and structural neuroimaging measures. *Behavioral Neuroscience, 121,* 602–613. doi:10.1037/0735-7044.121.3.602

Horsley, T.M. (2005). *Not all dyslexics are created equal: Neurocognitive evidence.* Amsterdam: VU dissertations.

Koster, C., Been, P., Krikhaar, E., Zwarts, F., Diepstra, H., & van Leeuwen, T. (2005). Differences at 17 months: Productive language patterns in infants at familial risk for dyslexia and typically developing infants. *Journal of Speech, Language, and Hearing Research, 48,* 426–438. doi:10.1044/1092-4388(2005/029)

Landerl, K., & Wimmer, H. (2008). Development of word reading fluency and spelling in a consistent orthography: An 8-year follow-up. *Journal of Educational Psychology, 100,* 150–161. doi:10.1037/0022-0663.100.1.150

Leonard, L.B. (1998). *Children with specific language impairment.* Cambridge, MA: MIT Press.

Locke, J.L., Hodgson, J., Macaruso, P., Roberts, J., Lambrecht-Smith, S., & Guttentag, C. (1997). The development of developmental dyslexia. In C. Hulme & M. Snowling (Eds.), *Dyslexia: Biology, cognition and intervention* (pp. 72–96). London: Whurr.

Lyytinen, H., Ahonen, T., Eklund, K., Guttorm, T., Kulju, P., Laakso, M.L., ... Voholainen, H. (2004). Early development of children at familial risk for dyslexia—Follow-up from birth to school age. *Dyslexia, 10,* 146–178. doi:10.1002/dys.274

Marshall, C.R., & van der Lely, H.K.J. (2009). Effects of word position and stress on onset cluster production: Evidence from typical development, Specific Language Impairment and dyslexia. *Language, 85,* 39–57. doi:10.1353/lan.0.0081s

McCandliss, B.M., & Noble, K.G. (2003). The development of reading impairment: A cognitive neuroscience model. *Mental Retardation and Developmental Disabilities Research Reviews, 9,* 196–205. doi:10.1002/mrdd.10080

Nation, K., & Hulme, C. (2010). Learning to read changes children's phonological skills: evidence from a latent variable longitudinal study of reading and nonword repetition. *Developmental Science, 14,* 649-659. doi: 10.1111/j.1467-7687.2010.01008

Pennington, B.F. (2006). From single to multiple deficit models of developmental disorders. *Cognition, 101,* 385–413. doi:10.1016/j.cognition.2006.04.008

Pennington, B.F., & Lefly, D.L. (2001). Early reading development in children at family risk for dyslexia. *Child Development, 72,* 816–833. doi:10.1111/1467-8624.00317

Raitano, N.A., Pennington, B.F., Tunick, R.A., Boada, R., & Shriberg, L.D. (2004). Pre-literacy skills of subgroups of children with speech sound disorders. *Journal of Child Psychiatry and Psychology, 45,* 821–835. doi:10.1111/j.1469-7610.2004.00275

Rispens, J., & Parigger, E. (2010). The relation between non-word repetition performance and reading problems in Dutch speaking children with Specific Language Impairment (SLI). *British Journal of Developmental Psychology, 28,* 177–188.

Robertson, E.K., Joanisse, M.F., Desroches, A.S., & Ng, S. (2009). Categorical speech perception deficits distinguish language and reading impairments in children. *Developmental Science, 12,* 753–767 doi:10.1111/j.1467-7687.2009.00806

Scarborough, H.S. (1990). Very early language deficits in dyslexic children. *Child Development, 61,* 1728–1743. doi:10.2307/1130834

Scheltinga, F., van der Leij, A., & van Beinum, F. (2003). Importance of phonological skills and underlying processes to reading achievement. *Proceedings of the Institute of Phonetic Sciences, 25,* 21–30.

Snowling, M.J. (2008). Specific disorders and broader phenotypes: The case of dyslexia. *Quarterly Journal of Experimental Psychology, 61,* 142–156. doi:10.1080/17470210701508830

Snowling, M.J., Gallagher, A., & Frith, U. (2003). Family risk of dyslexia is continuous: Individual differences in the precursors of reading skill. *Child Development, 74,* 358–373. doi:10.1111/1467-8624.7402003

Snowling, M.J., Muter, V., & Carroll, J. (2007). Children at family risk of dyslexia: A follow-up in early adolescence. *Journal of Child Psychology and Psychiatry, 48,* 609–618. doi:10.1111/j.1469-7610.2006.01725

Tallal, P., Allard, L., Miller, S., & Curtiss, S. (1997). Academic outcomes of language impaired children. In C. Hulme & M. Snowling (Eds.), *Dyslexia: Biology, cognition, and intervention* (pp. 167–181). London: Whurr.

Vaessen, A., Gerretsen, P., & Blomert, L. (2009). Naming problems do not reflect a second independent core deficit in dyslexia: Double deficits explored. *Journal of Experimental Child Psychology, 103,* 202–221. doi:10.1016/j.jecp.2008.12.004

van Alphen, P., de Bree, E., Gerrits, E., de Jong, J., Wilsenach, C., & Wijnen, F. (2004). Early language development in children with a genetic risk for dyslexia. *Dyslexia, 10,* 265–288. doi:10.1002/dys.272

van den Bos, K.P., Spelberg, H.C.L, Scheepstra, A.J.M., & de Vries, J.R. (1994). *De KLEPEL. Een test voor de leesvaardigheid van pseudo-woorden.* Nijmegen, The Netherlands: Berkhout Testmateriaal.

van den Bos, K.P., Zijlstra, J.B.H., & Spelberg, H.C. (2002). Life-span data on continuous naming speeds of numbers, letters, colors, and pictured objects, and word-reading speed. *Scientific Studies of Reading, 6,* 25–49.

van den Bosch, L., Gillijns, P., Krom, R.S.H., Moelands, F., Geurts, J.M., & Verhoeven, L. (1993). Leerling volg systeem : schaal vorderingen in spellingvaardigheid 1, groep 3-4. Hulpboek. Toets voor auditieve analyse, fonemendictee: handleiding (LVS SVS TAA). Arnhem, The Netherlands: CITO.

Vandewalle, E., Boets, B., Ghesquière, P., & Zink, I. (2010). Who is at risk for dyslexia? Phonological processing in five-to-seven-year-old Dutch-speaking children with SLI. *Scientific Studies of Reading, 14,* 58–84. doi:10.1080/10888430903242035

van Weerdenburg, M., Verhoeven, L. & van Balkom, H. (2006). Towards a typology of Specific Language Impairment. *Journal of Child Psychology and Psychiatry, 47,* 176–189. doi:10.1111/j.1469-7610.2005.01454

Wagner, R.K., & Torgesen, J.K. (1987). The nature of phonological processing and its causal role in the acquisition of reading skills. *Psychological Bulletin, 101,* 192–212. doi:10.1037//0033-2909.101.2.192

Wilsenach, C. (2006). *Syntactic processing in developmental dyslexia and in specific language impairment.* Utrecht, The Netherlands: LOT dissertation 128.

Wolf, M., & Bowers, P. (1999). The 'double deficit hypothesis' for the developmental dyslexias. *Journal of Educational Psychology, 91,* 415–438. doi:10.1037//0022-0663.91.3.415

Potential Neurobehavioral Markers and Biological Mechanisms of Specific Language Impairment and Dyslexia

Introduction

R. Holly Fitch

The chapters in Section I addressed key aspects of early brain development that scientists are working to link to the growing knowledge about genetic mechanisms, including the multifaceted manner in which genetic anomalies can alter parameters of neurodevelopment. These early characterizations can be "followed" through time to subsequent neural and behavioral phenotypes—and more specifically, to phenotypes associated with language disruptions and developmental language disability.

The chapters in Section II addressed research that has increasingly defined early measures that predict and/or underlie emergent language and, moreover, may be used in young populations to screen for risk and predict subsequent outcomes.

Building upon work presented in the first two sections, we now move toward the evaluation of behavioral and neuromorphological phenotypes driven by the knowledge of both early genetic factors, as well as early and/or underlying phenotypic (behavioral) risk factors associated with language disability (LD). Such approaches can capitalize on the study of core behavioral phenotypes associated with disabilities of language—for example, by providing an evaluation of neuromorphological and behavioral consequences of manipulating candidate dyslexia susceptibility genes

(CDSGs) in nonhuman species, as well as by allowing for fine-grained assessment of morphological–functional correlations in human behavior and imaging studies. Both of these approaches to the complex gene–brain–behavior relationship underlying dyslexia can move us beyond an exclusive focus on a general diagnostic category and toward the identification of specific neural anomalies (or patterns of anomalies) associated with specific behavioral deficits.

To address this goal, Section III begins to map how variations in the function of specific genes implicated in developmental language disruption (CDGSs, as described in Chapter 2) may alter structural and morphometric neural measures in animal models (Rosen, Chapter 10). This approach gives specific attention to the characterization of genetically modulated anomalies in "language-relevant" brain regions, such as the cerebral cortex. Next, the section addresses how core behavioral intermediate phenotypes associated with language disabilities in humans also can be studied in animal models (Chapter 11) using reverse-genetic approaches that cannot be applied to human studies (Chapter 10). Specifically, Chapter 11 describes animal studies that provide a venue to experimentally manipulate early developmental factors (with techniques such as embryonic RNAi transfection) and then assess subsequent behaviors as identified in human clinical research. In the final two chapters of this section, authors address how fine-grained analysis of neuroanatomical measures from diagnosed populations—along with cross-correlations to behavioral measures constituting intermediate phenotypes (or core behavioral deficits) of language disability—can provide new and more accurate insights to brain–behavior associations within dyslexia (Chapters 12 and 13). Indeed, as noted in Chapter 13, "[The] multiplicity of candidate genes [implicated in dyslexia] is likely to reflect the significant variability observed in dyslexia at the behavioral level...[and in turn] various brain phenotypes....This...highlights the need to link all levels of analysis (gene–brain–behavior) in a nondogmatic way..." Eventually such an approach may dramatically increase our ability to identify and characterize "subgroups" within heterogenous clinical populations, using combinations of genetic screening, neuroimaging, and behavioral analysis.

The integration of data from these multifaceted and cross-species approaches will—it is hoped—allow the identification of points of overlap and linkage across diverse scientific approaches to dyslexia, ranging from molecular genetics to neuroimaging to clinical psychological evaluation. By identifying these cross-level research links, and detailing the associations across these many levels of analysis (as well as across development), scientists may be able to join together from disparate fields to produce a more accurate and "testable" composite picture of dyslexia than has been generated through research conducted separately within each field. This approach can in turn allow us to work toward the goal of "combining measures of behavior, neuroimaging, genetics and environment...in clinical and educational practices" (Black & Hoeft, Chapter 12).

In keeping with the mission of The Dyslexia Foundation conference series, such steps will be invaluable to the goal of individualized assessment and intervention that will unlock the potential of each child struggling on the one hand with a unique set of challenges, but who on the other hand has been painted with the broad-brush label of dyslexia.

Cortical Phenotypes Associated with Developmental Dyslexia
Reverse and Forward Genetic
Approaches Using Animal Models
Glenn D. Rosen

One of the more encouraging trends for those who have been in the field of dyslexia research since the 1980s is the increasing number of research disciplines that are now employed to investigate this important and difficult issue. Whereas a mere 30 years ago, there were but a handful of researchers who were examining developmental dyslexia (DD) within a rigorous scientific framework. The field is now populated by exceptional researchers from an astonishing diversity of fields, including (but not limited to) education, cognitive science, linguistics, neuroscience, and genetics. Whereas this is obviously good news, there are a number of institutional barriers that can sometimes act to diminish the potential impact of this cross-disciplinary work. Primary among these are the issues of communication (researchers in disparate fields often speak different dialects) and access (scientists in different fields do not often find themselves reading the same journals or attending the same meetings). One advantage of the type of meeting that resulted in this volume is that its small size and focused topic helped to break down these impediments to better understanding and, hopefully, multidisciplinary collaborative investigation.

In this chapter, I discuss some of the ongoing work that has been conducted and strongly influenced by research being carried out in genetics and cognitive science laboratories. I also present a newly resurrected method for performing research on mice that, by its very nature, lends itself to multiscalar integration of data and hypotheses. These data are presented with the ultimate goal of providing a link back to DD by demonstrating some of the similarities in research approaches, as well as in the commonalities of discoveries.

DEVELOPMENTAL DYSLEXIA AND THE BRAIN

Developmental dyslexia, which is usually diagnosed during early school age, is a common reading disability that affects 5%–10% of the population.

All of the work described here is the result of collaborations with a spectacular group of scientists, including, but not limited to, Albert M. Galaburda, R. Holly Fitch, Joe LoTurco, and Robert W. Williams. This work was supported by grants from the National Institutes of Health, R01NS052397, P01 HD057853, and P01 HD20806.

The defining symptom of DD is a severe and specific difficulty in reading acquisition that is unexpected in relation to other cognitive abilities and educational circumstances (Lyon, Shaywitz, & Shaywitz, 2003). At the cognitive level, there is widespread agreement that a large majority of children with dyslexia suffer from what is commonly termed a "phonological deficit"—a problem with some aspects of the mental representation and processing of speech sounds (Snowling, 2000). Evidence for this phonological deficit comes from three main behavioral symptoms: 1) poor phonological awareness; 2) poor verbal short-term memory; and 3) slow lexical retrieval (Ramus, 2006; Wagner & Torgesen, 1987). In addition to phonological awareness, they may also have difficulties in the speed of processing as diagnosed by their performance on tests of rapid naming (Wolf & Bowers, 2000).

Other behavioral symptoms are often associated with dyslexia, including various types of auditory, visual, and motor deficits. Purely visual processing problems may explain reading disability in some children with dyslexia, although the various theories of visual dyslexia need to be reconciled (see Chapter 3; Stein, 2001a, 2001b; Valdois, Bosse, & Tainturier, 2004). Auditory and motor disorders are often suggested to be the underlying cause of the phonological deficit (Eckert, 2004; Fitch & Tallal, 2003; Nagarajan et al., 1999; Nicolson, Fawcett, & Dean, 2001; Stein & Walsh, 1997). Critics argue, however, that the prevalence of these sensorimotor disorders is too low to explain the phonological deficits and that the disorders are not specific to dyslexia (Nicolson et al., 2001; White et al., 2006). On the other hand, studies also show highly significant predictive relationships between early auditory indices, obtained both behaviorally and by magnetoencephalography, for later language performance (see Chapter 7; Benasich et al., 2006). Presently, it remains to be determined to what extent sensorimotor disorders are casual to the reading disability or to what extent the disorders comprise only comorbid symptoms. It is likely that some of the difficulty comes from the possibility that there are several subtypes of DD, and research efforts are confounded by our inability to classify them accurately, and thus associate them to specific biological underpinnings.

Since the mid 1980s, researchers have attempted to understand the biological substrates underlying DD. Initial examination of postmortem dyslexic brains revealed abnormalities in cerebral asymmetry, abnormalities of cortical development in the perisylvian cortex, and abnormalities in the thalamus and cerebellum (Galaburda & Kemper, 1979; Galaburda, Sherman, Rosen, Aboitiz, & Geschwind, 1985; Humphreys, Kaufmann, & Galaburda, 1990). More recent findings on living participants with dyslexia studied *in vivo* using imaging approaches such as structural and functional MRI have served to confirm these postmortem findings. Specifically, anomalies of cerebral asymmetry and other morphometric differences are seen in the dyslexic brain (see review by Eckert, 2004), and relatively large cortical developmental anomalies in individuals with language disorders were also reported (Chang et al., 2005, 2007; de Oliveira et al., 2005; Sokol, Golomb, Carvahlo, & Edwards-Brown, 2006). Our laboratory has focused on the presence of relatively large numbers of small malformations of the cerebral cortex in the brains of people with dyslexia. These malformations occur during the period when neurons are migrating from their proliferative zones to the cerebral cortex—a process that is completed by midgestation in humans. What makes these neuronal-migration disorders unique is their distribution (predominantly in the perisylvian cortices of the left hemisphere) and their relatively focal nature.

The location of these cerebral cortical malformations suggests that they could produce difficulties in both high-level and low-level processing, thereby affecting perceptual, cognitive, and even metacognitive functions. As an example, involvement of the auditory-related cortical areas could be responsible for the difficulties with rapid sound processing, whereas involvement of prefrontal, anterior temporal, temporo-occipital, or inferior parietal cortices could explain problems with memory and phonological awareness. Furthermore, functional deficits could result from the spread of anatomical disruption from the areas of disordered migration to regions connected to them. As an example, there are abnormalities in visual and auditory nuclei of the thalamus of people with dyslexia—the lateral and medial geniculate nuclei, respectively. In the lateral geniculate nucleus, neurons of the magnocellular layers were approximately 30% smaller in dyslexics than in control brains (Livingstone, Rosen, Drislane, & Galaburda, 1991). In the medial geniculate nucleus (MGN), there was no difference in the average neuronal size, but there was a significant shift of neuronal sizes toward smaller neurons in the dyslexic left hemisphere (Galaburda, Menard, & Rosen, 1994).

In summary, there are a variety of cortical malformations and thalamic changes seen in the brains of postmortem people with dyslexia. The functional and behavioral effects of these malformations are difficult to gauge in humans; my colleagues and I have therefore concentrated our efforts on the use of animal models to dissect the link between development, anatomy, and behavior.

ANIMAL MODELS

Animal experiments in our laboratory are designed to model the anatomical findings from postmortem dyslexic brains. Principally, they have mimicked specific types of neuronal-migration disorders—molecular layer ectopias that occur spontaneously in mice (Sherman, Morrison, Rosen, Behan, & Galaburda, 1990; Sherman, Rosen, Stone, Press, & Galaburda, 1992) or larger microgyria that are induced in rats (Herman, Galaburda, Fitch, Carter, & Rosen, 1997; Humphreys, Rosen, Press, Sherman, & Galaburda, 1991; Rosen, Sherman, Richman, Stone, & Galaburda, 1992). The study of developmentally induced microgyria has provided important insights into possible mechanisms by which an individual with dyslexia could have concomitant deficits in phonological processing. The induction of microgyria (by freeze injury of the developing cerebral cortex) in rodents caused striking plasticity-mediated changes in the architecture and connectivity of the cortex (Rosen, Burstein, & Galaburda, 2000), which especially affects thalamocortical and corticothalamic projections. This reorganization leads to deficits in auditory processing similar to those seen in individuals with dyslexia, and could (in humans) be related to phonological deficits. Specifically, a series of studies performed by Fitch and colleagues revealed that focal microgyria are associated with rapid auditory processing deficits in rodent models (see Fitch, Chapter 11; Clark, Rosen, Tallal, & Fitch, 2000; Fitch, Brown, Tallal, & Rosen, 1997; Fitch, Tallal, Brown, Galaburda, & Rosen, 1994; Peiffer, Rosen, & Fitch, 2004). In particular, male rats with induced focal microgyria were unable to perform a two-tone discrimination task when the stimulus duration was relatively short. In contrast, sham animals and microgyric females performed well at all stimulus durations (Fitch et al., 1994, 1997).

Although the link between these animal models and DD is potentially important, there are a number of uncertainties that remain. For one, the percentage of individuals with dyslexia that exhibit neuronal-migration disorders is unknown because they are mostly too small to be able to be visualized using noninvasive techniques such as MRI or CT. Moreover, the link between the rodent models that have been employed and the human disorder is, at best, indirect. The remarkable expansion of knowledge concerning the human and mouse genome suggests another pathway by which researchers can begin to understand the biological substrates of DD. In the following section, I review some of the recent evidence of the role of genes in DD, and their role in brain development.

MODELING THE GENETICS OF DEVELOPMENTAL DYSLEXIA USING FORWARD AND REVERSE GENETICS

Recent advances spurred by the Human Genome Project have enabled greater precision in forward genetic approaches to the study of genotype/phenotype correlations. Forward genetic approaches, such as linkage analysis and genome-wide association studies, allow researchers to isolate specific genetic variants by starting with the phenotype and looking for genetic associations. The results of these studies in the human dyslexic population are reviewed elsewhere in this volume (see Chapters 2 and 5). To briefly review, linkage analysis points to dyslexic susceptibility loci on chromosome (Chr) 1 (Tzenova et al., 2004), Chr 2 (Fagerheim et al., 1999; Francks et al., 2002; Kaminen et al., 2003; Raskind et al., 2005), Chr 3 (Nopola-Hemmi et al., 2001), Chr 6 (Cardon et al., 1994; Deffenbacher et al., 2004; Gayán et al., 1999; Grigorenko et al., 1997; Grigorenko et al., 2000), Chr 7 (Kaminen et al., 2003), Chr 11 (Hsiung et al., 2004), Chr 15 (Smith et al., 1983; Grigorenko et al., 1997; Schulte-Korne et al.,

1998; Nothen et al., 1999; Morris et al., 2000; Nopola-Hemmi et al., 2000), Chr 18 (Fisher et al., 2002; Schumacher et al., 2006b), and Chr Xq27.3 (de Kovel et al., 2004). Candidate dyslexia susceptibility genes have been proposed within these intervals, including ROBO1 on Chr 3 (Hannula-Jouppi et al., 2005), genes—DCDC2 and KIAA0319—on Chr 6 (Cope et al., 2005; Francks et al., 2004; Lind et al., 2010; Meng et al., 2005; Paracchini et al., 2006, 2008; Schumacher et al., 2006a, 2008; Velayos-Baeza, Toma, Paracchini, & Monaco, 2008; Wilcke et al., 2009), DYX1C1 (also known as EKN1) on Chr 15 (Bates et al., 2009; Brkanac et al., 2007; Chapman et al., 2004; Dahdouh et al., 2009; Marino et al., 2007; Massinen et al., 2009; Taipale et al., 2003; Wigg et al., 2004), as well as other candidates on Chr 2 (Anthoni et al., 2007) and Chr 21 (Poelmans et al., 2009).

Recent work using reverse genetic approaches has demonstrated that at least some of these genes modulate common pathways involved in neuronal-migration and axon growth. In contrast to forward genetic approaches, reverse genetics starts with the gene and then examines how phenotypes are affected following manipulation of the gene. The most common experimental paradigm that uses a reverse genetic approach is knockout, in which mouse genes are removed from the genome and the effect of this removal on certain phenotypes ascertained. There are other reverse genetic approaches as well, and we have adopted the RNAi strategy pioneered by LoTurco (see Chapter 2) of in utero electroporation of plasmids encoding short hairpin RNAs (shRNA). Specifically, shRNA plasmids targeted against dyslexia susceptibility genes (or, alternatively, plasmids designed to overexpress the gene) are injected into the cerebral ventricles of embryonic rats and then electroporated into the progenitor cells of the cerebral cortex. Subsequent examination of these transfected cells allow for the assessment of the effect of altering the expression of these genes on neuronal development.

Initial results from LoTurco's laboratory showed evidence that embryonic knockdown of the rodent homologs Dcdc2, Kiaa0319, and Dyx1c1 (Meng et al., 2005; Paracchini et al., 2006; Wang et al., 2006) resulted in the disruption of neuronal migration when examined 4–7 days after transfection. Work in our laboratory has concentrated on the effect of these disruptions on the eventual organization of the brain of these animals. We confirmed that embryonic transfections with shRNA targeted against Dyx1c1 disrupted neuronal migration (Rosen et al., 2007). We found that there were clusters of transfected cells located at the white matter border of the neocortex (heterotopia), which presumably failed to migrate to their adult position. It is interesting to note that, only a subset of these cells were transfected, which suggests that at least some of the neurons did not migrate because of secondary, noncell autonomous effects rather than a direct effect of Dyx1c1 RNAi transfection. My colleagues and I have recently confirmed this finding, as we have shown that GABAergic neurons, which are generated in a different portion of the brain from cortical neurons and are therefore not transfected, are also abundantly found in these heterotopias. There were other effects on neuronal migration that were not as evident as the heterotopias. For example, in controls, transfected neurons migrate mostly to layer 3 of the neocortex, whereas there were far more neurons scattered in the lower layers in *Dyx1c1* shRNA-transfected animals. It is interesting to note that those those that did migrate were found superficial to layer 3, a phenotype we have termed "overmigration."

Similar results were found following following *Kiaa0319*. As with *Dyx1c1*, there are essentially two populations of labeled cells in the neocortex. One population of cells was clustered around the white matter border, and another group of neurons had migrated (but did not overmigrate) to upper cortical layers. There was evidence of noncell autonomous effects as well, as there were large numbers of nontransfected neurons (both GABAergic and nonGABAergic) in the heterotopia. In the upper layers of the *Kiaa0319* shRNA transfection, all transfected cells had normal neuronal morphology and were radially oriented with respect to the pial surface. Of the deeper transfected neurons, there were large numbers that were not radially oriented as expected but instead showed apical dendrites that were aligned in seemingly random orientations. We found that neurons transfected with *Kiaa0319* shRNA had hypertrophy of apical, but not basal, dendrites. This supports the notion that *Kiaa0319* may have effects on neuronal development that range beyond the time period of neuronal migration (Peschansky et al., 2009).

Finally, my colleagues and I examined a series of brains that had been embryonically transfected with RNAi targeted against *Dcdc2* (Burbridge et al., 2008). Transfected cells were found either clustered around the white matter border with the neocortex, or overmigrated in the upper cortical layers. Some of the neurons terminated their migration in layer 1, which is a unique feature of this dyslexia susceptibility gene knockdown experiment. There was abnormal orientation of a portion of the transfected neurons in both the lower and upper cortical layers, and LoTurco's laboratory has shown that the dendritic outgrowth is disrupted in these cells (see LoTurco et al., Chapter 2 in this volume). Many of the abnormal cells had the morphology of pyramidal neurons, but their apical dendrites were not radially aligned with the neocortical surface.

These studies, as well as those described in Chapters 2 and 11, have demonstrated how one can use reverse genetic approaches to explore the function of genes originally identified using forward genetic approaches in the human population affected by dyslexia. In our case, my colleagues and I began with genes linked to the complex phenotype of DD and then concentrated our efforts on looking for functional effects on brain development. Other investigators can and have used the same genetic information to investigate how candidate dyslexia susceptibility function has an impact on any number of other phenotypes, including cognitive, behavioral, or physiological ones. In the next section, we discuss how we can use forward genetic approaches in mice to identify genes and gene networks that modulate the neuronal-migration phenotype. We suggest ways that this approach can be then used to further inform research on DD.

GENETIC REFERENCE POPULATIONS

Since the early 2000s, there has been a revitalizaion of the use of genetic reference panels of recombinant inbred (RI) strains in biomedical research. These strains were considered a research "backwater" that would soon be replaced by powerful reverse genetic methods, such as mutagenesis or conditional knockout technology. Now, genetic reference panels are regarded as a highly complementary companion to single gene perturbations. As researchers, we use the BXD recombinant inbred panel, which was created by breeding C57BL/6J and DBA/2J (as described in Figure 10.1). In brief, the parental strains generate an F1 generation that is isogenic, having inherited one chromosome from each parent. The progeny from this generation are bred to produce the F2 generation, which now incorporates recombinations of the parental chromosomes. Inbreeding starts with the F2, and after at least 20 generations of full brother–sister mating a set of isogenic and highly recombinant strains are generated. Each strain has a complex but fixed mixture of recombined chromosome segments inherited from the parent strains.

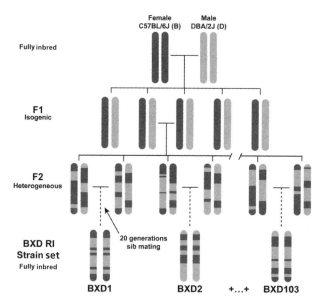

Figure 10.1. Breeding scheme used to generate the panel of BXD recombinant inbred strains. C57BL/6J females were mated with DBA/2J males. Pairs of chromosomes for the two inbred parents are shown in dark and light. F1 progeny are intercrossed. The F2 generation now incorporates recombinations of the parental chromosomes. Inbreeding starts with the F2 progeny. After at least 20 generations of full-sibling mating, a set of isogenic and highly recombinant strains, each with a complex but fixed mixture of recombined-chromosome segments inherited from the parent strains is generated. The number of BXDs in a panel is determined by the number of independent sibling matings at F2.

What are the advantages of this genetic reference panel? First, these panels of genetically diverse strains can be considered experimentally tractable surrogates for complex human populations. They provide "population models" that incorporate a controlled degree of genetic and phenotypic variation that corresponds more closely to those of human populations used in linkage and genome-wide association studies (GWAS). Second, the BXD line contains more than 80 strains, which allows more precise mapping of genetic traits. Third, the parent strains have now been fully genotyped at sufficient density such that individual single nucleotide polymorphisms (SNPs), insertions/deletions, and copy number variants are mapped for the entire genome. This allows the identification of specific gene variants associated with whatever phenotype we choose to measure. Finally, this RI line has been adopted as a research resource by more than 100 groups worldwide. What this means is that there is now an effective way to build a platform for a research community. Common data and tools can be shared across many domains (Williams, 2009), enabling a new type of data-centric, rather than concept-centric, collaboration.

As it turns out, this last advantage has provided a major boost toward exploiting this particular genetic reference panel as a tool for examination of systems genetics. Thus, the major promise of RI strains has always been in mapping quantitative trait loci (Belknap, 1992; Nesbitt, 1992; Neumann, 1992; Plomin, McClearn, Gora-Maslak, & Neiderhiser, 1991). Quantitative trait loci (QTLs) are normal genes or gene promoter regions that have relatively subtle quantitative effects on phenotypes (Lynch & Walsh, 1998) and are equivalent to susceptibility loci in humans. QTLs are often contrasted with Mendelian loci that have pronounced, and usually dichotomous, effects on phenotypes. In contrast, systems genetics is a relatively new branch of quantitative genetics that aims to understand complex networks of interactions across multiple levels. The goal is to predict risk and outcome on the basis of genotype, exposure history, and treatment. Whereas Mendelian genetics can be defined as the search for causal linkage between single traits and single gene variants (a one-to-one relation), and complex trait analysis can be defined as the search for linkages between single traits and sets of gene variants (one-to-many), systems genetics is the search for webs of causal interactions among sets of traits, networks of genes, and networks of developmental/environmental/epigenetic factors (many-to-many-to-many). In the following section, I detail some recent work in the laboratory that has taken advantage of some of these genetics tools to examine the systems genetics of neuronal-migration disorders.

GENOME-WIDE ASSOCIATION STUDY OF NEURONAL MIGRATION DISORDERS

As mentioned previously, disturbances of neuronal migration during the formation of the cerebral cortex have been associated with a wide variety of developmental disorders, ranging from severe intellectual disability to epilepsy to autism to DD (Andrade, 2009; Kuzniecky, 2006; Leventer, Guerrini, & Dobyns, 2008). I have discussed some rodent models that have proven to supply useful information as to the function of genes (in this particular case, dyslexia susceptibility genes) that are associated with neuronal migration. There are, of course, a number of other models that have been generated to investigate some of the genes involved in the complex process of neuronal migration, and a number of strains (knockout, mutant, and standard inbred) with neuronal-migration disorders have been identified. For example, approximately 25%–35% of C57BL/6J (B6) mice have ectopic collections of neurons in layer 1 of the neocortex (ectopias, see Figure 10.2.A). Because B6 mice are one of the parent strains of the BXD RI line, we examined the BXD set (and the parentals) for the presence of neocortical neuronal-migration disorders. This is essentially identical to performing a genome-wide association study in a human genetic reference population.

My colleagues and I screened the brains of more than 800 mice that represented 76 recombinant BXD inbred and 2 parental strains (approximately 10 mice per strain). Of these, 108 mice representing 43 strains had ectopias with the within-strain incidence ranging from 7%–100% (with a mean of approximately 28%). There were, therefore, 33 RI strains with no evidence of neocortical ectopias or other migration disturbances (Figure 10.2.B). We then used the percent incidence for each strain to map QTLs modulating neuronal-migration disorders.

We performed interval mapping, which is basically a regression of the strain phenotype (percent incidence) with the known genotypes for each strain. A significant linkage between genotype and phenotype indicates that there is a high likelihood that the phenotype is modulated by a gene lying within that interval. Mapping percent incidence of neuronal-migration disorders revealed a QTL on distal Chr 5 (Figure 10.3.A). We used bioinformatic resources to evaluate the 54 genes contained within this QTL interval. The first step in narrowing down the list of candidate genes was to select those genes that had allelic differences between the two parent strains. Recall that all BXD mice have inherited genes from the mother (B6) or father (D2). In order for there to be a significant relationship between our phenotype and a genotype, there has to be a difference between the B6 and D2 alleles at that interval. We therefore narrowed down the list of viable candidate genes by first choosing those that have missense SNPs between the two parent strains, indicating that there were allelic differences between the B6 and D2 version of this gene. We next used public databases, as well as our own databases, to find those genes that were expressed in the developing cerebral cortex. Finally, we performed a detailed literature search on each of the genes that had passed through this bioinformatic gauntlet. Using these criteria, we were able to isolate a likely candidate gene, *Sparcl1*, which has been previously shown to be involved in neuronal migration (Gongidi et al., 2004; Weimer et al., 2008; Yokota et al., 2007).

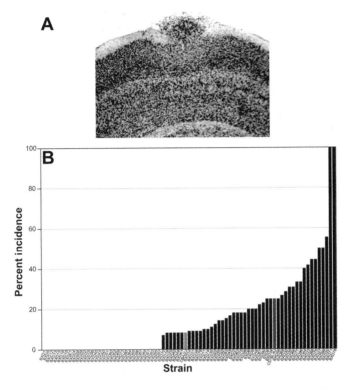

Figure 10.2. A) Ectopia collection of neurons in the upper layer of the cerebral cortex of a C57BL/6J mouse. B) Histogram showing the percent incidence of ectopias in 73 BXD strains (black bars) and parentals (grey bars).

Our next step was to see whether we could determine whether there were any genetic modulators of *Sparcl1* expression. To do this, we used a database of cortical gene expression in the BXD RI line that we had created using microarrays—a technology that allows us to simultaneously assay gene expression of virtually the entire mouse genome. We first looked to see whether there were any genes that modulated the expression of *Sparcl1* by performing a linkage analysis identical to that above but in this case using *Sparcl1* expression as the phenotype and seeing where in the genome its expression is modulated. We found that there was a significant expression QTL (eQTL) on Chr 7 that modulated the expression of Sparcl1 on Chr 5 (Figure 10.3.B). This is what is known as a trans-eQTL, meaning that one gene is modulating expression of a different gene. This is in contrast to a cis-eQTL, in which a gene modulates its own expression.

Further examination of this region on Chr 7 indicated that it was syntenic (i.e., homologous) to the region on human Chr 15 that has been linked to two related neurological disorders—Prader-Willi and Angelman syndromes—and contains genes that have been proposed as candidate genes for autism (Bucan et al., 2009). It is interesting to note that

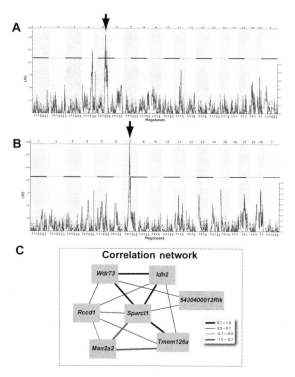

Figure 10.3. A) Likelihood ratio statistic (LRS) scores for percent incidence of ectopias across the entire genome. The x-axis represents the physical map of the chromosome; the y-axis and thick line provide the LRS of the association between the trait and the genotypes of markers. The two dashed horizontal lines are the suggestive and significance thresholds computed using 1,000 permutations. There is a QTL (arrow) on the distal end of Chr 5. B) LRS scores for *Sparcl1* expression across the entire genome. There is a significant eQTL on Chr 7. C) Highly significant intercorrelations with genes in the Chr 7 eQTL interval and *Sparcl1*. (*Key: Wdr73* = WD repeat domain 73; *Idh2* = isocitrate dehydrogenase 2 (NADP+), mitochondrial; *54050012Rik* = RIKEN cDNA 5430400D12 gene; *Tmem126a* = transmembrane protein 126A; *Man2a2* = mannosidase 2, alpha 2; *Rccd1* = RCC1 domain containing 1; *Sparcl1* = SPARC-like 1.)

this interval on Chr 7 modulates the expression of many other genes throughout the chromosome, which suggests that there may be either a single "master" gene (perhaps a transcription factor) that modulates the expression of many genes, or perhaps a well-integrated gene network that acts in the same capacity. We have preliminarily begun to dissect this gene network by correlating the strain distribution pattern for our *Sparcl1* expression against the expression of all the gene transcripts in our database. We found a number of genes whose expression is highly intercorrelated, and we have created a putative gene network map indicating how they relate (Figure 10.3.C). We are presently investigating exactly how these genes might interact to modulate the incidence of neuronal migration disorders.

What is most intriguing about these genetic reference panels is that we may no longer be limited to forward genetic approaches, which dramatically increases the power of reference panels (e.g., the BXD set). Now that both parental strains have been sequenced, it is possible to radically revise the way in which complex trait analysis is performed. Instead of starting from phenotypic differences and painstakingly working down to gene loci and QTLs, it is now possible to reverse the flow and to work upward from known sequence variants to phenotypes—in a manner similar to other reverse genetic approaches, such as those described in the first section of this chapter. In other words, once it is known that that are variations in sequence between the B6 and D2 parents, it is possible to isolate populations of BXD strains that contain one or the other variant, and then use these strains in a phenotype screen. Recent studies demonstrate the power of this approach (Carneiro et al., 2009; Ciobanu et al., 2010).

CONCLUSIONS

DD is a complex disorder, and there are a myriad of ways that a brain could be organized that would make learning to read difficult. As an example, the chapters in this volume suggest a number of plausible mechanisms whereby a brain can "become dyslexic." Given this fact, it is reasonable to suggest that the genes that modulate DD are going to reflect the complexity of the disorder. It is surely not that case that a single gene will explain all of dyslexia. In fact, it is highly likely that there are many genes that will underlie the disorder. Even more likely is the possibility that the complex phenotype we know as DD is regulated by a large and complex gene network comprised of scores of genes that interact in ways not yet amenable to easy dissection.

Because of our extended interest in the role of neuronal-migration disorders and dyslexia, my colleagues and I have naturally focused our research interests there. It is important to emphasize, however, that the genetic tools outlined in this chapter are amenable for the investigation of virtually any phenotype that can be modeled in animals. Thus, one could start with a particular brain or cognitive phenotype, and dissect the genetic modulation of that phenotype using forward genetic approaches. Having identified a gene locus by this approach, one could then perform linkage analysis in human populations to see if this gene variant is related to the disorder of interest (in our case, DD). Conversely, one could use reverse genetic approaches to isolate phenotypic differences that are related to DD and similarly confirm them in human populations. Finally, one can continue to investigate the function of known dyslexia susceptibility genes in animals with the intriguing possibility that they might lead to interesting biological or cognitive markers that could be investigated in human populations.

Clearly, one of the key problems for research on DD going forward is finding a way to integrate the findings from cognitive science, physiology, psychology, and neuroscience. Experimental genetics, using both forward and reverse approaches, has the potential to provide important insights into a wide variety of topics. Moreover, the experimental paradigms presented here offer unique opportunities for linking together research from disparate disciplines. Researchers recognize that this eventually has to translate to humans, but it is certainly the case that animal models can play a strong part in this effort.

REFERENCES

Andrade, D.M. (2009). Genetic basis in epilepsies caused by malformations of cortical development and in those with structurally normal brain. *Human Genetics, 126*(1), 173–193. doi:10.1007/s00439-009-0702-1

Anthoni, H., Zucchelli, M., Matsson, H., Muller-Myhsok, B., Fransson, I., Schumacher, J., ... Peyrard-Janvid, M. (2007). A locus on 2p12 containing the co-regulated MRPL19 and C2ORF3 genes is associated to dyslexia. *Human Molecular Genetics, 16*(6), 667–677. doi:10.1093/hmg/ddm009

Bates, T.C., Lind, P.A., Luciano, M., Montgomery, G.W., Martin, N.G., & Wright, M.J. (2009). Dyslexia and DYX1C1: Deficits in reading and spelling associated with a missense mutation. *Molecular Psychiatry, 15*(12), 1190–1196. doi:10.1038/mp.2009.120

Belknap, J.K. (1992). Empirical estimates of Bonferroni corrections for use in chromosome mapping studies with the BXD recombinant inbred strains. *Behavior Genetics, 22*(6), 677–684. doi:10.1007/BF01066638

Benasich, A.A., Choudhury, N., Friedman, J.T., Realpe-Bonilla, T., Chojnowska, C., & Gou, Z. (2006). The infant as a prelinguistic model for language learning impairments: predicting from event-related potentials to behavior. *Neuropsychologia, 44*(3), 396–411. doi:10.1016/j.neuropsychologia.2005.06.004

Brkanac, Z., Chapman, N.H., Matsushita, M.M., Chun, L., Nielsen, K., Cochrane, E., ... Raskind, W.H. (2007). Evaluation of candidate genes for DYX1 and DYX2 in families with dyslexia. *American Journal of Medical Genetics Part B: Neuropsychiatric Genetics, 144B*(4), 556–560.

Bucan, M., Abrahams, B.S., Wang, K., Glessner, J.T., Herman, E.I., Sonnenblick, L.I., ... Hakonarson, H. (2009). Genome-wide analyses of exonic copy number variants in a family based study point to novel autism susceptibility genes. *PLoS Genetics, 5*(6), e1000536. doi:10.1371/journal.pgen.1000536

Burbridge, T., Wang, Y., Volz, A., Peschansky, V., Lisann, L., Galaburda, A.M., ... Rosen, G.D. (2008). Postnatal analysis of the effect of embryonic knockdown and overexpression of candidate dyslexia susceptibility gene DCDC2. *Neuroscience, 152*(3), 723–733. doi:10.1016/j.neuroscience.2008.01.020

Cardon, L.R., Smith, S.D., Fulker, D.W., Kimberling, W.J., Pennington, B.F., & DeFries, J.C. (1994). Quantitative trait locus for reading disability on chromosome 6. *Science, 266*(5182), 276–279. doi:10.1126/science.7939663

Carneiro, A.M., Airey, D.C., Thompson, B., Zhu, C.B., Lu, L., Chesler, E.J., ... Blakely, R.D. (2009). Functional coding variation in recombinant inbred mouse lines reveals multiple serotonin transporter-associated phenotypes. *Proceedings of the National Academy of Sciences, USA, 106*(6), 2047–2052. doi:10.1073/pnas.0809449106

Chang, B.S., Katzir, T., Liu, T., Corriveau, K., Barzillai, M., Apse, K.A., ... Walsh, C.A. (2007). A structural basis for reading fluency: White matter defects in a genetic brain malformation. *Neurology, 69*(23), 2146–2154. doi:10.1212/01.wnl.0000286365.41070.54

Chang, B.S., Ly, J., Appignani, B., Bodell, A., Apse, K.A., Ravenscroft, R.S., ... Walsh, C.A. (2005). Reading impairment in the neuronal-migration disorder of periventricular nodular heterotopia. *Neurology, 64*(5), 799–803. doi:10.1212/01.WNL.0000152874.57180.AF

Chapman, N.H., Igo, R.P., Thomson, J.B., Matsushita, M., Brkanac, Z., Holzman, T., ... Raskind, W.H. (2004). Linkage analyses of four regions previously implicated in dyslexia: Confirmation of a locus on chromosome 15q. *American Journal of Medical Genetics Part B: Neuropsychiatric Genetics, 131B*(1), 67–75. doi:10.1002/ajmg.b.30018

Ciobanu, D.C., Lu, L., Mozhui, K., Wang, X., Jagalur, M., Morris, J.A., ... Williams, R.W. (2010). Detection, validation, and downstream analysis of allelic variation in gene expression. *Genetics, 184*(1), 119–128. doi:10.1534/genetics.109.107474

Clark, M.G., Rosen, G.D., Tallal, P., & Fitch, R.H. (2000). Impaired processing of complex auditory stimuli in rats with induced cerebrocortical microgyria: An animal model of developmental language disabilities. *Journal of Cognitive Neuroscience, 12*(5), 828–839. doi:10.1162/089892900562435

Cope, N., Harold, D., Hill, G., Moskvina, V., Stevenson, J., Holmans, P., ... Williams, J. (2005). Strong evidence that KIAA0319 on chromosome 6p is a susceptibility gene for developmental dyslexia. *American Journal of Human Genetics, 76*(4), 581–591. doi:10.1086/429131

Dahdouh, F., Anthoni, H., Tapia-Paez, I., Peyrard-Janvid, M., Schulte-Korne, G., Warnke, A., ... Zucchelli, M. (2009). Further evidence for DYX1C1 as a susceptibility factor for dyslexia. *Psychiatric Genetics, 19*(2), 59–63. doi:10.1097/YPG.0b013e32832080e1

de Kovel, C.G., Hol, F.A., Heister, J.G., Willemen, J.J., Sandkuijl, L.A., Franke, B., & Padberg, G.W. (2004). Genome-wide scan identifies susceptibility locus for dyslexia on Xq27 in an extended Dutch family. *Journal Medical Genetics, 41*(9), 652–657. doi:10.1136/jmg.2003.012294

de Oliveira, E.P., Guerreiro, M.M., Guimaraes, C.A., Brandao-Almeida, I.L., Montenegro, M.A., Cendes, F., & Hage, S.R. (2005). Characterization of the linguistic profile of a family with Perisylvian Syndrome. *Pro Fono, 17*(3), 393–402.

Deffenbacher, K.E., Kenyon, J.B., Hoover, D.M., Olson, R.K., Pennington, B.F., DeFries, J.C., & Smith, S.D. (2004). Refinement of the 6p21.3 quantitative trait locus influencing dyslexia: Linkage and association analyses. *Human Genetics, 115*(2), 128–138. doi:10.1007/s00439-004-1126-6

Eckert, M. (2004). Neuroanatomical markers for dyslexia: A review of dys-lexia structural imaging studies. *Neuroscientist, 10*(4), 362–371. doi:10.1177/1073858404263596

Fagerheim, T., Raeymaekers, P., Tonnessen, F.E., Pedersen, M., Tranebjaerg, L., & Lubs, H.A. (1999). A new gene (DYX3) for dyslexia is located on chromosome 2. *Journal of Medical Genetics, 36*(9), 664–669.

Fisher, S.E., Francks, C., Marlow, A.J., MacPhie, I.L., Newbury, D.F., Cardon, L.R., ... Monaco, A.P. (2002). Independent genome-wide scans identify a chromosome 18 quantitative-trait locus influencing dyslexia. *Nature Genetics, 30*(1), 86–91. doi:10.1038/ng792

Fitch, R.H., Brown, C.P., Tallal, P., & Rosen, G.D. (1997). Effects of sex and MK-801 on auditory-processing deficits associated with developmental microgyric lesions in rats. *Behavioral Neuroscience, 111*(2), 404–412. doi:10.1037//0735-7044.111.2.404

Fitch, R.H., & Tallal, P. (2003). Neural mechanisms of language-based learning impairments: Insights from human populations and animal models. *Behavioral and Cognitive Neuroscience Review, 2*(3), 155–178. doi:10.1177/1534582303258736

Fitch, R.H., Tallal, P., Brown, C., Galaburda, A.M., & Rosen, G.D. (1994). Induced microgyria and auditory temporal processing in rats: A model for language impairment? *Cerebral Cortex, 4*(3), 260–270. doi:10.1093/cercor/4.3.260

Francks, C., Fisher, S.E., Olson, R.K., Pennington, B.F., Smith, S.D., DeFries, J.C., & Monaco, A. (2002). Fine mapping of the chromosome 2p12-16 dyslexia susceptibility locus: Quantitative association analysis and positional candidate genes SEMA4F and OTX1. *Psychiatric Genetics, 12*(1), 35–41. doi:10.1097/00041444-200203000-00005

Francks, C., Paracchini, S., Smith, S.D., Richardson, A.J., Scerri, T.S., Cardon, L.R., ... Monaco, A.P. (2004). A 77-kilobase region of chromosome 6p22.2 is associated with dyslexia in families from the United Kingdom and from the United States. *American Journal of Human Genetics, 75*(6), 1046–1058. doi:10.1086/426404

Galaburda, A.M., & Kemper, T.L. (1979). Cytoarchitectonic abnormalities in developmental dyslexia: A case study. *Annals of Neurology, 6,* 94–100. doi:10.1002/ana.410060203

Galaburda, A.M., Menard, M.T., & Rosen, G.D. (1994). Evidence for aberrant auditory anatomy in developmental dyslexia. *Proceedings of the National Academy of Sciences, USA, 91*(17), 8010–8013. doi:10.1073/pnas.91.17.8010

Galaburda, A.M., Sherman, G.F., Rosen, G.D., Aboitiz, F., & Geschwind, N. (1985). Developmental dyslexia: Four consecutive cases with cortical anomalies. *Annals of Neurology, 18,* 222–233.

Gayán, J., & Olson, R.K. (1999). Reading disability: evidence for a genetic etiology. *European Child Adolescent Psychiatry, 8* Suppl 3, 52–55. doi: 10.1007/PL00010695

Gongidi, V., Ring, C., Moody, M., Brekken, R., Sage, E.H., Rakic, P., & Anton, E.S. (2004). SPARC-like 1 regulates the terminal phase of radial glia-guided migration in the cerebral cortex. *Neuron, 41*(1), 57–69. doi:10.1016/S0896-6273(03)00818-3

Grigorenko, E.L., Wood, F.B., Meyer, M.S., Hart, L.A., Speed, W.C., Shuster, A., & Pauls, D.L. (1997). Susceptibility loci for distinct components of developmental dyslexia on chromosomes 6 and 15. *American Journal of Human Genetics, 60*(1), 27–39.

Grigorenko, E.L., Wood, F.B., Meyer, M.S., & Pauls, D.L. (2000). Chromosome 6p influences on different dyslexia-related cognitive processes: Further confirmation. *American Journal of Human Genetics, 66*(2), 715–723. doi:10.1086/302755

Hannula-Jouppi, K., Kaminen-Ahola, N., Taipale, M., Eklund, R., Nopola-Hemmi, J., Kaariainen, H., & Kere, J. (2005). The axon guidance receptor gene ROBO1 is a candidate gene for developmental dyslexia. *PLoS Genetics, 1*(4), e50. doi:10.1371/journal.pgen.0010050

Herman, A.E., Galaburda, A.M., Fitch, R.H., Carter, A.R., & Rosen, G.D. (1997). Cerebral microgyria, thalamic cell size and auditory temporal processing in male and female rats. *Cerebral Cortex, 7,* 453–464. doi:10.1093/cercor/7.5.453

Hsiung, G.Y., Kaplan, B.J., Petryshen, T.L., Lu, S., & Field, L.L. (2004). A dyslexia susceptibility locus (DYX7) linked to dopamine D4 receptor (DRD4) region on chromosome 11p15.5. *American Journal of Medical Genetics, 125B*(1), 112–119. doi:10.1002/ajmg.b.20082

Humphreys, P., Kaufmann, W.E., & Galaburda, A.M. (1990). Developmental dyslexia in women: Neuropathological findings in three cases. *Annals of Neurology, 28,* 727–738.

Humphreys, P., Rosen, G.D., Press, D.M., Sherman, G.F., & Galaburda, A.M. (1991). Freezing lesions of the newborn rat brain: A model for cerebrocortical microgyria. *Journal of Neuropathic and Experimental Neurology, 50,* 145–160.

Kaminen, N., Hannula-Jouppi, K., Kestila, M., Lahermo, P., Muller, K., Kaaranen, M., … Kere, J. (2003). A genome scan for developmental dyslexia confirms linkage to chromosome 2p11 and suggests a new locus on 7q32. *Journal of Medical Genetics, 40*(5), 340–345. doi:10.1136/jmg.40.5.340

Kuzniecky, R.I. (2006). Malformations of cortical development and epilepsy, part 1: Diagnosis and classification scheme. *Reviews in Neurological Diseases, 3*(4), 151–162.

Leventer, R.J., Guerrini, R., & Dobyns, W.B. (2008). Malformations of cortical development and epilepsy. *Dialogues in Clinical Neurosciences, 10*(1), 47–62.

Lind, P.A., Luciano, M., Wright, M.J., Montgomery, G.W., Martin, N.G., & Bates, T.C. (2010). Dyslexia and DCDC2: Normal variation in reading and spelling is associated with DCDC2 polymorphisms in an Australian population sample. *European Journal of Human Genetics, 18*(6), 668–673. doi:10.1038/ejhg.2009.237

Livingstone, M., Rosen, G., Drislane, F., & Galaburda, A. (1991). Physiological and anatomical evidence for a magnocellular defect in developmental dyslexia. *Proceedings of the National Academy of Sciences, USA, 88*(18), 7943–7947. doi:10.1073/pnas.88.18.7943

Lynch, M., & Walsh, B. (1998). *Genetics and analysis of quantitative traits.* Sunderland, MA: Sinauer.

Lyon, G.R., Shaywitz, S.E., & Shaywitz, B.A. (2003). A definition of dyslexia. *Annals of Dyslexia, 53,* 1–14. doi:10.1007/s11881-003-0001-9

Marino, C., Citterio, A., Giorda, R., Facoett, I.A., Menozzi, G., Vanzin, L., … Molteni, M. (2007). Association of short-term memory with a variant within DYX1C1 in developmental dyslexia. *Genes, Brain and Behavior, 6*(7), 640–646. doi:10.1111/j.1601-183X.2006.00291

Massinen, S., Tammimies, K., Tapia-Paez, I., Matsson, H., Hokkanen,

M.E., Soderberg, O., ... Kere, J. (2009). Functional interaction of DYX1C1 with estrogen receptors suggests involvement of hormonal pathways in dyslexia. *Human Molecular Genetics, 18*(15), 2802–2812. doi:10.1093/hmg/ddp215

Meng, H., Smith, S.D., Hager, K., Held, M., Liu, J., Olson, R.K., ... Gruen, J.R. (2005). DCDC2 is associated with reading disability and modulates neuronal development in the brain. *Proceedings of the National Academy of Sciences, USA, 102*(47), 17053–17058. doi:10.1073/pnas.0508591102

Morris, D.W., Robinson, L., Turic, D., Duke, M., Webb, V., Milham, C., ... Williams, J. (2000). Family-based association mapping provides evidence for a gene for reading disability on chromosome 15q. *Human Molecular Genetics, 9*(5), 843–848. doi:10.1093/hmg/9.5.843

Nagarajan, S., Mahncke, H., Salz, T., Tallal, P., Roberts, T., & Merzenich, M.M. (1999). Cortical auditory signal processing in poor readers. *Proceedings of the National Academy of Sciences, USA, 96*(11), 6483–6488. doi:10.1073/pnas.96.11.6483

Nesbitt, M. (1992). The value of recombinant inbred strains in genetic analysis of behavior. In D. Goldowitz, D. Wahlsten, & R. Wimer (Eds.), *Techniques for the genetic analysis of brain and behavior: Focus on the mouse* (pp. 141–146). Amsterdam: Elsevier.

Neumann, P.E. (1992). Inference in linkage analysis of multifactorial traits using recombinant inbred strains of mice. *Behavior Genetics, 22*(6), 665–676. doi:10.1007/BF01066637

Nicolson, R., Fawcett, A.J., & Dean, P. (2001). Dyslexia, development and the cerebellum. *Trends in Neuroscience, 24*(9), 515–516. doi:10.1016/S0166-2236(00)01923-8

Nopola-Hemmi, J., Myllyluoma, B., Haltia, T., Taipale, M., Ollikainen, V., Ahonen, T., ... Widen, E. (2001). A dominant gene for developmental dyslexia on chromosome 3. *Journal of Medical Genetics, 38*(10), 658–664. doi:10.1136/jmg.38.10.658

Nopola-Hemmi, J., Taipale, M., Haltia, T., Lehesjoki, A.E., Voutilainen, A., & Kere, J. (2000). Two translocations of chromosome 15q associated with dys-lexia. *Journal of Medical Genetics, 37*(10), 771–775. doi:10.1136/jmg.37.10.771

Nothen, M.M., Schulte-Korne, G., Grimm, T., Cichon, S., Vogt, I.R., Muller-Myhsok, B., ... Remschmidt, H. (1999). Genetic linkage analysis with dyslexia: evidence for linkage of spelling disability to chromosome 15. *European Child Adolescent Psychiatry, 8* Suppl 3, 56–59. doi: 10.1007/PL00010696

Paracchini, S., Steer, C.D., Buckingham, L.L., Morris, A.P., Ring, S., Scerri, T., ... Monaco, A.P. (2008). Association of the KIAA0319 dyslexia susceptibility gene with reading skills in the general population. *American Journal of Psychiatry, 165*(12), 1576–1584. doi:10.1176/appi.ajp.2008.07121872

Paracchini, S., Thomas, A., Castro, S., Lai, C., Paramasivam, M., Wang, Y., ... Monaco, A.P. (2006). The chromosome 6p22 haplotype associated with dyslexia reduces the expression of KIAA0319, a novel gene involved in neuronal migration. *Human Molecular Genetics, 15*, 1659–1666. doi:10.1093/hmg/ddl089

Peiffer, A.M., Rosen, G.D., & Fitch, R.H. (2004). Sex differences in rapid auditory processing deficits in microgyric rats. *Developmental Brain Research, 148*(1), 53–57. doi:10.1016/j.devbrainres.2003.09.020

Peschansky, V.J., Burbridge, T.J., Volz, A.J., Fiondella, C., Wissner-Gross, Z., Galaburda, A.M., ... Rosen, G.D. (2009). The effect of variation in expression of the candidate dyslexia susceptibility gene Homolog Kiaa0319 on neuronal migration and dendritic morphology in the rat. *Cerebral Cortex, 20*(4), 884–897. doi:10.1093/cercor/bhp154

Plomin, R., McClearn, G.E., Gora-Maslak, G., & Neiderhiser, J.M. (1991). Use of recombinant inbred strains to detect quantitative trait loci associated with behavior. *Behavior Genetics, 21*(2), 99–116. doi:10.1007/BF01066330

Poelmans, G., Engelen, J.J., Van Lent-Albrechts, J., Smeets, H.J., Schoenmakers, E., Franke, B., ... Schrander-Stumpel, C. (2009). Identification of novel dyslexia candidate genes through the analysis of a chromosomal deletion. *American Journal of Medical Genetics Part B: Neuropsychiatric Genetics, 150B*(1), 140–147. doi:10.1002/ajmg.b.30787

Ramus, F. (2006). Genes, brain, and cognition: A roadmap for the cognitive scientist. *Cognition, 101*(2), 247–269. doi:10.1016/j.cognition.2006.04.003

Raskind, W.H., Igo, R.P., Chapman, N.H., Berninger, V.W., Thomson, J.B., Matsushita, M., ... Wijsman, E.M. (2005). A genome scan in multigenerational families with dyslexia: Identification of a novel locus on chromosome 2q that contributes to phonological decoding efficiency. *Molecular Psychiatry, 10*(7), 699–711. doi:10.1038/sj.mp.4001657

Rosen, G.D., Burstein, D., & Galaburda, A.M. (2000). Changes in efferent and afferent connectivity in rats with cerebrocortical microgyria. *Journal of Comparative Neurology, 418*(4), 423–440. doi:10.1002/(SICI)1096-9861 (20000320)418:4<423::AID-CNE5> 3.3.CO;2-X

Rosen, G.D., Sherman, G.F., Richman, J.M., Stone, L.V., & Galaburda, A.M. (1992). Induction of molecular layer ectopias by puncture wounds in newborn rats and mice. *Developmental Brain Research, 67*(2), 285–291. doi:10.1016/0165-3806(92)90229-P

Schulte-Korne, G., Grimm, T., Nothen, M.M., Muller-Myhsok, B., Cichon, S., Vogt, I.R., ... Remschmidt, H. (1998). Evidence for linkage of spelling disability to chromosome 15. *American Journal of Human Genetics, 63*(1), 279–282. doi:10.1086/301919

Schumacher, J., Anthoni, H., Dahdouh, F., Konig, I.R., Hillmer, A.M., Kluck, N., ... Kere, J. (2006a). Strong genetic evidence of DCDC2 as a susceptibility gene for dyslexia. *American Journal of Human Genetics, 78*(1), 52–62. doi:10.1086/498992

Schumacher, J., Konig, I.R., Plume, E., Propping, P., Warnke, A., Manthey, M., ... Preis, M. (2006b). Linkage analyses of chromosomal region 18p11-q12 in dyslexia. *Journal of Neural Transmission, 113*(3), 417–423. doi:10.1007/s00702-005-0336-y

Schumacher, J., Konig, I.R., Schroder, T., Duell, M., Plume, E., Propping, P., ... Nöthen, M. (2008). Further evidence for a susceptibility locus contributing to reading disability on chromosome 15q 15-q21. *Psychiatric Genetics, 18*(3), 137–142. doi:10.1097/YPG.0b013e3282fb7fc6

Sherman, G.F., Morrison, L., Rosen, G.D., Behan, P.O., & Galaburda, A.M.

(1990). Brain abnormalities in immune defective mice. *Brain Research, 532,* 25–33. doi:10.1016/0006-8993(90)91737-2

Sherman, G.F., Rosen, G.D., Stone, L.V., Press, D.M., & Galaburda, A.M. (1992). The organization of radial glial fibers in spontaneous neocortical ectopias of newborn New-Zealand black mice. *Developmental Brain Research, 67*(2), 279–283. doi:10.1016/0165-3806(92)90228-O

Smith, S.D., Kimberling, W.J., Pennington, B.F., & Lubs, H.A. (1983). Specific reading disability: Identification of an inherited form through linkage analysis. *Science, 219,* 1345–1347.

Snowling, M.J. (2000). *Dyslexia* (2nd ed.). Oxford: Blackwell.

Sokol, D.K., Golomb, M.R., Carvahlo, K.S., & Edwards-Brown, M. (2006). Reading impairment in the neuronal migration disorder of periventricular nodular heterotopia. *Neurology, 66*(2), 294.

Stein, J. (2001a). The magnocellular theory of developmental dyslexia. *Dyslexia, 7*(1), 12–36. doi:10.1002/dys.186

Stein, J. (2001b). The sensory basis of reading problems. *Developmental Neuropsychology, 20*(2), 509–534. doi:10.1207/ S15326942DN2002_4

Stein, J., & Walsh, V. (1997). To see but not to read: The magnocellular theory of dyslexia. *Trends in Neurosciences, 20*(4), 147–152. doi:10.1016/S0166-2236 (96)01005-3

Taipale, M., Kaminen, N., Nopola-Hemmi, J., Haltia, T., Myllyluoma, B., Lyytinen, H., ... Kere, J. (2003). A candidate gene for developmental dyslexia encodes a nuclear tetratricopeptide repeat domain protein dynamically regulated in brain. *Proceedings of the National Academy of Sciences, USA, 100*(20), 11553–11558. doi:10.1073/pnas.1833911100

Tzenova, J., Kaplan, B.J., Petryshen, T.L., & Field, L.L. (2004). Confirmation of a dyslexia susceptibility locus on chromosome 1p34-p36 in a set of 100 Canadian families. *American Journal of Medical Genetics, 127B*(1), 117–124. doi: 10.1002/ajmg.b.20139

Valdois, S., Bosse, M.L., & Tainturier, M.J. (2004). The cognitive deficits responsible for developmental dyslexia: Review of evidence for a selective visual attentional disorder. *Dyslexia, 10*(4), 339–363. doi:10.1002/dys.284

Velayos-Baeza, A., Toma, C., Paracchini, S., & Monaco, A.P. (2008). The dyslexia-associated gene KIAA0319 encodes highly N- and O-glycosylated plasma membrane and secreted isoforms. *Human Molecular Genetics, 17*(6), 859–871. doi:10.1093/hmg/ddm358

Wagner, R.K., & Torgesen, J.K. (1987). The nature of phonological processing and its causal role in the acquisition of reading skills. *Psychological Bulletin, 101,* 192–212. doi:10.1037//0033-2909.101.2.192

Weimer, J.M., Stanco, A., Cheng, J.G., Vargo, A.C., Voora, S., & Anton, E.S. (2008). A BAC transgenic mouse model to analyze the function of astroglial SPARCL1 (SC1) in the central nervous system. *Glia, 56*(9), 935–941. doi:10.1002/glia.20666

White, S., Frith, U., Milne, E., Rosen, S., Swettenham, J., & Ramus, F. (2006). A double dissociation between sensorimotor impairments and reading disability: A comparison of autistic and dyslexic children. *Cognitive Neuropsychology, 23*(5), 748–761. doi:10.1080/02643290500438607

Wigg, K.G., Couto, J.M., Feng, Y., Anderson, B., Cate-Carter, T.D., Macciardi, F., ... Barr, C.L. (2004). Support for EKN1

as the susceptibility locus for dyslexia on 15q21. *Molecular Psychiatry, 9*(12), 1111–1121. doi:10.1038/sj.mp.4001543

Wilcke, A., Weissfuss, J., Kirsten, H., Wolfram, G., Boltze, J., & Ahnert, P. (2009). The role of gene DCDC2 in German dyslexics. *Annals of Dyslexia, 59*(1), 1–11. doi:10.1007/s11881-008-0020-7

Williams, R.W. (2009). Herding cats: the sociology of data integration. *Frontiers in Neuroscience, 3*(2), 154–156. doi:10.3389/neuro.01.016.2009

Wolf, M., & Bowers, P.G. (2000). Naming-speed processes and developmental reading disabilities: An introduction to the special issue on the double-deficit hypothesis. *Journal of Learning Disabilities, 33*(4), 322–324. doi:10.1177/002221940003300404

Yokota, Y., Gashghaei, H.T., Han, C., Watson, H., Campbell, K.J., & Anton, E.S. (2007). Radial glial dependent and independent dynamics of interneuronal migration in the developing cerebral cortex. *PLoS ONE, 2*(8), e794. doi:10.1371/journal.pone.0000794

Using Animal Models to Dissociate Genetic, Neural, and Behavioral Contributors to Language Disability
R. Holly Fitch and Caitlin E. Szalkowski

anguage represents a complex and unique aspect of human neuro-cognitive processing that is vulnerable to disturbance through disruption of underlying neural systems. Developmental language disabilities are specifically the consequence of early disruptions to the initial establishment of neural systems needed to support emergent language. Disruptions can arise from general brain injury leading to global cognitive impairments such as mental retardation, learning disorders, or pervasive developmental disorders (Broman & Grafman, 1994; Pennington, 1991), but such effects are generally not labeled as language disability, and instead fall under the umbrella of cognitive disability. Other disruptions are *specific* to language systems (meaning overall intellect or IQ is intact), including impairments emergent during early acquisition of speech (specific language impairment, or SLI), as well as during the later acquisition of reading (dyslexia). Although language disorders have long been held as unique to humans, ongoing research has revealed that both SLI and dyslexia represent complex diagnoses that encompass underlying core impairments in fundamental processing systems that are utilized in language processing though not unique to language per se; As such, associated core phenotypic deficits (or intermediate phenotypes, see Chapter 4) have emerged as candidates for modeling outside of the human species. Moreover, when coupled with advances in the genetic etiology of language disability, new research opportunities using animal models can be pursued.

SPECIFIC LANGUAGE IMPAIRMENT, DYSLEXIA, AND LANGUAGE DISABILITY

The ability to understand and produce spoken words represents a profoundly complex process that most young children acquire with surprising ease, despite a lack of formal instruction—that is, most young children are not explicitly taught how to speak. Despite the language-ready predisposition of most typically developing children, some children experience delays reaching language milestones in the absence of known causal factors. When potential secondary impairments (such as epilepsy or other neurologic abnormalities, disorders of vision or hearing, psychiatric impairments, or environmental deprivation) are excluded, about 5%–10% of children exhibit unexplained impairments/ delays in language development (Beitchman, Nair, & Patel, 1986; Leonard, 1998). These language-specific problems occur despite a normal nonverbal IQ and are termed either language impairment (LI) or specific language impairment (SLI). Impairments associated with SLI can be further subdivided into receptive (SLI-R, comprehension), expressive (SLI-E, production), or combined impairments. SLI may also overlap with related conditions, such as autism spectrum disorder (ASD). ASD encompasses substantial communicative disabilities and includes a subpopulation with substantial language impairments termed by some as ASD-LI (Williams, Botting, & Boucher, 2008; see Chapter 18). Ongoing research in areas of phenotypic overlap will be helpful in ascertaining whether common mechanisms across disorders may account for similarities in language disturbance, or whether differing vectors of disruption to early brain development might exert common effects on fundamental (core) information processing systems, thus leading to similar phenotypes.

One of the most common comorbidities for SLI is a subsequent diagnosis of dyslexia or reading disability (also known as specific reading disability [RD], or developmental dyslexia [DD]). Much like SLI, dyslexia is defined by exclusionary criteria but in this case represents an unexpected delay or deficit in the acquisition and performance of reading despite a normal nonverbal IQ. The prevalent comorbidity between SLI and dyslexia likely reflects the fact that even though most children with SLI eventually learn to understand and produce speech, subsequent milestones in reading require new and demanding skills in the translation of learned phonemes (sounds) onto orthographic representation (letters). Because impairments in phonemic representation and/or phonologic processing comprise a core and persisting component of SLI, it is not surprising that a large portion (> 50%) of children with SLI go on to be diagnosed as dyslexic (Bishop & Snowling, 2004; Catts, Adlof, Hogan, & Weismer, 2005; Schuele, 2004; Sices, Taylor, Freebairn, & Hansen, 2007; Chapter 9). Researchers continue to debate whether those children who are initially diagnosed as SLI but overcome their disorder without further reading difficulties may represent a subtype of the SLI population, and whether a similar distinct subgroup within individuals with dyslexia includes older children/adults diagnosed with dyslexia absent any prior history of SLI (see Pennington & Bishop, 2009 and Bishop & Snowling, 2004, for discussion). In fact, it has been suggested that the latter subset of individuals with dyslexia— generally thought to correspond to a subcategory termed orthographic, or surface, dyslexics—exhibit primarily visual and higher-order reading impairments but lack the core phonological impairments characteristic of SLI. Conversely, remaining people with dyslexia do show core phonological impairments (hence termed phonologic dyslexics), and many people in this category have some history of SLI or language-related difficulties.

CORE BEHAVIORAL IMPAIRMENTS

Ongoing assessment of these various subgroups further reveals the existence of core functional features in both SLI and dyslexia, many of which overlap. For this reason, some researchers now refer to a "merged" diagnostic category of language disability (LD; also known as language-learning disabilities or language-learning impairments; Tallal, Miller, & Fitch, 1993; Peterson, McGrath, Shelley, Smith, & Pennington, 2007; see Bishop & Snowling, 2004, for an opposing view). Core behavioral features associated with this parent category of LD are further discussed next.

Core Behavioral Features of Language Disability

Behavior profiles in groups diagnosed with language disabilities vary, but are typically characterized by impairments in both lower order (e.g., sensory/motor) and higher order (e.g., grammatical, syntactic, and verbal memory) processes. The LD population includes individuals with deficiencies in some subset of the following functional core areas (along with other possible impairments not listed here): 1) oral-motor skills and articulation, as required for tasks such as rapid naming; 2) rapid auditory processing, as required to discriminate rapidly changing sounds (e.g., consonant–vowel syllables); 3a) phonemic awareness, as required to distinguish and identify phonemes (or subunits of words) and 3b) phonological processing, as required to manipulate phonemes within words and perform mapping to-and-from sounds to letters (as required for nonword reading); 4) short-term and/or working verbal memory and related auditory and phonological memory (as required for nonword repetition); and 5) visuo-spatial processing, visual memory, and/or visuo-spatial attention (as required for visual reading tasks). Evidence suggests that unique patterns of these core impairments may characterize specific subsets of individuals (i.e., SLI only, SLI+dyslexic, and dyslexic only; see Figure 11.1). For example, orthographic dyslexics are unlikely to show motor/articulation impairments, whereas SLI-only populations are unlikely to show visual processing and memory impairments. However, both groups (and the comorbid overlapping population) share strong evidence of common deficits in rapid auditory processing (Farmer & Klein, 1995; Fitch & Tallal, 2003), phonemic and phonological processing (Pennington & Bishop, 2009; Schuele, 2004; Shankweiler et al., 1995), and some aspects of short-term/working memory (Briscoe & Rankin, 2009; Montgomery, Magimairaj, & Finney, 2010). Each of these core functional features of LD (including SLI and dyslexia) are discussed in greater detail next.

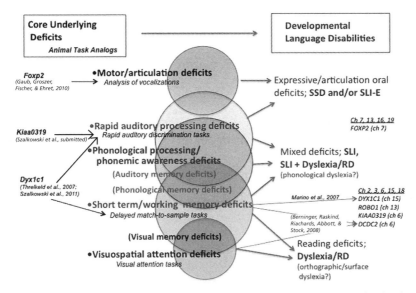

SSD= speech sound disorder; SLI=specific language impairment; SLI-E=SLI-expressive; RD=reading disorder

Figure 11.1. A proposed schematic diagram relating identified core function deficits associated with developmental language disability and clinically defined populations evidencing those underlying deficits.

Motor/Articulation Impairments

As young children learn to speak, it is normal to hear substitutions of letter sounds, lisps, or stutters. Most children outgrow these immature articulation patterns, but persistent difficulties may reflect chronic defects in oral musculature, vocal apparatus, palate formation, or general oral motor "weakness." These articulation impairments are not exclusively predictive of long-term language and literacy problems, but the chronic incorrect encoding of certain letter sounds may lead to some difficulties in their orthographic translation. Thus children exhibiting language difficulties such as phonemic omissions, substitutions, and other phonological processing difficulties display more marked impairment of articulation and expressive language. Such children have difficulty learning the sound systems of language, and may fail to recognize and identify specific sounds as unique (see Phonemic and Phonological Processing Impairments below).

Rapid Auditory Processing Impairments

A ground-breaking series of studies by Tallal and colleagues showed that SLI children are impaired in discriminating rapidly (but not slowly) presented sequential tones and consonant–vowel syllables with short,

rapidly changing formant transitions (e.g., /ba/, /da/, /pa/, /ta/; see Tallal, 1977, 1980; Tallal & Newcombe, 1978; Tallal & Piercy, 1973a, b; Tallal
& Piercy, 1975; Tallal & Stark, 1981; reviewed in Fitch & Tallal, 2003).
Additional studies showed that performance on these tasks correlated
with both speech perception and nonword reading scores (Tallal, 1980),
leading to the suggestion that defects in low-level auditory processing
may lead to cascading impairments in speech perception and phonology. Although this "bottom-up" model of LD is controversial (e.g., Mody,
Studdert-Kennedy, & Brady, 1997; Ramus, 2003; Rosen & Manganari,
2001), behavior and psychophysical studies continue to demonstrate
core deficits in rapid auditory processing in both SLI and populations
with dyslexia (Au & Lovegrove, 2007; Cardy, Flagg, Roberts, Brian, &
Roberts, 2005; Cohen-Mimran & Sapir, 2007; Corbera, Escera, & Artigas, 2006; Edwards et al., 2004; Farmer & Klein, 1995; Gaab, Gabrieli,
Deutsch, Tallal, & Temple, 2007; Hari & Kiesla, 1996; King, Wood, &
Faulkner, 2007; Kraus et al., 1996; McAnally & Stein, 1996, 1997; Mc-
Crosky & Kidder, 1980; Neville, Coffey, Holcomb, & Tallal, 1993; Reed,
1989; Renvall & Hari, 2002; Robin, Tomblin, Kearney, & Hug, 1989;
Sutter, Petkov, Baynes, & O'Connor, 2000; Watson, 1992; Witton et al.,
1998; Wright et al., 1997; Chapter 7). Although some critics argue that
it remains undetermined whether these auditory impairments represent causal versus comorbid (parallel but noncausal) impairments (see
McArthur & Bishop, 2001; Ramus, 2003; Rosen & Manganari, 2001), ongoing research has provided compelling evidence of longitudinal prediction from early acoustic processing to later language.

Benasich, Thomas, Choudhury, and Leppänen (2002) found that infants with a family history of language impairment or dyslexia—that is,
at an elevated risk for language problems (Tallal, 1980)—were impaired
relative to controls in their ability to discriminate two-tone sequences
separated by a short (but not long) interval. Prospective follow-up revealed that auditory processing threshold in infancy was predictive of
later language outcomes (Benasich et al., 2006; Choudhury, Leppänen,
Leevers, & Benasich, 2007). A similar relationship was seen for early
AERP/EEG scores and later language outcomes (Choudhury et al., 2007;
see Chapter 7). Predictive associations also exist between early auditory
processing skills and language performance later in life in normally developing samples. Trehub and Henderson (1996) found that children <
12 months with above-average performance on acoustic gap detection
tasks had larger vocabularies, used longer, more complex sentences,
and produced more irregular words later in childhood. These findings
are supported by Molfese and Molfese (1997), who found that ERPs to
consonant–vowel syllables recorded from newborn infants differed as
a function of later measures of verbal IQ. Infants with a family history of dyslexia also showed aberrant ERPs to consonant–vowel stimuli
(Leppänen & Lyytinen, 1997; Leppänen, Pihko, Eklund, & Lyytinen,
1999; Pihko et al., 1999). Collective data thus support the idea that rapid

auditory processing is strongly correlated with later language development, and that impairments in this function may impair higher-order processes seemingly distal to basic acoustic processing (e.g., reading; see also Chapter 3).

Phonemic and Phonological Processing Impairments

Many language-based developmental disorders also appear to encompass a central deficit in the ability to identify and discriminate individual speech sounds (phonemic awareness). SLI and populations with dyslexia both show impairments in phonemic awareness and phonological processing (using and manipulating phonemes and translating them to and from print). The consistency of impairments observed on tasks that tap these processes in both SLI and dyslexic populations has led to suggestions that phonological impairments may form a critical core deficit spanning diverse language disorders (e.g., Bradley & Bryant, 1983; Catts et al., 2005; reviewed in Vellutino, Fletcher, Snowling, & Scanlon, 2004). However, speculation persists regarding the causality of core phonemic and phonological difficulties. Some studies suggest that difficulties with phonological processing in LD populations reflect underlying deficits in rapid auditory processing, as described above, although others suggest that phonological impairments are parallel to separate auditory problems, but remain specific to linguistic systems (e.g., Ramus, 2003), whereas others ascribe these core phonological impairments to primary difficulties with phonological memory (e.g., Gathercole & Baddeley, 1990). A plausible explanation could be that the core demands of phonological processing are vulnerable to a variety of disruptions (bottom-up or top-down) that may create impairments in this and other key processes of language development and reading, and lead to overlapping phenotypes of language disruption.

Short-Term/Working Memory Impairments

There is also consistent evidence of working and/or verbal short-term memory impairments in LD populations when processing sentence morphology, syntax and/or semantics (Brady, Shankweiler, & Mann, 1983; Shankweiler & Crain, 1986; Shankweiler et al., 1995; Smith, Macaruso, Shankweiler, & Crain, 1989). The effective use of language requires the use of short-term memory to combine strings of letter sounds into meaningful words during word processing, as well as in processing complex semantic meaning within sentences, paragraphs, and narratives, whose meaning may be modified by early sentence structure that must be held in short-term memory. Tasks that tap these underlying capacities include digit span recall tasks, word memory tasks, and more complex assessments of active narrative comprehension during reading (see Montgomery et al., 2010, for a review). There is also evidence for short-term memory impairments specific to processing phonological information, such as required for repeating nonwords (Gathercole & Baddeley, 1990; see also Catts et al., 2005). In a recent review, Briscoe and Rankin (2009) concluded that evidence more strongly supports a deficit in core phonological memory processes (phonological loop) in SLI participants, as opposed to overall executive memory. However, findings by Smith-Spark and Fisk (2007) countered these assertions by demonstrating impairments in cross-modal executive working memory, as well as phonological memory, in individuals with dyslexia. Finally, a family based genetic association study revealed a linkage within a subset of individuals with dyslexia between variations in a segment of the dyslexia-risk gene *DYX1C1*, and short-term memory impairments (as measured by single letter backward span scores; Marino et al., 2007; see also Chapter 4). Studies support a similar linkage between composite measures of memory and the *DCDC2* gene (Berninger et al., 2008). Cumulative results thus support the view that ongoing genetic research on LD may eventually reveal correspondence between specific genes and specific core functional impairments such as short-term memory, and such associations may underlie more complex clinical diagnoses.

Visuospatial Processing, Visuospatial Memory, and/or Visuospatial Attention Impairments

A series of studies in the 1990s suggested that, in addition to deficits in rapid auditory processing, adults with dyslexia might also be impaired in processing rapidly changing visual information. This assertion was based on evidence of impairments in processing visual rapid change in people with dyslexia, and led to suggestions that LD may include a core deficit in magnocellular system processing, because rapidly changing visual information is processed in the magnocellular subsystem of the visual thalamic nucleus (Lehmkuhle, Garzia, Turner, Hash, & Baro, 1993; Livingstone, Rosen, Drislane, & Galaburda, 1991; Lovegrove, Garzia, & Nicholson, 1990; Slaghuis, Lovegrove, & Freestun, 1992; Stein, 2001; see Chapter 3).

A recent study of visual memory in adults with dyslexia and age/IQ-matched controls reported impairments in this group on both verbal and nonverbal (visuo-spatial) working memory-span tasks (Smith-Spark & Fisk, 2007). These latter studies were particularly interesting, showing that short-term memory impairments in populations with dyslexia are not exclusive to the phonological domain, and therefore may reflect a fundamental defect in neurological-memory systems that may impact language processing (as well as other functions; however see Briscoe & Rankin, 2009). Ongoing research also continues to explore the role of visual memory and/or attention as a feature of LD populations, and Shaywitz and Shaywitz (2008) have shown that attention plays a key role in reading for individuals with dyslexia as measured by fMRI.

Clearly, research has shown a range of core functional impairments associated with SLI and/or dyslexia, and research continues to refine these behavioral criteria for reliable subtyping. Though a strong impetus exists to establish genetic or neural markers to subdivide this heterogeneous LD population, reliable markers are first needed to identify homogenous sub-groups for testing that will yield significance in genetic linkage and neuroimaging studies. Recognizing these circular constraints and limitations, studies have proceeded by using heterogeneous populations (i.e. both SLI and dyslexic) with *post hoc* analysis of subgroups; by separating groups based on core behavioral features (e.g., those with/without phonologic impairments); by correlating one putative marker with another (e.g., memory scores and genetic mapping); by using longitudinal analyses of emergent language measures to segregate groups; and by assessing distinctions and overlaps with related disorders (such as ASD-LI and SLI). In the current chapter, we detail the use of core behavioral phenotypes identified above to study animal models in conjunction with manipulation of candidate language disability genes.

CANDIDATE LANGUAGE DISABILITY/ DYSLEXIA SUSCEPTIBILITY GENES

Numerous studies have examined the incidence of LD in families in order to determine estimates of heritability, and have used linkage analysis to assess genetic "markers" shared at above-chance levels among affected family members—as well as genetic association studies to examine correspondence between variations in specific genes and phenotypes within a group (generally a clinically defined group, such as individuals with dyslexia; see Chapters 4 and 5). Such studies have revealed that language disorders are characterized by a degree of heritability but do not conform to any single-gene models. Moreover, a degree of environmental influence seems to exist as well, because affected individuals can appear in families with no history of language disability. Cumulative studies implicate a role for regions on chromosomes 13, 16, and 19 in SLI, and on 1, 2, 3, 6, 15, 18, and X in dyslexia (reviewed in Bishop, 2009; Gibson & Gruen, 2008; Pennington & Bishop, 2009). Studies honing in on specific genes have revealed specific regions such as the *FOXP2* gene implicated in expressive oral praxis disorder (Fischer & Scharff, 2009), as well as 6 candidate dyslexia susceptibility genes (or CDSGs), including *DYX1C1, KIAA0319, DCDC2, ROBO1, MRPL19,* and *C2ORF3* (Anthoni et al., 2007; Brkanac et al., 2007; Cope et al., 2005; Francks et al., 2004; Hannula-Jouppi et al., 2005; Harold et al., 2006; McGrath, Smith, & Pennington, 2006; Meng et al., 2005; Parracchini et al., 2006; Schumacher et al., 2006; Taipale et al., 2003; see Fisher & Francks, 2006, for a review). It is interesting that research suggests that each of these genes may be involved in processes such as neuronal migration, axon growth, and synaptic plasticity (Wang et al., 2006). Because neurodevelopmental processes—such as neuronal

migration and axon growth—share several common features and requirements, including dependence upon coordinated changes in cell adhesion
and cytoskeletal restructuring, the overlapping functions implicated for
these genes is not surprising. The role of these various genes in modulating specific aspects of neurodevelopment is discussed in much greater
detail elsewhere in this text (see Chapters 2 and 10).

NOVEL ANIMAL MODELS OF LANGUAGE DISABILITY

Animal models have provided unique insight into the role of aberrant neurodevelopmental processes—as well as the specific role of "risk" genes in
these aberrations—by linking individual neurodevelopmental processes
and/or gene actions with core functional deficits characteristic of human
LD populations. Resulting findings are further discussed next.

Induced Neuronal Migration
Anomalies and Rapid Auditory Processing

Following the discovery of cellular-developmental anomalies in the
brains of dyslexics (Galaburda, Sherman, Rosen, Aboitiz, & Geschwind,
1985), rodent models were developed to simulate these anomalies
through perinatal injury. Humphreys, Rosen, Press, Sherman, and
Galaburda (1991) showed that focal-freezing lesions on the skull of
Postnatal day 1 (P1) rats led to the formation of neocortical microgyria
(a neuronal migration disorder) with histological similarity to neural
anomalies seen in *post mortem* human dyslexic brains (see also Dvorák
& Feit, 1977; Rosen, Press, Sherman, & Galaburda, 1992). Experiments
were then designed to assess whether processing impairments paralleling those seen in people with dyslexia would be seen in animals with
these induced microgyria. Results from our lab showed that microgyric male rats (but not females) exhibited significant auditory-processing impairments only at short stimulus durations (Fitch, Tallal, Brown,
Galaburda, & Rosen, 1994). This deficit was virtually identical to that
seen in children with language disabilities, using a similar two-tone
sequence discrimination task (Tallal & Piercy, 1973a, b), and has been
replicated in numerous subsequent rat studies (Clark, Rosen, Tallal, &
Fitch, 2000a, b; Peiffer, Friedman, Rosen, & Fitch, 2004; Peiffer, Rosen, &
Fitch, 2002; Peiffer, Rosen, & Fitch, 2004).

   Comparable studies of BXSB/MpJ and NZB/B1NJ mice (a subset of
which exhibits spontaneously forming focal-cortical neuronal-migration disruptions—that is, ectopias) showed similar evidence of rapid auditory processing (RAP) deficits, such as those seen in rats with induced
neuronal migration disruption (microgyria). In each case, ectopic male
mice were significantly worse than nonectopics in processing short (but
not long) duration stimuli (Clark, Sherman, Bimonte, & Fitch, 2000c;
Peiffer et al., 2001). Moreover, these behavioral data were paralleled by

auditory evoked response potential (AERP) data from adult male BXSB and NZB mice with ectopic mice showing a smaller negative deflection to the onset of a second acoustic stimulus following a short but not long tone (Frenkel, Sherman, Bashan, Galaburda, & LoTurco, 2000; Peiffer et al., 2001).

These convergent findings have critical implications in substantiating a robust relationship between developmental disruptions of neuronal migration in cortex and specific RAP impairments in both rats and mice. We have further reported that the above methods of auditory-discrimination assessment in rats—that is, modified startle reduction paradigm—are sensitive to age- and experience-based changes in threshold processing (Friedman, Peiffer, Clark, Benasich, & Fitch, 2004). Specifically, gap detection thresholds (which are considered a reliable index of auditory processing acuity) are seen to decrease (improve) with both increasing age and increasing auditory experience. Consistent with these data, we found that RAP impairments in male rats with induced neuronal migration disorders (as compared to shams) are most pronounced during the juvenile (prepubertal) time frame (P20–P40; Peiffer, McClure, Threlkeld, Rosen, & Fitch, 2004b; see also Threlkeld, McClure, Rosen, & Fitch, 2006). In adult rats, we found that disruptions of neuronal migration are associated with deficits on more complex rapid auditory processing tasks such as two-tone sequence processing at short durations and short frequency modulated (FM) sweep detection (see Clark et al., 2000a: Peiffer et al., 2002; Peiffer, Friedman, et al., 2004; Peiffer, Rosen, et al., 2004). These cross-task comparisons imply that stimulus complexity may interact with the threshold for processing defects in "impaired" animal models, with easier tasks eliciting processing deficits in younger animals, and more complex tasks required to elicit processing deficits in adult animals.

Neocortical Neuronal Migration Disorders and Short-Term Memory

The previously described findings reveal that focal cortical developmental disturbances clearly lead to RAP impairments in a rodent model, and also that these effects are exacerbated by increasingly complex and/or demanding task requirements. Such an interaction suggests that subjects with neuronal migration disorders may also exhibit deficits in higher-order cognitive domains, such as working (or short-term) memory. This assertion is consistent with findings by Denenberg and colleagues, who performed an exhaustive series of studies demonstrating significant deficits in working memory for ectopic (as compared to nonectopic) BXSB mice. These effects were seen for both spatial and nonspatial versions of a working memory (radial arm maze) task (Boehm et al., 1996a; Boehm, Sherman, Rosen, Galaburda, & Denenberg, 1996b; Hyde, Sherman, Hoplight, & Denenberg, 2000a, b). Recently we employed a delayed match to the sample radial arm maze task using adult male rats with induced microgyria and shams. The task required subjects to recall a target arm within an 8-arm radial maze. The target arm was altered daily and introduced in an initial trial followed by a delay interval of 1 hour and then a test trial. Results showed that all rats learned the task as indicated by a gradually decreasing number of errors (incorrect arms entered), but sham subjects performed significantly better as measured by fewer errors made. These results show that adult male rats with disruptions of neuronal migration exhibit impairments in the performance of a difficult short-term memory task (Fitch, Threlkeld, McClure, & Peiffer, 2008).

DYX1C1, Rapid Auditory Processing, and Short-Term Memory

Recent research has also used rodent models to transiently knockdown the function of identified dyslexia-risk genes, specifically through the transfection of short hairpin RNA (shRNA) into the cerebral ventricles of fetal rats. This shRNA is taken up by new neurons in the ventricular zone, thus deactivating the target genes in these specific cells (see Chapter 2 for more details). Behavior testing of rodents treated using this technology shows that male rats transfected with *Dyx1c1* shRNA exhibit impairments in complex/rapid auditory processing later in life (Threlkeld et al., 2007)—even though these animals perform comparably to shams on simple acoustic discrimination tasks. These results have intriguing implications for the possible role of *DYX1C1* in modulating phonemic/phonological impairments in human populations with dyslexia through potential disruption of neural mechanisms critical to the discrimination of complex and rapidly changing acoustic information.

More recently, we examined short-term memory performance on a delayed match to sample radial arm maze task in male rats transfected with *Dyx1c1* shRNA (Szalkowski et al., 2011). Results showed persistent short-term memory impairments in *Dyx1c1* knockdown rats, as indicated by higher numbers of errors—paralleling evidence of cross-modal short-term memory impairments in humans with dyslexia (Smith-Spark & Fisk, 2007), as well as evidence of associations between the *DYX1C1* gene and working memory impairments in the human population with dyslexia (Marino et al., 2007). These effects were seen despite parallel evidence that *Dyx1c1* shRNA rats do *not* show impairments on basic spatial maze learning (Morris maze) unless migrational anomalies specifically disrupted the hippocampus (as was seen in a small subset of subjects; Threlkeld et al., 2007). Again, this pattern of behavioral-genetic associations provides a relatively specific profile to model impairments seen in LD (i.e., impairments in short-term memory). Future work will continue to explore a role for animal models in evaluating these gene-brain-behavior relationships, including further behavioral assessment of a newly developed *Dyx1c1* knockout mouse (Chapter 2).

KIAA0319, Rapid Auditory Processing, and Short-Term Memory

More recent research has extended these findings to rodent models using another dyslexia risk gene, *KIAA0319*. Specifically, *Kiaa0319* shRNA transfected rats also showed significant impairments in rapid auditory processing as compared to sham controls (Szalkowski et al., in press). It is interesting to note that in this study, *Kiaa0319* subjects were found to perform comparably to shams on a complex FM sweep detection task—except when the stimulus was presented at the shortest duration. At this short duration (125 ms), *Kiaa0319* subjects performed significantly worse than shams—an effect that was subsequently replicated in another batch of animals (Szalkowski et al., in press). In this case, *Kiaa0319* effects appeared to be more specific to rapid acoustic processing per se, and these effects are interpreted to parallel evidence of rapid auditory processing impairments in LD populations. As an aside, it is important to note these animals were not categorically impaired in sound processing tasks, and they performed quite normally on discrimination tasks with easier/slower stimuli. This point is important when developing animal models for clinical conditions because a genetic defect resulting in comprehensive learning and cognitive impairments would provide a poor model for the specific pattern(s) of impairments seen within the LD phenotype.

When *Kiaa0319* shRNA subjects were tested as described previously on a complex working-memory task, it is interesting that no deficits were seen. In fact, *Kiaa0319* subjects had a trend toward (nonsignificantly) fewer errors than shams. These results stand in sharp contrast to the significantly higher number of errors made by *Dyx1c1* shRNAs rats on the very same task (Szalkowski et al., 2011).

Combined results suggest that *KIAA0319* may influence core component features of dyslexia through greater impact on rapid auditory processing, whereas *DYX1C1* may show a greater impact on working memory processes.

FOXP2 and Vocalizations

Finally, one extended family with an inherited form of expressive language impairment (also called verbal dyspraxia) has been particularly well studied (the KE family; Fischer & Scharf, 2009). Half the members of this family exhibit severe impairments in phonology and syntax, as well as oral praxis. Ongoing studies have led to the isolation of the gene *FOXP2*, which may be associated with the expressive and oral language impairments evidenced in this family. Animal studies of the *Foxp2* homolog have shown that disruptions of this gene lead to defects in motor learning. Specifically, studies have demonstrated that knockdown of the avian orthologue to *FOXP2* in birds leads to an impairment in the motor learning of birdsong, and also that *Foxp2* knockout mice show anomalous vocalizations (Gaub et al., 2010; Shu et al., 2005).

CONCLUSIONS

Animal studies provide a unique opportunity to test and assess some of the putative genetic-neural-behavioral links in an experimental manner that is virtually impossible to employ with human participants. Studies to date have begun to reveal that genes identified as candidate risk genes for dyslexia may affect global diagnosis through effects on different underlying component intermediate phenotypes. Specifically, disruptions to *KIAA0319* may exert deleterious effects on rapid auditory processing, whereas mutations to *DYX1C1* may show a greater impact on working memory processes. Effects of *FOXP2*, conversely, may be seen more for motor/articulation output (see Figure 11.1 for summary). Ongoing research following this cross-level experimental approach will continue to elucidate details in the complex gene-brain-behavior trajectory underlying the emergence of language disorders such as dyslexia.

REFERENCES

Anthoni, H., Zucchelli, M., Matsson, H., Muller-Myhsok, B., Fransson, I., Schumacher, J., ... Peyrard-Janvid, M. (2007). A locus on 2p12 containing the co-regulated MRPL19 and C2ORF3 genes is associated to dyslexia. *Human Molecular Genetics, 16,* 667–77. doi:10.1093/hmg/ddm009

Au, A., & Lovegrove, B. (2007). The contribution of rapid visual and auditory processing to the reading of irregular words and pseudowords presented singly and in contiguity. *Perception & Psychophysics, 69,* 1344–59. doi:10.3758/BF03192951

Beitchman, J.H., Nair, R., & Patel, P.G. (1986). Prevalence of speech and language disorders in 5-year-old kindergarten children in the Ottowa-Carlton region. *Journal of Speech and Hearing Disorders, 51,* 98–110.

Benasich, A.A., Choudhury, N., Friedman, J.T., Realpe-Bonilla, T., Chojnowska, C. & Gou, Z. (2006). Infants as a prelinguistic model for language learning impairments: Predicting from event-related potentials to behavior. *Neuropsychologia, 44,* 396–411.

Benasich, A.A., Thomas, J.J., Choudhury, N., & Leppanen, P.H.T. (2002). The importance of rapid auditory processing abilities to early language development: Evidence from converging methodologies. *Developmental Psychobiology, 40,* 278–292. doi:10.1002/dev.10032

Berninger, V.W., Raskind, W., Riachards, T., Abbott, R., & Stock, P. (2008). A multi-disciplinary approach to understanding developmental dyslexia within working-memory architecture: Genotypes, phenotypes, brain, and instruction. *Developmental Neuropsychology, 33,* 707–744.

Bishop, D.V.M. (2009). Genes, cognition and communication. Insights from neurodevelopmental disorders. *Annals of the New York Academy of Sciences, 1156,* 1–18.

Bishop, D.V.M., & Snowling, M.J. (2004). Developmental dyslexia and specific language impairment: Same or different? *Psychological Bulletin, 130,* 858–886. doi:10.1037/0033-2909.130.6.858

Boehm, G.W., Sherman, G.F., Hoplight, B J., Hyde, L.A., Waters, N.S., Bradway, D.M., ... Denenberg, V.H. (1996a). Learning and memory in the autoimmune BXSB mouse: Effects of neocortical ectopias and environmental enrichment. *Brain Research, 726,* 11–22. doi:10.1016/S0006-8993(96)00299-5

Boehm, G.W., Sherman, G.F., Rosen, G.D., Galaburda, A.M., & Denenberg, V.H. (1996b). Neocortical ectopias in BXSB mice: Effects upon reference and working memory systems. *Cerebral Cortex, 6,* 696–700. doi:10.1093/cercor/6.5.696

Bradley, L., & Bryant, P. (1983). Categorizing sounds and learning to read—A causal connection. *Nature, 301,* 419–421. doi:10.1038/301419a0

Brady, S., Shankweiler, D. & Mann, V. (1983). Speech perception and memory coding in relation to reading ability. *Journal of Experimental Child Psychology*, 35, 345–367. doi:10.1016/0022-0965(83)90087-5

Briscoe, J. & Rankin, P.M. (2009). Exploration of a "double-jeopardy" hypothesis within working memory profiles for children with specific language impairment. *International Journal of Language and Communication Disorders*, 44, 236–250. doi:10.1080/13682820802028760

Brkanac, Z., Chapman, N.H., Matsushita, M.M., Chun, L., Nielson, K., Cochrane, E., ... Raskind, W.H. (2007). Evaluation of candidate genes for DYX1 and DYX2 in families with dyslexia. *American Journal of Medical Genetics*, 144, 556–560.

Broman, S.H., & Grafman, J. (1994). *Atypical cognitive deficits in developmental disorders: Implications for brain function.* Hillsdale, NJ: Lawrence Earlbaum.

Cardy, J.E.O., Flagg, E.J., Roberts, W., Brian, J., & Roberts, T.P.L. (2005). Magnetoencephalography identifies rapid temporal processing deficit in autism and language impairment. *Neuroreport, 16*, 329–32.

Catts, H.W., Adlof, S.M., Hogan, T.P., & Weismer, S.M. (2005). Are specific language impairment and dyslexia distinct disorders? *Journal of Speech, Language, and Hearing Research, 48*, 1378–96. doi:10.1044/1092-4388(2005/096)

Choudhury, N., Leppannen, P.H.T., Leevers, H.J., & Benasich, A.A. (2007). Infant information processing and family history of specific language impairment: Converging evidence for RAP deficits from two paradigms. *Developmental Science, 10*, 213–36. doi:10.1111/j.1467-7687.2007.00546

Clark, M., Rosen, G., Tallal, P., & Fitch, R.H. (2000a). Impaired processing of complex auditory stimuli in rats with induced cerebrocortical microgyria. *Journal of Cognitive Neuroscience, 12*, 828–839. doi:10.1162/089892900562435

Clark, M., Rosen, G., Tallal, P., & Fitch, R.H. (2000b). Impaired two-tone processing at rapid rates in male rats with induced microgyria. *Brain Research, 871*, 94–97. doi:10.1016/S0006-8993(00)02447-1

Clark, M.G., Sherman, G.F., Bimonte, H.A., & Fitch, R.H. (2000c). Perceptual auditory gap detection deficits in ectopic male BXSB mice. *NeuroReport, 11*, 693–696.

Cohen-Mimran, R., & Sapir, S. (2007). Auditory temporal processing deficits in children with reading disabilities. *Dyslexia, 13*, 175–92. doi:10.1002/dys.323

Cope, N., Harold, D., Hill, G., Moskovina, V., Stevenson, J., Holmans, P., ... Williams, J. (2005). Strong evidence that KIAA0319 on chromosome 6p is a susceptibility gene for developmental dyslexia. *American Journal of Human Genetics, 76*, 581–91. doi:10.1086/429131

Corbera, S., Escera, C., & Artigas, J. (2006). Impaired duration mismatch negativity in developmental dyslexia. *NeuroReport, 17*, 10051–55. doi:10.1097/01.wnr.0000221846.43126.a6

Dvorák, K., & Feit, J. (1977). Migration of neuroblasts through partial necrosis of the cerebral cortex in newborn rats—Contribution to the problems of morphological development and developmental period of cerebral microgyria. *Acta Neuropathology (Berl), 38*, 203–212.

Edwards, V.T., Giaschi, D.E., Dougherty, R.F., Edgell, D., Bjornson, B.H., Lyons, C., & Douglas, R.M. (2004). Psychophysical indexes of temporal processing abnormalities in children with developmental dyslexia. *Developmental Neuropsychology, 25*, 321–54. doi:10.1207/s15326942dn2503_5

Farmer, M.E., & Klein, R.M. (1995). The evidence for a temporal processing deficit linked to dyslexia. *Psychonomic Bulletin and Review, 2*, 460–493. doi:10.3758/BF03210983

Fischer, S.E., & Francks, C. (2006). Genes, cognition and dyslexia: Learning to read the genome. *Trends in Cognitive Sciences, 10*(6), 250–257. doi:10.1016/j.tics.2006.04.003

Fischer, S.E., & Scharff, C. (2009). FOXP2 as a molecular window into speech and language. *Trends in Genetics, 25*, 166–177. doi:10.1016/j.tig.2009.03.002

Fitch, R.H. (in press). Language Impairments. In P. Rakic & J. Rubenstein (Eds.), *Comprehensive Developmental Neuroscience.* Oxford, U.K.: Elsevier.

Fitch, R.H., Tallal, P., Brown, C., Galaburda, A., & Rosen, G. (1994). Induced microgyria and auditory temporal processing in rats: A model for language impairment? *Cerebral Cortex, 4,* 260–270. doi:10.1093/cercor/4.3.260

Fitch, R.H., & Tallal, P. (2003). Neural mechanisms of language based learning impairments: Insights from human populations and animal models. *Behavioral and Cognitive Neuroscience Reviews, 2*(3), 155–178. doi:10.1177/1534582303258736

Fitch, R.H., Threlkeld, S.W., McClure, M.M., & Peiffer, A.M. (2008). Use of a modified prepulse inhibition paradigm to assess complex auditory discrimination in rodents. *Brain Research Bulletin, 76,* 1–7. doi:10.1016/j.brainresbull.2007.07.013

Francks, C., Paracchini, S., Smith, S.D., Richardson, A.J., Scerri, T.S., Cardon, L.R., … Monaco, A.P. (2004). A 77-kilobase region of chromosome 6p22.2 is associated with dyslexia in families in the United Kingdom and from the United States. *American Journal of Human Genetics, 75,* 1046–1058. doi:10.1086/426404

Frenkel, M., Sherman, G.F., Bashan, K.A., Galaburda, A.M., & LoTurco, J. (2000). Neocortical ectopias are associated with attenuated neurophysiological responses to rapidly changing auditory stimuli. *NeuroReport, 11,* 575–579. doi:10.1097/00001756-200002280-00029

Friedman, J.T., Peiffer, A., Clark, M., Benasich, A., & Fitch, R.H. (2004). Age and experience related improvements in gap detection in the rat. *Developmental Brain Research, 152,* 83–91. doi:10.1016/j.devbrainres.2004.06.007

Gaab, N., Gabrieli, J.D.E., Deutsch, G.K., Tallal, P., & Temple, E. (2007). Neural correlates of rapid auditory processing are disrupted in children with developmental dyslexia and ameliorated with training: An fMRI study. *Restorative Neurology and Neuroscience, 25,* 295–310.

Galaburda, A.M., Sherman, G.F., Rosen, G.D., Aboitiz, F., & Geschwind, N. (1985). Developmental dyslexia: Four consecutive cases with cortical anomalies. *Annals of Neurology, 18,* 222–233.

Gathercole, S.E., & Baddeley, A.D. (1990). Phonological memory deficits in language impaired children: Is there a causal connection? *Journal of Memory and Language, 29,* 336–360.

Gaub, S., Groszer, M., Fischer, S.E., & Ehret, G. (2010). The structure of vocalizations in Foxp2-deficient mouse pups.

Genes, *Brain and Behavior, 9*(4), 390–401. doi:10.1111/j.1601-183X.2010.00570

Gibson, C.J., & Gruen, J.R. (2008). The human lexinome: Genes of language and reading. *Journal of Communication Disorders, 41,* 409–420. doi:10.1016/j.jcomdis.2008.03.003

Hannula-Jouppi, K., Kaminen-Ahola, N., Taipale, M., Eklund, R., Nopola-Hemmi, J., Kaariainen, H., & Kere, J. (2005). The axon guidance receptor gene ROBO1 is a candidate gene for developmental dyslexia. *PLoS Genetics, 1,* e50. doi:10.1371/journal.pgen.0010050

Hari, R., & Kiesla, P. (1996). Deficit of temporal auditory processing in dyslexic adults. *Neuroscience Letters, 205,* 138–140. doi:10.1016/0304-3940(96)12393-4

Harold, D., Paracchini, S., Scerri, T., Dennis, M., Cope, N., Hill, G., … Monaco, A.P. (2006). Further evidence that the KIAA0319 gene confers susceptibility to developmental dyslexia. *Molecular Psychiatry, 11,* 1085–1091. doi:10.1038/sj.mp.4001904

Humphreys, P., Rosen, G.D., Press, D.M., Sherman, G.F., & Galaburda, A.M. (1991). Freezing lesions of the newborn rat brain: A model for cerebrocortical microgyria. *Journal of Neuropathology and Experimental Neurology, 50,* 145–160.

Hyde, L.A., Sherman, G.F., Hoplight, B.J., & Denenberg, V.H. (2000a). Non-spatial water radial-arm maze learning in mice. *Brain Research, 863,* 151–159. doi:10.1016/S0006-8993(00)02113-2

Hyde, L.A., Sherman, G.F., Hoplight, B.J., & Denenberg, V.H. (2000b). Working memory deficits in BXSB mice with neocortical ectopias. *Physiology & Behavior, 70,* 1–5. doi:10.1016/S0031-9384(00)00239-0

King, B., Wood, C., & Faulkner, D. (2007). Sensitivity to auditory stimuli in children with developmental dyslexia. *Dyslexia, 14,* 116–141. doi:10.1002/dys.349

Kraus, N., McGee, T.J., Carrell, T.D., Zecker, S.G., Nicol, T.G., & Koch, D.B. (1996). Auditory neurophysiologic responses and discrimination deficits in children with learning problems. *Science, 273,* 971–973. doi:10.1126/science.273.5277.971

Lehmkuhle, S., Garzia, R.P., Turner, L., Hash, T., & Baro, J.A. (1993). A defective visual pathway in children with reading disability. *New England Journal of Medicine, 328,* 989–996. doi:10.1056/NEJM199304083281402

Leonard, L.B. (1998). *Children with specific language impairment.* Cambridge, MA: MIT Press.

Leppänen, P.H.T., & Lyytinen, H. (1997). Auditory event-related potentials in the study of developmental language-related disorders. *Audiology and Neurotology, 2,* 308–340. doi:10.1159/000259254

Leppänen, P.H.T., Pihko, E., Eklund, K.M., & Lyytinen, H. (1999). Cortical responses of infants with and without a genetic risk for dyslexia: II. Group effects. *NeuroReport, 10,* 969–973.

Livingstone, M.S., Rosen, G.D., Drislane, F.W., & Galaburda, A.M. (1991). Physiological and anatomical evidence for a magnocellular defect in developmental dyslexia. *Proceedings of the National Academy of Sciences, USA, 88,* 7943–7947. doi:10.1073/pnas.88.18.7943

Lovegrove, W., Garzia, R., & Nicholson, S. (1990). Experimental evidence for a transient system deficit in specific reading disability. *Journal of the American Optometric Association, 2,* 137–146.

Marino, C., Citterio, A., Giorda, R., Facoetti, A., Menozzi, G., Vanzin, L., … Molteni, M. (2007). Association of short-term memory with a variant within DYX1C1 in developmental dyslexia. *Genes, Brain and Behavior, 6,* 640–646. doi:10.1111/j.1601-183X.2006.00291

McAnally, K.I., & Stein, J.F. (1996) Auditory temporal coding in dyslexia. *Proceedings of the Royal Society B: Biological Sciences, 263,* 961–5. doi:10.1098/rspb.1996.0142

McAnally, K.I., & Stein, J.F. (1997). Scalp potentials evoked by amplitude modulated tones in dyslexia. *Joural of Speech, Language and Hearing Research, 40,* 939–945.

McArthur, G.M., & Bishop, D.V.M. (2001). Auditory perceptual processing in people with reading and oral language impairments: Current issues and recommendations. *Dyslexia, 7,* 150–170. doi: 10.1002/dys.200

McCrosky, R., & Kidder, H. (1980) Auditory fusion among learning disabled, reading disabled and normal children. *Journal of Learning Disabilities, 13,* 69–76. doi:10.1177/002221948001300205

McGrath, L.M., Smith, S.D., & Pennington, B.F. (2006). Breakthroughs in the search for dyslexia candidate genes. *Trends in Molecular Medicine, 112,* 333–341. doi:10.1016/j.molmed.2006.05.007

Meng, H., Smith, S.D., Hager, K., Held, M., Liu, J., Olson, R.K., … Gruen, J.R. (2005). DCDC2 is associated with reading disability and modulates neuronal development in the brain. *Proceedings of the National Academy of Sciences, USA, 102,* 17053–17058.

Mody, M., Studdert-Kennedy, M., & Brady, S. (1997). Speech perception deficits in poor readers: Auditory processing or phonological coding? *Journal of Experimental Child Psychology, 64,* 199–231. doi:10.1006/jecp.1996.2343

Molfese, D.L., & Molfese, V.J. (1997). Discrimination of language skills at five years of age using event-related potentials recorded at birth. *Developmental Neuropsychology, 13,* 135–156. doi:10.1080/87565649709540674

Montgomery, J.W., Magimairaj, B.M., & Finney, M.C. (2010). Working memory and specific language impairment: An update on the relation and perspectives on assessment and treatment. *American Journal of Speech-Language Pathology, 19,* 78–94. doi:10.1044/1058-0360(2009/09-0028)

Neville, H.J., Coffey, S.A., Holcomb, P.J., & Tallal, P. (1993). The neurobiology of sensory and language processing in language-impaired children. *Journal of Cognitive Neuroscience, 5*(2), 235–253. doi:10.1162/jocn.1993.5.2.235

Paracchini, V., Seia, M., Coviello, D., Porcaro, L., Costantino, L., Capasso, P., … Colombo, C. (2006). The chromosome 6p22 haplotype associated with dyslexia reduces the expression of KIAA0319, a novel gene involved in neuronal migration. *Human Molecular Genetics, 73,* 346–352.

Peiffer, A.M., Dunleavy, C.K., Frenkel, M., Gabel, L.A., LoTurco, J.J., Rosen, G.D., & Fitch, R.H. (2001). Impaired discrimination of variable duration embedded tones in adult male ectopic NZB mice. *NeuroReport, 12,* 2875–2879.

Peiffer, A.M., Friedman, J.T., Rosen, G.D., & Fitch, R.H. (2004). Impaired gap detection in juvenile microgyric rats. *Developmental Brain Research, 152,* 93–98. doi:10.1016/j.devbrainres.2004.06.003

Peiffer, A.M., McClure, M.M., Threlkeld, S.W., Rosen, G.D., & Fitch, R.H. (2004). Severity of focal microgyria and associated rapid auditory processing deficits. *NeuroReport, 15*(12), 1923–1926. doi:10.1097/00001756-200408260-00018

Peiffer, A.M., Rosen, G.D., & Fitch, R.H. (2002). Rapid auditory processing and MGN morphology in rats reared in varied acoustic environments. *Developmental Brain Research, 138,* 187–193. doi:10.1016/S0165-3806(02)00472-8

Peiffer, A.M., Rosen, G.D., & Fitch, R.H. (2004c). Sex differences in auditory processing deficits in microgyric rats. *Developmental Brain Research, 148*(1), 53–57. doi:10.1016/j.devbrainres.2003.09.020

Pennington, B.F. (1991). Diagnosing learning disorders: A neuropsychological framework. New York, NY: The Guildford Press.

Pennington, B.F., & Bishop, D.V.M. (2009). Relations among speech, language, and reading disorders. *Annual Review of Psychology, 60,* 283–306.

Peterson, R.L., McGrath, L.M., Shelley, Smith, S.D., & Pennington, B.F. (2007). Neuropsychology and genetics of speech, language, and literacy disorders. *Pediatric Clinics of North America, 54,* 543–561. doi:10.1016/j.pcl.2007.02.009

Pihko, E., Leppänen, P.H.T., Eklund, K.M., Cheour, M., Guttorm, T.K., & Lyytinen, H. (1999). Cortical responses of infants with and without a genetic risk for dyslexia: I. Age effects. *NeuroReport, 10,* 901–905.

Ramus, F. (2003). Developmental dyslexia: Specific phonological deficit or general sensorimotor dysfunction? *Current Opinion in Neurobiology, 13,* 212–218. doi:10.1016/S0959-4388(03)00035-7

Reed, M.A. (1989). Speech perception and the discrimination of brief auditory cues in reading disabled children. *Journal of Experimental Child Psychology, 48,* 270–292. doi:10.1016/0022-0965(89)90006-4

Renvall, H., & Hari, R. (2002). Auditory cortical responses to speech-like stimuli in dyslexic adults. *Journal of Cognitive Neuroscience, 14,* 757–68. doi:10.1162/08989290260138654

Robin, D., Tomblin, J.B., Kearney, A., & Hug, L. (1989). Auditory temporal pattern learning in children with severe speech and language impairment. *Brain and Language, 36,* 604–613.

Rosen, S., & Manganari, E. (2001). Is there a relationship between speech and nonspeech auditory processing in children with dyslexia? *Journal of Speech, Language, and Hearing Research, 44,* 720–736.

Rosen, G.D., Press, D.M., Sherman, G.F., & Galaburda, A.M. (1992). The development of induced cerebrocortical microgyria in the rat. *Journal of Neuropathology and Experimental Neurology, 51,* 601–611. doi:10.1097/00005072-199211000-00005

Schuele, C.M. (2004). The impact of developmental speech and language impairments on the acquisition of literacy skills. *Mental Retardation and Developmental Disabilities Research Reviews, 10*(3), 176–83. doi:10.1002/mrdd.20014

Schumacher, J., Anthoni, H., Dahdouh, F., König, I.R., Hillmer, A.M., Kluck, N., … Kere, J. (2006). Strong genetic evidence of DCDC2 as a susceptibility gene for dyslexia. *American Journal of Human Genetics, 78,* 52–62. doi:10.1086/498992

Shankweiler, D., & Crain, S. (1986). Language mechanisms and reading disorder: A modular approach. *Cognition, 24,* 139–168. doi:10.1016/0010-0277(86)90008-9

Shankweiler, D., Crain, S., Katz, L., Fowler, E., Liberman, A., Brady, S.A. … Shaywitz, B.A. (1995). Cognitive profiles of reading-disabled children: Comparison of language skills in phonology, morphology and syntax. *Psychological Science, 6,* 149–156. doi:10.1111/j.1467-9280.1995.tb00324

Shaywitz, S.E., & Shaywitz, B.A. (2008). Paying attention to reading: The neurobiology of reading and dyslexia. *Development and Psychopathology, 20,* 1329–1349. doi:10.1017/S0954579408000631

Shu, W., Cho, J.Y., Jiang, Y., Zhang, M., Weisz, D., Elder, G.A., … Buxbaum, J.D. (2005). Altered ultrasonic vocalization in mice with a disruption in the Foxp2 gene. *Proceedings of the National Academy of Sciences, USA, 102,* 9643–9648. doi:10.1073/pnas.0503739102

Sices, L., Taylor, H.G., Freebairn, L., Hansen, A., & Lewis, B. (2007). Relationship between speech-sound disorders and early literacy skills in preschool-age children: Impact of comorbid language impairment. *Journal of Developmental and Behavioral Pediatrics, 28*(6), 438–447. doi:10.1097/DBP.0b013e31811ff8ca

Slaghuis, W.L., Lovegrove, W.J., & Freestun, J. (1992). Letter recognition in peripheral vision and metacontrast masking in dyslexic and normal readers. *Clinical Vision Sciences, 7,* 53–65.

Smith, S.T., Macaruso, P., Shankweiler, D., & Crain, S. (1989). Syntactic comprehension in young poor readers. *Applied Psycholinguistics, 10,* 429–454. doi:10.1017/S0142716400009012

Smith-Spark, J.H., & Fisk, J.E. (2007). Working memory functioning in developmental dyslexia. *Memory, 15,* 34–56. doi:10.1080/09658210601043384

Stein, J. (2001). The magnocellular theory of developmental dyslexia. *Dyslexia, 7,* 12–36. doi:10.1002/dys.186

Sutter, M.L., Petkov, C., Baynes, K., & O'Connor, K.N. (2000). Auditory scene analysis in dyslexics. *NeuroReport, 11,* 1967–1971. doi:10.1097/00001756-200006260-00032

Szalkowksi, C., Hinman, J., DiPinto, K., Malloy, D., Threlkeld, S.W., Wang, Y., ... Fitch, R.H. (2011). Assessment of episodic memory performance following early interference with a dyslexia-risk gene (Dyx1c1) in male Sprague-Dawley rats. *Genes, Brain and Behavior, 10,* 244–252.

Szalkowski, C.E., Fiondella, C.G., Galaburda, A.M., Rosen, G.D., LoTurco, J.J., & Fitch, R.H. Neocortical disruption and behavioral impairments in rats following in utero RNAi of candidate dyslexia risk gene Kiaa0319, *Brain Research Bulletin,* in review.

Taipale, M., Kaminen, N., Nopola-Hemmi, J., Haltia, T., Myllyluoma, B., Lyytinen, H., ... Kere, J. (2003). A candidate gene for developmental dyslexia encodes a nuclear tetratricopeptide repeat domain protein dynamically regulated in brain. *Proceedings of the National Academy of Sciences, USA, 100,* 11553–11558. doi:10.1073/pnas.1833911100

Tallal, P. (1977). Auditory perception, phonics and reading disabilities in children. *Journal of the Acoustical Society of America, 62,* S100. doi:10.1121/1.2016007

Tallal, P. (1980). Auditory temporal perception, phonics and reading disabilities in children. *Brain and Language, 9,* 182–198. doi:10.1016/0093-934X(80)90139-X

Tallal, P., Miller, S., & Fitch, R.H. (1993). Neurobiological basis of speech: A case for the preeminence of temporal processing. *Annals of the New York Academy of Sciences, 682,* 27–47. doi:10.1111/j.1749-6632.1993.tb22957

Tallal, P., & Newcombe, F. (1978). Impairment of auditory perception and language comprehension in dysphasia. *Brain and Language, 5,* 13–24. doi:10.1016/0093-934X(78)90003-2

Tallal, P., & Piercy, M. (1973). Defects of non-verbal auditory perception in children with developmental aphasia. *Nature, 241,* 468–469. doi:10.1038/241468a0

Tallal, P., & Piercy, M. (1973b). Developmental aphasia: Impaired rate of non-verbal processing as a function of sensory modality. *Neuropsychologica, 11,* 389–398. doi:10.1016/0028-3932(73)90025-0

Tallal, P., & Piercy, M. (1975). Developmental aphasia: The perception of brief vowels and extended stop consonants. *Neuropsychologia, 13,* 69–74. doi:10.1016/0028-3932(75)90049-4

Tallal, P., & Stark, R.E. (1981). Speech acoustic-cue discrimination abilities of normally developing and language-impaired children. *Journal of the Acoustical Society of America, 69*(2), 568–574. doi:10.1121/1.385431

Threlkeld, S.W., McClure, M.M., Bai, J., Wang, Y., Rosen, G.D., LoTurco, J.J., ... Fitch, R.H. (2007). Developmental disruptions and behavioral impairments in rats following in utero RNAi of Dyx1c1. *Brain Research Bulletin, 71,* 508–514. doi:10.1016/j.brainresbull.2006.11.005

Threlkeld, S.W., McClure, M.M., Rosen, G.D., & Fitch, R.H. (2006). Developmental timeframes for the induction of microgyria and rapid auditory processing deficits in the rat. *Brain Research, 1109,* 22–31. doi:10.1016/j.brainres.2006.06.022

Trehub, S.E,. & Henderson, J.L. (1996). Temporal resolution in infancy and subsequent language development. *Journal of Speech and Hearing Research, 39*(6), 1315–1320.

Vellutino, F.R., Fletcher, J.M., Snowling, M.J., & Scanlon, D.M. (2004). Specific reading disability (dyslexia): What have we learned in the past four decades? *Journal of Child Psychology and Psychiatry, 45,* 2–40. doi:10.1046/j.0021-9630.2003.00305

Wang, Y., Paramasivam, M., Thomas, A., Bai, J., Kaminen-Ahola, N., Kere, J., ... LoTurco, J.J. (2006). Dyx1c1 functions in neuronal migration in developing neocortex. *Neuroscience, 143,* 515–522. doi:10.1016/j.neuroscience.2006.08.022

Watson, B.U. (1992). Auditory temporal acuity in normally achieving and learning-disabled college students. *Journal of Speech and Hearing Research, 35,* 148–156.

Williams, D., Botting, N., & Boucher, J. (2008). Language in autism and specific language impairment: Where are the links? *Psychological Bulletin, 134,* 944–963. doi:10.1037/a0013743

Witton, C., Talcott, J., Hansen, P., Richardson, A., Griffiths, T., Rees, A., … Green, G. (1998). Sensitivity to dynamic auditory and visual stimuli predicts nonword reading ability in both dyslexic and normal readers. *Current Biology, 8,* 791–797. doi:10.1016/S0960-9822(98)70320-3

Wright, B., Lombardino, L., King, W., Puranik, C., Leonard, C., & Merzenich, M. (1997). Deficits in auditory temporal and spectral resolution in language-impaired children. *Nature, 387,* 176–178. doi:10.1038/387176a0

Prediction of Children's Reading Skills
Understanding the Interplay Among Environment, Brain, and Behavior
Jessica M. Black and Fumiko Hoeft

Learning to read is considered a milestone of childhood (Noble, Wolmetz, Ochs, Farah, & McCandliss, 2006), and fluent reading is increasingly important in a modern world (Snow, Burns, & Griffin, 1998). Between 5%–10% and up to 17% of children, however, are struggling readers, affected by developmental dyslexia (dyslexia), a disorder accounting for up to 80% of all learning disabilities (Shaywitz, 1998). Dyslexia (or specific reading disability) is a chronic condition characterized by marked, persistent and unexpected difficulty learning to read unexplained by poor cognition, motivation, or schooling (Bruck, 1992; Francis, Shaywitz, Stuebing, Shaywitz, & Fletcher, 1996; Lyon, 1995; Lyon, Shaywitz, & Shaywitz, 2003; Shaywitz, 1998; Shaywitz, Morris, & Shaywitz, 2008).

Certain children have an increased likelihood of developing dyslexia. Dyslexia has a genetic basis (Bates et al., 2009; Dennis et al., 2009; Fisher & Francks, 2006; McGrath, Smith, & Pennington, 2006; Nöthen et al., 1999; Paracchini et al., 2006; Taipale et al., 2003), and the median risk for a child of a parent with dyslexia is nine times greater than the population at large (Gilger, Pennington, & DeFries, 1991). It is widely held that dyslexia reflects an underlying weakness in phonological skills (Hoien, Lundberg, Stanovich, & Bjaalid, 1995; Noble, Farah, & McCandliss, 2006; Shaywitz, 1998; Shaywitz et al., 1999, 2008; Stanovich & Siegel, 1994). Specifically, the ability to master alphabetic reading strategies (that depend upon being able to match phonemes to letters) is compromised in children with dyslexia (for a review, see Hulme & Snowling, 2009). Impairments in phonological processing are associated with secondary consequences that can further impair children's reading fluency, comprehension, and growth of vocabulary and content knowledge (Lyon et al., 2003). Unfortunately, dyslexia is often diagnosed *after* commencement of formal schooling, and therefore children are likely to experience repeated academic failure *before* diagnosis

Funding for Fumiko Hoeft was provided by grants from NICHD HD054720, the Lucile Packard Foundation for Children's Health, the Dyslexia Foundation and NARSAD Young Investigator Award. Funding for Jessica M. Black was provided by an NIH-sponsored institutional research-training grant 5-T32-MH19908-17 to Dr. Allan L. Reiss in Center for Interdisciplinary Brain Sciences Research.

(Fletcher, Lyon, Fuchs, & Barnes, 2006; Shaywitz, Gruen, & Shaywitz, 2007). A host of problems (both social and emotional) secondary to reading difficulty (Brooks, 2001; Fletcher et al., 2006; Gerber et al., 1990) may affect dyslexic individuals with negative effects persisting into adulthood (Raskind, Goldberg, Higgins, & Herman, 1999).

Clearly, early identification of and intervention for dyslexia are critical to reduce the effect of the burden on the individual as well as society (Snow, Burns, & Griffin, 1998). In fact, there is reason to believe that through early identification and intervention, children with dyslexia can make substantive gains in reading (Fletcher et al., 2006; Fuchs & Fuchs, 2005; Shaywitz et al., 2008; Torgesen et al., 1999; Vellutino, Scanlon, Small, & Fanuele, 2006). One fifth of individuals with dyslexia manage to compensate and develop adequate reading skills by adulthood (Lyytinen, Aro, Erskine, & Richardson, 2007). Though dyslexia does not disappear and reading never becomes an automatic process in these individuals, they can become better decoders (Shaywitz, 1998).

Recent findings have raised an exciting possibility that one day neuroimaging (perhaps combined with measures of behavior, genes, and environment) may be a critical component of clinical and educational practices. Here we review current methods to predict reading outcome and we consider the potential benefit of using multiple modalities such as behavior and multimodal neuroimaging that may maximize the ability to circumscribe or at least ameliorate the potentially deleterious effects of dyslexia.

PREDICTION THROUGH STANDARD BEHAVIOR MEASURES

Similar to standard educational and clinical behavior-based diagnosis, efforts to quantify and predict current and future individual reading achievement have been primarily behavior based. Prediction models should be able to correctly identify affected children as having dyslexia (known as *sensitivity*) and accurately categorize unaffected children as not having the condition (known as *specificity*). As a benchmark, a strong prediction model should provide both sensitivity and specificity between 70%–80%, although even this leaves a large percentage of children incorrectly classified (Committee on Children with Disabilities, 2001). Extant behavioral studies have shown that many measures, such as phonological awareness (Elbro, Borstrom, & Petersen, 1998; Gallagher, Frith, & Snowling, 2000; Pennington & Lefly, 2001; Scarborough, 1990), letter knowledge (Elbro et al., 1998; Pennington & Lefly, 2001; Scarborough, 1989, 1990), rapid naming (Manis, Seidenberg, & Doi, 1999; Schatschneider, Carlson, Francis, Foorman, & Fletcher, 2002; Wolf & Bowers, 2000), and vocabulary (Flax, Realpe-Bonilla, Roesler, Choudhury, & Benasich, 2009; Nation & Snowling, 2004) are predictive of future reading ability. These studies have reported that behavior measures predict reading achievement (up to 3 years forward) with sensitivities/specificities ranging between

52%–92% to 80%–92% (for a review see Snow et al., 1998). Many of these studies have provided invaluable insight into the measures that best predict outcome. In certain cases, however, the findings may be limited because of the study design (lack of cross-validation and limited generalizability or not correcting for autoregressive effects of correlated predictors) (Wood, Hill, Meyer, & Flowers, 2005) or because of high false positive and negative rates (Torgensen, 1998).

Recently, investigators of one study sought to address these confounds and offered compelling results (Wood et al., 2005). In this study, efforts were made to predict third and eighth grade reading ability using four predictors from the first grade (phonemic awareness, picture vocabulary, rapid naming, and single word reading). Standard multiple regression analyses similar to other studies (N = 220, 51% male, tested at first, third, and eight grades; 69%–76% of variance explained, and 80%–85% accuracy in predicting poor readers) were used. Importantly, the authors employed a predictive model (i.e., predicting current reading ability) created from their first sample, and applied the regression weights to a new sample of kindergarten through third-grade students (N = 500). Although this latter component of the study predicted concurrent and not future reading ability, the models from the original sample predicted concurrent reading ability of a new sample with an impressive accuracy of well above 80%.

Clearly, behavioral measures have shed critical light on measures that predict reading outcome. Heretofore, however, no single measure or combination of measures has been able to reliably (above a minimum suggested threshold of 75%) (Gredler, 2000; Jansky, 1978; Kingslake, 1983)— and prospectively—predict who will develop dyslexia. Nor has any single measure or combination of measures been able to predict the trajectory of the disorder or its successful management (i.e., compensation). Moreover, relying solely on behavior measures often precludes the ability to test newborns and infants (except see, e.g., Benasich & Tallal, 2002). This is a significant methodological issue, for there is reason to believe that the neural topography of language processing already appears anomalous in infants and very young children at risk for dyslexia (Lyytinen et al., 2006; Molfese, Molfese, & Modgline, 2001). In sum, behavior measures provide integral components of prediction models, yet considering alternative or supplemental methods of prediction may lead to maximum benefit. Next we consider ways in which reading outcome may be better predicted through the addition of neuroimaging techniques coupled with behavior predictors.

PREDICTION THROUGH EVENT-RELATED POTENTIALS

Event-related potential (ERP), which measures electrical activity of the brain, has been used in the majority of neuroimaging studies in young populations, ranging from newborns to kindergarteners and older (Espy, Molfese, Molfese, & Modglin, 2004; Guttorm, Leppänen, Hämäläinen,

Eklund, & Lyytinen, 2009; Maurer et al., 2009; Maurer, Bucher, Brem, & Brandeis, 2003; Molfese, Modglin, & Molfese, 2003; Molfese & Molfese, 2002; Molfese et al., 2008; Molfese, Molfese, & Modgline, 2001). This wide usage of ERP, rather than magnetic resonance imaging (MRI) that we describe later in this chapter, may be due to ERP's accessibility (e.g., cost and portability, safety concerns, relative resistance to motion artifacts [though there are a few studies that used MRI to examine functional brain patterns in young populations; see Dehaene-Lambertz, Dehaene, & Hertz-Pannier, 2002; Wang et al., 2008]).

Findings from such ERP studies have improved our understanding of the brain basis of reading development, and add to increasing prediction efforts. For example, developmental change in ERP measures between 1 to 4 years of age, as well as 4 to 8 years of age, significantly differentiated those with good and poor decoding ability of pseudo words and real words, respectively, at age 8 years (Espy et al., 2004). In addition, discriminant function analyses showed high accuracy (65%–100%) in predicting diagnosis of poor versus typical readers (though findings are limited as the study did not include a cross-validation sample) (Molfese, 2000; Molfese et al., 2001). In a more recent study of children with high and low familial risk for dyslexia, Maurer et al. (2009) found that prediction using behavior measures of reading level in school (for Grades 2, 3, 5, and their mean) was significantly improved by combining them with ERP measures taken at the beginning of kindergarten (prior to any formal reading instruction). In this study, ERP measures explained an additional variance of up to 30%, and in some cases explained variance in which behavior measures did not. Finally, Lyytinen and colleagues in Finland found greater reliance on the right than the left hemisphere whereas processing of speech as a newborn was related to poorer language and prereading skills at age 6.5 (Guttorm et al., 2009) and that ERP measures explained an additional variance of up to 30% of reading ability at 9 years of age (out of a total of 60% of the variance explained by various behavioral and ERP measures) (Leppänen et al., 2010). As shown here, an exciting next step for ERP research (along with the majority of behavioral research on dyslexia) is to expand the validity of findings by the inclusion of methods using cross-validation or independent samples to support predictive models.

In sum, although prediction studies using imaging techniques are still in their infancy, these studies raise the hopeful possibility that future reading skills can be predicted in part by brain measures. ERP investigations are, however, not without limitations. Though the temporal resolution of EEG is better than neuroimaging, the spatial resolution is limited compared with methods such as functional MRI (fMRI). Furthermore, ERP and fMRI often rely on task-related brain responses that may be influenced by transient states such high emotionality or cognitive engagement (but see, e.g., Liu, Flax, Guise, Sukul, & Benasich, 2008, in which this is less likely to occur in functional neuroimaging). Conversely, structural

MRI (sMRI) may be less prone to such influences. Hence, fMRI and sMRI may provide valuable information that supplement behavior and ERP measures do not. Next, we examine how neuroimaging has been applied to predict outcome in nondyslexia disorders, and in a small number of dyslexia-specific studies.

PREDICTION THROUGH MAGNETIC RESONANCE IMAGING MEASURES

In the past several years, there has been increased interest in efforts to predict outcome and prognosis in various disorders, through the use of MRI. If successful, such measures may eventually support early identification of individuals most likely in need of intervention, and perhaps even point to intervention with maximum likelihood of effectiveness. Outside of dyslexia, MRI studies have been used to predict situations such as recovery from depression 8 months later (Canli et al., 2005), relapse in methamphetamine dependence 1 year later (Paulus, Tapert, & Schuckit, 2005), onset of psychosis in at-risk individuals (Koutsouleris et al., 2009), progression from health to Alzheimer's (Apostolva et al., 2006), outcome in depression (Davidson, Irwin, Anderle, & Kalin, 2003; Fu et al., 2004), anxiety (Whalen et al., 2008), and cognitive behavioral therapy in schizophrenia (Kumari et al., 2009).

Few known studies however, have examined the extent to which brain-related markers obtained from MRI can predict outcome in children with dyslexia. One may hypothesize that behavior and brain measures are two sides of the same coin, and hence MRI measures may add no additional information beyond what one could gain from administering standard behavior measures of reading and cognition. Furthermore, one may also predict that the ultimate goal of reading may be best predicted by the same measure, (i.e., behavior measures of reading). However, this does not address early diagnosis in infants and children.

Predicting Short-Term Reading Outcomes by Combining Neuroimaging and Behavior Measures

We undertook a study to directly examine these predictions and to see whether brain-imaging measures provide novel information above and beyond behavior in predicting reading outcome in children. We thus examined the usefulness of combining functional and structural neuroimaging measures with behavior to predict decoding ability one year later in 64 (37 female, 27 male) children ages 8–12 (Hoeft et al., 2007). All children were healthy, right-handed, native English-speakers. In our study, child participants were recruited from public schools after being identified by their teachers as poor readers.

We examined 1) how well voxel-based regional grey and white matter volumes and functional MRI (fMRI) brain activation during a real-word visual rhyme judgment task at the beginning of the school year predicted decoding skills at the end of the school year; 2) whether the prediction was improved by combining brain based and behavior measures over behavior measures alone using multiple regression, and 3) the validity of the regression models.

In answer to our first question posed, we found that neuroimaging measures (combination of VBM and fMRI) accounted for 57% of the variance in Time2 decoding skills. It is interesting to note that we found that a combination of only the behavior measures accounted for 65% of the variance of Time2 decoding performance, a finding consistent with previous regression-based studies of behavior. Although the combination of a standard battery of behavior measures performed slightly better than neuroimaging measures, there was no significant difference between the two modalities (Figure 12.1). It is important to note, however, by combining the behavior and neuroimaging predictors into one model, we found that 81% of the variance was explained—a percentage significantly better than behavior or neuroimaging alone. Results for the regression analyses were similar when we controlled for initial decoding skills, age, and IQ. We also controlled for the number of predictors used. All the aforementioned analyses (except for the selection of the predictors) were performed using various cross-validation methods, such as leave-one-out (i.e., creating the model using N-1 subjects and predicting outcome in the left-out subject, and rotating the left-out subject so that each subject is left out once), as well as split-half reliability (i.e., creating a model using half the sample and predicting outcome in the remaining half, and repeating this procedure 2,000 times).

Our results indicate that neuroimaging information provided non-redundant (i.e., new and important) information to behavior. As such, this study was the first to compare the ability to predict outcome between behavior and neuroimaging, and to combine these two modalities to see whether the prediction performance would be significantly enhanced.

Predicting Long-Term Compensation of Dyslexia Using Multivariate Pattern Analysis

As previously mentioned, there are some individuals for whom poor reading is remediated over time without specific interventions, yet there are currently no reliable predictors of this compensation (Lyytinen et al., 2007). Neuroimaging may serve to elucidate the underlying neuronal pathways by which individuals with dyslexia are able to compensate, developing adequate reading skills by adulthood. In a 2.5-year longitudinal study of children with ($N = 25$) and without ($N = 20$) dyslexia, we examined prospectively whether brain-based measures (fMRI [real word visual rhyme judgment task] as well as diffusion-tensor imaging [DTI; which reflects microstructural integrity]) predict who will gain in reading ability (Hoeft et al., 2011). Reading outcome was measured by increases in

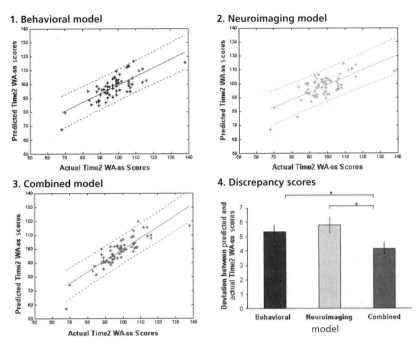

Figure 12.1. Predicting Time2 reading ability (Word Attack-standard score [WA-ss] one school year later) using neuroimaging and behavior measures. Parameters obtained from multiple regression analyses in the training set (*N* = 63) were applied to the omitted participant, which yielded one predicted value and was repeated 64 times for all possible permutations. Predicted values obtained from the omitted single test participants are plotted for the behavioral model (1), the neuroimaging model (2), and the combined model (3). Linear regression lines are obtained from the training sets and drawn as solid lines. Ninety-five percent prediction intervals of the expected individual Time2 WA-ss are in dotted curves (4). Deviation of predicted values from the actual Time2 WA-ss. Mean average of the 64 participants are plotted for the behavioral (dark grey), neuroimaging (light grey), and combined models (medium grey). Error bars represent standard error of the mean. *p* < .05. (From Hoeft, F., et al. [2007]. Prediction of children's reading skills using behavioral, functional, and structural neuroimaging measures. *Behavioral Neuroscience, 121*[3], pp. 602–613. Supplementary Figure D [APA]; reprinted with permission.)

single word reading ability. We also tested a composite measure of reading, as well as passage comprehension skills as outcome. We reasoned that the hyperactivation in dyslexia seen in various brain regions (most notably the right inferior frontal gyrus [IFG]) may reflect compensatory mechanisms by which poor readers attempt to overcome deficits in left posterior language centered regions (Shaywitz & Shaywitz, 2008). We included typical readers to examine whether improvement in reading skill was predicted by similar behavioral and neurobiological substrates in this sample, compared to children with dyslexia.

To extend our previous work, we performed cross-validation multivariate pattern analysis (MVPA) to examine whether a multivariate pattern of brain activation (elicited during the visual word rhyme judgment task) using a machine-learning algorithm, (i.e., linear support vector

machines [SVM] could predict future reading ability with high accuracy). This MVPA approach (in particular SVM) is becoming increasingly popular in neuroimaging research owing to its ability to deal with
high-dimensional data and to create models to predict outcome (Bray,
Chang, & Hoeft, 2009). Another advantage is that cross-validation is always performed in MVPA to avoid overfitting of the models, meaning
that it creates predictive models that have the potential to generalize to
independent samples.

Using univariate analysis, we found that none of the 17 behavioral or
composite scores predicted growth of reading skill in children with dyslexia (even using a very lenient threshold of $p = .05$, uncorrected) over the
2.5 years. Also using univariate analyses, fMRI findings of greater right
IFG activation during phonological processing predicted reading gains in
children with dyslexia but not in typical readers (controls). Results from
DTI analysis suggested that greater white matter integrity in the right
superior longitudinal fasciculus (SLF) (including arcuate fasciculus [AF])
predicted reading gains, but once again only for children with dyslexia
rather than control children. Our findings identified neural pathways potentially critical to compensation, and also suggested that the results were
specific to dyslexia rather than to reading in general. Finally, whole-brain
activation pattern from MVPA in children with dyslexia, which included the right frontal region, predicted which children would compensate
with over 90% accuracy in the cross-validation sample. Taken together,
our findings highlight the importance of right-frontal regions implicated
in successful compensation (Shaywitz & Shaywitz, 2008) and provide evidence that neuroimaging measures can predict outcome of reading skill
in children with impaired reading.

Interplay Among Brain, Environmental, and Genetic Factors in Reading Development

Although initial results from our research program (described above)
are promising, these methods should be extended to younger children
to assess the value of this model before children receive formal reading
instruction. We know from extensive ERP research that there are clear
differences between prereaders with and without familial risk for dyslexia, but publications from MRI research in this population are still
scarce. The only study to date, however, has in fact shown evidence of significant differences in brain activation patterns between prereaders with
and without familial risk for dyslexia (Specht et al., 2009). In summary,
although we know that there are structural and functional differences in
the brains of individuals with dyslexia via MRI techniques, we know very
little about how early and to what extent these structural deviations arise
in very young children.

Given evidence of functional anomalies present in pre- and early
readers at risk for dyslexia, it is conceivable that structural anomalies

exist in this timeframe as well. To examine individual differences in brain activation and structure, environmental, behavioral, and genetic patterns that would predict future reading outcome in at-risk and low-risk prereaders, we commenced a longitudinal MRI study in 5- and 6-year-old children ($N = 51$; 29 males; age $M = 5.59$, $SD = .42$) with varying degrees of family risk (i.e., a history of dyslexia in the family) and behavioral risk (i.e., poor ability in precursors of skills related to reading) for dyslexia (Black, et al., under review). Familial risk and behavioral risk have been robustly examined; however, this is the first known study to examine these risks simultaneously. We defined familial risk using the maternal and paternal Adult Reading History Questionnaire (ARHQ) scores (Lefly & Pennington, 2000). On this measure a score > .30 indicates history of reading impairment. We defined behavioral risk as the composite measure from measures of phonological awareness, rapid naming, and letter identification. We examined associations between regional grey and white matter volumes from VBM and either maternal familial risk, paternal familial risk, or behavioral risk, while controlling for the other risks.

Results show the first evidence (of which we are aware) of the influence of risk factors for developing dyslexia on brain morphometry in 5- and 6-year-old children. More specifically, dissociation between maternal and paternal familial risks as well as the child's behavioral risk was evident. The more severe the maternal (but not paternal) history of reading disability, the more reduced the child's bilateral prefrontal and parietotemporal grey matter regions. The trend for a significant negative correlation with white matter volume and maternal risk in the left parieto-temporal region (spatially adjacent to and statistically in the same direction as the grey matter finding) was no longer significant after controlling for behavioral risk, suggesting that it is the grey matter that appears most influenced by maternal reading-skill history. The brain regions implicated in this study are important for language processing (Vigneau et al., 2006) and other related cognitive skills (Alloway, Gathercole, Willis, & Adams, 2004; Bunge, Klingberg, Jacobsen, & Gabrieli, 2000; Smith & Jonides, 1999) and are also often reported as being atypical in dyslexia (Maisog, Einbinder, Flowers, Turkeltaub, & Eden, 2008; Richlan, Kronbichler, & Wimmer, 2009). It appears that maternal reading history is significantly related to brain structures implicated in fluent reading. Notably, in our study, mothers spent more time (generally and related to educational activities, such as reading) with their children than did fathers. Therefore, in this study we cannot disentangle genetics from environmental effects (e.g., exposure to mothers) and in fact posit that these two factors exert interactive effects. This conjecture is reflected in the findings of greater maternal affect, though it is noteworthy that regressing out environmental measures such as socioeconomic status (SES) and maternal education did not alter the results. Future studies disentangling whether the current results are due to environmental (e.g., mothers' current reading behaviors and activities with children) and/or genetic factors are warranted. Another important finding from our study is that significant associations with brain morphometry and behavioral risk were not identified. Thus, in this young age group, neuroanatomical patterns did not explain performance on measures known to be predictors of reading disability. Perhaps in young children, brain-based measures provide more sensitivity as traditional behavioral risk indices do not appear to play a large role in structural differences.

Finally, because the mass-univariate VBM analyses approach did not produce any significant associations with behavioral risk (a composite of prereading scores) and GM or WM regional brain volumes, we performed exploratory MVPA to examine whether a pattern of neuropsychological, environmental and neuroanatomical measures can predict behavioral risk. We found preliminary evidence of a pattern of environmental measures (e.g., parental reading history, mothers education level and IQ, home environment, and mothers perception of child) or neuroanatomical measures (e.g., bilateral parietotemporal, precentral, and occipitotemporal regions) being equally predictive to neuropsychological measures (e.g., phonological memory, processing speed, executive function, and sensorimotor function; Figure 12.2). Prediction accuracies of cross-validation analyses were all within the range of 86%–92%, and when combined, reached 100%.

IMPLICATIONS AND FUTURE DIRECTIONS

A large percentage of children could be aided by earlier identification and intervention for impaired reading. Standard educational and clinical practice relies on behavior measures of reading and cognition, and many of these measures explain a large portion of the variance in concurrent and future skill. An exciting new advance in the field of reading and dyslexia is the possibility of combining neuroimaging and behavior measures to enhance prediction of reading outcome and prognosis. This technique, however, is still in its nascent form, as most neuroimaging methods used to predict outcome in dyslexia have relied on retrospective, regression-based analyses without cross-validation. Recent research, however, is beginning to show that the combination of behavior and neuroimaging measures could build a stronger model to predict outcome of future reading abilities compared with either measure used alone. Studies are also starting to include cross-validation in which models are created from a training set independent from the data set to be tested (though not entirely because part of the total sample is set aside as the test set), which importantly allows these models to generalize to new samples. For example, Christiana Leonard's group (see Chapter 15) has played a pioneering role in this regard using anatomical patterns (anatomical risk index, ARI) to predict dyslexia and specific language impairment (SLI) in new samples (Leonard, Eckert, Given, Virginia, & Eden, 2006).

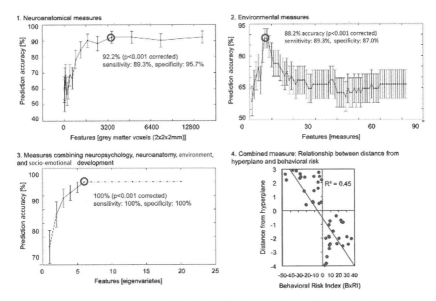

Figure 12.2. Predicting concurrent behavioral risk (inverse of prereading score) using neuropsychological (including demographic), neuroimaging, environmental, and social-emotional development measures. Multivariate pattern analyses (MVPA) were performed using leave-one-out linear support vector machine and by reducing features using recursive-feature elimination (RFE) [(1) and (2)] and data compression using principle component analysis (PCA) (3). Data compression was also used when combining modalities to roughly match the number of features. Circles indicate the number of features where maximal performance was obtained. Distance from the hyperplane for each child (i.e., plane that best dissects children with higher risk versus lower risk) correlates significantly with their behavioral risk, supporting the validity of the model combining neuropsychological, neuroanatomical, environmental, and social-emotional measures.

Findings reviewed here also point to the strong influence of possible environmental and genetic factors, such as maternal reading history on prereading children's anatomical patterns. Thus, it may be possible to elucidate the mechanisms by which fluent and impaired reading unfolds by combining behavior and neuroimaging measures with genetics as well as measures of environment. For example, although it is unlikely that dyslexia is X-linked (since father–son transmission has been reported) (Lewis, 1992), it would be important for future studies to examine sex-linked genes for further evidence. Findings of the importance of home environment (e.g., SES, measures of parental education and occupation), as well as schooling, should also be examined in future neuroimaging studies. Although substantial evidence points to a neurobiological origin subserving the phonological impairments observed in children with dyslexia, Fletcher et al. (2006) underscore the importance of examining the interplay of brain and environment on the development of reading. For example, one such environmental influence, SES (typically measured by a composite score of parental education, parental occupation, and family income; [Andreadis, Giannakakis, Papageorgiou, & Nikita, 2009;

Entwisle & Astone, 1994]) is strongly correlated with cognitive abilities, intelligence, and literacy (Bradley, 1993; Bradley & Corwyn, 2002; Molfese & Molfese, 2002), and rate of intellectual growth (Espy, Molfese, & Di-Lalla, 2001). Differences in reading achievement may thus also reflect differences in schooling and literacy-related activity in the home (Bradley, Corwyn, McAdoo, & Coll, 2001).

Findings presented here raise the remarkable possibility of combining measures of behavior, neuroimaging, genetics, and environment as critical components in clinical and educational practices. Before findings from research can have implications for the classroom, however, they will need to be validated using cross-validation methods with large samples of geographically diverse participants. Even then, there are many other issues that need to be overcome, such as ethical considerations ("Will children be discriminated against based on brain scans?") and cost effectiveness ("Is it worth paying several hundred dollars to improve a small amount of prediction accuracy?") to name a few. Nonetheless, dyslexia can have substantial deleterious effects on both individuals and society, and therefore it is paramount that future studies continue to examine mechanisms to improve predictors for early identification, thus allowing for earlier intervention and, in turn, benefiting a tremendous number of the world's children.

REFERENCES

Alloway, T.P., Gathercole, S.E., Willis, C., & Adams, A.M. (2004). A structural analysis of working memory and related cognitive skills in young children. *Journal of Experimental Child Psychology, 87*(2), 85–106. doi:10.1016/j.jecp.2003.10.002

Andreadis, I., Giannakakis, G.A., Papageorgiou, C., & Nikita, K.S. (2009). Detecting complexity abnormalities in dyslexia measuring approximate entropy of electroencephalographic signals. *Conference Proceedings IEEE Engineering in Medicine and Biology Society, 1*, 6292–6295.

Apostolva, L.G., Dutton, R.A., Dinov, I.D., Hayashi, K.M., Toga, A.W., & Cummings, J.L. (2006). Conversion from mild cognitive impairment to Alzheimer disease predicted by hippocampal atrophy maps. *Archives of Neurology, 63*, 693–699. doi:10.1001/archneur.63.5.693

Bates, T.C., Lind, P.A., Luciano, M., Montgomery, G.W., Martin, N.G., & Wright, M.J. (2009). Dyslexia and DYX1C1: Deficits in reading and spelling associated with a missense mutation. *Molecular Psychiatry, 15*, 1190–1196. doi:10.1038/mp.2009.120

Benasich, A.A., & Tallal, P. (2002). Infant discrimination of rapid auditory cues predicts later language impairment. *Behavioural Brain Research, 136*(1), 31–49. doi:10.1016/S0166-4328(02)00098-0

Black, J.M., Tanaka, H., Stanley, L., Nagamine, M., Zakerani, N., Thurston, A., ... Hoeft, F. Maternal history of reading difficulty is associated with reduced language-related grey matter in beginning readers. *NeuroImage.* doi:10.1016/j.neuroimage.2011.10.024

Bradley, R.H. (1993). Children's home environments, health, behavior, and intervention efforts: A review using the HOME inventory as a marker measure. *Genetic, Social, and General Psychology Monographs, 119*(4), 437–490.

Bradley, R.H., & Corwyn, R.F. (2002). Socioeconomic status and child development. *Annual Review of Psychology, 53*(1), 371–399.

Bradley, R.H., Corwyn, R.F., McAdoo, H.P., & Coll, C.G. (2001). The home environments of children in the United States part I: Variations by age, ethnicity, and poverty status.

Child Development, 72(6), 1844–1867. doi:10.1111/1467-8624.t01-1-00382

Bray, S., Chang, C., & Hoeft, F. (2009). Applications of multivariate pattern classification analyses in developmental neuroimaging of healthy and clinical populations. *Frontiers in Human Neuroscience, 3,* 32. doi:10.3389/neuro.09.032.2009

Brooks, R.B. (2001). Fostering motivation, hope and resilience in children with learning disorders. *Annals of Dyslexia, 51*(1), 9–20. doi:10.1007/s11881-001-0003-4

Bruck, M. (1992). Persistence of dyslexics' phonological awareness deficits. *Developmental Psychology, 28*(5), 874–886. doi:10.1037/0012-1649.28.5.874

Bunge, S.A., Klingberg, T., Jacobsen, R.B., & Gabrieli, J.D.E. (2000). A resource model of the neural basis of executive working memory. *Proceedings of the National Academy of Sciences, USA, 97*(7), 3573–3578. doi:10.1073/pnas.050583797

Canli, T., Cooney, R.E., Goldin, P., Shah, M., Sivers, H., Thomason, M.E., ... Gotlib, I. (2005). Amygdala reactivity to emotional faces predicts improvement in major depression. *Neuroreport, 16,* 1267–1270. doi:10.1097/01.wnr.0000174407.09515.cc

Committee on Children with Disabilities, American Academy of Pediatrics (2001). Developmental surveillance and screening of infants and young children. *Pediatrics, 108*(1), 192–196. doi:10.1542/peds.108.1.192

Davidson, R.J., Irwin, W., Anderle, M.J., & Kalin, N.H. (2003). The neural substrates of affective processing in depressed patients treated with venlafaxine. *American Journal of Psychiatry, 160,* 64–75. doi:10.1176/appi.ajp.160.1.64

Dehaene-Lambertz, G., Dehaene, S., & Hertz-Pannier, L. (2002). Functional neuroimaging of speech perception in infants. *Science, 298*(5600), 2013–2015. doi:10.1126/science.1077066

Dennis, M.Y., Paracchini, S., Scerri, T.S., Prokunina-Olsson, L., Knight, J.C., Wade-Martins, R., ... Monaco, A.P. (2009). A common variant associated with dyslexia reduces expression of the KIAA0319 gene. *PLoS Genetics, 5*(3). doi:10.1371/journal.pgen.1000436

Elbro, C., Borstrom, I., & Petersen, D.K. (1998). Predicting dyslexia from kindergarten: The importance of distinctness of phonological representations of lexical items. *Reading Research Quarterly, 33,* 36–60. doi:10.1598/RRQ.33.1.3

Entwisle, D.R., & Astone, N.M. (1994). Some practical guidelines for measuring youth's race/ethnicity and socioeconomic status. *Child Development, 65*(6), 1521–1540. doi:10.2307/1131278

Espy, K.A., Molfese, D.L., Molfese, V.J., & Modglin, A. (2004). Development of auditory event-related potentials in young children and relations to word-level reading abilities at age 8 years. *Annals of Dyslexia, 54,* 9–38. doi:10.1007/s11881-004-0002-3

Espy, K.A., Molfese, V.J., & DiLalla, L.F. (2001). Effects of environmental measures on intelligence in children: Growth curve modeling of longitudinal data. *Merrill-Palmer Quarterly, 47*(1), 42–73. doi:10.1353/mpq.2001.0001

Fisher, S.E., & Francks, C. (2006). Genes, cognition and dyslexia: Learning to read the genome. *Trends in Cognitive Sciences, 10*(6), 250–257. doi:10.1016/j.tics.2006.04.003

Flax, J.F., Realpe-Bonilla, T., Roesler, C., Choudhury, N., & Benasich, A. (2009). Using early standardized language measures to predict later language and early reading outcomes in children at high risk for language-learning impairments. *Journal of Learning Disabilities, 42*(1), 61–75. doi:10.1177/0022219408326215

Fletcher, J.M., Lyon, G.R., Fuchs, L.S., & Barnes, M. (2006). *Learning disabilities: From identification to intervention.* New York, NY: Guilford Press.

Francis, D.J., Shaywitz, S.E., Stuebing, K.K., Shaywitz, B.A., & Fletcher, J.M. (1996). Developmental lag versus deficit model of reading disability: A longitudinal, individual growth curves analysis. *Journal of Educational Psychology, 88,* 3–17. doi:10.1037//0022-0663.88.1.3

Fu, C.H., Williams, S.C., Cleare, A.J., Brammer, M.J., Walsh, N.D., Kim, J., ... Bullmore, E.T. (2004). Attenuation of the neural response to sad faces in major depression by antidepressant treatment: A prospective, event-related functional magnetic resonance imaging study. *Archives of General Psychiatry, 61,* 877–889. doi:10.1001/archpsyc.61.9.877

Fuchs, D., & Fuchs, L.S. (2005). Peer-assisted learning strategies: Promoting word recognition, fluency and reading comprehension in young children. *Journal of Special Education, 39*(1), 34–44. doi:10.1177/00224669050390010401

Gallagher, A., Frith, U., & Snowling, M.J. (2000). Precursors of literacy delay among children with genetic risk for dyslexia. *Journal of Child Psychology and Psychiatry, 41*(2), 203–213. doi:10.1017/S0021963099005284

Gerber, P.J., Schneiders, C.A., Paradise, L.V., Reiff, H.B., Ginsberg, R.J., & Popp, P.A. (1990). Persisting problems of adults with learning disabilities: Self-reported comparisons from their school-age and adult years. *Journal of Learning Disabilities, 23*(9), 570–573. doi:10.1177/002221949002300907

Gilger, J.W., Pennington, B.F., & DeFries, J.C. (1991). Risk for reading disability as a function of parental history in three family studies. *Reading and Writing, 3,* 205–217.

Gredler, G.R. (2000). Early childhood screening for developmental and educational problems. In B.A. Bracken (Ed.), *The Psychoeducational Assessment of Preschool Children* (pp. 399–411). Boston, MA: Allyn & Bacon.

Guttorm, T.K., Leppänen, P.H., Hämäläinen, J.A., Eklund, K.M., & Lyytinen, H.J. (2009). Newborn event-related potentials predict poorer pre-reading skills in children at risk for dyslexia. *Journal of Learning Disabilities, 43*(5), 391–401. doi:10.1177/0022219409345005

Hoeft, F., McCandliss, B., Black, J.M., Gantman, A., Zakerani, N., Hulme, C., ... Gabrieli, J.D. (2011). Neural systems predicting long-term learning of dyslexia. *Proceedings of the National Academy of Sciences, USA, 108*(1), 361–366.

Hoeft, F., Ueno, T., Reiss, A.L., Meyler, A., Whitfield-Gabrieli, S., Glover, G.H., ... Gabrieli, J.D.E. (2007). Prediction of children's reading skills using behavioral, functional, and structural neuroimaging measures. *Behavioral Neuroscience, 121*(3), 602–613. doi:10.1037/0735-7044.121.3.602

Hoien, T., Lundberg, I., Stanovich, K.E., & Bjaalid, I.K. (1995). Components of phonological awareness. *Reading and Writing: An Interdisciplinary Journal, 7*(2), 171–188.

Hulme, C., & Snowling, M.J. (2009). *Developmental disorders of language learning and cognition.* West Sussex, England: Wiley-Blackwell.

Jansky, J.J. (1978). A critical review of some developmental and predictor precursors of reading disabilities. In A.L. Benton & D. Pearl (Eds.), *Dyslexia: An appraisal of current knowledge* (pp. 331–347). New York, NY: Oxford University Press.

Kingslake, B.J. (1983). The predictive (in)accuracy of on-entry to school screening procedures when used to anticipate learning difficulties. *British Journal of Special Education, 10*(4), 23–26. doi:10.1111/j.1467-8578.1983.tb00184

Koutsouleris, N., Meisenzahl, E.M., Davatzikos, C., Bottlender, R., Frodl, T., Scheuerecker, J., ... Gaser, C. (2009). Use of neuroanatomical pattern classification to identify subjects in at-risk mental states of psychosis and predict disease transition. *Archives of General Psychiatry, 66*(7), 700–712. doi:10.1001/archgenpsychiatry.2009.62

Kumari, V., Peters, E.R., Fannon, D., Antonova, E., Premkumar, P., Anilkumar, A.P., ... Kuipers, E. (2009). Dorsolateral prefrontal cortex activity predicts responsiveness to cognitive-behavioral therapy in schizophrenia. *Biological Psychiatry, 66*(6), 594–602. doi:10.1016/j.biopsych.2009.04.036

Lefly, D.L., & Pennington, B.F. (2000). Reliability and validity of the Adult Reading History Questionnaire. *Journal of Learning Disabilities, 33*(3), 286–296. doi:10.1177/002221940003300306

Leonard, C., Eckert, M., Given, B., Virginia, B., & Eden, G. (2006). Individual differences in anatomy predict reading and oral language impairments in children. *Brain, 129*(12), 3329–3342. doi:10.1093/brain/awl262

Leppänen, P.H., Hämäläinen, J.A., Salminen, H.K., Eklund, K.M., Guttorm, T.K., Lohvansuu, K., ... Lyytinen, H. (2010). Newborn brain event-related potentials revealing atypical processing of sound frequency and the subsequent association with later literacy skills in children with familial dyslexia. *Cortex, 46*(10), 1362–1376. doi:10.1016/j.cortex.2010.06.003

Lewis, B.A. (1992). Pedigree analysis of children with phonology disorders. *Journal of Learning Disabilities, 25*(9), 586–597. doi:10.1177/002221949202500908

Liu, W.C., Flax, J.F., Guise, K.G., Sukul, V., & Benasich, A.A. (2008). Functional connectivity of the sensorimotor area in naturally sleeping infants. *Brain Research, 1223,* 42–49. doi:10.1016/j.brainres.2008.05.054

Lyon, G.R. (1995). Toward a definition of dyslexia. *Annals of Dyslexia, 45*(1), 1–27. doi:10.1007/BF02648210

Lyon, G.R., Shaywitz, S.E., & Shaywitz, B.A. (2003). A definition of dyslexia. *Annals of Dyslexia, 53*(1), 1–14. doi:10.1007/s11881-003-0001-9

Lyytinen, H., Aro, M., Erskine, J., & Richardson, U. (2007). Reading and reading disorders. In M. Shatz & E. Hoff (Eds.), *Handbook of Language Development.* (pp. 454–474). Malden, MA: Blackwell.

Lyytinen, H., Erskine, J., Tolvanen, A., Torppa, M., Poikkeus, A., & Lyytinen, P. (2006). Trajectories of reading development: A follow-up from birth to school age of children with and without risk for dyslexia. *Merrill-Palmer Quarterly, 52*(3), 514–546. doi:10.1353/mpq.2006.0031

Maisog, J.M., Einbinder, E.R., Flowers, D.L., Turkeltaub, P.E., & Eden, G.F. (2008). A meta-analysis of functional neuroimaging studies of dyslexia. *Annals of the New York Academy of Sciences, 1145,* 237–259. doi:10.1196/annals.1416.024

Manis, F.R., Seidenberg, M.S., & Doi, L.M. (1999). See Dick RAN: Rapid naming and the longitudinal prediction of reading subskills in first and second graders. *Scientific Studies of Reading, 3*(2), 129–157. doi:10.1207/s1532799xssr0302_3

Maurer, U., Bucher, K., Brem, S., Benz, R., Kranz, F., Schulz, … Brandeis, D. (2009). Neurophysiology in preschool improves behavioral prediction of reading ability throughout primary school. *Biological Psychiatry, 66*(4), 341–348. doi:10.1016/j.biopsych.2009.02.031

Maurer, U., Bucher, K., Brem, S., & Brandeis, D. (2003). Altered responses to tone and phoneme mismatch in kindergartners at familial dyslexia risk. *Neuroreport, 14*(17), 2245–2250. doi:10.1097/00001756-200312020-00022

McGrath, L.M., Smith, S.D., & Pennington, B.F. (2006). Breakthroughs in the search for dyslexia candidate genes. *Trends in Molecular Medicine, 12*(7), 333–341. doi:10.1016/j.molmed.2006.05.007

Molfese, D.L. (2000). Predicting dyslexia at 8 years of age using neonatal brain responses. *Brain and Language, 72*(3), 238–245. doi:10.1006/brln.2000.2287

Molfese, V.J., Modglin, A., & Molfese, D.L. (2003). The role of environment in the development of reading skills: A longitudinal study of preschool and school-age measures. *Journal of Learning Disabilities, 36*(1), 59–67. doi:10.1177/00222194030360010701

Molfese, V.J., & Molfese, D.L. (2002). Environmental and social influences on reading skills as indexed by brain and behavioral responses. *Annals of Dyslexia, 52*(1), 121–137. doi:10.1007/s11881-002-0009-6

Molfese, V.J., Molfese, D.L., Beswick, J.L., Jacobi-Vessels, J., Molfese, P.J., Molnar, A.E., … Brittany, L. (2008). Use of event-related potentials to identify language and reading skills. *Topics in Language Disorders, 28*(1), 28–45. doi:10.1097/01.adt.0000311414.69966.3f

Molfese, V.J., Molfese, D.L., & Modgline, A.A. (2001). Newborn and preschool predictors of second-grade reading scores: An evaluation of categorical and continuous scores. *Journal of Learning Disabilities, 34*(6), 545–554. doi:10.1177/002221940103400607

Nation, K., & Snowling, M.J. (2004). Beyond phonological skills: Broader language skills contribute to the development of reading. *Journal of Research in Reading, 27*(4), 342–356. doi:10.1111/j.1467-9817.2004.00238

Noble, K.G., Farah, M.J., & McCandliss, B.D. (2006). Socioeconomic background modulates cognition-achievement relationships in reading. *Cognitive Development, 21,* 349–368. doi:10.1016/j.cogdev.2006.01.007

Noble, K.G., Wolmetz, M.E., Ochs, L.G., Farah, M.J., & McCandliss, B.D. (2006). Brain-behavior relationships in reading acquisition are modulated by socioeconomic factors. *Developmental Science, 9*(6), 642–654. doi:10.1111/j.1467-7687.2006.00542

Nöthen, M.M., Schulte-Körne, G., Grimm, T., Cichon, S., Vogt, I.R., Müller-Myhsok, B., … Remschmidt, H. (1999). Genetic linkage analysis with dyslexia: Evidence for linkage of spelling disability to chromosome 15. *European Child & Adolescent Psychiatry, 8*(3), 56–59.

Paracchini, S., Thomas, A., Castro, S., Lai, C., Paramasivam, M., Wang, Y., … Monaco, A.P. (2006). The chromosome 6p22 haplotype associated with dyslexia reduces the expression of KIAA0319, a novel gene involved in neuronal migration. *Human Molecular Genetics, 15*(10), 1659–1666. doi:10.1093/hmg/ddl089

Paulus, M.P., Tapert, S.F., & Schuckit, M.A. (2005). Neural activation patterns of methamphetamine-dependent subjects during decision making predict relapse. *Archives of General Psychiatry, 62*(7), 761–768. doi:10.1001/archpsyc.62.7.761

Pennington, B.F., & Lefly, D.L. (2001). Early reading development in children at family risk for dyslexia. *Child Development, 72*(3), 816–833. doi:10.1111/1467-8624.00317

Raskind, M.H., Goldberg, R.J., Higgins, E.L., & Herman, K.L. (1999). Patterns of change and predictors of success in individuals with learning disabilities: Results from a twenty-year longitudinal study. *Learning Disabilities: Research & Practice, 14,* 35–50. doi:10.1207/sldrp1401_4

Richlan, F., Kronbichler, M., & Wimmer, H. (2009). Functional abnormalities in the dyslexic brain: A quantitative meta-analysis of neuroimaging studies. *Human Brain Mapping, 30*(10), 3299–3308. doi:10.1002/hbm.20752

Scarborough, H.S. (1989). Prediction of reading disability from familial and individual differences. *Journal of Educational Psychology, 81*(1), 101–108. doi:10.1037//0022-0663.81.1.101

Scarborough, H.S. (1990). Very early language deficits in dyslexic children. *Child Development, 61,* 1728–1743. doi:10.2307/1130834

Schatschneider, C., Carlson, C.D., Francis, D.J., Foorman, B.R., & Fletcher, J.M. (2002). Relationship of rapid automatized naming and phonological awareness in early reading development: Implications for the double-deficit hypothesis. *Journal of Learning Disabilities, 35*(3), 245–256. doi:10.1177/00222194020 3500306

Shaywitz, S.E. (1998). Dyslexia. *New England Journal of Medicine, 338*(5), 307–312. doi:10.1056/NEJM199801293380507

Shaywitz, S.E., Fletcher, J.M., Holahan, J.M., Shneider, A.E., Marchione, K.E., Stuebing, K.K., … Shaywitz, B.A. (1999). Persistence of dyslexia: The Connecticut longitudinal study at adolescence. *Pediatrics, 104*(6), 1351–1359. doi:10.1542/peds.104.6.1351

Shaywitz, S.E., Gruen, J.R., & Shaywitz, B.A. (2007). Managment of dyslexia, its rationale, and underlying neurobiology. *Pediatric Clinics of North America, 54,* 609–623. doi:10.1016/j.pcl.2007.02.013

Shaywitz, S.E., Morris, R., & Shaywitz, B.A. (2008). The education of dyslexic children from childhood to young adulthood. *Annual Review of Psychol-*ogy, 59, 451–475. doi:10.1146/annurev.psych.59.103006.093633

Shaywitz, S.E., & Shaywitz, B.A. (2008). Paying attention to reading: The neurobiology of reading and dyslexia. *Development and Psychopathology, 20*(4), 1329–1349. doi:10.1017/S0954579408000631

Smith, E.E., & Jonides, J. (1999). Storage and executive processes in the frontal lobes. *Science, 283*(5408), 1657–1661. doi:10.1126/science.283.5408.1657

Snow, C.E., Burns, M.S., & Griffin, P. (1998). *Preventing reading difficulties in young children.* Washington, DC: National Academy Press.

Specht, K., Hugdahl, K., Ofte, S., Nygård, M., Bjørnerud, A., Plante, E., & Helland, T. (2009). Brain activation on pre-reading tasks reveals at-risk status for dyslexia in 6-year-old children. *Scandavian Journal of Psychology, 50*(1), 79–91. doi:10.1111/j.1467-9450.2008.00688

Stanovich, K.E., & Siegel, L.S. (1994). Phenotypic performance profile of children with reading disabilities: A regression-based test of the phonological-core variable-difference model. *Journal of Educational Psychology, 86*(1), 24–53. doi:10.1037//0022-0663.86.1.24

Taipale, M., Kaminen, N., Nopola-Hemmi, J., Haltia, T., Myllyluoma, B., Lyytinen, H., … Kere, J. (2003). A candidate gene for developmental dyslexia encodes a nuclear tetratricopeptide repeat domain protein dynamically regulated in brain. *Proceedings of the National Academy of Sciences, USA, 100*(20). doi:10.1073/pnas.1833911100

Torgensen, J.K. (1998). Catch them before they fall: Identification and assessment to prevent reading failure in young children. *American Educator, 22*(1, 2), 32–39.

Torgesen, J.K., Wagner, R.K., Rashotte, C.A., Rose, E., Lindamood, P., Conway, T., & Garvan, C. (1999). Preventing reading failure in children with phonological processing difficulties: Group and individual responses to instruction. *Journal of Educational Psychology, 81,* 579–593.

Vellutino, F.R., Scanlon, D.M., Small, S., & Fanuele, D.P. (2006). Response to intervention as a vehicle for distinguishing between children with and without reading disabilities: Evidence for the role of kindergarten and first-grade interventions. *Journal of Learning Disabilities, 39*(2), 157–169. doi:10.1177/00222194060390020401

Vigneau, M., Beaucousin, V., Herve, P.Y., Duffau, H., Crivello, F., Houde, O., … Tzourio-Mazoyer, N. (2006). Meta-analyzing left hemisphere language areas: Phonology, semantics, and sentence processing. *NeuroImage, 30*(4), 1414–1432. doi:10.1016/j.neuroimage.2005.11.002

Wang, Z., Fernandez-Seara, M., Alsop, D.C., Liu, W.C., Flax, J.F., Benasich, A.A., & Detre, J.A. (2008). Assessment of functional development in normal infant brain using arterial spin labeled perfusion MRI. *NeuroImage, 39*(3), 973–978. doi:10.1016/j.neuroimage.2007.09.045

Whalen, P.J., Johnstone, T., Somerville, L.H., Nitschke, J.B., Polis, S., Alexander, A.L., … Kalin, N.H. (2008). A functional magnetic resonance imaging predictor of treatment response to venlafaxine in generalized anxiety disorder. *Biological Psychiatry, 63*(9), 858–863. doi:10.1016/j.biopsych.2007.08.019

Wolf, M., & Bowers, P.G. (2000). Naming-speed processes and developmental reading disabilities: An introduction to the special issue on the double-deficit hypothesis. *Journal of Learning Disabilities, 33*(4), 322–324. doi:10.1177/002221940003300404

Wood, F.B., Hill, D.F., Meyer, M.S., & Flowers, D.L. (2005). Predictive assessment of reading. *Annals of Dyslexia, 55*(2), 193–216. doi:10.1007/s11881-005-0011

CHAPTER 13

A Multifactorial Approach to Dyslexia
Cyril R. Pernet and Jean-François Démonet

BACK TO BASICS: WHAT IS DYSLEXIA?

According to the World Health Organization (1994), dyslexia is classified as a "specific reading impairment." Specific reading impairments are defined as problems in learning to read, spell, and write despite adequate intelligence, educational resources, and social background. It is important to note that in educational resources, dyslexia is defined as a "specific and significant impairment in the development of reading skills that is not solely accounted for by mental age, visual acuity problems, or inadequate schooling." Strikingly, these definitions rely mainly on exclusion criteria, that is, dyslexia is not diagnosed because of the reading impairment per se but because of learning difficulties that cannot be explained otherwise. Indeed, children are not diagnosed until they have tried and failed to learn to read (Heim & Benasich, 2006). Although children with dyslexia have no evident sensory impairments (i.e., poor visual or auditory acuity), poor literacy skills are often associated with various sensorimotor and cognitive dysfunctions (*DSM-IV, ICD-10*). Specific reading disorders have been associated with impairments in related domains such as oral language (dysphasia and specific language impairment), writing skills (dysgraphia), mathematical abilities (dyscalculia), motor coordination (dyspraxia), temporal orientation (dyschronia), visual abilities and attention-deficit/hyperactivity-disorder (Habib, 2000). For dyslexia, but also these other disorders, general intelligence is usually intact with normal or even above normal nonverbal IQ. In addition, although children with dyslexia have no primary psychological impairments, it has been shown that there is an association with an increased internalizing, anxious, and depressive symptomatology (Mugnaini, Lassi, La Malfa, & Albertni, 2009).

MULTIPLE IMPAIRMENTS IN DYSLEXIA?

There are many competing hypotheses aiming at explaining dyslexia, each one highlighting one type of behavioral impairment in relation to atypical brain structures and/or functional responses (Démonet, Taylor, & Chaix, 2004). We briefly summarized below the most influential ones.

Visual Hypotheses

Because reading is a visuo-attentional activity, many studies focus on finding some level of visual impairment in people with dyslexia. One major hypothesis posits the existence of low level visual disorders related to atypical thalamic magno cells (large neurons found in both the lateral and medial geniculate nuclei of the thalamus—Stein, 2001, and Chapter 3). These cells are involved in the processing of low contrast information and fast moving stimuli and would thus be important for reading activities related to saccadic eye movements. Favoring this hypothesis, a number of behavioral studies have shown increased thresholds on detection of low contrast, low spatial or high temporal frequencies (e.g., Lovegrove, Bowling, Badcock, & Blackwood, 1980), and poor sensitivity to visual motion (e.g., Demb, Boynton, & Heeger, 1998) in readers with dyslexia (see Skotun, 2000, for a critical review). Histological studies also revealed soma atrophies of magno cells in the lateral geniculate nuclei of the thalamus (Livingstone, Rosen, Drislane, & Galaburda, 1991) and cyto-architectonic impairments of the primary visual cortex (Jenner, Rosen, & Galaburda, 1999) have been observed alongside atypical functional brain responses of visual areas receiving magnocellular inputs (i.e., for motion territory [MT] and and dorsal regions, see Demb, Boynton, & Heeger, 1997; Demb et al., 1998; for electrophysiological evidences, see Schulter-Korne & Bruder, 2010). As an alternative or complementary explanation, the visuo-attentional hypothesis situates the impairment in the encoding of letter sequences. Visual-attention strongly relies on the integrity of the parietal cortex that receives magnocellular inputs, and visuo-attentional impairments have been observed in dyslexia (e.g., Facoetti, Paganoni, & Lorusso, 2000; Facoetti, Paganoni, Turatto, et al., 2000). One instantiation of this hypothesis is that readers with dyslexia have a shorter visuo-attentional span, that is, they cannot process simultaneously as many elements in an array as control readers (Bosse, Tainturier, & Valdois, 2007; Valdois et al., 2003). Although these visuo-attentional impairments are related to atypical inferior parietal responses, they can impact reading areas mediating orthographic and phonological lexicon. Such visuo-attentional impairments could thus explain altered brain responses in individuals with dyslexia in orthographic (inferior-temporal cortex) and phonological (angular/supramarginal gyri and inferior frontal gyrus) related brain areas (Démonet et al., 2004; Hoeft et al., 2007; Paulesu et al., 2001; Peyrin, Démonet, Baciu, Le Bas, & Valdois, 2010; Pugh et al., 2000).

Auditory and Phonological Hypotheses

Learning to read alphabetic languages depends on developing an awareness that printed characters (graphemes) correspond to meaningful units of sounds (phonemes). Indeed, it is admitted that one can predict which children are going to struggle to read on the basis of their ability to manipulate phonemes within spoken words (see Castles & Coltheart, 2004, for a critical review). It thus appears obvious to posit phonological impairments as the core impairments in dyslexia (e.g., Ramus, 2004; Shaywitz & Shaywitz, 2005; but see Boets et al., 2011). This hypothesis is supported by the frequently observed presence of phonological disorders in readers with dyslexia, for instance as seen in reduced performances for short-term verbal memory tasks, phonemic awareness (Ramus et al., 2003,) and/or impairments in phonemic categorization (Serniclaes, Sprenger-Charolles, Carre, & Démonet, 2001). Such behavioral impairments have been linked with impairments of the left superior temporal and inferior frontal cortex (Dufor, Serniclaes, Sprenger-Charolles, & Démonet, 2007). By contrast with the phonological hypothesis, the auditory processing deficit theory proposes that phonological impairments are secondary to a more basic impairment in rapid acoustic transition perception (Tallal, 2004; Tallal, Stark, & Mellits, 1985). Such impairments have been linked with microscopic impairments in the auditory cortex (Galaburda & Kemper, 1979), the frontal and perisylvian areas (Kaufman & Galaburda, 1989), and soma atrophies of magno-cells in the medial geniculate nuclei of the thalamus (Galaburda, Menard, & Rosen, 1994; see also Chapters 3, 10, and 11). Atypical functional responses to speech sounds have also been observed in the brainstem and the left inferior frontal cortex. For instance, Banai et al. (2009) showed atypical timing and harmonic information contents in the brainstem response to the sound /da/. Atypical responses of these types are likely to be due to altered interaction with other subcortical (thalamus) and cortical (auditory cortex) structures via cortico-fugal projections because no basic impairments are observed when using clicks rather than complex sounds (Song, Banai, Russo, & Kraus, 2006). Such impairments in temporal and spectral coding of auditory stimuli might underlie or contribute to the phonological impairments seen in populations with dyselxia. This hypothesis is further supported by the fact that slowing down the acoustic features in rolling /ma na/, /na ma/ stimuli (versus /ma ma/ /na na/) enhances the left inferior frontal cortex response of participants with dyslexia to a level comparable to controls in normal situations (Ruff, Cardebat, Marie, & Démonet, 2002).

Procedural Learning Hypothesis

The cerebellar hypothesis relates dyslexia to a general learning disorder that includes a failure to automatize reading and writing skills (Nicolson, Fawcett, & Dean, 2001), that is, dyslexia is regarded as an impaired automatization of high-order sensory-motor procedures essential in reading that would reflect atypical function in the lateral cerebellum (Doyon et al., 2002). Supporting this hypothesis, behavioral impairments in information processing speed, memory, motor skill, and balance, in addition to phonological and literacy skill, were observed (Nicolson, Fawcett, & Dean, 1995; Fawcett, Nicolson, & Dean; 1996, Fawcett & Nicolson, 1999). In addition, histological (Finch, Nicolson, & Fawcett, 2002), metabolic (Rae et al., 1998), structural (Pernet, Andersson, Paulesu, & Démonet, 2009; Pernet, Poline, Démonet, & Rousselet, 2009) and functional impairments (Nicolson et al., 2001) have been observed in the cerebellum of dyslexic readers. One attractive feature of this theory is that it reunites many developmental disorders that tend to co-occur within the same individuals (e.g., dyslexia, SLI, ADHD) under one general theory (Nicolson & Fawcett, 2007).

The General Magnocellular Hypothesis

The general magnocellular theory (Stein, 2001; Chapter 3 this volume) encompasses the basic auditory, basic visual, attentional, and cerebellar deficits by discussing each one as a consequence of a general multisystem magnocellular impairment. M-cells are found throughout the entire nervous system, including auditory, visual, and cutaneous sensory systems, as well as in memory and motor systems (Hockfield & Sur, 1990). The visual magnocellular pathway is involved in directing attention, eye movements, and visual search with all three processes being relevant to reading (Stein & Walsh, 1997). Although there is no such thing as an auditory magnocellular pathway, M-cells are observed in the medial lateral nuclei of the thalamus and play a role for analyzing auditory transients (changes in the frequency or amplitude of sounds). Therefore, M-defects would explain rapid acoustic transition and thus phonological impairments (being secondary in comparison to others). This idea of a multifocal cerebral impairment originating in magno cells is supported by histological impairments of M-cells cells in the lateral (Livingstone et al., 1991) and medial (Galaburda et al., 1994) geniculate nuclei of the thalamus and possibly other cerebellar/Purkinje cell impairments.

Multiple Dyslexias for One Reading Impairment?

The multiplicity of hypotheses aimed at explaining dyslexia reflects the multiplicity of behavioral impairments, which raises an obvious question: Are there different forms or subtypes of dyslexia? This question is not new, and several distinctions among readers with dyslexia have been proposed: 1) Boder in 1973 proposed to distinguish among children with dyslexia on the basis of their sensory impairment, that is, they would either be classified as dysphonetic (having phonological problems), or dyseidetic (having visual problems); 2) Castles and Coltheart (1993) proposed to distinguish phonological from surface developmental dyslexia in children, on the same basis as individuals with acquired dyslexia. Developmental dyslexics are thus split into individuals with assembling problems, or grapheme/phoneme association, versus individuals with addressing problem, or lexicon access; 3) Wolf and Bowers (1999) proposed, on the basis of what is referred to as the "double-deficit hypothesis" (Compton, De Fries, & Olson, 2001; Lovett, Steinbach, & Frijters, 2000; Wolf & Bowers 1999, 2000), three subtypes: phonological, rate, and phonological-rate. The double-deficit hypothesis asserts that impaired readers have some combination of two deficits. The first type of deficit corresponds to an impaired phonological awareness, whereas the second type corresponds to an impairment of rapid naming capacity (or visual naming speed), which involves the rapid access and retrieval of names of known objects or visual symbols, such as digits and letters. The double-deficit hypothesis therefore distinguishes readers with dyslexia based on phonological processes versus phonological lexical access.

However useful for clinical purposes, those classifications do not reflect the entire array of behavioral impairments and neural impairments mentioned above. In fact many authors agree that dyslexia is not pure even within subtypes (see, e.g., Ziegler et al., 2008). The literature is scarce, but several attempts have been made in order to characterize the heterogeneity of behavioral impairments. Many subtyping studies were performed in the 1980s, but these studies do not necessarily fit well with the theoretical cognitive frameworks proposed above. In order to address how one might best characterize the subtypes observed across many studies, we compiled here 10 articles (Heim et al., 2008; Ho, Chan, Lee, Tsang, & Luan, 2004; Katzir, Kim, Wolf, Morris, & Lovett, 2008; King, Giess, & Lombardina, 2007; Leinonen et al., 2001; Morris et al., 1998; Ramus et al., 2003; Reid, Szczerbinski, Iskierka-Kasperek, & Hansen, 2007; White et al., 2006; Ziegler et al., 2008) that examine subtypes and have results that fall within the theoretical approaches presented above. Percentages reported below reflect proportions taken from the samples with dyslexia only (i.e., percentages were recomputed when necessary by removing typical readers) and weighted by the sample size of each study. The first result from this minireview is that only 654 out of 763 participants with dyslexia were classified, leaving 14.28% of participants presenting with a literacy problem but no evidence of a clear perceptual or cognitive impairment. The second main result is that 41.47% of readers with dyslexia showed an impairment related to the phonological system (phonological awareness), with 14.11% of the sample having only this impairment. The remaining participants exhibited a mixture of associated impairments in the visual (magnocellular, letter-position encoding, orthographic), auditory, memory, and/or cerebellar (motor and/or sequential ordering) domains. Another major impairment, which does not appear prevalent when examining each study individually, is lexical impairment (defined as access to orthographic or to phonological stored information) with 21.64% of the participants with dyslexia showing at least one lexicon-level problem (19.44% having at least an impairment in the phonological lexicon). However, because not every study used the same tests and not all perceptual or cognitive aspects were investigated systematically, it is hard to estimate the prevalence of one indicator or another beyond these two very broad impairments (phonological processing and lexicon access). More specific impairments were infrequently assessed; for instance, not all studies investigated the presence of cerebellar impairments. For the sample as a whole, we obtained 9.13% of readers with dyslexia with what was defined as a cerebellar disorder. However, if we assume that rapid and sequential processing somehow relies on the cerebellum (Strick, Dum, & Fietz, 2009), then 13.56% of cases could be classified as cerebellar disorders, making cerebellar disorders a more common indicator. Overall, this minireview reveals that 1) subtyping studies are still necessary as no clear and consensual dyslexia subtype taxonomy has emerged so far, and 2) phonological and rapid serial processing (Wolf & Bowers, 1999) are common disorders observed in dyslexia but are also often seen in combination with other symptoms (see Figure 13.1). Because phonological and rapid, serial processing impairments can both be explained by more basic impairments and not all studies tested for basic impairments, one cannot (as yet) make firm conclusions regarding the neural origins of various forms of dyslexia. Together, these two findings highlight on one hand the need to fully investigate all perceptual and cognitive aspects related to reading (i.e., perform tests that tap each of the dimensions related to reading that are highlighted in the various theories), and on the other hand the lack of theoretical frameworks that can account for several co-occurring impairments.

Neurological Evidences for Multiple Forms of Dyslexia

No study to date (except for an attempt in Pernet, Poline et al., 2009) has examined sample heterogeneity in dyslexia from a brain perspective. However, because the studies reviewed, as well as others in the literature, found supporting evidence that fits one or more hypotheses, the view should shift toward a more multifactorial view of dyslexia.

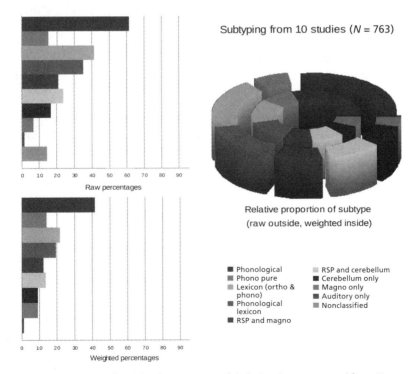

Figure 13.1.   Raw and weighted percentages of dyslexic subtypes counted from 10 subtyping studies.

As briefly reviewed (see also Eckert, 2004), a number of studies reveal that dyslexia is associated with cortical impairments in areas relevant to reading (lateral cerebellum, infero-temporal cortex, angular/supra marginal gyrus, auditory and superior temporal cortices, inferior frontal cortex). In the following paragraphs, we briefly present two studies from our laboratories illustrating how one can, on the one hand, study heterogeneity and, on the other hand, attempt to account for this heterogeneity by characterizing dyslexia using brain structures and/or responses.

Structural Heterogeneity

In the first study (Pernet, Andersson, et al., 2009), we investigated the relationship between grey matter volumes and behavioral performance in 77 participants (38 adult participants with dyslexia and 39 controls). All participants were tested on regular, irregular, "loan" (foreign words that are used in French and primarily call upon addressing, lexical reading procedure) and pseudoword reading, on rapid digit-strings reading, on phonological and metaphonological tasks (syllabic deletion, phoneme deletion, spoonerisms, phonologically incongruent word search, phonological-based rhyme decision from visual stimuli) and on spelling of irregular words and pseudowords (with diagnosis criteria as defined in Paulesu et al., 2001). MRI scans were acquired at 1.5 and 2 Tesla and preprocessed (segmented, normalized, and modulated) in order to compute a multiple regression among each grey matter voxel and RT/accuracy composite scores (see Pernet, Andersson et al., 2009, for details). Results (see Figure 13.2) revealed significant effects for phonemic deletion (metaphonology), irregular word spelling (orthographic lexicon), and pseudoword reading (grapheme–phoneme). While in control participants language performances correlated with grey matter volumes in many known language related areas (including the cerebellum), no correlations could be observed in participants with dyslexia, suggesting a strongly disorganized cortical architecture in dyslexia. We then hypothesized that the absence of within-group correlations could be partly explained by the existence of multiple dyslexia subtypes in the brain and thus developed a new methodology that allowed us to investigate brain heterogeneity (Pernet, Poline, et al., 2009). Briefly, we used the control group to construct a typical brain via bootstrapped confidence intervals, that is, we estimated for each voxel of brain what was the normal range of variation. Next, we classified each voxel of each dyslexic brain individually to see whether the participant showed brain regions that were out of the normal range. Finally, we pooled the results of each person with dyslexia to create a map indicating how the group with dyslexia differed from controls. The main advantage of this technique is of course that a brain region can be declared as showing a significant difference among groups, even if the group with dyslexia has half of the participants above the confidence interval and half below (i.e, this effect is nonlinear with regard to participant classification). Results of this study (see Figure 13.2) showed that 100% of participants with dyslexia had higher or lower grey matter volumes than controls over the right cerebellar declive, a cerebellar region showing systematic activation during language tasks (Stoodley & Schmahmann, 2009) and over the right striatum (lentiform nucleus). Importantly, about half of the participants had lower volumes than controls, and the other half had higher volumes, therefore revealing four clear-cut brain endo-phenotypes. In addition, these four subgroups showed significant behavioral differences in terms of phonological and lexicon access performance. Overall, our results suggest that different brain phenotypes exist and that brain phenotypes support different behavioral phenotypes. Furthermore, best language performance seems to be observed for optimal grey matter volumes (controls) and lower performances for lower or higher than average grey matter volumes.

Functional Heterogeneity

In a 2005 publication (Giraud et al.), we showed that at least two subtypes of individuals with dyslexia can be identified as showing atypical brain responses as compared with controls during the presentation of syllables /ba/ versus /pa/. Here, we expand this result, showing that other participants, despite showing reading impairments, can show a completely normal brain response to those stimuli.

In this experiment, participants were asked to read a book of their choice while passively listening to /ba/ and /pa/ syllables. Electrical activity over the scalp was recorded for each event and the averaged event-related potentials for /ba/ and /pa/ were then compared. The whole point of using these syllables is that, although phonologically different, they are acoustically close, differing mainly in their voice onset time (VOT—the time between a phonetically relevant supra-laryngeal event, such as release, and glottal pulsing (Lisker & Abramson, 1964). Intracerebral auditory evoked potentials (Liégeois-Chauvel, de Graaf, Laguitton, & Chauvel, 1999) showed that the VOT is processed in a time-locked fashion to the stimuli temporal cues at the level of the primary auditory cortex and, to a lesser degree, in the left planum temporale, two regions believed to be structurally and functionally impaired in dyslexia (Galaburda & Livingstone, 1993; Leonard et al., 2001). As presented in Figure 13.3, auditory evoked potentials (AEPs) for each syllable are clearly distinguishable in control participants (10 males, mean age: 26.5). Following the N1/P2 complex (peaks at 80 milliseconds [ms], 130 ms, and 180 ms), a negative component peaking at approximately 240 ms is observed for the syllable /ba/ but not /pa/, followed by an offset-response at approximately 334 ms. This component represents the electrophysiological signature of the neural processing of the consonant lip release burst that is therefore clearly distinguishable from the other and earlier components elicited by the preburst voice segment involved in the sound spectrum of phoneme /b/ in French.

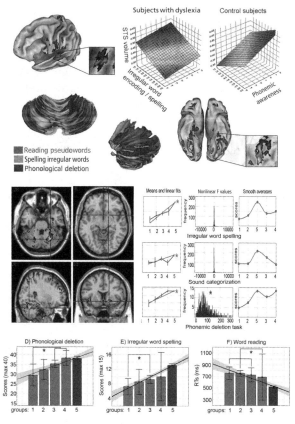

Figure 13.2. From top to bottom, illustration of cortcial grey matter areas with significantly different volumes in dyslexia. At the top, correlation across the dyslexic and control groups (pseudoword reading) and difference of correlations between groups (phoneme deletion, irregular word spelling). In the middle, right declive and lentiform nucleus as detected in Pernet, Poline, et al. (2009). Graphics show that among the four subgroups we could observe behavioral differences and that, together with controls, their performances varied as a function of a normal distribution of grey matter values (bottom). (*Source:* Pernet, Poline, Démonet, & Rousselet, 2009.)

From the 14 participants with dyslexia in this study (mean age: 32.7 years), three subgroups could be observed (Figure 13.3). In Subgroup 1, participants show a standard N1/P2 complex followed by an earlier than controls negative component (220 ms) followed by many other components without clear off-response. In Subgroup 2, participants show a standard N1/P2 complex but no release component for /ba/ could be observed, that is, /ba/ and /pa/ AEPs were not distinguishable on the basis of component number and latencies. Finally, in Subgroup 3 participants could not be distinguished from controls with a N1/P2 complex and a negative component (226 ms) followed by an off-response (326 ms). From a behavioral viewpoint these three subgroups can also be distinguished. In fact, participants in Subgroups 1 and 2 showed marked reading impairments (reading age < 10 years and/or overall spelling

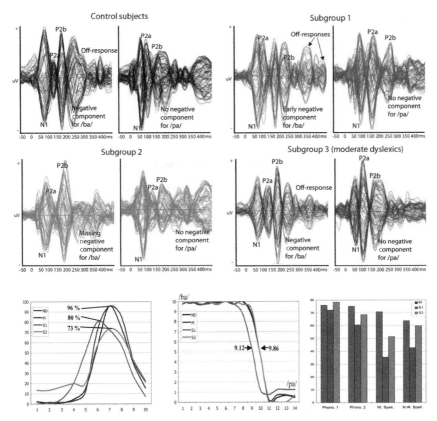

Figure 13.3. Example of functional heterogeneity: dyslexic participants (subgroups 1, 2, and 3) showed various degrees of functional deficits. For instance, subgroup 3 shows no deficit in phoneme perception and has normal auditory evoked potentials (AEPs). By contrast, subgroups 1 and 2 show impaired AEPs associated with impaired phonological perception but similar phoneme awareness skills. (*Source:* Giraud, Démonet, Habib, et al., 2005.)

< 60%), whereas participants of Subgroup 3 showed only moderate reading impairment (reading age > 10 years), suggesting that severe dyslexia only is associated with impairment of phoneme coding in the auditory cortex. Together these electro-physiological results show, just as structural data, that different brain functional endophenotypes can be observed, and that different endophenotypes support different behavioral phenotypes.

CONCLUSIONS: THE MULTIFACTORIAL APPROACH

There is no doubt, given the extensive literature as of 2011, that dyslexia is related to genetic impairments. In fact, genetic studies have revealed multiple loci for chromosomal impairments and, in particular, on chromosomes 16 and 6, but also on chromosomes 2, 3, and 18 (Brkanac et al., 2007; Chapman et al., 2004; Francks et al., 2003; Gayan & Olson, 2003; Raskind et al., 2005; Chapters 4 and 5 in this volume). Again, this multiplicity of candidate genes is likely to reflect the significant variability observed in dyslexia at the behavioral level. Thus, the multifactorial and polygenic nature of developmental dyslexia strongly suggests the existence of various brain phenotypes (Goldberg & Weinberger, 2004; Gottesman & Gould, 2003). Such brain phenotypes can be observed both at the structural and functional level and might be a better way to characterize dyslexia in the near future.

Developmental neurological and psychiatric disorders are often thought to be accounted for by genetic variation or mutation, although such associations are frequently not expressed in a straightforward fashion at the genotype/phenotype level. In many disorders, these associations can only be captured using a multifactorial-polygenic model that considers multiple genes, multiple interacting risk factors and comorbidities (See Chapters 4 and 5). This is particularly true for developmental dyslexia and other language disorders (Bishop, 2009). Such associations are also mediated by molecular and cellular mechanisms, which in turn affect and modulate behavior via the engagement of complex and adaptive neural circuitries (Bigos & Weinberger, 2010). Imaging the brain (MRI, fMRI, PET, EEG, MEG) is the only way, in humans, to link the behavioral and genetic levels while teasing apart various disease subtypes. For instance, an entire issue of the journal *Neuroimage* in 2010 was dedicated to brain imaging of genetics, that is, to a research strategy that applies anatomical or functional imaging technologies as phenotypic assays to evaluate genetic variations with the potential to understand the impact of such variations on behavior (Hariri & Weinberger, 2003). This approach highlights the need to link all levels of analyses (gene–brain–behavior) in a nondogmatic way, which ultimately will allow understanding and effective treatment of the various forms of dyslexia.

REFERENCES

Banai, K., Hornickel, J., Skoe, E., Nicol, T., Zecker, S., & Kraus, N. (2009). Reading and subcortical auditory function. *Cerebral Cortex, 19,* 2699–2707. doi:10.1093/cercor/bhp024

Bigos, K.L., & Weinberger, D.R. (2010). Imaging genetics, days of future past. *NeuroImage, 15,* 804–809. doi:10.1016/j.neuroimage.2010.01.035

Bishop, D.V.M. (2009). Genes, cognition, and communication. Insights from neurodevelopmental disorders. *Annals of the New York Academy of Science, 1156,* 1–18.

Boder, E. (1973). Developmental dyslexia: A diagnostic approach based on three atypical reading-spelling pattern. *Developmental Medical and Child Neurology, 15,* 663–687. doi:10.1111/j.1469-8749.1973.tb05180.x

Boets, B., Vandermosten, M., Poelmans, H., Luts, H., Wouters, J., & Ghesquière, P. (2001). Preschool impairments in auditory processing and speech perception uniquely predict future reading problems. *Research in Developemental Disabilities, 32,* 560–570. doi:10.1016/j.ridd.2010.12.020

Bosse, M.L., Tainturier, M.J., & Valdois, S. (2007). Developmental dyslexia: The visual attention span deficit hypothesis. *Cognition, 104,* 198–230. doi:10.1016/j.cognition.2006.05.009

Brkanac, Z., Chapman, N.H., Matsushita, M.M., Chun, L., Nielsen, K., Cochrane, E., … Raskind, W.H. (2007). Evaluation of candidate genes for DYX1 and DYX2 in families with dyslexia. *American Journal of Medicine Genetics: Neuropsychiatric Genetics, 144B,* 556–560.

Castles, A., & Coltheart, M. (1993). Varieties of developmental dyslexia. *Cognition, 47,* 149–180. doi:10.1016/0010-0277(93)90003-E

Castles, A., & Coltheart, M. (2004). Is there a casual link from phonological awareness to success in learning to read? *Cognition, 91,* 77–111.

Chapman, N.H., Igo, R.P., Thompson, J.B., Matsushita, M., Brkanac, Z., Holzman, T., ... Raskind, W.H. (2004). Linkage analyses of four regions previously implicated in dyslexia: Confirmation of a locus on chromosome 15q. *American Journal of Medical Genetics, 131B,* 67–75. doi:10.1002/ajmg.b.30018

Comptom, D.L., De Fries, J.C., & Olson, R.K. (2001). Are RAN- and phonological awareness–deficits additive in children with reading disabilities? *Dyslexia, 7,* 125–149. doi:10.1002/dys.198

Demb, J.B., Boynton, G.M., & Heeger, D.J. (1997). Brain activity in visual cortex predicts individual differences in reading performance. *Proceedings of the National Academy of Sciences, USA, 94,* 13363–13366. doi:10.1073/pnas.94.24.13363

Demb, J.B., Boynton, G.M., & Heeger, D.J. (1998). Functional magnetic resonance imaging of early visual pathways in dyslexia. *The Journal of Neuroscience, 18,* 6939–6951.

Démonet, J.F., Taylor, M.J. & Chaix, Y. (2004). Developmental dyslexia. *Lancet, 363,* 1451–1460. doi:10.1016/S0140-6736(04)16106-0

Doyon, J., Song, A.W., Karni, A., Lalonde, F., Adams, M.M., & Ungerleider, L.G. (2002). Experience-dependent changes in cerebellar contributions to motor sequence learning. *Proceedings of the National Academy of Sciences, USA, 99,* 1017–1022. doi:10.1073/pnas.022615199

Dufor, O., Serniclaes, W., Sprenger-Charolles, L., & Démonet, J.F. (2007). Top-down processes during auditory phoneme categorization in dyslexia: A PET study. *NeuroImage, 34,* 1692–1707. doi:10.1016/j.neuroimage.2006.10.034

Eckert, M. (2004). Neuroanatomical markers for dyslexia: A review of dyslexia structural imaging studies. *The Neuroscientist, 10,* 362–371. doi:10.1177/1073858404263596

Facoetti, A., Paganoni, P., & Lorusso, M.L. (2000). The spatial distribution of spatial attention in developmental dyslexia. *Experimental Brain Research, 132,* 531–538. doi:10.1007/s002219900330

Facoetti, A., Paganoni, P., Turatto, M., Marzola, V., & Mascetti, G.G. (2000). Visual-spatial attention in developmental dyslexia. *Cortex, 36,* 109–123. doi:10.1016/S0010-9452(08)70840-2

Fawcett, A.J. & Nicolson, R.I. (1999). Performance of dyslexic children on cerebellar and cognitive tests. *Journal of Motor Behavior, 31,* 68–78. doi:10.1080/00222899909601892

Fawcett, A.J., Nicolson, R.I. & Dean., P. (1996). Impaired performance of children with dyslexia on a range of cerebellar tasks. *Annals of Dyslexia, 46,* 259–283. doi:10.1007/BF02648179

Finch, A.J., Nicolson, R.I., & Fawcett, A.J. (2002). Evidence for a neuroanatomical difference within the olivo-cerebellar pathway of adults with dyslexia. *Cortex, 38,* 529–539. doi:10.1016/S0010-9452(08)70021-2

Francks, C., Fisher, S.E., Marlow, A.J., MacPhie, I.L., Taylor, K.E., Richardson, A.J., ... Monaco, A.P. (2003). Familial and genetic effects on motor coordination, laterality, and reading-related cognition. *American Journal of Psychiatry, 160,* 1970–1977. doi:10.1176/appi.ajp.160.11.1970

Galaburda, A.M., & Kemper, T.L. (1979). Cytoarchitectonic abnormalities in developmental dyslexia: A case study. *Annals of Neurology, 6,* 94–100. doi:10.1002/ana.410060203

Galaburda, A.M., & Livingstone, M. (1993). Evidence for a magnocellular defect in developmental dyslexia. *Annals of the New York Academy of Science, 682,* 70–82. doi:10.1111/j.1749-6632.1993.tb22960

Galaburda, A.M., Menard, M.T., & Rosen, G.D. (1994). Evidence for aberrant auditory anatomy in developmental dyslexia. *Proceedings of the National Academy of Sciences, USA, 91,* 8010–8013. doi:10.1073/pnas.91.17.8010

Gayan, J., & Olson, R.K. (2003). Genetic and environmental influences on individual differences on printed word recognition. *Journal of Experimental Child Psychology, 84,* 97–123. doi:10.1016/S0022-0965(02)00181-9

Giraud, K., Démonet, J.F., Habib, M., Marquis, P., Chauvel, P., & Liegeois-Chauvel, C. (2005). Auditory evoked potential patterns to voiced and voiceless speech sounds in adult developmental dyslexics with persistent deficits. *Cerebral Cortex, 15,* 1524–1534. doi:10.1093/cercor/bhi031

Goldberg, T.E., & Weinberger, D.R. (2004). Genes and the parsing of cognitive processes. *Trends in Cognitive Sciences, 8*, 325–335. doi:10.1016/j.tics.2004.05.011

Gottesman, L.I., & Gould, T.D. (2003). The endophenotype concept in psychiatry: Etymology and strategic intentions. *American Journal of Psychiatry, 160*, 636–645. doi:10.1176/appi.ajp.160.4.636

Habib, M. (2000). The neurological basis of developmental dyslexia. An overview and working hypothesis. *Brain, 123*, 2373–2399. doi:10.1093/brain/123.12.2373

Heim, S., & Benasich, A.A. (2006). Developmental disorders of language. In D. Cicchetti & D. Cohen (Eds.), *Developmental psychopathology: Risk, disorder and adaptation.* (2nd ed, vol. 3, pp. 268–316). Hoboken, NJ: John Wiley & Sons.

Heim, S., Tschierse, J., Amunts, K., Wilms, M., Vossel, S., Willmes, K., ... Huber, W. (2008). Cognitive subtypes of dyslexia. *Acta Neurobiologiae Experimentalis, 68*, 73–82.

Ho, C.S., Chan, D.W., Lee, S.H., Tsang, S.M., & Luan, V.H. (2004). Cognitive profiling and preliminary subtyping in Chinese developmental dyslexia. *Cognition, 91*, 43–75. doi:10.1016/S0010-0277(03)00163-X

Hockfield, S., & Sur, M. (1990). Monoclonal Cat-301 identifies Y cells in cat LGN. *Journal of Computational Neurology, 300*, 320–330.

Hoeft, F., Meyler, A., Hernandez, A., Juel, C., Taylor-Hill, H., Martindale, J.L., ... Gavrieli, J.D.E. (2007). Functional and morphometric brain dissociation between dyslexia and reading ability. *Proceedings of the National Academy of Sciences, USA, 104*, 4234–4239. doi:10.1073/pnas.0609399104

Jenner, A.R., Rosen, G.D., & Galaburda, A.M. (1999). Neuronal asymmetries in primary visual cortex of dyslexic and nondyslexic brains. *Annals of Neurology, 46*, 189–196. doi:10.1002/1531-8249(199908)46:2<189::AID-ANA8>3.0.CO;2-N

Katzir, T., Kim, Y.S., Wolf, M., Morris, R., & Lovett, M.W. (2008). The varieties of pathways to dysfluent reading: Comparing subtypes of children with dyslexia at letter, word, and connected text levels of reading. *Journal of Learning Disabilities, 41*, 47–66. doi:10.1177/0022219407311325

Kaufman, W.E., & Galaburda, A.M. (1989). Cerebrocortical microdysgenesis in neurologically normal subjects: A histopathologic study. *Neurology, 39*, 238–244.

King, W.M., Giess, S.A., & Lombardina, L.J. (2007). Subtyping of children with developmental dyslexia via bootstrap aggregated clustering and the gap statistic: Comparison with the double-deficit hypothesis. *International Journal of Language and Communication Disorders, 42*, 77–95. doi:10.1080/13682820600806680

Leinonen, S., Muller, K., Leppanen, P.H.T., Aro, M., Ahonen, T., & Lyytinen, H. (2001). Heterogeneity in adult dyslexic readers: Relating processing skills to the speed and accuracy of oral test reading. *Reading and Writing: An Interdisciplinary Journal, 14*, 265–296.

Leonard, C.M., Eckert, M.A., Lombardino, L.J., Oakland, T., Kranzler, J., Mohr, C.M., ... Freeman, A. (2001). Anatomical risk factors for phonological dyslexia. *Cerebral Cortex, 11*, 148–157. doi:10.1093/cercor/11.2.148

Liégeois-Chauvel, C., de Graaf, J.B., Laguitton, V., & Chauvel, P. (1999). Specialization of left auditory cortex for speech perception in man depends on temporal coding. *Cerebral Cortex, 9*, 484–496. doi:10.1093/cercor/9.5.484

Lisker, L., & Abramson A.S. (1964). A cross-language study of voicing in initial stops: Acoustical measurements. *Word, 20*, 384–422.

Livingstone, M.S., Rosen, G.D., Drislane, F.W., & Galaburda, A.M. (1991). Physiological and anatomical evidence for a magnocellular defect in developmental dyslexia. *Proceedings of the National Academy of Sciences, USA, 88*, 7943–7947. doi:10.1073/pnas.88.18.7943

Lovegrove, W.J., Bowling, A., Badcock, D., & Blackwood, M. (1980). Specific reading disability: Differences in contrast sensitivity as a function of spatial frequency. *Science, 210*, 439–440. doi:10.1126/science.7433985

Lovett, M.W., Steinbach, K.A., & Frijters, J.C. (2000). Remediating the core deficits of developmental reading disability: A double-deficit perspective. *Journal of Learning Disabilities, 33*, 334–358. doi:10.1177/002221940003300406

Morris, R.D., Stuebing, K.K., Fletcher, J.M., Schaywitz, S.E., Lyon, G.R., Shankweiler, D.P., ... Schaywitz, B.A.

(1998). Subtypes of reading disability: Variability around a phonological core. *Journal of Educational Psychology, 90,* 347–373. doi:10.1037//0022-0663.90.3.347

Mugnaini, D., Lassi, S., La Malfa, G., & Albertni, G. (2009). Internalizing correlates of dyslexia. *Word Journal of Pediatrics, 5,* 255–264. doi:10.1007/s12519-009-0049-7

Nicolson, R.I., & Fawcett, A.J. (2007). Procedural learning difficulties: Reuniting the developmental disorders? *Trends in Neurosciences, 30,* 135–141. doi:10.1016/j.tins.2007.02.003

Nicolson, R.I., Fawcett, A.J., & Dean, P. (1995). Time-estimation deficits in developmental dyslexia—Evidence for cerebellar involvement. Proceedings of the Royal Society B: *Biological Sciences, 259,* 43–47. doi:10.1098/rspb.1995.0007

Nicolson, R.I., Fawcett, A.J., & Dean, P. (2001). Developmental dyslexia: The cerebellar deficit hypothesis. *Trends in Neurosciences, 24,* 508–511. doi:10.1016/S0166-2236(00)01896-8

Paulesu, E., Démonet, J.F., Fazio, F., Mc-Crozy, E., Chanoine, V., Brunswick, N., ... Frith, U. (2001). Dyslexia: Cultural diversity and biological unity. *Science, 291,* 2165–2167. doi:10.1126/science.1057179

Pernet, C.R., Andersson, J., Paulesu, E., & Démonet, J.F. (2009). When all hypotheses are right: A multifocal account of dyslexia. *Human Brain Mapping, 30,* 2278–2292. doi:10.1002/hbm.20670

Pernet, C.R., Poline, J.B., Démonet, J.F., & Rousselet, G.A. (2009). Brain classification reveals the right cerebellum as the best biomarker of dyslexia. *BMC Neuroscience, 10,* 67. doi:10.1186/1471-2202-10-67

Peyrin, C., Démonet, J.F., Baciu, M., Le Bas, J.F., & Valdois, S. (2011). Superior parietal lobe dysfunction in a homogeneous group of dyslexic children with a single visual attention span disorder. *Brain and Language, 118*(3), 128–138. doi:10.1016/j.bandl.2010.06.005

Pugh, K.R., Mencl, W.E., Jenner, A.R., Katz, L., Frost, S.J., Lee, J.R., ... Shawititz, B.A. (2000). Functional neuroimaging studies of reading and reading disability (developmental dyslexia). *Developmental Disability Research Review, 6,* 207–213. doi:10.1002/1098-2779(2000)6:3<207::AID-MRDD8>3.3.CO;2-G

Rae, C., Lee, M.A., Dixon, R.M., Blamire, A.M., Thompson, C.H., Styles, P., ...

Stein, J.F. (1998). Metabolic abnormalities in developmental dyslexia detected by H-1 magnetic resonance spectroscopy. *Lancet, 351,* 1849–1852.

Ramus, F. (2004). Neurobiology of dyslexia: A reinterpretation of the data. *Trends in Neurosciences, 27,* 720–726. doi:10.1016/j.tins.2004.10.004

Ramus, F., Rosen, S., Dakinm S.C., Day, B.L., Castellote, J.M., White, S., & Frith, U. (2003). Theories of developmental dyslexia: Insights from a multiple case study of dyslexic adults. *Brain, 126,* 841–865. doi:10.1093/brain/awg076

Raskind, W.H., Igo, R., Jr., Chapman, N.H., Berninger, V.W., Matsushita, M., Brkanac, Z., ... Wijsman, E.M. (2005). A genome scan in multigenerational families with dyslexia: Identification of a novel locus on chromosome 2q that contributes to phonological decoding efficiency. *Molecular Psychiatry, 10,* 699–711. doi:10.1038/sj.mp.4001657

Reid, A.A., Szczerbinski, M., Iskierka-Kasperek, E., & Hansen, P. (2007). Cognitive profiles of adult developmental dyslexics: Theoretical implications. *Dyslexia, 13,* 1–24. doi:10.1002/dys.321

Ruff, S., Cardebat, D., Marie, N., & Démonet, J.F. (2002). Enhanced response of the left frontal cortex to slowed down speech in dyslexia: An fMRI study. *Neuroreport, 13,* 1285–1289. doi:10.1097/00001756-200207190-00014

Schulter-Korne, G., & Bruder, J. (2010). Clinical neurophysiology of visual and auditory processing in dyslexia: A review. *Clinical Neurophysiology, 121,* 1794–1809. doi:10.1016/j.clinph.2010.04.028

Serniclaes, W., Sprenger-Charolles, L., Carre, R., & Démonet, J.F. (2001). Perceptual discrimination of speech sounds in developmental dyslexia. *Journal of Speech, Language and Hearing Research, 44,* 384–399. doi:10.1044/1092-4388(2001/032)

Shaywitz, S.E., & Shaywitz, B.A. (2005). Dyslexia (specific reading disability). *Biological Psychiatry, 57,* 1301–0309. doi:10.1016/j.biopsych.2005.01.043

Skotun, B.C. (2000). The magnocellular deficit theory of dyslexia: Evidence from contrast sensitivity. *Vision Research, 40,* 111–127. doi:10.1016/S0042-6989(99)00170-4

Song, J., Banai, K., Russo, N., & Kraus, N. (2006). On the relationship between speech- and non-speech evoked brainstem responses. *Audiology and Neurotology, 11,* 233–241.

Stein, J.F. (2001). The magnocellular theory of developmental dyslexia. *Dyslexia, 7,* 12–36. doi:10.1002/dys.186

Stein, J.F., & Walsh, V. (1997). To see but not to read: The magnocellular theory of dyslexia. *Trends in Neuroscience, 20,* 147–151. doi:10.1016/S0166-2236(96)01005-3

Stoodley, C.J., & Schmahmann, J.D. (2009). Functional topography in the human cerebellum: A meta-analysis of neuroimaging studies. *NeuroImage, 44,* 489–501. doi:10.1016/j.neuroimage.2008.08.039

Strick, P.L., Dum, R.P., & Fiez, J.A. (2009). Cerebellum and nonmotor function. *Annual Review of Neuroscience, 32,* 413–434. doi:10.1146/annurev.neuro.31.060407.125606

Tallal, P. (2004). Improving language and literacy is a matter of time. *Nature Reviews Neuroscience, 5,* 721–728. doi:10.1038/nrn1499

Tallal, P., Stark, R.E., & Mellits, E.D. (1985). Identification of language impaired children on the basis of rapid perception and production skills. *Brain and Language, 25,* 314–322. doi:10.1016/0093-934X(85)90087-2

Valdois, S., Bosse, M.L., Ans, B., Zorman, M., Carbonnel, S., David, D., & Pellat, J. (2003). Phonological and visual processing deficits are dissociated in developmental dyslexia: Evidence from two case studies. *Reading and Writing, 16,* 543–572.

White, S., Milne, E., Rosen, S., Hansen, P., Swettenham, J., Frith, U., & Ramus, F. (2006). The role of sensorimotor processing in dyslexia: A multiple case study of dyslexic children. *Developmental Science, 9,* 237–265.

Wolf, M., & Bowers, P.G. (1999). The double deficit hypothesis for the developmental dyslexias. *Journal of Educational Psychology, 91,* 415–438. doi:10.1037//0022-0663.91.3.415

Wolf, M., & Bowers, P.G. (2000). Naming speed processes and developmental reading disabilities: An introduction to the special issue on the double-deficit hypothesis. *Journal of Learning Disabilities, 33,* 322–324. doi:10.1177/002221940003300404

World Health Organization (1994). *The International Classification of Diseases, vol. 10: Classification of mental and behavioral disorders.* Geneva, Switzerland.

Ziegler, J.C., Castel, C., Pech-Georgel, C., George, F., Alario, F.X., & Perry, C. (2008). Developmental dyslexia and the dual route model of reading: Simulating individual differences and subtypes. *Cognition, 107,* 151–178. doi:10.1016/j.cognition.2007.09.004

Using Developmental Neuroimaging for Identification, Intervention, and Remeditation

Introduction

April A. Benasich

Similar to the revolution in genetics, advances in neuroimaging have led to a deeper understanding of the brain–behavior interface. Such advances have also helped foster identification of putative neurobiological markers for various disorders and offer the opportunity to assess the earliest effects of remediation and intervention. In particular, the broad range of cutting-edge imaging techniques available and increasing sophistication in acquiring converging structural, physiological, and functional data have provided a unique opportunity to study progressively younger populations and to link morphometric changes and age-specific patterns of functional connectivity across neurodevelopment. In the area of language and reading development, these advances have supplied the means to test specific hypotheses regarding the neurobiological bases of language development and disorder. This is of particular importance for disorders such as dyslexia that are hypothesized to have their origins early in development (see Sections I and II), given the progressive accommodation and plasticity of cortical and subcortical regions as a child develops from birth through early language acquisition to prereading and then to school age and accomplished reading skills.

All the chapters in this section discuss research that utilized structural or functional neuroimaging techniques to examine neural substrates of linguistic and literacy acquisition (and dysfunction) and/or anatomical biomarkers. Such neuroimaging techniques provide a dynamic look at the working brain and allow localization of brain areas, mapping of functional organization, and in particular, of circuits and white matter tracts (as characterized by diffusion tensor imaging [DTI] and tractography) that may be critical to language development and/or to the acquisition of reading skills. Significant progress has been made in using neuroimaging approaches to examine language, reading, and reading disability in older children from about the age of 5 years. However, periods early in infancy characterized by exuberant brain growth and increases in synaptic connectivity, as well as times of the most rapid language acquisition (~16–36 months), have been virtually unstudied in nonclinical populations. A number of factors are implicated in the lack of data for this age group, including the inability of very young children to cooperate with task demands within the scanner, the slowness of MRI acquisition and thus the necessity of sophisticated algorithms that enable prospective motion correction, and the challenging techniques necessary to achieve accurate brain segmentation in young infants (in Chapters 14, 16, and 17).

A more fundamental explanation, however, for the dearth of information across these early years, when vast transformations in brain volume and connectivity are occurring, has to do with the inherent limitations in imaging. Although the field is moving forward at a dizzying pace, image resolution is not yet adequate in human applications to allow examination of important parameters, such as synaptogenesis versus pruning, which appear to be crucial variables in defining developmental deviations of many developmental disorders, not just learning language disorders (LLD). Yet, it will be critical to focus on this still-elusive goal, because even the most fine-grained study of the adult phenotype cannot demonstrate how things came to be. For example, if a structure is found to be smaller in LLD versus typical adults, this could occur through 1) reduced neurogenesis, 2) normal neurogenesis but reduced synaptogenesis (reduced arbor and thus decreased grey matter), or 3) normal neurogenesis and synaptogenesis but excessive pruning. Nonetheless, these different developmental trajectories would all lead to a similar end result. The ability to follow what is actually happening in the brain of at-risk infants, coupled with knowledge of what the genes involved are controlling (i.e., regulating proliferation, synapse formation, and so on) will ultimately solve this puzzle. But this aspect is critical to the understanding of the adult phenotype and is currently missing from most experimental approaches.

In the first chapter in this section, Grant addresses these issues and further provides a comprehensive overview of the evolution of pediatric neuroimaging, emphasizing the untapped potential of imaging techniques in the characterization and understanding of neurodevelopmental disorders (Chapter 14). Although Grant does not directly address dyslexia per se, the points so beautifully made in this chapter set the stage for those that follow (as well as recapitulating issues raised in earlier sections). Grant reinforces the importance of capturing growth trajectories across age, given that they reflect processes including neurogenesis, neuronal migration, axonal connectivity and pruning, neuronal specification, and myelination—all of which are in turn influenced by genes, gene expression, and environmental factors.

Subsequent chapters address a variety of topics that have been frequently discussed in the dyslexia arena. One of these concerns the role of neural specializations, such as asymmetries of the planum temporale, within the dyslexia phenotype, and more specifically the diagnostic strength of this and other easily assessed anatomical markers alone and in combination with variables such as passage comprehension and processing speed. Leonard (Chapter 15) presents a critical review of this literature and then details a series of studies that explores the utility of an anatomical risk index (ARI) as a predictor of later reading and verbal skill. Her findings suggest that the ARI is not a good predictor of dyslexia (when defined as "poor decoding skills"), but rather may index successful compensation even with severe decoding deficits.

Converging onto the topic of anatomical markers and volumetrics, as well as comorbidity, the wide-ranging contribution from Herbert (Chapter 18) examines the striking increase in brain volume, specifically in white matter volume, in children with autism spectrum disorders as well as those diagnosed with LLD. As did Leonard, Herbert observed rightward cortical asymmetries in both autism and childhood LLD and suggests both developmental and widely distributed epigenetic factors. As is proposed in many chapters across sections in this volume, the suggestion is raised of sensory processing precursors and subsequently altered underlying cellular physiology.

Another long-debated issue is the role phonological processing plays in the core deficits of dyslexia. Phonological processing (often assessed via nonword repetition or pseudoword reading) has been shown to be impaired across disorders, and a deficit in phonological representation is the most reliable marker of dyslexia in school-age children (e.g., Gathercole, 2006). Plante (Chapter 16) suggests that an alternative approach to assessing what individuals with LLD know and can demonstrate (e.g., phonological representation) is to examine learning itself, and specifically the learning mechanisms that language-typical children as well as children with LLD use to acquire language. Plante reviews studies that illustrate the critical role receptive capabilities have in effectively using these implicit learning mechanisms and raises the issue of control and maintenance of attention and of memory. The creative fMRI studies described in Plante's chapter examine the intersection of language, attention, and memory. These studies are focused on acquiring physiological data in an attempt to visualize processing components as learning takes place and eventually, it is hoped, to image the dynamic processes associated with learning.

Studies that have used fMRI to investigate phonological processing in adults and children with developmental dyslexia have found atypical activation, primarily hypoactivation within the left parietotemporal and occipitotemporal cortex as well as in perisylvian areas. All these regions are typically activated during phonological tasks. However, as Raschle, Lee, Stering, Zuk, and Gaab (Chapter 17) observe, a critical step is to determine if the differences in behavioral markers, brain structure, and neural correlates of phonological or rapid auditory processing, widely reported in school-age children and adults diagnosed with dyslexia, are already present in children at risk for dyslexia prior to reading onset. Raschle and colleague's preliminary findings are of great interest given that the reduced activation within perisylvian, occipitotemporal, and parietotemporal cortical regions, seen in their prereaders with a familial history of dyslexia, echo what is seen in older children and adults. This suggests, as do the findings reported in Section II (Chapters 6, 7, and 8) that differences in individuals with LLD are either present at birth or develop within the first years of life.

A somewhat more specific functional specialization, that of the characteristic left-lateralized neural activity that emerges in the fusiform gyrus (visual word form area, or VWFA) for skilled readers, and its role in experience-dependent tuning of perceptual expertise for reading is added to this discussion by McCandliss and Yoncheva (Chapter 19). The research detailed here, which makes use of converging imaging modalities including DTI, investigates how this interactive, left-lateralized functional network might develop and which aspects of the reading experience, and, correspondingly, the functional network recruited by these experiences, drives the characteristic left lateralization of the VWFA system. Individual variation that might affect the development of perceptual expertise for reading is studied as well, including the atypical reading development associated with dyslexia. Given that these and other areas concerned with phonological processes interact functionally, McCandliss and Yoncheva hypothesize that preexisting individual differences in anatomy or acquisition of phonology might shape this interactive process very early on, as is suggested in the findings reported by Leonard (Chapter 15), Raschle and colleagues (Chapter 17), and Herbert (Chapter 18), as well as the studies reported in Sections I and II. Overall it is clear that across the contributions in this volume, many themes are sounded repeatedly and the knowledge gained from this unique cross-disciplinary symposium may well point the way toward new directions that could illuminate dyslexia precursors, identification, and remediation.

REFERENCE

Gathercole, S. (2006). Nonword repetition and word learning: The nature of the relationship. *Applied Psycholinguistics, 27,* 513–543. doi:10.1017/S0142716406060383

CHAPTER 14
Evolution of Pediatric Neuroimaging and Application of Cutting-Edge Techniques

P. Ellen Grant

W
ith the increasing sophistication of image analysis methods and the widespread availability of magnetic resonance (MR) scanners, neuroimaging is beginning to play a major role in the understanding of many neurodevelopmental disorders, including dyslexia.

Imaging has the potential to provide an important window into the physiology and molecular events that underlie brain development and function and to provide an important bridge from animal to human studies. However, to fully realize this potential, technology needs to be optimized so that this exploration can begin at the earliest possible time point, the fetus. In addition, it is important to have technology focused on the infants and young children whose brains are vastly different in size and composition to the mature brain. This is particularly important for dyslexia and related developmental language disorders given the increasing evidence that the earliest precursors of such disorders may be identified very early in development. The technological advances detailed in this chapter will increase the ability to scan children from birth onwards without sedation and get higher quality data. The volumetric, surface data combined with tractography and resting state functional connectivity data allows the search for networks of involvement, provides the potential to develop early biomarkers of atypical network development, and affords the opportunity to monitor response to therapy.

As researchers, moving forward in our studies of early brain development, it is also important to realize that we cannot study only one or two time points, we need to study developmental trajectories. As has been long recognized with studies of head circumference, developmental trajectories are critically important to understanding risk profiles. Thus if two children have identical head circumferences at 6 months, but one had a percentile that dropped by more than 50 points, the risk of an atypical neurodevelopmental outcome is much higher. In other words, the brain contains history—it is not only important where you are on a developmental trajectory but also how you got there. It is likely that these concepts apply to all neuroimaging measures of brain development, including structure, physiology, and connectivity.

Clinical neuroimaging has failed to meet the needs of the neuro-developmental community due to the inherent shortcomings of visual perception. Visual perception cannot accurately capture growth trajectories, as at every age there is a wide range of biological diversity that results in a wide spread of features. Reliable quantitative neuroimaging techniques need to be created to more accurately characterize these rapid developmental changes. We need to exploit these rapid temporal changes that occur early in life to differentiate typical from atypical developmental trajectories. After about 3 years of age, these temporal changes rapidly reach asymptotes, making differences among individuals more difficult to detect. The time period between fetal life and 3 years is arguably the most important phase of brain development, as it captures neurogenesis, neuronal migration, and axonal connectivity, as well as the vast majority of pruning through apopotosis, neuronal specification, and myelination. During this early brain growth activity dependent connections increase, and axonal connections decrease. Genes, gene expression, and environmental factors influence this process. How the brain is put together is likely to determine its later function, its vulnerability and, ultimately, the risk of cognitive decline in old age.

In this chapter I provide a basic overview of available and developing neuroimaging tools to monitor brain growth and development. The only viable tools to monitor human brain health and development are noninvasive and present no significant risk of harm. The three modalities that best fit these criteria and provide complimentary information are (Figure 14.1)

1. Magnetic resonance imaging (MRI)
2. Near infrared spectroscopy (NIRS)
3. Magnetoencephalography (MEG)

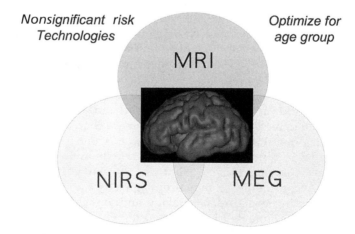

Figure 14.1. Modalities for in vivo imaging of children must present no significant risks. Magnetic resonance imaging, magnetoencephalography, and near infrared spectroscopy meet meet these requirements, but hardware designs and data analysis software must be optimized for the size and unique tissue properties of the developing brain.

Each of these modalities provides a different perspective on brain structure, metabolism, and neural activity (Figure 14.2). MRI is the most popular modality for studying the brain due to its relatively easy accessibility. High-resolution T1 weighted volumetric data sets provide information on regional brain volumes and shapes, regional cortical thickness, gyral patterns, and cortical curvature. Diffusion imaging provides information on tissue coherence that in turn reflects the organization of major axonal bundles in the white matter. Arterial Spin Labeling (ASL) provides more physiological information as it provides a quantitative measure of regional cerebral perfusion that is closely linked to cerebral metabolism. These MR methods are of relative high spatial resolution and provide whole head coverage. New frequency domain methods for near infrared spectroscopy (FD-NIRS) approaches provide regional quantitative cerebral oxygen saturation and cerebral blood volume. Even newer diffuse correlation spectroscopy (DCS) approaches provide regional cerebral blood flow indices. When the DCS is combined with FD-NIRS, regional cerebral oxygen consumption can be calculated. These NIRS methods provide low spatial but high temporal resolution information that compliments MR methods. Finally, magnetoencephalography (MEG) provides information on neural activity by detecting resulting fluctuations in magnetic fields.

MAGNETIC RESONANCE IMAGING

Methods for Studying Children without Sedation

A small number of groups have developed expertise in imaging infants and young children without sedation (Gao et al., 2009; Ortiz-Mantilla, Choe, Flax, Grant, & Benasich, 2010). This situation typically occurs in research settings, and often the expertise resides in a transient postdoctoral fellow or a small team of individuals removed from routine MR

- Volume and Surface (Structural MRI)
- Tissue coherence (Diffusion MRI)
- Physiology
  - Cerebral blood flow (Arterial Spin Labeling MRI)
  - Cerebral oxygen saturation (FD-NIRS)
  - Cerebral blood volume (FD-NIRS)
  - Cerebral rate of oxygen consumption (FD-NIRS, DCS)
- Neuronal activity (MEG)

Figure 14.2. Magnetic resonance imaging, magnetoencephalography, and near infrared spectroscopy provide complementary information on brain development, physiology, and neuronal activity.

practice. However, to make significant advances in imaging nonsedated infants and young children, these advances need to become common-place and part of a high volume practice. Child-life specialists are the ideal repository for this knowledge and the ideal nexus for future de-velopments. In routine pediatric care, child–life specialists use their knowledge of child development to assist in physician and parent–child interaction and help educate, prepare, and support children and their families through medical tests, therapies, and interventions. By empow-ering child-life specialists and using allied subspecialties such as de-velopmental cognitive neuroscience to improve approaches, the ability to routinely guide children and their families through nonsedated MR imaging studies will significantly increase. A model in which child-life specialists are part of the team with the MR technologist when ordering MR studies, clinical or research, would facilitate the rapid increase of nonsedated studies.

Volume and Surface Analysis

Volumetric analysis of volumetric T1 brain MR images provides a means to characterize the complex orchestration of regional brain growth. Re-gional differences in growth trajectories have profound implications for the coordination of neuronal circuit development. In addition, given the concept of increased vulnerability during times of rapid growth, regional growth trajectories may provide information on time periods of increased selective vulnerability. The potential of volumetric studies to provide relevant information on cognitive development is illustrated in the recent report of amygdala size at 6 months predicting language performance at 2, 3, and 4 years of age (Ortiz-Mantilla et al., 2010). The ability to predict infants at risk for later disabilities is key to identifying those in need of early intervention and to beginning treatment before disabilities are manifest. Ideally, interventions would occur prior to the completion of neuronal pruning and myelination (before approximately 2 years of age) as plasticity is likely to be significantly reduced after this time. However, most developmental disorders, including dyslexia, are not diagnosed until later in life when the maximal phase of plasticity has already passed.

Ideally, all infants would undergo assessment of regional volumes to move from head circumference measures to more specific regional volumes. However, this is currently not possible due to the differences in the contrast and geometry between the infant and adult brain (Fig-ure 14.3). In addition, the difficulty in scanning unsedated infants and young children makes it difficult to acquire typical data. As a result there is little data available on volumetric growth before 5 years of age and almost no information before 1 year of age. However, this stage is the most important, as it is the phase of most rapid brain growth in which regional differences in growth rates are clearly evident but disappear

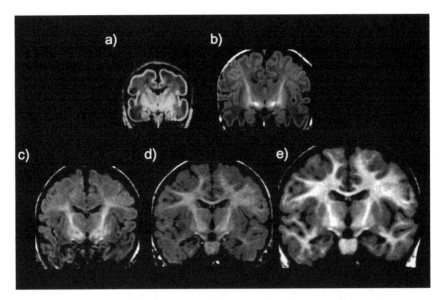

Figure 14.3. Coronal volumetric T1 weighted images at a) 7 weeks preterm, b) term, c) 3 months, d) 6 months, and e) 12 months show the changing size, topology, and composition of the developing brain.

as asymptotes in brain growth are reached. Many groups are working on methods not only to semiautomatically or automatically segment the developing brain but also to capture the changes in topology and tissue character that are a reflection of developmental stage (Habas et al., 2010; Knickmeyer et al., 2008; Weisenfeld & Warfield, 2009) .

Another major reason there is little data available in the early ages is the fact that MRI is very slow. The long scan times result in unavoidable motion, which degrades image quality. New hardware developments of high density phased array coils with 32 channel arrays now

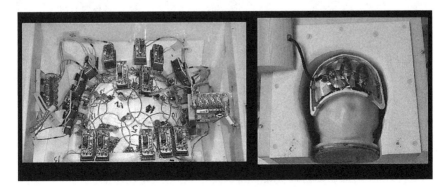

Figure 14.4. Custom built neonatal head coil form fit to the size of a term neonatal head. (*Source:* Keil et al., 2011.)

commercially available for adults have resulted in image acceleration factors of 2 to 4 times. However, the lack of coils tailor made for the smaller size of the infant brain make such increases in acceleration unavailable to this most needy population. The development of 32 channel phased array coil prototypes tailored to the infant head has started to provide similar increases in infant brain image acquisition possible (Figure 14.4). The improvements in image acceleration combined with novel prospective motion correction techniques for volumetric structural images have significantly improved image quality in the pediatric population (Figure 14.5) (Keil et al., 2011; Tisdall, Hess, & van der Kouwe). As we move to 7T and still higher numbers of elements are constructed, even greater accelerations may be possible.

MR image volumetric analysis does not capture the full complexity of brain growth. During the third trimester, dramatic changes in surface topology occurs as gyrification takes place. With gyrification representing the brain's solution to allowing increased radial columns in a contained volume and improved functional compartmentalization, there is a need to meaningfully quantify and compare gyral structure. Using software tools, triangulated meshes representing the complex 2D surface topology in 3D can be created and measures on these surfaces performed (Figure 14.6) (Dale, Fischl, & Sereno, 1999; Fischl, Sereno, & Dale, 1999). Many measures have been proposed, such as the maximal and minimal curvature, sharpness, mean curvature, bending energy, and Gaussian curvature (Pienaar, Fischl, Caviness, Makris, & Grant, 2008). In addition, sulcal pits, the deepest part of the sulci, have been shown to be the most invariant component of the gyral pattern, suggesting they are under tighter genetic control (Lohmann, von Cramon, & Colchester, 2008). Using sulcal pits, gyral patterns can be compared to explore the relationship of gyral structure to cognitive function or genetic disorders (Im et al., 2011). Wavelet decompositions have also been used to provide a global mathematical

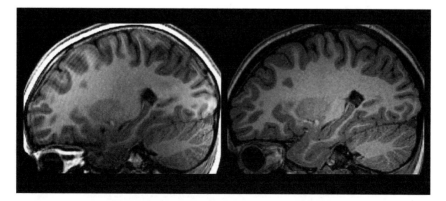

Figure 14.5. Sagittal magnetization prepared rapid acquisition gradient echoa without (left) and with (right) prospective motion correction in a 4-year-old unsedated child.

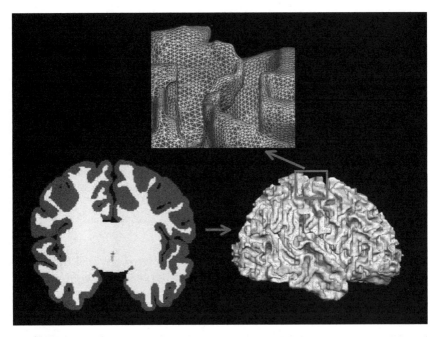

Figure 14.6. Volumetric T1 weighted images of a term neonate with the cortex represented as grey and everything else as white. The grey-white matter interface can be reconstructed as a triangulated mesh on which measures can be obtained.

description of an individual brain's gyral pattern and a means to express gyral folding over time (Yu et al., 2007).

Diffusion Measures of Tissue Coherence

Diffusion imaging provides a method to interrogate the structural coherence of brain tissue. There are two major types of diffusion acquisition schemes: diffusion tensor imaging (DTI) and high angular resolution diffusion imaging (HARDI). DTI is usually performed at lower diffusion gradient strengths (lower b values) and with fewer diffusion gradient directions. When the directional diffusion is calculated using DTI, only one major direction is allowed and, as a result, crossing axonal bundles within a voxel cannot be resolved. In contrast, HARDI is usually performed at higher diffusion gradient strengths (higher b values) with many more diffusion gradient directions. In HARDI reconstructions, diffusion directions are represented as orientation distribution functions that allows peaks in multiple directions and hence the possibility to resolve crossing axonal bundles (Tuch, 2004). The most sophisticated and time-consuming method for characterizing diffusion properties is diffusion spectrum imaging (DSI), in which not only a large number of diffusion gradient directions but also multiple b values are sampled (Wedeen, Hagmann,

Tseng, Reese, & Weisskoff, 2005). This provides the most complete information about tissue diffusion properties, but imaging times are currently prohibitive for routine use in the pediatric population.

Once the diffusion images have been acquired, tissue coherence from voxel to voxel can be tracked using a number of postprocessing methods. The most comment method is the FACT algorithm in which axonal bundles are assumed to exist between two voxels if the fractional anisotropy (FA) is above and the angular deviation of the major diffusion direction between the two voxels is below ad hoc values (Mori, Crain, Chacko, & van Zijl, 1999). Typically the FA threshold is set between 0.15 and 0.2 with the assumption that values below the threshold are in the noise. However, FA is a ratio whose value is given as:

$$= \sqrt{\frac{1}{2}} \frac{\sqrt{(\lambda_1 - \lambda_2)^2 + (\lambda_1 - \lambda_3)^2 + (\lambda_2 - \lambda_3)^2}}{\sqrt{(\lambda_1^2 + \lambda_2^2 + \lambda_3^2)}}$$

in which $\lambda 1$, $\lambda 2$, $\lambda 3$ are the eigenvalues in three orthogonal directions. When diffusivity is high, the eigenvalues are larger and therefore it may be possible to have an FA value below 0.15 and still be able to resolve the

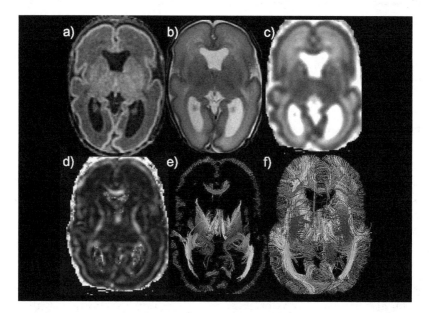

Figure 14.7.   30-week corrected gestational age neonate with an absent septum pellucidum. a) T1; b) T2 fast spin echo, c) apparent diffustion coefficient map, d) fractional anistropy map, e) diffusion tensor imaging, reconstruction with fiber assignment by continuous tracking tractography, fractional anistropy, threshold of 0.15 and angular threshold of 35 degrees; f) high angular resolution diffusion imaging reconstruction with Runge-Kutta 2nd Order tractography no fractional anistropy threshold and angular threshold of 35 degrees. The image obtained in f) matches our expectations for the underlying anatomy of unmyelinated axonal pathways.

difference between the different eigenvalues. In other words, the minimal FA value that should be used as a threshold is not clear. When FA thresholds are removed, anatomically plausible results are often obtained (Figure 14.7). In addition, when FA thresholds are removed, tract reconstructions move beyond the mainstream of the axonal bundles into the more divergent regions in which much of the individual variability is likely to occur. Angular thresholds are also ad hoc and typically values around 35 degrees are chosen. In reality, there are many examples in which axonal bundles make sharp turns but as the angular threshold is increased, reconstruction times increase and more spurious results are obtained.

Diffusion imaging with pathological specimens is increasing the understanding of the meaning and limitations of diffusion tractography. Tissue coherence and tracts can arise due to cellular or axonal organization and therefore care must be taken when interpreting results, particularly in the second and third trimester brain and in pathological conditions (Figure 14.8) (Takahashi et al., 2010; Takahashi, Folkerth, Galaburda, & Grant, 2011). Although diffusion coherence can be used to gather information about cortical structure and connectivity, it must be kept in mind that "tracts" are not axons. Whereas in most reconstructions the size of the tract is likely to be related to the overall size of the axonal bundles, the diameter of the tracts is not related to the axonal diameter.

Cerebral Perfusion with Arterial Spin Labeling

Arterial spin labeling (ASL) provides a method to obtain regional cerebral perfusion in mL/100g/min using MRI without the need to inject

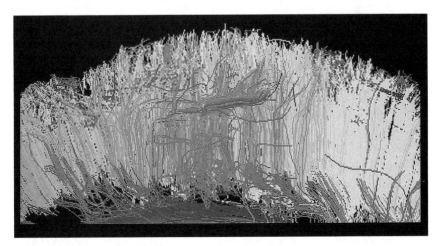

Figure 14.8. High angular resolution diffusion imaging reconstruction and streamline tractography on a 20-week gestational age fetal specimen. Sagittal image of the 3D tract reconstruction focused on the cerebral mantel with the ventricular margin at the bottom and the pial surface at the top. Left is rostral and right is caudal. (*Source:* Takahashi, Folkerth, Galaburda, & Grant, 2011.)

exogenous contrast. Typically, ASL sequences are between approximately 2 and 8 minutes, depending on the type of ASL sequence, the coverage, and the field strength of the MRI. Although, as with any quantitative method, there are assumptions that are made to obtain quantitative data, ASL provides very useful information on brain perfusion. With cerebral perfusion tightly linked to neuronal metabolism, cerebral perfusion as measured with ASL provides an important window into cerebral metabolism during development and in disease (Figure 14.9) (Wang et al., 2003). Areas in which particular caution should be applied in ASL quantitation are in the infant and in cases in which treatment or disease results in particularly low or high cerebral perfusion and where hematocrit varies.

NEAR INFRARED SPECTROSCOPY

Frequency Domain Near Infrared Spectroscopy

Continuous wave near infrared spectroscopy (CW-NIRS) has been used to monitor cerebral oxygenation since the mid-1980s. Wide adoption of these systems has been hampered by the lack of quantitation and the high variability of the results. In addition, commercial systems typically provide only estimates of regional cerebral tissue oxygenation, and recent studies suggest that oxygenation may not be the most sensitive marker of development or injury (Franceschini et al., 2007; Grant et al., 2009). New frequency domain near infrared spectroscopy (FD-NIRS) methods offer advantages over CW-NIRS approaches in that not only is

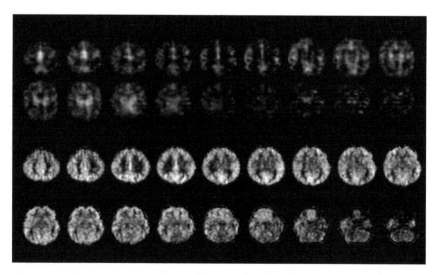

Figure 14.9. Pseudocontinuous arterial spin labeling on a term infant (top 2 rows) and a 6-month-old child (bottom 2 rows) showing the marked increases in cerebral perfusion that occur with early development.

regional cerebral tissue oxygenation determined but also regional absolute cerebral blood volumes can be calculated if hematocrit is known. If multiple frequencies and source detector distances are used with FD-NIRS systems, objective data inclusion criteria can be used to increase data quality and decrease variability due to noise. Regional cerebral blood volumes appear to be more sensitive markers of development and injury than regional oxygen saturation (Franceschini et al., 2007; Grant et al., 2009; Roche-Labarbe, Grant, & Franceschini, in press).

Diffuse Correlation Spectroscopy

Diffuse correlation spectroscopy is a new method to estimate blood flow using near infrared light without the need for an oxygen or indocyanine green bolus. DCS estimates a regional blood flow index based on the movement of red blood cells inside the tissue. Although not yet an absolute measure, DCS systems provide a flow index that over a least a reasonable range of flows appear to be linearly related to ASL perfusion measures (Durduran et al., 2010; Roche-Labarbe et al., in press).

Combined Measures

The biggest advantage of NIRS systems, in my opinion, comes with the combination of FD-NIRS and DCS systems, as the combination enables calculation of regional cerebral metabolic rate of oxygen consumption (CMRO2) (Roche-Labarbe et al., 2010, in press). With oxygen a major substrate for neuronal metabolism, this combination provides a bedside regional evaluation of neuronal metabolism. CMRO2 appears to be a sensitive marker for development, gestational age, acute brain injury, and in initial studies, response to therapeutic hypothermia. I believe that FD-NIRS combined with DCS will prove extremely useful in monitoring trajectories of growth and development.

Continuous Wave Near Infrared Spectroscopy

CW-NIRS offers the advantage of higher temporal resolution compared with the FD-NIRS methods but the disadvantage of lack of absolute quantitation. CW-NIRS is therefore typically used to study functional responses. When using CW-NIRS in functional studies, most optical research groups use many wavelengths. In pediatric studies, it is helpful to have baseline values of cerebral blood flow first to help contextualize responses and determine if changes may be affected by changes in baseline flow.

MAGNETOENCEPHALOGRAPHY

The ability to detect and monitor the development of neuronal activity is also critically important to understanding the developing brain and the emergence of cognitive or behavior disorders. The changing skull and scalp thickness, as well as the closing of sutures and fontanels, affect longitudinal EEG studies but have little impact on MEG studies. However, to study emergence of impairments during infancy, higher spatial resolution and smaller helmet sizes are needed. Such advances are currently under development.

CONNCECTIVITY ANALYSIS

Coordinating and integrating information from different brain regions is an important part of typical brain function. Therefore, methods to capture dynamic network properties are gaining popularity as many mental health disorders, including dyslexia, are thought to arise from atypical network activity. Diffusion imaging methods are used to measure structural connectivity and blood oxygen level dependent (BOLD) methods are used to assess resting state functional connectivity (Hagmann et al., 2008; Vogel, Power, Petersen, & Schlaggar, 2010). Since 2010, initial estimates of myelin maturation effects on structural connectivity have been explored (Hagmann et al., 2010). However, the most robust method for multisite connectivity analysis is resting state functional connectivity. Measures of resting state functional connectivity have allowed identification of multiple typical functional networks, estimates of brain maturational stage, and differences in developmental disorders. Currently, many investigators from diverse backgrounds enthusiastically support such connectivity approaches to the diagnosis and understanding of developmental disorders.

CONCLUSION

Although in neurodevelopmental disorders such as dyslexia neuroimaging studies are typically read clinically as "normal", quantitative neuroimaging analysis promises to provide important insights into and the opportunity to investigate the earliest precursors of language-based learning disorders. As the ability to study unsedated infants and young children increases, so too will the ability to detect the early divergence of developmental trajectories in those destined to develop dyslexia from typical controls. Such approaches are necessary to begin separating out causative epigenetic factors and potential environmental triggers from compensatory or secondary effects. Advances in multimodal imaging provide additional tools to explore potential hypotheses for physiological mechanisms and new approaches in connectivity analysis promise to capture changes developing network properties. Finally, as the ability to rapidly process and provide analysis results on individual subject increases, there is the potential to eventually move beyond group analysis approach to exploring the meaning of results in each individual.

REFERENCES

Dale, A.M., Fischl, B., & Sereno, M.I. (1999). Cortical surface-based analysis. I. Segmentation and surface reconstruction. *NeuroImage, 9*(2), 179–194. doi:10.1006/nimg.1998.0395

Durduran, T., Zhou, C., Buckley, E.M., Kim, M.N., Yu, G., Choe, R., ... Licht, D.J. (2010). Optical measurement of cerebral hemodynamics and oxygen metabolism in neonates with congenital heart defects. *Journal of Biomedical Optics, 15*(3), 037004. doi:10.1117/1.3425884

Fischl, B., Sereno, M.I., & Dale, A.M. (1999). Cortical surface-based analysis. II: Inflation, flattening, and a surface-based coordinate system. *NeuroImage, 9*(2), 195–207. doi:10.1006/nimg.1998.0396

Franceschini, M.A., Thaker, S., Themelis, G., Krishnamoorthy, K.K., Bortfeld, H., Diamond, S.G., ... Grant, P.E. (2007). Assessment of infant brain development with frequency-domain near-infrared spectroscopy. *Pediatric Research, 61*(5 Pt 1), 546–551. doi:10.1203/pdr.0b013e318045be99

Gao, W., Lin, W., Chen, Y., Gerig, G., Smith, J.K., Jewells, V., & Gilmore, J.H. (2009). Temporal and spatial development of axonal maturation and myelination of white matter in the developing brain. *American Journal of Neuroradiology, 30*(2), 290–296. doi:10.3174/ajnr.A1363

Grant, P.E., Roche-Labarbe, N., Surova, A., Themelis, G., Selb, J., Warren, E.K., ... Franceschini M.A. (2009). Increased cerebral blood volume and oxygen consumption in neonatal brain injury. *Journal of Cerebral Blood Flow and Metabolism, 29*(10), 1704–1713. doi:10.1038/jcbfm.2009.90

Habas, P.A., Kim, K., Corbett-Detig, J.M., Rousseau, F., Glenn, O.A., Barkovich, A.J., & Studholme, C. (2010). A spatiotemporal atlas of MR intensity, tissue probability and shape of the fetal brain with application to segmentation. *NeuroImage, 53*(2), 460–470. doi:10.1016/j.neuroimage.2010.06.054

Hagmann, P., Cammoun, L., Gigandet, X., Meuli, R., Honey, C.J., Wedeen, V.J., & Sporns, O. (2008). Mapping the structural core of human cerebral cortex. *PLoS Biology, 6*(7), e159. doi:10.1371/journal.pbio.0060159

Hagmann, P., Sporns, O., Madan, N., Cammoun, L., Pienaar, R., Wedeen, V.J., ... Grant, P.E. (2010). White matter maturation reshapes structural connectivity in the late developing human brain. *Proceedings of the National Academy of Sciences, USA, 107*(44), 19067–19072. doi:10.1073/pnas.1009073107

Im, K., Choi, Y.Y., Yang, J.J., Lee, K.H., Kim, S.I., Grant, P.E., Lee, J.-M. (2011). The relationship between the presence of sulcal pits and intelligence in human brains. *NeuroImage, 55*(4), 1490–1496. doi:10.1016/j.neuroimage.2010.12.080

Keil, B., Alagappan, V., Mareyam, A., McNab, J., Fujimoto, K., Tountcheva, V., Triantafyllou, C., Dilks, D.D., ... Wald, L.L. (2011). Size-optimized 32-channel brain arrays for 3T pediatric imaging. *Magnetic Resonance in Medicine.* Advance online publication. Retrieved June 7, 2011. doi:10.1002/mrm.22961.

Knickmeyer, R.C., Gouttard, S., Kang, C., Evans, D., Wilber, K., Smith, J.K., ... Gilmore, J.H. (2008). A structural MRI study of human brain development from birth to 2 years. *Journal of Neuroscience, 28*(47), 12176–12182. doi:10.1523/JNEUROSCI.3479-08.2008

Lohmann, G., von Cramon, D.Y., & Colchester, A.C. (2008). Deep sulcal landmarks provide an organizing framework for human cortical folding. *Cerebral Cortex, 18*(6), 1415–1420. doi:10.1093/cercor/bhm174

Mori, S., Crain, B.J., Chacko, V.P., van Zijl, P.C. (1999). Three-dimensional tracking of axonal projections in the brain by magnetic resonance imaging. *Annals of Neurology, 45*(2), 265–269. doi:10.1002/1531-8249(199902)45:2<265::AID-ANA21>3.0.CO;2-3

Ortiz-Mantilla, S., Choe, M.S., Flax, J., Grant, P.E., & Benasich, A.A. (2010). Associations between the size of the amygdala in infancy and language abilities during the preschool years in normally developing children. *Neuroimage, 49*(3), 2791–2799. doi:10.1016/j.neuroimage.2009.10.029

Pienaar, R., Fischl, B., Caviness, V., Makris, N., Grant, P.E. (2008). A Methodology for analyzing curvature in the developing brain from preterm to adult. *International Journal of Imaging Systems and Technology, 18*(1), 42–68. doi:10.1002/ima.20138

Roche-Labarbe, N., Carp, S.A., Surova, A., Patel, M., Boas, D.A., Grant, P.E., &

Franceschini, M.A. (2010). Noninvasive optical measures of CBV, StO(2), CBF index, and rCMRO(2) in human premature neonates' brains in the first six weeks of life. *Human Brain Mapping, 31*(3), 341–352.

Roche-Labarbe, N., Grant, P., & Franceschini, M. (in press). Part 11: Neurology, 48. Assessment of infant brain development. In J. Popp, V.V. Tuchin, A. Chiou, & S.H. Heinemann (Eds.), *Handbook of biophotonic: Vol. 2: Photonics for health care.* Weinheim, Berlin: Wiley-VCH.

Takahashi, E., Dai, G., Wang, R., Ohki, K., Rosen, G.D., Galaburda, A.M., ... Weeden, V.J. (2010). Development of cerebral fiber pathways in cats revealed by diffusion spectrum imaging. *NeuroImage, 49*(2), 1231–1240. doi:10.1016/j.neuroimage.2009.09.002

Takahashi, E., Folkerth, R.D., Galaburda, A.L., & Grant, P.E. (in press). Emerging cerebrak connectivity in the human fetal brain: an MR tractography study. *Cerebral Cortex.*

Tisdall, M., Hess, A., & van der Kouwe, A. (Eds.). (2009, April). *MPRAGE using EPI navigators for prospective motion correction.* Paper presented at the 17th meeting of the ISMRM, Honolulu, Hawaii.

Tuch, D.S. (2004). Q-ball imaging. *Magnetic Resonance in Medicine, 52*(6), 1358–1372. doi:10.1002/mrm.20279

Vogel, A.C., Power, J.D, Petersen, S.E., & Schlaggar, B.L. (2010). Development of the brain's functional network architecture. *Neuropsychology Review, 20*(4), 362–375. doi:10.1007/s11065-010-9145-7

Wang, J., Licht, D.J, Jahng, G.H., Liu, C.S., Rubin, J.T, Haselgrove, J., ... Detre, J.A. (2003). Pediatric perfusion imaging using pulsed arterial spin labeling. *Journal of Magnetic Resonance and Imaging, 18*(4), 404–413. doi:10.1002/jmri.10372

Wedeen, V.J, Hagmann, P., Tseng, W.Y., Reese, T.G., & Weisskoff, R.M. (2005). Mapping complex tissue architecture with diffusion spectrum magnetic resonance imaging. *Magnetic Resonance in Medicine, 54*(6), 1377–1386. doi:10.1002/mrm.20642

Weisenfeld, N.I., & Warfield, S.K. (2009). Automatic segmentation of newborn brain MRI. *NeuroImage, 47*(2), 564–72. doi:10.1016/j.neuroimage.2009.04.068

Yu, P., Grant, P.E., Qi, Y., Han, X., Segonne, F., Pienaar, R., et al. (2007). Cortical surface shape analysis based on spherical wavelets. *IEEE Transactions on Medical Imaging, 26*(4), 582–597. doi:10.1109/TMI.2007.892499

CHAPTER 15

Anatomical Risk Factors for Reading Comprehension

Christiana M. Leonard

The ability to rapidly decode auditory and printed symbols is a unique human specialization. All human cultures communicate with oral language, but written language only developed after humans passed through an evolutionary bottleneck, approximately 50,000 years ago (Tishkoff & Verrelli, 2003). Since writing emerged so recently in human evolution, many have assumed that there can be no genetic foundation for this skill. Recent research on human origins is now casting doubt on this assumption. Powerful genomic changes can be attributed to the emergence of agricultural culture 10,000 years ago (Peng et al., 2010; Quintana-Murci et al., 2008; Verginelli, Aru, Battista, & Mariani-Costantini, 2009). On an evolutionary time scale, the development of reading and writing occurred almost simultaneously with the development of agriculture. By analogy, it seems possible that fluent reading also depends on genetically fostered neural specializations.

The neural specialization that has drawn the most attention in dyslexia studies is planar asymmetry. In an overwhelming majority of people, the left Sylvian fissure is longer and less sloped in the left hemisphere than the right (see Figure 15.1). This asymmetry is visible with the naked eye and was first quantified in a large sample with caliper measurements (Geschwind & Levitsky, 1968). These authors suggested that this asymmetry was the foundation for language lateralization, but this suggestion has not been born out by subsequent large-scale studies (Dorsaint-Pierre et al., 2006; Eckert, Leonard, Possing, & Binder, 2006). Geschwind also proposed that a failure to develop planar asymmetry might be associated with dyslexia, and early work provided some support (see review by Hynd & Semrud-Clikeman, 1989).

The advent of modern MRI techniques and generous funding by the National Institutes of Health stimulated a brief surge of studies on planar asymmetry and dyslexia, as well as other developmental disorders such as autism and schizophrenia. In a series of studies, our laboratory found no support for diagnostic differences in planar symmetry (Leonard, Eckert, Givens, Virginia, & Eden, 2006; Leonard et al., 1993, 1999, 2001, 2004, 2008, 2011).

The work described in this chapter was conducted in association with Kytja Voeller, Linda Lombardino, Mark Eckert, John Kuldau, Virginia Berninger, Todd Richards, Guinevere Eden, Christine Chiarello, Christian Beaulieu, and Linda Siegel. We thank the families who participated in these studies and the many students who assisted in collecting and analyzing the data. Preparation of this chapter was performed with support from the Evelyn F. & William L. McKnight Brain Institute of the University of Florida.

241

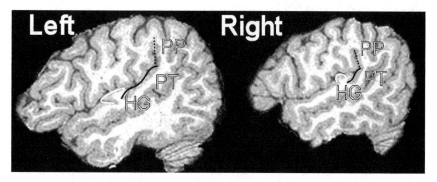

Figure 15.1 Sagittal MRI images of the left and right hemisphere illustrating typical planar asymmetry. The planum temporale (PT), outlined in black, extends between Heschl's gyrus (HG), outlined in white, and the planum parietale (PP), outlined in grey. Both PT and HG are typically larger on the left.

Confirmatory work by other groups is summarized by Eckert (2004). Paradoxically, we did, however, find an association between reading skills and planar asymmetry in typically developing children (Eckert, Lombardino, & Leonard, 2001; Leonard et al., 1996).

In many of these studies, the associations between planar asymmetry and reading skills were strengthened if the group were subdivided in some way—by hand preference, by age, by reading profile, or diagnosis. Eventually, a group of additional anatomical measures was identified that strengthened the structure/function association. These measures were: 1) gross cerebral volume, 2) the surface areas of Heschl's gyrus (containing primary and secondary auditory cortex), 3) a second Heschl's gyrus (if present), and 4) a group of asymmetries, including the summed asymmetry of planum temporale and planum parietale, asymmetry of the cerebral hemispheres, and asymmetry of the anterior lobe of the cerebellar vermis.

When these seven measures were entered into a discriminant analysis, they separated children and adults with dyslexia (a specific impairment in decoding) from children with specific language impairment (SLI), a developmental disorder in which *all* verbal skills are impaired (Leonard et al., 2002). When the seven measures were combined using the discriminant formula into an anatomical risk index (ARI), it was found that 1) children with specific language impairment (SLI) had strongly negative values (low cerebral volume and symmetrical plana temporale), 2) children and adults with dyslexia had strongly positive values (high cerebral volume and leftward asymmetry of the planum), and 3) a group of 103 typical children had intermediate values, centering around zero.

The 2002 paper emphasized the fact that children with language impairments and dyslexia had anatomical profiles deviating from typical ones in *opposite* directions. Subsequent studies in children, however, identified very few individuals with dyslexia with large positive ARI. However, the association between ARI and verbal skills in individuals with a variety of diagnoses has been repeatedly confirmed.

PROCESSING SPEED

One variable with a powerful relation to reading fluency (but not to ARI) is a variable referred to as processing speed, or focused attention (Altemeier, Abbott, & Berninger, 2008; Wolf & Bowers, 2000). This construct is assessed with two very different tests—rapid automatized naming (RAN; Denckla & Rudel, 1976), and Visual Matching (Woodcock & Mather, 1989; Woodcock, McGrew, & Mather, 2001b). A recent sample of Canadian individuals with dyslexia provided by Linda Siegel and Christian Beaulieu (Leonard et al., 2011) provided the opportunity to explore the relationship between these two tests ARI and reading ability.

In this sample, the two tests correlated better with each other than they did with any of the reading and cognitive assessments, and there was a powerful interaction between speed and ARI. In children with negative ARI (characterizing children with SLI and low verbal IQ), speed predicted all reading and cognitive abilities. In children with positive ARI, there was no relationship between processing speed and any cognitive score (Leonard et al., 2011). A hierarchical-multiple regression in which ARI, speed, and an interaction variable were entered predicted a startling 53% of the variance in real word reading.

This chapter reports the investigation of the relation between different reading skills and ARI and the strength of the interaction between ARI and reading in a large data archive.

Method

Consent was obtained according to the Declaration of Helsinki and the Ethical Committees of the participating universities that approved the work. A brain scan archive was searched for all participants whose reading skills had been assessed with the Word Attack (pseudoword reading), Letter Word Identification (real word reading), and Passage Comprehension tests from the Woodcock Johnson III (WJ III) Tests of Achievement (Woodcock, McGrew, & Mather, 2001a), and whose processing speed has been assessed with either rapid automatized naming (RAN, $n = 183$) or the Woodcock Johnson R (WJR) Visual Matching subtest (match, $n = 185$). Both RAN and Visual Match had been administered to 215 individuals. The selected individuals had participated in studies of typical development, dyslexia, and schizophrenia.

Each study provided an estimate of verbal IQ. The tests varied from study to study and included Verbal Comprehension from the WJ III, Similarities and Vocabulary from the Wechsler Intelligence Scale for Children (WISC), and Picture Vocabulary from the WJ R. The CTOP (Wagner, Torgesen, & Rashotte, 1999), the original Denckla and Rudel plates (Denckla & Rudel, 1976), and purpose designed variants were used to estimate RAN. Colors, objects, letters, numbers, and alternating numbers and letters were used in different samples. Each RAN score was corrected for age, z scored for the sample, and the results inspected to ensure that the range and variance were comparable across all the samples. A single "speed" variable was formed from whichever scores were available for each individual.

Table 15.1 provides means and standard deviations for the entire sample, grouped by age and diagnosis. Dyslexia was defined as a WJ R or WJ III pseudoword reading score in the bottom 25th percentile. Thirty-nine individuals (whose means are omitted from this table although they were included in the analyses) were classified as borderline. They had either been recruited as controls but had word reading scores below 90, or had been identified as having dyslexia in individual studies but had pseudo- and real-word reading scores above 90.

High-resolution T1 weighted volumetric scans were obtained on a variety of scanners. Voxel dimensions ranged from 1.0 to 1.5 mm in size. All scans were preprocessed with FSL scripts (http://www.fmrib.ox.ac.uk/) (Smith et al., 2004). Extraction of the brain parenchyma from scalp and skull was performed with BET (Smith, 2002) before registration (FLIRT) (Jenkinson & Smith, 2001) to a 1 mm isometric voxel study-specific template image aligned into the Talairach planes without warping. Grey and white matter volumes and surface areas were measured on sagittal images according to published methods (Leonard et al., 2008) using scripts written in PVWave. Intra rater reliabilities for all measures were > 0.90; inter rater reliabilities were > 0.85. Cerebral volumes were normalized for sex using means obtained in the present sample.

Calculation of Anatomical Risk Index

The anatomical risk index was calculated with weights from the empirically derived discriminant equation that separated individuals with mild from severe language disabilities (Leonard et al., 2002). The equation for calculating the anatomical risk index is

> 0 .95*normalized cerebral volume + 0.7*left Heschl's (1) + 1.25*planum temporale asymmetry + 0.63*left Heschl's (2) + 0.55*summed planum temporale and planum parietale asymmetry + 3.1*anterior cerebellar vermis asymmetry - 13.8*cerebral asymmetry - 4.31.

The brains of individuals with positive anatomical risk indices are characterized by 1) higher cerebral volume, and relatively more rightward asymmetry of the hemispheres; 2) relatively more leftward asymmetry of the planum temporale and cerebellar anterior lobe; and 3) larger surface areas of the first and second Heschl's gyri in the left hemisphere. Individuals with negative anatomical risk indices have 1) lower cerebral volume and relatively less rightward asymmetry of the hemispheres, 2) relatively less leftward asymmetry of the planum temporale and cerebellar anterior lobe, and 3) smaller surface areas of the first and second Heschl's gyri in the left hemisphere. Because cerebral volume is well known to predict variance in cognitive ability, this variable can be subtracted from the anatomical risk

Table 15.1. A comparison of means and standard deviations for selected measures in subgroups.

	Controls				Diagnosis			
	Children		Adult		Dyslexia		Schizophrenia	
n	113 (65M 48F)		49 (41M 8F)		64 (42M 22F)		43 (34M 9F)	
	Mean	Std	Mean	Std	Mean	Std	Mean	Std
Age	10.4	2.45	36.1	11.9	14.0	5.2	41.1	9.8
Cognitive and reading-related measures								
Verbal estimate	110	13	106	12	105	15	*92*	15
Speed estimate	102	12	110	12	*84*	14	88	11
Real word	114	13	116	14	82	12	101	16
Pseudoword	111	13	116	12	83	10	102	19
Passage comp	113	13	119	13	95	19	*93*	16
Neuroanatomical measures								
ARI	-0.07	1.6	0.09	1.45	-0.34	1.87	-0.51	1.48
Cerebral volume	0.10	1.0	0.23	0.93	-0.24	1.11	0.04	1.16
Asymmetry of planum temporale	0.30	0.46	0.45	0.51	0.39	0.64	0.37	0.43
HG	-0.17	1.3	-0.14	1.10	-0.10	1.64	-0.47	1.03

Key: Italic values are significantly different from controls; bolded values are significantly different from the means of other three groups; italic values are significantly different from two control groups ($p < .05$, corrected for multiple comparisons). ARI: anatomical risk index, HG: Heschl's gyri, M: mean, Std: standard deviation.

index to create a variable that represents the contribution of variation in the six remaining variables—the hemispheric gradient (HG).

RESULTS AND DISCUSSION

Effect of Diagnosis on Behavioral and Anatomical Profile

Diagnosis significantly affected all reading scores (F's > 30, $p < .0001$). Post hoc, Bonferroni corrected t-tests ($P < .05$) showed that the group with dyslexia differed significantly from both child and adult controls on all reading scores, as well as the speed composite, but not on the verbal estimate. The schizophrenia group, by contrast, differed from the control groups on the verbal and speed estimates as well as passage comprehension, but not the two word reading scores. The groups did not differ on mean planar asymmetry, cerebral volume, the hemispheric gradient, or the anatomical risk index. The two groups with diagnoses also had different reading profiles. The schizophrenia group could be characterized as "poor comprehenders" whose comprehension was worse than their decoding skills (Cutting, Materek, Cole, Levine, & Mahone, 2009; Nation, Cocksey, Taylor, & Bishop, 2010). In the group with dyslexia, by contrast, comprehension was better than decoding.

In the sample as a whole (Table 15.2), the reading scores were strongly intercorrelated (Pearson r's > .56). The word reading scores were weakly associated with the verbal estimate (r's of .29, .26), but moderately strongly associated with the speed estimate (r's of .51, .48). Passage comprehension was moderately strongly associated with both the verbal ($r = .47$) and the speed estimate ($r = .55$), whereas the verbal and speed estimates were only weakly associated with each other (.22). All correlations were significant at $p < .0001$.

Table 15.3 shows the Pearson r for the association between reading and cognitive scores, as well as the ARI. The association was only significant in the groups with diagnoses. In the group with dyslexia, ARI was strongly associated with passage comprehension, weakly associated with the verbal and speed estimates, and not at all associated with the word

Table 15.2.   Pearson r for associations between behavioral values in 308 children and adults with a wide range of reading skill.

Variable	Pseudo word	Passage comp	Verbal estimate	Speed estimate	Age
Real word	.80	.64	.29	.51	.09
Pseudoword		.56	.26	.48	.09
Comprehension			.47	.55	-.05
Verbal estimate				.22	-.22
Speed estimate					-.03

Key: For this and subsequent tables, bold values are significant, $p < 0.0001$, italic values significant, $p < 0.05$.

Table 15.3. Pearson *r* for associations between behavioral variables and anatomical risk index ARI in control and diagnosed groups.

Group	Child controls	Adult controls	Dyslexia	Schizo-phrenia	Border-line	All
n	113	49	64	43	39	308
Real word	.19	-.16	.22	.38	.21	.18
Pseudoword	.04	-.14	.02	.41	-.03	.11
Passage comprehension	.16	-.03	.49	.59	.29	.32
Verbal estimate	.18	-.20	.34	.58	.08	.23
Speed estimate	-.11	-.10	.28	.22	.04	.10

The "Pearson *r* for association with ARI" spans all columns.

reading scores. In the schizophrenic group, by contrast, ARI was associated with word reading and comprehension, as well as the verbal estimate, but was not significantly associated with the speed estimate.

To summarize, the data presented (consistent with the individual studies published previously) suggest that children and adults with low ARI (i.e., low brain volume and reduced cerebral asymmetries) are at risk for poor reading comprehension *only if* they also have a diagnosis. But many children and adults with exactly the same brain measures develop perfectly adequate reading ability. The ARI is sensitive, but not at all specific, for reading problems.

Analyses in the Canadian study identified a possible moderating variable. An examination of the differences between children in whom ARI was and was not predictive of reading problems revealed that children with low ARI were more affected by processing speed. In children with negative ARI, regardless of diagnosis, processing speed predicted 45% of the variance in the reading composite. In children with positive ARI, by contrast, there was no relation at all between processing speed and reading (Leonard et al., 2011).

We were interested in whether this interaction between anatomy and processing speed could be detected in our data archive with the Canadian sample removed ($n = 265$). First, we performed a two factor analysis of variance, dividing the group into four anatomy/speed combinations using the median speed composite and ARI = 0 as cut offs. These analyses were all significant, explaining 26% of the variance for passage comprehension, 20% for real word naming, 18% for pseudoword naming, and 9% for the verbal estimate. The interaction between speed and anatomy was significant ($p < .01$) for both passage comprehension and the verbal estimate but was not significant (t's < 1.0) for either of the word naming scores.

The interaction between anatomy and speed was much weaker than that found in the sample of Canadian children. In that sample, the speed

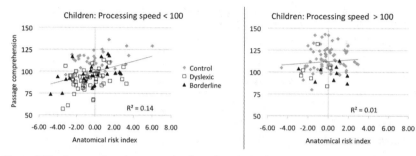

Figure 15.2. Scatter plots demonstrating how the relation between the anatomical risk index and passage comprehension changes as a function of processing speed in children.

composite predicted no variance in reading scores in children with positive ARI (high brain volume and cerebral asymmetries). In the data archive, only the verbal estimate showed this effect (i.e., no effect of speed in individuals with positive ARI). There was a weak interaction effect on passage comprehension, but not on word reading scores.

Figure 15.2 shows scatter plots of the relation between the anatomical risk index and passage comprehension in children. When processing speed scores are above 100, all groups—dyslexic, control, and borderline—show the same positive slope. On the right side of Figure 15.2 it can be seen that no relation between the anatomical risk index and passage comprehension exists in children with above average processing speed. Figure 15.3 shows that the relationship between anatomy and passage comprehension is even stronger in adults with below average processing speed. Again, no relationship exists between these variables when processing speed is above average.

A median split is a relatively low-power technique for studying the interaction of processing speed and anatomy. The large size of the data archive made it possible to look at how the location of the speed cutoff affected this relationship. Figure 15.4 shows that the relationship between passage comprehension and anatomy in children with speeds below the cutoff is relatively insensitive to the location of the cutoff.

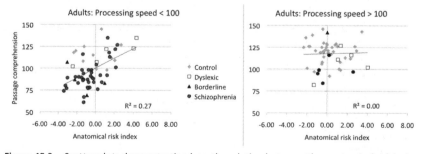

Figure 15.3. Scatter plots demonstrating how the relation between the anatomical risk index and passage comprehension changes as a function of processing speed in adults.

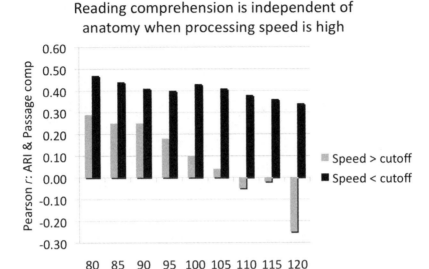

Figure 15.4. Bar graph showing the effect of processing speed threshold on the relation between Woodcock Johnson R passage comprehension and the anatomical risk index index (Woodcock, McGrew, & Mather, 2001b). The light bars represent the correlation coefficients in individuals with processing speed scores below the cutoff listed on the y axis. The correlation coefficient in those with low processing speed is not particularly sensitive to the location of the cutoff. The light bars show the correlation coefficients in individuals with processing speeds above the cutoff. The relation between anatomy and passage comprehension is highly dependent on the location of the cutoff. Individuals with processing speeds above 95 show no relation between anatomy and reading comprehension and the relation becomes negative at processing speed cutoffs above 105.

In children with high processing speed, by contrast, the relation between anatomy and passage comprehension is highly dependent on the location of the cutoff (Table 15.4). Specifically, individuals with processing speeds above 95 showed no relation between anatomy and reading comprehension, and the relation became negative at processing speed cutoffs above 105. The numbers of individuals in each group are given in Table 15.5.

Table 15.4. Pearson *r* for associations between anatomical and behavioral variables in entire sample.

Variable	Cerebral volume	Hemispheric gradient	Coefficient of planar asymmetry
Real word	*0.19*	0.09	0.04
Pseudoword	*0.17*	0.01	0.03
Passage Comprehension	**0.27**	*0.18*	0.12
Verbal estimate	**0.26**	0.09	-0.09
Speed estimate	0.1	0.05	0.02

Table 15.5. Numbers of individuals in each group depicted in Figure 15.4.

Speed cutoff	80	85	90	95	100	105	110	115	120
n above cutoff	269	244	206	169	136	88	67	39	22
% Dyslexia	16	14	13	12	9	6	4	3	5
% Verbal estimate < 90	11	10	8	8	7	8	9	3	0
n below cutoff	39	64	102	139	172	220	241	269	286
% Dyslexia	56	47	37	31	30	27	25	23	22
% Verbal estimate < 90	28	27	25	20	19	15	15	15	14

Conclusions

An analysis of 308 individuals with a range of reading skills has revealed the following:

1. Passage comprehension is the reading and verbal skill most sensitive to the effect of auditory cortex size and cerebral asymmetry (indexed as hemispheric gradient). Cerebral volume is associated with all reading skills (both decoding and comprehension), but the hemispheric gradient explains additional variance in comprehension.

2. These anatomical variables explain substantial variance in passage comprehension in individuals with low processing speed. All reading skills are relatively insensitive to these measures in individuals with average or high processing speed

GENERAL DISCUSSION

An immense amount of time and effort has been devoted to identifying neural markers of dyslexia. Postmortem findings of ectopias and planar symmetry and the theories of Geschwind and Galaburda (1987) initially stimulated this effort. Although there have been no independent confirmations of these postmortem findings, they have been widely cited and are frequently cited as the only anatomical signatures of dyslexia (Pennington & Bishop, 2009, and multiple presentations, this conference).

Traditional imaging protocols cannot identify ectopias in the living brain. Planar asymmetry, on the other hand, can be assessed in an MRI scan that takes less than five minutes. Thus there have been many attempted replications of the postmortem work. The present reanalysis of a data archive, like many independent studies reviewed in Eckert (2004) and Shapleske, Rossell, Woodruff, and David (1999) have failed to demonstrate any single anatomical signature of dyslexia. The modern consensus is that dyslexia is heterogeneous and multidetermined (Pernet, Andersson, Paulesu, & Démonet, 2009).

In a novel and promising approach, Pernet identified voxel clusters that, in French adults with dyslexia, had grey matter volumes that were outside the confidence limits of those in a series of typical individuals (Pernet, Poline, Démonet, & Rousselet, 2009). Two regions were identified, neither of them in the neocortical mantle. Small clusters of voxels in the right globus pallidus (identified as lentiform nucleus) and right cerebellum were outside the typical range in every single individual with dyslexia. The results are convincing because they were robust to changes in confidence limits, smoothing kernel, and threshold. They are, however, somewhat hard to interpret, because some individuals with dyslexia had smaller volumes in both, some had larger volumes in both, and some had the other two possible combinations.

It is interesting to note that individuals with dyslexia with lower grey matter volumes in both regions performed more poorly on a number of phonological and reading tests than those with higher grey matter volumes in both. This latter group (half the total sample of individuals with dyslexia) performed similarly to controls on a number of measures. It is intriguing to speculate that this latter group might have contained "low comprehenders," poor readers whose word reading scores are typical but who still have difficulty extracting meaning from text (Nation et al., 2010). No comprehension scores were reported.

These results are somewhat reminiscent of those reported in Leonard et al. (2002). In that study, individuals with poor decoding *and* poor comprehension had anatomical measures on one side of the typical distribution, whereas individuals with poor decoding but good comprehension were on the other side. The distribution of typical children peaked in between the distributions of the two diagnosed groups. In contrast to the findings by Pernet and his colleagues, the two diagnosed groups were distinguished from each other by cortical measures and their comprehension skill. In Pernet's study, however, the two diagnosed groups were separated by striatal and cerebellar measures, and differences in their comprehension skill remain unknown. It would clearly be of interest to perform both types of analysis on a sample in which comprehension and rapid automatized naming had both been assessed.

The main point to be emphasized here is that the cortical measures that have long been emphasized in dyslexia studies may be more predictive of comprehension skills than the core decoding deficits of dyslexia. Although many studies have reported grey matter loss in dyslexia, few have attempted to show that this loss is specific for decoding skills rather than a correlate of lower comprehension and verbal intelligence (Betjemann et al., 2010; Eckert et al., 2003; Kibby, Pavawalla, Fancher, Naillon, & Hynd, 2009; Phinney, Pennington, Olson, Filley, & Filipek, 2007). Pernet's results support long standing suggestions (Nicolson & Fawcett, 1990; Stoodley & Stein, 2011; see also Chapter 3) that the cerebellum, not the neocortex, is the site of atypical development in dyslexia.

It is interesting to note that passage comprehension—the skill that is most robustly predicted by the anatomical risk index—is frequently not included in the assessment of dyslexia. The test is not a pure measure of reading comprehension, because it requires executive function skills and a verbal response. It is an untimed measure of the ability to generate appropriate responses based on one's memory of a text. When we started these studies almost 20 years ago, we hypothesized, based on Tallal's rapid auditory processing theory (Tallal, 1980), that measures of Heschl's gyrus and planar asymmetry would be related to measures of phonological decoding and auditory processing. The first findings appeared supportive of this theory. But, according to Spearman (1904), auditory discrimination predicts general intelligence not just phoneme decoding and reading. In studies in which decoding and comprehension were dissociated, as they are in compensated individuals with dyslexia (Chiarello, Lombardino, Kacinik, Otto, & Leonard, 2006; Leonard et al., 2001), measures related to the auditory cortex did not predict decoding skill. In fact, they predicted the reverse relationship. Students with good comprehension and poor decoding actually had greater planar asymmetry and larger Heschl's gyri than students who had good decoding skills (Leonard et al., 2001).

In subsequent studies, we have identified very few individuals with dyslexia with large discrepancies between comprehension and decoding. Even so, the anatomical risk index (ARI) continued to be associated with reading skills. Instead of predicting the discrepancy between passage comprehension and decoding, as originally reported, evidence gradually accumulated that the more the skill tapped verbal learning and memory skills, the more closely it was associated with the anatomical risk index. It appeared that ARI was not an index of discrepancy; it was an index of comprehension, per se.

The fact that a measure of cerebral volume and auditory cortex asymmetry predicts comprehension rather than decoding skills means that the ARI is not a good predictor of dyslexia when defined as decoding skills that are unexpectedly low given typical intelligence. What the ARI may measure is the potential of the individual with dyslexia to compensate and gain an education and a successful place in life even when confronted with severe impairments in decoding. A case study with an ARI of 3.41 reported in Chiarello et al. (2006) failed English all four years in high school, yet completed a Ph.D. in psychology, specializing in statistics. Another student with a high ARI in an earlier study was a resident in surgery. Only future longitudinal studies will show whether a high ARI is a significant predictor of successful compensation.

Moderating Variable

The studies previously described consistently failed to find a relationship between the ARI and any reading or verbal skill in typically developing individuals. The present analysis suggests a tentative explanation. The effect of the anatomical risk index may be moderated by processing speed (Figures 15.2–15.4). Individuals with high processing speed are apparently protected from negative effects of low brain volume and cerebral symmetry. This finding fits with conceptions of a multiple risk model in which both general and specific risk factors must be present for the expression of a disorder.

Yeo, Gangestad, and Thoma have proposed that developmental disorders arise as a result of both specific and general risk factors. They decry the traditional "constrained, disorder-specific perspective" (Yeo et al., 2007, p. 245). They hypothesize that families with "developmental instability," that is, genetic variants that render them liable to suboptimal brain development, have a lower threshold for the development of complex behavior disorders such as nonsyndromal mental retardation, schizophrenia, autism, attention deficit disorder, and dyslexia. Specific rare genetic variants (Reich & Lander, 2001) would then determine which particular disorder would develop. This model provides an explanatory framework for the findings described in this chapter. Low cerebral volume and reduced brain asymmetries may arise as a result of common variants associated with developmental instability. These common variants would be associated with poor auditory temporal processing (Benasich & Tallal, 2002; Chandrasekaran, Hornickel, Skoe, Nicol, & Kraus, 2009; Choudhury, Leppanen, Leevers, & Benasich, 2007) and verbal facility (i.e., oral and reading comprehension) across a variety of disorders. The specific disordered neural mechanisms underlying dyslexia are distinct from these general risk factors for slowed development and low IQ, and may involve procedural learning modules associated with the cerebellum and striatum (Pernet, Poline, et al., 2009; Stoodley & Stein, 2011). Future work should incorporate research designs that distinguish between the effects of general and specific risk factors.

REFERENCES

Altemeier, L.E., Abbott, R.D., & Berninger, V.W. (2008). Executive functions for reading and writing in typical literacy development and dyslexia. *Journal of Clinical and Experimental Neuropsychology, 30,* 588–606. doi:10.1080/13803390701562818

Benasich, A.A., & Tallal, P. (2002). Infant discrimination of rapid auditory cues predicts later language impairment. *Behavioural Brain Research, 136,* 31–49. doi:10.1016/S0166-4328(02)00098-0

Betjemann, R.S., Johnson, E.P., Barnard, H., Boada, R., Filley, C.M., Filipek, P.A., ... Pennington, B. (2010). Genetic covariation between brain volumes and IQ, reading performance, and processing speed. *Behavior Genetics, 40,* 135–145. doi:10.1007/s10519-009-9328-2

Chandrasekaran, B., Hornickel, J., Skoe, E., Nicol, T., & Kraus, N. (2009). Con-

text-dependent encoding in the human auditory brainstem relates to hearing speech in noise: Implications for developmental dyslexia. *Neuron, 64,* 311–319. doi:10.1016/j.neuron.2009.10.006

Chiarello, C., Lombardino, L.J., Kacinik, N.A., Otto, R., & Leonard, C.M. (2006). Neuroanatomical and behavioral asymmetry in an adult compensated dyslexic. *Brain and Language, 98,* 169–181.

Choudhury, N., Leppanen, P.H., Leevers, H.J., & Benasich, A.A. (2007). Infant information processing and family history of specific language impairment: Converging evidence for RAP deficits from two paradigms. *Developmental Science, 10,* 213–236. doi:10.1111/j.1467-7687.2007.00546

Cutting, L.E., Materek, A., Cole, C.A., Levine, T.M., & Mahone, E.M. (2009). Effects of fluency, oral language, and executive function on reading comprehension performance. *Annals of Dyslexia, 59,* 34–54. doi:10.1007/s11881-009-0022-0

Denckla, M., & Rudel, R. (1976). Rapid 'automatized' naming (R.A.N.). Dyslexia differentiated from other learning disabilities. *Neuropsychologia, 14,* 471–479. doi:10.1016/0028-3932(76)90075-0

Dorsaint-Pierre, R., Penhune, V.B., Watkins, K.E., Neelin, P., Lerch, J.P., Bouffard, M., Zatorre, R.J. (2006). Asymmetries of the planum temporale and Heschl's gyrus: Relationship to language lateralization. *Brain, 129,* 1164–1176. doi:10.1093/brain/awl055

Eckert, M.A. (2004). Neuroanatomical markers for dyslexia: A review of dyslexia structural imaging studies. *Neuroscientist, 10,* 362–371. doi:10.1177/1073858404263596

Eckert, M.A., Leonard, C.M., Possing, E.T., & Binder, J.R. (2006). Uncoupled leftward asymmetries for planum morphology and functional language processing. *Brain and Language, 98,* 102–111. doi:10.1016/j.bandl.2006.04.002

Eckert, M.A., Leonard, C.M., Richards, T.L., Aylward, E.H., Thomson, J., & Berninger, V.W. (2003). Anatomical correlates of dyslexia: Frontal and cerebellar findings. *Brain, 126,* 482–494. doi:10.1093/brain/awg026

Eckert, M.A., Lombardino, L.J., & Leonard, C.M. (2001). Planar asymmetry tips the phonological playground and environment raises the bar. *Child Development, 72,* 988–1002. doi:10.1111/1467-8624.00330

Geschwind, N., & Galaburda, A. (1987). *Cerebral lateralization: Biological mechanisms, association and pathology.* Cambridge, MA: MIT Press.

Geschwind, N., & Levitsky, W. (1968). Human brain: Left-right asymmetries in temporal speech region. *Science, 161,* 186–187. doi:10.1126/science.161.3837.186

Hynd, G.W., & Semrud-Clikeman, M. (1989). Dyslexia and brain morphology. *Psychological Bulletin, 106,* 447–482.

Jenkinson, M., & Smith, S.M. (2001). A global optimisation method for robust affine registration of brain images. *Medical Image Analysis, 5,* 143–156. doi:10.1016/S1361-8415(01)00036-6

Kibby, M.Y., Pavawalla, S.P., Fancher, J.B., Naillon, A.J., & Hynd, G.W. (2009). The relationship between cerebral hemisphere volume and receptive language functioning in dyslexia and attention-deficit hyperactivity disorder (ADHD). *Journal of Child Neurology, 24,* 438–448. doi:10.1177/0883073808324772

Leonard, C.M., Eckert, M., Givens, B., Virginia, B., & Eden, G. (2006). Individual differences in anatomy predict reading and oral language impairments in children. *Brain, 129,* 3329–3342. doi:10.1093/brain/awl262

Leonard, C.M., Eckert, M., Lombardino, L.J., Oakland, T., Kranzler, J., Mohr, C.M., ... Freeman, A. (2001). Anatomical risk factors for phonological dyslexia. *Cerebral Cortex, 11,* 148–157. doi:10.1093/cercor/11.2.148

Leonard, C.M., Kuldau, J.M., Breier, J.I., Zuffante, P.A., Gautier, E.R., Heron, D.C., ... DeBose, C. (1999). Cumulative effect of anatomical risk factors for schizophrenia: An MRI study. *Biological Psychiatry, 46,* 374–382. doi:10.1016/S0006-3223(99)00052-9

Leonard, C.M., Kuldau, J.M., Maron, L., Ricciuti, N., Mahoney, B., Bengtson, M., & DeBose, C. (2008). Identical neural risk factors predict cognitive deficit in dyslexia and schizophrenia. *Neuropsychology, 22,* 147–158. doi:10.1037/0894-4105.22.2.147

Leonard, C.M., Lombardino, L.J., Mercado, L.R., Browd, S.R., Breier, J.I., & Agee, O.F. (1996). Cerebral asymmetry and cognitive development in children: A magnetic resonance imaging study. *Psychological Science, 7,* 79–85. oi:10.1111/j.1467-9280.1996.tb00335

Leonard, C.M., Lombardino, L.J., Walsh, K., Eckert, M.A., Mockler, J.L., Rowe, L.A., ... DeBose, C. (2002). Anatomical risk factors that distinguish dyslexia from SLI predict reading skill in normal children. *Journal of Communication Disorders, 35,* 501–531. doi:10.1016/S0021-9924(02)00120-X

Leonard, C.M., Low, P., Jonczak, E., Schmutz, K.M., Siegel, L.S., & Beaulieu, C. (2011). Anatomy, processing speed and reading in children. *Developmental Neuropsychology, 36,* 828–846.

Leonard, C.M., Voeller, K.S., Lombardino, L.J., Morris, M.K., Alexander, A.W., Andersen, H.G., ... Staab, E.V. (1993). Anomalous cerebral structure in dyslexia revealed with magnetic resonance imaging. *Archives of Neurology, 50,* 461–469.

Nation, K., Cocksey, J., Taylor, J.S., & Bishop, D.V. (2010). A longitudinal investigation of early reading and language skills in children with poor reading comprehension. *Journal of Child Psychology and Psychiatry, 51*(9), 1031–1039. doi:10.1111/j.1469-7610.2010.02254

Nicolson, R.I., & Fawcett, A.J. (1990). Automaticity: A new framework for dyslexia? *Cognition, 35,* 159–182. doi:10.1016/0010-0277(90)90013-A

Peng, Y., Shi, H., Qi, X.B., Xiao, C.J., Zhong, H., Ma, R.L., & Sue, B. (2010). The ADH1B Arg47 His polymorphism in east Asian populations and expansion of rice domestication in history. *BMC Evolutionary Biology, 10,* 15. doi:10.1186/1471-2148-10-15

Pennington, B.F., & Bishop, D.V. (2009). Relations among speech, language, and reading disorders. *Annual Review of Psychology, 60,* 283–306. doi:10.1146/annurev.psych.60.110707.163548

Pernet, C.R., Andersson, J., Paulesu, E., & Démonet, J.F. (2009). When all hypotheses are right: A multifocal account of dyslexia. *Human Brain Mapping, 30,* 2278–2292. doi:10.1002/hbm.20670

Pernet, C.R., Poline, J.B., Démonet, J.F., & Rousselet, G.A. (2009). Brain classification reveals the right cerebellum as the best biomarker of dyslexia. *BMC Neuroscience, 10,* 67. doi:10.1186/1471-2202-10-67

Phinney, E., Pennington, B.F., Olson, R., Filley, C.M., & Filipek, P.A. (2007). Brain structure correlates of component reading processes: Implications for reading disability. *Cortex, 43,* 777–791. doi:10.1016/S0010-9452(08)70506-9

Quintana-Murci, L., Quach, H., Harmant, C., Luca, F., Massonnet, B., Patin, E., ... Behar, D.M. (2008). Maternal traces of deep common ancestry and asymmetric gene flow between Pygmy hunter-gatherers and Bantu-speaking farmers. *Proceedings of the National Academy of Sci-*ences, USA, 105, 1596–1601. doi:10.1073/pnas.0711467105

Reich, D.E., & Lander, E.S. (2001). On the allelic spectrum of human disease. *Trends in Genetics, 17,* 502–510. doi:10.1016/S0168-9525(01)02410-6

Shapleske, J., Rossell, S.L., Woodruff, P.W., & David, A.S. (1999). The planum temporale: A systematic, quantitative review of its structural, functional and clinical significance. *Brain Research Reviews, 29,* 26–49. doi:10.1016/S0165-0173(98)00047-2

Smith, S.M. (2002). Fast robust automated brain extraction. *Human Brain Mapping, 17,* 143–155. doi:10.1002/hbm.10062

Smith, S.M., Jenkinson, M., Woolrich, M.W., Beckmann, C.F., Behrens, T.E., Johansen-Berg, H., ... Matthews, P.M. (2004). Advances in functional and structural MR image analysis and implementation as FSL. *NeuroImage, 23 Supplement 1,* S208–S219. doi:10.1016/j.neuroimage.2004.07.051

Spearman, C. (1904). "General intelligence," objectively determined and measured. *American Journal of Psychology, 15,* 201–293. doi:10.2307/1412107

Stoodley, C.J., & Stein, J.F. (2011). The cerebellum and dyslexia. *Cortex, 47,* 101–116. doi:10.1016/j.cortex.2009.10.005

Tallal, P. (1980). Auditory temporal perception: Phonics and reading disabilities in children. *Brain and Language, 9,* 182–198. doi:10.1016/0093-934X(80)90139-X

Tishkoff, S.A., & Verrelli, B.C. (2003). Patterns of human genetic diversity: Implications for human evolutionary history and disease. *Annual Review of Genomics and Human Genetics, 4,* 293–340.

Verginelli, F., Aru, F., Battista, P., & Mariani-Costantini, R. (2009). Nutrigenetics in the light of human evolution. *Journal of Nutrigenetics and Nutrigenomics, 2,* 91–102. doi:10.1159/000228251

Wagner, R., Torgesen, J., & Rashotte, C. (1999). *Comprehensive test of phonological processing.* Austin TX: Pro-Ed.

Wolf, M., & Bowers, P.G. (2000). Naming-speed processes and developmental reading disabilities: An introduction to the special issue on the double-deficit hypothesis. *Journal of Learning Disabilities, 33,* 322–324. doi:10.1177/002221940003300404

Woodcock, R.W., & Mather, N. (1989). WJ-R tests of cognitive ability-standard and supplemental batteries: Examiner's manual. In R.W. Woodcock & M.B. Johnson (Eds.), *Woodcock-Johnson Psycho-Educational Battery* revised. Chicago, IL: Riverside Publishing.

Woodcock, R.W., McGrew, K., & Mather, M. (2001a). *Woodcock-Johnson III Tests of Achievement.* Itasca, IL: Riverside Publishing.

Woodcock, R.W., McGrew, K., & Mather, M. (2001b). *Woodcock-Johnson III Tests of Cognitive Abilities.* Itasca, IL: Riverside Publishing.

Yeo, R.A., Gangestad, S.W., & Thoma, R.J. (2007). Developmental instability and individual variation in brain development. *Current Directions in Psychological Science, 16,* 245–249. doi:10.1111/j.1467-8721.2007.00513

CHAPTER 16
Windows into Receptive Processing
Elena Plante

Specific language impairment (SLI) is frequently a precursor or a comorbid condition for specific reading impairments such as dyslexia (de Bree et al., Chapter 9; Flax et al., 2003; McArthur, Hogben, Edwards, Heath, & Mengler, 2000). Further, striking overlaps in core impairments, including deficits in phonological processing, have been repeatedly demonstrated across these and related disorders (e.g., Bishop & Snowling, 2004; Catts, Adlof, Hogan, & Weismer, 2005; Pennington, 2006). For both SLI and dyslexia, receptive-language skills have received sparse attention compared with the more overt signs of these disorders. Recent behavioral research in language learning disorders (LLD) such as SLI and dyslexia holds promise for illuminating problems involving language processing that would be missed with standard clinical testing. Examination of the functional brain correlates of language processing can be accomplished via creative imaging paradigms that allow examination of how the brain changes as individuals learn language. Insights from imaging data that span these disorders can identify and elucidate common pathways that may underlie various forms of language disability.

SLI is typically classified as involving either expressive impairments only (the majority of cases) or expressive plus receptive impairments (a minority of cases). It is important to note, however, that this classification is largely based on communication skills measured in preschool children who carry the SLI diagnosis. Conversely, tests that identify SLI status during adulthood measure receptive syntax and single word vocabulary (Fidler, Plante, & Vance, 2011; Poll, Betz, & Miller, 2010; Tomblin, Freese, & Records, 1992), suggesting that once these impairments emerge, they are persistent. The discrepancy between preschoolers with predominantly expressive impairments and their older counterparts with stronger receptive impairments may reflect a "growing into the impairment" phenomenon commonly seen as the demands on language skills increase with age. If true, then the receptive-language impairments seen at older ages are likely to reflect the increasing ease and accuracy of assessment at older ages, rather than a sudden appearance of a "new" impairment. The implication of this scenario is that early receptive impairments, which could undermine efforts to remediate these children's more obvious expressive impairments, may actually go undetected. However, both behavioral and imaging approaches are capable of offering new insights into the prevalence and nature of receptive processing impairments. Early findings using these methods suggest that receptive impairments are much more pervasive than assumed.

Meaningful evaluation of receptive processing will require the field of speech-language pathology (and probably also the field of reading disabilities) to abandon the notion that current standardized tests provide anything resembling adequate or informative measures of receptive processing skills. Furthermore, a more productive approach to receptive language will require a finer-grained analysis of the various skills that support language processing. However, forward progress will not happen in a vacuum. The extant literature provides a starting point for understanding receptive impairments.

THE CURRENT STATE OF AFFAIRS

Auditory Processing

There are now four decades of research concerning how children with impaired language process sublexical information. This is perhaps the most well studied aspect of receptive processing in developmental-language disorders. Early work by Tallal and Piercy (1973) has been replicated and extended (e.g., Elliot, Hammer, Scholl, & Carrell, 1989; Tallal, Stark, & Mellits, 1985; Wright, Lombardino, King, & Puranik, 1997). Behavior and physiological studies suggest that the rapid temporal processing impairment extends to the visual modality as well (Tallal, Stark, Kallman, & Mellits, 1981).

That these auditory processing impairments exist is not in dispute. The role of this phenomenon in the language impairments of SLI, however, remains controversial. For example, studies of children with attention deficit disorder and childhood aphasia have shown dissociations between language impairments and rapid temporal processing impairments using stimuli developed by Tallal (Aram & Ekelman, 1988; Ludlow, Cadahy, Bassich, & Brown, 1983). Likewise, rapid temporal processing impairments early in childhood do not necessarily persist over time despite the persistent language impairments (Bernstein & Stark, 1985; Bishop, Carlyon, Deeks, & Bishop, 1999; Lincoln, Dickstein, Courchesne, Elmasian, & Tallal, 1992). Finally, individuals with impaired language show impairments in auditory tasks for which processing of rapid transitions is not necessary for task performance. For example, individuals with language impairment also have difficulty processing prosodic cues (e.g., Bahl, Plante, & Gerken, 2009; Courtright & Courtright, 1983; Fisher, Plante, Vance, Gerken, & Glattke, 2007; Trauner, Ballantyne, Chase, & Tallal, 1993). Unlike phonemes, prosodic cues have a long temporal envelope. However, the sublexical information provided by prosody is used by listeners to assist in such linguistic processing tasks as word identification and chunking words into syntactic units.

Some have sought to explain poor performance on auditory processing tasks as one of poor auditory attention, rather than auditory processing per se (Helzer, Champlin, & Gillam, 1996; Stevens, Fanning, Coch,

Sanders, & Neville, 2008). This notion is gaining new support with more recent reports of subtle difficulties in the control of attention by children with SLI (e.g., Finneran, Francis, & Leonard, 2009; Noterdaeme, Amorosa, Mildenberger, Sitter, & Minow, 2000; Spaulding, Plante, & Vance, 2008). Particularly compelling is electrophysiologic evidence that suggests that cortical change affected by training temporal aspects of auditory processing is related to changes in auditory attention rather than specifically to the temporal aspects of sound processing (Stevens et al., 2008).

Phonological Processing

Phonological processing can be thought of as existing at "a layer above" the more basic cognitive processes of auditory attention and acoustic processing. Although phonological processing rests on these more basic cognitive capabilities, processing at this higher level suggests recognition of the language-specific aspects of sounds. In fact, there is strong evidence that the ability to process phonological information is weak in cases of SLI (e.g., Aguilar-Mediavilla, Sanz-Torrent, & Serra-Raventos, 2002; Maillart, Schelstraete, & Hupet, 2004; Nobury, Bishop, & Briscoe, 2002; Owen, Dromi, & Leonard, 2001).

Phonological processing is likewise weak in other diagnostic conditions that typically include some degree of impaired language, such as learning disabilities and dyslexia (e.g., Catts et al., 2005; Gray & McCutchen, 2006; Savage & Frederickson, 2006). Perhaps the most widely used measure of phonological processing is nonword repetition (see Gathercole, 2006, or Graf Estes, Evans, & Else-Quest, 2007, for extensive reviews). Performance on these measures, although certainly influenced by several factors, is thought to reflect the ability to hold phonological information in working memory, a factor originally proposed to undermine the ability of those with SLI to learn new words (Gathercole & Baddeley, 1990). However, we know that performance on nonword repetition tasks is influenced by the phonotactic probabilities of the sounds that comprise the nonwords tested. For example, Munson, Kurtz, and Windsor (2005) showed that the inclusion of nonwords for which sound sequences reflected high probability English phonotactics boosted performance on a nonword repetition task for typically developing children. This finding is also consistent with studies of word learning that indicate better mapping of the sounds that comprise word labels, if those labels contained sounds that are high probability for English (e.g., Alt & Plante, 2006; Nash & Donaldson, 2005; Plante, Bahl, Vance, & Gerken, 2011). These studies all indicate that, despite weak skills in this area, children with SLI still benefit from the phonotactic information that comes with prior language experience.

Morphosyntax

In contrast to phonological processing, relatively little is known about the ability of impaired individuals to process other aspects of language form.

A few exceptions that deal with sentence processing have appeared in the more recent literature. Several of these studies have suggested that children with SLI are using semantic cues rather than syntactic cues to process complex sentences (e.g., Nobury et al., 2002; Bishop, Bright, James, Bishop, & Van der Lely, 2000; Van der Lely & Stollwerck, 1996), rather than simply failing to grasp syntactic principles (e.g., "binding"). There is also evidence to support this notion for children with learning disabilities as well (Windsor, 1999). The problem with overreliance on semantics is that it may lead to erroneous interpretations, as cues to meaning derived from syntax are missed.

The results of these studies also beg the question of why children adopt a semantic-based strategy, rather than attending to cues to syntactic structure. Deevy and Leonard (2004) suggested processing capacity limitations may account for differential performance in processing "Wh" questions in long sentences, relative to short sentences. However, other studies (Nobury et al., 2002; Bishop et al., 2000; Van der Lely & Stollwerck, 1996) have found that difficulty with processing other sentence forms, such as passives, can occur independently of sentence length. Although other forms of evidence support the idea of cognitive capacity limitations in SLI (e.g., Ellis Weismer et al., 2000; Gathercole & Baddeley, 1990; Leonard, McGregor, & Allen, 1994), the notion that capacity limits fully account for difficulty in processing language form cannot be correct, given evidence of poor processing under low capacity conditions. However, capacity limits may exacerbate other types of processing problems. Therefore, it may be the case that capacity limits come into play when those with language impairment confront sentences that are already inherently difficult for other reasons. If this is the case, the field needs a better understanding of the types of information about sentence structure individuals with impairment do and do not utilize. The literature does not index what elements of language form impaired individuals are sensitive to, nor why they do not make better use of other aspects.

A PARADIGM SHIFT

An alternate means for addressing receptive skills involves a departure from asking what individuals with impaired language can demonstrate they "know" about their language and instead asking how language impaired individuals learn. Bishop (2009) has suggested that exploring the nature of "learning" in specific language impairment may be a more practical and illuminating approach to this disorder compared with the study of domain-specific impairments. To address this goal, it may be useful to turn to learning theory in order to move beyond the global examination of receptive language that has characterized the majority of the literature on language impairment. When applied to the area of language acquisition, this theoretical perspective holds that children extract the properties of their language from the properties of the input they receive. Therefore, language is acquired not by the unfolding of innate programs, but rather by the application of general cognitive mechanisms. This type of learning is largely implicit, and is shaped by the constraints of the cognitive resources the individual brings to the learning task (Gómez, 2006; Newport & Aslin, 2004; Saffran, 2003).

This perspective posits that children come equipped with a number of general "mechanisms for learning" that are applied to the task of acquiring language. These mechanisms include things such as categorical perception, the ability to notice and remember how frequently elements in their sensory environment co-occur, to consider co-occurring phenomena to be units, the ability to recognize statistical dependencies among units, and the ability to develop categories based on regularities in the input. Perhaps most important for the case of language, learners have the ability to abstract beyond the specifics of the exemplars they hear (or see) to broader principles that permit generalization.

Artificial languages are frequently used to study learning phenomena. Unlike natural language stimuli, that necessarily present multiple and sometimes redundant cues to support receptive processing, artificial languages can be constructed in ways that allow the experimenter to constrain the input to the learner so that learning can be attributed to the particular phenomena under experimental control. For example, artificial languages use nonwords that effectively prevent processing of semantic information to mask processing of morphosyntactic patterns. Likewise, input can be constrained to examine learning of a specific cue to language form (e.g., word order, affixation, stress markers). These constraints, although necessary for identifying specific mechanisms for learning, do not necessarily mean that the findings have no relevance for the more complex context of natural languages. Indeed, there are now several studies (e.g., Gerken, Wilson, & Lewis, 2005; Kittleson, Aguilar, Tokerud, Plante, & Asbjørnsen, 2010; Pelucchi, Hay, & Saffran, 2009; Richarson, Harris, Plante, & Gerken, 2006) demonstrating that principles that first emerged in artificial language studies have explanatory power for natural language learning.

To guide new studies in the area of language impairment, there is already a large and growing literature from typical language learners. This work demonstrates the early abilities of learners to track information contained in the speech stream in ways that build implicit knowledge of language form. For example, infants are known to track the statistical properties of the input they receive. By 8 months, this sensitivity allows infants to notice when sounds co-occur as a set, signaling the presence of an individual word within an otherwise continuous acoustic stream (Aslin, Saffran, & Newport, 1998; Johnson & Jusczyk, 2001; Saffran, Aslin, & Newport, 1996). This is a critical first step for identifying word forms, to which meaning can then be attached. Infants will use other cues (stress, coarticulation) in addition to phoneme co-occurrence if those cues are available (e.g., Johnson & Jusczyk, 2001; Mattys, Jusczyk, Luce, & Morgan, 1999). In addition, infants appear to be influenced by the phonotactic patterns of their native language in making word segmentations (Mattys et al., 1999). Identification of words is a prerequisite skill for learning how words can be ordered within a grammar, and infants can perform both tasks by 12 months of age (Saffran & Wilson, 2003). Furthermore, infants of this age can learn more complex artificial grammars that involve multiple possible combinations of novel words (Gómez & Gerken, 1999). By 15 months, infants are able to track nonadjacent contingencies (Gómez & Maye, 2005), a cue necessary for learning such features as noun–verb agreement, or present progressive verb tense. At 17 months, they can learn a system of bound morphemes in an unfamiliar language (Gerken et al., 2005).

Parallel studies in typical adult participants indicate that learners do not necessarily lose sensitivity to the cues to language form as they mature. For example, adults and children can both use the transitional probabilities for phonemes to identify words in running speech (Saffran, Newport, Aslin, Tunick, & Barrueco, 1997). Adults can learn to recognize novel systems of stress assignment (Bahl et al., 2009). Like their younger counterparts, adult learners can also learn syntax-like features, including word order constraints (Plante, Gómez, & Gerken, 2002), dependent relations that can signal phrase structure (Gómez, 2002; Morgan & Newport, 1981; Saffran, 2001, 2002), and categorical distinctions that parallel open- and close-class words (Monaghan, Chatera, & Christiansen, 2005; Valian & Coulson, 1988). Finally, adults retain the ability to learn systems of bound morphemes through implicit means alone (Richarson et al., 2006).

There is also accumulating evidence that each new learning episode is not approached with a blank slate. Infants at 7.5 months, for example, are able to learn an artificial linguistic rule that does not occur in natural languages. But only a few months later at 9 months, infants appear to resist this type of learning (Gerken & Bollt, 2008). Similarly, adults may learn to recognize stress patterns consistent with those of an artificial language but also do not extract the underlying principles those patterns reflect with the same ease as infants or children (compare Gerken, 2004, and Plante et al., 2011, with Bahl et al., 2009, and Guest, Dell, & Cole, 2000).

Even when adult and child learners perceive the same cues in the input, they may weigh these cues differently. For example, although infant learners appear to weight stress patterns heavily as a cue to language structure, adults can override stress cues in favor of statistical information (Saffran, Newport, & Aslinm, 1996). This differential weighting by children and adults may reflect the learner's relative experience with the different types of cues and their overall reliability in signaling language form. For example, one might hypothesize that prenatal hearing makes prosodic cues available early on but also continued experience may indicate that other cues are more reliable (cf. Bates & MacWhinney, 1987).

LEARNING IN THE CONTEXT OF LANGUAGE IMPAIRMENT

It has only been relatively recently that the dynamics of learning have been explored for individuals with language impairment. Therefore, the view of learning in the context of language impairment is still limited. However, some principles are emerging. First, it is the case that those with disordered language can demonstrate significant learning of underlying linguistic patterns after brief exposures to informative exemplars. This learning occurs without direct instruction or expressive practice. Therefore, this learning is a direct reflection of receptive capabilities. However, those with language disorders frequently show poorer learning of many of the aspects of language compared with their typical-language peers (Alt & Plante, 2006; Bahl et al., 2009; Evans & Saffran, & Robe-Torres, 2009; Grunow, Spaulding, Gómez, & Plante, 2006; Plante, Gómez et al., 2002; Richardson et al., 2006). This is true even when study participants are not selected for the presence of documented receptive-language impairments.

Consistent with the more general learning theory, the impairments demonstrated by learners with poor language skills are not specific to the domain of language. For example, Evans and Saffran have demonstrated that children with language impairment are not as proficient in tracking the statistical information within verbal input. Likewise, Tomblin, Mainela Arnold, and Zhang (2007) demonstrated a poor ability to track this information in a visual learning task. Furthermore, individuals with impaired language may not "catch up" with their language-typical peers in terms of their learning abilities. Indeed, there are now several studies that demonstrate poor learning in adults who were selected for poor language skills (Alt & Gutmann, 2009; Bahl et al., 2009; Grunow et al., 2006).

Finally, it is the case that receptive and expressive learning seem to be intertwined, even for those with language disorders. For example, it is well known that phonotactic frequency affects children's ability to learn and pronounce novel lexical labels (Graf Estes et al., 2007). Richtsmeier, Gerken, Goffman, and Hogan (2009) extended this work to show that typical children's learning of novel lexical items could be affected by the phonotactic frequency of sounds in the child's native language, as well as the frequency with which those sounds were presented within the context of an experiment. In fact, high experimental frequency could enhance performance, even when phonotactic frequency was low. Plante et al. (2011) demonstrated that this effect could also be elicited for children with language impairments. This result established that manipulations of input alone were sufficient to drive changes in expressive performance. Conversely, Camarata, Nelson, Gillum, and Camarata (2009) showed that expressive training of language targets resulted in incidental improvements in receptive language for children who had both expressive and receptive impairments. Taken as a whole, these findings suggest that input to the child, whether accompanied by expressive practice or not, serves to alter the internal representation of the structure of the language. This strengthened representation can then support language in multiple modalities.

The most prevalent outcome across studies is that conditions that promote learning in language-typical individuals will also produce learning for those with poor language skills. However, their learning tends to be less robust. After a period of familiarization with a novel language, impaired learners accept fewer items that are consistent with the input and reject fewer items that are inconsistent with the input compared with their language-typical peers. This is the pattern of results that one would expect if one set of learners had received less input overall than the other. This raises the question of whether disordered learners functionally receive less input because of problems maintaining their attention to—and/or processing—the stimuli. This question parallels the discussion of the potential role of attention in auditory processing, and is supported by separate reports of problems with the control or maintenance of attention by individuals with developmental-language disorders (e.g., Finneran et al., 2009; Noterdaeme et al., 2000; Spaulding et al., 2008).

Occasionally, the outcome of a learning study will suggest that learners with impaired language are using learning strategies that are different than their typical-language peers. In Richardson et al. (2006), learners were familiarized with Russian lexical items and their gender markings. In Russian, gender markers take the form of phonological suffixes. Gender may be either single-marked (one suffix) or double marked (two adjacent suffixes). The redundant information available for double-marked suffixes made them easier to learn for both typical and atypical learners. Learners were also asked to generalize their knowledge of the gender marking system to items they had not previously heard inflected. Typical learners were highly accurate in accepting new lexical items that were correctly inflected and rejected items that were incorrectly inflected. Those in the disordered group, however, showed a different pattern of response. The more phonological overlap between the generalization items and the training items, the more likely the impaired learners were to accept these items as correct. They preferred all double-marked items over single marked items; whether these items were correctly or incorrectly inflected appeared to be a secondary influence on performance.

This outcome suggests that impaired learners rely on their memory for familiar phonological forms more than abstraction of a more global pattern that signals the underlying "rules" for gender marking. Similar overattention to phonological forms at the expense of broader patterns has been seen in other artificial learning paradigms (Bahl et al., 2009; Plante et al., 2011). This learning strategy may be particularly inefficient for two reasons. First, exclusive reliance on memory for items heard would preclude generalization to new items that conform to the global pattern but also were not actually heard. Indeed, lack of generalization is a pervasive and long recognized problem for individuals with SLI. Second, reliance on memorization may be particularly inefficient given that individuals with language impairment tend to have a reduced memory capacity compared with their typical peers (e.g., Ellis Weismer et al., 2000; Gathercole & Baddeley, 1990; Marton & Schwartz, 2003). So, even if some memory for items heard is a prerequisite for learning and generalization, the memory limitations of those with language impairment may be placing constraints on learning.

The issue of whether memory or attention plays a key role in learning outcome is not simply an intellectual exercise. Language therapy is fundamentally an attempt to improve learning of linguistic features that were not acquired typically during the period of language acquisition. Therapy that considers both the linguistic and nonlinguistic factors that inhibit learning is likely to be more effective than that which does not. At this point, however, the behavioral literature offers a plethora of impairments that are linked to poor learning through theory rather than direct evidence. For this type of evidence, we need to turn to techniques that permit visualization of processing components that are invisible to behavioral assessment methods.

Imaging Language Disorders

Although a series of MRI studies have documented structural differences in the brains of individuals with developmental-language disorder relative to typical language controls (e.g., Clark & Plante, 1998; Jackson & Plante, 1997; see also Black and Hoeft, Chapter 12; Pernet and Démonet, Chapter 13; and Leonard, Chapter 15), there is much less corresponding physiologic data. The two available functional MRI (fMRI) studies employed auditory tasks in which both language impaired and control participants were asked to listen to brief narratives and to remember the information presented (Ellis Weismer, Plante, Jones, & Tomblin, 2005; Plante, Ramage, & Maglöire, , 2006). One study included children age 14 who had been identified as SLI at age 5 and followed longitudinally and matched control participants (Ellis Weismer et al., 2005). The second included young adults (18–19 years of age) with language-based learning disability and matched controls with typical language skills. Although each study included both listening and recall tasks, here we are most concerned with the listening component as a reflection of receptive-language processing.

During the listening portion of both studies, activation differences occurred not only in temporal cortex (classically associated with receptive language) but also in dorsolateral prefrontal and parietal regions during initial encoding of information. Dorsolateral prefrontal–parietal coactivations occur routinely in language processing studies but also in studies that have focused on memory (Chien, Ravizza, & Fiez, 2003; Wagner & Smith, 2003) or attention (Corbetta & Shulman, 2002; Hopfinger et al., 2001; Kan & Thompson-Schill, 2004). In fact, variations in parietal activation have been described in response to attention to specific characteristics of the stimuli (Shaywitz et al., 2001) or when attention is directed to one stimulus stream relative to another (Christensen, Antonucci, Lockewood, Kittleson, & Plante, 2008; Jäncke, Specht, Shah, & Hugdahl, 2003). Dorsolateral prefrontal activation is strongly associated with executive processes, including the control of attention (Christensen et al., 2008; Kan & Thompson-Schill, 2004; Yantis & Serences, 2003) and memory encoding (Buckner, 2003).

These fMRI data provide support for the idea that the behavioral impairments of individuals with developmental-language disorders reflect not only core language ability but also the intersection among language, attention, and memory. However, this interpretation must be considered preliminary. The two available fMRI studies both used tasks that emphasized verbal memory. It is not clear how much the areas outside of classic language cortex would be engaged if participants were not told explicitly that they would be asked about the input later (see Plante, Creusere, & Sabin, 2002; Plante, Holland, & Schmithorst, 2006). One could argue that both attention to the auditory stream and memory for the speech components represent integral features of language processing (Just & Carpenter, 1992), with the contributions of these cognitive capacities being simply a matter of degree. Indeed, when participants without language impaimrents are asked to passively process sentences without expectation that they should remember the sentences, small regions of frontal activity can still be found (Plante, Creusere, & Sabin, 2002; Plante, Holland, & Schmithorst, 2006).

The types of imaging paradigms discussed so far can be thought of as static tests of current skill levels and are characteristic of the majority of the cognitive imaging literature. There have been several approaches used to visualize the dynamic processes associated with learning. One tactic to do so is to image children either longitudinally (Szaflarski et al., 2006) or at cross-section ages over the period of language acquisition (e.g., Karunanayaka et al., 2007; Plante, Holland, et al., 2006; Schmithorst, Holland, & Plante, 2007). Such studies have demonstrated that by age 5, areas of activation for children are largely similar to what is seen in studies of adults (e.g., compare Plante, Cruesere, & Sabin, 2002 with Plante, Holland, & Schmithorst, 2006; Plante, Ramage, & Maglöire, 2006, with Schmithorst et al., 2007). However, early left-hemisphere lateralization tends to strengthen with time (Holland et al., 2007; Szaflarski et al., 2006), and the strength of individual regional activations and the degree of functional connectivity among regions can change as well (e.g., Karunanayaka et al., 2007; Schmithorst et al., 2007).

Although imaging of language during the childhood years has been illuminating, there are several limitations for using studies of language processing during childhood as a model for understanding language learning. First, the extant literature largely focuses on children age 5 and above. This is largely reflective of the ability of very young children to comply with task demands in the scanner environment. Although there are a few studies of passive processing by sleeping infants (Arichi et al., 2010; Dehaene-Lambertz, Dehaene, & Hertz-Pannier, 2002; Morita et al., 2000), there is a notable gap between the ages of 1 and 4 years, considered the most critical for describing language acquisition. Second, the available cross-sectional and longitudinal studies can more properly be considered a snapshot of the cumulative effect of children's learning up until the point of the scan, rather than a view of the process of learning. In other words, these studies provide insight into the outcome of this learning, rather than imaging learning as it is happening.

It is possible to adapt previous behavior studies of learning to the scanner environment. However, this approach has been taken in only a handful of studies, and only for typical learners to date. Of these, only a very few focused on learning specific aspects of oral language (e.g., Breitenstein et al., 2005; Fletcher, Büchel, Josephs, Friston, & Dolan, 1999; McNealy, Mazziotta, & Dapretto, 2006; Newman-Norlund, Frey, Petitto, & Grafton, 2006; Raboyeau, Marcotte, Adrover-Roig, & Ansaldo, 2010). Each of these used methods that were different in noteworthy ways. For example, three studies employed artificial languages consistent with behavioral research paradigms described previously. One trained participants on an auditory task outside the scanner and then scanned the outcome of that learning at four time points over the course of a four-week learning period (Newman-Norland et al., 2006). Another involved auditory learning inside the scanner within a single session (McNealy et al., 2006). The third involved a visual learning paradigm that incorporated feedback as part of the learning paradigm (Fletcher et al., 1999). With these types of methodological differences, it is not surprising that the results across studies showed little overlap in terms of regions of activation that changed with learning. In fact, some regions, such as the superior temporal gyrus and dorsolateral prefrontal cortex, showed an increase in activation in one learning study (Fletcher et al., 1999) and a decrease in another (McNealy et al., 2006).

Despite these incongruities, each of the studies contains some of the elements critical to the study of learning. First, McNealy et al. (2006) included conditions in which the input to the participant was unlearnable as well as input that was learnable. In the "learnable" conditions (there were two), nonword strings were combined using rules for ordering the elements, whereas in the "unlearnable" condition, nonwords were randomly arranged so no pattern could be detected. This contrast between learnable and unlearnable input is critical for differentiating change associated with learning from other processes such as habituation. The McNealy et al. (2006) study was the only study to include a learnable versus unlearnable contrast. On the other hand, two other studies (Newman-Norlund et al., 2006; Raboyeau et al., 2010) did incorporate the element of change over time. However, the tasks tapped the outcome of learning (test performance) rather than resource allocation during learning itself.

In addition, two studies have used natural language stimuli (phonological contrast [Golestani & Zatorre, 2004], lexical-semantic learning [Raboyeau et al., 2010]), and recent behavior studies have shown that typical learners also demonstrate rapid learning of aspects of language form in natural language contexts (Kittleson et al., 2010; Pelluchi & Saffran, 2009; Richardson et al., 2006). This raises the possibility of using natural language stimuli to study additional aspects of language learning in the context of a neuroimaging study.

CONCLUSION

The study of receptive impairments in developmental-language disorders has lagged behind the study of expressive impairments. Although there is a substantial body of work concerning acoustic and phonological processing, much less is known concerning the full receptive processing of language form. This has been due, in part, to a paucity of sensitive methods. Adaptation of paradigms based on learning theory offers the potential for new insights into the receptive processing of individuals with language disorders. Behaviorally, these methods also offer potential insights into learning strategies that can be applied across the entire range of LLD and allow common mechanisms and/or substrates that lead to developmental language and reading disorders to be elucidated. Finally, these evolving techniques can be adapted to a scanner environment and in this context, offer the potential to visualize the dynamics of learning as it unfolds. This may offer unparalleled insights into developmental-language disorders by illuminating the extent to which poor learning specifically reflects differences in the activation of classic language cortex versus the interaction of linguistic and nonlinguistic capacities.

REFERENCES

Aguilar-Mediavilla, E.M., Sanz-Torrent, M., & Serra-Raventos, M. (2002). A comparative study of the phonology of pre-school children with specific language impairment (SLI), language delay (LD) and normal acquisition. *Clinical Linguistics & Phonetics, 16,* 573–596. doi:10.1080/02699200210148394

Alt, M., & Gutmann, M. (2009). Fast mapping semantic features: Performance of adults with normal language, history of disorders of spoken and written language, and attention deficit hyperactivity disorder on a word learning task. *Journal of Communication Disorders, 42,* 347–364. doi:10.1016/j.jcomdis.2009.03.004

Alt, M., & Plante, E. (2006). Factors that influence lexical and semantic fast-mapping of young children with specific language impairment. *Journal of*

Speech, Language, and Hearing Research, 49, 941–954. doi:10.1044/1092-4388(2006/068)

Aram, D., & Ekelman, B. (1988). Auditory temporal perception of children with left or right brain lesions. *Neuropsychologia, 26,* 931–935. doi:10.1016/0028-3932(88)90061-9

Arichi, T., Moraux, A., Melendez, A., Doria, V., Groppo, M., Merchant, N., ... Edwards, A.D. (2010). Somatosensory cortical activation identified by functional MRI in preterm and term infants. *NeuroImage, 49*(3), 2063–2071. doi:10.1016/j.neuroimage.2009.10.038

Aslin, R., Saffran, J., & Newport, E. (1998). Computational of conditional probability statistics by 8-month old infants. *Psychological Science, 9,* 321–324. doi:10.1111/1467-9280.00063

Bahl, M., Plante, E., & Gerken, L.A. (2009). Processing prosodic structure by adults with language-based learning disability. *Journal of Communication Disorders, 42,* 313–323. doi:10.1016/j.jcomdis.2009.02.001

Bates, E., & MacWhinney, B. (1987). Competition, variation, & learning. In B. MacWhinney (Ed.), *Mechanisms of language acquisition* (pp. 157–193). Hillsdale, NJ: Lawrence Erlbaum.

Bernstein, L.E., & Stark, R.E. (1985). Speech perception development in language-impaired children: A 4-year follow-up study. *Journal of Speech and Hearing Research, 30,* 21–30.

Bishop, D.V.M. (2009). Specific language impairment as a language learning disability. *Child Language Teaching and Therapy, 25*(2), 163–165. doi:10.1177/0265659009105889

Bishop, D.V.M., Bright, P., James, C., Bishop, S., & Van der Lely, H. (2000). Grammatical SLI: A distinct subtype of developmental language impairment? *Applied Psycholinguistics, 21,* 159–181. doi:10.1017/S0142716400002010

Bishop, D.V.M., Carlyon, R., Deeks, J., & Bishop, S. (1999). Auditory temporal processing impairments: Neither necessary nor sufficient for causing language impairments in children. *Journal of Speech, Language, and Hearing Research, 42,* 1295–1310.

Bishop, D.V.M., & Snowling, M.J. (2004). Developmental dyslexia and specific language impairment: Same or different? *Psychological Bulletin, 130,* 858–886. doi:10.1037/0033-2909.130.6.858

Breitenstein, C., Jansen, A., Deppe, M., Foerster, A.F, Sommer, J., Wolbers, T., & Knecht, S. (2005). Hippocampus activity differentiates good from poor learners of a novel lexicon. *NeuroImage, 25,* 958–968. doi:10.1016/j.neuroimage.2004.12.019

Buckner, R.L. (2003). Functional-anatomic correlates of control processes in memory. *The Journal of Neuroscience, 23,* 3999–4004.

Camarata, S., Nelson, K., Gillum, H., & Camarata, M. (2009). Incidental receptive language growth associated with expressive grammar intervention in SLI. *First Language, 29*(1), 51–63. doi:10.1177/0142723708098810

Catts, H.W., Adlof, S.M., Hogan, T.P., & Weismer, S.E. (2005). Are specific language impairment and dyslexia distinct disorders? *Journal of Speech, Language, and Hearing Research, 48,* 1378–1396. doi:10.1044/1092-4388(2005/096)

Chien, J.M., Ravizza, S.M., & Fiez, J.A. (2003). Using neuroimaging to evaluate models of working memory and their implications for language processing. *Journal of Neurolinguistics, 16,* 315–339. doi:10.1016/S0911-6044(03)00021-6

Christensen, T., Antonucci, S., Lockwood, J.L., Kittleson, M., & Plante, E. (2008). Cortical and subcortical contributions to the attentive processing of speech. *NeuroReport, 19,* 1101–1105. doi:10.1097/WNR.0b013e3283060a9d

Clark, M.M. & Plante, E. (1998). Morphology of the inferior frontal gyrus in adults with developmental language disorders. *Brain and Language, 61,* 288–303. doi:10.1006/brln.1997.1864

Corbetta, M., & Shulman, G.L. (2002). Control of goal-directed and stimulus-driven attention in the brain. *Nature Reviews Neuroscience, 3,* 201–215. doi:10.1038/nrn755

Courtright, J.A., & Courtright, I.C. (1983). The perception of nonverbal vocal cues of emotional meaning by language disordered and normal children. *Journal of Speech and Hearing Research, 26,* 412–417.

Deevy, P., & Leonard, L. (2004). The comprehension of Wh-questions in children with specific language impairment. *Journal of Speech, Language, and Hearing Research, 47,* 802–815. doi:10.1044/1092-4388(2004/060)

Dehaene-Lambertz, G., Dehaene, S., & Hertz-Pannier, L. (2002). Functional neuroimaging of speech perception in infants. *Science, 298,* 2013–2015. doi:10.1126/science.1077066

Elliot, L., Hammer, M., Scholl, M., & Carrell, T. (1989). Discrimination of rising and falling simulated single-formant frequency transitions: Practice and transition duration effects. *Journal of the Acoustical Society of America, 86*(3), 945–953.

Ellis Weismer, S., Plante, E., Jones, M., & Tomblin, J.B. (2005). A functional magnetic resonance imaging investigation of verbal working memory in adolescents with specific language impairment. *Journal of Speech, Language, and Hearing Research, 48,* 405–425.

Ellis Weismer, S., Tomblin, J.B., Zhang, X., Buckwalter, P., Chynoweth, J.G., & Jones, M. (2000). Nonword repetition

performance in school-age children
with and without language impairment.
*Journal of Speech, Language, and Hearing
Research, 43,* 865–878.

Evans, J.L., Saffran, J.R., & Robe-Torres,
K. (2009). Statistical learning in children with specific language impairment. *Journal of Speech, Language,
and Hearing Research, 52*(2), 321-335.
doi:10.1044/1092-4388(2009/07-0189)

Fidler, L.J., Plante, E., & Vance, R. (2011).
Identification of adults with developmental language impairments. *American Journal of Speech-Language Pathology.*
doi:10.1044/1058-0360(2010/09-0096)

Finneran, D., Francis, A., & Leonard, L.
(2009). Sustained attention in children with specific language impairment (SLI). *Journal of Speech, Language,
and Hearing Research, 52*(4), 915–929.
doi:10.1044/1092-4388(2009/07-0053)

Fisher, J., Plante, E., Vance, R., Gerken,
LA., & Glattke, T.J. (2007). Do children and adults with language impairment recognize prosodic cues?
*Journal of Speech, Language, and Hearing
Research, 50,* 746–758. doi:10.1044/1092-
4388(2007/052)

Flax, J.F., Realpe-Bonilla, T., Hirsch,
L.S., Brzustowitz, L.M., Bartlett, C.W.,
& Tallal, P. (2003). Specific language
impairment in families: Evidence for
co-occurrence with reading impairments. *Journal of Speech, Language,
and Hearing Research, 46,* (3), 530–543.
doi:10.1044/1092-4388(2003/043)

Fletcher, P., Büchel, C., Josephs, O., Friston, K., & Dolan, R. (1999). Learn-
ing-related neuronal responses in
prefrontal cortex studied with functional neuroimaging. *Cerebral Cortex, 9,*
168–178. doi:10.1093/cercor/9.2.168

Gathercole, S. (2006). Nonword repetition and word learning: The nature
of the relationship. *Applied Psycholinguistics, 27,* 513–543. doi:10.1017/
S0142716406060383

Gathercole, S., & Baddeley, A. (1990). Phonological memory deficits in language
disordered children: Is there a causal
connection? *Journal of Memory and Language, 29,* 336–360. doi:10.1016/0749-
596X(90)90004-J

Gerken, L. (2004). Nine-month-olds extract structural principles required for
natural language. *Cognition, 93*(3), B89–
B96. doi:10.1016/j.cognition.2003.11.005

Gerken, L., & Bollt, A., (2008). Three exemplars allow at least some linguistic

generalizations: Implications for generalization mechanisms and constraints.
Language Learning and Development, 4,
228–248. doi:10.1080/15475440802143117

Gerken, L.A., Wilson, R., & Lewis, W.
(2005). Infants can use distributional
cues to form syntactic categories.
Journal of Child Language, 32, 249–268.
doi:10.1017/S0305000904006786

Golestani, N., & Zatorre, R.J. (2004).
Learning new sounds of speech: Re-
allocation of neural substrates. *NeuroImage, 21,* 494–506. doi:10.1016/j.
neuroimage.2003.09.071

Gómez, R. (2002). Variability and detection of invariant structure. *Psychological
Science, 13,* 431–436. doi:10.1111/1467-
9280.00476

Gómez, R. (2006). Dynamically guided
learning. In Y. Munakata & M. Johnson (Eds.), *Attention & performance XXI:
Processes of change in brain and cognitive
development* (pp. 87–110). New York:
Oxford University Press.

Gómez, R., & Gerken, LA. (1999). Artificial grammar learning by 1-year-olds
leads to specific and abstract knowledge. *Cognition, 70,* 109–135. doi:10.1016/
S0010-0277(99)00003-7

Gómez, R., & Maye, J. (2005). The developmental trajectory of nonadjacent de-
pendency learning. *Infancy, 7,* 183–206.
doi:10.1207/s15327078in0702_4

Graf Estes, K., Evans, J.L., & Else-Quest,
N.M. (2007). Differences in the nonword
repetition performance of children with
and without specific language impairment: A meta-analysis. *Journal of Speech,
Language, and Hearing Research, 50,* 177–
195. doi:10.1044/1092-4388(2007/015)

Gray, A., & McCutchen, D. (2006). Young
readers' use of phonological information: Phonological awareness, memory, and comprehension. *Journal of
Learning Disabilities, 39,* 325–333. doi:1
0.1177/00222194060390040601

Grunow, H., Spaulding, T.J., Gómez,
R.L., & Plante, E. (2006). The effects of
variation on learning word order rules
by adults with and without language-
based learning disabilities. *Journal of
Communication Disorders, 39,* 158–170.
doi:10.1016/j.jcomdis.2005.11.004

Guest, D.J., Dell, G.S., & Cole, J.S. (2000).
Violable constraints in language production: Testing the transitivity assumption of optimality theory. *Journal
of Memory and Language, 42,* 272–299.
doi:10.1006/jmla.1999.2679

Helzer, J.R., Champlin, C.A., & Gillam, R.B. (1996). Auditory temporal resolution in specifically language impaired and age-matched children. *Perceptual and Motor Skills, 83,* 1171–1181.

Holland, S.K., Vannest, J., Mecoli, M., Jacola, L.M., Tillema, J.M., Karunanayaka, P.R., ... Byars, A.W. (2007). Functional MRI of language lateralization during development in children. *International Journal of Audiology, 46,* 533–551. doi:10.1080/14992020701448994

Hopfinger, J.B., Woldorff, M.G., Fletcher, E.M., & Mangun, G.R. (2001). Dissociating top-down attentional control from selective perception and action. *Neuropsychologia, 39,* 1277–1291. doi:10.1016/S0028-3932(01)00117-8

Jackson, T., & Plante, E. (1997). Gyral morphology in the posterior sylvian region in families affected by developmental language disorder. *Neuropsychology Review, 6,* 81–94. doi:10.1007/BF01875369

Jäncke, L., Specht, K., Shah, J.N., & Hugdahl, K. (2003) Focused attention in a simple dichotic listening task: an fMRI experiment. *Cognitive Brain Research, 16,* 257–266. doi:10.1016/S0926-6410(02)00281-1

Johnson, E.K., & Jusczyk, P.W. (2001). Word segmentation by 8-month-olds: When speech cues count more than statistics. *Journal of Memory and Langauge, 44,* 548–567. doi:10.1006/jmla.2000.2755

Just, M.A., & Carpenter, P.A., (1992). A capacity theory of sentence comprehension: Individual differences in working memory. *Psychological Review, 99,* 122–149.

Kan, I.P., & Thompson-Schill, S.L. (2004). Selection from perceptual and conceptual representations. *Cognitive, Affective, & Behavioral Neuroscience, 4,* 466–482. doi:10.3758/CABN.4.4.466

Karunanayaka, P.R., Holland, S.K., Schmithorst, V.J., Solodkin, A., Chen, E.E., Szaflarski, J.P., & Plante, E. (2007). Age-related connectivity changes in fMRI data from children during listening to stories. *NeuroImage, 34,* 349–360. doi:10.1016/j.neuroimage.2006.08.028

Kittleson, M.M., Aguilar, J.M., Tokerud, G.L., Plante, E., & Asbjørnsen, A.E. (2010). Implicit language learning: Adults' ability to segment words in Norwegian. *Bilingualism: Language and Cognition, 13,* 513–523. doi:10.1017/S1366728910000039

Leonard, L.B., McGregor, K.K., & Allen, G.D. (1994). Grammatical morphology and speech perception in children with specific language impairment. *Journal of Speech and Hearing Research, 35,* 1076–1085.

Lincoln, A.J., Dickstein, P., Courchesne, E., Elmasian, R., & Tallal, P. (1992). Auditory processing abilities in nonretarded adolescents and young adults with developmental receptive language disorder and autism. *Brain and Language, 43,* 613–622. doi:10.1016/0093-934X(92)90086-T

Ludlow, C.L., Cadahy, E.A., Bassich, C., & Brown, C.L. (1983). Auditory processing skills of hyperactive, language impaired and reading disabled boys. In E.Z. Lasky & J. Katz (Eds.), *Central auditory processing disorders* (pp. 163–184). Baltimore: University Park Press.

Maillart, C., Schelstraete, M., & Hupet, M. (2004). Phonological representations in children with SLI: A study of French. *Journal of Speech, Language, and Hearing Research, 47,* 187–198. doi:10.1044/1092-4388(2004/016)

Marton, K., & Schwartz, R.G. (2003). Working memory capacity and language processes in children with specific language impairment. *Journal of Speech, Language, and Hearing Research, 41*(7), 1138–1153. doi:10.1044/1092-4388(2003/089)

Mattys, S.L., Jusczyk, P.W., Luce, P.A., & Morgan, J.L. (1999). Phonotactic and prosodic effects on word segmentation in infants. *Cognitive Psychology, 38,* 465–494. doi:10.1006/cogp.1999.0721

McArthur, G.M., Hogben, J.H., Edwards, V.T., Heath, S.M., & Mengler, E.D. (2000). On the "specifics" of specific reading disability and specific language impairment. *Journal of Child Psychology and Psychiatry, 41*(7), 869–874. doi:10.1111/1469-7610.00674

McNealy, K., Mazziotta, J.C., & Dapretto, M. (2006). Cracking the language code: Neural mechanisms underlying speech parsing. *The Journal of Neuroscience, 26,* 7629–7629. doi:10.1523/JNEUROSCI.5501-05.2006

Monaghan, P., Chatera, N., & Christiansen, M.H. (2005). The differential role of phonological and distributional cues in grammatical categorization. *Cognition, 96,* 143–182.

Morgan, J.L., & Newport, E.L. (1981). The role of constituent structure in the induction of an artificial language. *Journal of Verbal Learning and Verbal Behavior, 20,* 67–85. doi:10.1016/S0022-5371(81)90312-1

Morita, T., Kochiyama, T., Yamada, H., Konishi, Y., Yonekura, Y., Matsumura, M., & Sadato, N. (2000). Difference in the metabolic response to photic stimulation of the lateral geniculate nucleus and the primary visual cortex of infants: A fMRI study. *Neuroscience Research, 38*(1), 63–70. doi:10.1016/S0168-0102(00)00146-2

Munson, B., Kurtz, B.A., & Windsor, J. (2005). The influence of vocabulary size, phonotactic probability, and wordlikeness on nonword repetitions of children with and without specific language impairment. *Journal of Speech, Language, and Hearing Research, 48*(5), 1033–1047. doi:10.1044/1092-4388(2005/072)

Nash, M., & Donaldson, M.L. (2005). Word learning in children with vocabulary deficits. *Journal of Speech, Language, and Hearing Research, 48,* 439–458. doi:10.1044/1092-4388(2005/030)

Newman-Norlund, R.D., Frey, S.H., Petitto, L.A., & Grafton, S.T. (2006). Anatomical substrates of visual and auditory miniature second-language learning. *Journal of Cognitive Neuroscience, 18,* 1984–1997. doi:10.1162/jocn.2006.18.12.1984

Newport, E., & Aslin, R. (2004). Learning at a distance: I Statistical learning of non-adjacent dependencies. *Cognitive Psychology, 48,* 127–162. doi:10.1016/S0010-0285(03)00128-2

Nobury, C.F., Bishop, D.V.M., & Briscoe, J. (2002). Does impaired grammatical comprehension provide evidence for an innate grammar module? *Applied Psycholinguistics, 23,* 247–268.

Noterdaeme, M., Amorosa, H., Mildenberger, K., Sitter, S., & Minow, F. (2000). Evaluation of attention in children with autism and children with a specific language disorder. *European Child and Adolescent Psychiatry, 10,* 58–66. doi:10.1007/s007870170048

Owen, A.J., Dromi, E., & Leonard, L.B. (2001). The phonology-morphology interface in the speech of Hebrew-speaking children with specific language impairment. *Journal of Communication Disorders, 34,* 323–337. doi:10.1016/S0021-9924(01)00053-3

Pelucchi, B., Hay, J.F., & Saffran, J.R. (2009). Statistical learning in a natural language by 8-month-old infants. *Child Development, 80,* 674–685. doi:10.1111/j.1467-8624.2009.01290

Pennington, B.F. (2006). From single to multiple deficit models of developmental disorders. *Cognition, 101,* 385–413. doi:10.1016/j.cognition.2006.04.008

Plante, E., Bahl, M., Vance, R., & Gerken, L.A. (2011). Beyond phonotactic frequency: Presentation frequency effects word productions in specific language impairment. *Journal of Communication Disorders, 44,* 91–102. doi:10.1016/j.jcomdis.2010.07.005

Plante, E., Creusere, M., & Sabin, C. (2002). Dissociating sentential prosody from sentence processing: Activation interacts with task demands. *NeuroImage, 17,* 401–410. doi:10.1006/nimg.2002.1182

Plante, E., Gómez, R., & Gerken, L.A. (2002). Sensitivity to word order cues by normal and language/learning disabled adults. *Journal of Communication Disorders, 35,* 453–462. doi:10.1016/S0021-9924(02)00094-1

Plante, E., Holland, S.K., & Schmithorst, V.J. (2006). Prosodic processing by children: An fMRI study. *Brain and Langauge, 97,* 332–342. doi:10.1016/j.bandl.2005.12.004

Plante, E., Ramage, A., & Maglöire, J. (2006). Processing narratives for verbatim and gist information by adults with language learning disabilities: A functional neuroimaging study. *Learning Disabilities Research and Practice, 21,* 61–76. doi:10.1111/j.1540-5826.2006.00207

Plante, E., & Vance, R. (1994). Selection of preschool language tests: A data-based approach. *Language, Speech, and Hearing Services in Schools, 25,* 15–24.

Plante, E., & Vance, R. (1995). Diagnostic accuracy of two tests of preschool language. *American Journal of Speech-Language Pathology, 4,* 70–76.

Poll, G.H., Betz, S.K., & Miller, C.A. (2010). Identification of clinical markers of specific language impairment in adults. *Journal of Speech, Language, and Hearing Research, 53,* 414–429. doi:10.1044/1092-4388(2009/08-0016)

Raboyeau, G., Marcotte, K., Adrover-Roig, D., & Ansaldo, A. (2010). Brain activation and lexical learning: The impact of learning phase and word type. *NeuroImage, 49*(3), 2850–2861. doi:10.1016/j.neuroimage.2009.10.007

Richardson, J., Harris, L., Plante, E., & Gerken, L.A. (2006). Subcategory learning in normal and language learning-disabled adults: How much information do they need? *Journal of Speech, Language, and Hearing Research, 49,* 1257–1266. doi:10.1044/1092-4388(2006/090)

Richtsmeier, P.T., Gerken, L.A., Goffman, L., & Hogan, T. (2009). Statistical frequency in perception affects children's lexical production. *Cognition. 111,* 372–377. doi:10.1016/j.cognition.2009.02.009

Saffran, J.R. (2001). The use of predictive dependencies in language learning. *Journal of Memory and Language, 44,* 493–515. doi:10.1006/jmla.2000.2759

Saffran, J.R. (2002). Contraints on statistical language learning. *Journal of Memory and Language, 47,* 172–196. doi:10.1006/jmla.2001.2839

Saffran, J.R. (2003). Statistical language learning: Mechanisms and constraints. *Current Directions in Psychological Science, 12,* 110–114. doi:10.1111/1467-8721.01243

Saffran, J.R., Aslin, R.N., & Newport, E.L. (1996). Statistical learning by 8-month-old infants. *Science, 274,* 1026–1928. doi:10.1126/science.274.5294.1926

Saffran, J.R., Newport, E.L., & Aslin, R.N. (1996). Word segmentation: The role of distributional cues. *Journal of Memory and Language, 35,* 606–621. doi:10.1006/jmla.1996.0032

Saffran, J.R., Newport, E.L., Aslin, R.N., Tunick, R.A., & Barrueco, S. (1997). Incidental language learning: Listening (and learning) out of the corner of your ear. *Psychological Science, 8,* 101–105.

Saffran, J.R., & Wilson, D.P. (2003). From syllables to syntax: Multilevel statistical learning by 12-month-old infants. *Infancy, 4,* 273–284. doi:10.1207/S15327078IN0402_07

Savage, R.S., & Frederickson, N. (2006). Beyond phonology: What else is needed to describe the problems of below-average readers and spellers? *Journal of Learning Disabilities, 39,* 399–413. doi:10.1177/00222194060390050301

Schmithorst, V.J., Holland, S.K., & Plante, E. (2007). Development of effective connectivity for narrative comprehension in children. *NeuroReport, 18,* 1411–1415. doi:10.1097/WNR.0b013e3282e9a4ef

Shaywitz, B.A., Shaywitz, S.E., Pugh, K.R., Fulbright, R.K., Skudlarski, P., Mencl, W.E., … Gore, C. (2001). The functional neural architecture of components of attention in language-processing tasks. *NeuroImage, 13,* 601–612. doi:10.1006/nimg.2000.0726

Spaulding, T., Plante, E., & Vance, R. (2008). Sustained selective attention skills of preschool children with specific language impairment: Evidence for separate attentional capacities. *Journal of Speech, Language, and Hearing Research, 51*(1), 16–34. doi:10.1044/1092-4388(2008/002)

Stevens, C., Fanning, J., Coch, D., Sanders, L., & Neville, H. (2008). Neural mechanisms of selective auditory attention are enhanced by computerized training: Electrophysiological evidence from language-impaired and typically developing children. *Brain Research, 1205,* 55–69. doi:10.1016/j.brainres.2007.10.108

Szaflarski, J.P., Schmithorst, V.J., Altaye, M., Byars, A.W., Rett, J., Plante, E., & Holland, S.K. (2006). FMRI study of longitudinal language development in children age 5-1. *Annals of Neurology, 59,* 796–807.

Tallal, P., & Piercy, M. (1973). Developmental aphasia: Impaired rate of non-verbal processing as a function of sensory modality. *Neuropsychologia, 11*(4), 389–398. doi:10.1016/0028-3932(73)90025-0

Tallal, P., Stark, R., Kallman, C., & Mellits, D. (1981). A reexamination of some nonverbal perceptual abilities of language-impaired and normal children as a function of age and sensory modality. *Journal of Speech & Hearing Research, 24*(3), 351–357.

Tallal, P., Stark, R., & Mellits, E. (1985). Identification of language-impaired children on the basis of rapid perception and production skills. *Brain and Language, 25*(2), 314–322. doi:10.1016/0093-934X(85)90087-2

Tomblin, J.B., Freese, P., & Records, N. (1992). Diagnosis of specific language impairments in adults for the purpose of pedigree analysis. *Journal of Speech and Hearing Research, 35,* 832–843.

Tomblin, J.B., Mainela-Arnold, E., & Zhang, X. (2007). Procedural learning and adolescents with and without specific language impairment. *Language Learning and Development, 3*(4), 269–293. doi:10.1080/15475440701377477

Trauner, D., Ballantyne, A., Chase, C., & Tallal, P. (1993). Comprehension and expression of affect in language-impaired children. *Journal of Psycholinguistic Research, 22*(4), 445–452. doi:10.1007/BF01074346

Valian, V., & Coulson, S. (1988). Anchor points in language learning: The role of marker frequency. *Journal of Memory and Language, 27,* 71–86. doi:10.1016/0749-596X(88)90049-6

Van der Lely, H.K.J., & Stollwerck, L. (1996). A grammatical specific language impairment in children: An autosomal dominant inheritance. *Brain and Language, 52,* 484–504. doi:10.1006/brln.1996.0026

Wagner, T.D., & Smith, E.E. (2003). Neuroimaging studies of working memory: A meta-analysis. *Cognitive, Affective, & Behavioral Neuroscience, 3,* 255–274.

Windsor, J. (1999). Effect of semantic inconsistency on sentence grammaticality judgements for children with and without language-learning disabilities. *Language Testing, 16,* 293–313. doi:10.1191/026553299668713774

Wright, B., Lombardino, L., King, W., & Puranik, C. (1997). Deficits in auditory temporal and spectral resolution in language-impaired children. *Nature, 387*(6629), 176–178. doi:10.1038/387176a0

Yantis, S., & Serences, J.T. (2003). Cortical mechanisms of space-based and object-based attentional control. *Current Opinion in Neurobiology, 13,* 187–193. doi:10.1016/S0959-4388(03)00033-3

Neural Correlates of Reading-Related Processes Examined with Functional Magnetic Resonance Imaging Before Reading Onset and After Language/Reading Remediation

Nora Maria Raschle, Michelle YH Chang,
Patrice L. Stering, Jennifer Zuk, and Nadine Gaab

L anguage-based learning problems are among the most prevalent developmental disabilities, with epidemiological studies demonstrating that approximately 20% of children are affected (Beitchman, Nair, Clegg, Ferguson, & Patel, 1986). Of these, developmental dyslexia (DD) is one of the most prominent specific learning disabilities, affecting 5%–17% of children. DD is characterized by difficulties with accurate and/or fluent word recognition, poor spelling, and poor decoding performance and is disproportionate to other cognitive abilities. It cannot be explained by poor vision or hearing or lack of adequate motivation or educational opportunities (Critchley, 1970; World Health Organization, 1992). DD can be diagnosed only around the second or third grade, and most children with a diagnosis of DD exhibit enduring reading impairments throughout adolescence and into adulthood (e.g., Flowers, 1994).

PHONOLOGICAL-PROCESSING IMPAIRMENTS IN DEVELOPMENTAL DYSLEXIA

The majority of researchers who study DD agree that the central difficulty in DD is based within the language system. Specifically, a large proportion of individuals with DD are unable to access the underlying sound structure of words and map these onto their written counterparts (e.g., letter combinations; Liberman, Shankweiler, & Liberman, 1989; Shaywitz, 1998). In support of this, an impairment in these phonological representations is the most reliable marker of DD in school-age children (e.g., Snowling, 2000; Wagner & Torgesen, 1987). Based on strong evidence from intervention studies, structural equation modeling, and path analysis, it has been suggested that phonological processing skills may have a causal relationship with reading (e.g., Shaywitz et al., 2004).

Children who enter first grade with weak knowledge about the phonological features of words and poor phonemic awareness are at high risk for developing difficulties with reading. As many as 80% of poor readers in the early years of elementary school are still classified as such in fourth grade (Francis, Shaywitz, Stuebing, Shaywitz, & Fletcher, 1996; Juel, 1988; Torgesen & Buress, 1998). Phonological processing measures also contribute most to the discrimination of readers with DD and those of average ability and between those of average and superior ability (Shaywitz et al., 1999).

RAPID TEMPORAL PROCESSING
IMPAIRMENTS IN DEVELOPMENTAL DYSLEXIA

The ability to discriminate and manipulate syllables relies on the ability to discriminate rapid changes in sound. Several researchers have suggested that DD and its characteristic phonological-processing impairments may be caused by a more fundamental impairment in this skill (Ahissar, Protopapas, Reid, & Merzenich, 2000; Gaab, Gabrieli, Deutsch, Tallal, & Temple, 2007; Tallal & Gaab, 2006). Studies have shown that children with DD are significantly impaired in their ability to manipulate, discriminate, sequence, or remember rapidly changing stimuli that differ only in their acoustic frequency (Tallal, 2004; Tallal & Gaab, 2006). These skills are fundamental to the perception of syllables. In line with this, individuals with DD have difficulties discriminating between consonant–vowel pairs (e.g., ba/da) that mainly differ in the first 40 milliseconds but not between syllables incorporating longer duration acoustic differences (Reed, 1989; Tallal & Piercy, 1974). Other studies have failed to find a rapid auditory temporal processing impairment in DD (e.g., Chiappe, 2002; McArthur, 2009). A few studies have directly linked the auditory rapid temporal-processing impairment to phonological measures (e.g., Tallal & Piercy, 1973) and a review of 10 studies in individuals with DD estimated the incidence of auditory deficits to be approximately 40% (Ramus, 2003).

NEURAL CORRELATES OF READING
DEVELOPMENT IN THE TYPICALLY DEVELOPING BRAIN

Several cross-sectional functional magnetic resonance imaging (fMRI) studies have examined reading development in the typically developing brain by comparing beginning and skilled readers. Shaywitz and colleagues (Shaywitz, Gruen, & Shaywitz, 2007) examined phonological processing skills in 119 typically developing children between the ages of 7 and 18. The authors observed increased activation within the left anterior lateral occipitotemporal area as a function of age, whereas right superior and middle frontal regions showed decreased activation with age. Turkeltaub, Gareau, Flowers, Zeffiro, and Eden (2003) reported a different developmental pattern during implicit reading in children and young adults between the ages of 6 and 22. The authors observed increased activation in the left middle temporal and inferior frontal gyri and decreased activation in right inferotemporal regions. In addition, activation in left posterior superior temporal regions was positively correlated with phonological processing abilities in beginning readers. Schlaggar et al. highlighted the importance of controlling for performance differences in fMRI tasks by comparing 7- to 10-year-olds with adult readers (Schlaggar et al., 2002). Some differences in frontal and posterior brain correlates between the two groups were directly related to maturational differences, but others could be explained by discrepancies in performance.

To date, no study has employed a longitudinal design to examine the development of reading-related processes (e.g., phonological processing or rapid auditory processing [RAP]) in prereading children using fMRI. In addition, brain changes accompanying reading–fluency development in children or adolescents remain largely unexamined.

NEURAL CORRELATES OF DEVELOMENTAL DYSLEXIA: PHONOLOGICAL PROCESSING

There is considerable evidence for neurological impairments in children and adults with DD (Schlaggar & McCandliss, 2007). Multiple fMRI studies of phonological processing have revealed dysfunction within the left parietotemporal and occipitotemporal cortex of adults and children with DD, as well as reduced or absent activation in perisylvian, occipitotemporal, and parietotemporal cortical regions (Horowitz, Rumsey, & Donohue, 1998; Paulesu et al., 1996; Shaywitz et al., 2002; Simos, Breier, Fletcher, Bergman, & Papanicolaou, 2000; Wagner & Torgesen, 1987). The consistent hypoactivation of the left perisylvian, occipitotemporal, and parietotemporal cortices in individuals with DD, along with increased activation in these regions following successful remediation, support the notion that these areas are essential for phonological processing and reading (Eden et al., 2004; Simos et al., 2002). Children with DD display this pattern of hypoactivation when compared with age-matched average readers but also when compared with younger children who have equivalent reading skills (Hoeft et al., 2007). This suggests that the observed alterations are not due to delayed maturation but seem characteristic of DD. Research has documented increased activity in anterior language regions in individuals with DD compared with controls, during tasks that demand increasing phonological analysis (Paulesu et al., 1996; Shaywitz et al., 1998; Zeffiro & Eden, 2000). However, Hoeft et al. (2007) show that these differences appear to reflect reading ability rather than a characteristic of DD, because no differences between children with DD and younger reading-matched children were observed in these regions.

NEURAL CORRELATES OF
DEVELOPMENTAL DYSLEXIA: RAPID AUDITORY PROCESSING

An fMRI study revealed that typically developing adults display left prefrontal activation in response to rapidly changing acoustic stimuli relative to slowly changing acoustic stimuli (Temple et al., 2000). Individuals with DD showed no differential left frontal response for the same contrast, suggesting a dysfunction of the brain circuit that processes rapidly changing nonlinguistic auditory percepts. Two of the participants with DD took part in a remediation program that resulted in increased left prefrontal cortex activation, demonstrating the possibility of establishing changes within the left prefrontal regions after intensive training.

To date only one study has examined the neural correlates of rapid auditory temporal processing in school-age children with DD using fMRI (Gaab et al., 2007). Twenty-two children with DD and 23 control children underwent fMRI while listening to nonlinguistic acoustic stimuli with either rapid or slow transitions. Typical readers showed activation for rapid transitions, compared with slow transitions, in the left prefrontal cortex (Figure 17.1A). Children with DD did not show a differential response in these regions (Figure 17.1). After 8 weeks of remediation focused primarily on RAP, children with DD showed significant improvements in language and reading skills and exhibited activation for rapid relative to slow transitions in the left prefrontal cortex (Figure 17.1D). These results suggest an important role for RAP in reading development.

MORPHOLOGICAL MARKERS OF DEVELOPMENTAL DYSLEXIA

The functional differences observed between individuals with dyslexia and without DD have been related to differences in brain morphology. Measures of brain volume have revealed structural differences in regions that previously demonstrated functional differences, such as the occipitotemporal, parietotemporal, inferior frontal, and cerebellar regions (Eckert, 2004). When assessed using voxel-based morphometry, individuals with DD show decreased grey matter volume indices (relative to controls) in left occipitotemporal and temporoparietal cortices, bilateral fusiform (Brambati et al., 2004; Kronbichler et al., 2008), and lingual gyri (Silani et al., 2005). Grey matter volume indices in these areas are positively correlated with reading subskills such as rapid automatized naming (RAN) and phonological processing (e.g., Kronbichler et al., 2008). A study in 2010 from our laboratory revealed significantly reduced grey matter volume indices in prereading children with—compared with children without—a family history of DD in left occipitotemporal and bilateral parietotemporal regions and in the left fusiform and right lingual gyri. Grey matter volume indices in left hemispheric occipitotemporal and parietotemporal regions also correlated positively with RAN skills prior to reading onset (Raschle, Chang, & Gaab, 2010).

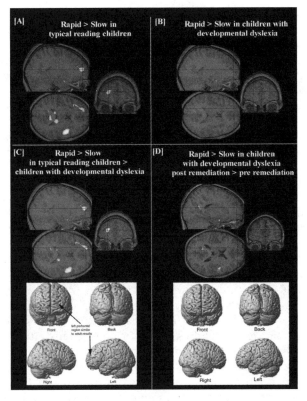

Figure 17.1. Brain activation in response to rapid versus slow auditory stimuli in children with and without developmental dyslexia (DD). Typical readers showed activation for rapid compared to slow transitions in the left prefrontal cortex (A). Children with DD did not show a differential response in these regions (B). A direct comparison between the two groups can be seen in C. After 8 weeks of remediation focused primarily on rapid auditory processing, children with DD showed significant improvements in language and reading skills and exhibited activation for rapid relative to slow transitions in the left prefrontal cortex (D). (From Gaab, N., Gabrieli, J.D., Deutsch, G.K., Tallal, P., & Temple, E. [2007]. Neural correlates of rapid auditory processing are disrupted in children with developmental dyslexia and ameliorated with training; an fMRI study. *Restorative Neurology and Neuroscience, 25*[3–4], pp. 295–310. © 2007, with permission from IOS Press.)

Similarly, white matter structure, as characterized by diffusion tensor imaging, appears less organized in the left posterior brain regions of children with DD. This difference in organization is indexed, for example, by reduced fractional anisotropy (FA) in adults and children with DD or reading impairment (e.g., Niogi & McCandliss, 2006). FA values are also positively correlated with standardized reading scores in adults and children with DD and among typical readers (e.g., Deutsch et al., 2005).

FAMILY RISK OF DEVELOPMENTAL DYSLEXIA

Genetics seem to play a key role in susceptibility to DD. Many studies conducted since 1990 have identified chromosomal sites related to

DD susceptibility (for a review, see Galaburda, LoTurco, Ramus, Fitch, & Rosen, 2006). Strong evidence of heredity derives from molecular–genetic studies (e.g., Cardon et al., 1994; Grigorenko et al., 1997), twin studies (e.g., DeFries, Plomin, & LaBuda, 1987), and family studies (e.g., Pennington, 1991; Wolff & Melngailis, 1994). It is interesting to note that all reported candidate genes for DD susceptibility are thought to participate in brain development (Galaburda et al., 2006) and impairments in brain development have been observed in children with a diagnosis of DD (see Morphological Markers of Developmental Dyslexia).

Risk for reading disability has been shown to be greater among relatives of those with DD than in the general population (Olson, Forsberg, Gayan, & DeFries, 1999; Pennington, 1991). Approximately 18% of girls and 40% of boys who have at least one parent with a diagnosis of DD exhibit DD themselves (Pennington & Smith, 1988). However, others have reported higher increases with no gender discrepancies (Pennington & Lefly, 2001; Puolakanaho et al., 2007; Scarborough, 1990; Snowling, Gallagher, & Frith, 2003). Approximately 35% of adults who had reading problems in childhood reported that one or more of their children experience reading difficulties (Finucci, Whitehouse, Isaacs, & Childs, 1984). Similarly, a prospective study on children who have at least one parent with DD reported that about 30% of these children go on to exhibit reading difficulties in second grade. This rate increased to approximately 60% when reading difficulties were defined using more stringent psychometric methods (described in Grigorenko, Wood, Meyer, & Pauls, 2000). In summary, studies of families with DD suggest that it is strongly heritable, occurring in up to 68% of identical twins and up to 50% of individuals who have a first-degree relative with DD (Finucci et al., 1984; Volger, DeFries, & Decker, 1985). Although some of these results are controversial due to the genetic heterogeneity of the disorder, available evidence suggests that DD could be the result of atypical migration and maturation of neurons during early development (Galaburda et al., 2006).

BEHAVIORAL PREDICTORS OF
DEVELOPMENTAL DYSLEXIA PRIOR TO READING ONSET

Studies that focus on behavioral premarkers of DD have revealed a broad range of linguistic impairments in preschoolers and kindergartners who later exhibit weak reading scores. These early linguistic impairments include phonological processing/awareness (e.g., Nation & Hulme, 1997; Snowling, Gallagher, & Frith, 2003), phonological production (Tunmer, 1989), speech perception (Flax, Realpe-Bonilla, Roesler, Choudhury, & Benasich, 2009; Pennington & Lefly, 2001), syntax production (Butler et al., 2001), syntactic awareness (Tunmer, 1989), syntax comprehension (Share, McGee, & Silva, 1989), language comprehension (Flax et al., 2009), object naming (Share et al., 1989; Wolf & Goodglass,

1986), and receptive vocabulary (Share et al., 1989; Stanovich & Siegel, 1994). Several studies also reported that RAN abilities, letter name knowledge, and verbal short-term memory abilities prior to kindergarten predict later reading disability (Badian, 1992; Gallaghar, Frith, & Snowling, 2000; Snowling et al., 2003).

The first large-scale prospective study in children with and without a family history of DD was conducted by Scarborough et al. (1990). Children who were later diagnosed with reading impairments were compared with children not diagnosed with reading difficulty on a range of measures gathered from 2½ years of age. The study revealed that DD is characterized by early deficits in phonological processing and oral language difficulties in the preschool years.

A similar study conducted within the Finnish language system (Puolakanaho et al., 2008) identified that the key childhood predictors of reading problems were phonological awareness, short-term memory, RAN, expressive vocabulary, pseudoword repetition, and letter naming (Puolakanaho et al., 2007).

NEURAL PREDICTORS OF
DEVELOPMENTAL DYSLEXIA PRIOR TO READING ONSET

Several studies have investigated the neural correlates of language and prereading skills in infants and children with a family history of DD or language impairment. Using electroencephalography (EEG), for example, Guttorm et al. (2005) exposed newborn infants to syllabic sounds and reported a slower bilateral shift in polarity, from positive to negative, in infants at risk for DD compared with control infants. Differences observed in the left hemisphere were associated with verbal memory skills at age 5, and differences observed in the right hemisphere were correlated with poorer receptive skills at age 2½.

Similar predictors of language skills based on newborn event-related potentials (ERPs) have been reported (Molfese, 2000). Differences between 6-month-olds with a family history of DD compared with those without a family history have been found for consonant–duration changes (Leppänen et al., 2002) and syllabic sounds (e.g., Guttorm et al., 2005) in both hemispheres. Benasich and Tallal (2002) showed that impairments in RAP abilities at age 6–9 months both preceded and predicted subsequent language delays at ages 12–16, 24, and 36 months (Benasich & Tallal, 2002; Choudhury, Leppänen, Leevers, & Benasich, 2007). Additional electrophysiological measurements in the same infants showed differences for rapidly, but not slowly, presented tone sequences in infants with a family history of language impairments (Benasich et al., 2006). These differences, observed selectively in the frontal and central areas of the left hemisphere, were consistent with other electrophysiological studies in newborn infants at risk for language or reading impairments (e.g., Lyytinen et al., 2004).

As of 2011, only a few studies have reported neural predictors of reading abilities (Maurer et al., 2009) in children with and without a familial risk of DD. In a 5-year longitudinal study, neurophysiologic and behavior measures obtained in kindergarteners with and without a family history of DD predicted reading outcome after reading instruction. Neurophysiologic measures in kindergarten improved reading prediction in comparison to behavior measures alone and were the only predictor for reading success in fifth grade.

Furthermore, Specht et al. (2009) compared 6-year-old readers at risk for DD to controls using fMRI and observed activation differences within the posterior reading network for visual stimuli, which differed in their demands for literacy processing.

WHY IT IS IMPORTANT TO PREDICT DYSLEXIA IN PREREADERS

Finding accurate predictors of DD has crucial clinical, psychological, and social implications. Others often perceive children with DD as "lazy," and their struggle to learn is often misinterpreted as the result of a negative attitude or poor behavior (Beitchman et al., 1986; Wagner, Blackorby, Cameto, Hebbeler, & Newman, 1993). Negative classroom experiences can intensify anxiety, frustration, and confusion and lead to decreased self-esteem (Humphrey & Mullins, 2004; Riddick, Sterling, Farmer, & Morgan, 1999). Thus, children with DD and other learning disabilities are more likely to drop out of high school (Marder & D'Amico, 1992), are less likely than their peers to go on to programs of higher education (Quinn, Rutherford, & Leone, 2001), and are more apt to enter the juvenile justice system (Wagner et al., 1993)

Early identification of predictors for reading ability and disability in prereading children offers a chance to eliminate or at least reduce significant personal and social costs. Early predictors of reading ability can help educators and scientists find ways to support the academic and cognitive growth of children with DD potentially through implementation of new remediation programs. The development and extension of supportive social networks for parents and children may lead to improved psychosocial development and experiences for these children. Social networks for those at risk may also lead to strategies that will reduce the severity of DD after reading onset, as well as reduce child and parental stress and improve the overall family dynamic.

Many clinicians, educators, and parents believe that DD cannot be identified reliably until third grade, after children have already exhibited substantial reading difficulty. However, when the identification and diagnosis of a child with reading abilities occur in mid elementary school, the delayed development of reading has already affected his or her vocabulary skills and motivation to read (Pihko et al., 1999), thus leading to missed opportunities for the development of much-needed comprehension strategies (Guttorm, Leppänen, Richardson, & Lyytinen, 2001). Children who are weak readers at the end of first grade remain poor readers by the end of elementary school (Snowling, 2000; Wagner, Torgesen, & Rashotte, 1999). Studies have shown that reading remediation is most effective in kindergarten and first grade. Specifically, when beginning readers identified as at risk were provided with intensive instruction, approximately 60%–90% showed average reading ability following intervention (Vellutino, Fletcher, Snowling, & Scanlon, 2004). However, there are issues with both the sensitivity and specificity with which children with reading problems are identified or misidentified. Criteria that are too conservative may lead to low sensitivity, leaving many children with DD unidentified. Liberal criteria will lead to low specificity and potentially to children mistakenly identified as at risk. The ability to assign individualized education programs for children prior to reading onset is most useful in implementing customized curriculums for children at true risk for DD and so distribute available funds to children who really need it.

ADVANCES IN PEDIATRIC NEUROIMAGING ENABLE STUDY OF THE PREREADING BRAIN

Since the mid 1990s, there has been a significant increase in the use of MRI to investigate the neural basis of human perception, cognition, and behavior (Boecker et al., 2008). This noninvasive imaging method has allowed researchers to investigate typical and atypical brain development. Although advances in neuroimaging tools and techniques are evident, fMRI in pediatric populations continues to be used relatively infrequently (Bookheimer, 2000). Challenging factors associated with fMRI include time constraints, movement restriction, scanner background noise, and general unfamiliarity with the MR scanner environment (e.g., Poldrack, Pare-Blagoev, & Grant, 2002). A progressive use of neuroimaging in younger age groups, however, will further understanding of brain development and early detection of children at risk for developmental disorders such as DD. Various techniques to ensure comfort and cooperation of young children during neuroimaging sessions have been reported. Play therapy (Pressdee, May, Eastman, & Grier, 1997), behavioral approaches (e.g., Slifer, Koontz, & Cataldo, 2002), scanning simulation (Rosenberg et al., 1997), the use of mock scanners (de Amorim e Silva, Mackenzie, Hallowell, Stewart, & Ditchfield, 2006), and basic relaxation techniques (Lukins, Davan, & Drummond, 1997) have all led to improvements in children's compliance and MRI data quality. These strategies also increase the comfort of the children's families (Pressdee et al., 1997). Our research team has published a pediatric neuroimaging video protocol with guidelines that have proven successful in young children. This protocol presents hands-on solutions that address the main practical challenges that may prevent research groups from performing fMRI experiments on young children (Raschle et al., 2009).

PRELIMINARY RESULTS FROM THE
BOSTON LONGITUDINAL DYSLEXIA STUDY

To what extent the brain differences are related to the cause versus the consequence of DD is unknown because all fMRI studies as of 2012 have been performed with children who have already experienced years of reading failure. The brain differences seen in children with a history of reading failure could be the root biological cause of DD; however, it may instead be the brain's adaptation to years of struggling to read. In our on-going Boston Longitudinal Dyslexia Study (BOLD), we aim to determine if previously observed differences in behavioral markers, brain structure, and neural correlates of phonological processing or RAP observed in school-age children and adults with DD are already present in children at risk for DD prior to reading onset.

In the BOLD study, healthy, native English-speaking children with (FHD+) and without (FHD-) a family history of DD participate in a behavioral and fMRI/MRI session prior to their first year of kindergarten. Approximately 1 year after the initial session, a reading evaluation screen is conducted. Matched for age, gender, and nonverbal IQ (Kaufman Brief Intelligence Test, Second Edition; KBIT-2; Kaufman & Kaufman, 2004), children are tested on language and prereading skills using assessments such as the Clinical Evaluation of Language Fundamentals Preschool Second Edition (CELF/Preschool-2; Semel, Wiig, & Secord, 2003), the Comprehensive Test of Phonological Processing (CTOPP; Gallaghar et al., 2000), and the Rapid Automatized Naming Test (RAN; Wolf & Denckla, 2005). In addition to an eligibility questionnaire, the Word Identification subtest of the Woodcock Reading Mastery Test (WRMT; Woodcock, 1987) is used to determine that all children are prereaders. Two questionnaires are used to describe each child's home literacy environment and socioeconomic status. RAP skills are also tested using a temporal order judgment task and a rise time of amplitude envelope onset task. Children will be retested for 4 consecutive years using functional imaging and behavior measures until a positive or negative diagnosis of DD can be established.

In the preliminary sample presented here, 27 children (14 FHD+ and 13 FHD-; mean age 67.3 months) (Table 17.1) completed the initial visit and 13 children (7 FHD+ and 6 FHD-) have completed their follow-up visit (within 50–54 weeks after their initial visit; Table 17.2). In the second year, the same battery of tests was used with a few additions: spelling (Wide Range Achievement Test; WRAT; Wilkinson, 1993), passage comprehension (Woodcock Reading Mastery Test; WRMT; Woodcock, 1987), reading fluency (Woodcock-Johnson Tests of Achievement; WJ; Woodcock, McGrew, & Mather, 2001), and speeded sight word efficiency and phonemic decoding (Test of Word and Reading Efficiency; TOWRE; Turgescent, Wagner, & Reshot, 1999).

In our initial year of testing, significantly lower scores on several language measures, phonological processing, and RAN were observed for

Table 17.1. Preliminary psychometric results for Year 1 of the Boston Longitudinal Dyslexia Study (BOLD) (all children are prereaders at this point).

		FHD+	FHD-	Sig. 2-tailed
		Mean ± SD	Mean ± SD	FDH+ vs. FHD-
N		14	13	
Age (months)		68.9	65.7	0.101
Behavioral measures				
CELF	Core language	101.9 ±12.31	110.5 ± 11.4	0.075
	Receptive language	101.8 ± 17.11	109.8 ± 10.8	0.171
	Expressive language	98.9 ± 10.01	110.9 ± 12.1	0.009
	Language content	98.2 ± 12.71	109.8 ± 11.1	0.020
	Language structure	101.2 ± 13.61	110.7 ± 11.9	0.069
CTOPP	Elison	8.8 ± 1.7	10.5 ± 2.2	0.031
	Blending	10.6 ± 2.1	11.9 ± 1.4	0.070
	Non-word repetition	9.8 ± 2.2	10.8 ± 1.9	0.185
RAN	Objects	86.4 ± 12.3	105.7 ± 12.1	0.000
	Colors	87.9 ± 15.1	108.3 ± 9.8	0.000
	Numbers	79.3 ± 12.4	102.9 ± 9.2	0.000
KBIT	Verbal ability	109.1 ± 9.5	114.6 ± 7.7	0.115
	Nonverbal activity	97.9 ± 9.5	102.5 ± 11.8	0.229
RAP	Rapid auditory prcocessing (two tones), % correct	54.42 ± 17.3	71.16 ± 14.8	0.051
Dino	Rise Time of envelope onset ms	34.20 ± 3.78	32.46 ± 3.92	0.291

Key: CELF, Clinical Evaluation of Language Fundamentals Expressive Language (Semel, Wiig, & Secord, 1986); CTOPP, Comprehensive Test of Phonological Processing (Wagner, Torgesen, & Rashotte, 1999); RAN, Rapid Automatized Naming Test (Wolf & Denckla, 2005); KBIT, Kaufman Brief Intelligence Test (Kaufman & Kaufman, 1997); Dino, Rise Time perception; FHD+, family history of dyslexia; FHD-, no family history of dyslexia.

FHD+ children compared to FHD- children. A trend was also observed for RAP ($p = 0.051$). Our preliminary results from the longitudinal follow-up indicate significantly lower scores for FHD+ children for timed and untimed single-word reading, passage comprehension, and spelling (Table 17.2).

During our first-year neuroimaging session, each child performed (among other components) one RAP and one phonological processing task in the MR scanner. We examined the neural correlates of RAP employing the same stimuli and task design as previously used in children and adults with a diagnosis of DD (Tallal, 2004; Temple et al., 2000). Preliminary analysis using 20 of the 27 children (12 FHD+ and 8 FHD-) revealed increased activation in the prefrontal, inferior parietal, inferior temporal, and auditory regions in FHD- children for fast compared with slow transitions. The same contrast revealed increased activation

Raschle et al.

Table 17.2. Preliminary psychometric results for Year 2 of the Boston Longitudinal Dyslexia Study (BOLD).

		FHD+	FHD-	Sig. 2-tailed
		Mean ± SD	Mean ± SD	FDH+ vs. FHD-
N		7	6	
Behavioral Measures				
CELF	Core language	105.7 ± 13.3	110.5 ± 7.5	0.454
	Receptive language	104.1 ± 14.0	109.0 ± 7.2	0.461
	Expressive language	103.3 ± 11.6	112.0 ± 8.7	0.196
	Language content	99.5 ± 12.4	109.3 ± 10.3	0.156
	Language structure	105.0 ± 14.7	116.2 ± 8.0	0.165
CTOPP	Elison	9.8 ± 1.6	11.8 ± 2.2	0.095
	Blending	10.5 ± 1.5	11.3 ± 1.0	0.320
	Non-word repetition	8.7 ± 2.1	9.5 ± 1.8	0.499
RAN	Objects	96.8 ± 21.0	103.8 ± 10.5	0.527
	Colors	97.7 ± 19.4	110.6 ± 10.2	0.139
	Numbers	92.8 ± 27.5	109.5 ± 11.4	0.193
KBIT	Verbal ability	120.5 ± 6.3	124.5 ± 12.2	0.718
	Nonverbal activity	103.0 ± 9.8	104.0 ± 21.9	0.938
TOWRE	Sight word reading efficiency	87.1 ± 10.4	114.2 ± 10.2	0.002
	Phonemic decoding	94.8 ± 8.3	112.0 ± 11.4	0.018
WRAT	Spelling	95.4 ± 8.3	107.6 ± 4.9	0.023
WRMT	Word ID	95.85 ± 14.0	128.6 ± 13.9	0.001
	Word attack	106.2 ± 14.4	117.4 ± 6.7	0.155
	Passage comprehension	97.0 ± 7.8	117.4 ± 7.9	0.004

Key: CELF, Clinical Evaluation of Language Fundamentals Expressive Language (Semel, Wiig, & Secord, 1986); CTOPP, Comprehensive Test of Phonological Processing (Wagner, Torgesen, & Rashotte, 1999); RAN, Rapid Automatized Naming Test (Wolf & Denckla, 2005); KBIT, Kaufman Brief Intelligence Test (Kaufman & Kaufman, 1997); TOWRE, Test of Word Reading Efficiency (Turgescent, Wagner, & Reshot, 1999); WRAT, Wide Range Achievement Test (Wilkinson, 1993); WRMT, Woodcock Reading Mastery Tests (Woodcock, 1987); FHD+, family history of dyslexia; FHD-, no family history of dyslexia.

in FHD+ children in the inferior frontal, inferior temporal, and inferior parietal regions. Direct comparison between the two groups showed increased activation (FHD- > FHD+) in the left prefrontal, bilateral auditory, and bilateral inferior parietal regions (Figure 17.2). These preliminary results suggest that prereading FHD+ children already show a disrupted response to rapid acoustic stimuli in brain regions similar to those seen in children and adults with a diagnosis of DD.

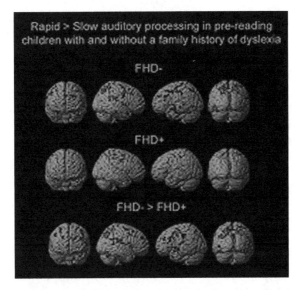

Figure 17.2. Preliminary imaging results for the contrast rapid transition > slow transition for children without a family history (FHD-), with a family history (FHD +), and a direct comparison between the two groups.

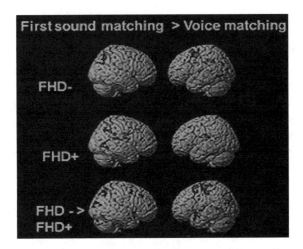

Figure 17.3. The contrast of first sound matching > voice matching (phonological processing) in children without a family history (FHD-), with a family history (FHD+), and a direct comparison between the two groups.

To determine if previously observed alterations in the functional neural correlates of phonological processing in school-aged children and adults (e.g., Shaywitz et al., 2002) can be detected in children prior to reading onset, a phonological processing task was added to the neuroimaging session. Preliminary analysis on this first sound-matching task, compared with a voice-matching control task, assessed performance of 11 of the 27 children (6 FHD+ and 5 FHD-). Activation within the left-hemispheric parietotemporal, occipitotemporal, and perisylvian regions was observed for FHD- children, whereas FHD+ children displayed more right-lateralized activations within the parietotemporal, occipitotemporal, and perisylvian regions. Direct comparison between the two groups revealed increased activation within the left-hemispheric parietotemporal, occipitotemporal, and perisylvian regions for FHD- children (Figure 17.3).

These early results suggest that prereading FHD+ children already show reduced activation within the perisylvian, occipitotemporal, and parietotemporal cortical regions when compared to FHD- children. These results are consistent with previous studies in children and adults with a diagnosis of DD.

As a third part of our neuroimaging session, we examined if the previously observed structural differences in school-age children and adults with DD were already observable in children prior to reading onset. Our results indicate that grey matter alterations in children and adults with DD in the parietotemporal and occipitotemporal brain regions and the left fusiform and right lingual gyri are already observable in prereading FHD+ children and correlate with prereading skills such as RAN (Raschle et al., 2010), suggesting that structural alterations in DD may be present at birth or develop in early childhood.

CONCLUSION

Overall, prereading children with a family history of DD display behavioral, functional, and structural differences relative to prereading children without a family history of DD. These results suggest that differences in individuals with DD are most likely present at birth or develop within the first years of life and thus are not due to experience-dependent brain changes resulting from DD itself. Our longitudinal design (BOLD study) will determine how these networks develop and whether these behavioral, functional, and structural alterations may be used as premarkers to identify young children at risk for DD prior to reading onset.

REFERENCES

Ahissar, M., Protopapas, A., Reid, M., & Merzenich, M.M. (2000). Auditory processing parallels reading abilities in adults. *Proceedings of the National Academy of Sciences, USA, 97*(12), 6832–6837. doi:10.1073/pnas.97.12.6832

Badian, N.A. (1992). Nonverbal learning disability, school behavior, and dyslexia. *Annals of Dyslexia, 42*(1), 159–178. doi:10.1007/BF02654944

Beitchman, J.H., Nair, R., Clegg, M., Ferguson, B., & Patel, P.G. (1986). Prevalence of psychiatric disorders in children with speech and language disorders. *Journal of the Amerocam Academy of Child Psychiatry, 25*(4), 528–535. doi:10.1016/S0002-7138(10)60013-1

Benasich, A.A., Choudhury, N., Friedman, J.T., Realpe-Bonilla, T., Chojnowska, C., & Gou, Z. (2006). The infant as a prelinguistic model for language learning impairments: Predicting from event-related potentials to behavior. *Neuropsychologia, 44*(3), 396–411. doi:10.1016/j.neuropsychologia.2005.06.004

Benasich, A.A., & Tallal, P. (2002). Infant discrimination of rapid auditory cues predicts later language impairment. *Behavioural Brain Research, 136*(1), 31–49. doi:10.1016/S0166-4328(02)00098-0

Boecker, H., Scheef, L., Jankowski, J., Zimmermann, N., Born, M., & Heep, A. (2008). Current stage of fMRI applications in newborns and children during the first year of life. *Rofo, 180*(8), 707–714.

Bookheimer, S.Y. (2000). Methodological issues in pediatric neuroimaging. *Mental Retardation and Developmental Disabilities Research Reviews, 6*(3), 161–165. doi:10.1002/1098-2779(2000)6:3<161::AID-MRDD2>3.3.CO;2-N

Brambati, S.M., Termine, C., Ruffino, M., Stella, G., Fazio, F., Cappa, S.F., & Perani, D. (2004). Regional reductions of grey matter volume in familial dyslexia. *Neurology, 63*(4), 742–745.

Butler, P.D., Schechter, I., Zemon, V., Schwartz, S.G., Greenstein, V.C., Gordon, J., ... Javitt, D.C. (2001). Dysfunction of early-stage visual processing in schizophrenia. *American Journal of Psychiatry, 158*(7), 1126–1133. doi:10.1176/appi.ajp.158.7.1126

Cardon, L.R., Smith, S.D., Fulker, D.W., Kimberling, W.J., Pennington, B.F., & DeFries, J.C. (1994). Quantitative trait locus for reading disability on chromosome 6. *Science, 266*(5183), 276–279. doi:10.1126/science.7939663

Chiappe, P. (2002). Why the timing deficit hypothesis does not explain reading disability in adults. *Reading and Writing: An Interdisciplinary Journal, 15,* 73–107.

Choudhury, N., Leppänen, P.H., Leevers, H.J., & Benasich, A.A. (2007). Infant information processing and family history of specific language impairment: Converging evidence for RAP deficits from two paradigms. *Developmental Science, 10,* 213–236. doi:10.1111/j.1467-7687.2007.00546

Critchley, M. (1970). The dyslexic child. In C.C. Thomas (Ed.), *Behavior* (pp. 169–176). San Diego, CA: Academic.

de Amorim e Silva, C.J., Mackenzie, A., Hallowell, L.M., Stewart, S.E., & Ditchfield, M.R. (2006). Practice MRI: Reducing the need for sedation and general anaesthesia in children undergoing MRI. *Australasian Radiology, 50*(4), 319–323. doi:10.1111/j.1440-1673.2006.01590

DeFries, J.C., Plomin, R., & LaBuda, M.C. (1987). Genetic stability of cognitive development from childhood to adulthood. *Developmental Psychology, 23*(1), 4–12.

Deutsch, G.K., Dougherty, R.F., Bammer, R., Siok, W.T., Gabrieli, J.D., & Wandell, B. (2005). Children's reading performance is correlated with white matter structure measured by diffusion tensor imaging. *Cortex, 41*(3), 354–363. doi:10.1016/S0010-9452(08)70272-7

Eckert, M. (2004). Neuroanatomical markers for dyslexia: A review of dyslexia structural imaging studies. *Neuroscientist, 10*(4), 362–371. doi:10.1177/1073858404263596

Eden, G.F., Jones, K.M., Cappell, K., Gareau, L., Wood, F.B., Zeffiro, T.A., ... Flowers, D.L. (2004). Neural changes following remediation in adult developmental dyslexia. *Neuron, 44*(3), 411–422. doi:10.1016/j.neuron.2004.10.019

Finucci, J.M., Whitehouse, C.C., Isaacs, S.D., & Childs, B. (1984). Derivation and validation of a quantitative definition of specific reading disability for adults. *Developmental Medicine and Child Neurology, 26*(2), 143–153. doi:10.1111/j.1469-8749.1984.tb04425

Flax, J.F., Realpe-Bonilla, T., Roesler, C., Choudhury, N., & Benasich, A. (2009). Using early standardized language measures to predict later language and early reading outcomes in children at high risk for language-learning impairments. *Journal of Learning Disabilities, 42*(1), 61–75. doi:10.1177/0022219408326215

Flowers, D.L. (1994). Neuropsychological profiles of persistent reading disability and reading improvement. In R.M. Joshi & C.K. Leong (Eds.), *Developmental and aquired dyslexia: Neuropsychological and neurolinguistic perspectives* (pp. 61–78). Boston, MA: Kluwer Academic Publishers.

Francis, D.J., Shaywitz, S.E., Stuebing, K.K., Shaywitz, B.A., & Fletcher, J.M. (1996). Developmental lag versus deficit models of reading disability: A longitudinal, individual growth curves analysis. *Journal of Educational Psychology, 88*(1), 3–17. doi:10.1037//0022-0663.88.1.3

Gaab, N., Gabrieli, J.D., Deutsch, G.K., Tallal, P., & Temple, E. (2007). Neural correlates of rapid auditory processing are disrupted in children with developmental dyslexia and ameliorated with training: An fMRI study. *Restorative Neurology and Neuroscience, 25*(3–4), 295–310.

Galaburda, A.M., LoTurco, J., Ramus, F., Fitch, R.H., & Rosen, G.D. (2006). From genes to behavior in developmental dyslexia. *Nature Neuroscience, 9*(10), 1213–1217. doi:10.1038/nn1772

Gallaghar, A., Frith, U., & Snowling, M.J. (2000). Precursors of literacy delay among children at genetic risk of dyslexia. *Journal of Child Psychology and Psychiatry, 41*(2), 203–213. doi:10.1017/S0021963099005284

Grigorenko, E.L., Wood, F.B., Meyer, M.S., Hart, L.A., Speed, W.C., Shuster, A., & Pauls, D.L. (1997). Susceptibility loci for distinct components of developmental dyslexia on chromosomes 6 and 15. *American Journal of Human Genetics, 60*(1), 27–39.

Grigorenko, E.L., Wood, F.B., Meyer, M.S., & Pauls, D.L. (2000). Chromosome 6p influences on different dyslexia-related cognitive processes: Further confirmation. *American Journal of Human Genetics, 66*(2), 715–723. doi:10.1086/302755

Guttorm, T.K., Leppänen, P.H., Poikkeus, A.M., Eklund, K.M., Lyytinen, P., & Lyytinen, H. (2005). Brain event-related potentials (ERPs) measured at birth predict later language development in children with and without familial risk for dyslexia. *Cortex, 41*(3), 291–303. doi:10.1016/S0010-9452(08)70267-3

Guttorm, T.K., Leppänen, P.H., Richardson, U., & Lyytinen, H. (2001). Event-related potentials and consonant differentiation in newborns with familial risk for dyslexia. *Journal of Learning Disabilities, 34*(6), 534–544. doi:10.1177/002221940103400606

Hoeft, F., Ueno, T., Reiss, A.L., Meyler, A., Whitfield-Gabrieli, S., Glover, G.H., ... Gabrieli, J. (2007). Prediction of children's reading skills using behavioral, functional, and structural neuroimaging measures. *Behavioral Neuroscience, 121*(3), 602–613. doi:10.1037/0735-7044.121.3.602

Horowitz, B., Rumsey, J.M., & Donohue, B.C. (1998). Functional connectivity of the angular gyrus in normal reading and dyslexia. *Proceedings of the National Academy of Sciences, USA, 95*(15), 8939–8944. doi:10.1073/pnas.95.15.8939

Humphrey, N., & Mullins, P.M. (2004). Self-concept and self-esteem in developmental dyslexia. *Journal of Research in Special Education Needs, 2*(2). doi:10.1111/j.1471-3802.2002.00163

Juel, C. (1988). Learning to read and write: A longitudinal study of 54 children from first through fourth grades. *Journal of Educational Psychology, 80*(4), 437–447. doi:10.1037//0022-0663.80.4.437

Kaufman, A.S., & Kaufman, N.L. (2004). *KBIT-2: Kaufman brief intelligence test* (2nd ed.). Minneapolis, MN: NCS Pearson.

Kronbichler, M., Wimmer, H., Staffen, W., Hutzler, F., Mair, A., & Ladurner, G. (2008). Developmental dyslexia: Grey matter abnormalities in the occipito-temporal cortex. *Human Brain Mapping, 29*(5), 613–625. doi:10.1002/hbm.20425

Leppänen, P.H., Richardson, U., Pihko, E., Eklund, K.M., Guttorm, T.K., Aro, M., & Lyytinen, H. (2002). Brain responses to changes in speech sound durations differ between infants with and without familial risk for dyslexia. *Developmental Neuropsychology, 22*(1), 407–422. doi:10.1207/S15326942dn2201_4

Liberman, I.Y., Shankweiler, D., & Liberman, A.M. (1989). The alphabetic principle and learning to read. In D. Shankweiler & I.Y. Liberman (Eds.), *Phonology and reading disability: Solving the reading puzzle* (pp. 1–33). Ann Arbor, MI: University of Michigan Press.

Lukins, R., Davan, I.G., & Drummond, P.D. (1997). A cognitive behavioural approach to preventing anxiety during magnetic resonance imaging. *Journal of Behavior Therapy and Experimental Psychiatry, 28*(2), 97–104. doi:10.1016/S0005-7916(97)00006-2

Lyytinen, H., Aro, M., Eklund, K., Erskine, J., Guttorm, T., Laakso, M.L., ... Richardson, U. (2004). The development of children at familial risk for dyslexia: Birth to early school age. *Annals of Dyslexia, 54*(2), 184–220. doi:10.1007/s11881-004-0010-3

Marder, C., & D'Amico, R. (1992). *How well are youth with disabilities really do-*

ing? A comparison of youth with disabilities and youth in general. Menlo Park, CA: SRI International.

Maurer, U., Bucher, K., Brem, S., Benz, R., Kranz, F., Schulz, E., ... Brandeis, D. (2009). Neurophysiology in preschool improves behavioral prediction of reading ability throughout primary school. Biological Psychiatry, 66, 341–348. doi:10.1016/j.biopsych.2009.02.031

McArthur, G.M. (2009). Auditory processing disorders: Can they be treated? Current Opinion in Neurology, 22(2), 137–143. doi:10.1097/WCO.0b013e328326f6b1

Molfese, D.L. (2000). Predicting dyslexia at 8 years of age using neonatal brain responses. Brain and Language, 72(3), 238–245. doi:10.1006/brln.2000.2287

Nation, K., & Hulme, C. (1997). Phonemic segmentation, not onset-rime segmentation, predicts early reading and spelling skills. Reading Research Quarterly, 32(2), 154–167. doi:10.1598/RRQ.32.2.2

Niogi, S.N., & McCandliss, B.D. (2006). Left lateralized white matter microstructure accounts for individual differences in reading ability and disability. Neuropsychologia, 44(11), 2178–2188. doi:10.1016/j.neuropsychologia.2006.01.011

Olson, R.K., Forsberg, H., Gayan, J., & DeFries, J.C. (1999). A behavioral-genetic analysis of reading disabilities and component processes. In R.M. Klein & P.A. McMullen (Eds.), Converging methods for understanding reading and dyslexia (pp. 133–153). Cambridge, MA: MIT Press.

Paulesu, E., Frith, U., Snowling, M., Gallagher, A., Morton, J., Frackowiak, R.S., & Frith, C.D. (1996). Is developmental dyslexia a disconnection syndrome? Evidence from PET scanning. Brain, 119 (Pt 1), 143–157.

Pennington, B.F. (1991). Annotation: The genetics of dyslexia. Journal of Child Psychology and Psychiatry, 31, 193–201.

Pennington, B.F., & Lefly, D.L. (2001). Early reading development in children at family risk for dyslexia. Child Development, 72(3), 816–833. doi:10.1111/1467-8624.00317

Pennington, B.F., & Smith, S.D. (1988). Genetic influences on learning disabilities: An update. Journal of Consulting and Clinical Psychology, 56(6), 817–823. doi:10.1037//0022-006X.56.6.817

Pihko, E., Leppänen, P.H., Eklund, K.M., Cheour, M., Guttorm, T.K., & Lyytinen, H. (1999). Cortical responses of infants with and without a genetic risk for dyslexia: I. Age effects. NeuroReport, 10(5), 901–905.

Poldrack, R.A., Pare-Blagoev, E.J., & Grant, P.E. (2002). Pediatric functional magnetic resonance imaging: Progress and challenges. Topics in Magnetic Resonance Imaging, 13(1), 61–70. doi:10.1097/00002142-200202000-00005

Pressdee, D., May, L., Eastman, E., & Grier, D. (1997). The use of play therapy in the preparation of children undergoing MR imaging. Clinical Radiology, 52(12), 945–947. doi:10.1016/S0009-9260(97)80229-2

Puolakanaho, A., Ahonen, T., Aro, M., Eklund, K., Leppänen, P.H., Poikkeus, A.M., ... Lyytinen, H. (2007). Very early phonological and language skills: Estimating individual risk of reading disability. Journal of Child Psychology and Psychiatry, 48(9), 923–931. doi:10.1111/j.1469-7610.2007.01763

Puolakanaho, A., Ahonen, T., Aro, M., Eklund, K., Leppänen, P.H., Poikkeus, A.M., ... Lyytinen, H. (2008). Developmental links of very early phonological and language skills to second grade reading outcomes: Strong to accuracy but only minor to fluency. Journal of Learning Disabilities, 41(4), 353–370. doi:10.1177/0022219407311747

Quinn, M.M., Rutherford, R.B., & Leone, P.E. (2001). Students with disabilities in correctional facilities. ERIC Digest. Arlington, VA: ERIC Clearinghouse on Disabilities and Gifted Education. (ERIC Identification No. ED461958).

Ramus, F. (2003). Developmental dyslexia: Specific phonological deficit or general sensorimotor dysfunction? Current Opinion in Neurobiology, 13(2), 212–218. doi:10.1016/S0959-4388(03)00035-7

Raschle, N.M., Chang, M., & Gaab, N. (2010). Structural brain alterations associated with dyslexia predate reading onset. Neuroimage, 57, 742–749. doi:10.1016/j.neuroimage.2010.09.055

Raschle, N.M., Lee, M., Buechler, R., Christodoulou, J.A., Chang, M., & Vakil, M. (2009). Making MR imaging child's play—Pediatric neuroimaging protocol, guidelines and procedure.

Journal of Visualized Experiments, 29, e1309. doi:10.3791/1309

Reed, M.A. (1989). Speech perception and the discrimination of brief auditory cues in reading disabled children. *Journal of Experimental Child Psychology, 48*(2), 270–292. doi:10.1016/0022-0965(89)90006-4

Riddick, B., Sterling, C., Farmer, M., & Morgan, S. (1999). Self-esteem and anxiety in the educational histories of adult dyslexic students. *Dyslexia, 5*(4), 227–248. doi:10.1002/(SICI)1099-0909(199912)5:4<227::AID-DYS146>3.3.CO;2-Y

Rosenberg, D.R., Sweeney, J.A., Gillen, J.S., Kim, J., Varanelli, M.J., O'Hearn, K.M., … Thulborn, K.R. (1997). Magnetic resonance imaging of children without sedation: preparation with simulation. *Journal of the American Academy of Child and Adolescent Psychiatry, 36*(6), 853–859. doi:10.1097/00004583-199706000-00024

Scarborough, H.S. (1990). Very early language deficits in dyslexic children. *Child Development, 61*(6), 1728–1743. doi:10.2307/1130834

Schlaggar, B.L., Brown, T.T., Lugar, H.M., Visscher, K.M., Miezin, F.M., & Petersen, S.E. (2002). Functional neuroanatomical differences between adults and school-age children in the processing of single words. *Science, 296*(5572), 1476–1479. doi:10.1126/science.1069464

Schlaggar, B.L., & McCandliss, B.D. (2007). Development of neural systems for reading. *Annual Review of Neuroscience, 30,* 475–503. doi:10.1146/annurev.neuro.28.061604.135645

Semel, E., Wiig, E., & Secord, W. (2003). CELF/Preschool-2: *Clinical evaluation of language fundamentals* (4th ed.). San Antonio, TX: Harcourt Assessment.

Share, D.L., McGee, R., & Silva, P.A. (1989). IQ and reading progress: A test of the capacity notion of IQ. *Journal of the American Academy of Child and Adolescent Psychiatry, 28*(1), 97–100. doi:10.1097/00004583-198901000-00018

Shaywitz, A., Shaywitz, S., Blachman, B.A., Pugh, K., Fulbright, R., Skudlarski, P., … Gore, J.C. (2004). Development of left occipitotemporal systems for skilled reading in children after a phonologically-based intervention. *Biological Psychiatry, 55*(9), 926–933. doi:10.1016/j.biopsych.2003.12.019

Shaywitz, B.A., Shaywitz, S.E., Pugh, K.R., Mencl, W.E., Fulbright, R.K., Skudlarski, P., … Gore, J.C. (2002). Disruption of posterior brain systems for reading in children with developmental dyslexia. *Biological Psychiatry, 52*(2), 101–110. doi:10.1016/S0006-3223(02)01365-3

Shaywitz, S. (1998). Dyslexia. *New England Journal of Medicine, 338*(5), 307–312. doi:10.1056/NEJM199801293380507

Shaywitz, S., Shaywitz, B., Pugh, K., Fulbright, R., Constable, R., Mencl, W., … Gore, J.C. (1998). Functional disruption in the organization of the brain for reading in dyslexia. *Proceedings of the National Academy of Sciences, USA, 95*(5), 2636–2641. doi:10.1073/pnas.95.5.2636

Shaywitz, S.E., Fletcher, J.M., Holahan, J.M., Schneider, A.E., Marchione, K.E., Stuebing, K.K., … Shaywitz, B.A. (1999). Persistence of dyslexia: The Connecticut longitudinal study at adolescence. *Pediatrics, 104,* 1351–1359. doi:10.1542/peds.104.6.1351

Shaywitz, S.E., Gruen, J.R., & Shaywitz, B.A. (2007). Management of dyslexia, its rationale, and underlying neurobiology. *Pediatric Clinics of North America, 54*(3), 609–623. doi:10.1016/j.pcl.2007.02.013

Silani, G., Frith, U., Démonet, J.F., Fazio, F., Perani, D., Price, C., … Paulesu, E. (2005). Brain abnormalities underlying altered activation in dyslexia: A voxel based morphometry study. *Brain, 128*(10), 2453–2461. doi:10.1093/brain/awh579

Simos, P.G., Breier, J.I., Fletcher, J.M., Bergman, E., & Papanicolaou, A.C. (2000). Cerebral mechanisms involved in word reading in dyslexic children: A magnetic source imaging approach. *Cerebral Cortex, 10*(8), 809–816. doi:10.1093/cercor/10.8.809

Simos, P.G., Fletcher, J.M., Bergman, E., Breier, J.I., Foorman, B.R., Castillo, E.M., … Papanicolaou, A.C. (2002). Dyslexia-specific brain activation profile becomes normal following successful remedial training. *Neurology, 58*(8), 1209–1213.

Slifer, K.J., Koontz, K.L., & Cataldo, M.F. (2002). Operant-contingency-based preparation of children for functional magnetic resonance imaging. *Journal of Applied Behavioral Analysis, 35*(2), 191–194. doi:10.1901/jaba.2002.35-191

Snowling, M.J. (2000). *Dyslexia.* Oxford, England: Blackwell.

Snowling, M.J., Gallagher, A., & Frith, U. (2003). Family risk of dyslexia is continuous: Individual differences in the precursors of reading skill. *Child Development, 74*(2), 358–373. doi:10.1111/1467-8624.7402003

Specht, K., Hugdahl, K., Ofte, S., Nygard, M., Bjornerud, A., Plante, E., & Helland, T. (2009). Brain activation on pre-reading tasks reveals at-risk status for dyslexia in 6-year-old children. *Scandinavian Journal of Psychology, 50*(1), 79–91. doi:10.1111/j.1467-9450.2008.00688

Stanovich, K.E., & Siegel, L.S. (1994). Phenotypic performance profile of children with reading disabilities: A regression-based test of phonological-core variable-difference model. *Journal of Educational Psychology, 86*(1), 24–53. doi:10.1037//0022-0663.86.1.24

Tallal, P. (2004). Improving language and literacy is a matter of time. *Nature Reviews Neuroscience, 5*(9), 721–728. doi:10.1038/nrn1499

Tallal, P., & Gaab, N. (2006). Dynamic auditory processing, musical experience and language development. *Trends in Neurosciences, 29*(7), 382–390. doi:10.1016/j.tins.2006.06.003

Tallal, P., & Piercy, M. (1973). Developmental aphasia: Impaired rate of non-verbal processing as a function of sensory modality. *Neuropsychologia, 11*(4), 389–398. doi:10.1016/0028-3932(73)90025-0

Tallal, P., & Piercy, M. (1974). Developmental aphasia: Rate of auditory processing and selective impairment of consonant perception. *Neuropsychologia, 12*(1), 83–93. doi:10.1016/0028-3932(74)90030-X

Temple, E., Poldrack, R.A., Protopapas, A., Nagarajan, S., Salz, T., Tallal, P., … Gabrieli, J.D.E. (2000). Disruption of the neural response to rapid acoustic stimuli in dyslexia: Evidence from functional MRI. *Proceedings of the National Academy of Science, USA, 97*(25), 13907–13912. doi:10.1073/pnas.240461697

Torgesen, J.K., & Buress, S. (1998). Consistency of reading-related phonological processes throughout early childhood: Evidence from longitudinal-correlational and instructional studies. In J. Metsala & L. Ehri (Eds.), *Word recognition in beginning reading* (pp. 161–188). Hillsdale, NJ: Erlbaum.

Tunmer, W.E. (1989). The role of language related factors in reading disability. In

D. Shankweiler & I.Y. Liberman (Eds.), *Phonology and reading disability: Solving the reading puzzle* (pp. 91–131). Ann Arbor, MI: University of Michigan Press.

Turgescent, J.K., Wagner, R.K., & Reshot, C.A. (1999). *Test of word and reading efficiency.* Austin, TX: PRO-ED.

Turkeltaub, P.E., Gareau, L., Flowers, D.L., Zeffiro, T.A., & Eden, G.F. (2003). Development of neural mechanisms for reading. *Nature Neuroscience, 6*(7), 767–773. doi:10.1038/nn1065

Valas, H. (1999). Students with learning disabilities and low-achieving students: Peer acceptance, loneliness, self-esteem, and depression. *Social Psychology of Education, 3*(3), 173–192.

Vellutino, F.R., Fletcher, J.M., Snowling, M.J., & Scanlon, D.M. (2004). Specific reading disability (dyslexia): What have we learned in the past four decades? *Journal of Child Psychology and Psychiatry, 45*(1), 2–40. doi:10.1046/j.0021-9630.2003.00305

Volger, G.P., DeFries, J.C., & Decker, S.N. (1985). Family history as an indicator of risk for reading disability. *Journal of Learning Disabilities, 18*(7), 419–421.

Wagner, M., Blackorby, J., Cameto, R., Hebbeler, K., & Newman, L. (1993). *The transition experiences of young people with disabilities. A summary of findings from the national longitudinal transition study of special education students.* Menlo Park, CA: SRI International.

Wagner, R.K., & Torgesen, J.K. (1987). The nature of phonological processing and its causal role in the aquisition of reading skills. *Psychological Bulletin, 101*, 192–212. doi:10.1037//0033-2909.101.2.192

Wagner, R.K., Torgesen, J.K., & Rashotte, C.A. (1999). *The comprehensive test of phonological processing.* Austin, TX: PRO-ED.

Wilkinson, G.S. (1993). *The wide range achievement test* (3rd ed.). Tampa, FL: Wide Range.

Wolf, M., & Denckla, M.B. (2005). *RAN/RAS: Rapid automatized naming and rapid alternating.* Austin, TX: PRO-ED.

Wolf, M., & Goodglass, H. (1986). Dyslexia, dysnomia, and lexical retrieval: A longitudinal investigation. *Brain and Language, 28*(1), 154–168. doi:10.1016/0093-934X(86)90098-2

Wolff, P.H., & Melngailis, I. (1994). Family patterns of developmental dyslexia: Clinical findings. *American Journal of*

Medical Genetics, 54(2), 122–131. doi:10. 1002/ajmg.1320540207

Woodcock, R.W. (1987). *Woodcock reading mastery test: Revised.* Circle Pines, MN: American Guidance Service.

Woodcock, R.W., McGrew, K.S., & Mather, N. (2001). *Woodcock-Johnson III tests of cognitive ability.* Itasca, IL: Riverside Publishing.

World Health Organization. (1992). *The ICD-10 classification of mental and behavioral disorders: Clinical descriptions and diagnostic guidelines.* Geneva, Switzerland.

Zeffiro, T., & Eden, G. (2000). What's the matter? White matter? *Neuron, 25*(2), 257–259. doi:10.1016/S0896-6273 (00)80890-9

CHAPTER 18

Transcending Gaps Among Disciplines in Neurodevelopmental Disorders

From Brain Volumetrics to Collaborative Multisystem Assessment

Martha R. Herbert

Reflection upon a rich dataset can allow the elaboration of many dimensions of the data. It can also lead to a realization that the findings point beyond the domains envisioned during data collection. In this chapter, I describe several unexpected volumetric magnetic resonance imaging (MRI) findings common to both autism spectrum disorder (ASD) and developmental-language disorder (DLD). Moreover, I show how they call for brain investigations including not only volumetrics, but also tissue characterization and temporally sensitive functional measures. I review parallel developments in the literature supporting systemic considerations, and describe how these developments led to a shift in my research program from volumetrics to multimodal imaging and an intensive multisystem approach to subject assessment and research design.

This journey began with an "inheritance" of nearly 100 T1-weighted MRI scans (Filipek, Center for Morphometric Analysis, Massachusetts General Hospital). These scans had been acquired during the early 1990s as part of the Autism and Language Disorders Nosology Project, headed by Rapin (1996). The project examined children with ASD and DLD, as well as "nonautistic" low IQ children (NALIQ), at multiple levels. The overall intent was to examine the consistency of groupings and their features over time, and to identify predictors of outcome. Assessments began with preschool children, with reassessment at school age when MRI became available and was performed.

I was preparing for my fellowship when I joined this project, and was given the MRI data and assigned the task of parcellating the cerebral cortex and linking neuropsychological testing data with specific brain regions. However, the data did not cooperate with this goal structure. In fact, my colleagues and I found only a few minimally significant brain-regional volume differences associated with any diagnostic category. Instead, what was much more striking was a pattern of brain enlargement in the ASD and DLD groups, which was widely distributed within the radiate (outer) white matter, and most pronounced in prefrontal white matter. Effects in the DLD group were more pronounced in girls, whereas in the ASD groups there were not enough females to assess sex differences. Although the current findings need to be replicated by further imaging work, they also call for reflection and explanation.

AUTISM SPECTRUM DISORDER AND LANGUAGE DISORDERS CONSIDERED TOGETHER

The Nosology Project data set us on the path of looking at language disorder and ASD in the same setting. DLD was defined as an impairment of language in the absence of low IQ, physical problems with the vocal apparatus, or social circumstances that could account for this language impairment (Aram, Morris, & Hall, 1993). ASD was defined conventionally as impairments in social interaction and communication and a repetitive, restricted repertoire of behaviors and interests; communication challenges often include language impairment (American Psychiatric Association, 1994).

Beyond (or beneath) the simple definitions of each of these disorders, however, lurks a wealth of further considerations. In particular, neither disorder defines a specific condition with specific and consistent features across the board. Instead, a substantial heterogeneity of language phenotypes characterizes both ASD and DLD, along with a substantial heterogeneity in other features in ASD. For example, conditions beyond those included in the disorder definitions are commonly found for both disorders. In fact, the majority of children with DLD (including those with typical intelligence required by DLD definition) exhibit impairments, albeit subtle ones, in multiple other domains, (e.g., cognition, emotion, and motor performance; Leonard, 1998). Indeed, there are many reports of multiple, subtle, nonlinguistic impairments in children with DLD, including impairments on cognitive tasks (Johnston, 1994; Johnston & Weismer, 1983; Kamhi, Catts, Mauer, Apel, & Gentry, 1988; Kamhi, Gentry, Mauer, & Gholson, 1990; Rescorla & Goosens, 1992), processing of social and emotional stimuli (Shields, Varley, Broks, & Simpson, 1996), crossed localization (implying impaired callosal information transfer; Fabbro, Libera, & Tavano, 2002), and motor and neurological impairments (Hill, 2001; Noterdaeme, Mildenberger, Minow, & Amorosa, 2002; Owen & McKinlay, 1997; Trauner, Wulfeck, Tallal, & Hesselink, 2000), including slow performance of fine motor tasks, balance, and limb praxis (Bradford & Dodd, 1994; Gonen & Grossman, 2000). In ASD, all these domains and many more (e.g., sensory dysregulation, sleep disturbance, gastrointestinal and immune disturbances, and frequent infections) are common, though not universal. DLD participants also manifest various functional difficulties when greater demands are placed on the nervous system (Gillam, Hoffman, Marler, & Wynn-Dancy, 2002). This would also be expected with a generalized systems impairment, and should lead to a profile of greater weakness in tasks (e.g., linguistic domains) requiring more associational, cross-modal, or integrative activity (Boucher, Lewis, & Collis, 2000; Mesulam, 1999;Weismer & Evans, 2002).

This clinical picture begins to shed doubt on the idea that either condition represents a "selective" neural systems disorder. The anatomical literature also contains findings inconsistent with a selective neural systems model. For example, in DLD, volumetric or neuropathological differences in the peri-Sylvian region of the dominant hemisphere (central to language function; Mesulam, 1990), are not consistently found and are sometimes noted in unaffected relatives, even when they are absent in the affected individuals themselves (Price, 2000). Thus, focal anatomical correlates identified to date remain nondeterministic—that is, documented anatomical variants are neither necessary nor sufficient to the condition. Moreover, anatomical findings in areas of the brain that are not primarily language-associated—such as the cerebellum (Bishop, 1989; Geschwind & Galaburda, 1987), the caudate , and other nonlanguage areas (Galaburda, Sherman, Rosen, Aboitiz, & Geschwind, 1985); (Humphreys, Kaufmann, & Galaburda, 1990);—suggest influences on language function that are not language specific but may simultaneously be affecting other domains.

Brain Volumetric Investigations of Autism and Developmental Language Disorder

These considerations strongly informed our approach to analyzing our whole-brain volumetric MRI data. The nondeterministic character of neuroanatomical differences, the findings of structural brain differences outside areas whose known functions related specifically to the core features of the disorders, and the prevalence of accompanying subtle nonlinguistic disorders, all supported our endeavor. Neuroconstructivists have ably argued that being developmental (rather than acquired through some insult to a previously intact brain), these conditions may reasonably be expected to be widespread, and thus to involve realms beyond language areas of the brain (Bishop, 1998; Karmiloff-Smith, 1998; Leonard, 1998; Paterson, Brown, Gsodl, Johnson, & Karmiloff-Smith, 1999). Rather than manifesting pronounced local findings, they may involve widely distributed but locally subtle anatomical shifts (Herbert & Ziegler, 2005), leading to widely distributed functional compromises (Williams, Goldstein & Minshew, 2006), and in fact might be detectable only by using quantitative parameters that have not been part of standard clinical neuroradiology practice.

Brain Volume   In both our ASD and DLD samples, the most striking finding was an increase in total brain volume. For the group with autism, this was consistent with a large body of literature documenting an increase in average brain size, head size, or brain weight in autism (Redcay & Courchesne, 2005). In fact, about 20% of those diagnosed with ASD have head circumference measures above the 90th percentile, and most are above average (Bauman & Kemper, 1985); Herbert, 2005; Rapin, 1996), although there is little analogous literature in DLD. Our own research was (to our knowledge) the first reported documentation of increased brain volume in DLD . Specifically, the volume hierarchy was high IQ autistic > DLD = low IQ autistic > controls > nonautistic low IQ (Filipek 1992). One prior study of head circumference in autism and se-mantic-pragmatic disorder found more children with language disorders but not autism than controls with macrocephalic head circumference. The only MRI volumetric study to report brain volume of which we are aware found forebrain volume 7% smaller in DLD than in controls (Preis, Steinmetz, Knorr, & Jancke, 2000). Of note, large brains do not appear to be found in other disorders, such as bipolar disorder and schizophrenia (Ward, Friedman, Wise, & Schulz, 1996).

White Matter and Brain Enlargement It appears that increased brain volume in both autism and DLD is largely driven by an increase in white matter. For example, in a study of 2 to 16-year-olds, white matter enlargement was found in 2 to 3-year-old children with autism, whereas 12 to 16-year-old children with autism had less white matter than con-trols. In the younger children, moreover, although the group with autism had 18% more cerebral white matter, in the cerebellum the white matter volume increase in cerebellum was 38%. This volume increase in autism increase appears to occur postnatally, as meta-analysis of cross-sectional studies of differently aged cohorts suggests a very rapid increase during the first 2 years and a sharp fall-off after 2 years in growth rate relative to controls (Redcay & Courchesne, 2005). When they measured brain vol-umes in a cohort at risk for autism from age 2 years, Hazlett et al. (2005) found enlargement of cerebral grey and white matter but not of cerebel-lum. Aylward, Minshew, Field, Sparks, and Singh (2002), who measured both head circumference and brain volume, found both measures to be larger in children with autism under 12, whereas only head circumfer-ence but not brain size was larger in older individuals with autism, sug-gesting an early rapid brain growth not maintained through life, and possibly suggesting some modest volume loss with age.

The one report of grey and white matter volumes in children with DLD (Kabani, MacDonald, Evans, & Gopnik, 1997), which does not in-clude any age-matched controls, does show that the adult group with language impairments had a decreased grey/white ratio compared with adult controls, with more white matter and less grey matter. Although this was attributed to generalized atrophy, it is not obvious why atrophy would be associated with (or result in) increased white matter volume.

In our own study population, white matter was the only region that both absolutely and proportionally increased in both our ASD and our DLD samples. Specifically, white matter was 15% larger in boys with autism than in controls, whereas in DLD it was 8% larger in boys and 18% larger in girls. (Given the difficulty in finding high-functioning girls with autism to enroll in imaging studies and the great difficulties involved in scanning low functioning participants with autism, very little is known about the volumetrics of autism in girls, although a national effort to pool the small samples from multiple studies is underway). In summary, white matter alterations constitute a disproportionate 66% of the total brain volume increase in ASD and 88% of the brain volume increase in DLD for our sample. For DLD, the increase in both unadjusted and adjusted white matter volume thus means that the 3.7% increase in overall brain volume is almost entirely due to the 11.7% volume increase in central white matter.

Within the white matter, volume differences were also nonuniform; radiate white matter (i.e., subjacent to the cortex) was significantly enlarged in both groups, whereas deep sagittal, bridging and descending tracts were not. Radiate white matter was affected in all lobes in ASD (though in DLD parietal was spared). However, in both disorders the prefrontal lobe was affected most prominently, being 36% larger in autism and 26% larger in DLD as compared with controls. Analysis of volumetric findings in relation to developmental trajectories of myelination by region showed that areas myelinating later (or for a longer period of time) showed greater enlargement.

The interpretation of these findings is challenging. It is tempting to make sense of the contribution of large brain volume to observed functional impairments by looking for areas in which brain volume overlaps with relevant distributed neural systems. However, this ultimately begs the question of the functional impact of the rest of the enlargement in which the areas impacted do not so clearly associate with functional domains specifically pertinent to either ASD or DLD. An alternative approach that can encompass the overall pattern of enlargement is to consider the network impacts of disruption of long-tract connectivity (Herbert, 2005), an approach that has taken off strongly because of the initial pathbreaking contribution of Just, Cherkassky, Keller, and Minshew (2004).

Corpus Callosum   The corpus callosum (CC) has been of interest in both DLD and autism, because interhemispheric transfer is relevant to various hypotheses about the functional impairments (including asymmetry) in both disorders. In autism, two studies have found the CC to be smaller, mostly posteriorly (Egaas, Courchesne, & Saitoh, 1995; Piven, Bailey, Ranson, & Arndt, 1997). A further study of participants with autism and intellectual disabilities found volume reduction mostly in the body of the CC. Yet another study found volume reduction in the anterior (Hardan, Minshew, & Keshavan, 2000). In DLD, one study found no difference in midsagittal CC area, although another measured the CC to be thicker in children with familial dysphasia/dyslexia (Njiokiktjien, de Sonneville, & Vaal, 1994). In our own samples, we found no difference in either DLD or autism in midsagittal area of the CC, either as a whole or in any of the specific subregions delineated according to the methods of Witelson. However, it is notable that the lack of volume increase occurred in the context of larger brain and white matter volume, which ought to have led to a larger corpus callosum, given that corpus callosum typically covaries to the two third power of brain volume (Jancke, Staiger, Schlaug, Huang, & Steinmetz, 1997).

Asymmetry The populational predominance of leftward lateralization of language functions has made the study of asymmetry attractive in both ASD and DLD because it is known that there is a higher frequency of ambidextrousness or left-handedness and/or right hemisphere language dominance in individuals with both disorders. In both the ASD and DLD literature, large-scale asymmetries have been a modest but persistent theme in the literature, and were among the first differences from controls to be documented. Computerized tomographic scans were found to reveal "unfavorable" anatomical asymmetries in ASD (Hier, LeMay, & Rosenberger, 1979). The same authors also found reversed asymmetry by CT in participants with speech delay (Rosenberger & Hier, 1980). A large-scale rightward shift in ASD and a childhood speech disorder (dysphasia) had been previously reported in two functional studies, with resting regional cerebral blood flow asymmetry shifted from predominantly left to predominantly right in both a group with ASD and a group with dysphasia. However, this ratio shift had a different origin in each group. In the group with ASD, this reversal of right:left ratio was driven by regional cerebral blood flow that was no different from controls on the right but also diminished on the left. In the group with dysphasia, the left rCBF was largely unchanged whereas the right was increased. Taken together, these two studies suggested less overall cerebral blood flow in the sample with autism and more in the dysphasic one.

Notwithstanding the studies mentioned previously, there remain few comprehensive studies of asymmetries throughout the brain in the ASD and DLD brain research literatures. Indeed, most studies have examined asymmetries in areas of specific interest. However, our own group reported a whole-brain investigation of volumetric asymmetries, including anatomical structures and regions in a nested hierarchy in a comparison of high-functioning boys with ASD (with previously reported reversed inferior frontal asymmetry; Herbert et al., 2002), boys with DLD, and age-matched controls (Herbert et al., 2005). No group showed asymmetry at the level of total hemispheric volumes. In fact, lobar asymmetry was manifested only in the controls (with a leftward asymmetry in the frontal lobes). However, in cortical regions there was a marked increase in rightward asymmetry in both autism and DLD. This effect was widely and similarly distributed in both groups, and was especially prominent in higher-order associational areas. The striking similarity in asymmetry alterations between these two groups suggests that 1) asymmetries may be significant far beyond language regions, 2) the alterations may be systematic rather than random, and 3) asymmetry alterations in language-associated regions may be a subcomponent of a more pervasive pattern of anatomical perturbation. These similarities also raise the question of whether there may be other widespread changes in both anatomical and functional domains in these populations. Moreover, the greater degree of asymmetry alterations in higher-order associational areas—in which development is more experience-expectant—suggests a potentially important role for epigenetic factors in the emergent asymmetry. In fact, a magnetoencephalography study of late childhood and adolescent participants reported an age-based increase in participants with ASD and leftward asymmetry in controls (Flagg, Cardy, Roberts, & Roberts, 2005), supporting this notion.

The Challenges of Pervasive Brain Differences   To summarize the above imaging findings from the Nosology project, we had entered the volumetric investigations expecting to find a classical brain region—neurocognitive correlations—a selective neural systems disorder—but what we found instead was larger brains, nonuniformity of regional contributions to this enlargement, strong predominance of white matter in driving this enlargement, predominance of radiate and frontal/prefrontal white matter within the white matter enlargement, and widely distributed shifts in cortical asymmetry so similar between ASD and DLD as to seem strongly likely to be meaningful rather than random.

This set of changes was so at variance with our expectation that it gave us pause, and called out for investigation in several directions: 1) What are the tissue underpinnings of these changes and what is their functional significance? 2) Given the wide anatomical distribution and the broad range of subtle (or sometimes not so subtle) clinical problems, are the additional impacted areas functionally significant, or are they "caught in the crossfire" of an underlying process whose impacts include, but do not specifically target, the functional areas that have attracted the most attention? 3) In what ways and to what extent could distributed rather than localized brain disturbances be contributing to the specific and defining functional impairments?

Tissue Underpinnings of Brain Enlargement

If brain and white matter enlargement are due to a greater number and density of neurons and axons (e.g., from "failure to prune"), then one would predict either no difference from controls or an increase in neuronal and/or white matter integrity. Magnetic resonance spectroscopy and diffusion weighted imaging studies suggesting that this prediction is not borne out, as well as brain pathophysiology potentially consistent with these imaging findings, will be reviewed in the following sections.

Magnetic Resonance Spectroscopy and Neuronal Integrity   The metabolite N-Acetyl-aspartate (NAA), detectable by proton magnetic resonance imaging (1H-MRS) and produced more in mitochondria than in the cytoplasm, is a measure of neuronal integrity or neuronal function, and is sometimes considered a measure of neuronal density—which the increased cell density theory predicts should increase. Several 1H-MRS studies have been performed to test this prediction; however their findings have contradicted the increased cell density hypothesis. Out of 22 magnetic resonance imaging papers in the ASD literature, 80 measures of NAA were performed. In all studied brain regions combined, 25 found reductions in NAA, 1 found an increase, and 54 showed no change (Shetty, Ratai, Ringer, & Herbert, 2009). Methodological problems including low field strength magnet and cohorts with very wide age range may have contributed to the failure to detect difference in some of the studies. Reduced NAA suggests either reduced neuronal density, a lower level of neuronal functioning, impaired mitochondrial function, or less elaborate neuronal architecture (e.g., less dendritic arborization). Moreover, in the overall body of ASD spectroscopy literature in children, all of the metabolites measured are generally lower rather than higher in ASD than controls, suggesting a lower rather than a higher density of cells and metabolic components (DeVito et al., 2007); this matter is exceedingly well reviewed in Dager, Friedman, Petropoulos, and Shaw (2008). This is quite different from what would be predicted were the enlargement due to greater cellular proliferation.

Imaging White Matter Integrity   In the setting of higher density of myelinated axons, the findings predicted by the increased cell density theory would be increased fractional anisotropy (FA)—that is, more heavily restricted diffusion of water around axonal fibers, and reduced diffusivity (ADC, apparent diffusion coefficient)—less diffusion of fluids. But a number of studies have shown the opposite—more freely diffusing water, suggesting reduced white matter integrity. Sundaram et al. (2008) reported reduced FA and increased ADC in short-range cortico-cortical white matter fibers similar in distribution to the radiate white matter that we reported as enlarged, as described previously (Herbert et al., 2004). They also noted that their findings were not consistent with white matter volumetric enlargement in this area being composed of a larger number of myelinated axons. Cheung et al. (2009), who noted that lower FA correlated with greater severity of ASD, also explicitly ponder how to reconcile lower FA with greater white matter volume, which they described as counterintuitive. They suggest that white matter volumetric indices are rather nonspecific, and that given their findings, volume increase might even be due to nonneuronal proliferative processes, such as activation and cell swelling of microglia and astroglia that has been reported by Vargas (Vargas, Nascimbene, Krishnan, Zimmerman, & Pardo, 2005), which will be discussed in the following section. The finding that increased motor cortex white matter volume predicts motor impairment in ASD, not enhanced motor performance (Mostofsky, Burgess, & Gidley Larson, 2007), could conceivably be interpreted in relation to these reflections on tissue underpinnings—that is, reduced white matter integrity could be consistent with lower efficiency in motor systems.

Underlying Pathophysiological Processes with Widespread and Functionally Nonspecific Impact

Neuropathology: Neuroinflammation and Oxidative Stress Several studies have now identified markers consistent with innate immune activation, or neuroinflammation, in ASD. The first study, by Pardo and colleagues (Vargas et al., 2005) has now been followed by two more (Li et al., 2009; Morgan et al., 2010). Altered expression of immune genes has also been identified in brain tissue with ASD (Garbett et al., 2008; Lintas, Sacco, & Persico, 2010; Voineagu et al., 2011). A much larger number of studies have identified a range of systemic immune differences (Ashwood & Van de Water, 2004; Ashwood, Wills, & Van de Water, 2006), although the specific details of the immune profiles are not identical between central nervous system and the organism systemically. Innate immune activation is a prominent feature of a variety of neurodegenerative diseases, such as Alzheimer's, however it is not detectable by MRI scan or by other clinically available in vivo imaging techniques. Oxidative stress, another feature commonly identified in neurodegenerative diseases and a common fellow traveler with inflammation, has been measured in brains with ASD (Evans et al., 2008; Sajdel-Sulkowska, Ming & Koibuchi, 2009; Sajdel-Sulkowska, Ming, McGinnis, & Koibuchi, 2010; Lintas, Sacco, & Persico, 2010) as well as systemically in a growing number of studies (Chauhan, Chauhan, & Brown, 2009; James, 2008).

Impact of Distributed Processes on Specific Functions

Functional Impacts of Immune Activation and Oxidative Stress An emerging field of literature relates to the active roles played by glial cells (astroglial, microglial, and oligodendroglial cells) in signal transmission in the brain (Fields, 2006; Fields, 2008; Fields, 2009; Halassa, Fellin, & Haydon, 2007). However, the impact of immune activation of these cells on their signal transmission functions is not well studied. Inflammation and oxidative stress may alter the neurochemical milieu by impairing the astroglial reuptake of glutamate and leading to excessive extracellular glutamate (Pardo & Eberhart, 2007), an excitatory neurotransmitter, which may secondarily affect connectivity through increasing the excitation/inhibition ratio that could also have cascading developmental effects. This may be a contributor to the abundant documentation of cerebral perfusion differences (predominantly reduction) in at least 18 papers studying ASD cohorts. Cerebral perfusion refers to the quantity of blood flow in the brain. Atypical regulation of cerebral perfusion is found in a range of severe medical conditions, including tumors, vascular disease, and epilepsy, and has also been found in a range of psychiatric disorders (Theberge, 2008). In ASD, hypoperfusion has been identified in frontal regions (e.g., Gupta & Ratnam, 2009), temporal lobes (e.g., as well as a variety of subcortical regions, including basal ganglia, cerebellum, limbic structures, and thalamus—that is, in a widely distributed set of brain regions. Even with this heterogeneous localization, it is interesting to note that 17 of the 18 publications showed substantial reduction of cerebral perfusion. In addition the white matter hyperintensities commonly reported in ASD clinical scans (Boddaert et al., 2009) may be signs of localized hypoperfusion.

These perfusion studies were generally psychologically oriented and contained little to no reflection upon tissue underpinnings of the perfusion changes. However, inflammation, oxidative stress, and other pathophysiological features identified in ASD might contribute to reduced perfusion by a range of mechanisms: 1) *Altered vascular function.* Astroglia are part of the blood-brain barrier, and the swelling they undergo with activation can reduce capillary lumen by as much as 50%, impairing perfusion. Byproducts of oxidative stress are associated with platelet activation and vasoconstriction; and 2) *Increased blood viscosity.* Oxidative stress can contribute to increased blood viscosity by decreasing red-cell membrane fluidity (Chauhan, Chauhan, Cohen, Brown, & Sheikh, 2004), decreasing membrane elasticity, increasing red-cell plastic viscosity (Liu, Qin, & Yin, 2004), and decreasing red cell deformability, as well as increased viscosity from platelet activation (Flynn, Johnson, & Allen, 1981). It is notable that many of these factors are dynamic and potentially reversible.

Potential Pathophysiological Contributions to Rightward Brain Asymmetry in Development   A disturbed neurochemical and neuroimmune milieu belongs to a set of factors that in the broader neuroscience literature have been shown to have some influence on brain asymmetry. A prediction of asymmetry can be made mathematically on the basis of efficiencies of cross-hemispheric communication in which lateralization becomes more efficient with larger brain size (Ringo, 1991; Ringo, Doty, Demeter, & Simard, 1994). However, this does not account for the specifically rightward predominance of asymmetry alterations in language-related disorders. In the broader neuroscience literature, there are papers documenting the influence on brain asymmetry, and in particular a shift toward rightward asymmetry, from various visceral and regulatory factors, including autonomic (Craig, 2005), neuropeptides (Ramirez, Prieto, Vives, de Gasparo, & Alba, 2004), gonadal steroids (Wisniewski, 1998), and immune (Kang et al., 1991; Shen, Hebert, Moze, Li, & Neveu, 2005; Wittling, 1995); but at present although all these factors have some documented pertinence to ASD and DLD, their connection to asymmetry in these conditions has not been pursued.

Plasticity and Loss of Diagnosis in Autism Spectrum Disorder: Pathophysiology and Static versus Dynamic Encephalopathy   Although prognosis is not part of the definition of ASD, loss of ASD diagnosis seems to many to be unthinkable. Yet in addition to anecdoctal reports, there has for decades also been a small amount of academic documentation of improvement, loss of diagnosis, and recovery. Early reports of improved outcome include the Case #1 in the 1943 paper by Kanner, in which autism was first described and named (Kanner, 1943). This individual improved markedly and became an independent adult after gold salts treatment for juvenile rheumatoid arthritis (Donvan & Zucker, 2010; Kanner, 1968, 1971; Olmsted, 2005), suggesting that treatment of an immune disorder may have had unintended but substantial impacts on aspects of the ASD. Early documentation of improvement and recovery also includes papers coauthored in 1967 by Rutter (Rutter, Greenfeld, & Lockyer, 1967), in 1974 by Gajzago and Prior (Gajzago & Prior, 1974), in 1981 by DeMyer, Hingtgen and Jackson (DeMyer, Hingtgen, & Jackson, 1981), and in 1987 by Lovaas (Lovaas, 1987). Fein and colleagues have produced a further review of outcome studies and the notion of autism recovery, including documentation of residual neurodevelopmental impairments such as attention deficit disorder or language impairment (Fein, Dixon, Paul, & Levin, 2005). The loss of diagnosis and transient improvement in and fluctuation of core features raise intriguing questions about what kinds of underlying neurobiological basic features and changes could enable such variability and improvement to occur (Herbert & Anderson, 2008; Mehler & Purpura, 2009). Among various possible routes to brain plasticity may be reversal of some of the tissue-based pathophysiology alluded to previously. Recovery of depressed NAA in secondarily affected areas after epilepsy surgery also suggests plasticity (Hugg et al., 1996).

Low IQ may be in part artifactual; Dawson et al. (2007) found 70% mental retardaion with the Weschler scales of intelligence and only 20% with Raven's Progressive Matrices in the same cohort. An interesting potentially related phenomenon is an increasing recognition of an often substantial discrepancy between expressive and receptive-language impairment, as well as the presence of high IQ in nonverbal individuals with ASD, some of whom can read and use keyboards to express themselves (sometimes showing great creativity and nuance), but cannot produce speech. Some attribute this discrepancy to oro-motor apraxia and others focus on sensory processing issues. Such phenomena could suggest that "obstruction" of potential rather than "impairment" or "absence" of capability may better describe at least some of the ASD phenotype.

CONCLUSIONS: FROM VOLUMETRICS THROUGH MULTIMODAL IMAGING TO MULTISYSTEMS ASSESSMENT

What I have described in the current chapter includes evidence that 1) brain imaging findings outside of volumetrics have shed light on mechanisms that could be driving some unanticipated widely distributed, but neurocognitively enigmatic, macroanatomical findings such as brain enlargement, 2) neuropathological findings suggest that tissue pathophysiology, particularly innate immune activation or inflammation, could be a parsimonious explanation tying together these findings, and 3) systemic pathophysiology could further contribute to some of the potentially dynamical features measured in the ASD brain, such as cerebral hypoperfusion, which has also been documented in language impairment.

Considering these issues, and strongly suspecting that the route to useful medical interventions in ASD and perhaps other neurodevelopmental disorders such as DLD would pass through addressing these issues forthrightly, my colleagues and I developed a research collaborative called TRANSCEND, an acronym for Treatment Research And NeuroSCience Evaluation of Neurodevelopmental Disorders. This multidisciplinary, physiologically oriented research program provides infrastructure for multidisciplinary investigation of research participants, with a common neurocognitive core around which we can acquire and coregister data with several imaging modalities (MRI, MEG and/or electroencephalography, depending on age and capacity of the subject to stay still). TRANSCEND also has in development a biomarker project to collect biomaterials for analysis of metabolic, immune, toxicant, nutritional, and genetic factors as covariates.

TRANSCEND is organized around the hypothesis that language problems have sensory processing precursors, and that underlying cellular physiology (when altered by metabolic or immune disturbances such as are being identified in ASD) can affect synaptic functioning and thereby sensory processing and functions downstream. We also take a "middle-out" approach (Noble, 2008), arguing that signaling and physiological activity mediates between genes and function, but cannot be fully predicted by genes due to emergent properties not determined by genes. Thus we argue for the integration of functional and pathophysiological brain investigations. Our core questions are as follows:

1. Does anatomical change relate to functional change? Our approach to this question is multimodal MRI scanning and obtaining and coregistering volumetric, diffusion, and spectroscopy data to convergently characterize tissue properties in white matter in ASD, dyslexia, and DLD.

2. Do sensory problems have similar signaling signatures across modalities, and do sensory and social problems also have similar signaling signatures? Our approach here is MEG studies of auditory, visual, and somatosensory processing on children with ASD, dyslexia, and DLD, along with controls, who have received MRI scans.

3. Does the severity of sensory processing impairment correlate with metabolic or immune markers? By obtaining blood, urine, and salivary samples for metabolic and immune biomarker analysis, we hope to address whether selected systemic markers correlate with CNS dysfunction, because it is becoming increasingly appreciated that peripheral inflammation can modulate central neuronal excitability.

4. How early can we detect these problems in development? And what is the coupling in development between systemic and brain physiology and between pathophysiology and neurocognitive function? Our study entitled "A Prospective Multisystem Assessment of Infants at Risk for Autism," which involves prenatal-sample collection and

seven intensive multidisciplinary evaluations between 2 weeks and 30 months of age, is to our knowledge the first to take a whole-body approach (Herbert, 2011) to prospective monitoring of systemic (metabolic, immune, lipids, minerals, toxics) and brain/EEG (autonomic nervous system [ANS]/EEG/event related potentials [ERP]/electrodermal activity [EDA], development in addition to behavioral and neuromotor assessments in infants at risk for ASD.

Because about 15%–20% of younger siblings of children with autism develop ASD themselves (Ozonoff et al., 2011), and because about half of the remainder manifest a neurodevelopmental impairment such as attention deficit disorder or indeed language impairment, our pilot study is laying the foundation for studying what we hypothesize will be the continuous distribution of disturbances across physiological as well as functional levels. We argue that descriptive in-depth case studies of developing at-risk infants will provide both single-subject repeated measures data on development and natural history observations that will inform further detailed future studies and also have strong clinical relevance.

If our collaborative multidisciplinary research approach allows us to identify 1) tissue pathophysiology features of brain enlargement that point to medical treatment targets, 2) early medical or electrophysiological features of ASD (and possibly DLD if some of the infants in our at-risk study develop language impairment but not ASD) that may be partly or fully ameliorable by interventions that might thereby reduce severity, or 3) features of brain function over time that are dynamic or amenable to treatment, we will have made a clinical contribution that may increase the quality of life for many affected individuals.

REFERENCES

American Psychiatric Association. (1994). *Diagnostic and Statistical Manual of Mental Disorders* (4th ed, DSM IV). Washington, DC.

Aram, D.M., Morris, R., & Hall, N.E. (1993). Clinical and research congruence in identifying children with specific language impairment. *Journal of Speech and Hearing Research, 36*(3), 580–591.

Aschner, M., Allen, J.W., Kimelberg, H.K., LoPachin, R.M., & Streit, W.J. (1999). Glial cells in neurotoxicity development. *Annual Review of Pharmacology and Toxicology, 39,* 151–173.

Ashwood, P., & Van de Water, J. (2004). A review of autism and the immune response. *Clinical and Developmental Immunology, 11*(2), 165–174. doi:10.1080/10446670410001722096

Ashwood, P., Wills, S., & Van de Water, J. (2006). The immune response in autism: A new frontier for autism research. *Journal of Leukocyte Biology, 80*(1), 1–15. doi:10.1189/jlb.1205707

Aylward, E.H., Minshew, N.J., Field, K., Sparks, B.F., & Singh, N. (2002). Effects of age on brain volume and head circumference in autism. *Neurology, 59*(2), 175–183.

Bauman, M.L., & Kemper, T.L. (1985). Histoanatomic observations of the brain in early infantile autism. *Neurology, 35,* 866–874.

Bishop, D.V. (1989). Autism, Asperger's syndrome and semantic-pragmatic disorder: Where are the boundaries? *International Journal of Language and Communication Disorders, 24*(2), 107–121. doi:10.3109/13682828909011951

Bishop, D.V.M. (1998). *Uncommon understanding: Devlopment and disorders of language comprehension in children.* New York, NY: Psychology Press.

Boddaert, N., Zilbovicius, M., Philipe, A., Robel, L., Bourgeois, M., Barthelemy, C., ... Chabane, N. (2009). MRI findings in 77 children with non-syndromic autistic disorder. *PLoS One, 4*(2), e4415. doi:10.1371/journal.pone.0004415

Boucher, J., Lewis, V., & Collis, G.M. (2000). Voice processing abilities in children with autism, children with specific language impairments, and young typically developing children. *Journal of Child Psychology and Psychiatry, 41*(7), 847–857. doi:10.1111/1469-7610.00672

Bradford, A., & Dodd, B. (1994). The motor planning abilities of phonologically disordered children. *International Journal of Language and Communication Disorders, 29*(4), 349–369. doi:10. 3109/13682829409031288

Brickman, A.M., Zahra, A., Muraskin, J., Steffener, J., Holland, C.M., Habeck, C., ... Stern, Y. (2009). Reduction in cerebral blood flow in areas appearing as white matter hyperintensities on magnetic resonance imaging. *Psychiatry Research: Neuroimaging, 172*(2), 117–120. doi:10.1016/j.pscychresns.2008.11.006

Burroni, L., Orsi, A., Monti, L., Hayek, Y., Rocchi, R., & Vattimo, A.G. (2008). Regional cerebral blood flow in childhood autism: A SPET study with SPM evaluation. *Nuclear Medicine Communications, 29*(2), 150–156. doi:10.1097/MNM.0b013e3282f1bb8e

Chauhan, A., Chauhan, V., & Brown, T. (Eds.). (2009). *Autism: Oxidative stress, inflammation and immune abnormalities.* Boca Raton, FL: Taylor & Francis/CRC Press.

Chauhan, V., Chauhan, A., Cohen, I.L., Brown, W.T., & Sheikh, A. (2004). Alteration in amino-glycerophospholipids levels in the plasma of children with autism: A potential biochemical diagnostic marker. *Life Sciences, 74*(13), 1635–1643. doi:10.1016/j.lfs.2003.08.024

Cheung, C., Chua, S.E., Cheung, V., Khong, P.L., Tai, K. S., Wong, T.K., ... McAlonan, G.M. (2009). White matter fractional anisotrophy differences and correlates of diagnostic symptoms in autism. *Journal of Child Psychology and Psychiatry, 50*(9), 1102–1112. doi:10.1111 /j.1469-7610.2009.02086

Chiron, C., Leboyer, M., Leon, F., Jambaque, I., Nuttin, C., & Syrota, A. (1995). SPECT of the brain in childhood autism: Evidence for a lack of normal hemispheric asymmetry. *Developmental Medicine and Child Neurology, 37*(10), 849–860. doi:10.1111/j.1469-8749.1995.tb11938

Chiron, C., Pinton, F., Masure, M.C., Duvelleroy-Hommet, C., Leon, F., & Billard, C. (1999). Hemispheric specialization using SPECT and stimulation tasks in children with dysphasia and dystrophia. *Developmental Medicine and Child Neurology, 41*(8), 512–520. doi:10.1017/S0012162299001139

Courchesne, E., Karns, C.M., Davis, H.R., Ziccardi, R., Carper, R.A., Tigue, Z.D., ... Courchesne, R.Y. (2001). Unusual brain growth patterns in early life in patients with autistic disorder: An MRI study. *Neurology, 57*(2), 245–254. doi:10.1212/01.wnl.0000399191.79091.28

Craig, A.D. (2005). Forebrain emotional asymmetry: A neuroanatomical basis? *Trends in Cognitive Sciences, 9*(12), 566–571. doi:10.1016/j.tics.2005.10.005

Dager, S.R., Friedman, S.D., Petropoulos, H., & Shaw, D.W.W. (2008). Imaging evidence for pathological brain development in Autism Spectrum Disorders. In A. Zimmerman (Ed.), *Autism: Current theories and evidence* (pp. 361–389). Totowa, NJ: Humana Press.

Dawson, M., Soulieres, I., Gernsbacher, M. A., & Mottron, L. (2007). The level and nature of autistic intelligence. *Psychol Sci, 18*(8), 657-662. doi: PSCI1954 [pii] 10.1111/j.1467-9280.2007.01954.x

Degirmenci, B., Miral, S., Kaya, G.C., Iyilikci, L., Arslan, G., Baykara, A., ... & Durak, H. (2008). Technetium-99m HMPAO brain SPECT in autistic children and their families. *Psychiatry Research: Neuroimaging, 162*(3), 236–243. doi:10.1016/j.pscychresns.2004.12.005

DeMyer, M.K., Hingtgen, J.N., & Jackson, R.K. (1981). Infantile autism reviewed: A decade of research. *Schizophrenia Bulletin, 7*(3), 388–451.

DeVito, T.J., Drost, D.J., Neufeld, R.W., Rajakumar, N., Pavlosky, W., Williamson, P., & Nicolson, R. (2007). Evidence for cortical dysfunction in autism: A proton magnetic resonance spectroscopic imaging study. *Biological Psychiatry, 61*(4), 465–473. doi:10. 1016/j.biopsych.2006.07.022

Donvan, J., & Zucker, C. (2010, October). *Autism's first child.* Retrieved from http://www.theatlantic.com/magazine/archive/2010/2010/autism-8217-s-first-child/8227/

Egaas, B., Courchesne, E., & Saitoh, O. (1995). Reduced size of corpus callosum in autism. *Archives of Neurology, 52*(8), 794–801.

Evans, T.A., Siedlak, S.L., Lu, L., Fu, X., Wang, Z., McGinnis, W.R., ... Zhu, X. (2008). The autistic phenotype exhibits a remarkably localized modification of brain protein by products of free radical-induced lipid oxidation. *American Journal of Biochemistry and Biotechnology, 4*(2), 61–72. doi:10.3844/ajbbsp.2008.61.72

Fabbro, F., Libera, L., & Tavano, A. (2002). A callosal transfer deficit in children with developmental language disorder. *Neuropsychologia, 40*(9), 1541–1546. doi:10.1016/S0028-3932(02)00026-X

Fein, D., Dixon, P., Paul, J., & Levin, H. (2005). Pervasive developmental disorder can evolve into ADHD: Case illustrations. *Journal of Autism and Developmental Disorders, 35,* 525–534. doi:10.1007/s10803-005-5066-3

Fields, R.D. (2006). Advances in understanding neuron-glia interactions. *Neuron Glia Biology 2*(1), 23–26. doi:10.1017/S1740925X05000335

Fields, R.D. (2008). Oligodendrocytes changing the rules: Action potentials in glia and oligodendrocytes controlling action potentials. *Neuroscientist, 14*(6), 540–543. doi:10.1177/1073858408320294

Fields, R.D. (2009). The Other Brain: From Dementia to Schizophrenia, How New Discoveries about the Brain Are Revolutionizing Medicine and Science. New York, NY: Simon and Schuster.

Filipek, P., Richelme, C., Kennedy, D., Rademacher, J., Pitcher, D., Zidel, S., & Caviness, V. (1992). Morphometric analysis of the brain in developmental-language disorders and autism (abstract). *Annals of Neurology, 32,* 475.

Flagg, E.J., Cardy, J.E., Roberts, W., & Roberts, T.P. (2005). Language lateralization development in children with autism: Insights from the late field magnetoencephalogram. *Neuroscience Letters, 386*(2), 82–87. doi:10.1016/j.neulet.2005.05.037

Flynn, T.P., Johnson, G.J., & Allen, D.W. (1981). Mechanisms of decreased erythrocyte deformability and survival in glucose 6-phosphate dehydrogenase mutants. *Progress in Clinical Biological Research, 56,* 231–249.

Gajzago, G., & Prior, M. (1974). Two cases of "recovery" in Kanner syndrome. *Archives of General Psychiatry, 31*(2), 264–268.

Galaburda, A.M., Sherman, G.F., Rosen, G.D., Aboitiz, F., & Geschwind, N. (1985). Developmental dyslexia: Four consecutive patients with cortical anomalies. *Annals of Neurology, 18*(2), 222–233. doi:10.1002/ana.410180210

Garbett, K., Ebert, P.J., Mitchell, A., Lintas, C., Manzi, B., Mirnics, K., & Persico, A.M. (2008). Immune transcriptome alterations in the temporal cortex of subjects with autism. *Neurobiology of Disease, 30*(3), 303–311. doi:10.1016/j.nbd.2008.01.012

Geschwind, N., & Galaburda, A.M. (1987). *Cerebral lateralization.* Cambridge, MA: MIT Press.

Gillam, R.B., Hoffman, L.M., Marler, J.A., & Wynn-Dancy, M.L. (2002). Sensitivity to increased task demands: Contributions from data-driven and conceptually driven information processing deficits. *Topics in Language Disorders, 22*(3), 30–48.

Gonen, O., & Grossman, R.I. (2000). The accuracy of whole brain N-acetylaspartate quantification. *Magnetic Resonance Imaging, 18*(10), 1255–1258. doi:10.1016/S0730-725X(00)00221-6

Gupta S.K., & Ratnam B.V. (2009). Cerebral perfusion abnormalities in children with autism and mental retardation: A segmental quantitative SPECT study. *Indian Pediatrics, 46*(2), 161–164.

Halassa, M.M., Fellin, T., & Haydon, P.G. (2007). The tripartite synapse: Roles for gliotransmission in health and disease. *Trends in Molecular Medicine, 13*(2), 54–63. doi:10.1016/j.molmed.2006.12.005

Hardan, A.Y., Minshew, N.J., & Keshavan, M.S. (2000). Corpus callosum size in autism. *Neurology, 55*(7), 1033–1036.

Hazlett, H.C., Poe, M., Gerig, G., Smith, R.G., Provenzale, J., Ross, A., ... Piven, J. (2005). Magnetic resonance imaging and head circumference study of brain size in autism: Birth through age 2 years. *Archives of General Psychiatry, 62*(12), 1366–1376. doi:10.1001/archpsyc.62.12.1366

Helt, M., Kelley, E., Kinsbourne, M., Pandey, J., Boorstein, H., Herbert, M., & Fein, D. (2008). Can children with autism recover? If so, how? *Neuropsychology Review, 18*(4), 339–366. doi:10.1007/s11065-008-9075-9

Herbert, M.R. (2005). Large brains in autism: The challenge of pervasive abnormality. *Neuroscientist, 11*(5), 417–440. doi:10.1177/0091270005278866

Herbert, M.R. (in press). A whole-body systems approach to ASD. In D.A. Fein (Ed.), *The neuropsychology of autism* (pp. 511–526). New York, NY: Oxford University Press.

Herbert, M.R., & Anderson, M.P. (2008). An expanding spectrum of autism models: From fixed developmental defects to reversible functional impairments. In A. Zimmerman (Ed.), *Autism: Current theories and evidence* (pp. 429–463). Totowa, NJ: Humana Press.

Herbert, M.R., Harris, G.J., Adrien, K.T., Ziegler, D.A., Makris, N., Kennedy, D.N., ... Caviness, V.S. Jr. (2002). Abnormal asymmetry in language association cortex in autism. *Annals of Neurology, 52*(5), 588–596. doi:10.1002/ana.10349

Herbert, M.R., & Ziegler, D.A. (2005). Volumetric neuroimaging and low-dose early-life exposures: Loose coupling of pathogenesis-brain-behavior links. *NeuroToxicology, 26*(4), 565–572. doi:10.1016/j.neuro.2005.01.002

Herbert, M.R., Ziegler, D.A., Deutsch, C.K., O'Brien, L.M., Kennedy, D.N., Filipek, P.A. ... Caviness, V.S., Jr. (2005). Brain asymmetries in autism and developmental language disorder: A nested whole-brain analysis. *Brain, 128*(1), 213–226. doi:10.1093/brain/awh330

Herbert, M.R., Ziegler, D.A., Deutsch, C.K., O'Brien, L.M., Lange, N., Bakardjiev, A., ... Caviness, V.S. (2003). Dissociations of cerebral cortex, subcortical and cerebral white matter volumes in autistic boys. *Brain, 126*(5), 1182–1192. doi:10.1093/brain/awg110

Herbert, M.R., Ziegler, D.A., Makris, N., Bakardjiev, A., Hodgson, J., Adrien, K.T., ... Caviness, V.S. (2003). Larger brain and white matter volumes in children with developmental language disorder. *Developmental Science, 6*(4), F11–F22. doi:10.1111/1467-7687.00291

Herbert, M.R., Ziegler, D.A., Makris, N., Filipek, P.A., Kemper, T.L., Normandin, J.J., ... Caviness, V.S. Jr. (2004). Localization of white matter volume increase in autism and developmental language disorder. *Annals of Neurology, 55*(4), 530–540. doi:10.1002/ana.20032

Hier, D.B., LeMay, M., & Rosenberger, P.B. (1979). Autism and unfavorable left-right asymmetries of the brain. *Journal of Autism and Developmental Disorders, 9*(2), 153–159. doi:10.1007/BF01531531

Hill, E.L. (2001). Non-specific nature of specific language impairment: A review of the literature with regard to concomitant motor impairments. *International Journal of Language and Communication Disorders, 36*(2), 149–171. doi:10.1080/13682820010019874

Hugg, J.W., Kuzniecky, R.I., Gilliam, F.G., Morawetz, R.B., Fraught, R.E., & Hetherington, H.P. (1996). Normalization of contralateral metabolic function following temporal lobectomy demonstrated by 1H magnetic resonance spectroscopic imaging. *Annals of Neurology, 40*(2), 236–239.

Humphreys, P., Kaufmann, W.E., & Galaburda, A.M. (1990). Developmental dyslexia in women: Neuropathological findings in three patients. *Annals of Neurology, 28*(6), 727–738. doi:10.1002/ana.410280602

Ito, H., Mori, K., Hashimoto, T., Miyazaki, M., Hori, A., Kagami, S., & Kuroda, Y. (2005). Findings of brain 99mTc-ECD SPECT in high-functioning autism-3-dimensional stereotactic ROI template analysis of brain SPECT. *The Journal of Medical Investigation, 52*(1, 2), 49–56. doi:10.2152/jmi.52.49

James, S.J. (2008). Oxidative stress and the metabolic pathology of autism. In A. Zimmerman (Ed.), *Autism: Current theories and evidence* (pp. 245–268) Totowa, NJ: Humana Press.

Jancke, L., Staiger, J.F., Schlaug, G., Huang, Y., & Steinmetz, H. (1997). The relationship between corpus callosum size and forebrain volume. *Cerebral Cortex, 7*(1), 48–56. doi:10.1093/cercor/7.1.48

Johnston, J. (1994). Cognitive abilities of children with language impairment. In R. Watkins & M. Rice (Eds.), *Specific lanuage impairments in children* (pp. 107–121). Baltimore, MD: Paul H. Brookes Publishing Co.

Johnston, J.R., & Weismer, S.E. (1983). Mental rotation abilities in language-disordered children. *Journal of Speech & Hearing Research, 26*(3), 397–403.

Just, M.A., Cherkassky, V.L., Keller, T.A., & Minshew, N.J. (2004). Cortical activation and synchronization during sentence comprehension in high-functioning autism: Evidence of underconnectivity. *Brain, 127*(8), 1811–1821. doi:10.1093/brain/awh199

Kabani, N.J., MacDonald, D., Evans, A., & Gopnik, M. (1997). Neuroanatomical correlates of familial language impairment: A preliminary report. *Journal of Neurolinguistics, 10*(2–3), 203–214. doi:10.1016/S0911-6044(97)00009-2

Kamhi, A.G., Catts, H.W., Mauer, D., Apel, K., & Gentry, B.F. (1988). Phonological and spatial processing abilities in language- and reading-impaired children. *Journal of Speech and Hearing Disorders, 53*(3), 316–27.

Kamhi, A.G., Gentry, B., Mauer, D., & Gholson, B. (1990). Analogical learning and transfer in language-impaired children. *Journal of Speech and Hearing Disorders, 55*(1), 140–148.

Kang, D.H., Davidson, R.J., Coe, C.L., Wheeler, R.E., Tomarken, A.J., & Ershler, W.B. (1991). Frontal brain asymmetry and immune function. *Behavioral Neuroscience, 105*(6), 860–869. doi:10.1037//0735-7044.105.6.860

Kanner, L. (1943). Autistic disturbances of affective contact. *Nervous Child, 10,* 217–250.

Kanner, L. (1968). Early infantile autism revisited. *Psychiatry Digest, 29*(2), 17–28.

Kanner, L. (1971). Follow-up study of eleven autistic children originally reported in 1943. *Journal of Autism and Childhood Schizophrenia, 1*(2), 119–145. doi:10.1007/BF01537953

Karmiloff-Smith, A. (1998). Development itself is the key to understanding developmental disorders. *Trends in Cognitive Sciences, 2*(10), 389–398. doi:10.1016/S1364-6613(98)01230-3

Kelley, E., Paul, J.J., Fein, D., & Naigles, L.R. (2006). Residual language deficits in optimal outcome children with a history of autism. *Journal of Autism and Developmental Disorders, 36*(6), 807–828. doi:10.1007/s10803-006-0111-4

Leonard, L.B. (1998). *Children with specific language impairment.* Cambridge, MA: MIT Press.

Li, X., Chauhan, A., Sheikh, A.M., Patil, S., Chauhan, V., Li, X.M., ... Malik, M. (2009). Elevated immune response in the brain of autistic patients. *Journal of Neuroimmunology, 207,* 111–116. doi:10.1016/j.jneuroim.2008.12.002

Lintas, C., Sacco, R., & Persico, A.M. (2010). Genome-wide expression studies in autism spectrum disorder, Rett syndrome, and down syndrome. *Neurobiology of Diseases.* doi:10.1016/j.nbd.2010.11.010

Liu, X., Qin, W., & Yin, D. (2004). Biochemical relevance between oxidative/carbonyl stress and elevated viscosity of erythrocyte suspensions. *Clinical Hemorheology and Microcirculation Journal, 31*(2), 149–56.

Lovaas, O.I. (1987). Behavioral treatment and normal educational and intellectual functioning in young autistic children. *Journal of Consulting and Clinical Psychology, 55*(1), 3–9. doi:10.1037//0022-006X.55.1.3

Manes, F., Piven, J., Vrancic, D., Nanclares, V., Plebst, C., & Starkstein, S.E. (1999). An MRI study of the corpus callosum and cerebellum in mentally retarded autistic individuals. *Journal of Neuropsychiatry and Clinical Neuroscience, 11*(4), 470–474.

Mehler, M.F., & Purpura, D.P. (2009). Autism, fever, epigenetics and the locus coeruleus. *Brain Research Review, 59*(2), 388–392. doi:10.1016/j.brainresrev.2008.11.001

Mesulam, M.M. (1999). Spatial attention and neglect: Parietal, frontal and cingulate contributions to the mental representation and attentional targeting of salient extrapersonal events. *Philosophical Transactions of the Royal Society B: Biological Sciences, 354*(1387), 1325–1346. doi:10.1098/rstb.1999.0482

Mesulam, M.M. (1990). Large-scale neurocognitive networks and distributed processing for attention, language, and memory. *Annals of Neurology, 28,* 597–613. doi:10.1002/ana.410280502

Ming, X., Stein, T.P., Brimacombe, M., Johnson, W.G., Lambert, G.H., & Wagner, G.C. (2005). Increased excretion of a lipid peroxidation biomarker in autism. *Prostaglandins Leukotrienes and Essential Fatty Acids, 73*(5), 379–384. doi:10.1016/j.plefa.2005.06.002

Morgan, J.T., Chana, G., Pardo, C.A., Achim, C., Semendeferi, K., Buckwalter, J., ... Everall, I. P. (2010). Microglial activation and increased microglial density observed in the dorsolateral prefrontal cortex in autism. *Biological Psychiatry, 68*(4), 368–376. doi:10.1016/j.biopsych.2010.05.024

Mostofsky, S.H., Burgess, M.P., & Gidley Larson, J.C. (2007). Increased motor cortex white matter volume predicts motor impairment in autism. *Brain, 130*(8), 2117–2122. doi:10.1093/brain/awm129

Nicolson, R.I., Fawcett, A.J., Berry, E.L., Jenkins, I.H., Dean, P., & Brooks, D.J. (1999). Association of abnormal cerebellar activation with motor learning difficulties in dyslexic adults. *The Lancet, 353*(9165), 1662–1667. doi:10.1016/S0140-6736(98)09165-X

Njiokiktjien, C., de Sonneville, L., & Vaal, J. (1994). Callosal size in children with learning disabilities. *Behavioural Brain Research, 64*(1–2), 213–218. doi:10.1016/0166-4328(94)90133-3

Noble, D. (2008). *The music of life.* New York: Oxford University Press.

Noterdaeme, M., Mildenberger, K., Minow, F., & Amorosa, H. (2002). Quantitative and qualitative evaluation of neuromotor behaviour in children with a specific speech and language disorder. *Infant and Child Development, 11*(1), 3–15. doi:10.1002/icd.234

Ohnishi, T., Matsuda, H., Hashimoto, T., Kunihiro, T., Nishikawa, M., Uema, T., & Sasaki, M. (2000). Abnormal regional cerebral blood flow in childhood autism. *Brain, 123*(9), 1838–1844. doi:10.1093/brain/123.9.1838

Olmsted, D. (2005). The age of autism: Case 1 revisited. American Chronicle. Retrieved from http://www.americanchronicle.com/articles/view/1872

Owen, S.E., & McKinlay, I.A. (1997). Motor difficulties in children with developmental disorders of speech and language. *Child: Care, Health and Development, 23*(4), 315–325. doi:10.1046/j.1365-2214.1997.864864

Ozonoff, S., Young, G.S., Carter, A., Messinger, D., Yirmiya, N., Zwaigenbaum, L., . . . Stone, W.L. (2011). Recurrence risk for autism spectrum disorders: A baby siblings research consortiums study. *Pediatrics, 128*(3), e488–e495. doi:10.1542/peds.2010-2825

Pardo C.A., & Eberhart C.G. (2007). The neurobiology of autism. *Brain Pathology 17*(4), 434–447. doi:10.1111/j.1750-3639.2007.00102

Paterson, S.J., Brown, J.H., Gsodl, M.K., Johnson, M.H., & Karmiloff-Smith, A. (1999). Cognitive modularity and genetic disorders. *Science, 286*(5448), 2355–2358. doi:10.1126/science.286.5448.2355

Piven, J., Bailey, J., Ranson, B.J., & Arndt, S. (1997). An MRI study of the corpus callosum in autism. *American Journal of Psychiatry, 154*(8), 1051–1056.

Preis, S., Steinmetz, H., Knorr, U., & Jancke, L. (2000). Corpus callosum size in children with developmental language disorder. *Cognitive Brain Research, 10*(1–2), 37–44. doi:10.1016/S0926-6410(00)00020-3

Price, C.J. (2000). The anatomy of language: Contributions from functional neuroimaging. *Journal of Anatomy, 197*(3), 335–359. doi:10.1046/j.1469-7580.2000.19730335

Rae, C., Lee, M.A., Dixon, R.M., Blamire, A.M., Thompson, C.H., Styles, P., ... Stein, J.F. (1998). Metabolic abnormalities in developmental dyslexia detected by 1H magnetic resonance spectroscopy. *The Lancet, 351*(9119), 1849–1852. doi:10.1016/S0140-6736(97)99001-2

Ramirez, M., Prieto, I., Vives, F., de Gasparo, M., & Alba, F. (2004). Neuropeptides, neuropeptidases and brain asymmetry. *Current Protein and Peptide Science, 5*(6), 497–506. doi:10.2174/1389203043379350

Rapin, I. (1996). *Preschool children with inadequate communication: Developmental language disorder, autism, low IQ* (Clinics in Developmental Medicine No. 139). London, England: Mac Keith Press.

Redcay, E., & Courchesne, E. (2005). When is the brain enlarged in autism? A meta-analysis of all brain size reports. *Biological Psychiatry, 58*(1), 1–9. doi:10.1016/j.biopsych.2005.03.026

Rescorla, L., & Goossens, M. (1992). Symbolic play development in toddlers with expressive specific language impairment (SLI-E). *Journal of Speech and Hearing Research, 35*(6), 1290–302.

Ringo, J.L. (1991). Neuronal interconnection as a function of brain size. *Brain, Behavior and Evolution, 38*(1), 1–6. doi:10.1159/000114375

Ringo, J.L., Doty, R.W., Demeter, S., & Simard, P.Y. (1994). Time is of the essence: A conjecture that hemispheric specialization arises from interhemispheric conduction delay. *Cerebral Cortex, 4*(4), 331–343. doi:10.1093/cercor/4.4.331

Rosenberger, P.B., & Hier, D.B. (1980). Cerebral asymmetry and verbal intellectual deficits. *Annals of Neurology, 8*(3), 300–304. doi:10.1002/ana.410080313

Rutter, M., Greenfeld, D., & Lockyer, L. (1967). A five to fifteen year follow-up study of infantile psychosis. II. Social and behavioural outcome. *The British Journal of Psychiatry, 113*(504), 1183–1199. doi:10.1192/bjp.113.504.1183

Ryu, Y.H., Lee, J.D., Yoon, P.H., Kim, D.I., Lee, H.B. , & Shin, Y.J. (1999). Perfusion impairments in infantile autism on technetium-99m ethyl cysteinate dimer brain single-photon emission tomography: Comparison with findings on magnetic resonance imaging. *The European Journal of Nuclear Medicine and Molecular Imaging, 26*(3), 253–259. doi:10.1007/s002590050385

Sajdel-Sulkowska, E.M., Ming, X., Koibuchi, N. (2009). Increase in brain neurotrophin-3 and oxidative stress in autism. *Cerebellum, 8,* 366–372.

Sajdel-Sulkowska, E.M., Ming, X., McGinnis, W., Koibuchi, N. (2010). Brain region-specific changes in oxidative stress and neurotrophin levels in autism spectrum disorders (ASD). *Cerebellum.*

Shen, Y.Q., Hebert, G., Moze, E., Li, K. S., & Neveu, P.J. (2005). Asymmetrical distribution of brain interleukin-6 depends on lateralization in mice. *Neuroimmunomodulation, 12*(3), 189–194. doi:10.1159/000084852

Shetty, N., Ratai, E., Ringer, A., & Herbert, M. (2009, May). *Magnetic resonance studies in ASD: Review of regions investigated, findings, potential influence of methodology, and directions for future research.* Poster session presented at the International Meeting for Autism Research, Chicago, IL.

Shields, J., Varley, R., Broks, P., & Simpson, A. (1996). Hemispheric function in developmental language disorders and high-level autism. *Developmental Medicine & Child Neurology, 38*(6), 473–486. doi:10.1111/j.1469-8749.1996.tb12108

Starkstein, S.E., Vazquez, S., Vranic, D., Nanclares, V., Manes, F., Piven, J., & Plebst, C. (2000). SPECT findings in mentally retarded autistic individuals. *Journal of Neuropsychiatry, 12*(3), 370–375. doi:10.1176/appi.neuropsych.12.3.370

Sundaram, S.K., Kumar, A., Makki, M.I., Behen, M.E., Chugani, H.T., & Chugani, D.C. (2008). Diffusion tensor imaging of frontal lobe in autism spectrum disorder. *Cerebral Cortex, 18*(11), 2659–2665. doi:10.1093/cercor/bhn031

Sutera, S., Pandey, J., Esser, E.L., Rosenthal, M.A., Wilson, L.B., Barton, M., … Fein, D. (2007). Predictors of optimal outcome in toddlers diagnosed with autism spectrum disorders. *Journal of Autism and Developmental Disorders, 37*(1), 98–107. doi:10.1007/s10803-006-0340-6

Theberge, J. (2008). Perfusion magnetic resonance imaging in psychiatry. *Topics in Magnetic Resonance Imaging, 19*(2), 111–130. doi:10.1097/RMR.0b013e3181808140

Trauner, D., Wulfeck, B., Tallal, P., & Hesselink, J. (2000). Neurological and MRI profiles of children with developmental language impairment. *Developmental Medicine and Child Neurology, 42*(7), 470–475. doi:10.1017/S0012162200000876

Voineagu, I., Wang, X., Johnston, P., Lowe, J. K., Tian, Y., Horvath, S., … Geschwind, D. H. (2011). Transcriptomic analysis of autistic brain reveals convergent molecular pathology. *Nature, 474*(7351), 380–384. doi: 10.1038/nature10110

Vargas, D.L., Nascimbene, C., Krishnan, C., Zimmerman, A.W., & Pardo, C.A. (2005). Neuroglial activation and neuroinflammation in the brain of patients with autism. *Annals of Neurology, 57*(1), 67–81. doi:10.1002/ana.20315

Wang, X., Wu, Z., Song, G., Wang, H., Long, M., & Cai, S. (1999). Effects of oxidative damage of membrane protein thiol groups on erythrocyte membrane viscoelasticities. *Clinical Hemorheology and Microcirculation Journal, 21*(2), 137–146.

Ward, K.E., Friedman, L., Wise, A., & Schulz, S.C. (1996). Meta-analysis of brain and cranial size in schizophrenia. *Schizophrenia Research, 22*(3), 197–213. doi:10.1016/S0920-9964(96)00076-X

Watkins, K.E., Vargha-Khadem, F., Ashburner, J., Passingham, R.E., Connelly, A., Friston, K.J., … Gadian, D.G. (2002). MRI analysis of an inherited speech and language disorder: Structural brain abnormalities. *Brain, 125*(3), 465–478. doi:10.1093/brain/awf057

Weismer, S.E., & Evans, J.L. (2002). The role of processing limitations in early identification of specific language impairment. *Topics in Language Disorders, 22*(3), 15–29. doi:10.1097/00011363-200205000-00004

Williams, D.L., Goldstein, G., & Minshew, N.J. (2006). Neuropsychologic functioning in children with autism: Further evidence for disordered complex information-processing. *Child Neuropsychology, 12*(4–5), 279–298. doi:10.1080/09297040600681190

Wisniewski, A.B. (1998). Sexually-dimorphic patterns of cortical asymmetry, and the role for sex steroid hormones in determining cortical patterns of lateralization. *Psychoneuroendocrinology, 23*(5), 519–547. doi:10.1016/S0306-4530(98)00019-5

Witelson, S.F. (1989). Hand and sex differences in the isthmus and genu of the corpus callosum: A postmortem morphological study. *Brain, 112,* 799–835.

Wittling, W. (1995). Brain asymmetry in the control of autonomic-physiologic activity. In R.J. Davidson & K. Hugdahl (Eds.), *Brain asymmetry* (pp. 305–357). Cambridge, MA: MIT Press.

Woodhouse, W., Bailey, A., Rutter, M., Bolton, P., Baird, G., & Le Couteur, A. (1996). Head circumference in autism and other perva-sive developmental disorders. *Journal of Child Psychology and Psychiatry, 37*(6), 665–671. doi:10.1111/j.1469-7610.1996.tb01458.x

Yao, Y., Walsh, W.J., McGinnis, W.R., & Pratico, D. (2006). Altered vascular phenotype in autism: correlation with oxidative stress. *Archives of Neurology, 63*(8), 1161–1164 doi:10.1001/archneur.63.8.1161

CHAPTER 19

Integration of Left-Lateralized Neural Systems Supporting Skilled Reading
Bruce D. McCandliss and Yuliya N. Yoncheva

E arly educational experiences with reading lead to remarkable changes in children's cognitive abilities to recognize the sight, sounds, and meaning of visual words. The emergence of this novel form of perceptual expertise brings representations of visual features and spoken language together in a fundamentally new way. This emerging ability requires functional reorganization of the visual system's cortical circuitry, specifically reflected in changes in the response properties of a left mid-fusiform region of the ventral object recognition pathway (for a review, see McCandliss, Cohen, & Dehaene, 2003). What are the critical factors at the cognitive, functional, and structural levels that drive this left-lateralized functional reorganization of the visual system and thus enable it to support fluent word recognition? How might individual variation in brain networks that are implicated in developmental dyslexia affect this experience-dependent process of cortical reorganization?

In this chapter, we review recent neuroimaging findings that illuminate the rise of perceptual expertise for reading, as well as the nature of individual differences in brain structure and functional organization that render such changes challenging for individuals with developmental dyslexia. In considering these questions, we draw upon the theoretical framework of interactive specialization (Johnson, 2000, 2001), which posits that postnatal functional changes in developing cortical regions are primarily driven not by maturation, but rather by patterns of interactivity with other cortical regions. Extending this framework to reading development, we propose that reading experience promotes novel interactivity among the visual system and other cortical systems, such as left-lateralized systems involved in processing the phonology of language. In this process, the specialization for reading within the visual system manifests in increasingly left-lateralized responses to visual word forms (Schlaggar & McCandliss, 2007). In keeping with the interactive specialization framework, we propose that top-down attention processes play a central role in establishing the necessary patterns of interactivity between visual and phonological cortical systems. Considering the

This work was supported by NIH R01DC007694, NSF REESE 0956855, and the James S. McDonnell Foundation.

implications of this framework for understanding individual differences in reading ability and dyslexia, we examine emerging evidence that links atypicalities in the left lateralization of phonological processing systems to atypicalities in the development of functional specialization for visual word recognition in left-lateralized regions of the visual system.

PERCEPTUAL EXPERTISE FOR VISUAL WORDS

Understanding the cognitive and neural processes that support perceptual expertise for visual word recognition requires integrating observations across converging methods (Posner & McCandliss, 1993). Functional magnetic resonance imaging (fMRI) studies reveal that when skilled adult readers view visual words, neural activity increases in a left-lateralized region of the ventral visual system near the mid-fusiform gyrus, referred to as the visual word form area (VWFA) or the visual word form system (Cohen et al., 2002; McCandliss et al., 2003). Converging evidence from lesion studies relate damage to this left-lateralized region (Cohen et al., 2003) to loss of the ability to fluently read visual words. Similarly, event-related potential (ERP) studies demonstrate that skilled readers' viewing of a visual word (relative to a control, visually matched stimulus, such as a symbol string) leads to a larger negative deflection over left posterior occipito-temporal regions within 170 milliseconds, termed the visual word form N170 response. This N170 response has been linked via intracranial recordings (Allison, McCarthy, Nobre, Puce, & Belger, 1994), source localization (Maurer, Brem, Bucher, & Brandeis, 2005), and joint ERP-fMRI experiments (Brem et al., 2006, 2010) to recruitment of the VWFA (for a review, see McCandliss et al., 2003; Schlaggar & McCandliss, 2007). Together, these findings of increased functional activity in response to visual words suggest a form of functional specialization, or experience-dependent tuning of response properties that support perceptual expertise.

Various lines of evidence link this form of neural specialization to the specific educational experience of learning to read one's own language. Cross-cultural studies that compare skilled adult readers of different scripts have demonstrated that both the left-lateralized mid-fusiform fMRI response (Baker et al., 2007) and the left-lateralized N170 response over posterior visual regions (Maurer, Zevin, & McCandliss, 2008; Wong, Gauthier, Woroch, DeBuse, & Curran, 2005) are highly 'tuned' to the specific properties of the script one has learned over multiple years relative to an unfamiliar script in another language. Furthermore, cross-sectional and even longitudinal studies that track preliterate children as they progress through the early years of literacy have demonstrated experience-related changes in N170 ERP responses to eventually exhibit sensitivity to visual words presented in native script and take on the characteristic left lateralization observed in adult skilled readers (e.g., Brem et al., 2009; Maurer et al., 2006).

Findings of experience-dependent changes in the functional properties of fusiform gyrus fMRI blood oxygen level-dependent (BOLD) responses and related N170 ERP effects are not unique to reading. N170 perceptual expertise effects have been demonstrated across a wide range of visual object categories, including faces (Maurer, Rossion, & McCandliss, 2008), birds, cars, and laboratory induced expertise in identifying novel "greeble" figures (for a review, see Bukach, Gauthier, & Tarr, 2006; Gauthier, Williams, Tarr, & Tanaka, 1998). Perceptual experiences of this sort can progressively tune fusiform gyrus and N170 responses and typically yield effects predominantly in the right, or across both hemispheres. Reading-related perceptual expertise effects, in contrast, consistently lead to left lateralization of both mid-fusiform fMRI and posterior occipito-temporal N170 ERP responses. Such left lateralized responses reach such a high degree of automaticity in skilled readers that they have been found even under conditions where subjects view words but focus all available perceptual resources on rapid streams of superimposed pictures (Ruz et al., 2005). This contrast in the lateralization of perceptual expertise for words versus other visual objects raises the question: Which aspects of the reading experience, and correspondingly, which regions of the functional network recruited by these reading experiences, drive the characteristic left lateralization of the visual word form system?

THE INTERACTIVE SPECIALIZATION FRAMEWORK AND TYPICAL READING DEVELOPMENT

Reading Acquisition in the Context of Interactive Specialization

One influential theoretical account of functional brain development, interactive specialization, provides a useful framework for understanding how experience-dependent processes lead to the left lateralization of the visual word form system by motivating hypotheses regarding the influence of individual differences in brain structure, function, and learning dynamics on the development of the reading system. This framework, proposed by Johnson and colleagues (Johnson, 2000, 2001), posits that the emergence of functional specialization within a given cortical region is shaped primarily by experience-dependent interactions with other specific cortical systems.

Applying the interactive specialization framework to reading acquisition may provide an account of the processes that lead to the emergence of the hallmark left lateralization of the functional specialization of the visual word form system. This framework is related to our previously proposed phonological mapping hypothesis (Maurer & McCandliss, 2007), which suggests that the left lateralization of visual word form processing is largely driven by the processing demands inherent in reading an alphabetic writing system, which requires extensive coactivation of systems involved in the visual analysis of print and systems involved in the phonological analysis of the sounds of language, which are largely left-lateralized (Joanisse, McCandliss, & Zevin, 2007). In the following sections, we provide evidence for three important aspects of the cortical dynamics of reading that are essential to the interactive specialization account. First, we propose that activation of left-lateralized phonological regions and their related connections to the left-lateralized visual word form area can be recruited by top-down task demands in skilled adult readers. Second, we propose that during the process of learning to read, top-down attention to phonology drives left lateralization of visual word form responses to stimuli learned under such task demands. Finally, we suggest that individual variation or atypicalities in the organization of the phonological system lead to atypicalities in the development of the left-lateralized visual word form area.

Selective Attention to Phonology in Skilled Reading

How a voluntary mental activity such as learning to read can drive functional reorganization within a cortical region is a fundamental issue in cognitive neuroscience accounts of reading. By the interactive specialization account, functional changes observed in a cortical region are driven by increased interactivity with other functional cortical systems. What are the top-down processes that might drive such increased interactivity among regions? To examine this, we investigated the voluntary, top-down impact of selective attention to phonology on cortical activity using fMRI in skilled adults, while controlling for all bottom-up stimulus effects (Yoncheva, Zevin, Maurer, & McCandliss, 2010). Participants performed a rhyme judgment on spoken word pairs, while ignoring three-note melodies superimposed on each word. An equally challenging control condition directed attention to the same auditory stimuli, but required focusing on the melodies in the service of a matching task. A left-lateralized network including frontal and superior temporal regions typically associated with phonological processes showed greater activation when attention was focused on phonology rather than on melodies (Figure 19.1). Thus, attention to phonology enhanced activation in left-lateralized phonological networks, and such increased activity in reading related tasks may be an important prerequisite for interactive specialization.

Even though no visual words were presented, focusing attention on the phonology of spoken words also produced increased activation of the left mid-fusiform gyrus, a region associated with the VWFA. A spatial analysis directly contrasting anatomically defined left and right hemisphere regions of interest (ROIs) provided direct evidence that this top-down effect was left-lateralized and isolated to mid-fusiform gyrus. Related findings in children (mean age: 12 years) have demonstrated that left lingual/fusiform activity in a rhyme task correlates with the speed of making rhyme judgments, and notably that this correlation

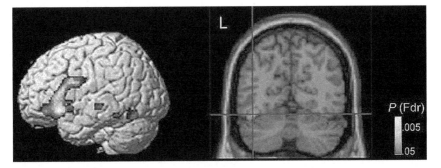

Figure 19.1. Functional magnetic resonance imaging results demonstrating regions of increased activation associated with selectively attending to phonological codes within spoken words relative to attending to embedded melodies. Crosshairs indicate an anatomically defined region of interest in the left mid-fusiform gyrus (the visual word form area). (Reprinted from Yoncheva, Y.N., Zevin, J.D., Maurer, U., & McCandliss, B.D. Auditory Selective Attention to Speech Modulates Activity in the Visual Word Form Area, *Cerebral Cortex,* 2010, 20, 3, 622–632, by permission of Oxford University Press.)

grows stronger as children approach adulthood. Furthermore, activation of the left fusiform gyrus by such an auditory rhyme task is absent in children with reading difficulties in contrast to age-matched typical readers (Desroches et al., 2010). Taken together, these results lend support to the notion that top-down attention to phonological codes, such as those elicited by the task demands of the early phases of reading acquisition, may lead to increased functional interactivity between the left-lateralized phonological circuitry and the left-lateralized mid-fusiform regions specialized for processing visual words.

Selective Attention to Phonology During Visual Word Learning

A second implication of the interactive specialization framework applied to reading is that increased interactivity between phonological and visual processes during learning should lead to sustained changes in lateralization of visual responses to learned visual words. This hypothesis was investigated in an N170 ERP study of skilled adult readers learning an artificial orthography (Yoncheva, Blau, Maurer, & McCandliss, 2010). Selective attention to phonology was manipulated between two groups of skilled adult readers who otherwise engaged in identical learning trials. The whole-word group learned to associate glyph-like word symbols with familiar, meaningful, spoken English words. The grapheme–phoneme group learned the same material, but instructions directed them to attend to hidden novel visual letters embedded within the glyphs and to learn to associate each with consonants and vowels within the spoken words. In a subsequent ERP experiment, both groups viewed trained glyphs within a reading verification (audio-visual matching) task and their N170 responses were contrasted. Results demonstrated that focusing attention on subsyllabic phonology during visual word learning has an impact on subsequent encounters with the learned visual word forms. For participants who focused attention on phonology during learning, N170 responses to trained words were significantly left-lateralized over left posterior inferior visual regions. Conversely, the whole-word focus group exhibited a right-lateralized N170 topography to these same visual words learned under conditions that did not explicitly focus attention on associated phonological codes (Figure 19.2).

A related artificial orthography training study examined whether N170 lateralization would reflect learning strategy even when the same student had to master whole-word mappings for some words versus grapheme–phoneme mappings for others (Yoncheva, Wise, & McCandliss, 2011). Reading words trained with a focus on phonology again elicited a left-lateralized N170 topography, in stark contrast to the right-lateralized N170 response to words learned with a focus on whole words. It is interesting to note that reading novel but decodable (based on learned grapheme–phoneme mappings) words led to a further differential recruitment of left-lateralized networks later in the processing stream during the late posterior positivity complex starting at approximately 400 ms after viewing the word. Whereas latency of the late posterior positivity complex ERP response has commonly been linked to domain-general aspects of task performance, the current lateralization modulation might reflect reading-specific processes as learners actively engage in decoding letter-to-sound mappings. Overall, the reproducible patterns of lateralization bias across the two artificial orthography training experiments reinforce the notion that the act of directing attention to phonology during learning of visual words likely sets up lasting patterns of left-lateralized N170 responses, which can be evoked even when these words are presented under different task conditions.

Similar findings have been obtained in fMRI studies of left-lateralized inferior occipitotemporal regions near the VWFA, demonstrating functional changes in this area when novel visual symbols were learned in association with speech sounds, but not in association with nonspeech control sounds (Hashimoto & Sakai, 2004). As expected in light of the

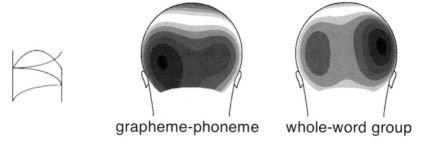

grapheme-phoneme   whole-word group

Figure 19.2.   N170 responses to novel visual word forms from an artificial orthography, following training that directs subjects' attention to grapheme–phoneme versus whole-word associations. (*Source:* Yoncheva, Blau, Maurer, & McCandliss, 2010.)

phonological mapping hypothesis, even an intensive, 2-week visual training in an artificial script, when administered in isolation of phonological instruction, failed to recruit left-lateralized fusiform responses on subsequent encounters of this visual script despite proficiency in identifying these symbols (Xue, Chen, Jin, & Dong, 2006). These findings reinforce the pivotal point differentiating interactive specialization accounts from other, more general "experience-dependent" accounts. Although in all of the previously reviewed studies participants obtained equivalent visual experience with the learned stimuli, the critical factor that mediated functional changes in VWFA-related regions was how these visual experiences were associated with other systems, namely the systems associated with phonological codes in speech.

Individual Differences and Interactive Specialization

The interactive specialization account of systems-level changes in function and anatomy associated with reading holds potentially important implications for predicting how individual differences in cortical systems that are present prior to reading experience might influence one another later during reading acquisition. This framework provides an account of how individual variations in the left lateralization of cortical systems associated with phonology, including atypicalities associated with dyslexia (for a review, see McCandliss & Noble, 2003), and poor phonological abilities in early readers from low socioeconomic status backgrounds (Noble, Farah, & McCandliss, 2006; Noble, Wolmetz, Ochs, Farah, & McCandliss, 2006) might affect the development of perceptual expertise for reading and the eventual left lateralization of the visual word form system. A recent example lending support to this notion investigated the left lateralization of kindergarten children's late mismatch negativity ERP response to auditory contrasts, including phonemic contrasts to speech stimuli (Maurer et al., 2009). Greater left lateralization of responses to phoneme deviants in kindergarten was found to be a strong predictor of future gains in reading and was significantly predictive of individual differences in reading skill later exhibited by these same children in second to fifth grade across a range of children with and without familial risk for dyslexia. It is interesting to note that predictions based on left lateralization of electrophysiological responses to phonemic contrasts captured unique variance above and beyond that provided by behavioral measures alone.

Future studies that combine early measures of individual differences in cortical systems that exist before reading onset with longitudinal studies of functional changes may provide even more direct tests of the hypothesis that functional changes in the visual regions crucial to reading are driven by the nature of the systems they interact with during learning, such that individual differences in a property such as the left lateralization in one system becomes "inherited" by the other system (see Chapter 12).

THE INTERACTIVE SPECIALIZATION FRAMEWORK AND DYSLEXIA

Differences in Left Lateralization
Revealed by Functional Magnetic Resonance
Imaging and Positron Emission Tomography

How is this left-lateralized visual specialization altered in individuals
with dyslexia? A recent study that examined the convergence of findings
of reduced activations in readers with dyslexia relative to unimpaired
readers revealed that the largest cluster of significant overlap was centered in a left occipito-temporal region that included the VWFA (see Figure 19.3; McCandliss & Wolmetz, 2004). Similar findings were reported
in a more inclusive meta-analysis using a related technique for specifying
ROIs (Maisog, Einbinder, Flowers, Turkeltaub, & Eden, 2008). As predicted, based on these functional meta-analyses, the N170 expertise effect
for visual words in individuals with dyslexia is also specifically compromised. This is the case for both children in their early stages of reading
acquisition (Maurer et al., 2007) and reading-impaired adults (Helenius,
Tarkiainen, Cornelissen, Hansen, & Salmelin, 1999).

Together these observations support the proposition that the processes critical for the left-lateralized specialization of fusiform gyrus regions
in skilled adults are compromised in dyslexia, further highlighting the importance of elucidating the causal factors at the cognitive, functional, and
structural levels responsible for this developmental process going awry.

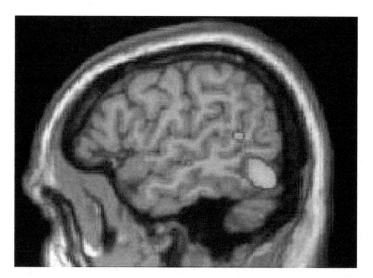

Figure 19.3. Quantitative meta-analysis of eight functional magnetic resonance
imaging and positron emission tomography findings that differentiate brain activity in skilled and readers with dyslexia viewing visual letters, pseudowords, or
real words.

White Matter Tract Studies of
Individual Differences in Left Lateralization

Next we consider how structural atypicalities in the left lateralization of cortical systems may pose unique challenges to the experience-dependent processes that typically shape the left-lateralized organization of the visual word form system. Diffusion tensor imaging (DTI) measures have recently demonstrated a set of well-replicated results relevant to children's individual differences in several cognitive domains including short-term memory (Niogi et al., 2006), mathematics (van Eimeren et al., 2008), and reading skill. Individual differences in diffusion properties of white matter tracts were first reported to differentiate individuals with dyslexia from controls and to correlate with individual differences in reading ability. The most robust findings emerged in a left temporo-parietal region at the level of the corpus calosum (Klingberg et al., 2000). Studies of typically developing children (Beaulieu et al., 2005; Deutsch et al., 2005), as well as children with development dyslexia (Niogi & McCandliss, 2006; Odegard, Farris, Ring, McColl, & Black, 2009), have found strikingly similar results, several of which have isolated this region to superior-inferior projection fibres in the left superior corona radiata (SCR). Converging findings across all these investigations demonstrate a strong correlation between microstructural (i.e., fractional anisotropy) properties in this white matter tract structure and children's standardized reading scores in the Woodcock Johnson Word Identification test. Remarkably, across multiple studies, properties of this left hemisphere white matter tract region account for between 30% and 50% of the variance in children's reading scores. Although no other structure has been reported to demonstrate such consistency in patterns of correlation with reading skill, several reports have found correlations between right hemisphere regions and reading skill (Beaulieu et al., 2005; Odegard et al., 2009; Rimrodt, Peterson, Denckla, Kaufmann, & Cutting, 2010).

In light of the well-established functional significance of left-lateralized cortical systems contributing to reading function, Niogi and McCandliss (2006) directly investigated the influence of lateralization in the SCR fiber tract via a semi-automated region of interest approach (Niogi, Mukherjee, & McCandliss, 2007). To normalize overall main effects that affect FA variations from one child to the next and to extract a sensitive index of individual differences, a lateralization index for each child was computed by subtracting the FA values in the left SCR from the FA values in the right SCR and diving by the sum of the two (thus, a negative index corresponds to left lateralization). Correlating individual's lateralization index with their respective standardized reading scores yielded robust results, suggesting that children who scored in the dyslexic range were characterized by reduced FA scores in the left SCR relative to their own FA scores in the right hemisphere SCR (see Figure 19.4).

The pattern of a positive brain–behavior correlation between FA scores in the left SCR and reading-related skills held also true for phonological

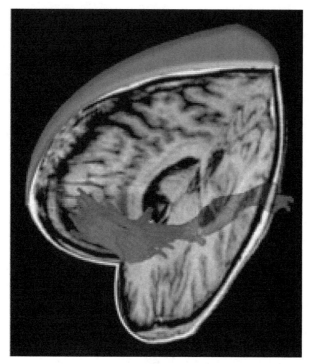

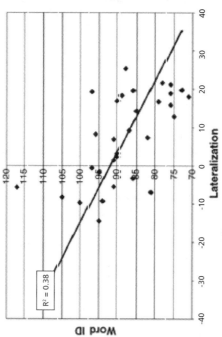

Figure 19.4. Lateralization index of fractional anisotropy scores in superior corona radiata (SCR) correlates strongly with reading performance, as indexed by Word Identification scores (left panel); Fibrotractography of the left SCR (right panel). (*Source:* Niogi & McCandliss, 2006.)

decoding abilities (Odegard et al., 2009) and phonological awareness measures, specifically demonstrating a strong correlation with Elision scores (r = .67, $p < .01$), a measure that captures the form of synthesis and analysis that is most relevant for subsyllabic phonological processes. Other forms of phonological awareness, such as memory for digits and rapid automatized naming, were uncorrelated with SCR measures in the same population. These findings converge to support the interactive specialization prediction in that the degree of left lateralization of systems involved in phonological processing is functionally linked to the emergence of visual word recognition skills. It should be noted, however, that these studies provide no evidence bearing on the direction of causality among these observations, especially as findings are beginning to emerge of reading-related experience-driven changes in white matter tract properties (Keller & Just, 2009).

FUTURE DIRECTIONS

Skilled readers' perceptual expertise in fluently recognizing visual word forms has been attributed to experience-dependent tuning of extrastriate regions reflected in a characteristically left-lateralized pattern of neural activity. In this chapter, we consider the origins of the left-lateralized signature of reading expertise in the context of an interactive specialization account and propose that it arises due to interactivity between the visual system and left-lateralized systems engaged in phonological language processing. Within this framework, we suggest that specific structural and functional sources of individual differences influence the course of reading expertise development.

Methodological strides in pediatric neuroimaging over the past decade now allow direct longitudinal tracking of experience-driven changes as children become literate. This renders the theoretical perspective of interactive specialization valuable in generating testable predictions at the level of individual learners. First, consider the degree to which top-down phonological recruitment takes place prior to and during reading acquisition. Concurrently tracing the lateralization of preexisting phonological and emerging reading functions in the same child would inform the extent to which lateralization of the visual word form system can be predicted by lateralization of phonology. As illustrated by Gaab and colleagues (Chapter 17), atypicalities in the lateralization of preliterate's phonological processing can be related to risk factors—for example, familial history of dyslexia—further motivating investigations of the interactions between risk factors and the rise of reading expertise. Second, consider anatomical variation in the lateralization of the white matter tracts that are typically linked to phonological skills as a factor potentially biasing the interactive specialization process leading to the lateralization of the visual word form system. Given that individual differences in left SCR FA have been consistently shown to correlate with reading performance, the association between extrastriate regions, which subserve reading expertise and left-lateralized white matter tracts beckons a direct investigation. Indeed, extending these questions beyond typical development, Leonard and colleagues (Chapter 15) have completed a series of studies delineating profiles of anatomical asymmetry relevant to dyslexia as opposed to fluent reading. It is interesting to note that relations between reading performance and anatomical indices were moderated by executive functions, implicating top-down processes as players in the practice of gaining perceptual expertise for reading.

Future studies of the neural systems that support reading acquisition across typical and atypical development ought to combine insights regarding preexisting individual differences relevant to language function that might bias specialization, individual differences in learning dynamics shaping the corresponding patterns of interactivity, and the phenomena arising out of the learning process, such as the left-lateralized perceptual expertise for reading. With headway made in addressing these questions, shaping a learner's experience through education holds a brighter than ever potential (McCandliss, 2010; Varma, McCandliss, & Schwartz, 2008).

REFERENCES

Allison, T., McCarthy, G., Nobre, A., Puce, A., & Belger, A. (1994). Human extrastriate visual cortex and the perception of faces, words, numbers, and colors. *Cerebral Cortex, 4,* 544–554. doi:10.1093/cercor/4.5.544

Baker, C.I., Liu, J., Wald, L.L., Kwong, K.K., Benner, T., & Kanwisher, N. (2007). Visual word processing and experiential origins of functional selectivity in human extrastriate cortex. *Proceedings of the National Academy of Sciences, USA, 104,* 9087–9092. doi:10.1073/pnas.0703300104

Beaulieu, C., Plewes, C., Paulson, L.A., Roy, D., Snook, L., Concha, L., & Phillips, L. (2005). Imaging brain connectivity in children with diverse reading ability. *Neuroimage, 25,* 1266–1271. doi:10.1016/j.neuroimage.2004.12.053

Brem, S., Bach, S., Kucian, K., Guttorm, T.K., Martin, E., Lyytinen, H., … Richardson, U. (2010). Brain sensitivity to print emerges when children learn letter-speech sound correspondences. *Proceedings of the National Academy of Sciences, USA, 107,* 7939–7944. doi:10.1073/pnas.0904402107

Brem, S., Bucher, K., Halder, P., Summers, P., Dietrich, T., Martin, E., & Brandeis, D. (2006). Evidence for developmental changes in the visual word processing network beyond adolescence. *Neuroim-*

age, 29, 822–837. doi:10.1016/j.neuroimage.2005.09.023

Brem, S., Halder, P., Bucher, K., Summers, P., Martin, E., & Brandeis, D. (2009). Tuning of the visual word processing system: Distinct developmental ERP and fMRI effects. *Human Brain Mapping, 30,* 1833–1844. doi:10.1002/hbm.20751

Bukach, C.M., Gauthier, I., & Tarr, M.J. (2006). Beyond faces and modularity: The power of an expertise framework. *Trends in Cognitive Sciences, 10,* 159–166. doi:10.1016/j.tics.2006.02.004

Cohen, L., Lehericy, S., Chochon, F., Lemer, C., Rivaud, S., & Dehaene, S. (2002). Language-specific tuning of visual cortex? Functional properties of the visual word form area. *Brain, 125,* 1054–1069. doi:10.1093/brain/awf094

Cohen, L., Martinaud, O., Lemer, C., Lehericy, S., Samson, Y., Obadia, M., … Dehaene, S. (2003). Visual word recognition in the left and right hemispheres: Anatomical and functional correlates of peripheral alexias. *Cerebral Cortex, 13,* 1313–1333. doi:10.1093/cercor/bhg079

Desroches, A.S., Cone, N.E., Bolger, D.J., Bitan, T., Burman, D.D., & Booth, J.R. (2010). Children with reading difficulties show differences in brain regions associated with orthographic processing during spoken language processing. *Brain Research, 1356,* 73–84. doi:10.1016/j.brainres.2010.07.097

Deutsch, G.K., Dougherty, R.F., Bammer, R., Siok, W.T., Gabrieli, J.D., & Wandell, B. (2005). Children's reading performance is correlated with white matter structure measured by diffusion tensor imaging. *Cortex, 41,* 354–363. doi:10.1016/S0010-9452(08)70272-7

Gauthier, I., Williams, P., Tarr, M.J., & Tanaka, J. (1998). Training 'greeble' experts: A framework for studying expert object recognition processes. *Vision Research, 38,* 2401–2428. doi:10.1016/S0042-6989(97)00442-2

Hashimoto, R., & Sakai, K.L. (2004). Learning letters in adulthood: Direct visualization of cortical plasticity for forming a new link between orthography and phonology. *Neuron, 42,* 311–322.

Helenius, P., Tarkiainen, A., Cornelissen, P., Hansen, P.C., & Salmelin, R. (1999). Dissociation of normal feature analysis and deficient processing of letter-strings in dyslexic adults. *Cerebral Cortex, 9,* 476–483. doi:10.1093/cercor/9.5.476

Joanisse, M., Zevin, J.D., & McCandliss, B.D. (2007). Brain mechanisms implicated in the preattentive categorization of speech sounds revealed using fMRI and short interval habituation trials. *Cerebral Cortex, 17,* 2084–2093. doi:10.1093/cercor/bhl124

Johnson, M.H. (2000). Functional brain development in infants: Elements of an interactive specialization framework. *Child Development, 71,* 75–81. doi:10.1111/1467-8624.00120

Johnson, M.H. (2001). Functional brain development in humans. *Nature Reviews Neuroscience, 2,* 475–483. doi:10.1038/35081509

Keller, T.A., & Just, M.A. (2009). Altering cortical connectivity: Remediation-induced changes in the white matter of poor readers. *Neuron, 64,* 624–631. doi:10.1016/j.neuron.2009.10.018

Klingberg, T., Hedehus, M., Temple, E., Salz, T., Gabrieli, J.D., & Moseley, M.E. (2000). Microstructure of temporo-parietal white matter as a basis for reading ability: Evidence from diffusion tensor magnetic resonance imaging. *Neuron, 25,* 493–500.

Maisog, J.M., Einbinder, E.R., Flowers, D.L., Turkeltaub, P.E., & Eden, G.F. (2008). A meta-analysis of functional neuroimaging studies of dyslexia. *Annals of the New York Academy of Sciences, 1145,* 237–259. doi:10.1196/annals.1416.024

Maurer, U., Brem, S., Bucher, K., & Brandeis, D. (2005). Emerging neurophysiological specialization for letter strings. *Journal of Cognitive Neuroscience, 17,* 1532–1552. doi:10.1162/089892905774597218

Maurer, U., Brem, S., Bucher, K., Kranz, F., Benz, R., Steinhausen, H.C., & Brandeis, D. (2007). Impaired tuning of a fast occipito-temporal response for print in dyslexic children learning to read. *Brain, 130,* 3200–3210. doi:10.1093/brain/awm193

Maurer, U., Brem, S., Kranz, F., Bucher, K., Benz, R., Halder, P., … Brandeis, D. (2006). Coarse neural tuning for print peaks when children learn to read. *Neuroimage, 33,* 749–758. doi:10.1016/j.neuroimage.2006.06.025

Maurer, U., Bucher, K., Brem, S., Benz, R., Kranz, F., Schulz, E., … Brandeis, D. (2009). Neurophysiology in preschool improves behavioral prediction of reading ability throughout primary school. *Biological Psychiatry, 66,* 341–348. doi:10.1016/j.biopsych.2009.02.031

Maurer, U., & McCandliss, B.D. (2007). The development of visual expertise for words: The contribution of electrophysiology. In E.L. Grigorenko & A.J. Naples (Eds.), *Single-word reading: Biological and behavioral perspectives* (pp. 43–64). Mahwah, NJ: Lawrence Erlbaum.

Maurer, U., Rossion, B., & McCandliss, B.D. (2008). Category specificity in early perception: Face and word N170 responses differ in both lateralization and habituation properties. *Frontiers in Human Neuroscience, 2*(18). doi:10.3389/neuro.09.018.2008

Maurer, U., Zevin, J.D., & McCandliss, B.D. (2008). Left-lateralized N170 effects of visual expertise in reading: evidence from Japanese syllabic and logographic scripts. *Journal of Cognitive Neuroscience, 20,* 1878–1891. doi:10.1162/jocn.2008.20125

McCandliss, B.D. (2010). Educational neuroscience: The early years. *Proceedings of the National Academy of Sciences, USA, 107,* 8049–8050. doi:10.1073/pnas.1003431107

McCandliss, B.D., Cohen, L., & Dehaene, S. (2003). The visual word form area: Expertise for reading in the fusiform gyrus. *Trends in Cognitive Sciences, 7,* 293–299. doi:10.1016/S1364-6613(03)00134-7

McCandliss, B.D., & Noble, K.G. (2003). The development of reading impairment: A cognitive neuroscience model. *Mental Retardation & Developmental Disabilities Research Reviews, 9,* 196–204. doi:10.1002/mrdd.10080

McCandliss, B.D., & Wolmetz, M. (2004). Developmental psychobiology of reading disability. In B.J. Casey (Ed.), *Developmental Psychobiology* (Vol. 23, pp. 69–110). Washington, DC: American Psychiatric Publishing.

Niogi, S.N., & McCandliss, B.D. (2006). Left lateralized white matter microstructure accounts for individual differences in reading ability and disability. *Neuropsychologia, 44,* 2178–2188. doi:10.1016/j.neuropsychologia.2006.01.011

Niogi, S.N., Mukherjee, P., & McCandliss, B.D. (2007). Diffusion tensor imaging segmentation of white matter structures using a Reproducible Objective Quantification Scheme (ROQS). *NeuroImage, 35,* 166–174 doi:10.1016/j.neuroimage.2006.10.040

Noble, K.G., Farah, M., & McCandliss, B.D. (2006). Socioeconomic background modulates cognition-achievement relationships in reading. *Cognitive Development, 21,* 349–368. doi:10.1016/j.cogdev.2006.01.007

Noble, K.G., Wolmetz, M.E., Ochs, L.G., Farah, M., & McCandliss, B.D. (2006). Brain-behavior relationships in reading acquisition are modulated by socioeconomic status factors. *Developmental Science, 9*(6), 642–654.

Odegard, T.N., Farris, E.A., Ring, J., McColl, R., & Black, J. (2009). Brain connectivity in non-reading impaired children and children diagnosed with developmental dyslexia. *Neuropsychologia, 47,* 1972–1977. doi:10.1016/j.neuropsychologia.2009.03.009

Posner, M.I., & McCandliss, B.D. (1993). Converging methods for investigating lexical access. *Psychological Science, 4,* 305–309. doi:10.1111/j.1467-9280.1993.tb00569.x

Rimrodt, S.L., Peterson, D.J., Denckla, M.B., Kaufmann, W.E., & Cutting, L.E. (2010). White matter microstructural differences linked to left perisylvian language network in children with dyslexia. *Cortex, 46,* 739–749. doi:10.1016/j.cortex.2009.07.008

Ruz, M., Worden, M.S., Tudela, P., & McCandliss, B.D. (2005). Inattentional amnesia to words in a high attentional load task. *Journal of Cognitive Neuroscience, 17*(5), 768–776. doi:10.1162/0898929053747685

Schlaggar, B.L., & McCandliss, B.D. (2007). Development of neural systems for reading. *Annual Review of Neuroscience, 30,* 475–503. doi:10.1146/annurev.neuro.28.061604.135645

Varma, S., McCandliss, B.D., & Schwartz, D.L. (2008). Scientific and pragmatic challenges for bridging education and neuroscience. *Educational Researcher, 37,* 140–152. doi:10.3102/0013189X08317687

Wong, A.C.N., Gauthier, I., Woroch, B., DeBuse, C., & Curran, T. (2005). An early electrophysiological response associated with expertise in letter perception. *Cognitive, Affective & Behavioral Neuroscience, 5,* 306–318. doi:10.3758/CABN.5.3.306

Xue, G., Chen, C., Jin, Z., & Dong, Q. (2006). Language experience shapes fusiform activation when processing a logographic artificial language: An fMRI training study. *Neuroimage, 31,* 1315–1326. doi:10.1016/j.neuroimage.2005.11.055

Yoncheva, Y.N., Blau, V.C., Maurer, U., & McCandliss, B.D. (2010). Attentional focus during learning impacts N170 responses to an artificial script. *Developmental Neuropsychology, 35,* 423–445. doi:10.1080/87565641.2010.480918

Yoncheva, Y.N., Zevin, J.D., Maurer, U., & McCandliss, B.D. (2010). Auditory selective attention to speech modulates activity in the visual word form area. *Cerebral Cortex, 20,* 622–632. doi:10.1093/cercor/bhp129

Yoncheva, Y.N., Wise, J., & McCandliss, B.D. (2011). Attentional focus during learning impacts N170 lateralization to novel visual word forms. *Journal of Cognitive Neuroscience,* Supplement ISSN 1096-8857, 229.

van Eimeren, L.V., Niogi, S., McCandliss, B.D., Holloway, I.D., & Ansari, D. (2008). White matter microstructures underlying mathematical abilities in children. *NeuroReport, 11,* 1117–1121. doi:10.1097/WNR.0b013e328307f5c1

Conclusion/Next Steps
Critical Research Directions and Priorities
Peggy McCardle and Brett Miller

T he 12th Extraordinary Brain Symposium of The Dyslexia Foundation
(TDF) focused on biological substrates and potential early precursors
of language disorders and developmental dyslexia (DD) and on new
approaches to investigating neural and genetic mechanisms that might contribute to and potentially be used to predict patterns of disability in these
conditions. As can be seen in the contents of this book, the participants
of this meeting represented various disciplines and approaches, including
behavioral science, genetics, neurobiology (including neuroimaging), and
both animal models and studies of children. At issue throughout the symposium, and in fact throughout the field of those studying dyslexia and other developmental difficulties that are multifactorial, is whether the same
or similar behavioral profiles can be caused by a variety of different etiologies, or whether the same genetic and/or neurobiological conditions can
produce a variety of different developmental problems. Clearly both can
occur, but to what extent, and how and why? Is it possible to predict, based
on genetic mechanisms, how neuroanatomical and/or neurophysiological
development might go awry, and how would that make a difference for
not only earlier identification but also to develop more targeted and earlier
treatments? Is there a better way to explore early precursors of language
disorders and dyslexia, and what controls or influences comorbidities?

The 12th Extraordinary Brain Symposium explored these issues. In
this chapter, we briefly review the specific future research recommendations made by the chapter authors and then summarize key themes
that were discussed at the symposium and that we see as overarching for
the field and for the future of research into the genetics, neurobiology,
and behavior of dyslexia. Although we know that such distinctions are
artificial, we present the chapters and their recommendations through
our triumvirate—genetics, neurobiology, and behavior—the three linked
facets of the interdisciplinary science we see as critical to moving forward
in understanding dyslexia.

GENETICS
The chapters in Section I of this book and a few from other sections focus primarily on genetic mechanisms regulating brain development and

The opinions and assertions contained herein are the private opinions of the authors
and are not to be construed as official or reflecting the views of the U.S. Department of
Health and Human Services or the National Institutes of Health.

individual variation, in both animal and human models. In Chapter 1, Nowakowski lays out some basics of early brain development in a mouse model, indicating that he sees using genetic differences in inbred strains of mice (with potential to extend this approach to humans) as a "Rosetta Stone" to link across traits, pathologies, and even behaviors. He sees the extensive homology between the mouse and human genomes as a potential bridge between basic and translational research and advocates using a combination of genome-wide and other genetic approaches to understanding brain development and function. Approaches using both human genetics and animal models (e.g., mouse knockouts and knockins; LoTurco, Chapter 2) should in the near future significantly increase our understanding of both the genetics and neurophysiology of dyslexia and other disorders of reading and language. Alongside ongoing work in humans, LoTurco recommends continued work with animal genetic models to specifically define cellular neurophysiology and circuitry changes to better understand the disruptions caused by dyslexia candidate genes and ultimately to help determine the timing and targets for optimal educational interventions.

Fitch and Szalkowski (Chapter 11 in Section III) examine the use of core behavioral phenotypes and the manipulation of candidate language disability genes, highlighting the unique opportunity that animal models provide. They suggest that cross-level experimental work is important to uncovering the details of the complex genes–brain–behavior links and the trajectory underlying the emergence of language disorders. Marino, Mascheretti, Facoetti, and Molteni (Chapter 4), in calling for further research, raise three questions: how to best conceptualize pleiotropy (how do genes come together to influence overexpression and comorbidities, additively or interactively?), how to address the explanatory gap between the statistical association of a gene variant and a disorder and our understanding of pathogenesis, and how genes confer increased susceptibility in light of environmental factors. They urge future researchers addressing the genetics of dyslexia and language disorders to consider environmental influences (socioeconomic status, familial structure, parental education, and home literacy) on neuropsychological phenotypes as well as genetic pleiotropic effects on multiple neural systems.

In the capstone of the genetics chapters, Grigorenko (Chapter 5) explores the links between reading disability research and genetics, differentiating between definitive and tentative findings, and outlines connections between the new field of public health genomics and reading disability. Both seek to personalize/individualize their current research findings and impact; both make use of technology and multimedia to disseminate information; both have over time changed their definition of problems; but public health genomics has focused on using genomic information to improve health, whereas education has largely ignored such information. Grigorenko gives three stages for translating genomic discoveries into public health application: discovery (analytical validity stage), clinical validity (which includes ethical and social considerations), and implementation (which also establishes the short- and long-term net benefits). She offers an approach to using this model for education and genomics, beginning with public education, then provider education, and finally and most importantly, the engagement of the professional and lay communities in a discussion about the issues of where and how public health, genomics, and education can and should meet.

NEUROBIOLOGY

Neurobehavioral markers and biological mechanisms are a clear theme of this book and are addressed using both animal and human models. Stein (Chapter 3) discusses the visual magnocellular system and impairments of it found in many dyslexics, asserting that the most fruitful areas of future research may be a combination of genetics, immunology, and nutrition. He advocates examining nutrition in populations known to have a high prevalence of reading difficulties (incarcerated youth) as a potential basis for cost-effective yet potentially powerful intervention, which he believes will improve social functioning, although a direct connection with reading ability has yet to be established.

Rosen (Chapter 10) describes his work with animal models designed to examine the neurolobiology–behavior links thought to underlie aspects of dyslexia. He asserts that the genes modulating DD will reflect the complexity of the disorder itself and that this complex phenotype is probably regulated by a large complex network of genes that interact in ways that can not yet be deciphered. He cites the integration of findings from various disciplines (neuroscience, cognitive science, physiology, and psychology) across human and animal models as a key problem facing the field. This is a key theme for this book and in fact for many of TDF's symposia.

Several chapters of this book address early brain development, how it can be studied, and how studies can and must examine the interactions of perception, learning, and neurobiological development (both structural and functional). Grant (Chapter 14) emphasizes the importance of developmental trajectories in brain development from birth to 3 years. She offers a basic overview of neuroimaging tools, technologies, and challenges in their use with infants and young children. (Note that the NIH has two major resources available that can facilitate such research[1].) Grant points out that,

---

[1]The National Institutes of Health (NIH) Blueprint for Neuroscience Research has established the Neuroimaging Informatics Tools and Resources Clearinghouse (NITRC), which facilitates finding and comparing neuroimaging resources for functional and structural neuroimaging analyses; NITRC can be found at http://www.nitrc.org/. In addition, the NIH Magnetic Resonance Imaging (MRI) Study of Normal Brain Development has been completed; the Pediatric MRI Data Repository web site at https://nihpd.crbs.ucsd.edu/ nihpd/info/index.html provides information on the study and on how the data can be obtained by qualified researchers. The overarching goal of the Pediatric MRI Study is to foster a better understanding of normal brain maturation as a basis for understanding atypical brain development associated with a variety of disorders and diseases. In addition, the National Institute of Child Health & Human Development (NICHD) supports the ongoing development of a pediatric functional MRI database similar to the structural data repository, which will be made available to the field upon completion.

as structural and functional imaging techniques improve, so too does the ability to move from group studies to studies of individual differences and potentially to predict future problems such as dyslexia.

Addressing the importance of neuroanatomy, Leonard (Chapter 15) reports on a study of more than 300 individuals from which she and colleagues determined that passage comprehension seems more closely associated than other reading or language skills to the size of the auditory cortex and to cerebral asymmetry. She speculates that this finding is potentially moderated by processing speed and urges future research to examine reading comprehension skills and processing speed in conjunction with anatomic brain measures.

Herbert (Chapter 18) presents volumetric MRI findings of increased white matter common to both autism and developmental language disorders and calls for studies to include and link volumetric, tissue characterization (looking for possible tissue pathophysiology), and functional measures. She raises several important questions, such as whether and how anatomic and functional change are related, suggesting multimodal approaches to tease apart the many suggestive findings to date and break new ground; whether sensory problems manifest similarly across auditory, visual, and somatosensory modalities; whether severity of these sensory problems correlates with metabolic or immune function biomarkers; and how early it might be possible to detect all this.

The Link to Behaivor

Seeking to link neurophysiological function to prediction, Black and Hoeft (Chapter 12) review current behavioral methods used to predict reading outcome and discuss the potential for doing so using multiple neuroimaging modalities. They cite the need for future studies that will disentangle the interactive effects of maternal education, environmental factors (e.g., parental reading and other parent–child interactions), and genetics in relation to neuroimaging results, stating that such studies should eventually guide clinical and educational interventions, and further, note the importance of cross-validating findings with large, geographically diverse samples. Similarly, Pernet and Démonet (Chapter 13), in reviewing recent studies on possible dyslexia subtypes, highlight the need to continue to study, in depth, all perceptual and cognitive skills related to reading and to develop a theoretical framework that can account for the several co-occurring deficits that have been noted in various studies since the mid 1990s. These authors suggest that structural and functional brain phenotypes might actually provide a viable characterization of dyslexia in the near future and see this as a promising approach to linking behavioral, genetic, and neurobiological data.

In Chapter 8, Maassen, van der Leij, Maruits, and Zwarts describe findings from the Dutch Dyslexia Project, showing clear differences as early as 2 months of age in neurophysiological and neurocognitive measures between children at familial risk for dyslexia compared with those without such risk. They indicate that their own future research will continue to follow this well-documented cohort, but also they call for similar studies that would permit cross-linguistic comparisons and cite the need to address the role of orthographic transparency in reading and dyslexia[2]. In Chapter 9, de Bree, Snowling, Gerrits, van Alphen, van der Leij, and Wijnen specifically tackle the issue of whether children with specific language impairments (SLI) all have phonological deficits or whether this is specific to dyslexia and therefore only found in SLI when it is comorbid with dyslexia. They address the issue using data from the Utrecht longitudinal study, which compares children with SLI to children at familial risk of dyslexia and typically developing children without familial risk. To disentangle alternative explanations and continue to deepen our understanding of these two conditions, de Bree et al. call for more longitudinal studies addressing phonological development, oral language, decoding and spelling ability, and their underlying mechanisms, and for careful study of domain-general skills required for literacy. They also urge examination of individual differences and developmental trajectories.

Focusing on early precursors of SLI and the role this and other language problems might play in dyslexia, Chandrasekaran and Kraus (Chapter 6) examine the implications of various theories regarding core deficits underlying dyslexia, seeking to understand the complex bidirectional interactions between cognitive and sensory processing in poor readers. They indicate findings on deficits in subcortical processing (neural timing, representation of higher harmonics, resistance to background noise, and ability to use prior experience) and reduced cortical asymmetry. These authors offer as issues for future research the refinement of work in three areas: the subcortical neural signature, the developmental trajectory for reading, and brainstem activity as an early neurobiomarker of reading—as well as further work on the integration of data from various neuroimaging technologies in examining individual differences and subcortical physiology. Benasich and Choudhury (Chapter 7) describe longitudinal work beginning in infancy, using converging measures (initially dense-array electroencephalography and event related potentials and later fMRI and behavioral measures). This work reveals differences in early rapid auditory processing and in developmental trajectories between children with and without familial risk for language-based learning disorders. These authors highlight the importance of studying the developmental process, because later outcomes do not necessarily reflect the path(s) that led to language or reading problems. They present as important future research topics the patterns of oral language disorders, which may predict later reading disorders, and clues those patterns might reveal as to etiology, as well as to

---

[2]We note that the issue of the role of orthography in dyslexia was addressed in the prior Extraordinary Brain Symposium, reported in McCardle, Miller, Lee, and Tzeng (2011).

whether language-based learning disorders may be points on a continuum or arise from different precursors, etiologies, or profiles of deficit.

Raschle, Lee, Stering , Zuk, and Gaab (Chapter 17) also emphasize the importance of early detection. They agree that imaging studies of younger children (before they have experienced reading failure) are needed. Based on their own findings that young children (5½–6¼ years) with a family history of dyslexia show behavioral, functional, and structural differences relative to prereading peers without this family history, they conclude that these differences are not dependent on experience but appear to be present prior to reading exposure. In addition, it is noted that other studies have shown the potential for such predictions: Researchers have shown that ERPs could be used to distinguish infants who later, at age 8 years of age, read well or poorly (Molfese, 2000); that ERPs revealed hemispheric processing differences to speech stimuli between infants at risk for dyslexia and infants not at risk (Guttorm, Alho, Richardson, & Lyytinen, 2011); and that ERPs indicated poorer auditory speech sound perception in at-risk infants at 2 months of age (Van Leeuwen et al., 2006, as cited in Chapter 8).

Plante (Chapter 16) raises the controversy of the role of auditory processing deficits in SLI, advocating a paradigm shift from assessing what individuals with language impairment *know* to asking *how they learn*. Reviewing both behavioral and neuroimaging data, Plante asserts that the deficits associated with developmental language disorders reflect not only core language abilities but the interactions of language, memory, and attention. She concludes that studying receptive language deficits in conjunction with neuroimaging, in light of learning theory, can offer potential insights into learning strategies and can enable us to study learning in these children as it progresses.

Finally, McCandliss and Yoncheva (Chapter 19) address experience-dependent changes in functional properties of specific brain regions. They discuss the phonological mapping hypothesis (Maurer & McCandliss, 2007), which asserts that lateralization of functional specialization for both visual and phonological abilities in reading results from the demands for interaction of these two systems made by learning to read. These authors suggest that two things may be sources of observed individual differences in readers in both phonological and visual word-form processing: 1) the degree to which top-down activation of phonological processes occurs during reading acquisition and 2) anatomical variations in white matter tracts associated with phonological processes. They note the need for more direct evidence linking white matter tracts to differences in lateralization and for work examining the role of executive function in possibly modulating these effects as reading development progresses. In a closing statement that nicely confirms Plante's plea for greater attention to learning, McCandliss and Yoncheva state that future studies ought to combine findings on preexisting individual differences with those on learning processes that shape patterns of interactivity and newly emerging phenomenon such as how learning processes influence lateralization specialization.

THE NEXT STEPS

In addition to the research directions summarized from the chapters in this book, it is possible to note various themes that, in the final conference session, participants agreed were essential to moving forward on these important topics. They emphasized the importance of connecting human findings and animal models, especially in the area of systems neuroscience (the auditory, visual, magnocellular and motor systems, attention, and prelinguistic memory). This can be fostered through greater communication and even collaboration across labs and research teams. As observers to the discussions and enthusiastic participants, we would add that it will be important that teams working on early precursors to the various aspects of language disorders also communicate with those examining early predictors of reading disabilities (RD) as it is clear that RD are complex and multifactorial; although precursors of language disorders likely play a role in at least some cases of RD, work on subtypes or profiles of RD indicates that it is necessary to take a more inclusive view, focusing broadly on a range of factors that critically includes, but is not limited to, oral language processing precursors.

Both electrophysiological measures such as ERPs and various types of functional and structural neuroimaging were invoked as important tools. A plea was made to use these types of measures across studies, including bilingual and second-language learning families, as neuroimaging may reveal commonalities that may not be revealed in behavioral and language testing alone. (See McCardle, Miller, Lee, and Tzeng [2011], for information on dyslexia across languages, which includes studies of neuroimaging of bilinguals and those learning to read in languages with nonalphabetic orthographies.)

The development and use of common measures and converging paradigms could help to move the field forward faster, and participants called for some common *practices* as well: Researchers should include explicit definitions in writing up their results, because not everyone adopts the same inclusion or exclusion criteria or the same definitions of what constitute, for example, language disorders or RD. Descriptions of tasks used and the constructs they are measuring would make research reports more comprehensible as well as more replicable, as would agreement on and use of a standard core battery of tests and tasks. These procedures would also allow more cross-study comparisons.

As has been noted earlier in summarizing the specific suggestions from various chapters, conference participants heartily agreed that more longitudinal research is needed. Cross-sectional work, with larger samples, is also crucial and offers real advantages in timing and what can be learned overall. However, the need to study students in depth—to examine change in learning over time, examine response to instruction and intervention, and develop trajectories and profiles of both language disorders and RD—is essential to more fully understanding these disorders. These deeper more detailed data are also essential to developing phenotypes and their stability—how they change over time—and to being able to more closely examine individual differences as they contribute to all of these issues.

Combining efforts synergistically was a recurring theme. Participants asked for collaborations in testing key theories with multiple techniques and from different theoretical perspectives, for data sets that could be shared and for data sets that could be integrated (including integration of genetic, behavioral, and neurobiological data, as well as integrating data across coordinated studies, where possible). This combining of resources and data could allow for larger scale, in-depth investigations and examination of underlying factors, both differences and commonalities, between RD and SLI to help inform the etiology of both conditions and of language-based disabilities more generally.

An applied theme was translation and dissemination: how to link what is known about the behavior, neuroscience, and genetics of language disability and dyslexia to education at various levels, and how to translate what is known for teachers and families and disseminate it in usable forms. There is a need to inform education decision makers (superintendents, administrators, principals, and policy makers) about these disorders, the science that underlies them, and interventions that have been developed and tested. Related to this is the importance of partnering with schools in data collection—to find assessments that are useful for teachers to inform their instructional practices but that also tap key underlying constructs related to literacy and oral language development and related cognitive and/ or neural processing. Such assessments should gather essential behavioral data that researchers can use to further our understanding of these disorders and of learning in general and to close the feed forward–feedback loop from research to practice.

As noted in each of the earlier sections, it is difficult if not impossible to study genetics or neurobiology without considering behavior, be it in animals or humans. Certainly for the study of developmental disabilities involving language, behavior is the defining goal of genetic and neurobiological investigations. A key feature that recurs in these research recommendations is the importance of the environment. Genes are important, but they are not the whole story; they are not a final determination. The environment in which a child is raised, the parenting, nutrition, healthcare, peer relations, and education (including child care, preschool, and elementary and later grades) can influence the expression of those genes. These factors can also influence in ways that are not fully understood the plasticity of the nervous system set in motion by those genes.

Studying early precursors of language disorders and RD, including the basic processes associated with early language development (perception,

cognition) and the timing of gene expression and neurological development, is key to more fully understanding both types of disorders. Much
has been accomplished, but more work is needed on identification, classification, prediction, prevention, and intervention for these fascinating
but troublesome conditions. The accomplishments reported at the 12th Extraordinary Brain Symposium and in this book offer hope that the field is
moving toward these goals in the focal areas of early language and brain
development, perception and processing, and the research directions that
the conference participants called for should help move us further in that
direction.

REFERENCES

Guttorm, T., Alho-Naveri, L., Richardson, U., & Lyytinen, H. (2011). Brain
activation measures in predicting
reading skills and evaluating intervention effects in children at risk for
dyslexia. In P. McCardle, B. Miller, J.R.
Lee, & O. Tzeng (Eds.), *Dyslexia across
languages: Orthography and the gene–
behavior link* (pp. 133–140). Baltimore,
MD: Paul H. Brookes Publishing Co.

Maurer, U., & McCandliss, B.D. (2007).
The development of visual expertise for
words: The contribution of electrophysiology. In E.L. Grigorenko & A.J. Naples
(Eds.), *Single-word reading: Biological and
behavioral perspectives* (pp. 43–64). Mahwah, NJ: Lawrence Erlbaum Associates.

McCardle, P., Miller, B., Lee, J.R., & Tzeng, O. (2011). *Dyslexia across languages: Orthography and the gene–behavior
link.* Baltimore, MD: Paul H. Brookes
Publishing Co.

Molfese, D. (2000). Predicting dyslexia
at 8 years of age using neonatal brain
responses. *Brain and Language, 72,* 238–
245. doi:10.1006/brln.2000.2287

Van Leeuwen, T.H., Been, P.H., Kuijpers, C., Zwarts, F., Maassen, B., &
Van der Leij, A. (2006). Mismatch
response is absent in 2-month-old
infants at risk for dyslexia. *Neuro-
Report, 17,* 351–355. doi:10.1097/01.
wnr.0000203624.02082.2d

Index

Tables and figures are indicated by *t* and *f*, respectively.